ADVANCED MANAGERIAL ACCOUNTING

ADVANCED MANAGERIAL ACCOUNTING

Robert P. Magee
Kellogg Graduate School of Management
Northwestern University

1817
HARPER & ROW, PUBLISHERS, New York
Cambridge, Philadelphia, San Francisco,
London, Mexico City, São Paulo, Singapore, Sydney

Sponsoring Editor: Peter Coveney
Project Editor: Steven Pisano
Cover Design: Tomoko Miho
Text Art: Fineline Illustrations, Inc.
Production: Willie Lane
Compositor: Waldman Graphics, Inc.
Printer and Binder: R. R. Donnelley and Sons Company

ADVANCED MANAGERIAL ACCOUNTING

Library of Congress Cataloging-in-Publication Data

Magee, Robert P.
Advanced managerial accounting.

Includes index.
1. Managerial accounting. I. Title.
HF5635.M2165 1986 658.1′511 85-21948
ISBN 0-06-044162-3

86 87 88 89 9 8 7 6 5 4 3 2 1

To my parents,
C. Robert and Rosemond J. Magee

Contents

Preface to the Instructor

By writing this text, my objective has been to overcome a shortcoming I have experienced in teaching quantitative methods for managerial accounting, that is, the lack of a consistent focus on what I consider to be the substance of managerial accounting—the making of information choices. For instance, in cost variance material one finds a description of variance calculations and a quantitative model for deciding when to investigate a cost variance. Yet the managerial accountant's role extends beyond these issues to include the choice among flexible budgeting models as well as the choice of frequency of and level of aggregation in the variance reports, and available materials did not help the students to understand or attack such questions. Similarly, the use of contribution margin information in a linear programming model of the product mix decision is seldom followed by an analysis of that model's implications for the process of estimating contribution margins.

This text uses decision theory (and in later chapters, agency theory) to provide a consistent framework for approaching information choices. Therefore, the focus of the book is on the influence that information has on the decisions made by a manager and on an assessment of the benefits that the information produces. After the first chapter (which introduces the parameters of information choices), the remaining chapters can be roughly grouped into three areas. Three chapters (2, 3, and 11) provide the basics of the decision theory and agency theory analysis of information and provide the groundwork for assessing the benefits of different accounting information systems. Two chapters (5 and 6) cover the techniques a managerial accountant can use to estimate cost behavior (including a section on simulation), while the remaining chapters apply the frameworks and techniques in managerial decision settings which proceed from simpler to more complex. Simple cost–volume–profit analysis under uncertainty and issues related to the value of cost information in this setting are introduced in Chapter 4, and this is expanded to the analysis of information regarding learning curves and multiple products in Chapter 7. Chapter 8 covers the influence of competition and competitive bidding on the value of information about costs. Variances and an investigation model are introduced in Chapter 9, while Chapter 10 considers explicitly information issues such as the timing and aggregation of variance reports and the assessment of benefits from different flexible budgeting models. The use of information for performance evaluation in an agency setting is introduced in Chapter 11. The concept of "informativeness" is covered, and two appendices to the chapter analyze the effects of various factors on the optimal linear incentive contract and the use of relative performance evaluation. Budgets and participation are covered in Chapter 12, with clear recognition that the person being evaluated can have better information than the person doing the evaluation. Finally, the accounting measurement issues in performance evaluation are divided into allocations across activities and allocations over time, and these topics are covered in Chapters 13 and 14, respectively.

In addition to a consistent framework for information decisions, I have also attempted to achieve a reasonably consistent level of mathematical complexity throughout the text, so there are no rigorously mathematical chapters followed by totally intuitive chapters. (Although the intuition behind the quantitative results is important for the student, and has not been neglected.) The level of mathematical training required is higher than most managerial accounting texts, and a knowledge of probability and statistics is important to understanding the material in the book. An understanding of calculus and, to a lesser extent, matrix algebra will also be helpful to the student. In addition to training in quantitative methods, the student is expected to have an understanding of the accounting process and basic cost accounting procedures as covered in Horngren's *Cost Accounting* (Prentice-Hall, 1982) or Moriarity and Allen's *Cost Accounting* (Harper & Row, 1984). The text is intended for use by advanced undergraduate and master's students, since it stops short of the technical detail and extensive referencing necessary for a doctoral student.

To reduce the amount of effort needed to apply the quantitative methods described in the text, a number of computer programs (written in the BASIC language for microcomputers) appear at the end of the book. For instance, there is a program for service department cost allocation, for estimating a learning curve, for computing an optimal incentive contract, and so on. The students can learn the principles of information analysis in computationally simple problems and then apply those principles in more complex settings by letting the computer do the tedious work. These programs are also available on a diskette (IBM only), free to instructors upon adoption. Like the text, the problem material emphasizes the assessment of the benefits of information in a variety of settings, and a number of cases from HBS Case Services are suggested for supplementary material in the Instructor's Manual.

In preparing an accounting student for the types of information decisions that he or she will have to make in the future, there are three things that a text should provide. First, the odds that the information situation faced in real life will duplicate one faced in class are remote, so the text should provide a framework with principles that can be applied in a wide variety of situations. Second, the text's examples and problem materials should provide an opportunity to apply the principles so that they are not learned only in the abstract, but as a working, usable framework. Finally, a text should provide enough information that it can serve as a reference for the future, rather than pointing out a problem and leaving it at that. It has been my objective to write a text which provides these three things for students of managerial accounting, and I hope that you (and they) find it useful.

ACKNOWLEDGMENTS

A project such as this cannot be completed (or even started) without the support and influence of a number of persons. The ways in which I view accounting information problems, and therefore my objectives in writing this book, have been significantly influenced by three people. I would like to express my thanks to Tom Dyckman of Cornell University, Nick Dopuch of Washington University, and Joel Demski of Yale University. Also, a number of faculty members have reviewed all or part of the text at various stages, and I would like to thank Professor William Baber of Columbia University, Professor Edward Blocher of the University of North Carolina, Timothy Crichfield of Ernst & Whinney, Professor Thomas Hedges of Southern Methodist University, Professor Jack Hughes of the University of British Columbia, Professor Michael Maher of the University of Michigan, Professor Gary Sundem of the University of Washington, and Professor Ralph Benke, Jr. of James Madison University. Professor Ronald Hilton of Cornell University reviewed the manuscript at all stages, and I would like to express a special thanks for his thoughtful suggestions (and endurance).

The Institute for Management Accounting of the National Association of Accountants allowed me to use and adapt material from the Certificate of Management Accounting examination, and these problems are identified by (C.M.A.) or (C.M.A., adapted). In addition, some problems are based on papers written by students in my course on advanced managerial accounting, and my debt to them is acknowledged in the credits given for the problems.

A number of typists have worked on the manuscript over the years, with Kathy Smith, Phyllis Van Hooser, and Wilbert Kellogg doing the most significant portions. Judy Rothman and Peter Coveney of Harper and Row, Publishers, Inc. saw the project through the final stages and I am grateful to the entire staff of Harper & Row for their help in bringing this project to fruition.

Finally, I would like to thank my wife, Peggy, and our sons, Paul and Michael, for their patience and support and for keeping me in touch with the important things in life.

ROBERT P. MAGEE

Preface to the Student

The modern business world is giving increasing recognition to the importance of information. Companies, even industries, have been created to produce, disseminate, and manage this resource called information. But the value of this resource is frequently difficult to estimate, and may vary with the environment and situation. Changes in technology may cause the ''best'' amount of information to change dramatically over time, so an organization's information decisions must be frequently reviewed and evaluated.

This text focuses on the role of information within organizations and on a framework for making information decisions in that environment. In particular, we focus on information produced by the accounting system for use by decision makers in the organization. Examples of these decision situations are short-term planning (cost–volume–profit), control (variance interpretation and investigation), and performance evaluation (budget setting, responsibility accounting). In each such situation, there are information decisions that must be made. How accurate should the information be? How often should the decision maker receive a report from the accounting system? How much aggregation should there be in the report? In making these information decisions, our objective should be the same as it is in making other decisions (investment decisions, marketing decisions)—to further the goals of the organization.

This approach requires that we estimate the costs of an information alternative, and assess the benefits that it produces through more effective decision making by people in the organization. The objective of this text is to help you further those skills by providing a consistent framework for estimating the benefits of information (costs are more easily identified), and demonstrating the application of that framework in the planning, control, and evaluation settings mentioned above. In addition, there is some material on the production of information about costs using engineering and statistical methods.

The increasing awareness of the importance of information in business, and the rapidity of changes in the business world in general, and in the technology of information in particular, require that a managerial accountant know more than the techniques that are in use today. He or she should have an understanding of the ways in which information affects an organization, and be able to apply that understanding to new problems and situations that arise. My goal in this text is to help you develop an understanding and ability that will be useful in approaching and resolving both current information decisions and those that will be faced in the future.

Chapter 1

Managerial Accounting Choices

1.1 THE ROLE OF ACCOUNTING

Information has long been recognized as a key component in decision making, but in recent years there has been increasing awareness of information as a commodity. We are accustomed to thinking of automobiles as coming in various shapes, colors, and sizes, and as capable of different speeds, providing a variety of comforts, and costing different amounts of money. Likewise, information can come with different speeds, different accuracies, different contents, and different costs. For instance, in managing an investment portfolio you could choose from a variety of investment advisory services—each with different characteristics and costs. We make such information decisions on a regular basis, yet it is often difficult to estimate the value of information in decision making. In this book, we will develop frameworks for the analysis of information, including the estimation of its benefits.

Accounting may be defined as the collection, processing, and reporting of information about the activities and events that affect an organization. The purpose of this information is to enable decision makers to allocate their resources (or resources entrusted to them) more efficiently. For example, the general-purpose financial statements found in a firm's annual report provide information to current and potential shareholders and creditors to aid them in their decision making.

We can classify accounting activities according to the audience for which the accounting outputs (reports) are intended. Almost every organization must prepare accounting reports for some external user group. For example, companies whose shares are publicly held must issue an annual report at the end of their fiscal year; borrowers must provide a financial and credit history, and perhaps additional information, to lenders; hospitals must supply cost records to third-party payers such as Blue Cross; and all organizations that are not tax-exempt must file income reports with the Internal Revenue Service.

It should be obvious that the objectives of these various reports differ, and that the accounting measurement rules and levels of detail used in one report are not necessarily best for another. The report that minimizes a company's tax burden does not necessarily provide the fairest presentation of a firm's financial position, and the level of detail provided in general-purpose financial statements may not be sufficient for a major lender. Therefore, the evaluation of alternative accounting measurements cannot be separated from the way the measurements will be used.

1.2 MANAGERIAL ACCOUNTING

In this book, we focus on one group of accounting information users—the management of an organization. Generally speaking, the objective of *managerial accounting* is to improve different types of decision making within the organization. But even within this one user group (management), there are a variety of decision settings in which a change in information can affect the organization. We can categorize the ways in which managerial accounting information affects the organization as *decision facilitating* and *decision influencing*.[1] The purpose of decision facilitating information is to improve the manager's allocation of resources, while the purpose of decision influencing information is to improve the organization's control over decisions made by its employees.

In the chapters that follow, we will be looking at the common decision settings faced in most organizations: short-term planning (pricing and product mix decisions); control (variance investigation decisions); and performance evaluation situations (performance measures, transfer pricing, budget setting). In each of these situations, the accounting system and the information it provides can have an influence on the decisions that are made, and the managerial accountant may find it desirable to depart from the accounting methods used to report to those outside the organization. For instance, the cost allocations used to report to investors may make product mix planning more difficult, or the revenue reported in a firm's tax return may not be the best measure of a sales manager's accomplishments. Therefore, the process of making accounting/information decisions involves understanding how other managerial decisions will be influenced by changes in information.

Most generally, the objective of managerial accounting should be no different than the objective of any other decisions made in the organization (product mix decisions, investment decisions, etc.). The goals chosen by the organization—maximize expected profits, maximize share price, provide quality service at low cost, and so on—should form the basis of the yardstick by which the managerial accounting system's effectiveness is measured. If we accept this role for managerial accounting, the process of *information planning* becomes very important. That is, when we consider alternative accounting information systems, we should make an assessment of their effect on the organization's performance. This information planning process can be a difficult one, because in the case of decision facilitating, we must make an estimate of the effect of the information on a manager's decision making and then make an estimate of the effects of changes in

[1]The terms "decision facilitating" and "decision influencing" were first used by Demski and Feltham (1976).

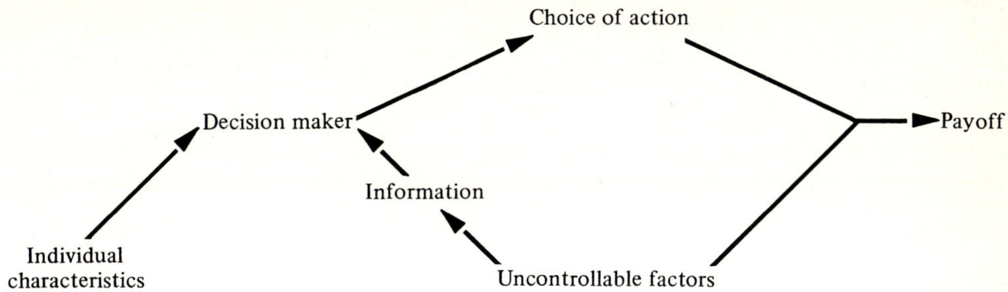

Figure 1.1

the manager's decision making on the organization's performance. A simple schematic of the individual decision maker appears in Figure 1.1. The decision maker has a set of characteristics—risk aversion, time horizon, etc.—and he or she must choose a course of action from a set of alternatives. This decision, along with factors that the decision maker cannot control, influences the outcome of the decision process (e.g., profit). In this situation, the primary purpose of information is to improve the decision maker's assessments of the factors that are not controllable, but which influence the results of his or her decision making. In Chapters 2 and 3 we will explore in more detail frameworks for this type of information planning.

Planning for decision influencing information is even more complex, since the information is used to influence human behavior rather than to improve resource allocation directly. A simple schematic of this situation appears in Figure 1.2. Again, the decision maker chooses a course of action, but now he or she is inside an organization where his or her performance measures and incentive function (bonuses, promotions, etc.) replace the payoff in Figure 1.1. The central administration must try to set the performance system (performance measure and incentive function) so as to encourage the decision maker to select the course of action that results in the best outcome for the

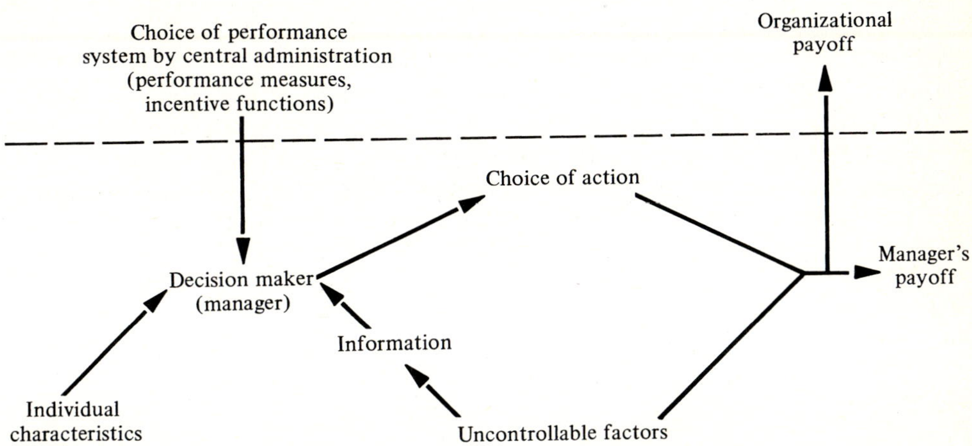

Figure 1.2

organization. One of the roles of managerial accounting is to design performance measures and budgeting processes which facilitate this process. An approach to information planning in these situations is introduced in Chapter 11, and is used in subsequent chapters to explore budget setting and some performance measurement issues.

1.3 INFORMATION ATTRIBUTES

The basis of information planning is that we should try to treat information as a commodity—weighing the costs and benefits of more information versus less information. One difficulty that we encounter in adopting this view is that the *quantity* of information in a given accounting system is difficult to envision. But just as we can measure the "quantity" of an automobile by assessing the attributes of performance, gas mileage, size, color, etc., so can we identify four informational attributes that help us to define the quantity of information that a given accounting system provides.

The first informational attribute is *content,* which reflects the number and variety of activities and events that are recorded and processed by the measurement/reporting system. For instance, when a manager is making a product pricing decision, one accounting system might provide the historical cost of making the product, while another system might report both the historical cost and the current replacement cost of production. Or, when evaluating the performance of the manager of a central service department, the performance report from one system might only cover costs, while another information system might also include some measures of the benefits and services provided by the department. Increasing the content of an accounting information system makes it more likely that important information will be included, although unimportant information is also more likely to be included.

A second informational attribute is the *level of aggregation* in the accounting reports. That is, how many items are reported separately, and how many (and which ones) are added together and reported in aggregate. We know that aggregation is a necessary part of accounting measurement, but differing levels of aggregation can have differing effects on management decision making. For instance, when a manager makes activity level decisions, a cost report that separates fixed and variable costs is more useful than one that does not. When a manager receives a cost variance report, the level of detail will affect the identification of those areas that appear to require management attention. As reports become less aggregated, there is less chance that a problem situation will be "buried" by being aggregated with information on other aspects of the operation.

In addition to the scope and detail of accounting measurements, the *accuracy* of the measurements is also an attribute which the managerial accountant may choose. Accuracy is affected by the procedures by which the accounting information is originally recorded by the system. For instance, suppose that cost and production reports are issued at the end of every month, but the local utility reads the electric meter on the fifth day of every month, and then issues a bill to the company. The firm could use the billed amount as the cost for the previous month, but that amount would not be totally accurate. As an alternative, the firm could read the meter on the last day of the month and determine its monthly cost from that reading. After entry of information into the accounting system, its accuracy can be affected by aggregation procedures, if detail that was originally recorded is lost through aggregation.

The final attribute of information is the *timing* of the reports, although we might divide it into two subattributes—*frequency* and *delay*. In a dynamic environment, where management should revise and adjust their plans, more frequent reports facilitate the timely response to changing conditions. In addition, the speed with which accounting reports are made available after an operating period will influence the level of control that a manager can achieve. If monthly cost and production reports are delayed until three weeks after the month's end, their usefulness in controlling operations may be less than if they had been available two weeks earlier.

While these attributes help to define the quantity of information provided by a given system, we should recognize that it is not possible to compare all accounting systems on each attribute. For instance, a report that includes both historical and replacement cost information has more information content than a report that has only historical cost information. However, we cannot compare directly the information content of a report with only replacement costs to one with only historical costs. Although they have different information content, neither has greater information content. The same comparison difficulties can occur with the other informational attributes. In these cases, there is no way to assess the benefits of alternative accounting information systems without making reference to the decision making context, as we will do in Chapters 2, 3, and 11.

These attributes are related to one another. Disaggregated reports may take longer to prepare, as may those that contain more types of data; and all of the attributes of the quantity of information in a given system are related to the *cost* of the system. As the accounting information system covers more activities and events, retains more detail, measures more accurately, and reports more frequently, its cost will increase. Therefore, the managerial accountant is faced with the difficult, and interesting, problem of discovering the combination of quantity and cost attributes of information that will best achieve the organization's goals.

1.4 THE NATURE OF MANAGERIAL ACCOUNTING DECISIONS

While the attributes described in the preceding section are helpful in assessing the impact of information, it's probably useful at this point to be a little more specific about what we mean by "accounting decisions." We can readily identify product mix decisions, pricing decisions, investment decisions, financing decisions, and so on. Information decisions or accounting decisions are more difficult to envision, and their impact is less easily seen. But it is important that we have a clear grasp of these decisions before proceeding further. Without this understanding, the material in the following chapters will not be as meaningful. Therefore, we will explore some examples in this section.

One basic area of accounting decision making is the allocation of financial results (revenues, costs, etc.) to the various activities that are being carried on in the organization. In terms of concrete examples: "How should we allocate costs to product lines?" or "How should we allocate revenues and expenses to responsibility centers?" In attempting to answer these questions, our objective may be to assist the managers in assessing the desirability of future plans, or to motivate the managers to control costs and to further the organization's goals.

Suppose that a department has just completed the three jobs described in Exhibit

1.1, and its costs of production were as listed. The costs have been traced *directly* to the individual jobs, and we can see that Job 1 cost $150, Job 2 cost $155, and Job 3 cost $190. With this detailed information, we can then evaluate the profitability of each job (assuming that there is a separate price for each product), and we can also assess the level of cost control achieved by the foreman assigned to each job. But let's stop and think about the accounting system that was needed to trace the various costs directly to the individual jobs. Some costs (direct material and direct labor) are traced rather easily by recording them on a "job ticket," but others are not so easily assigned. For instance, an employee that went to the stock room to get parts or supplies for two jobs would have to record which parts and supplies went to which job, and then would have to allocate his own time to the two jobs. Such accuracy and detail would represent one extreme in costing systems. At the other extreme, the company may know only that its costs were $495, and that Jobs 1, 2, and 3 were completed. In this situation, we might allocate one-third of the $495 to each job, but we probably wouldn't feel confident basing any decisions on this allocation.[2] Between these two extreme cost allocation systems, there are a variety of cost allocations which employ varying degrees of "tracing" and "allocating," and some of these are shown in Exhibit 1.1.

The different costing systems result in different costs being assigned to the three jobs. For instance, Job 2's assigned cost varies from $135.56 to $173.25, and the other jobs experience similar fluctuations. None of these cost allocations are as "accurate" as those from (i) direct tracing, but they also require less input and therefore should cost less. For instance, in allocation (iii) the cost of supplies and machine time are allocated on the basis of direct labor hours. Therefore, there is no reason to keep track of the supplies that were used by each job or of the exact amount of time spent on each machine. This should decrease the input cost of the accounting information system. Obviously, the differences in costs assigned to the individual jobs might affect some of the decisions made within the firm, for example, the expansion or deletion of Job 2's product line, or the evaluation of the employees who produced Job 2.

Not all "systematic cost allocations" cause the products' assigned costs to differ significantly from the direct tracing cost. In many situations, the systematic allocation procedures can produce essentially the same cost numbers as a direct tracing of costs. This could occur when two different allocation bases vary closely with each other from job to job. For instance, if it always takes exactly two production employees to run a machine, then it shouldn't make much difference whether we base the cost allocations on direct labor hours or machine hours or both.

There are other examples where accountants must choose how to allocate financial results across different activities. The costs of a centralized service department might be allocated to operating departments in a number of ways. (We will explore this topic in Chapters 5 and 13.) Also, the concept of responsibility accounting involves the allocation of an organization's costs and revenues to the decision makers who are responsible for them.

Another basic area of accounting decision making is the allocation of financial results (revenues, expenses, etc.) across time periods. In the last section, we described

[2]Unless the three jobs were identical, in which case the $165 (⅓ of $495) might represent the expected cost of producing a similar job in the future.

EXHIBIT 1.1

	Job 1	Job 2	Job 3	Total
Direct material cost	$50	$70	$80	$200
Direct labor hours	6	4	8	18
Direct labor cost	$30	$25	$35	$ 90
Machine hours	6	4	6	16
Machine cost	$60	$40	$60	$160
Supplies	$10	$20	$15	$ 45

(i) ''Extreme'' job order system: Direct tracing

Job	Cost
1	$50 + 30 + 60 + 10 = $150.00
2	$70 + 25 + 40 + 20 = $155.00
3	$80 + 35 + 60 + 15 = $190.00
	$495.00

(ii) Allocate ''supplies'' based on direct material cost

Job	Cost
1	$50 + 30 + 60 + (0.25)45 = $151.25
2	$70 + 25 + 40 + (0.35)45 = $150.75
3	$80 + 35 + 60 + (0.40)45 = $193.00
	$495.00

(iii) Allocate ''supplies'' and ''machine cost'' based on direct labor hours

Job	Cost
1	$50 + 30 + (0.33)(160 + 45) = $148.33
2	$70 + 25 + (0.22)(160 + 45) = $140.55
3	$80 + 35 + (0.45)(160 + 45) = $206.11
	$495.00

(iv) Allocate ''supplies,'' ''machine cost,'' and ''direct labor cost'' based on direct labor hours

Job	Cost
1	$50 + (0.33)(90 + 160 + 45) = $148.33
2	$70 + (0.22)(90 + 160 + 45) = $135.56
3	$80 + (0.45)(90 + 160 + 45) = $211.11
	$495.00

(v) Allocate all costs based on direct material cost

Job	Cost
1	(0.25)$495 = $123.75
2	(0.35)$495 = $173.25
3	(0.40)$495 = $198.00
	$495.00

the timing attribute of accounting information. More frequent, more timely accounting reports make it possible for managers to reassess plans and spot problem areas at an earlier stage. But the increased frequency means that an accounting decision must be made as to the costs and/or revenues that will be allocated to a specific period. For instance, suppose that a sales representative spends a year developing a small, growing business as a potential new customer for the firm. Starting the next year, the customer makes purchases of increasing amounts as his business grows. Financial accounting reports would recognize the costs of development as expenses in the first year, followed by the recognition of revenues (and costs of goods sold) as the goods are shipped to the customer in following years. Yet this pattern does not reflect the contributions of the sales representative at the time of achievement, making the use of this information to influence his or her decisions more difficult.

There are a variety of other managerial accounting issues which fall into this same category. For instance, a standard-cost system values inventories at the cost that has been agreed to be the "norm." Any favorable or unfavorable variances from this norm are not included in the inventory value, but are recognized in the income statement of the period in which they occur. Therefore, the choice of actual versus standard costing is a choice of the way in which variations from the cost standards are recognized over time.[3] Other intertemporal allocation decisions include the choice of depreciation schedules, the choice of FIFO versus LIFO for inventory costing, and the choice of capitalization versus expensing for costs such as advertising and research and development.[4]

There are many other accounting information decisions that affect the "quantity" of information that is provided to an organization's management, and we will discuss examples in the later chapters. In order to make information decisions successfully, a managerial accountant must be able to evaluate the informational characteristics of different accounting systems and to assess their impacts on people, on decision making, and on the organization.

1.5 PLAN OF THE BOOK

The central theme of this book is the evaluation of managerial accounting information. There is no such thing as a universally "best" managerial accounting system, but there are frameworks that can be used to identify the benefits of alternative systems. We have three goals: (1) to present these frameworks for informational planning; (2) to present "tools" with which we can produce estimates of the effects of alternative courses of action; and (3) to examine the impacts of information on common managerial situations. Each chapter contains some elements of each of these three areas, but the central themes of the chapters are described below.

As we noted above, there are two dimensions in which managerial accounting information affects the organization—decision facilitating and decision influencing. Chapters

[3]Within the standard cost system, the intertemporal allocation is also influenced by the choice of standard. That is, an easier (higher) cost standard will produce higher income in a period of production (no selling) and lower income in a period of selling (no production).

[4]While these costs are invariably expensed in financial accounting reports, we may choose to capitalize them for internal purposes if it improves the decision making within the organization.

2 and 3 provide a framework for evaluating information from a decision facilitating perspective, weighing the benefits of improved decision making against the costs of better information. The decision influencing aspect of managerial accounting is explored in Chapter 11, with a framework that builds on the decision making models of Chapters 2 and 3. In addition to these "framework" chapters, Chapters 5 and 6 provide a review of forecasting and estimation techniques that the managerial accountant can use in analyzing costs. Each of these topics is worthy of a course of study in itself—engineering measurement, analytic methods, simulation, and statistical estimation. The objective of Chapters 5 and 6 is to provide an introduction to the use of these methods in managerial accounting, and to describe the limitations of their usefulness.

The remaining chapters explore common managerial decision situations, with the objective of understanding how these situations are affected by the managerial accounting system. The sequence of these decision situations is from the simpler, to the more complex. We begin with the single-product, single-period, single-decision case in Chapter 4, with the examination of cost–volume–profit under uncertainty. After exploring cost estimation techniques in Chapters 5 and 6, we study short-term planning with learning curves and with multiple products in Chapter 7. Chapter 8 explores the effects of increased competition and other factors on the value of managerial accounting information. In Chapter 8 we also explore the possibility that better information could make a manager worse off. In Chapter 9, we consider decision making in a multiperiod situation, where a manager is responsible for the control of ongoing operations. The effects of changes in the managerial accounting information system on these control decisions are explored in Chapter 10, where the benefits of more accurate, more timely, and less aggregated information are estimated. Finally, the last four chapters of the book explore the decision influencing role of managerial accounting. After establishing a framework in Chapter 11, issues of budget setting and participation in budget setting are analyzed in Chapter 12, while Chapters 13 and 14 explore the performance measurement topics of responsibility accounting and incentives for investment, respectively.

The objective of this book is to develop a *process* that can be used in *information planning*. There are no standard answers for managerial accounting decisions. The best managerial accounting system depends on the decision setting at hand, the organization's goals, and many more factors. However, there are frameworks and tools that the managerial accountant can utilize to make decisions in a variety of situations he or she may face, and the goal of the succeeding chapters is to make those frameworks and tools both familiar and comfortable for those who make managerial accounting decisions.

PROBLEMS

1.1. The following data pertain to four jobs produced during the same time period, and to costs incurred in that period. The costs are those that are usually termed "indirect," and are allocated to jobs in a systematic manner.

Indirect labor	\$ 750
Electricity	1,400
Material handling	950

Job	Direct material cost	Direct labor hours	Machine hours
403	2,000	28	21
404	1,500	20	15
405	3,000	24	18
406	1,000	20	15
	7,500	92	69

Required

A. Allocate costs to jobs using only direct labor hours as an allocation base.

B. Distribute costs to jobs using (i) direct material cost to allocate material handling costs and (ii) direct labor hours to allocate indirect labor and electricity costs.

C. Same as B, but use machine hours instead of direct labor hours.

D. Obviously, different allocations produce different cost applications. Give some thought as to how you might judge the ''accuracy'' of alternative allocations.

1.2. The Acme Green Bean Co. has a plant where truckloads of green beans are processed and canned in the following way. The unprocessed beans are first cut into the proper size, and then spices are added prior to cooking. After cooking, the beans are put into tin cans, sealed, and processed to insure product quality. Acme uses a process costing system which assumes that conversion costs are incurred uniformly throughout the process, spices are added one-quarter of the way through the process, and the canning operation occurs four-fifths of the way through the process.

The following data pertain to the month of September:

Beginning inventory	0 tons
Green bean cost	$75,000
Spice cost	$ 8,000
Can costs	$35,000
Conversion costs	$60,000
Goods completed	10,000 tons
Ending inventory	2,000 tons

Required

A. Acme assumes that all ending inventory is one-half complete. Compute the cost of goods completed.

B. Suppose Acme were to assume that spices were added at the beginning of the process. Would the cost of goods completed be affected?

C. In actual fact, Acme's ending inventory is spread uniformly throughout its production process. (For example, one-quarter of the ending inventory is between one-quarter and one-half of the way through the process.) How would the cost of goods completed be affected by taking this into account?

1.3. David Robertson was reviewing the monthly budgeting process for a department that produces and sells a single item. The revenue was $150 per unit, and the variable costs of production were $50 per unit. The department's fixed costs were $1,000,000 per month. To maintain economies, production was kept close to 20,000 units per month, but sales could fluctuate from month to month. These fluctuations were largely the result of factors beyond the department's control, although sales usually responded positively to the efforts of the department's sales personnel.

In trying to analyze the problem, Robertson wanted to forecast the department's operating profits at sales levels of 18,000, 20,000, and 22,000 units, using two different profit measurements.

(a) A *gross margin* approach, where the cost of goods sold are measured at the standard, full (or absorption) cost.

(b) A *contribution margin* approach, where the standard variable cost of goods sold and all fixed costs are deducted from revenues to find a measure of operating profit.

Required Using each of the above approaches, make the forecasts that Robertson would like to have for the three levels of sales.

1.4. The Geographic Company has two divisions, one on the east coast and one on the west coast, and a central administration in Chicago. The divisions are responsible for production and sales in their geographic areas, while the central headquarters handles general administration, financing, and personnel administration and benefits. The following information relates to the 1985 operating results.

	Central headquarters	Eastern division	Western division
Sales revenue		$200,000	$400,000
Cost of goods sold		100,000	250,000
Division selling and administration		20,000	30,000
Division profit		80,000	120,000
General administration	$100,000		
Interest	30,000		
Personnel administration and benefits	40,000		
TOTAL	($170,000)	$80,000	$120,000
Net assets		$300,000	$300,000
Number of employees		100	150

Required

A. Determine the divisional profits after allocation of central administration costs based on *each* of the following alternatives.

(a) All central costs allocated based on divisional sales revenue.

(b) All central costs allocated based on divisional profit.

(c) All central costs allocated based on divisional assets.

(d) General administrative costs allocated based on divisional sales revenue; interest costs allocated based on divisional assets; and central personnel costs allocated based on the number of employees.

B. How might decisions at the division be affected by the method used to allocate central administration costs?

1.5. "We're trying to decide on a depreciation schedule for a new set of equipment that has just been installed. The cost was $1,000,000, and the equipment has an expected life of 10 years. For each of those years, we project that the revenues, less out-of-pocket expenses, will be $150,000 from this equipment. Before purchasing the new equipment, we had an income of $150,000 before taxes, and assets of $500,000. Those levels would continue regardless of the new assets."

Required

A. Assuming straight-line depreciation, calculate (i) the income before taxes and (ii) the return on investment (income before taxes divided by net assets) for the first five years of usage of the new equipment.

B. Same as A, but use sum-of-years'-digits depreciation.

C. How might the allocation of equipment costs to periods (i.e., depreciation) affect decision making in the organization?

1.6. The Speedflow Corporation has adopted a standard cost system for its only product. The total material, labor, and variable overhead standard costs have been set at $250 per unit, and the inventory carrying value is set at this amount. Any variances are charged to income in the period in which they occur. The selling price of each unit is $500, and unit selling and production data for the last three months are given below.

	March	April	May
Opening inventory (units)	0	2,000	1,000
Production (units)	4,000	5,000	3,000
Sales (units)	2,000	6,000	4,000
Ending inventory (units)	2,000	1,000	0
Variable production costs	$1,200,000	$1,200,000	$800,000

Required

A. Determine the contribution margin (including cost variances) for each of the three months. (There are no variable selling costs.)

B. Same as A, but use a standard cost of $260 per unit.

C. Same as A, but use a standard cost of $240 per unit.

1.7. Chandler & Thorpe is a large accounting firm with a staff of 200 in the Chicago office. The firm is engaged in three types of activities—auditing (80 people), tax advisory services (70 people), and management advisory services (50 people). There is a food service operation which operates in space rented by Chandler & Thorpe to provide lunch service for employees. A local catering service runs the food operation, charging $8,000 per month plus $5 for every meal served. These costs are to be allocated to each of the three activities. Two months of data are presented below.

	Number of lunches served	
	Month 1	Month 2
Auditing	1,200	1,200
Tax services	1,000	800
Management advisory	300	500
Food service cost	$20,500	$20,500

Required

A. Determine the cost to be assigned to each of the three areas of activity for each of the two months.

(a) Assume all costs are allocated based on lunches served.

(b) Assume all costs are allocated based on number of employees.

(c) Assume that the fixed costs are allocated based on the number of employees, while the variable costs are allocated based on the number of lunches served.

B. For which of the allocations above is the information cost minimized? What would be the additional costs that would be incurred to implement the other cost allocations?

1.8. The 21st Century Desk Company was incorporated and began operations on January 1, 1984. The company is a distributor of a line of desks that are specially designed for microcomputer users. The purchases and sales of desks for the first two years were as follows:

Purchases	
January 8, 1984	100 desks @ $250
May 23, 1984	150 desks @ $275
February 16, 1985	100 desks @ $300
September 16, 1985	100 desks @ $350
Yearly sales	
1984	200 desks @ $450
1985	200 desks @ $500

In addition to the costs of goods sold, the company incurred expenses of $30,000 in 1984 and $32,000 in 1985. At the end of 1984, the company had assets (other than inventory) of $20,000. These assets had increased to $23,000 by the end of 1985.

Required

A. Using first-in, first-out inventory costing, determine the income before taxes for 1984 and 1985. In addition, calculate the before-tax return on end-of-period assets.

B. Same as A, but use last-in, first-out inventory costing, applied on a periodic basis.

C. Suppose that in December a manager must purchase units for inventory (i.e., none of these units will be sold this year). The manager could go to the normal supplier and pay the usual price, or he could expend some resources and time to search for a better price. The manager is scheduled to be transferred to another position in January. How might the inventory valuation (LIFO versus FIFO) affect his willingness to search for a lower price? Think of other decisions that might be influenced by the inventory valuation method.

1.9. Two different monthly reports are shown below for a regional sales office that consists of two territories. The sales office is responsible for sales of a wide range of products to customers located in the region.

Report #1: Monthly Regional Sales Office Report—September 1986

Sales revenue	$200,000

Report #2: Monthly Regional Sales Office Report—September 1986

	Territory A		Territory B	
	Sept. 1–15	Sept. 16–30	Sept. 1–15	Sept. 16–30
Sales revenue	$40,000	$45,000	$60,000	$55,000
Selling expense	2,000	2,200	4,000	4,500
Contribution margin	15,000	16,500	18,000	13,000

Required

A. Compare these two reports on the informational attributes of timing, content, and aggregation.

B. What are the differences in the costs of producing the two reports? That is, what resources are required to produce the increases in content, timing, and disaggregation? Try to be as specific as you can.

1.10. As the manager of the data processing department for a large company, Elizabeth Bond is responsible for the level of efficiency achieved by the department's personnel. About twenty of the department's employees are engaged in the entry of information into the company's computer system. Customer orders, purchases, wage and salary information, accounting adjustments, and other items are received as ''hard copy'' and are entered into the company's data processing system via terminals. Subsequent operating and accounting reports are based on the information entered.

The efficiency of the data-entry group is assessed by comparing the department's personnel costs (salaries plus overtime plus any part-time wages) to a ''flexible budget.'' This flexible budget is computed by multiplying a standard cost per item entered times the number of information items that were entered into the system. For example, the number of customer orders processed is multiplied by the standard, or ''average,'' cost per order, and this calculation is repeated for the different types of items that are processed. These standards had been developed by studies done by the costing standards department of the company.

''In part, my performance is evaluated based on the cost variance for the data-entry group,'' said Elizabeth Bond. ''But there are a number of factors that I cannot control. For instance, if the computer system goes down, we can't enter any data until it's fixed by the company from which we bought it (with a service contract). Also, the standards don't take into account the uneven arrival of items to be entered. At the end of the month, we have a lot of salary-related items plus a large number of sales orders that arrive just in time for the salespeople to make their monthly targets.''

Required

A. The flexible budget described above is based on the number of items processed by the data-entry group. Develop a flexible budget that is based on *additional* information (i.e., has more information content). Does this alternative budget produce variances that are more accurate?

B. What are the additional costs that would be incurred to produce the flexible budget you developed in A?

REFERENCES

Demski, J., and G. Feltham. *Cost Determination: A Conceptual Approach*. Ames, IA: Iowa State University Press. 1976.

Eiler, R., W. Goletz, and D. Keegan. ''Is Your Cost Accounting System Up to Date?'' *Harvard Business Review*. July–August 1982.

Horngren, C. *Cost Accounting: A Managerial Emphasis,* 5th Ed. Englewood Cliffs, NJ: Prentice-Hall. 1982. Chapters 4, 14, 15, 16, 17.

Moriarity, S., and C. Allen. *Cost Accounting*. New York: Harper & Row. 1984. Chapters 2, 10, 11, 12, 13, 14.

Possett, R. ''Measuring Production Costs in the Service Sector,'' *Management Accounting*. October 1980.

Chapter 2

Managerial Decision Making

In Chapter 1, we illustrated a few of the information choices that the managerial accountant must address in determining the content, aggregation, accuracy, timeliness, and cost of accounting reports. In evaluating the information alternatives, the objective is to improve the decision making within the organization, either by providing more valuable information or by achieving greater congruence between the individual manager's objectives and those of the organization. Therefore, an essential step in information planning is a study of managerial decision making. Once this basis is established, we can turn our attention to the impact of information on decisions in Chapter 3 (for decision facilitating situations) and in Chapter 11 (for decision influencing situations).

One conclusion we will arrive at is that there are no universally "best" managerial accounting systems. The decision problem, the environment, and the organizational structure can all influence the value of accounting information. Moreover, these factors change over time and as the organization changes. For example, technological developments in electronic data processing cause continual changes in the cost of acquiring information, so that a report that is "too expensive" today may become common in two years. Changes in uncertainty or in the competitive environment may make information on costs more or less valuable.

Since we cannot hope to provide a system that is universally applicable, our objective is to become familiar with a general framework for making managerial accounting decisions, and then to apply this framework to a number of common situations to become comfortable with its application. This understanding should enable a managerial accountant to better attack the unique problems he or she may face in a given organization.

2.1 A DECISION-THEORETIC APPROACH

The need to make a decision arises when a manager is confronted with a choice between two or more alternative courses of action. In this section, we will describe this choice using *decision theory,* an approach that formalizes the decision making process. An important feature of the decision-theoretic approach is that it explicitly incorporates uncertainty (or risk) into the decision making model. This feature is important for two reasons. First, managers are seldom able to choose a course of action and know exactly the ultimate outcome of the action. For example, the effects of launching a new product line, buying a new piece of equipment, and most other managerial decisions, are uncertain, and it is an advantage if our model of decision making incorporates this uncertainty. In addition, if there is no uncertainty in the decision model, then there can be no decision facilitating role for managerial cost accounting. That is, if in the absence of any cost accounting system, there is no uncertainty concerning the decision maker's impact on costs, then a cost accounting system has little to add. Fortunately (for cost accountants and textbook writers) such cases occur infrequently.

We now turn to the five parts of our decision making model. To make the notation (which is rather cumbersome at first) somewhat easier to interpret, a simple example will be developed simultaneously.

1. Courses of Action The objective of our decision making model is to choose *one* course of action from among the set of alternatives. Therefore, we must have a list or *set* of alternative actions. We shall call this set A, and the ith action in the set A shall be called a_i. The term $a_i \in A$, means that "a_i is a member (or element) of the set A" or simply that a_i is on the list of alternatives. One restriction is that the list of alternatives must be *mutually exclusive* and *collectively exhaustive,* which means that all possible actions have been included, and there is no "overlap" in the actions. Therefore, exactly one course of action will be chosen. (We will return to this requirement a little later.)

Example. A customer has approached the firm with an offer to purchase an order of 1,000 special widgets and is willing to pay $20,000 for the order. The offer is a one-time-only order and will not affect any other business if accepted. In this case the actions list would look like the following.

$$\begin{aligned} &a_1\text{:} \quad \text{accept the special order} \\ &a_2\text{:} \quad \text{reject the special order} \\ &A = (a_1; a_2) = (\text{accept; reject}) \end{aligned} \tag{2.1}$$

If the firm received two independent special orders, say order 1 and order 2, then the mutually exclusive list of actions would have to be the following.

$$\begin{aligned} &a_1\text{:} \quad \text{accept order 1; accept order 2} \\ &a_2\text{:} \quad \text{accept order 1; reject order 2} \\ &a_3\text{:} \quad \text{reject order 1; accept order 2} \\ &a_4\text{:} \quad \text{reject order 1; reject order 2} \end{aligned} \tag{2.2}$$

2. States of Nature The term "state of nature" describes the vehicle by which uncertainty is introduced into the decision making process. That is, the "state of nature" reflects everything that affects the outcome of the decision process but that is not controllable by the decision maker. For instance, in oil exploration the rock and soil formations and the existence or nonexistence of recoverable oil are the possible "states of nature.'' Before any exploration is done, the actual state of nature is uncertain. As with the courses of action, we must first form a list or set of mutually exclusive and collectively exhaustive states of nature. This set is called S, and its jth element is termed s_j. When all the uncertainty is resolved, there will be exactly one state that will turn out to be true.

Example. While the firm has produced regular widgets before, it has little experience with special widgets, and therefore there is some uncertainty as to the incremental costs that will be incurred to fill the order. (The uncertainty could be due to possible production problems, unpredictable learning effects, or many other factors.) We will assume that there are three possible costs and that the uncertainty arises because we are unsure as to how overhead costs will change when the additional order is produced. The states of nature could be the following.

$$\begin{aligned} &s_1\text{: Incremental cost} = \$17{,}000 \text{ (low overhead)} \\ &s_2\text{: Incremental cost} = \$19{,}000 \text{ (medium overhead)} \\ &s_3\text{: Incremental cost} = \$21{,}000 \text{ (high overhead)} \\ &S = (s_1; s_2; s_3) = (\$17{,}000; \$19{,}000; \$21{,}000) \end{aligned} \tag{2.3}$$

3. Outcomes (Payoffs) When the action choice is made and the true state of nature is revealed, these factors combine to produce the decision outcome that we shall refer to as $x(a, s)$. (That is, the outcome x is a function of the action a and the state s.) Usually this outcome will be some measure of performance, such as profit or incremental profit. However, our decision making model is general enough to allow other types of outcomes. For instance, a hospital administrator may be concerned with outcomes such as the number of patients successfully treated and the cost of that treatment. We assume that the decision maker can go through a *budgeting* process which translates actions and assumptions about the state of nature into outcomes to form a payoff table or outcome table of the following form. (We assume there are n courses of action and m states of nature.)

States of nature

		s_1	s_2	$\cdots$	s_j	$\cdots$	s_m
	a_1	$x(a_1, s_1)$	$x(a_1, s_2)$	$\cdots$	$x(a_1, s_j)$	$\cdots$	$x(a_1, s_m)$
	a_2	$x(a_2, s_1)$	$x(a_2, s_2)$	$\cdots$	$x(a_2, s_j)$	$\cdots$	$x(a_2, s_m)$
	$\cdot$	$\cdot$	$\cdot$		$\cdot$		$\cdot$
Actions	$\cdot$	$\cdot$	$\cdot$		$\cdot$		$\cdot$
	$\cdot$	$\cdot$	$\cdot$		$\cdot$		$\cdot$
	a_i	$x(a_i, s_1)$	$x(a_i, s_2)$	$\cdots$	$x(a_i, s_j)$	$\cdots$	$x(a_i, s_m)$
	$\cdot$	$\cdot$	$\cdot$		$\cdot$		$\cdot$
	$\cdot$	$\cdot$	$\cdot$		$\cdot$		$\cdot$
	$\cdot$	$\cdot$	$\cdot$		$\cdot$		$\cdot$
	a_n	$x(a_n, s_1)$	$x(a_n, s_2)$	$\cdots$	$x(a_n, s_j)$	$\cdots$	$x(a_n, s_m)$

(2.4)

Example. We assume that the firm's decision outcome is a measure of incremental profit due to the decision. That is, the payoff function is

$$x(a, s) = \begin{cases} \$20{,}000 - C(s) \text{ if } a \text{ is ``accept''} \\ \$0 \text{ if } a \text{ is ``reject''} \end{cases} \tag{2.5}$$

where $C(s)$ is the incremental cost if state s occurs. This function may be expressed in table form as follows.

a	Low overhead	Medium overhead	High overhead
Accept	\$3,000	\$1,000	−\$1,000
Reject	\$0	\$0	\$0

4. Probabilities We assume that the decision maker can assign probabilities to the possible states of nature. We call $\phi(s_j)$ the probability assigned to state s_j, and we require that each of the probabilities be greater than or equal to zero and that they sum to 1.

$$\phi(s_j) \geq 0, \qquad \text{each } s_j \in S \tag{2.6}$$
$$\sum_{s_j \in S} \phi(s_j) = \phi(s_1) + \phi(s_2) + \cdots + \phi(s_m) = 1$$

If a random variable (e.g., an incremental cost) has an associated probability distribution $\phi(s_j)$, then we define an *expected value* function $E[\cdot]$ as

$$E[f(s_j)] = \sum_{s_j \in S} f(s_j)\phi(s_j) \tag{2.7}$$

For example, if s_j is the outcome of a roll of a die, and if $f(s_j) = s_j$, the expected outcome would be $1/6(1 + 2 + 3 + 4 + 5 + 6) = 3\frac{1}{2}$. If $C(s_j)$ is the cost that results when state s_j occurs, then the expected cost would be

$$E[C] = \sum_{s_j \in S} C(s_j)\phi(s_j) \tag{2.8}$$

This *expected cost* may be thought of as a weighted average value. If the cost also depends on the action chosen by the decision maker $C(a,s)$, then an expected cost, conditional on the action a, may be found:

$$E[C|a] = \sum_{s_j \in S} C(a,s_j)\,\phi(s_j) \tag{2.9}$$

Example. The firm's manager believes that the relative likelihoods of low, medium, or high incremental overhead costs are reflected in the following probabilities.

$$\begin{aligned} \phi(s_1) &= \phi(\text{low overhead}) = 0.3 \\ \phi(s_2) &= \phi(\text{medium overhead}) = 0.4 \\ \phi(s_3) &= \phi(\text{high overhead}) = 0.3 \\ E[\text{cost}|\text{accept}] &= \$17{,}000(0.3) + \$19{,}000(0.4) + \$21{,}000(0.3) \\ &= \$5{,}100 + 7{,}600 + 6{,}300 \\ &= \$19{,}000 \end{aligned} \tag{2.10}$$

If the manager cannot assign probabilities to the states of nature, then one possible strategy would be to choose the action that provides the *maximum minimum* (or "maximin'') payoff. In other words, ''Given that the worst happens, what is the best action?'' (In our example, this strategy would reject the order.) In contrast to this pessimistic approach is a ''maximax'' strategy which asks, ''Given that the best happens, what is the best action?'' (This strategy would accept the order.) But neither of these strategies take account of the likelihoods of the best and worst states occurring. If the decision maker can form the likelihoods, then the manager's action will be that which maximizes his expected utility, as described below in part 5.

*5. **The Decision Maker's Preferences*** With the first four components of the decision theory model, we could compute the expected outcome for each course of action. However, if our objective is to describe a decision maker's behavior, we must recognize the possibility that the decision maker's preferences for the outcomes are not the same as the outcomes themselves. For instance, the decision maker may be *risk-averse,* and when presented with two alternatives with the same expected outcome, he or she will always choose the less risky alternative. In addition, the manager may have preferences over the alternatives that are independent of the outcomes. For instance, in Chapters 11–14 we consider situations in which different courses of action may require different levels of effort by the decision maker, affecting his or her well-being.

Under specific conditions,[1] we can define a *preference function* or *utility function,* $U(x(a,s))$, which can be used to describe the decision maker's preferences over possible outcomes (payoffs). Then the values of $x(a,s)$ in payoff table (2.4) in part 3 can be replaced with $U(x(a,s))$. With the utility function, we may calculate the expected utility of each course of action and use it as a measure of desirability for that course of action. Examples of utility curves for risk aversion, risk neutrality, and risk seeking are presented in Figure 2.1. Other possibilities are considered in Chapter 11.

2.2 THE DECISION

We now have all the parts necessary to determine the action the decision maker would prefer. For each possible action alternative a, the decision maker's preferences, or more precisely his or her expected preferences, will be reflected in the following.

$$E[U(x(a,s))|a] = \sum_{s_j \in S} U(x(a,s_j))\, \phi(s_j) \tag{2.11}$$

Therefore, the outcome of the decision, or planning process, can be described by calculating the expected utility for all possible actions, and noting the action with the highest expected utility. However, it is important to remember that the decision maker doesn't choose the action to maximize his or her expected utility. Rather, the expected utility *reflects* the decision maker's choice.

$$\max_{a \in A}\{E[U(x(a,s)|a)]\} \tag{2.12}$$

[1]Suppose there are n possible outcomes $(x_1, \ldots, x_n)$ and a ''gamble'' on the outcomes is $P = (p_1, \ldots, p_n)$, where p_i is the probability of outcome x_i. Then the utility function $U(\cdot)$ exists if (1) for every possible pair of gambles P and P' either P is at least preferred as P', or P' is at least as preferred as P, or both; and (2) if gamble P is at least as preferred as P' and if P' is at least as preferred as gamble P'', then P is at least as preferred as P''. See Demski (1980) for a further discussion.

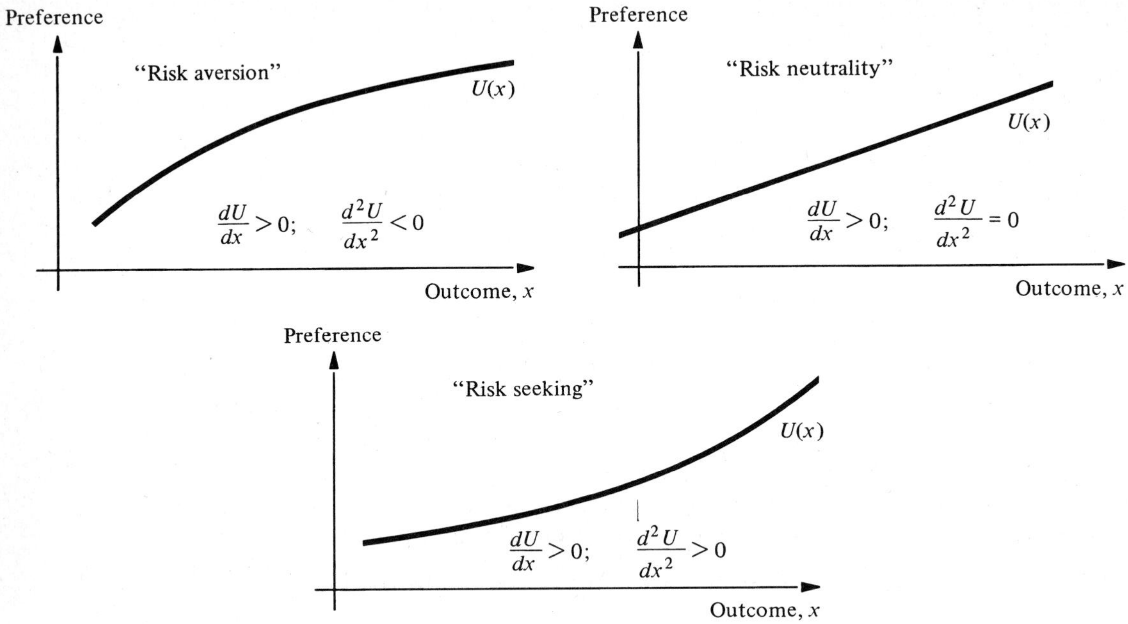

Figure 2.1

Example. We assume that the decision maker's goal is to maximize the firm's expected incremental profit. That is, $U(x(a,s)) = x(a,s)$.

$$\begin{aligned} E[x(a,s)|\text{accept}] &= \$3{,}000(0.3) + \$1{,}000(0.4) - \$1{,}000(0.3) \\ &= \$1{,}000 \\ E[x(a,s)|\text{reject}] &= 0 \end{aligned} \tag{2.13}$$

The maximum expected payoff of $1,000 occurs with the action "accept," and that is the outcome of our decision making process.

At this point, we have a model of decision making that combines the decision maker's alternative courses of action, his or her beliefs about uncertain factors, and his or her objectives. The model is quite general, in that it could be used to describe a variety of decision situations, performance measures, and managerial behavior, by changing the set of actions, the "payoff" outcomes, and the manager's preference function. For instance, if a risk-averse manager's preference for incremental profit is reflected by $[1{,}500 + x(a,s)]^{1/2}$, the decision choice would be evaluated as follows.

$$\begin{aligned} E[U(x(a,s))|\text{accept}] &= (4{,}500)^{1/2}(0.3) + (2{,}500)^{1/2}(0.4) + (500)^{1/2}(0.3) \\ &= 46.83 \\ E[U(x(a,s))|\text{reject}] &= (1{,}500)^{1/2} = 38.73 \end{aligned} \tag{2.14}$$

Therefore, even though the decision "accept" exposes the (risk-averse) manager to more risk, it appears to be preferred. That is, the contribution margin "gamble" is preferred to a certain contribution of zero.

This model of decision making can be used in evaluating accounting information in two ways. First, we can use this model to consider the changes in a manager's beliefs about costs and the subsequent effect on decisions. This approach will be examined in the next chapter. In addition, the impact of the management control system can be incorporated through the payoffs $x(a,s)$ to the manager. Changes in performance measures, budgeting systems, and so on, can be considered in the decision theory model.

In the above example, we assumed that the manager's objective was to maximize the firm's expected incremental profit. But suppose that the management control system is set up so that the manager receives a bonus of $2,000 if sales are greater than $500,000, and the current level of sales (without the special order) is $485,000. If this is the case, then the manager will most likely accept the offer, because the relevant outcome $x(a,s)$ is the bonus, rather than the incremental profit. The payoff table becomes the following.

a	Low overhead	Medium overhead	High overhead
Accept	2,000	2,000	2,000
Reject	0	0	0

In this particular situation, there is no question that the order should be accepted and that the decision will also increase the expected incremental profit for the firm. However, if high overhead costs were $25,000 instead of $21,000, then the expected incremental profit would be *negative* (−$200), but the manager with the sales bonus would still prefer to accept the order. These issues will be explored much more fully in Chapters 11–14, but we introduce them here to underscore the importance of a model or description of decision making in evaluating accounting systems.

A variety of embellishments are possible to show the generality of the decision model. We could allow the manager to choose among alternative jobs, rather than simply accept/reject. The jobs could use varying amounts and types of overhead. The uncertainties could be expanded to include other factors such as raw material cost, labor productivity, the arrival of other, more profitable offers, and so on. But rather than embellish the present example, we examine one in a different context.

2.3 ILLUSTRATION

A hospital administrator is trying to determine nurse staffing policies for the various sections of the hospital. His objective is to keep costs low, but at the same time to provide an adequate level of service for patients. In one particular section of the hospital, there are forty beds and one nursing station, and the administrator must decide how many nurses should be regularly scheduled for a given 8-hour shift. The incremental cost of a nurse who is regularly scheduled is $8.00/hr, but if additional staff are necessary for a shift, the hospital's costs are $11.00/hr. The primary source of uncertainty is the number of patients in the section at any one time. Of course, the administrator has some data from the past year on the number of patients in the section on an individual day, and this data is presented in Exhibit 2.1.

In addition to costs, the administrator is also concerned with the level of service that patients receive. Of course, this is a hard concept to quantify and measure, and we would expect that the number of nurses required to provide adequate service would vary from section to section (e.g., between intensive care and obstetrics). In this particular

EXHIBIT 2.1
LAST YEAR'S PATIENT DATA

No. of patients	No. of days
1–5	5
6–10	20
11–15	25
16–20	25
21–25	50
26–30	50
31–35	50
36–40	25
	250
Average number of patients = 23.9	

section, the administrator and his staff feel that no less than one nurse for every five patients should be sufficient to provide adequate care.

How many nurses should be regularly scheduled for the shift?

An Analysis This decision problem can be addressed using alternative frameworks. First, we could observe a large set of hospital administrators and try to find out how they make decisions of this sort. This approach will be discussed later in the chapter.

Alternatively, the administrator could list the available courses of action, the states of nature, and the outcomes.

Actions: a = number of nurses permanently staffed (minimum 1, maximum 8)

$$A = \{a\} = \{1,2,3,4,5,6,7,8\}$$

States: s = number of nurses needed to ensure adequate care

$$S = \{s\} = \{1,2,3,4,5,6,7,8\}$$

The probabilities for the different states could be estimated from the past data.

$$\begin{aligned} &\phi(1) = 5/250 = 0.02;\ \phi(2) = 20/250 = 0.08 \\ &\phi(3) = \phi(4) = \phi(8) = 25/250 = 0.10 \\ &\phi(5) = \phi(6) = \phi(7) = 50/250 = 0.20 \end{aligned} \tag{2.15}$$

Outcomes: $x(a,s)$ = incremental cost per hour if a nurses are permanently staffed and s nurses are required

$$x(a,s) = \begin{cases} \$8a, & \text{if } s \leq a \\ \$8a + \$11(s - a), & \text{if } s > a \end{cases}$$

Permanent staff	Staff needed 1	2	3	4	5	6	7	8
1	$ 8	$19	$30	$41	$52	$63	$74	$85
2	16	16	27	38	49	60	71	82
3	24	24	24	35	46	57	68	79
4	32	32	32	32	43	54	65	76
5	40	40	40	40	40	51	62	73
6	48	48	48	48	48	48	59	70
7	56	56	56	56	56	56	56	67
8	64	64	64	64	64	64	64	64

Now if the hospital administrator's objective were to minimize the worst cost outcome, he would choose $a = 8$, because the worst cost outcome would be \$64/hr. We assume that the administrator wants to minimize the expected hourly nursing costs for the section. Then we could determine the expected cost for each possible action

$$E[x(a,s)] = \sum_s x(a,s)\,\phi(s) \tag{2.16}$$

For instance,

$$\begin{aligned} E[x(4,s)] &= 32(0.02) + 32(0.08) + 32(0.10) + 32(0.10) \\ &\quad + 43(0.20) + 54(0.20) + 65(0.20) + 76(0.10) \\ &= \$49.6 \\ E[x(6,s)] &= 48(0.02) + 48(0.08) + 48(0.10) + 48(0.10) \\ &\quad + 48(0.20) + 48(0.20) + 59(0.20) + 70(0.10) \\ &= \$52.4 \end{aligned} \tag{2.17}$$

All the staffing alternatives could be evaluated this way, and the hospital administrator would end up choosing $a = 4$ because it has the lowest expected cost per hour.

This illustration serves a dual purpose. In addition to providing an example of the decision-theoretic approach, it also illustrates that the basic framework of decision making is applicable in a variety of institutional settings. The same is true of the types of accounting information problems we will address. While we will often use a "for-profit" illustration, the basic issues also apply in "not-for-profit" settings. However there are some particular measurement problems in the not-for-profit analyses. For instance, suppose that our hospital administrator was not able to hire temporary help to cover peak demand. Then the manager must make tradeoffs between the costs of staffing and the possible costs of not being able to provide facilities for patients' treatment. Unless such a tradeoff or weighting can be achieved (explicitly or implicitly), no decision can be reached.

2.4 SIMPLIFICATION

We should recognize that the decision theory model presented in the preceding section contains a number of simplifications. For instance, it assumes that the sets of actions and states of nature have already been identified. Therefore, it ignores the parts of the decision making process where alternatives are identified and major sources of uncertainty are discovered, and concentrates on the consistent evaluation of the alternatives already identified.

Even for the part of the decision making process that is described by decision theory, it is necessary to make some simplifications in its application. In fact, simplifications could be made in each of the components of the decision theory model. The action set may be simplified by only considering major courses of action, since a complete listing of each possible action may be time consuming. For instance, if there are ten product proposals, each of which can be accepted or rejected, there are $2^{10} = 1{,}024$ possible combinations! Moreover, in making product mix decisions we usually don't consider whether to purchase life insurance for key executives or whether to account for inventory on a LIFO basis or a FIFO basis. In cases where an omitted action affects all the variables in the payoff table equally, its inclusion is less likely to affect the decision.[2] Or if there are two actions a and b, and if the payoff function is $x(a,b,s) = x_1(a,s) + x_2(b,s)$, then the manager can maximize the expected value of $x(\cdot)$ by first choosing a to maximize the expected value of $x_1(\cdot)$, and then choosing b to maximize the expected value of $x_2(\cdot)$. For instance, if there are two completely independent products and the manager's objective is to maximize the expected contribution margin, he or she could consider each product separately. (However, if the manager was risk-averse or if there were constraints on productive capacity, the two products should be considered jointly. We will explore these issues in more depth in Chapter 7.)

The state set may also be simplified by considering only those sources of uncertainty that have a major impact on the outcomes of the action alternatives being considered. For instance, in making an accept/reject decision on a special order, we could ignore the possibility that the plant might burn down or that a supplier could go bankrupt. The effects of such simplifications must be considered in much the same way as action simplifications. If there are two state variables s and t, and if the payoff function is $x(a,s,t) = x_1(a,s) + x_2(t)$, then the manager can maximize the expected value of $x(\cdot)$ by maximizing the expected value of $x_1(\cdot)$ and ignoring $x_2(\cdot)$ and t. However, if the manager is risk averse, the risks of $x_2(\cdot)$ may influence the amount of risk the manager will be willing to bear in his or her choice of action a.

Other simplifications have to do with the outcome function $x(\cdot)$ and the probabilities $\phi(\cdot)$. Usually we will measure outcomes in financial terms such as costs or profits, but there are often other outcomes that impact on the decision maker's well-being. Examples might be ecological considerations or the provision of favorable working conditions for employees. If such matters play a significant role in the manager's decision making (as in the previous section's hospital example), then we must consider them in assessing the effects of information on the decision making. Probability distributions may also be simplified if the payoff to the decision maker depends not only on his or her own action and on nature, but also on the actions of another decision maker. This second decision maker does not choose randomly, but rather to obtain his or her own objectives, complicating the decision setting and perhaps altering decisions and the demand for information. For the next few chapters, we assume that there is only one decision maker, but we will consider multiperson situations in Chapters 8 and 11–14.

2.5 DESCRIPTIONS OF DECISION MAKING

Throughout this book, we will be analyzing the effects of information on decision making. Therefore, a description of decision making is essential to the analysis. In the preceding sections of this chapter we explored a decision-theoretic model of decision making. The primary strengths of this model are its internal consistency and its generality. That is, the model is general enough to encompass a wide range of situations, and in each of these situations it should predict the action to be taken.

While the decision-theoretic model has a "normative" tone in its terminology, it

[2]As long as the decision maker's risk preferences are properly adjusted.

should not be regarded as the way in which decisions *should* be made. Its usefulness in information planning comes from its ability to predict decisions that will be made in given situations. If the decision setting has been carefully analyzed, the decision maker does not choose an action because it maximizes his or her expected utility. The expected utilities are *reflections* of the manager's preferences over actions, not the causes of the preferences.

More concretely, it is perfectly possible for us to develop a decision-theoretic model that does not reflect the decision maker's preferences. We may assume state probabilities, utility function, etc., that are not descriptive of the decision maker's beliefs and tastes. Such a model is not very useful in information planning, since the model will not accurately predict the effects of information on decision making. Therefore, internal consistency is necessary but not sufficient for a model of managerial decision making.

There are a variety of methods to describe the behavior of an actual decision maker. Some approaches do not try to describe the decision making process, but rather search for a model that predicts the decisions. For instance, suppose that we observe a manager who receives cost reports and marketing reports and then makes product price decisions. For each product i, we could record the cost estimate C_i, the market competitiveness measure M_i, and the price chosen P_i. Based on the data from the products, we might estimate (using techniques discussed in Chapter 6) the relationship between the variables.[3]

$$P_i = \beta_0 + \beta_1 C_i + \beta_2 M_i \tag{2.18}$$

As an illustration, suppose we had gathered the following data.

Product	Cost estimate	Measure of competitiveness	Price
1	\$50	100	\$ 75
2	\$80	80	\$130

One relationship based on this data would be $P_i = 1.75C_i - 0.125M_i$.[4]

Another approach to describing decision behavior would involve the manager in formulating the description. We might ask the manager which variables he or she considers first and how he or she uses them in arriving at a decision. The result of this process would be a *flow chart* diagram or a *decision network* which would reflect the manager's perception of how he or she makes decisions.[5] An advantage of this approach over the previous one is that it allows for more complexity in the use of information (e.g., "If $M_i > 150$, we don't get into the market"). However, the usefulness of the decision network is dependent on the manager's level of self-insight.

The decision-theoretic and behavioral approaches to describing managerial decisions should not be seen as competing, but rather as complementary to each other. The behavioral approach uses data based on experienced managers' decisions in real-life situations. The advantage of this approach is that it is based on analysis of real-world phenomena rather than on a situation that may be totally hypothetical. On the other hand,

[3]See Libby (1981).

[4]We would need more observations to be confident about the model, since there are others which describe these two decisions [e.g., $P_i = C_i(1 + 50/M_i)$].

[5]For an example, see Larcker and Lessig (1983).

the behavioral approaches are limited by the decision maker's expertise and level of self-insight, and by the availability of valuable managerial time needed for data collection. The primary strength of the decision-theoretic approach is its internal consistency—given the objectives and the situation, the best alternative is identified. The shortcoming is that the assumed objectives and probability beliefs may not correspond to those of the actual decision maker.

It would appear that a melding of the two approaches would be most fruitful. For instance, we might begin with a decision-theoretic analysis of a situation and compare its result with the decision actually made. There are many reasons why these may differ—for example, the manager's shortcomings as a decision maker and inaccurate assumptions made in the decision theory model. Over time (and in a variety of situations), the objective is to develop a model that fits the decision situation reasonably well. Such a realistic model enables the information analyst to *predict* the effects of a change in the managerial accounting system. Without these predictions, it is much more difficult to make accounting decisions that are beneficial to the organizations.

People and situations change over time, so reconciling the decision-theoretic and behavioral models of decision making is an ongoing task that is never completed. But a decision-theoretic model which never comes close to predicting actual decisions is of little use in forecasting the effects of information on an organization, so some attempt must be made to inject realism into the assumed goals and beliefs.

2.6 SUMMARY

We now have a description of decision making under uncertainty, and when analyzing a decision problem we could try to fit it into this framework by identifying courses of action, the sources of uncertainty, the outcome of the decision problem, the probabilities of different outcomes, and the preferences of the decision maker. This framework is fairly general, and can be used in planning, control, or performance evaluation decisions, with some modifications. Its primary advantage is that it allows us to do information planning ''on paper,'' rather than by experimenting continually with the decision maker. However, it is important to remember that the usefulness of the decision-theoretic model depends on its descriptive validity as much as on its internal consistency. In Chapter 3, we examine the role that accounting information can play in this decision making process, and describe the analysis that allows us to make the tradeoffs among the informational characteristics described in Chapter 1.

PROBLEMS

2.1. Jay Crihfield has inherited a trucking company of modest size, and after a month in the driver's seat, is in need of some assistance. The company is a moderate-sized operation which operates entirely within the state, and mostly within the city. The majority of its business is on a contract basis with specified hauls at specified intervals. For instance, regular trips are made from a local box producer to the box company's regular customers. The trucking company's salesforce keeps abreast of contracts that are offered for bids as well as trying to persuade firms that Crihfield's Trucking Company (CTC) could do a better job than their existing trucker. The actual amount to be bid was always left to Jay's uncle, a fantastic businessman, but very secretive, so no one knows how he used to make bids. Jay is left with two alternatives: trying to guess what the costs of a contract will be, or attempting to plow through past accounting reports to see what he can find.

To start, Crihfield poses a problem for you that is meant to shed some light on the value of getting better cost information.

Suppose he is trying to decide how much to bid on a contract, either $10,000 or $12,000, and the actual costs could be $9,000, $11,000, or $13,000, all with equal probability. Of course, one other possibility would be to not bid at all.

Required What action should be taken?

2.2. The Hotshot Company is considering whether or not to accept an outside order for a special item. The selling price of the item will be $.50 with direct labor and material costs of $.30. However, the variable overhead may be either $.10 or $.25 with equal probability. The contract is a rather unusual one, since the company may contract to supply a small amount (1 million items) or a large amount, (10 million items). If the small amount is chosen, the outside buyer will go elsewhere for the remaining items, and there will be no opportunity to sell more than 1 million items. However, if the large contract is signed, Hotshot has the option to get out of the contract after supplying 2 million items by paying a penalty of $100,000 to the outsider. After supplying that many items, Hotshot will know exactly the variable overhead per unit.

Assume Hotshot wants to maximize its expected profit.

Required What action should Hotshot take?

2.3. Kevin Bond was recently appointed the president and chief operations officer of a medium-sized manufacturing firm whose stock is publicly held. One of his first tasks is to appoint a new general manager for the Chicago plant and a new controller. Both jobs require skills in dealing with people and skills in problem solving. "Personnel" skills are more important in the general manager job, while the controller's job is more concerned with analytic, or problem-solving, skills. For simplicity, let's say that an individual can have one of two levels for each of these skills—high or low. The expected payoff (over the next five years) for each type, for each job, is given below:

Personnel skills	Analytic skills	Expected payoff[a] if general manager	Expected payoff[a] if controller
High	High	10,000	4,000
High	Low	8,000	2,500
Low	High	6,000	3,000
Low	Low	4,000	1,000

[a]In thousands of dollars.

There are two job candidates. B. Lunder has been with the firm for fifteen years, and it is clear that his personnel skills are high, however, Bond figures there's only a 0.2 probability that he has a high level of analytic skill. C. M. Pute has been with the firm for only two years. After graduating from a prestigious graduate school of management, she worked in the management services division of a C.P.A. firm, then for an independent consulting concern before being hired by the firm. It's clear that Pute has a high level of analytic skill, but there is only a 0.5 probability that her personnel skill level is high.

Required Who should get which job?

2.4. Laura Lambert has been approached by a mini-computer salesman to see whether she would like to consider leasing a system at $4,000 per month (assume a four-week month). The system would handle the data processing of orders, billing, payroll, and so on, all of which are currently done by four clerks. Each clerk earns $5/hr and works a 40-hr week. While the clerks' wages are known, some of the fringe benefit costs are uncertain. When an employee is ill, he or she receives sick pay, and a part-time replacement is hired at the usual rate. (A table of statistics on this is provided.) In addition, the company provides a modest pension program for full-time employees, but the long-term costs are uncertain. The present value of these costs are either $.20/hr (with probability 0.6) or $.30/hr (with probability 0.4). Other fringe benefit costs are negligible.

Data on sick days per month

Sick days month	Frequency (probability)
10	0.3
15	0.4
20	0.3

Required If Laura Lambert wants to minimize the expected monthly cost of the data processing function, should she lease the computer system?

2.5. A small electronics business currently has fixed costs of $200,000 per year, with variable costs averaging 50% of sales revenue. A proposal for new equipment is being considered that would increase fixed costs by $48,000 per year and decrease variable costs by 20% (to 40% of sales revenue). The uncertain economic environment makes it difficult for the firm to forecast its next year's sales, other than to say they will be between $450,000 and $550,000.

Required

A. Make what you feel is a reasonable assumption about the probabilities of different sales levels. If the decision maker's objective is to maximize the firm's expected profit, should the investment be made?

B. The firm's manager receives a bonus of $10,000 if this year's profits exceed last year's profits. Last year, the firm made $24,000 in profit. Will the manager be willing to make the investment?

2.6. Blackjack, or "21," is a relatively simple card game between a dealer and a player. After shuffling the standard, 52-card pack, the dealer gives two cards to the player and two cards to himself. For each of the persons, one card is concealed and the other is dealt "face-up." The object of the game is to achieve a point total as close to 21 as possible, but a total which exceeds 21 loses. An "ace" may be counted as 1 or 11, while the "court cards" (K, Q, J) are counted as 10.

After the initial deal, the player must decide whether to "stand" with the point total of the initial two cards, or to ask for an additional card. After receiving this card (face-up), the player has the option to continue to request cards until the total is "close enough" to

21, or if it exceeds 21 he or she loses. The dealer then can take additional cards, if he or she desires.

Below are ten blackjack situations where you are asked to decide whether to request an additional card.

Hand no.	Your concealed card	Your revealed card	Dealer's revealed card
1	Q	5	2
2	2	Ace	3
3	K	10	3
4	8	5	J
5	9	Q	4
6	J	Q	7
7	6	K	Q
8	4	Ace	3
9	Q	7	9
10	3	K	5

Required

A. In each of the situations above, would you request an additional card or not?

B. Try to develop a "decision net" or flow diagram that describes the way that you have arrived at the decisions in A.

C. Exchange your list of decisions with someone. Try to develop a decision net based on the other person's decisions. Compare your perception of their decision process to their own.

2.7. Listed below are last month's materials budgets and material usage variances for nine separate cost centers.

Cost center	Budget	Variance
1	$40,000	$3,000 Unfavorable
2	20,000	3,000 Unfavorable
3	38,000	4,000 Favorable
4	65,000	6,000 Unfavorable
5	70,000	4,000 Favorable
6	25,000	1,000 Favorable
7	42,000	5,000 Unfavorable
8	72,000	6,000 Unfavorable
9	19,000	500 Unfavorable

Required

A. Investigating a variance can use up between $500 and $1,500 of resources. Decide which costs centers you would investigate.

B. Try to explain in writing the decision process you used to arrive at the decisions in A.

C. In class, exchange your *decisions* (not the decision process of B) with another student. Without making any judgments about whether the other student's decisions are "right," try to discern his or her decision making process. What items of information appear to be most important?

D. Compare your description of the other student's decision process with their own description from B.

2.8. The manager of a manufacturing operation has just received a copy of the material scrap reports for the past week. From this information. he assesses that there is a 0.3 probability that one of the plant's machines is out of adjustment. The machine is already scheduled for maintenance to begin one week from now when it will be modified to manufacture a different product. If the machine is out of adjustment, it will waste material valued at $1,300 over the next week, but it will cost some overtime and parts to realign the machine.

Required If the costs of realigning the machine are $350, would you recommend realignment? If the costs were $500?

2.9. Think of a simple decision that you make on a regular basis, for example, what route to follow when driving home, whether to subscribe to a magazine, etc. Use decision theory to model the decision by defining actions, states, outcomes, probabilities, etc. Which course of action is predicted by the decision-theoretic model? What simplifications did you make in your analysis?

2.10. Boy Scout Troop 29 has decided to sell Christmas wreaths as a fundraising project. They will order the wreaths from a supplier in October with delivery at the beginning of December. (If the troop gets its order in early, the supplier only charges $5 per wreath.) The scouts will take orders for the wreaths in October and November up to the point where they have commitments for as many as they will receive from the supplier. The scouts will charge $10 for every wreath sold.

The scoutmaster, Jerry Beam, must decide how many wreaths to order next week. He isn't certain of the number of wreaths that the scouts would be able to sell, but he thinks it would be 100, 125, 150, 175, or 200, all with equal likelihood. Of course, the scouts cannot sell more than he orders, and if he orders more than they sell, the excess wreaths have no value.

Required

A. Assume that Jerry Beam can order wreaths in multiples of 25, and his objective is to maximize the expected value of the net funds raised. How many wreaths should he order?

B. Assume that Jerry Beam is risk averse, and that his preferences for the amount of funds raised is reflected in the square root function. That is, $U(\text{funds}) = \text{funds}^{1/2}$. What is the number of wreaths that would be ordered?

2.11. Listed below are four "gamble" situations in which a manager may choose to receive an amount for certain or a risky payment.

Gamble no.	Certain payment	Risky payment: Payment	Probability	Payment	Probability
1	$1,000	$500	0.5	$1,500	0.5
2	1,000	450	0.5	1,500	0.5
3	1,000	800	0.5	1,200	0.5
4	1,000	0	0.2	1,300	0.8

Required For each of the utility functions listed below, determine whether the certain payment or the risky payment would be preferred by the decision maker. In addition, determine the maximum amount that the decision maker would be willing to pay in order to receive the risky payment.

(a) $U(\text{payment}) = \text{payment}$
(b) $U(\text{payment}) = (\text{payment})^{1/2}$
(c) $U(\text{payment}) = (\text{payment})^2$
(d) Your choice

REFERENCES

Demski, J. *Information Analysis,* 2nd Ed. Reading, MA: Addison-Wesley. 1980.

Larcker, D., and V. P. Lessig. "An Examination of the Linear and Retrospective Process Tracing Approaches to Judgment Modeling," *Accounting Review*. January 1983.

Libby, R. *Accounting and Human Information Processing: Theory and Applications*. Englewood Cliffs, NJ: Prentice-Hall. 1981.

Roussel, P. "Cutting Down the Guesswork in R & D," *Harvard Business Review*. September–October 1983.

Ulvila, J., and R. Brown. "Decision Analysis Comes of Age," *Harvard Business Review*. September–October 1982.

Vanacek, M. "An Overview of Decision Theory for Management Accountants," *Management Accounting*. January 1978.

Chapter 3

Information Decisions

As discussed in Chapter 1, the major responsibility of managerial accounting is the choice of accounting information that is used in planning, control, and evaluation decisions within the organization. In this chapter we will concentrate on the decision facilitating role of managerial accounting. Information factors such as content, accuracy, timing, aggregation, and cost must be balanced to meet the goals that the organization has chosen. As a result, we need to have a framework that allows us to prepare a budget of the *effects of information* and to engage in the planning necessary for effective information decisions. In choosing a level of production, we compare revenues with costs; in choosing the level of capital improvement, we compare the value of the future cash flows with the investment required. The same sorts of comparisons are necessary for successful information planning. That is, the benefits of improved decision making should be compared with the costs of improved information. These comparisons are not always easy to make, but the frameworks presented here should help to direct the comparisons.

Of course, a major part of the framework is our description of managerial decision making, since it is through this description that the effects of different information alternatives can be seen. To examine the effects of information on decision making, we can look to the decision-theoretic description that we explored in Chapter 2. This framework is a complex one, but it does offer us guidance in estimating a value of information, so that we can produce budgets for alternative accounting information systems and thereby make information decisions.

3.1 SYSTEMS, STATES, AND SIGNALS

In Chapter 2 the decisions depended on the decision maker's alternatives and objectives, and on his or her beliefs about the uncertain factors incorporated in the probability distribution over the states of nature, for example, the incremental overhead due to the special order. Since the objective of information, including accounting information, is to alter the decision maker's beliefs (and thereby alter the decisions), we must somehow connect the accounting information system with the states of nature.

At the level of our notation, this link is a fairly simple matter. We can develop a list of alternative information systems H, whose members are accounting systems η_k with different characteristics, for example, different content, levels of aggregation, accuracy, etc. An accounting system ''interfaces'' with the state of nature and produces signals, or reports. We let y be a report or signal and Y be the set of all possible signals. (The report may have more than one component.) This relationship is depicted in Figure 3.1. If we receive the accounting report, and know something about the information system, we may be able to infer something about the state of nature that actually exists.

Before going too far with notation, let's look at an example. Suppose that our decision maker is uncertain about the incremental overhead that will be incurred if a special order is accepted. To simplify things we'll assume that the true state is that incremental overhead is \$4 for each additional direct labor hour and \$3 for each additional machine hour. But this firm allocates overhead using a single-cost pool with direct labor hours as the allocation base, and this information system will be called η_1. If, over the long run, the average job uses labor and machine hours in a 4.5:7.33 ratio, the variable overhead rate could be \$4 + \$3(7.33/4.5) = \$8.89 per direct labor hour. This system would produce the following types of reports.

Job no.	Direct labor hours	Machine hours	Actual incremental overhead (state of nature)	Reported incremental overhead
1	1	1	\$ 7	\$ 8.89
2	1	2	10	8.89
3	1	3	13	8.89
4	$1\frac{1}{2}$	$1\frac{1}{3}$	10	13.33

The first three reports show us that different states of nature can produce the same accounting report, while the second and fourth show that the same state of nature can produce different accounting reports. In such situations it is not immediately obvious how to use the accounting reports to refine our information about the state of nature.

Nevertheless, such revisions are possible using a relationship known as Bayes'

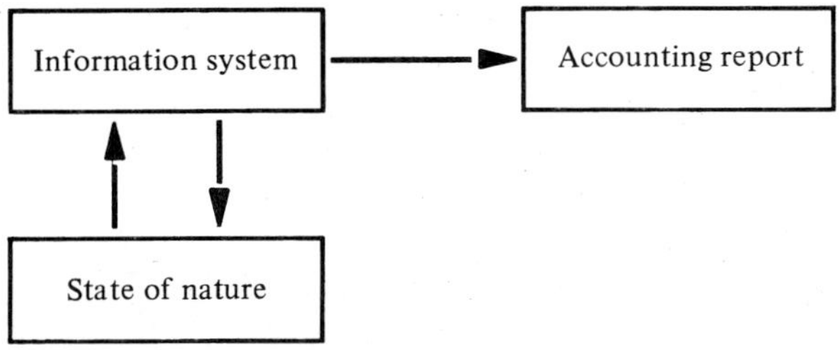

Figure 3.1

theorem. We have now described how the information system η and the state of nature s combine to produce a signal or report y, as depicted in Figure 3.1. In order to revise probabilities, we must define a new probability distribution $\phi(y|s,\eta)$ to describe this relationship. For the four jobs above, we would have

$$\phi(y|s = \$7, \eta_1) = \begin{cases} 1, & \text{for } y = \$8.89 \\ 0, & \text{for all other } y \end{cases}$$
$$\phi(y|s = \$10, \eta_1) = \begin{cases} 1/2, & \text{for } y = \$8.89 \\ 1/2, & \text{for } y = \$13.33 \\ 0, & \text{for all other } y \end{cases} \qquad (3.1)$$
$$\phi(y|s = \$13, \eta_1) = \begin{cases} 1, & \text{for } y = \$8.89 \\ 0, & \text{for all other } y \end{cases}$$

If all four jobs are equally likely to occur in the short run, then the probability distribution over the states of nature before receiving any information would be

$$\begin{aligned} \phi(s = \$7) &= \text{probability of job \#1} = 1/4 \\ \phi(s = \$10) &= \text{probability of job \#2 or job \#4} = 1/4 + 1/4 = 1/2 \\ \phi(s = \$13) &= \text{probability of job \#3} = 1/4 \end{aligned} \qquad (3.2)$$

With these probabilities we can determine the revision in the decision maker's beliefs that will occur when he or she receives a cost estimation report from the accounting system. The new probabilities will depend on the old probabilities and the likelihood of the report under the different possible states. This revision is based on the relationships between conditional probability distributions. (For instance, the probability of A and B is equal to the conditional probability of A given B times the unconditional probability of B. It is also equivalent to the conditional probability of B given A times the unconditional probability of A.) In the context of our decision problem, we can use these relationships to find the probability of state s given that signal y has been received.

$$\begin{aligned} \phi(s \text{ and } y|\eta) &= \phi(s|y,\eta)\phi(y|\eta) \\ &= \phi(y|s,\eta)\phi(s|\eta) = \phi(y|s,\eta)\phi(s) \end{aligned} \qquad (3.3)$$

The two terms on the right-hand side can be rearranged to form Bayes' theorem of probability revision.

$$\begin{aligned} \phi(s|y, \eta) &= \frac{\phi(y|s\,\eta)\phi(s)}{\phi(y|\eta)} \\ &= \frac{\phi(y|s, \eta)\phi(s)}{\sum_{s_j \in S} \phi(y|s_j, \eta)\phi(s_j)} \end{aligned} \qquad (3.4)$$

In our information example, there are two possible signals or reports, $y = \$8.89$ or $y = \$13.33$, and for each of these signals we can calculate the revision in beliefs that would occur.

s	$\phi(s)$	$\phi(s \mid y = \$8.89, \eta_1)$	$\phi(s \mid y = \$13.33, \eta_1)$
\$ 7	0.25	$\frac{(1)(0.25)}{(1)(0.25) + (0.5)(0.5) + (1)(0.25)} = \frac{1}{3}$	$\frac{0}{0 + 1(0.5) + 0} = 0$
\$10	0.50	$\frac{(0.5)(0.5)}{(1)(0.25) + (0.5)(0.5) + (1)(0.25)} = \frac{1}{3}$	$\frac{1(0.5)}{0 + 1(0.5) + 0} = 1$
\$13	0.25	$\frac{(1)(0.25)}{(1)(0.25) + (0.5)(0.5) + (1)(0.25)} = \frac{1}{3}$	$\frac{0}{0 + 1(0.5) + 0} = 0$

These revised probabilities confirm our intuition that if the cost report is "\$8.89," then we can infer that the costs \$7, \$10, and \$13 are equally likely. But if the report is "\$13.33," we know it is job #4 with a cost of \$10. (You should note that the decision maker does not take the accounting reports at face value, but instead interprets them in light of his or her knowledge of the underlying system.)

3.2 REVISED DECISIONS AND INFORMATION CHOICE

When the decision maker receives a signal or report prior to making the choice of action, the revised probability distribution is used in the decision model in place of the original or prior distribution. (For example, when the morning weather forecast says rain, we utilize revised probabilities in deciding whether to take an umbrella.) That is, when the impact of a particular action is considered, the expected preference is calculated as

$$E[U(x(a,s,\eta)) \mid a,y,\eta] = \sum_{s_j \in S} U(x(a,s_j,\eta))\phi(s_j \mid y,\eta)$$

You should note two changes in this expression from its counterpart, Eq. (2.11), in Chapter 2. Of course, the probability distributions have changed to account for the receipt of signal y from accounting system η. But, in addition, the outcome, or payoff function, x, now includes the information system as a variable so that the cost of the information system may be deducted from the payoff.

The decision, or choice, can be predicted by finding that action which provides the highest expected preferences, given the report y from system η. We call this optimal action $a^*(y, \eta)$, and we must find this optimal action for each possible signal y from the information system. In this way we develop a policy or strategy composed of the best action for each possible report.

$$\max_{a_i \in A} \{E[U(x(a_i,s,\eta)) \mid a_i,y,\eta]\} \equiv E[U \mid a^*(y,\eta),y,\eta] \tag{3.5}$$

If we knew exactly what report would come from the accounting system, then we would know exactly what would be the impact on the decision and the expected utility. But that is not the case, and therefore we develop the decision policy described above. When we choose an information system η, we can only have a probability distribution over the reports that will be received $\phi(y \mid \eta)$. [In our example above $\phi(y = \$8.89 \mid \eta_1) = \frac{3}{4}$ and $\phi(y = \$13.33 \mid \eta_1) = \frac{1}{4}$.] And since the revised action and expected utility depend on the report y, we have a probability distribution for these as well. Therefore, the expected utility of the decision maker with accounting information system η is

$$E[U|\eta] = \sum_{y \in Y} E[U|a^*(y, \eta), y, \eta]\phi(y|\eta) \tag{3.6}$$

This expression for $E[U|\eta]$ is based on the optimal use of the information produced by η in revising beliefs and decisions. It also incorporates the cost of the information system in the payoff to the decision maker. Therefore, if we calculate, or budget, this value for alternative information systems, we have a criterion for choosing among them.

$$E[U|\eta^*] = \max_{\eta_k \in H}\{E[U|\eta_k]\} \tag{3.7}$$

The effects of information on decision making can be seen graphically in Figures 3.2 and 3.3. Figure 3.2 depicts a simple decision situation with no information: the alternatives are evaluated using the manager's initial probabilities, $\phi(s_j)$. The initial fork in the decision tree is an *action fork,* followed by an *event* (or state) *fork* at the end of each action branch. (Utilities are left out for simplicity.) In comparison, the decision tree in Figure 3.3 begins with an *information fork,* and at the end of each report branch (for y_1 or y_2) there is a tree structure that is essentially similar to that in Figure 3.2. The only differences are that the probabilities have changed to $\phi(s_j|y_i,\eta)$, reflecting the new information; and the outcomes have now included the cost of the information system. There is not just one decision in Figure 3.3, but a policy consisting of decisions for each possible accounting report. We can say, "If the accounting report says y_i, then the best course of action is $a^*(y_i)$." The idea that the optimal action will depend on the signal is an important one. If it does not depend on the signal, then the information does not

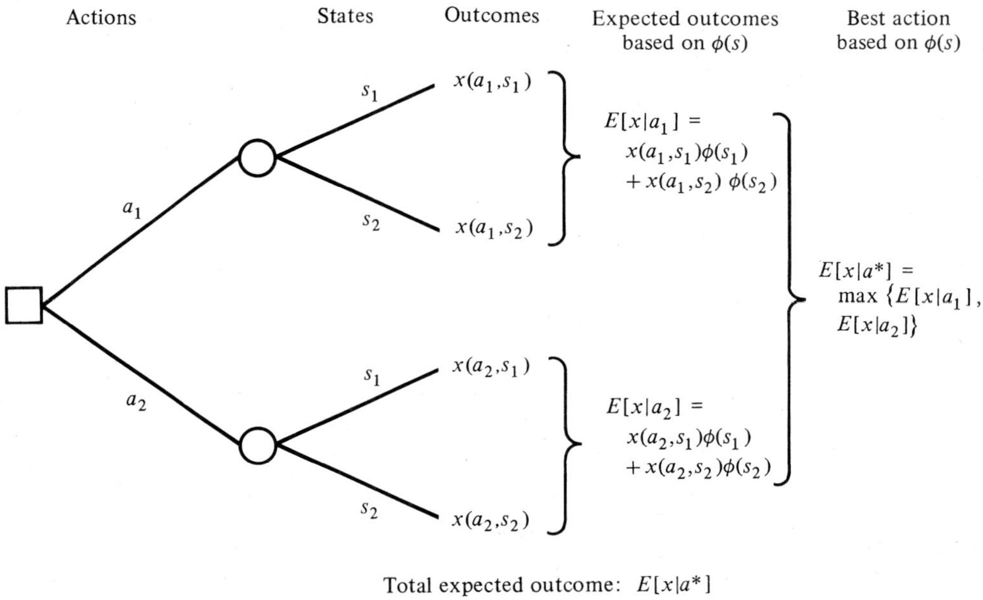

Figure 3.2 Decision with no information.

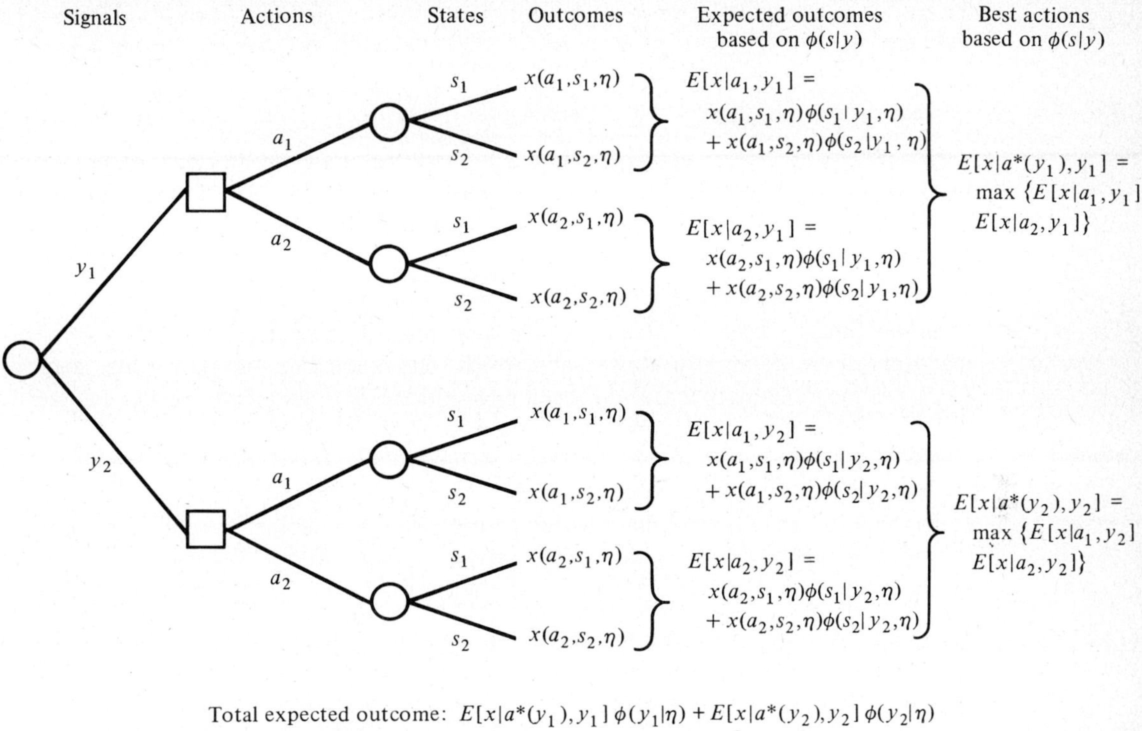

Figure 3.3 Decision with information, η.

affect (improve) decision making, and thus the information has no value. Finally, the "total expected outcomes" in Figures 3.2 and 3.3 can be compared to determine whether it is desirable to obtain the information system η.

We now have a framework for choosing among accounting information alternatives for managerial decision making. An important feature of this framework is that it does not involve the use of terms such as "information needs" and "information requirements," but rather treats information like any other commodity and explicitly weighs the costs and benefits of its acquisition.

Example Let us return to our example of Chapter 2 where the decision maker had to accept or reject the special order, and faced uncertainty about the incremental costs. The best decision, based on the decision maker's beliefs, was to accept the order and achieve an expected incremental profit of $1,000. However, there was a 0.3 probability that the firm would lose money on the order, so the decision maker might want to acquire some information from one of two sources.

The simpler of the two systems to evaluate is a *special cost study,* where the decision maker conducts (or pays for someone else to conduct) an extensive study of the special widget's specifications and the firm's production facilities to determine exactly how costs will change if the special order is accepted. The output of this information system, which we'll call η_1, is a report such as "Incremental costs will be low, i.e., $17,000." The conditional probabilities for this information system are quite simple, as

TABLE 3.1 VALUES OF $\phi(y|s, \eta_1)$

	State of nature		
Reports	s_1 (low)	s_2 (medium)	s_3 (high)
y_1 (low)	1	0	0
y_2 (medium)	0	1	0
y_3 (high)	0	0	1

$\phi(y_1|\eta_1) = 0.3$; $\phi(y_2|\eta_1) = 0.4$; $\phi(y_3|\eta_1) = 0.3$

shown in Tables 3.1 and 3.2, because we assume that this is a perfect information system that will tell the decision maker exactly which state is the true one. If the true state is low, then the probability that "low" will be reported is 1.0; no other report ("medium" or "high") has a positive probability of occurring, as long as the true state is that costs will be low. Corresponding relationships hold if the true states are medium or high. As a result, receipt of a signal, say "medium," means that the probability that the signal is correct is 1.0 (i.e., costs would indeed be medium). Yet another feature of the perfect information case is that $\phi(y_i|\eta_1) = \phi(s_i)$ if y_i is "s_i will occur." We can now consider the revised decision making that would take place for each of the different signals.

		Expected profit if		
Signal, y	Probability of signal	Accept	Reject	$a^*(y, \eta_1)$
Low	0.3	<u>3,000</u>	0	Accept
Medium	0.4	<u>1,000</u>	0	Accept
High	0.3	−1,000	<u>0</u>	Reject

The expected payoff with system η_1 will be the following:

$$E[x|\eta_1] = \sum_{y \in Y} E[x|a^*, y, \eta_1]\phi(y|\eta_1) \tag{3.8}$$
$$= 3{,}000(0.3) + 1{,}000(0.4) + 0(0.3) = \$1{,}300$$

This amount is the expected payoff with perfect information before any information costs. The expected *value,* or benefit, of the information is the expected payoff increase due to the information, or

$$\text{Expected value of perfect information (EVPI)} = E[x|\eta_1] - E[x] \tag{3.9}$$
$$= \$1{,}300 - \$1{,}000 = \$300$$

TABLE 3.2 VALUES OF $\phi(s|y, \eta_1)$

	Reports		
States of nature	y_1 (low)	y_2 (medium)	y_3 (high)
s_1 (low)	1	0	0
s_2 (medium)	0	1	0
s_3 (high)	0	0	1

That is, having η_1 increases our expected payoff by \$300,[1] and this amount constitutes an upper limit on what we would be willing to pay for any information system. In other words, if the cost of a proposed information system exceeds the EVPI, then we can say, without further analysis, that the system is not desirable.

The \$1,300 amount above does not include the cost of conducting the special cost study. Let us assume that the study costs \$200 so that the revised value of $E[x|\eta_1]$ would be

$$E[x|\eta_1] = (3{,}000 - 200)(0.3) + (1{,}000 - 200)(0.4) + (-200)(0.3) \qquad (3.10)$$
$$= \$1{,}100$$

We have now evaluated two information alternatives: the first is the "null" information system, η_0, where we acquire no further information and have an expected payoff of \$1,000; the other system, η_1, is a special cost study with an expected payoff of \$1,100. There may be other alternatives the decision maker could consider. Suppose that by using some past cost data and statistical analysis the decision maker could obtain some additional information about incremental overhead costs. While this alternative does not produce the perfect information of a special cost study, it only costs \$50. The conditional probabilities for this information alternative (which we will call η_2) could be similar to those in Tables 3.3 and 3.4. If the true state is s_1, there is a 0.8 probability that the statistical analysis will report that overhead costs will be low, but there is also a 0.2 probability that the report will say medium. If the true state is s_2, the probabilities of the report being low, medium, or high are 0.1, 0.8, and 0.1, respectively. Regardless of the state, there is always a 20% chance that the report will be inaccurate. As a result, when the statistical cost study reports that costs will be medium, the probability that the state is s_2 is 0.728, as seen in the middle entry in Table 3.4. (The probabilities of s_1 and s_3 are each 0.136, if the cost study reports medium.) Using these revised probabilities, we now look at the revised decision making that may result from this information system. (The \$50 information cost will be deducted from the expected payoffs.)

Signal, y	Probability of signal	Expected payoff, if accept	Expected payoff, if reject	$a^*(y,\eta_2)$
Low	0.28	[0.857(3,000) + 0.143(1,000) − 50] = 2,664	−50	Accept
Medium	0.44	[0.136(3,000) + 0.728(1,000) + 0.136(−1,000) − 50] = 950	−50	Accept
High	0.28	[0.143(1,000) + 0.857(−1,000) − 50] = −764	−50	Reject

In essence, we have formed a plan where the action on the special order depends on the results from the statistical cost study. If it reports "low" or "medium," then we would accept the order, while the order will be rejected if the report says "high." The expected payoff from this information system can be calculated by multiplying the probability of a given report by the expected payoff if that report occurs, and then summing over all the reports possible from η_2.

[1] One way to interpret this \$300 is that the improved information will let us avoid accepting the order when the costs are high. Thus we avoid a loss of \$1,000, which would have occurred with probability 0.3.

TABLE 3.3 VALUES OF $\phi(y|s, \eta_2)$

	State of nature		
Reports	s_1 (low)	s_2 (medium)	s_3 (high)
y_1 (low)	0.8	0.1	0
y_2 (medium)	0.2	0.8	0.2
y_3 (high)	0	0.1	0.8

$\phi(y_1|\eta_2) = 0.3(0.8) + 0.4(0.1) = 0.28 = \phi(y_3|\eta_2)$
$\phi(y_2|\eta_2) = 0.3(0.2) + 0.4(0.8) + 0.3(0.2) = 0.44$

$$E[x|\eta_2] = 0.28(2{,}664) + 0.44(950) + 0.28(-50) \qquad (3.11)$$
$$= \$1{,}149.92$$

We've now considered three information alternatives: (1) no further information; (2) a special cost study; and (3) a statistical analysis of past cost data. For each of these we have considered the net effects of benefits and costs on the expected payoff to the firm, with the result that the statistical cost study appears most desirable.

Of course this conclusion is not generalizable. By changing the costs, probabilities, or revenue we could change the optimal information system. (For example, see what happens if the revenues increase to $22,000.) As a result, we shall not find any general rules for managerial accounting: each new problem will have to be considered individually, and the same information system may have very different values for different decision makers. As a day-to-day example, consider the information source known as a weather forecast. The value of that information may be negligible for a person who lives and works in a commercial/residential complex. But a person who commutes from the suburbs to the city and then must walk half a mile from parking lot to office may go to some length to obtain a forecast of the day's weather.

TABLE 3.4 VALUES OF $\phi(s|y, \eta_2)^a$

	Reports		
States of nature	y_1 (low)	y_2 (medium)	y_3 (high)
s_1(low)	$\frac{(0.8)(0.3)}{(0.8)(0.3) + (0.1)(0.4)} = 0.857$	$\frac{(0.2)(0.3)}{(0.2)(0.3) + (0.8)(0.4) + (0.2)(0.3)} = 0.136$	0
s_2(medium)	$\frac{(0.1)(0.4)}{(0.8)(0.3) + (0.1)(0.4)} = 0.143$	$\frac{(0.8)(0.4)}{(0.2)(0.3) + (0.8)(0.4) + (0.2)(0.3)} = 0.728$	0.143
s_3(high)	0	0.136	0.857

[a]Based on Bayes' theorem: $\phi(s|y,\eta) = \phi(y|s,\eta)\phi(s)/\phi(y|\eta)$.

3.3 EFFECTS OF RISK AVERSION ON THE VALUE OF INFORMATION

One factor that influences the value of information is the decision maker's risk aversion. Moreover, the introduction of risk aversion makes it more difficult to calculate the value of information directly. To illustrate this point, we'll use the special widget example with the utility function of $[1500 + x(a,s)]^{1/2}$ that was used in Chapter 2. In this case, the optimal decision was to accept the order with a resulting expected utility of 46.83.

If we consider the perfect information system η_1, the decision policy for each cost report y will be the same as the risk-neutral case. But to illustrate the effect of risk aversion, assume that the cost of η_1 is \$305.

Signal, y	Probability of signal	Utility if accept	Utility if reject	$a^*(y,\eta_1)$
Low	0.3	$(1{,}500 + 3{,}000 - 305)^{1/2} = \underline{64.77}$	$(1{,}500 - 305)^{1/2} = 34.57$	Accept
Medium	0.4	$(1{,}500 + 1{,}000 - 305)^{1/2} = \underline{46.85}$	$= 34.57$	Accept
High	0.3	$(1{,}500 - 1{,}000 - 305)^{1/2} = 13.96$	$\underline{34.57}$	Reject

$$E[U|\eta_1] = (64.77)(0.3) + (46.85)(0.4) + (34.57)(0.3) = 48.54$$

The conclusion is that even though the information costs more than \$300, the decision maker's expected utility is higher with the information than it is without the information (48.54 versus 46.83). In this case, the manager's risk aversion has made the information more valuable than it was when he or she was risk-neutral, but this result is not a general one. Risk aversion can make information less valuable.[2]

There is no way to calculate directly the maximum amount that the decision maker would be willing to pay for the information system. However, we could repeat the analysis above for different costs (\$310, \$315, etc.) until the expected utility *with* the information equaled the expected utility of 46.83 that can be achieved without the information. (Try a few costs. You'll find that the information is worth more than \$450 to the decision maker.)

3.4 ILLUSTRATION

The Acme Co. plant had been operating at capacity until recently, when a customer firm was purchased by a bigger firm which had its own suppliers. As a result, about 200 labor hours of capacity became available, and the plant manager could use that available

[2]For an analysis, see Hilton (1981).

capacity to produce more of one of his three existing products, A, B, or C. Some information on the products is presented below.

Per-unit data	Product A	Product B	Product C
Selling price	$60	$90	$130
Material cost	$13	$16	$ 24
Labor cost	$12	$24	$ 30
Labor hours	2	4	5
Machine hours	3	2	5

The onc additional cost that the plant manager wants to consider is the variable overhead costs of the various products. But there is some uncertainty as to how these costs are affected by changing labor hours (LH) and machine hours (MH). Since LH and MH have tended to vary together in the recent past, it is difficult to separate the effects of each. (We'll return to this problem in Chapter 6.) The plant manager is willing to assume that there are two possibilities: either variable overhead is \$6(LH) + 4(MH), or it is \$4(LH) + 6(MH). However, the former possibility is twice as likely as the latter.

In the absence of further information, which product should be produced? How much would it be worth to find out exactly how overhead costs behave?

Solution We can use the decision-theoretic framework to attempt to answer the questions facing the plant manager. The first step is to solve the decision under the uncertainty he currently faces.

Actions

$$\begin{aligned} a_1&: \text{ Expand product A by } (200/2) = 100 \text{ units} \\ a_2&: \text{ Expand product B by 50 units} \\ a_3&: \text{ Expand product C by 40 units} \end{aligned} \tag{3.12}$$

States

$$\begin{aligned} s_1&: \text{ Variable overhead is \$6(LH) + 4(MH)} \\ s_2&: \text{ Variable overhead is \$4(LH) + 6(MH)} \end{aligned} \tag{3.13}$$

Probabilities

$$\begin{aligned} &\phi(s_1) = 2\phi(s_2) \\ &\phi(s_1) + \phi(s_2) = 1 \text{ (probability law)} \\ &\rightarrow \phi(s_1) = 2/3; \qquad \phi(s_2) = 1/3 \end{aligned} \tag{3.14}$$

Payoffs (incremental profit)

	States	
Actions	s_1	s_2
a_1	100(60 − 13 − 12 − 24) = \$1,100	100(60 − 13 − 12 − 26) = \$900
a_2	50(90 − 16 − 24 − 32) = \$900	50(90 − 16 − 24 − 28) = \$1,100
a_3	40(130 − 24 − 30 − 50) = \$1,040	40(130 − 24 − 30 − 50) = \$1,040

If we can presume that the plant manager wants to maximize the expected incremental profit, then we can compare the alternative actions.

$$
\begin{aligned}
E[\text{payoff}|a_1] &= (2/3)(1{,}100) + (1/3)(900) = \$1{,}033.33 \\
E[\text{payoff}|a_2] &= (2/3)(900) + (1/3)(1{,}100) = \$966.67 \\
E[\text{payoff}|a_3] &= (2/3)(1{,}040) + (1/3)(1{,}040) = \$1{,}040.00
\end{aligned} \tag{3.15}
$$

It appears that, in the absence of additional information about variable overhead costs, we would predict that the plant manager would choose to expand product C by 40 units, with an expected incremental profit of $1,040.

What if a special cost study would tell exactly how the variable overhead costs behave? We could describe this information system in the following way.

Signals

$$
\begin{aligned}
y_1&: \text{``Variable overhead is \$6(LH) + 4(MH)''} \\
y_2&: \text{``Variable overhead is \$4(LH) + 6(MH)''}
\end{aligned} \tag{3.16}
$$

Signal Probabilities

$$
\begin{aligned}
\phi(y_1|s_1) &= 1 \\
\phi(y_2|s_2) &= 0 \\
\phi(y_1|s_2) &= 0 \\
\phi(y_2|s_2) &= 1 \\
\phi(y_1) &= \phi(y_1|s_1)\phi(s_1) + \phi(y_1|s_2)\phi(s_2) \\
&= 1(2/3) + 0(1/3) = 2/3 \\
\phi(y_2) &= \phi(y_2|s_1)\phi(s_1) + \phi(y_2|s_2)\phi(s_2) \\
&= 0(2/3) + 1(1/3) = 1/3
\end{aligned} \tag{3.17}
$$

Revised Probabilities

$$
\begin{aligned}
\phi(s_1|y_1) &= \frac{\phi(y_1|s_1)\phi(s_1)}{\phi(y_1)} = \frac{1(2/3)}{2/3} = 1 \\
\phi(s_2|y_2) &= \frac{\phi(y_2|s_2)\phi(s_2)}{\phi(y_2)} = \frac{1(1/3)}{1/3} = 1 \\
\phi(s_2|y_1) &= \phi(s_1|y_2) = 0
\end{aligned} \tag{3.18}
$$

Revised Decisions

Signal, y	Probability	Expected payoff a_1	a_2	a_3	$a^*(y)$
y_1	2/3	1,100	900	1,040	a_1
y_2	1/3	900	1,100	1,040	a_2

We can see that if the special cost study reports that the variable overhead cost relationship is 6(LH) + 4(MH), the manager will choose a_1 and expand product A with resulting incremental profit $1,100. If the report tells him that the variable overhead is

4(LH) + 6(MH), he will produce more of product B, with an incremental profit of \$1,100. The expected payoff is

$$\begin{aligned} &E[\text{payoff} \mid \text{special cost study}] \\ &\quad = E[\text{payoff}|y_1, a^*(y_1)]\phi(y_1) + E[\text{payoff}|y_2, a^*(y_2)]\phi(y_2) \\ &\quad = \$1{,}100(2/3) + \$1{,}100(1/3) = \$1{,}100 \end{aligned} \tag{3.19}$$

So, if the special cost study is performed, the incremental profit will be \$1,100. Since an expected incremental profit of \$1,040 could be achieved without the study, the manager would pay no more than \$60 (1,100 − 1,040) for the study. (The EVPI is \$60.)

3.5 USING PAST DATA TO ESTIMATE EVPI

When a manager makes a large number of similar decisions, and where sufficient feedback exists, it may be desirable to explore ways of empirically estimating the EVPI. Suppose the manager faces a decision situation in which he or she chooses action a, state s then occurs, and the outcome realized is $x(a,s)$. However, if the manager had known that s was going to occur, he or she would have chosen $\overline{a}$, with a resulting outcome of $x(\overline{a},s)$. Then the opportunity loss (from not knowing s ahead of time) is $x(\overline{a},s) - x(a,s)$. In the case where $a = \overline{a}$, the opportunity loss is zero, because he or she made the right decision based on hindsight. If we can observe these variables in n situations, then we can calculate the average opportunity loss (AOL) as an estimate of the EVPI.

$$\text{AOL} = \frac{1}{n}\sum_{i=1}^{n} [x(\overline{a}_i, s_i) - x(a_i, s_i)] \tag{3.20}$$

Of course, there are limits to the usefulness of this approach. The smaller the number of situations (n), the less reliable the estimation of the EVPI; if future decision situations will differ significantly from those in the past, the estimate would not be useful in information planning; and, if the decision maker is risk-averse, the estimate will not reflect the value of the information.

Perhaps the greatest limitation in many situations is the difficulty in obtaining complete feedback information. In some cases, the choice of action may make it difficult or even impossible to determine which state actually occurs. For instance, suppose that the decision is whether to launch a new product and the uncertainty involves the costs of long production runs. If we decide to go ahead with the new product, then we will be able to find out which state occurs (i.e., what the costs are). But if the new product is not launched, there will be no production runs, no cost data, and therefore no measure of the profits (or losses) we *would* have made *had* we launched the product. Thus, we may be able to measure opportunity loss on errors of commission, but not on errors of omission. Therefore, this empirical approach to estimating the EVPI may help in some situations, but it has limitations that should be recognized.

3.6 A SEPARATE INFORMATION EVALUATOR

The decision-theoretic model described above has a number of strong points. It is internally consistent, it can describe a wide variety of situations, and it allows us to treat information as a commodity, comparing benefits with costs. However, the model is based on a single decision maker who chooses the information system and then receives the signal and chooses a course of action. In most organizations, a separate individual (e.g., the managerial accountant) plays the role of information evaluator.[3]

Separation of the information evaluator and decision maker roles creates greater complexity. We might assume that the information evaluator would choose the information system so as to maximize the decision maker's expected utility. Then the information evaluator would estimate the decision maker's utility function, prior probability beliefs, and so on. The choice of information system would proceed as we've described it above, using these estimates. If the estimates are accurate, then the information system choice would be similar to that which the decision maker would prefer.

There are a variety of difficult issues that could arise in this situation. For instance, suppose the information evaluator disagrees with the decision maker's prior beliefs. Then he or she might choose the information system so as to manipulate the decision maker's actions. More significantly, the information evaluator has his or her own payoffs that are affected by the information system. Going one step further, the decision maker could set the incentives for the information evaluator, so as to influence the information choice.

It should be clear that going from a one-person analysis to a two-person analysis can add a significant amount of complexity to the information planning problem. We will not pursue the issue further at this point, but Chapters 11–14 address information issues in organizations, and we will address similar problems at that point.

3.7 DESCRIPTIONS OF INFORMATION DECISIONS

In Chapter 2 we hypothesized a situation in which a manager used cost and competition data to make pricing decisions, and we had the opportunity to observe the decisions that were made by the manager. Suppose we wanted to know whether different types of cost information would yield different decisions. Instead of simply giving the manager a single, total cost estimate C_i, for product i, we could break it out by reporting raw material costs R_i, labor costs L_i, variable overhead costs V_i, and a fixed overhead allocation F_i. After observing the manager's decisions, the separate effect of each type of cost could be estimated. For instance, the decisions made could be those in Exhibit 3.1. If we try to estimate a relationship between price, total cost, and competitiveness, we find the following.[4] Both cost and competition appear to influence the manager's pricing decisions.

$$P_i = -15.7 + 1.17C_i - 0.125M_i \tag{3.21}$$

On the other hand, a relationship based on the disaggregated cost data yields

$$P_i = 1.5R_i + 1.5L_i + 1.0V_i + 0.0F_i - 0.25M_i \tag{3.22}$$

What interpretations could a managerial accountant make from these results? Rather than say that "the decision maker appears to use cost data in pricing decisions," we can be more specific. We might ask whether we need to report material and labor costs sepa-

[3]Demski and Feltham (1970).

[4]This equation does not fit the data exactly, but it comes about as close as possible with a linear model.

EXHIBIT 3.1
RECORD OF PAST DECISIONS

Product	Material ($)	Labor ($)	Variable overhead ($)	Fixed overhead ($)	Total	Measure of competitiveness	Price chosen
1	10	30	20	10	70	100	55
2	20	20	15	15	70	80	55
3	30	40	20	20	110	88	103
4	30	20	10	20	80	40	75
5	20	30	20	10	90	60	80

rately. Since they both have the same coefficient (1.5) in the equation above, it appears that we might simply report the total "prime cost" $R_i + L_i$ since it would have had no effect on the decisions. On the other hand, the estimated decision model indicates that it *does* matter whether we separate the costs or report a total cost, $C_i = R_i + L_i + V_i + F_i$. The fixed cost allocation appears to receive no weight in the decision maker's pricing decisions. Therefore the manager's decisions would be unaffected if we didn't bother to report the fixed cost allocation.

As a practical matter, the results of a study of a manager's decision making will not be so unambiguous. If the coefficients on R_i and L_i were 1.54 and 1.47, respectively, does this represent a significant difference, or can we still report $R_i + L_i$ with no loss? Is the coefficient of 1.0 on V_i significantly different from the coefficients on R_i and L_i? If so, then we might separate them in our cost reports. We will find measures of statistical significance that will answer these questions when we get to Chapter 6, but you should realize that statistical significance is not necessarily the same as economic significance.

The behavioral or empirical approach to describing information decisions can be a useful tool for the managerial accountant, but we should recognize its limitations. It can help us discover whether a manager uses an item of information and whether the manager attaches different weights to items that could be aggregated. But we have to be careful in interpreting the results of this analysis for a variety of reasons. As we've stated, this approach will not yield measures of economic significance, but there is also the potential problem that the decision maker's behavior may be more complex than we imagined. Suppose that the fixed cost allocation only becomes important when it exceeds $25/unit, but our decision making data does not include these cases. Then the conclusion that F_i is unimportant would be an incorrect one. In addition, there is no consideration of the *quality* of decisions made by the manager.

3.8 KEY QUESTIONS

While the decision-theoretic model of information choice is a fairly complete one, there can be little dispute that it is complex, rather difficult to understand, and often difficult to apply. But it does provide a benchmark for information decision making, and if we depart from it, we should do so knowingly.

The model does provide us with a set of key questions that we can use when doing an initial analysis of an accounting information problem. After these have been answered, it may not be necessary to conduct an extensive information analysis, but that will depend on how clear-cut the answers are.

What decisions are currently being made, and on what information are they based?

In what situations does the existing information system lead managers to make inappropriate decisions? How often do these situations occur? When they do occur, how serious are the consequences of the decisions?

How will the reports from the proposed information system differ from those of the current information system?

How will the proposed information system increase the effectiveness of the decisions made? If the optimal decision policy $a^*(y,\eta)$ doesn't depend on y, then the information has no value.

What is the incremental cost of the proposed information system?

These questions, and similar ones, can be very useful in making an initial assessment of an information problem. They help to cast the problem in our decision theory/information economics framework, and that can be an important step in finding solutions to accounting information problems.

PROBLEMS

3.1. Refer back to problem 2.1.

Required

A. What is the expected value of perfect information about the contract costs?

B. After looking at your analysis, Jay Crihfield points out that you have oversimplified the problem. "I'm not the only one that's bidding on a contract. What happens if a competitor bids $11,000 on the contract? What's the value of cost information?"

If there is another bid for $11,000, what is the expected value of perfect cost information?

3.2. Refer back to problem 2.3.

Required

A. What is the expected value of perfect information about Pute's skills?

B. What is the expected value of perfect information about both Pute's *and* Lunder's skills?

3.3. Refer back to problem 2.4. What is the expected value of perfect information about the pension costs per hour?

3.4. Refer to the illustration in Section 3.4 of Chapter 3. Suppose the plant manager could get a "quick cost study" for $20 that would give the following signal probabilities

$$\phi(y_1|s_1) = 0.75$$
$$\phi(y_2|s_1) = 0.25$$
$$\phi(y_1|s_2) = 0.25$$
$$\phi(y_2|s_2) = 0.75$$

Would this cost study be preferable to making the product choice with no further cost information?

3.5. Refer to the illustration in Section 3.4. Suppose the plant manager receives a bonus of $2,000 when his profits exceed $20,000, and his current profit level is $19,000 without expansion into product A, B, or C.

Required If the plant manager wants to maximize his expected bonus, what is the value of the special cost study?

3.6. As Michael Davidson considered the problem facing him, he wished he had better information on the costs of the proposed project. There were a number of technical problems to be resolved in designing the client's information system, so the best that his staff could do was the probability distribution of costs listed below.

Cost	Probability
$100,000	1/6
$110,000	1/3
$120,000	1/3
$130,000	1/6

Davidson had to present the client with a bid by the end of next week.

Required

A. What is the EVPI about the project costs if

1. the client will accept any price up to $125,000?
2. the client will accept any price up to $115,000?
3. the client will accept any price up to $105,000?

B. What does this analysis tell you about the effect of margin on EVPI?

3.7. Refer to the illustration in Section 3.4. Suppose that the three products, A, B, and C had unit selling prices of $80, $130, and $180, respectively.

Required Is the EVPI greater or less than the $60 found in the illustration? Why?

3.8. The Chandler Electronics Company has been approached by a large manufacturer of electronic equipment to see if it would be interested in supplying 500,000 integrated circuit components in the next six months. The potential customer has offered to pay $625,000 for the components. However, the manufacturing office at Chandler is not sure how fast the employees will be able to ''get down the learning curve'' and reduce production costs to a minimum. The following probabilistic forecast was made.

Cost of filling the order	Probability
$500,000	1/6
$550,000	1/3
$600,000	1/3
$650,000	1/6

Required

A. Should the order be accepted?

B. What is the EVPI on the cost of the order?

C. Suppose that the customer had offered to pay Chandler a fixed fee of $58,333 and to reimburse all costs up to $600,000. What would be the EVPI (to Chandler) on the costs of filling the order?

3.9. The Hapless Chemical Company uses a chemical in one of its processes that is very difficult to transport and store. Every delivery of the chemical costs $500 for special equipment and labor, and once delivered the chemical deteriorates and becomes unusable after 5 days. On Friday of each week, the production supervisor forecasts the number of gallons that will be needed the next week, and the purchasing manager phones in an order for this amount to be delivered early Monday morning. Quantities delivered on Monday remain usable until Friday, but over the weekend the entire processing system is emptied and cleaned. Any unused material is discarded during this cleaning process. During the week additional material can be ordered but the $500 delivery charge will be incurred. The chemical itself is not very expensive—$5/gal—but it is crucial to the process in which it is used. Data from the previous 10-week period appear below.

Week	Quantity forecast and ordered (gals)	Quantity needed in production (gals)
1	500	525
2	450	475
3	600	550
4	550	525
5	500	475
6	500	550
7	550	500
8	450	400
9	400	425
10	600	650

Required

A. What is the *average opportunity loss* (AOL) from not knowing the amount that would be needed in production?

B. How does this AOL relate to the EVPI on the production needs for the following week? Are they identical?

3.10. "We have a new product that a number of people in the organization are anxious to launch. I can see that there is a good possibility that it will be more profitable than our present products, but we haven't worked out all the production bugs, and the degree of market acceptance is by no means certain. Let's say that the incremental production costs might be $25,000, $30,000, $35,000, or $40,000, all with equal probability (1/4). On the revenue side, it could be $50,000 (with probability 1/2) or $55,000 (with probability 1/2). Obviously, these are simplified numbers, but they're the best I can do right now."

"As things stand, I don't feel comfortable going ahead with the product without more information—either a cost study or a marketing study or both. Each study would cost about $2,000, but let's say it would resolve the uncertainty in the area which it investigated."

"What I'd like to know is which study I should do—marketing or cost? Or maybe I should do both. Or maybe get one and then perhaps get the other. This project isn't a big part of our business, so don't worry about risk. Oh, by the way, if we don't go ahead with this project, we would be able to use the production capacity to produce our existing products with a contribution margin of about $20,000."

Required Analyze the situation described above and write a recommendation.

3.11. Refer to problem 2.10.

Required

A. Suppose that Jerry Beam could perfectly forecast the demand for Christmas wreaths. How much would that forecasting ability be worth if he is risk-neutral as in problem 2.10(A)? How much would it be worth if he is risk-averse as in problem 2.10(B)?

B. How would the value of the information change if there were a third course of action? Wreaths could be ordered now at a cost of $5, and additional wreaths costing $8 could be ordered at the beginning of December when all the orders are in.

3.12. Refer to the decision problem you described in Problem 2.9.

Required

A. Describe potential sources of information that might affect the uncertainty in the decision problem.

B. Compare these sources on the informational attributes of content, accuracy, timeliness, and cost.

3.13. The variable overhead spending variances for seven different departments are listed below for the current month and the same month a year ago. It costs approximately $500 to investigate and determine the cause of a variance.

Budget	April 1986	April 1985
$40,000	$3,000 Unfavorable	$1,000 Unfavorable
20,000	3,000 Unfavorable	2,000 Favorable
30,000	3,000 Favorable	500 Unfavorable
60,000	5,000 Unfavorable	3,500 Unfavorable
70,000	5,000 Favorable	500 Unfavorable
45,000	3,200 Unfavorable	1,000 Favorable
55,000	3,000 Favorable	5,000 Favorable

Required

A. For each of the variances above, determine whether you would conduct an investigation based on the information available.

B. Did you use the variance from last year in making the investigation decision?

C. Look at the decisions made by another person. Can you determine how that person used the last year's variance? Based on your observation, would that person's decisions be altered if you stopped reporting last year's variances? Would the decisions be altered if the budget amounts were not reported?

3.14. Megan Moulden is in charge of raw materials purchasing for a manufacturing operation. One of her suppliers has offered a two-month supply of a basic raw material for $10 per unit. The plant needs 10,000 units for *each* of the next two months, and the usual procedure would be for Moulden to purchase a one-month supply at the start of each month. If a two-month supply is purchased, the inventory holding costs would increase from \$2,000 to \$3,000 for the first month. If Moulden purchases just one month's supply, she will have to make another purchase of 10,000 units at the start of the second month. However, the price per unit at that time is uncertain and could be \$9, \$10, or \$11, with equal probability.

Required

A. If Megan Moulden wants to minimize the expected cost of raw materials and holding inventory for the next two months, what is the EVPI about next period's price per unit?

B. Assume that Moulden's utility for different cost outcomes over the two months can be described by the following function.

$$U(\text{material and holding cost}) = (250{,}000 - \text{material cost} - \text{holding cost})^{1/2}$$

What is the most that Moulden would pay for perfect information about next month's price per unit?

C. Same as **B**, but with the following utility function:

$$U(\text{material and holding cost}) = \log_e(250{,}000 - \text{material cost} - \text{holding cost})$$

REFERENCES

Demski, J., and G. Feltham. "Forecast Evaluation," *Accounting Review*. July 1972.

Feltham, G. "The Value of Information," *Accounting Review*. October 1968.

Feltham, G. "Cost Aggregation: An Information Economic Analysis," *Journal of Accounting Research*. Spring 1977.

Feltham, G., and J. Demski. "The Use of Models in Information Evaluation," *Accounting Review*. October 1970.

Hilton, R. "Integrating Normative and Descriptive Theories of Information Processing," *Journal of Accounting Research*. Autumn 1980.

Hilton, R. "The Determinants of Information Value: Synthesizing Some General Results," *Management Science*. January 1981.

Mock, T. "The Value of Budget Information," *Accounting Review*. July 1973.

Mock, T., and M. Vasarehlyi. "A Synthesis of the Information Economics and Lens Models," *Journal of Accounting Research*. Autumn 1978.

Chapter 4

Short-Term Planning

To this point, we have discussed the types of information decisions that managerial accountants make, and examined frameworks for making those decisions. For the remainder of this book we will be somewhat more specific about the decision setting and/or types of accounting decisions to be made. In general, we will proceed from simpler situations to more complex ones. In this chapter, we will explore a very simple situation where a single manager makes a single decision that affects a single period. As we progress, this decision setting will expand to multiple decisions, multiple periods, and finally to multiperson situations involving performance measurement, budgeting, and so on.

The basic cost information issue in short-term planning involves the identification of those costs that are fixed with respect to changes in output and those that vary with output. This distinction will continue to have importance in a variety of decision settings, as will be seen in later chapters. (The cost estimation methods discussed in the following two chapters will also apply in these later situations.) Of course, the distinction between fixed and variable costs depends on a variety of factors, including the time horizon under consideration. In the very short run, most costs are fixed, while almost all costs are variable in the very long run. Our definition of *short-term planning* is that some costs (usually materials, direct labor, and some overhead) will be variable, while some overhead costs will be fixed. This definition can be easily altered to different time horizons by altering the fixed/variable classification.

4.1 AN ECONOMIC ANALYSIS

The short-term planning decisions we will focus on for the moment are decisions on the level of *activity*[1] that the organization undertakes. More specifically, we want to answer

[1]Usually, the term "level of activity" will refer to the number of units produced. However, where the units are not homogeneous (e.g., in a job shop operation) the level of activity may be measured by direct labor hours, raw material usage, etc.

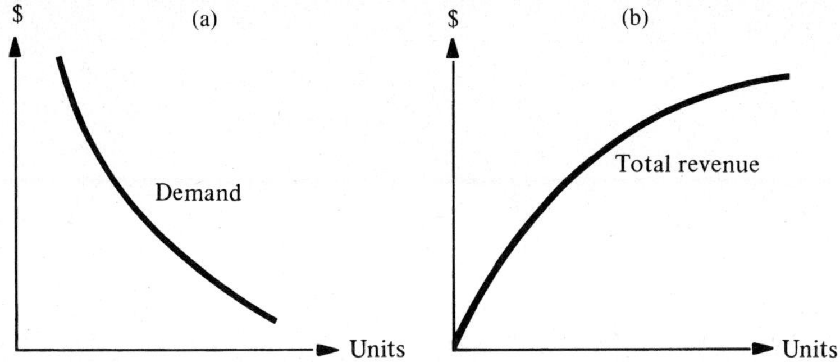

Figure 4.1

questions such as, "How much should I produce?" or "What price should I charge?" These same questions may take other forms, such as, "Should I accept that special order to utilize my spare capacity?", but the issues involved are essentially the same.

These questions have been examined by economists for a long time, and a variety of models have been developed to answer them. One basic approach is to assume that the firm's objective is profit maximization, and that the revenue and cost curves are known. For instance, in Figure 4.1a, we see a demand function where the amount demanded (sold) depends on the price charged. This relationship produces a total revenue relationship as seen in Figure 4.1b, where the sale of additional units requires a lowering of the price and, eventually, even a reduction in total revenues. The shape of these curves depends on the consumers' preferences for the product and on the competition from other producers. (We will explore a different competitive situation in the next section.) In addition to the revenue considerations, the company also incurs the costs of production. In the short run the company has a given production facility that cannot be changed. The costs of these facilities are fixed with respect to the number of units produced, and are depicted in Figure 4.2a. In addition, production requires materials, labor, power, etc., and these costs will increase as production increases, perhaps as shown in Figure 4.2b. Combining these to obtain total costs, the result is seen in Figure 4.2c.

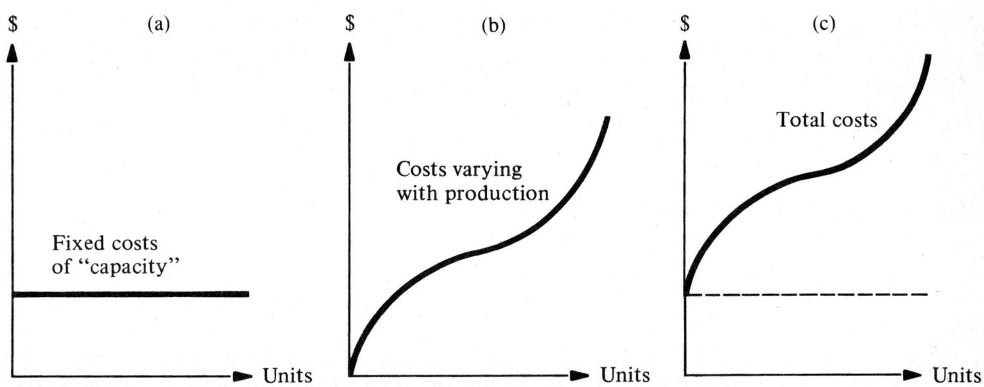

Figure 4.2

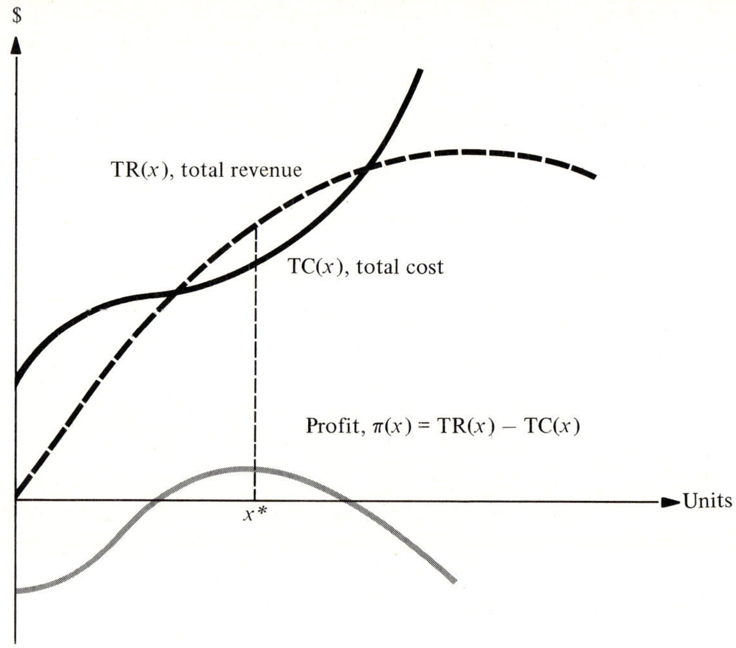

Figure 4.3

If Figures 4.1b and 4.2c are combined, it is possible to determine which level of production produce profits (revenues in excess of costs), and which level of production produces the highest profit. In Figure 4.3, we can see that there are two breakeven points where revenue equals cost, and we can identify the level of production x^*, where profits are maximized (or perhaps where losses are minimized). This graphical analysis leads to the familiar result that profits are maximized at the point where marginal revenue equals marginal cost.[2]

There are a number of simplifying assumptions that have been made in this analysis, but before we begin to examine them in more detail, we turn to a yet more simple version which is often applied in practice.

4.2 BASIC COST–VOLUME–PROFIT ANALYSIS

Cost–volume–profit (CVP) analysis highlights the relationship between the firm's volume of activity and its profit. In contrast to the graphs in the previous section, CVP analysis usually assumes that the revenue and cost relationships are *linear*. It is assumed implicitly that the market for the firm's product is such that the firm can sell as much as it wishes at a price determined in the market. If the price per unit is p and the number of units produced is x, the total revenues are px. (See Figure 4.4a.) A similar assumption is made

[2] $\max_x\{\text{profit}\} \leftrightarrow \max_x\{\text{revenue} - \text{cost}\} \leftrightarrow \max_x[\text{TR}(x) - \text{TC}(x)]$

Using calculus, this maximization occurs when the derivative equals zero. $\text{TR}'(x) - \text{TC}'(x) = 0$ or $\text{TR}'(x) = \text{TC}'(x)$, or marginal revenue = marginal cost.

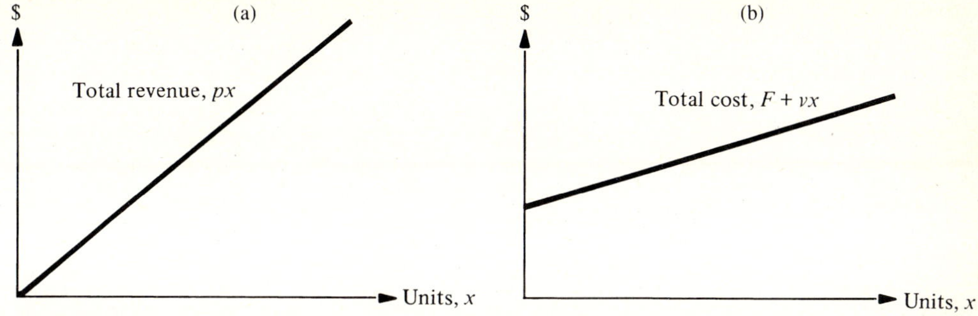

Figure 4.4

about the variable costs of production: Each unit produced has exactly the same variable cost v, as all other units, yielding a total cost of $F + vx$. (See Figure 4.4b.)

The combination of these two curves into profit as a function of volume leads to the familiar profit–volume curve in Figure 4.5. In addition, notions such as *breakeven volume* $F/(p - v)$ and *breakeven sales* $pF/(p - v)$ can be found. The *contribution margin* $(p - v)x$ and the *unit contribution margin* $(p - v)$ can be used to determine the marginal impact of an additional unit of output.

In comparing Figure 4.5 with Figure 4.3, it is evident that CVP analysis will not directly answer the question, "How much should I produce?" The profits in Figure 4.5 always increase with increased output, so it appears that production should always be kept at the maximum. The advantage of this *incremental approach* or *contribution approach* is its improvement over the *absorption cost* system, which is used for financial reporting to shareholders and other outsiders. The absorption cost approach used in financial accounting unitizes the fixed cost component and applies this portion of the costs in a manner similar to a variable cost. If $\bar{x}$ is the budgeted output, then the full cost assigned to each unit is $F/\bar{x} + v$, and the *gross margin* attributed to a unit of output will be $(p - v - F/\bar{x})$. This amount is less than the unit contribution margin. The gross margin is depicted in Figure 4.6, where it is contrasted with the profit curve from Figure 4.5.

It should be clear that if the contribution margin depicts the actual impact of output on the firm, a manager who uses gross margin information will tend to underestimate

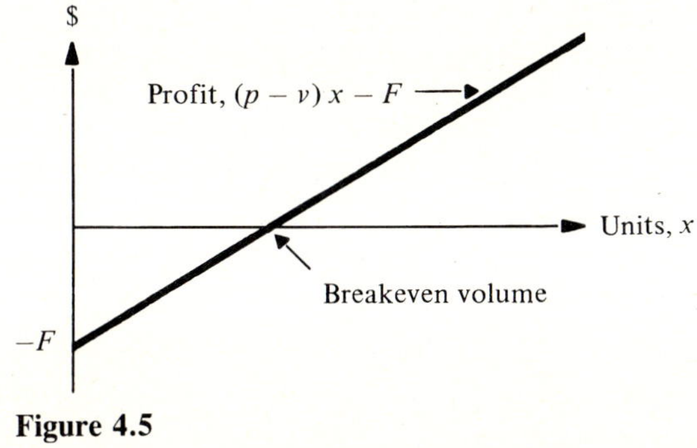

Figure 4.5

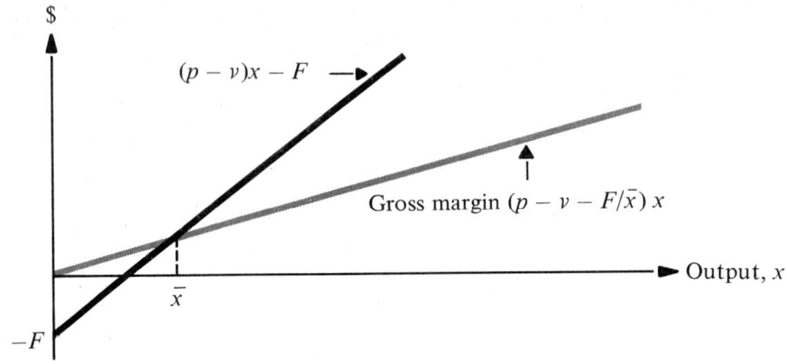

Figure 4.6

the incremental impact of a unit of production on the firm's profits (because $p - v$ is greater than $p - v - F/\bar{x}$). For instance, if a customer were to offer to purchase 100 additional units at a reduced price p', it is possible that the contribution margin $(p' - v)$ would be positive, while the gross margin $(p' - v - F/\bar{x})$ would be negative. Thus, a gross margin manager could reject an offer that would increase the company's profits. Of course, the manager may try to make some estimate of the contribution margin, but that may be difficult to do if he or she only has gross margin information.

4.3 LIMITATIONS OF CVP ANALYSIS

While CVP analysis represents an improvement over the use of gross margins in evaluating alternative courses of action, there are still a number of limitations that need to be noted. For instance, the analysis assumes that all units produced are sold, with no inventory carried forward.

A further assumption involves the linearity of the revenue and cost curves. (See Figures 4.4 and 4.5). On the revenue side, this assumes a perfectly competitive market, where all output can be sold at a known unit price p. On the cost side, linearity implies that there are no economies or diseconomies of scale in production given the level of fixed (capacity) costs. Either of these assumptions may be violated for a firm's situation, and could lead to alternative curves as depicted in Figure 4.3. Whether the linearity assumption is warranted for costs is an issue that we will address in more detail in the chapters on cost estimation. Of course, we know that costs do not behave in a precisely linear fashion, but the essential issue is whether the linearity assumption is a costly one, and we shall return to this matter later in this chapter.

Finally, traditional CVP analysis assumes that the manager knows what the variable cost per unit will be. That is, there is no uncertainty regarding the cost structure and the impact of a decision on the firm's costs. This assumption may be valid in some situations, but there are many others where it will not hold. When the manager faces uncertainty in the costs of producing a unit of product or service, this uncertainty can affect the decisions that are made and the value of information about those costs.

4.4 CVP UNDER UNCERTAINTY

The first limitation that we will deal with is the assumption of certain costs. In most operations, whether manufacturing or service, there are some costs that are clearly fixed or clearly variable. But there may be many other costs that are difficult to classify. Therefore, it is likely that the manager will not be absolutely certain how costs will change with a change in the level of activity.

Actually, the example that was used to illustrate the decision-theoretic approach in Chapters 2 and 3 was an accept/reject form of short-term decision making. The *actions* represented different levels of output, and the *states* reflected the uncertainty in the incremental costs that would be incurred if output was increased. The *payoffs* were the levels of incremental profit that would arise from the possible output/cost combinations. If the manager can assign probabilities to the different possible incremental costs, then the expected profit for each level of output can be calculated, and (assuming the manager is risk-neutral) the best level of output can be found. But rather than repeat another example such as that in Chapters 2 and 3, we will look at a situation where the manager must choose the price and quantity jointly.

Suppose that a firm faces a demand for its product such as that in Figure 4.7a. The amount sold (over the time period under consideration) decreases as the price increases. The total revenue that results from a particular price–quantity combination is derived by simply multiplying the price by the quantity, yielding the curve in Figure 4.7b. The (unavoidable) fixed costs of production are known to be \$450 for the period of time under consideration, but the variable cost per unit produced is not certain. The most optimistic estimate is \$25 per unit, and the most pessimistic is \$35 per unit. Each of these possibilities has about 1/4 chance of occurring, according to the manager. The remaining, and most likely, possibility is that costs will turn out to be \$30 per unit. This cost uncertainty may be due to the possibility of purchasing problems, unforeseen production problems, unknown learning effects, or other factors. Additionally, the uncertainty may result from the manager's receiving estimates based on absorption costing and having to make some "guesstimates" of variable costs. The actions available to the manager are the levels of output x (and price p). We will explore five different alternatives and combine them with the states (variable costs) to get the payoff table shown in Table 4.1. The best price–quantity combination depends on the variable cost, but the variable

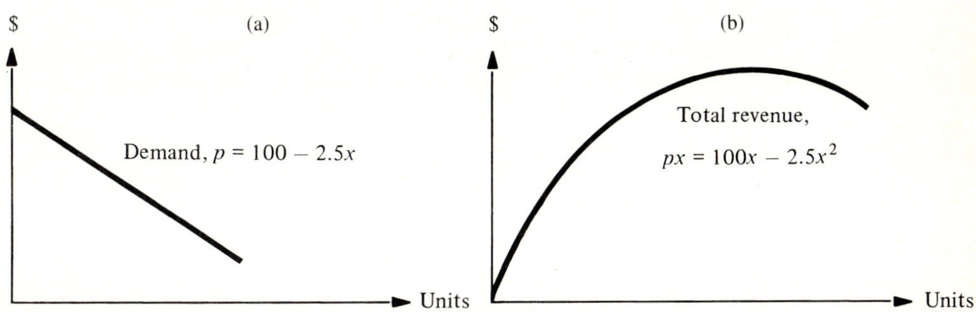

Figure 4.7

TABLE 4.1 EVALUATION OF PRICE–QUANTITY LEVELS[a]

Price; quantity (p;x)	Variable cost, v			Expected profit
	25	30	35	
\$70.00;12	\$90.00	\$30.00	(\$30.00)	\$30.00
\$67.50;13	102.50	37.50	(27.50)	37.50
\$65.00;14	110.00	40.00	(30.00)	40.00
\$62.50;15	112.50	37.50	(37.50)	37.50
\$60.00;16	110.00	30.00	(50.00)	30.00
Probability	1/4	1/2	1/4	

[a]Payoff = revenue − cost = $px - 450 - vx = 100x - 2.5x^2 - 450 - vx$.

cost is uncertain. Therefore, the decision might be based on the expected profit which indicates that $p = \$65.00$ and $x = 14$ is the best combination.

One could also explore the value of information to resolve the cost uncertainty. If the cost turned out to be \$25, we would produce fifteen units and achieve a profit of \$112.50. If costs were \$30 and \$35, we would produce fourteen and thirteen units, respectively, and achieve profits of \$40.00 and (\$27.50), respectively.

$$\begin{aligned} &E[\text{payoff} \mid \text{perfect information}] \\ &\quad = 1/4(112.50) + 1/2(40.00) + 1/4(-27.50) \\ &\quad = 41.25. \end{aligned} \tag{4.1}$$

Therefore, the value that the manager would attach to resolving the cost uncertainty is only \$41.25 − \$40.00 = \$1.25. In other words, further information about variable costs isn't worth much in this situation: decision making would be improved, but the incremental payoff is small. Thus, we might choose to leave the information system as it is, instead of incurring costs to change it. This conclusion should not be surprising, since the best managerial accounting system will vary from situation to situation. In fact, this result highlights the importance of doing the information budgeting described in Chapter 3.

4.5 RISK AND MEASURES OF RISK

The analysis of the short-term planning problem in the previous section has been based on the assumption that the manager was risk-neutral. (Refer back to Figure 2.1.) A risk-neutral manager would rank the \$70 price and the \$60 price alternatives in Table 4.1 as equivalent. Both have an expected payoff of \$30. But we can see that the range of outcomes is larger for the \$60 price than for the \$70 price, and hence this could be considered the more risky alternative. In most situations, decision makers tend to be risk-averse (Figure 2.1) and to choose the alternative with lower risk. In other words, the \$70 price alternative would be ranked more highly than the \$60 alternative, even though they have the same expected payoff.

The most direct way to incorporate the manager's risk attitudes into the short-term planning situation would be to modify Table 4.1 so that the profit numbers in the table

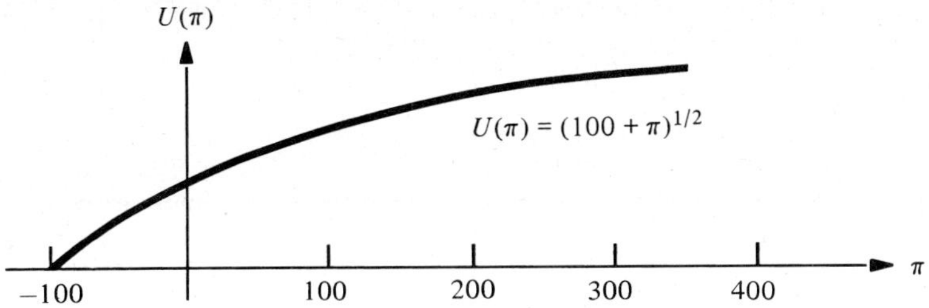

Figure 4.8

are replaced by the utility of the profit numbers. Of course, this requires that the utility or preference function can be approximated, and for this example we assume that the manager's utility of profit π is reflected in the function $(100 + \pi)^{1/2}$ (see Figure 4.8).

This preference function can be incorporated into our pricing problem as in Table 4.2. Before making the calculations we know that the \$62.50 price alternative will not be more attractive than \$65.00, because it lowers the expected payoff and increases risk at the same time. But it might be possible for the \$67.50 alternative to be more attractive, since it reduces the risk somewhat. In fact, Table 4.2 shows us that the \$65.00 price is still the preferred alternative, since it has the highest expected utility. (Of course, this conclusion depends on the risk preference that we have assumed. What happens if the manager's preferences are reflected in $U(\pi) = (30 + \pi)^{1/2}$? You should be able to verify that the \$67.50 price will be preferred to the \$65.00 price.)

This utility analysis is the most complete way to incorporate risks and uncertainties into the analysis of short-term decision alternatives. But we can also see that it is a very individualistic analysis, because we have incorporated the preferences of a particular manager and have applied those preferences to each combination of action and state. An alternative approach to this situation would be to try to formulate some measures that convey the uncertainties of the situation and the risks of different alternatives, without reference to the manager's specific preferences. In essence, we might try to separate *risk measurement* from *risk attitude*. This separation is not always totally successful, but it is worth exploring.

Although our concern is with profits, we will begin by analyzing the source of the uncertainty—variable costs v. We might try to describe the cost uncertainty in a variety

TABLE 4.2 REVISED EVALUATION OF PRICE–QUANTITY LEVELS[a]

Price; quantity (p;x)	Variable cost, v: 25	30	35	Expected utility
\$70.00; 12	13.784	11.402	8.367	11.239
\$67.50; 13	14.230	11.726	8.515	11.549
\$65.00; 14	14.491	11.832	8.367	11.631
\$62.50; 15	14.577	11.726	7.906	11.484
\$60.00; 16	14.491	11.402	7.071	11.091
Probability	1/4	1/2	1/4	

[a]Utility of payoff $= (100 + \text{revenue} - \text{cost})^{1/2} = (100 + px - 450 - vx)^{1/2}$.

of ways. "What is the *expected value* of the cost?" We have answered this question before, in Chapter 2. If there are n different possible values of $v - v_1, \ldots, v_n$, and each has a probability $\phi_1, \ldots, \phi_n$ of occurring, the expected value is

$$E[v] = v_1\phi_1 + v_2\phi_2 + \cdots + v_n\phi_n$$

$$= \sum_{i=1}^{n} v_i\phi_i \qquad (4.2)$$

$$E[v] = 25(1/4) + 30(1/2) + 35(1/4) = \$30$$

In a sense, this means that the *weighted average* variable cost is \$30. Another question is, "How large is the uncertainty?" We might answer this question by calculating the *range* of possible outcomes. In our example, the range is 35 − 25, or 10, but this amount does not reflect the probabilities assigned to the different outcomes. Two common statistical measures of uncertainty are the *variance* and the *standard deviation*. In calculating the variance $\sigma^2[v]$, we measure the difference between each possible outcome v_i and the expected value $E[v]$, square this difference $(v_i - E[v])^2$ so that positive and negative differentials don't cancel each other out, then weight this amount by the probability of v_i occurring, ϕ_i.

$$\sigma^2[v] = (v_1 - E[v])^2\phi_1 + \cdots + (v_n - E[v])^2\phi_n$$

$$= \sum_{i=1}^{n} (v_i - E[v])^2\phi_i \qquad (4.3)$$

$$\sigma^2[v] = (25 - 30)^2(1/4) + (30 - 30)^2(1/2) + (35 - 30)^2(1/4)$$

$$= 12.5$$

The standard deviation $\sigma[v]$ is simply the square root of the variance. In the example, $\sigma[v] = (12.5)^{1/2} = 3.536$.

There are other measures of risk that might be used, but before examining them, we can translate cost risk into profit risk and see how these are affected by the activity level decision. In other words, we translate $E[v]$ and $\sigma[v]$ into information about profit risk such as $E[\pi]$ and $\sigma[\pi]$, using the following relationships.[3]

$$\pi = px - F - vx$$
$$E[\pi] = px - F - E[v]x = (p - E[v])x - F \qquad (4.4)$$
$$\sigma[\pi] = x\sigma[v]; \qquad \sigma^2[\pi] = x^2\sigma^2[v]$$

These relationships suggest that the effect of volume on expected profit is essentially the same as in Figures 4.3 and 4.5, depending on the competitiveness of the market for the firm's product. However, we can see that risk, as measured by the standard deviation and variance, increases as the volume of production increases. (See Figure 4.9.) We can also see this in our example. For each price–quantity combination, we can

[3]More generally, if p and F are also uncertain (but independent of v and each other), the formulas would be

$$E[\pi] = (E[p] - E[v])x - E[F]$$
$$\sigma^2[\pi] = x^2(\sigma^2[p] + \sigma^2[v]) + \sigma^2[F]$$
$$\sigma[\pi] = (\sigma^2[\pi])^{1/2}$$

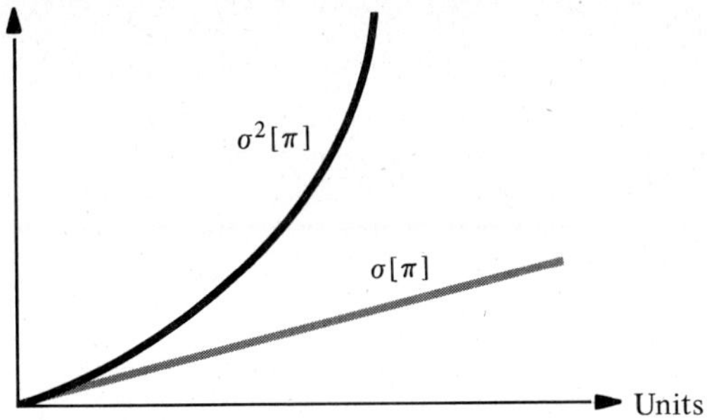

Figure 4.9

now calculate the standard deviation of profit in addition to the expected profit. This could yield a summary such as that in Table 4.3 where the measures of expected profit and risk are provided for each alternative. The exact tradeoffs would then have to be made by the manager, for without knowing his or her preferences, we can go no further.

4.6 OTHER MEASURES OF RISK

While the variance and standard deviation are common measures of the degree of uncertainty, there are other risk measures that may be more meaningful to a manager. For instance, if the organization is short of cash and the manager wishes to minimize the risk of not breaking even, then the appropriate risk measure might be the probability of a profit less than zero. The manager may weigh this risk against expected profit, and, in the extreme, could choose the alternative that minimizes the probability of not breaking even. As we can see from Table 4.1, the probability of not breaking even is equal to 1/4 for each of the alternative courses of action.

An alternative to this may occur when a manager has been given a profit target, say π_T, and his or her performance will be judged as bad if profits fall short of the target, and good if profits exceed the target. In this case the manager's preference is induced by the evaluation system and would look like that in Figure 4.10. As a result, the manager's objective would be to maximize the likelihood of a good evaluation, and to

TABLE 4.3 EXPECTED PROFIT AND STANDARD DEVIATION FOR PRICE–QUANTITY LEVELS

Price; quantity (p; x)	Expected profit[a]	Standard deviation of profit[b]
$70.00; 12	$30.00	42.43
$67.50; 13	$37.50	45.96
$65.00; 14	$40.00	49.50
$62.50; 15	$37.50	53.03
$60.00; 16	$30.00	56.57

[a]From Table 4.1.
[b]$\sigma[\pi] = (\Sigma_{i=1}^{n} (\pi_i - E[\pi])^2\phi_i)^{1/2}$, or $\sigma[\pi] = x\sigma[v]$.

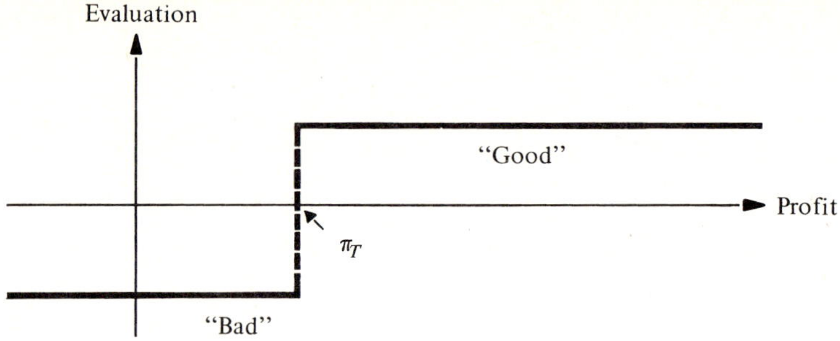

Figure 4.10

minimize the probability that profits are lower than π_T. Thus, the appropriate measure of risk for this manager would be the probability that profits will fall short of π_T.

Can risk measures such as these be derived from information on the expected profit and the standard deviation of profit? Only sometimes. There are some probability distributions that can be completely described by the expected value and the standard deviation. The most well-known of these is the *normal distribution,* which has a familiar, bell-shaped probability density function. (See Figure 4.11.) The distribution is symmetric, centered around the expected value $E[\pi]$. The degree of uncertainty is measured by $\sigma[\pi]$; the larger $\sigma[\pi]$, the flatter and more spread-out the probability distribution. The probability that profit will fall between two points, say π_L and π_H, is represented by the area under the probability function between π_L and π_H. (See Figure 4.12). The probability of profit being between $E[\pi] - \sigma[\pi]$ and $E[\pi] + \sigma[\pi]$ (that is, within one standard deviation of $E[\pi]$), is about 0.6826, regardless of the values of $E[\pi]$ and $\sigma[\pi]$.[4]

If we are willing to assume that profits are distributed normally with expected value $E[\pi]$ and standard deviation $\sigma[\pi]$, can we deduce the probability that profits will fall short of a target π_T? We can, by using a fact about normal probabilities and a standard table based on a normal probability distribution with expected value 0 (zero) and standard deviation 1 (one). In Figure 4.13a, there appears the probability distribution of profit π, and the risk that profit will fall below the target π_T is represented by the shaded area to the left of π_T. It is this area that we are interested in measuring. In Figure 4.13b, there is a *standardized normal distribution* with expected value 0 and standard deviation 1.

[4]The probability that profit will be within two standard deviations of $E[\pi]$ is about 0.9544.

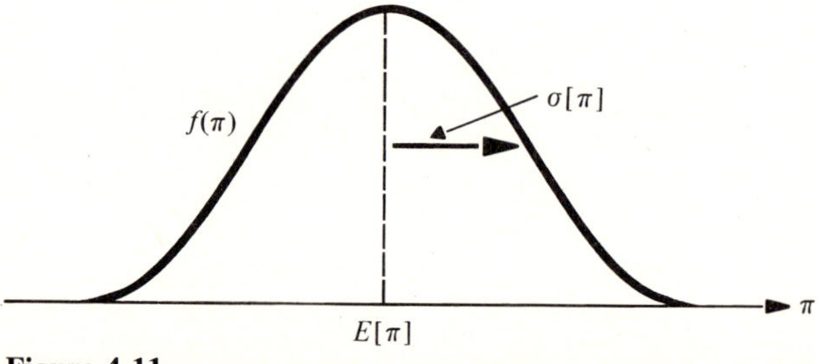

Figure 4.11

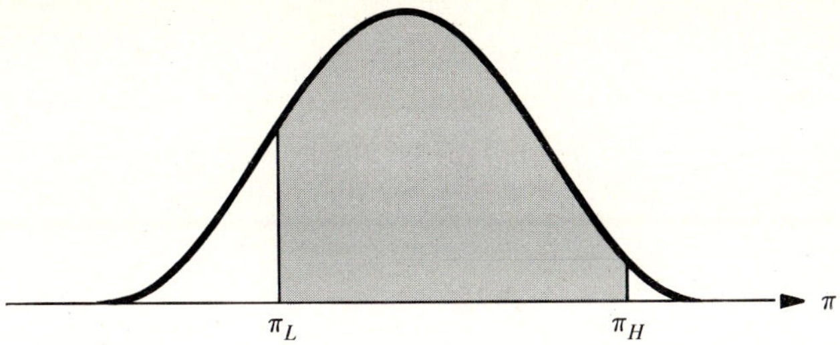

Figure 4.12

A new point has been calculated, which we might call the *standardized target* $(\pi_T - E[\pi])/\sigma[\pi]$. It is a fact of the normal probability distribution that the shaded area to the left of the standardized target in Figure 4.13b is *equal* to the shaded area in Figure 4.13a. Therefore, the probability that profits will fall below a target can be found by computing a standardized target and then using a table such as Appendix 4.1 to find the probability of an outcome below this target.

As an example, we found in Table 4.3 that a price–quantity combination of ($65; 14) led to an $E[\pi]$ of 40 and a $\sigma[\pi]$ of 49.50. If the profit target is set to zero, $\pi_T = 0$, then what is the probability of missing this target (i.e., the probability of not breaking even)? The standardized target will be $(0 - 40.00)/49.50 = -0.81$, and we can look in Appendix 4.1 to find the probability of an outcome less than -0.81. From the table, it looks to be between 0.1841 and 0.2119. This amount is not the actual probability of not breaking even, which we know from Table 4.1 to be 0.25. This discrepancy occurs because the probabilities of 0.1841 and 0.2119 are based on the assumption that profits follow a normal distribution, when in fact profits in our example follow a discrete distribution with only three possible values.

There are a number of embellishments that could be made to this risk analysis. For instance, in addition to the probability of not exceeding the target and the probability of not breaking even, the manager might also want to know the probability of not making the target, but at least breaking even. This would simply be the probability that profits will fall short of the target, less the probability that profits will fall short of breakeven. Yet other extensions are aimed at the assumption of a normal distribution of profit. If

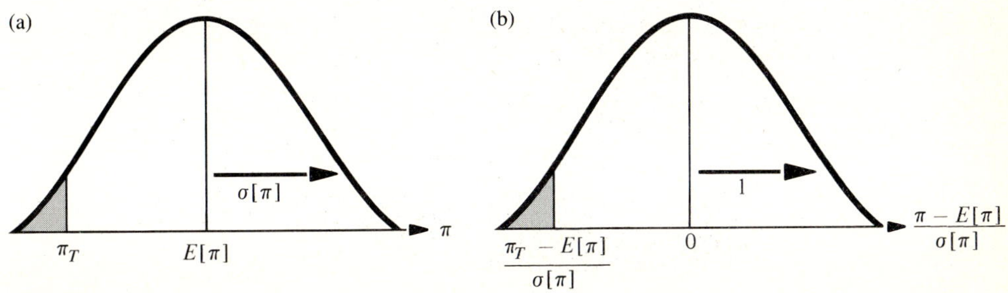

Figure 4.13

$\pi = (p - v)x - F$, then π will follow a normal distribution if: (i) p, v, and F follow normal distributions and x is a decision factor known with certainty; *or* (ii) x and F follow normal distributions and $p - v$ is known with certainty. If neither of these cases holds, then we cannot say that profits will be normally distributed. Some researchers have attempted to overcome this limitation by making other assumptions about the probability distributions[5] or by resorting to simulation techniques[6] that we will discuss in the next chapter.

4.7 THE LINEARITY ASSUMPTION

Throughout the discussion so far, we have assumed that the costs of production have a *linear* relationship with the volume of activity. That is, there is a fixed cost F, and a variable cost per unit v, which remains the same if one unit or one thousand units is produced. In practice, we would expect that the incremental cost of the first few units could be high because we would have to have employees at the different stations of the production process, even though they wouldn't be very busy. Expanding output further, the employees can handle additional volume without substantial difficulty, so that the incremental labor costs will be reduced. But at some level of volume, the incremental costs begin to increase again as the practical capacity is reached, and the operation encounters *diseconomies of scale*. The linear situation is portrayed in Figure 4.14a, and a nonlinear case appears in Figure 4.14b. While the linear cost line can be represented as $C = F + vx$, the nonlinear cost requires a more complex formula including x^2 and x^3. In portraying the type of line shown in Figure 4.14b, we would expect (i) v_1 to be greater than zero, reflecting the variable cost of the first units; (ii) v_2 to be less than zero, reflecting the reduction in variable costs from economies of scale; and (iii) v_3 to be greater than zero, reflecting the diseconomies of scale when x gets larger.

Clearly, the nonlinear cost form is more complex, and more difficult to estimate. We will have to find estimates of four cost parameters, F, v_1, v_2, and v_3, as opposed to two parameters, F and v. An appropriate question is whether the additional complexity produces significantly better decisions even if, in fact, costs are nonlinear. Suppose that

[5] Hilliard and Leitch (1975).

[6] Liao (1975).

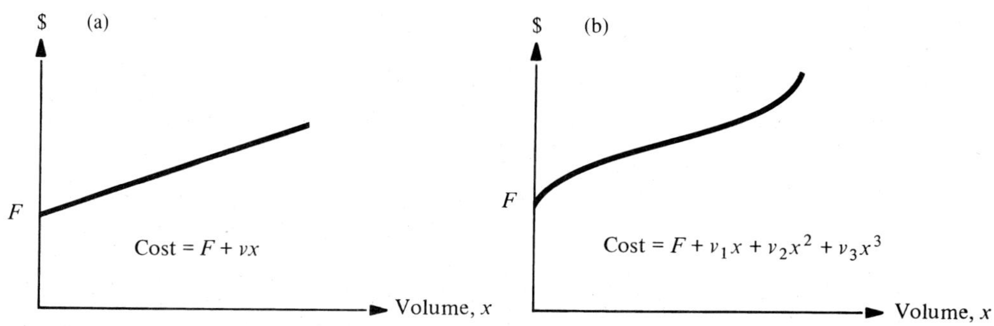

Figure 4.14

TABLE 4.4 TABLE OF INCREMENTAL COST[a]

Current output	Current cost	Additional unit incremental cost	Additional 5-units incremental cost (per unit)	Additional 10 units incremental cost (per unit)
20	11,680	\$71.61	\$351.25 (70.25)	\$690 (\$69)
30	12,370	\$66.91	\$333.75 (66.75)	\$670 (\$67)
40	13,040	\$68.21	\$346.25 (69.25)	\$710 (\$71)
50	13,750	\$75.51	\$388.75 (77.75)	\$810 (\$81)

[a]Cost = $10{,}000 + 100x - x^2 + 0.01x^3$.

a manager is in the position of having to accept or reject additional business. How often will he or she make a mistake using a simple linear cost curve to make decisions? Suppose that the firm is currently producing x units and has received an order for an additional y units at a price (per unit) of p. The incremental profits can be calculated in the following ways:

	Linear	Nonlinear
Additional revenue	py	py
Cost of producing $x + y$	$F + v(x + y)$	$F + v_1(x + y) + v_2(x + y)^2 + v_3(x + y)^3$
Cost of producing x	$F + vx$	$F + v_1x + v_2x^2 + v_3x^3$
Incremental cost	vy	$v_1y + v_2[(x + y)^2 - x^2] + v_3[(x + y)^3 - x^3]$
Incremental profit	$\pi_L = (p - v)y$	$\pi_N = py - v_1y - v_2[(x + y)^2 - x^2] - v_3[(x + y)^3 - x^3]$

The manager who uses π_L will be making a mistake when π_L is less than zero, but π_N is greater than zero, *or* when π_L is greater than zero, but π_N is less than zero.

To look at a simple example, suppose that the actual costs are nonlinear and follow the relationship: Cost $= 10{,}000 + 100x - x^2 + 0.01x^3$. The additional costs of different-sized orders at different levels of production are seen in Table 4.4. The cost of an additional unit is \$71.61 at $x = 20$. This amount first decreases to \$66.91 at $x = 30$, has begun to rise again by $x = 40$, and then continues to increase beyond that.[7] If a manager were to make the simplifying assumption that $v = \$70$, would he or she make mistakes? We can see from Table 4.4 that the answer depends on both the current level of operation and the price that was offered. If the price offered was \$100 per unit (or \$40 per unit), there would be no difference between the decisions based on the linear and nonlinear costs in the production range of Table 4.4. If the price is reduced to \$75 per unit, then there are a number of cases in the table where π_N would be negative, while π_L is positive. (The reverse can be true as well. If $p = \$69$, then π_L is negative, but there are places where π_N is positive. These situations would occur more readily if the linear model assumed a $v = \$75$ or some higher value.)

Attempting to estimate how costs vary with respect to activity is not an easy task. We shall consider a number of possible techniques in Chapters 5 and 6. But before conducting an extensive analysis of cost behavior, an analysis such as that in Table 4.4 should provide some insight into the cost of the linearity assumption and into the expected

[7]Actually, the lowest incremental cost is at $x = 33$, where an additional unit costs \$66.67.

benefit of further analysis. (For instance, we could find the expected value of perfect information as to whether costs were linear or not.)

4.8 DIFFERENCES BETWEEN DEMAND AND PRODUCTION

While there are many assumptions implicit in traditional CVP analysis, we will examine only one more—the assumption that the amount sold is equal to the amount produced. That is, demand is known with certainty, or at least becomes known in time to adjust production so that there are no stockouts or excess inventory. However, there are a number of situations, particularly in service industries, where a manager must decide on the number of units to provide before the actual demand is known. If the demand turns out to be less than the number provided, then the excess units may be kept in inventory to be sold at a later date. If the product is subject to spoilage (e.g., food) or obsolescence (e.g., a daily newspaper), then the revenue on these excess units may be very low (even negative if it costs something to dispose of them). On the other hand, if the demand exceeds the number produced, then the additional sales will be lost unless the manager can purchase some extra units from some other supplier.[8] In general, the profits will be of the following form.

$$\pi(x_p,x_d) = \begin{cases} (p - v_p)x_p + (p - v_B)(x_d - x_p) - F, & \text{if } x_d > x_p \\ px_d + (p - i)(x_p - x_d) - v_p x_p - F, & \text{if } x_p \geq x_d \end{cases} \tag{4.5}$$

where x_p = number of units produced

x_d = number of units demanded

p = selling price per unit

v_p = variable cost of producing a unit

v_B = variable cost of buying a unit to meet excess demand

i = the cost of holding a unit until the next period, including the decline in value due to obsolescence

F = fixed costs of production

This equation encompasses many different situations through different parameters. The parameter i may be equal to p, reflecting the fact that the leftover units are worthless, or, alternatively, i may simply equal a normal inventory carrying charge if the leftover units can be sold the next period without penalty. If the company must go into the regular market to purchase units to meet excess demand, then it may be that v_B will equal p, and no profit will be made on these units.

The various situations can be studied in more depth in inventory control courses, and we will look at the simple situation where there is no way to purchase additional units to satisfy excess demand, and leftover units (or service potential) cannot be sold and must be thrown away. In this case, the profit equation is

[8] It is tempting to say that the manager should adjust his price until demand equals supply. However, in a situation that is repeated, it may be better for the price to stay constant. For instance, what would happen to the demand pattern of a newspaper vendor if he announced that after 6 p.m. all newspapers would be sold at half price?

$$\pi(x_p,x_d) = \begin{cases} (p - v_p)x_p - F, & \text{if } x_d > x_p \\ px_d - v_px_p - F, & \text{if } x_p \geq x_d \end{cases} \tag{4.6}$$

In a sense, the manager's choice of x_p, the amount produced, is like choosing a capacity. Each unit of capacity costs v_p, and gives the capability of selling an additional unit if demand materializes. Graphically, the situation may be seen in Figure 4.15. If x_p units are produced, the costs incurred are $F + v_px_p$ and the profit–volume line goes up as revenues increase until x_p units are sold. If demand exceeds this, no additional revenues will be forthcoming, so the profits are flat after x_p. If $x_p'(>x_p)$ are produced then additional capacity costs are incurred, but the profit line rises beyond x_p until x_p' is reached.

The basic decision problem is how many units to produce, and this may be formulated as a decision theory problem with x_d as the state, x_p as the action, and $\pi(x_p, x_d)$ as the outcome. As an illustration, suppose that the fixed costs F are \$40,000, the unit price p is \$2,000, and the variable costs of production are \$1,000 per unit. For simplicity, assume that demand follows the distribution below.

Demand (in units)	Probability
45	0.15
50	0.20
55	0.30
60	0.20
65	0.15

Of course, there are a large number of possible courses of action to consider, and a computerized spreadsheet program could be used to compute the outcomes, expected outcomes, and risk measures for each possible action as shown in Table 4.5. From this table, we can see that the expected payoff is highest if 55 units are produced, but that the risk increases as x_p increases beyond 45.

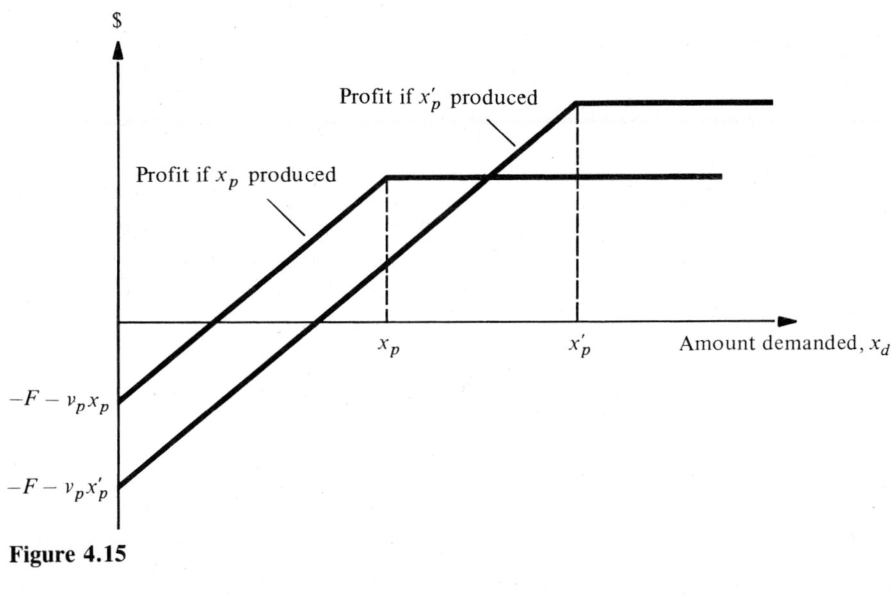

Figure 4.15

TABLE 4.5 PROFIT STATISTICS

Level of production	Expected profit	Standard deviation of profit	Probability of a loss
45	$5,000	0	0
50	$8,500	3,571	0
55	$10,000	7,416	0.15
60	$8,500	10,618	0.15
65	$5,000	12,649	0.35

This analysis could also be used to get an estimate of the value of different kinds of information. If the manager could discern the exact demand prior to production, the amount produced would always equal the amount demanded, and the expected profit would be $15,000.[9] Therefore, a risk-neutral manager would be willing to pay up to $15,000 − $10,000, or $5,000, for a marketing report that would forecast demand perfectly. Additionally, we can analyze the effect of different variable costs on the payoffs and decision. Lower variable costs will tend to make higher levels of production more desirable, and vice versa. For instance, suppose that the above example were modified so that there was a 1/2 probability that v was $900 and a 1/2 probability that v was $1,100. What would be the expected value of resolving this cost uncertainty? (You should be able to verify that the value is zero.)

There are a number of extensions to this analysis that could be explored. For instance, we might consider other, more general, types of demand distributions[10] or other measures of risk.[11] Factors such as seasonality and customer goodwill could also be brought into the analysis. The action could become a multiperiod production *strategy* rather than a specific amount to be produced at present. In these more complex settings, the framework for evaluating alternatives may remain the same—identifying actions, uncertainties, and outcomes. In addition, the analysis can be used to determine the value of increased efforts to resolve the uncertainty related to costs.

4.9 SUMMARY

In this chapter, we have explored a basic decision situation in which a manager must determine a level of activity for the short run. It should be obvious that not all such situations have been covered, but we will explore more complex situations in later chapters. For instance, in Chapter 5 we consider the case where a manager receives project proposals over time, and he or she must decide which to accept without knowing whether a better proposal will arrive the next day. In Chapter 7, we explore the choice of a product mix rather than the level of production for an individual product. In Chapter 8 we examine the effects of competition and cases where the manager must submit a bid to obtain a contract to supply a good or service. In general, we will follow the same framework: identify alternatives, uncertainties, and objectives, and then choose an appropriate course of action.

[9] (0.15)(5,000) + (0.2)(10,000) + (0.3)(15,000) + (0.2)(20,000) + (0.15)(25,000).

[10] Shih (1979).

[11] Magee (1975).

However, before moving on to these more complex situations, the next two chapters describe a variety of techniques that might be used to estimate costs and cost behavior. To this point, we have identified the impact of costs on decision making and have examined ways to put a value on improved cost information. In the following chapters we turn to those techniques that may be used to produce the improved cost information.

APPENDIX 4.1
CUMULATIVE NORMAL FREQUENCY DISTRIBUTION

Z	P(Z)[a]	Z	P(Z)	Z	P(Z)	Z	P(Z)
−4.0	0.0000	−2.0	0.0228	0.0	0.5000	2.0	0.9772
−3.9	0.0000	−1.9	0.0287	0.1	0.5398	2.1	0.9821
−3.8	0.0001	−1.8	0.0359	0.2	0.5793	2.2	0.9861
−3.7	0.0001	−1.7	0.0446	0.3	0.6179	2.3	0.9893
−3.6	0.0002	−1.6	0.0548	0.4	0.6554	2.4	0.9918
−3.5	0.0002	−1.5	0.0668	0.5	0.6915	2.5	0.9938
−3.4	0.0003	−1.4	0.0808	0.6	0.7257	2.6	0.9953
−3.3	0.0005	−1.3	0.0968	0.7	0.7580	2.7	0.9965
−3.2	0.0007	−1.2	0.1151	0.8	0.7781	2.8	0.9974
−3.1	0.0010	−1.1	0.1357	0.9	0.8159	2.9	0.9981
−3.0	0.0013	−1.0	0.1587	1.0	0.8413	3.0	0.9987
−2.9	0.0019	−0.9	0.1841	1.1	0.8643	3.1	0.9990
−2.8	0.0026	−0.8	0.2119	1.2	0.8849	3.2	0.9993
−2.7	0.0035	−0.7	0.2420	1.3	0.9032	3.3	0.9995
−2.6	0.0047	−0.6	0.2743	1.4	0.9192	3.4	0.9997
−2.5	0.0062	−0.5	0.3085	1.5	0.9332	3.5	0.9998
−2.4	0.0082	−0.4	0.3446	1.6	0.9452	3.6	0.9998
−2.3	0.0107	−0.3	0.3821	1.7	0.9554	3.7	0.9999
−2.2	0.0139	−0.2	0.4207	1.8	0.9641	3.8	0.9999
−2.1	0.0179	−0.1	0.4602	1.9	0.9713	3.9	1.000
						4.0	1.000

[a]$P(Z)$ = area under the standard normal curve from $-\infty$ to Z = probability of an outcome less than or equal to Z.

PROBLEMS

4.1. (CMA adapted). Anchor Company manufactures several different styles of jewelry cases. Management estimates that during the third quarter of 1985 the company will be operating at 80 percent of normal capacity. Because the company desires a higher utilization of plant capacity, the company will consider a special order.

Anchor has received a special order inquiry from JCP Inc., which would like to market a jewelry case similar to one of Anchor's cases. The JCP jewelry case would be marketed under JCP's own label. JCP Inc. has offered Anchor $5.75 per jewelry case for 20,000 cases to be shipped by October 1, 1985. The cost data for the Anchor jewelry case, which would be similar to the specifications of the JCP special order, are as follows:

Regular selling price per unit	$9.00
Costs per unit	
Raw materials	$2.50
Direct labor 0.5 hr @ $6.00/hr	3.00
Overhead 0.25 machine hr @ $4.00/hr	1.00
Total costs	$6.50

According to the specifications provided by JCP Inc., the special order case requires less-expensive raw materials. Consequently, the raw materials will only cost $2.25 per case. Management has estimated that the remaining costs, labor time, and machine time, will be the same as the Anchor jewelry case.

The Anchor manufacturing capabilities are limited to the total machine hours available. The plant capacity under normal operations is 90,000 machine hours per year or 7,500 machines hours per month. The budgeted fixed overhead for 1985 amounts to $216,000. All manufacturing overhead costs are applied to production on the basis of machine hours at $4.00 per hour.

Anchor will have the entire third quarter to work on the special order. Management does not expect any repeat sales to be generated from a special order. Company practice precludes Anchor from subcontracting any portion of an order when special orders are not expected to generate repeat sales.

Required Should Anchor Company accept JCP's special order? Justify your answer and show your calculations.

4.2. (CMA Adapted). Aplet Inc. purchased Avcont Company in 1975 during Aplet's expansion period. The subsidiary has been quite profitable until recently. Beginning in 1983 the market share dropped, costs increased primarily due to increased prices of inputs, and the profits

AVCONT COMPANY
INCOME STATEMENT FOR YEARS ENDING DECEMBER 31
(000 Omitted)

	1983	1984	1985 (Est.)
Industry unit sales	1,300	1,200	1,200
Avcont unit sales	120	110	110
Sales	$1,200	$1,100	$1,100
Less: Variable expenses			
Raw materials	$ 175	$ 170	$ 175
Labor	210	215	225
Manufacturing overhead	100	99	100
Selling	125	115	120
Administrative	50	50	60
	$ 660	$ 649	$ 680
Variable contribution margin	$ 540	$ 451	$ 420
Less: Fixed expenses			
Manufacturing[a]	$ 200	$ 210	$ 230
Selling[a]	125	140	145
Administration[a]	135	145	145
	$ 460	$ 495	$ 520
Net income (loss)	$ 80	$ (44)	$ (100)

[a]Depreciation and amortization included in fixed expenses.

Manufacturing	$ 60	$ 70	$ 70
Selling	5	6	6
Administration	8	8	9
	$ 73	$ 84	$ 85

turned into losses. The income statements for 1983 and 1984 are presented along with an estimate of the 1985 income made in October 1985.

The subsidiary management is optimistic about the volume of sales for 1986. Recent sales promotion efforts seem to be beneficial, and Avcont expects to increase unit sales 10 percent during 1986 even though industry volume is expected to decline to 1,100,000 units. However, Avcont management also knows its variable cost rates will increase 10 percent in 1986 over 1985 levels.

Avcont management wants to take action to reverse the unsatisfactory results the company has been experiencing. One proposal under consideration is to increase the price of Avcont's product. Some members of management believe that the market might accept an 8 percent increase in prices at this time without affecting the expected 10 percent increase in unit sales volume because no price increases have taken place in this market since 1982. Several other companies are also considering price increases for 1976.

Other members of Aplet management question the feasibility of a price increase because Avcont is operating in an industry that is experiencing declining sales. In addition, the marketing department believes a price increase will have an impact on the expected increase in unit sales volume during 1986. Its estimates of the possible outcomes on unit sales and the related probabilities for the 8 percent price increase are as follows.

Increase (decrease) in 1986 unit sales volume	Probability
10%	0.4
5	0.3
0	0.2
(5)	0.1
	1.0

Required

A. Calculate Avcont's profits for 1986 if the 8 percent price increase takes place and unit sales volume increases 10 percent.

B. What are Avcont's expected profits for 1986 if the probabilistic sales data assembled by the marketing department are used?

C. A member of the analysis team made the following observation to support his recommendation for a price increase: ''Inflationary pressures make it reasonable for a company to forecast increased costs, increased product prices, and increased, or at least constant, volume because consumers can be expected to accept the product price increases.'' Comment on the validity of this statement for planning purposes.

4.3. (CMA Adapted). Jackston Inc. manufactures and distributes a line of Christmas toys. The company had neglected to keep its doll house line current. As a result sales have decreased to approximately 10,000 units per year from a previous high of 50,000 units. The doll house has been redesigned recently and is considered by company officials to be comparable to its competitors' models. The company plans to redesign the doll house each year in order to compete effectively. John Blocke, the sales manager, is not sure how many units can be sold next year, but he is willing to place probabilities on his estimates. Blocke's estimates of the number of units that can be sold during the next year and the related probabilities are as follows:

Estimated sales in units	Probability
20,000	0.10
30,000	0.40
40,000	0.30
50,000	0.20

The units would be sold for $20 each.

The inability to estimate the sales more precisely is a problem for Jackston. The number of units of this product is small enough to schedule the entire year's sales in one production run. If the demand is greater than the number of units manufactured, then sales will be lost. If demand is below supply, the extra units cannot be carried over to the next season and would be given away to various charitable organizations. The production and distribution cost estimates are listed below.

	Units manufactured			
	20,000	30,000	40,000	50,000
Variable costs	$180,000	$270,000	$360,000	$450,000
Fixed costs	140,000	140,000	160,000	160,000
Total costs	$320,000	$410,000	$520,000	$610,000

The company intends to analyze the data to facilitate making a decision as to the proper size of the production run.

Required Prepare a payoff table for the different sizes of production runs required to meet the four sales estimates prepared by John Blocke for Jackston Inc. If Jackston Inc. relied solely on the expected monetary value approach to make decisions, what size of production run would be selected?

4.4. Jeffrey Allen has recently taken over a plant in a large, decentralized firm. As plant manager, he has considerable autonomy to make decisions about which orders to accept, production scheduling, investments in equipment, and so on. A plantwide measure of profit is used in evaluating a plant manager's performance.

After a month on the job, Allen feels that he has become fairly familiar with the day-to-day operations of the plant, and would like to see if he can improve his decision making (and profitability). Over lunch, he describes the following problem.

"Every week I get a summary of the orders that we have received during the week from the plant sales manager, Al S. Miles. For each order, the production engineer, W. E. Macom, has estimated the labor and material costs, and then adds an overhead cost. I feel pretty comfortable with the direct costs, but the overhead cost allocation is something I'm not so sure about. We operate on some pretty low margins and we have had excess capacity for the last eighteen months, so I think these costs are really important. I hate to turn down orders that could be profitable if I know what the incremental overhead would be. On the other hand, I don't want to increase sales at the cost of my own profitability.

"Suppose, for the sake of argument, that I have two orders like the following to accept or reject. I could accept either one or both.

Order #	Revenue − direct material and labor cost	Direct labor hours	Direct machine hours
1	$1,290	150	100
2	$1,230	100	150

I believe that the variable overhead depends on the number of direct labor hours and machine hours, but I am unsure about the exact rates. Suppose the rates could be either $6/DLH and $4/MH *or* $4/DLH and $6/MH, and each of these alternatives is equally likely.''

Required How much would it be worth to find out which overhead behavior is the true one?

4.5. Kelsey Meredith works for a large firm that operates job shops at various locations in the Midwest. Each of these shops is run by a shop manager who, to some extent, is responsible for the profits of the shop. That is, the shop manager has considerable latitude in determining which jobs to do, production scheduling, labor relations, material purchasing, and so on. However, the accounting function is centralized in the firm, with input and access through remote, time-sharing computer terminals. Meredith's responsibility is the part of this accounting information that is supposed to aid the shop managers in planning their operations. One of the most often used planning tools is a *cost estimation module* (CEM), where a shop manager can provide certain characteristics of a proposed job, and the CEM will provide an estimate of how the job will affect costs. (For simplicity, we assume that the manager provides an estimate of the direct labor hours and machine hours for the job. The CEM then provides estimates of labor costs and overhead costs.)

Initially, Meredith has turned her attention to the estimation of overhead costs. In the present CEM, variable overhead is allocated on the basis of direct labor hours, but she is concerned that other factors also affect the overhead costs. An analysis of the incremental overhead for past jobs indicates that this type of cost could equal $5 per direct labor hour, plus $3 per machine hour, for each job.

However, the CEM assumes that incremental overhead depends only on direct labor hours, and the rate used by the CEM is $6.50 per direct labor hour. In order to see whether the overhead estimation had any affect on the shop manager's decisions, Meredith decided to run a ''mini-simulation.'' She asked a shop manager to give her the characteristics of four ''representative'' job proposals, including the price that the customer would be willing to pay for each job.

Job	Direct labor hour	Machine hour	Price less estimated direct costs
101	50	40	$ 400
102	100	35	640
103	100	40	600
104	150	110	1,050

Required

A. Compute the estimated incremental overhead and incremental profit for these four jobs, once using the CEM's method, and once using the actual cost behavior. For each job, and each allocation method, is the best action to accept or reject?

B. What is the actual expected payoff if variable overhead is $5 per direct labor hour and

$3 per machine hour, and the CEM method is used for accept/reject decisions? What is the expected payoff if the actual overhead rates are used in decision making?

C. How does the analysis you did in A and B help to determine the potential benefits of a change in the cost estimation module?

4.6. The Beechnut Box Company (BNB Co.) is a multiplant producer of corrugated fiberboard containers. Since the box business is very competitive (the largest firm in the industry accounts for 6% of industry sales) the sales manager must approve bids for customer orders that have a very low expected margin. Of course the expected margin depends on the cost estimate on the order, so that if costs are underestimated, BNB can lose a fair amount of money. The problem is compounded by the policy of BNB President, I. M. Thebos, that the prices charged customers should only be changed when the raw material costs (mostly paper costs) change. This "price stability" policy means that the loss from underestimation is compounded, since these orders are of a recurring type. For example, a particular type of box (e.g., for a given television set) may be ordered every month, so if paper costs don't change for 8 months, BNB is stuck with the stated order price for 8 orders.

As orders are received they are sent to the production scheduler, who takes note of the requested delivery date as well as the order specifications. Then, on the scheduled day, the production order is sent to the production area where four operations occur. While the operation is a fairly simple one, there are a number of places where the costs are uncertain.

As a result, the sales manager is very uneasy about his existing cost estimation system, particularly since BNB does not use a job cost system to measure the cost of each job. Therefore, the only feedback to the cost estimating system is at the plant level, not at the order level. To start, he poses a problem for you that is meant to shed some light on the value of getting better cost information.

Suppose the sales manager is trying to decide how much to bid on an order, either $2,300 or $2,650 (or no bid at all), and the actual costs may be $2,200 or $2,600, both with equal probability.

Required

A. What would be the expected value of perfect *cost* information?

After reviewing your analysis, the sales manager points out that you have oversimplified the problems. "We operate in a competitive environment, and there will be others bidding on the contract. I know that Oak Box Company will be bidding." After some consultation, you arrive at the following. *If* the true cost is $2,200, then Oak Box Company will either bid $2,250 or $2,350 with equal probability. *If* the true cost is $2,600, then Oak Box Company will either bid $2,550 or $2,700 with equal probability.

B. What is the expected value of perfect *cost* information in this case? (In essence, you are assuming something about a competitor's cost estimation system and bidding strategies, and seeing what effect it has on the value of information. We study this further in Chapter 8.)

4.7. Andrew Eubank owns and operates a custom furniture operation in a large midwestern city. The company's activities include the restoration of antique furniture as well as the design and manufacture of high-quality wood furniture. When a customer approaches Andrew to design and produce a new piece, he must decide how many copies of the piece to produce. For instance, if a customer wants a particular style of oak cabinet, there are substantial fixed costs to the design and production set-up. Therefore, Andrew might decide to produce a limited number of additional copies, perhaps in walnut or cherry, and keep these in inventory to sell to future customers. He says, "If I design and sell just one piece, then the design and set-up costs are about a quarter of the direct costs of production. Materials and finishing are each a third, on average, with the rest being the direct labor involved in cutting the wood according to design. I continually face the choice of how many to produce in addition to the one ordered. The material costs are substantial, and I don't like to have a lot of capital tied up in pieces that don't get sold."

Required

A. Prepare a list of information that you would want in order to help Andrew Eubank establish a systematic approach to determining how many additional pieces to produce.

B. The price set by Andrew for a piece of custom designed furniture is usually four times the price of the materials. If he believes that the probabilities of additional demand are the following, how many additional pieces should he produce?

Additional demand	Probability
1	0.2
2	0.3
3	0.3
4	0.1
5	0.1

C. As a percentage of selling price, what would be the expected value of perfect information about the number of additional units that will be demanded?

4.8. Suzanne Robbins has the responsibility for determining the pricing and production of her company's major product. A substantial amount of market research has already been conducted to estimate the consumer response to the product, so one period's demand curve is believed to be reflected in the following relationship.

$$\text{Revenue} = 7 \times (\text{units sold}) - 0.001 \times (\text{units sold})^2$$

The production cost behavior is less certain, because the speed with which diseconomies of scale occur is not known. For simplicity, assume that there are two possible cost relationships, each equally likely.

$$\text{Possibility 1: Cost} = 1 \times (\text{units produced})$$
$$\text{Possibility 2: Cost} = 1 \times (\text{units produced}) + 0.002 \times (\text{units produced})^2$$

Required

A. If costs are linear (possibility 1), what is the best level of production and sales? What is the level of profit expected from this choice? (Assume for all questions that the quantity produced equals the quantity sold.)

B. If costs are nonlinear (possibility 2), what is the best level of production and sales? What level of profit is expected?

C. If Suzanne Robbins's objective is to maximize expected profit, what level of production should she choose? What is the expected profit from that action?

D. What is the expected value of perfect information concerning the behavior of production costs?

4.9. Michael Davidson has the responsibility for determining the pricing and production of his company's major product. A substantial amount of market research has already been conducted to estimate the consumer response to the product, so one period's demand curve is believed to be reflected in the following relationships.

$$\text{Demand, in units} = (8{,}000 - 1{,}000 \times \text{price})$$
$$\text{Revenue} = 8 \times (\text{units sold}) - 0.001 \times (\text{units sold})^2$$

The production cost behavior is less certain. The period's fixed costs will be $10,000, but the variable cost per unit is not known. For simplicity, assume that there are three possible cost relationships, each equally likely.

$$\text{Possibility 1: Cost} = 10{,}000 + 1.00 \times (\text{units produced})$$
$$\text{Possibility 2: Cost} = 10{,}000 + 1.05 \times (\text{units produced})$$
$$\text{Possibility 3: Cost} = 10{,}000 + 1.10 \times (\text{units produced})$$

Required

A. For *each* of the above cost possibilities, determine the optimal price, output, and profit, assuming that all units produced are sold.

B. Given the current level of uncertainty and an objective of maximizing expected profit, what is the best price–output combination? What is the expected profit?

C. What is the expected value of perfect information about the variable cost per unit, assuming an objective of maximizing expected profit?

D. As an alternative to perfect information, there is an imperfect information system available, with signal probabilities as shown below. What is the most that you would pay for a report from this information system?

	Actual variable cost		
Signals	1.00	1.05	1.10
$v = 1.00$	0.80	0.10	0.00
$v = 1.05$	0.20	0.80	0.20
$v = 1.10$	0.00	0.10	0.80

4.10. Consider a situation in which a manager must choose between two levels of production—either 1,000 units or 1,500 units. The fixed costs of production and administration will be $80,000, and the variable cost of production has an expected value of $100 per unit with a standard deviation of 10. If 1,000 units are produced, the revenues will be $200,000, but if production is increased to 1,500 units, price reductions will cause the revenues to go up only to $260,000.

Required

A. For each level of production, compute the following: (i) expected profit; (ii) standard deviation of profit; (iii) variance of profit.

B. Assume that the variable cost per unit follows a normal probability distribution. Compute the probability of breaking even for each level of production.

C. Suppose that the manager receives a bonus if profits exceed the budgeted level of $20,000. Which production level maximizes the probability of receiving the bonus?

4.11. Christopher Patrick must determine the level of production for one of his company's major products in preparation for the holiday selling season. At this point, the price per unit and the variable cost per unit are uncertain, but the best estimates are the following:

	Expected value	Standard deviation
Price per unit	$5.00	$0.05
Variable cost per unit	$3.00	$0.10

Required

A. Graph the expected contribution margin and the variance of the contribution margin against the level of production.

B. Christopher Patrick recognizes that both the expected contribution and its variance increases as the level of production increases. Suppose that he is willing to increase production to the point where the increase in expected contribution from an additional unit is exceeded by the increase in the variance on the contribution multiplied by a factor of 0.01. Determine the level of production he should choose

(i) graphically;

(ii) analytically.

4.12. Gwinn & Hall is a management consulting firm specializing in cultural orientation programs for multinational corporations. When a U.S.-based company plans to send a manager overseas for an extended period of time, there is normally a cultural adjustment for the manager and family. Gwinn & Hall provides orientation services prior to the manager's departure for the assignment, with programs designed to familiarize the manager with business practices, protocols, and the economic environment. Cultural orientations for the manager and family, including language courses if necessary, are designed to ease the transition into the new assignment. In describing the current situation of the business, Joanna Gwinn made the following remarks.

"As you know, most of our clients are small- to medium-sized businesses that can't afford their own cultural orientation staff like the very large multinationals. Up to this point, we've had a single office just outside of Chicago, and that has served our needs quite well. However, our business is growing at a significant rate and the travel cost has reached the level where we're considering opening a second office on the West Coast. Since we don't want to be big consumers of our own services, we would transfer few personnel from the Chicago office, hiring most of the new staff from the new area. A significant issue is whether to open the new office, and if we do, how many people should we hire. Demand is uncertain, and we cannot adjust the level of staff in the short run, since the skill combinations we require are not easy to find, and once we do find them, we don't let them go lightly. I've put together some of the information that should be relevant below. You can assume that the new office would handle only West Coast business, and no Chicago office personnel would be used in West Coast business. Don't worry about the Chicago office. Its business is growing quickly enough to keep us all busy around here."

Maximum billable hours per employee per year: 1,500

Yearly salary (and fringes) cost per employee: $37,500

Average billing rate: $80 per hour

Last year's hours billed on West Coast: 6,000

Last year's transportation and lodging costs on West Coast: $180,000 (roughly variable with hours billed)

Fixed costs of running new office: $225,000

Forecast of West Coast billable hours for coming year:

Hours	Probability
7,000	0.25
8,000	0.30
9,000	0.25
10,000	0.20

Required

A. Assuming that the West Coast office is opened, what is your recommendation for the level of staff? You may assume that having the office on the West Coast cuts the transportation costs by half.

B. Can you make a recommendation as to whether the West Coast office should be opened? Would any additional information be helpful in making such a recommendation?

REFERENCES

Adar, Z., A. Barnea, and B. Lev. ''A Comprehensive Cost–Volume–Profit Analysis Under Uncertainty,'' *Accounting Review*. January 1977.

Cohen, M., and R. Halperin. ''Optimal Inventory Order Policy for a Firm Using the LIFO Inventory Costing Methods,'' *Journal of Accounting Research*. Autumn 1980.

Dickenson, J. ''Cost–Volume–Profit Analysis Under Uncertainty,'' *Journal of Accounting Research*. Spring 1974.

Dillon, R., and J. Nash. ''The True Relevance of Relevant Costs,'' *Accounting Review*. January 1978.

Jaedicke, R., and A. Robichek. ''Cost–Volume–Profit Analysis Under Conditions of Uncertainty,'' *Accounting Review*. October 1964.

Hilliard, J., and R. Leitch. ''Cost–Volume–Profit Under Uncertainty: A Lognormal Approach,'' *Accounting Review*. January 1975.

Liao, M. ''Model Sampling: A Stochastic Cost–Volume–Profit Analysis,'' *Accounting Review*. October 1975.

Magee, R. ''Cost–Volume–Profit Analysis, Uncertainty, and Capital Market Equilibrium,'' *Journal of Accounting Research*. Autumn 1975.

Shih, W. ''A General Decision Model for Cost–Volume–Profit Analysis Under Uncertainty,'' *Accounting Review*. October 1979.

Singh, P., and G. Chapman. ''Is the Linear Approximation Good Enough?'' *Management Accounting*. January 1978.

Chapter 5

Cost Estimation: Engineering Methods

In the chapters that precede these on cost estimation, we have studied a model of managerial decision making, and the role that accounting information plays in furthering the organization's objectives. We now have a framework for evaluating different information systems, including estimations of cost behavior, and we have explored the types of information that may be used in a short-term planning situation. In this chapter and the one that follows, we will review a variety of methods for estimating costs: engineering measurement, simulation, statistical methods, and so on. Of course, to do complete justice to these methods would require at least a course for each. Therefore, our purpose here is to become familiar with cost estimation situations in which these techniques can be applied, and with some common problems encountered in their application, rather than to study them in great depth.

In most cases, the initial source of information about costs is the manager who is most familiar with the activity under consideration, and we usually start with this information. For instance, in our decision-theoretic model, the initial probabilities could be the result of the manager's assessments. However, there are a variety of limitations in relying solely on managerial expertise for information used in budgeting and planning. For instance, if the manager will be evaluated based on budgets that are, in turn, based on his or her information, there is the possibility that the budgets will be padded. (We will return to this problem of budget participation in a later chapter.) In addition, if a production process is new, and no one is familiar with its operation, or if the cost estimates of numerous experts must be integrated, we may wish to use a set of estimation methods that we will call *engineering* methods. These techniques include engineering measurement as well as analytic and simulation techniques for integrating other measurements together.

5.1 ENGINEERING MEASUREMENT

When determining the direct material and labor costs for a unit of final output, we could make a list of all the different types of material and labor. For example, we could examine the product specifications to make a list of all the parts and labor that were required to build an automobile. Then for each direct input we could find the quantity of units used and the cost per unit, and therefore the cost of that input [e.g., one horn purchased from Acme Electric @ $11.50; 12 min (0.2 hr) of K. Smith's time to connect horn @ $12.25/hr]. With a complete list of these direct inputs we could determine the direct cost of the automobile, but we need to know both the cost per unit of input and the amount of input needed per unit of output. It is the latter factor that engineering measurement methods address.

Estimation of the types and amounts of direct materials needed to produce a unit of output may be accomplished by studying the chemical, physical, and/or mechanical relationships that characterize the production process. For instance, we could get a list of the parts necessary to construct an automobile by studying the product specifications developed by the engineering department. The chemical reactions in petroleum refining are known, and the materials necessary to obtain a given output, or set of outputs, can be determined. Losses due to scrap, waste, or shrinkage would have to be taken into account. For instance, in a sheet metal stamping operation, the unit of output is typically punched out of a sheet of metal, with the remaining metal being scrap, which may be salvaged or sold. Engineering methods would attempt to minimize the amount of scrap, and could estimate the costs (net of scrap salvage) of the stamping operation's output.

Direct labor cost relationships can be more difficult to estimate, since the physical laws of nature are more constant than human nature. That is, identical materials put through identical production processes ought to yield identical outputs. But we seldom expect different people to react the same way in identical situations. There are two common methods of determining the amount of labor necessary to perform a specified task. The first, *time and motion study,* has two related purposes: (i) to determine the most efficient way in which to complete the task by eliminating unnecessary elements; and (ii) to measure the amount of time necessary to complete the task. The latter purpose is accomplished by breaking down the task into basic movements or elements, recording the time necessary for each element, and then using these measurements to estimate normal and standard production rates. These studies require an in-depth examination of a task, and close observation of an individual (or individuals) performing the task. As a result, time and motion studies are rather expensive to conduct, and our information analysis would suggest that they would be employed only when the expected benefit was high (e.g., if the task were to be repeated frequently). In addition, one must be careful of *observation effects,* since the presence of an observer can alter an employee's behavior. It is also possible to engineer all of the interest out of a job, resulting in bored employees, and the cost engineer must try to avoid such a situation.

The cost estimator can average the observed times to forecast the expected time necessary to complete a step, but the short-term planning model of Chapter 4 also used information on the variability of cost (employee time, in this case). If the analyst has taken n observations of the amount of time necessary to complete a step, $t_1, t_2, \ldots, t_n$, then the estimated mean and variance would be

$$\bar{t} = \frac{t_1 + \cdots + t_n}{n}$$
$$s_t^2 = \frac{(t_1 - \bar{t})^2 + \cdots + (t_n - \bar{t})^2}{n - 1} \tag{5.1}$$

If the time is measured in minutes and if w is the cost of a minute of direct labor, the estimated mean and standard deviation of the direct labor cost would be $w\bar{t}$ and ws_t, respectively.

As an example, suppose that the maintenance foreman has observed a particular repair operation ten times, and has recorded the time that was needed for each repair.

Repair ticket no.	Time needed (in man-minutes)
1046	700
1072	780
1110	690
1131	730
1134	760
1162	800
1179	710
1208	740
1221	720
1255	750

The average time per repair is 738 man-minutes, and the standard deviation is 35.2. If we are willing to assume that repair time is normally distributed, we can use the techniques described in Chapter 4 to analyze the probability that repair time will exceed a given amount.

An alternative approach to measuring the amount of direct labor necessary to complete a task is called *work sampling*. Over a given time period, a number of random observations are made and the activity observed is recorded. Let us say that over a 40-hour work week we observe an employee n times and for n_i of those, he is typing invoices. We would then estimate that he spent $40(n_i/n)$ hours typing invoices, and if there were k invoices typed by this employee over the course of the week, we could estimate the time-per-invoice to be the following.

$$t = \frac{40(n_i/n)\text{ hr}}{k\text{ invoices}} \tag{5.2}$$

Of course, the accuracy of this estimate will increase as the number of observations made over the week increases.

Engineering measurement methods are a major source of information in the estimation of costs for decision making, particularly when there is little past data for statistical techniques such as those described in Chapter 6. However, the manager making decisions about cost estimation techniques should keep in mind that engineering measurement studies are usually expensive. And one must use care to account for observation effects: employee behavior under observation may be quite different than under normal operating conditions.

5.2 ANALYTICAL INTEGRATIVE METHODS (DETERMINISTIC)

In most organizations there are many different types of costs that are incurred, and for a particular decision, a number of them may be relevant. For instance, in our example of Chapters 2 and 3, the relevant costs were the incremental costs of producing 1000 special widgets, including incremental material, labor, and overhead costs. But there is no reason to expect that we will go to the same source for all three types of costs. For instance, the materials costs may be estimated using engineering measurement, the labor costs by the production supervisor's subjective estimate, and the variable overhead by an analysis of past data, and so on. Having obtained these estimates, we *integrate* them by simply adding them together to get the total incremental cost.

In many cases the integration of various cost estimates will be as simple as adding them together, but this is not always true. For instance, there may be diverse departments within the organization: some are directly a part of the production process, while others provide services to the production departments. Examples of such *service departments* may be an accounting department, a maintenance department, a computer services department, a power plant, and so on. At first blush it may appear that the integration of these indirect costs into the costs of production is simply a matter of taking the intermediate step of first allocating the service department costs to the production departments. This is true, but incomplete, since we need to consider the method of allocation.

As an example, consider the simple system depicted in Figure 5.1a. The completion of a unit of product in operating department 1 requires 1 unit of service from service department 1. The completion of a unit of product in operating department 2 requires 2 units of service from service department 2. This situation is complicated by the fact that a unit of service 1 requires one-quarter unit of service 2, while a unit of service 2 requires one-half unit of service 1. If production departments 1 and 2 decide to produce 70 units each, then service departments 1 and 2 must produce 160 and 180 units, respectively, to support this level of activity. The flows of services are depicted in Figure 5.1b.

How shall the costs of the service departments be allocated to the production departments? A naive answer would be to allocate the costs of service department 1 to operating department 1 only, and to allocate the costs of service department 2 to operating department 2. That this scheme will create problems becomes evident when we consider what happens when operating department 1 increases production to 77 units. To support

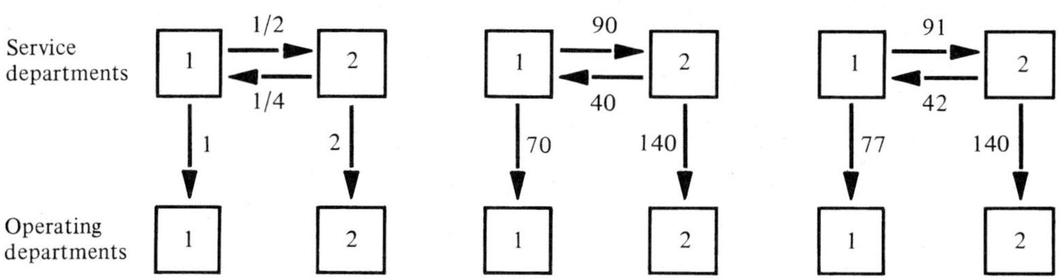

Figure 5.1 (a) Service Flows on a per-unit basis. (b) Total service flows if departments 1 and 2 produce 70 each. (c) Total service flows if department 1 increases to 77 units.

this level of activity, service departments 1 and 2 must increase their levels of service to 168 and 182 units, respectively. (See Figure 5.1c.) This represents an increase of 8 units in service department 1 and 2 units in service department 2, but operating department 1 would only be allocated the cost of the additional 8 units in service department 1, while the costs of the extra 2 units in service department 2 would be allocated to operating department 2.

This *direct method* of allocation can affect decision making in two adverse ways. First, the manager of operating department 1 will not be bearing the entire cost of his or her decisions, will tend to underestimate the variable cost of services, and therefore will tend to accept additional business that might not be profitable to the firm as a whole. At the same time, the costs that are allocated to operating department 2 are influenced by operating department 1's decisions, and this ''uncontrollability'' could lead to difficulties in motivation and performance evaluation which we will consider in later chapters. At any rate, the direct method of allocating service costs would probably lead the operating departments to mis-estimate the variable cost of a unit of service, and to alleviate these problems, we must use an allocation technique that accounts for the reciprocal service department usages.[1] The technique is a complex one, but a number of organizations have decided that the information it provides is worth the cost. (In fact, one large midwestern bank uses this technique to allocate the costs of 500 service departments every month.)

Suppose we have an organization with n service departments and m production or operating departments. Let q_j be the quantity of service demanded from (and supplied by) service department j, $j = 1, \ldots, n$. These demands on service department j come from two sources—its fellow service departments and the operating departments. Let a_{ij} be the units of service j required to produce a unit of service i, and let p_{kj} be the units of service j required to produce a unit of product in operating department k. Finally, let u_k be the number of units produced in operating department k. Now we can determine the number of units of service that must be produced by setting the quantity supplied equal to the quantity demanded.

$$\begin{array}{l} q_1 = a_{11}q_1 + a_{21}q_2 + \cdots + a_{n1}q_n + p_{11}y_1 + \cdots + p_{m1}u_m \\ \quad\vdots \\ q_n = a_{1n}q_1 + a_{2n}q_2 + \cdots + a_{nn}q_n + p_{1n}u_1 + \cdots + p_{mn}u_m \end{array} \tag{5.3}$$

In our example in Figure 5.1a, the relationships can be expressed in two equations. In words, the first equation states that the quantity of service 1 supplied must equal one-half the level of activity in service department 2 plus one times the level of activity in operating department 1. The second equation describes the supply–demand relationships for service department 2.

$$\begin{array}{l} q_1 = (1/2)q_2 + 1u_1 \\ q_2 = (1/4)q_1 + 2u_2 \end{array} \tag{5.4}$$

[1]A thorough analysis is given in Kaplan (1973).

If we know the values of the a_{ij}'s, the p_{kj}'s, and the u_k's, then we have n equations and n unknowns, and we ought to be able to find the q_j's that will support the proposed level of production. This would allow us to accurately budget the services that would be necessary to fulfill the plans of managers in operating departments. We can solve these to get an expression for q_1 in terms of u_1 and u_2, and a similar one for q_2. These would be the following.[2]

$$\begin{aligned} q_1 &= \frac{8}{7}u_1 + \frac{8}{7}u_2 \\ q_2 &= \frac{2}{7}u_1 + \frac{16}{7}u_2 \end{aligned} \tag{5.5}$$

From these we can see that if production department 2 increases u_2 by one unit, this will require an additional 8/7 units of q_1 and 16/7 units of q_2.

More generally, we can use matrix notation to describe the service demand–supply relationships and to solve for the effects of production levels on service levels.

$$Q \equiv [q_1 q_2 \cdots q_n] \qquad U \equiv [u_1 u_2 \cdots u_m]$$

$$A \equiv \begin{bmatrix} a_{11} \cdots a_{1n} \\ \cdot \quad\quad \cdot \\ \cdot \quad\quad \cdot \\ \cdot \quad\quad \cdot \\ a_{n1} \cdots a_{nn} \end{bmatrix} \qquad P \equiv \begin{bmatrix} p_{11} \cdots p_{1n} \\ \cdot \quad\quad \cdot \\ \cdot \quad\quad \cdot \\ \cdot \quad\quad \cdot \\ p_{m1} \cdots p_{mn} \end{bmatrix} \tag{5.6}$$

Then the set of equations in (5.1) can be restated and solved in the following way.

$$\begin{aligned} Q &= QA + UP \\ Q - QA &= UP \\ Q(I - A) &= UP \end{aligned} \tag{5.7}$$

where I is an identity matrix with 1's on the diagonal and 0's elsewhere. Multiplying any matrix by an identity matrix leaves the original matrix unchanged.

$$Q = UP(I - A)^{-1} \tag{5.8}$$

where the exponent of -1 represents the *inverse* matrix. When a matrix is multipled by its inverse matrix, the result is an identity matrix. That is, $(I - A)(I - A)^{-1} = I$ by definition of $(I - A)^{-1}$ as the inverse of $(I - A)$.

While the matrix notation may be somewhat unfamiliar, the operations above are exactly what we would have done if there were only one or two service departments. (Besides, once we understand the process, it is a fairly simple matter to allow a computer to do the calculations using a computer program like the one that appears at the end of the book.)

Before going further, let us examine how this model relates to the example in Figure 5.1a. We have already noted that the relationships between the four departments

[2]These are found by substituting the expression for q_2 into the expression for q_1. That is $q_1 = 1/2[(1/4)q_1 + 2u_2] + 1u_1 \rightarrow q_1 = (1/8)q_1 + u_1 + u_2 \rightarrow (7/8)q_1 = u_1 + u_2 \rightarrow q_1 = 8/7(u_1 + u_2)$. The expression for q_2 is found similarly.

can be expressed in two equations.

$$q_1 = (1/2)q_2 + 1u_1 \qquad (5.9)$$
$$q_2 = (1/4)q_1 + 2u_2$$

These same relationships can be found using the matrix approach where

$$A = \begin{pmatrix} 0 & 1/4 \\ 1/2 & 0 \end{pmatrix} \quad P = \begin{pmatrix} 1 & 0 \\ 0 & 2 \end{pmatrix} \quad I = \begin{pmatrix} 1 & 0 \\ 0 & 1 \end{pmatrix} \qquad (5.10)$$
$$I - A = \begin{pmatrix} 1 & -1/4 \\ -1/2 & 1 \end{pmatrix} \quad (I - A)^{-1} = \begin{pmatrix} 8/7 & 2/7 \\ 4/7 & 8/7 \end{pmatrix}$$

With these matrices,[3] the identical relationships are found between q_1, q_2, u_1, and u_2.

$$Q = UP(I - A)^{-1}$$
$$(q_1 \quad q_2) = (u_1 \quad u_2)\begin{pmatrix} 1 & 0 \\ 0 & 2 \end{pmatrix}\begin{pmatrix} 8/7 & 2/7 \\ 4/7 & 8/7 \end{pmatrix} \qquad (5.11)$$
$$= \{[(8/7)(u_1 + u_2)]\,[(2/7)u_1 + (16/7)u_2]\}$$

or

$$q_1 = (8/7)(u_1 + u_2) \qquad (5.12)$$
$$q_2 = (2/7)u_1 + (16/7)u_2$$

You should refer back to Figures 5.1b and 5.1c to verify that the budgeted levels of service there are consistent with the relationships we've just derived. For instance, when the level of activity in operating departments 1 and 2 are 77 and 70, respectively, service department 1 must produce (8/7) (77 + 70), or 168 units.

Once we have determined how the quantities of service change with respect to production decisions, it is a simple step to determining how service department *costs* vary with production. If we let v_j be the variable costs that can be traced to a unit of service j, the expression for the total variable service department cost C is the following, where V is a vector of variable costs.

$$C = q_1v_1 + q_2v_2 + \cdots + q_nv_n$$
$$= (q_1q_2 \cdots q_n)\begin{pmatrix} v_1 \\ v_2 \\ \cdot \\ \cdot \\ \cdot \\ v_n \end{pmatrix} \qquad (5.13)$$
$$= QV = UP(I - A)^{-1}V$$

In our example, suppose that the variable cost of producing a unit of service was \$10 in service department 1 and \$15 in service department 2. Using the relationships

[3] The inverse of a 2 × 2 matrix can be found using the following formula.

$$\begin{pmatrix} a & b \\ c & d \end{pmatrix}^{-1} = \frac{1}{ad - bc}\begin{pmatrix} d & -b \\ -c & a \end{pmatrix}$$

that we have derived so far, we can find the total service cost as a function of u_1 and u_2.

$$\begin{aligned} C &= \$10q_1 + \$15q_2 = 10[(8/7)(u_1 + u_2)] + 15[(2/7)u_1 + (16/7)u_2)] \\ &= \left[\frac{(10)(8) + (15)(2)}{7}\right]u_1 + \left[\frac{(10)(8) + (15)(16)}{7}\right]u_2 \\ &= \$15.7u_1 + \$45.7u_2 \end{aligned} \tag{5.14}$$

Using this relationship, we can take budgeted activity levels in the production departments and derive budgeted costs for the service departments.

In addition, this relationship lets us avoid the problems inherent in the direct cost allocation technique discussed earlier. If the manager of production department 1 decides to increase production, he or she will be allocated \$15.7 for the service required for each additional unit of output. This is the actual variable service cost of a unit of product 1, so the manager will have the information to make the appropriate activity level decisions. Further, the costs allocated to production department 2 will be unaffected by the activity in production department 1. These variable costs are relatively important for decision making, and can also be derived from the matrix notation.

$$\begin{aligned} C_u &\equiv \begin{pmatrix} \text{marginal service cost with respect to } u_1 \\ \text{marginal service cost with respect to } u_2 \end{pmatrix} \\ &= \begin{pmatrix} c_{u_1} \\ c_{u_2} \end{pmatrix} = P(I - A)^{-1}V \\ &= \begin{pmatrix} 1 & 0 \\ 0 & 2 \end{pmatrix} \begin{pmatrix} 8/7 & 2/7 \\ 4/7 & 8/7 \end{pmatrix} \begin{pmatrix} \$10 \\ \$15 \end{pmatrix} = \begin{pmatrix} \$15.7 \\ \$45.7 \end{pmatrix} \end{aligned} \tag{5.15}$$

There is one other decision setting in which this sort of allocation procedure can be of value. Suppose that an outside supplier would be willing to provide service 2 at a cost of \$20 per unit. Should this offer be accepted, or should we continue to produce service 2 in-house? One way to answer this question would be to go through the analysis that we have just completed, but with service 2 supplied by the outsider. What affect would this have on the variable service costs C_u? The new values of $\hat{A}$ and $\hat{V}$ would be the following. (P would be unchanged.)

$$\begin{aligned} \hat{A} &= \begin{pmatrix} 0 & 1/4 \\ 0 & 0 \end{pmatrix} \qquad \hat{V} = \begin{pmatrix} \$10 \\ \$20 \end{pmatrix} \\ I - \hat{A} &= \begin{pmatrix} 1 & -1/4 \\ 0 & 1 \end{pmatrix} \qquad (I - \hat{A})^{-1} = \begin{pmatrix} 1 & 1/4 \\ 0 & 1 \end{pmatrix} \\ C_u &= \begin{pmatrix} 1 & 0 \\ 0 & 2 \end{pmatrix} \begin{pmatrix} 1 & 1/4 \\ 0 & 1 \end{pmatrix} \begin{pmatrix} \$10 \\ \$20 \end{pmatrix} = \begin{pmatrix} \$15 \\ \$40 \end{pmatrix} \end{aligned} \tag{5.16}$$

We can see from this that the purchase of service 2 outside would *reduce* the variable service costs of the production departments, even though the outside costs of \$20 exceeded the traceable variable costs of \$15 per unit. Of course, the reason for this is that the \$15 did not consider the reciprocal service department usages.

Before moving on to the methods for integrating probabilistic forecasts, we should recognize the accounting information issues inherent in the above allocation techniques. While we have been concentrating on the technique to use in allocating costs from service department cost pools to production cost pools, we have not considered (i) the choice of the number of cost pools, or (ii) the unit of measurement for the quantity of service supplied. Of course, these issues are not unrelated. For instance, suppose that the costs of a computer service department were associated with three factors—CPU usage, peripheral device (tapes, discs, printers) usage, and personnel time. Should these costs be all thrown into one cost pool and allocated on, say, the number of CPU hours used by a department? The problem with this alternative is that different jobs may require differing ratios of the peripheral usage to CPU time or of personnel time to CPU time. Therefore a job that uses a higher than average ratio of peripherals will be "undercharged" for this use. Are these problems serious enough to warrant separate cost pools for the three factors with three different measures of service? There is no one answer to this problem: it will depend on the variety[4] of jobs that pass through the system and on the margins (benefits less costs) for the jobs. If the variety of jobs is low and/or if the margins on jobs are large enough that a slight change in cost allocations will not alter many decisions, then a single cost pool may be cost-effective.

5.3 ANALYTICAL INTEGRATIVE METHODS (PROBABILISTIC)

Most managerial decision making occurs under conditions of uncertainty, and the probability distribution of costs influences the action chosen. But in the previous section, various cost estimates were integrated deterministically. That is, there was no consideration of the possibility that the traceable service department cost might be uncertain. In reality, there are a number of uncontrollable factors such as employee productivity, material prices, machine breakdowns, and so on, which can affect the actual costs and whose outcomes are not known at the time a decision must be made.

If we have cost probability distributions for certain types of costs, we can sometimes aggregate or integrate these to obtain a probability distribution for the total cost. For instance, suppose that v_M and v_L are the uncertain direct material and labor costs for a special order. If we want to find out about the probability distribution for direct cost $(v_M + v_L)$ we can do so by taking advantage of the following statistical relationships.

$$E[v_M + v_L] = E[v_M] + E[v_L] \tag{5.17}$$
$$\sigma^2[v_M + v_L] = \sigma^2[v_M] + \sigma^2[v_L] + 2\rho_{ML}\sigma[v_M]\sigma[v_L]$$

That is, the expected value of the sum is the sum of the expected values. The variance of the sum (which measures dispersion) is the sum of the variances plus a factor that depends on ρ_{ML}, the correlation between v_M and v_L. This correlation coefficient ρ_{ML}, can take on values between -1 and $+1$, and indicates the degree to which the two costs vary together. Positive values of ρ_{ML} would indicate that the two costs tend to vary together, for example, when an employee wastes time he wastes material as well. Nega-

[4]"Variety" is meant in a particular sense. A lack of variety would mean that all jobs use the three factors in the same proportions.

tive values of ρ_{ML} occur when the two costs vary inversely with each other, for example, when an employee takes more time he uses less material than when he rushes the job. As you can see from the expressions for the expected direct cost and the variance of direct cost above, the correlation between v_M and v_L has no effect on the expected cost, while the variance increases as the correlation increases. That is, there is more risk associated with the direct costs if v_M and v_L vary together (i.e., are positively correlated), and less risk if they are negatively correlated.

If the incremental overhead v_{OH} depends on the direct labor costs as $v_{OH} = a + bv_L$, then we can find the expected value and variance of incremental overhead as follows.

$$E[v_{OH}] = E[a + bv_L] = a + bE[v_L] \tag{5.18}$$
$$\sigma^2[v_{OH}] = \sigma^2[a + bv_L] = b^2\sigma^2[v_L]$$

Using these relationships we can find the expected value and variance of more and more complex integrations of cost estimates.[5] For example, we could apply this technique to the reciprocal cost allocation in the previous section (although to do so would be rather complex).

For some decision making, the mean and variance of cost is all the information necessary. As we saw in Chapter 4, the normal probability distribution is completely dependent on mean and variance. But in many cases these two parameters don't completely describe the possible behavior of costs. At this point we run into a problem. While some probability distributions combine nicely (the sum of two normally distributed variables is itself normally distributed), most are not very flexible. For instance, the *product* of two normally distributed variables is not normally distributed. And if we shift to a distribution that multiplies "nicely," it does not add "nicely." This problem is further compounded by the fact that some managerial action may affect the shape of the probability distribution. That is, when activity falls to a certain level, or costs rise to a specified level, some managerial control action occurs that cuts off a part of the probability distribution, and these truncated distributions may be difficult to work with analytically. In some cases we may be able to make an estimate of the expected value of cost, but for some decisions it may be beneficial to get more information about the distribution of costs. For instance, the decision maker may want information on the probability of breaking even for different levels of production.

5.4 SIMULATION METHODS

When analytical methods can no longer provide the information we desire, then we may resort to a form of artificial experimentation called *simulation*. With simulation we try to model both the relationships between different types of costs, and the managerial decision process and its effects on costs. Then we generate random costs from the

[5]The conversion cost $v_C = v_L + v_{OH}$ would have an expected value of $E[v_L] + E[v_{OH}] = a + (1 + b)E[v_L]$, but the variance of the conversion costs must take the correlation of v_L and v_{OH} into account. If $v_{OH} = a + bv_L$, the correlation is a perfect, positive one ($b > 0$), so the correlation coefficient ρ is equal to 1.

$$\begin{aligned}\sigma^2[v_C] &= \sigma^2[v_L] + \sigma^2[v_{OH}] + 2\rho_{L,OH}\sigma[v_L]\sigma[v_{OH}] \\ &= \sigma^2[v_L] + b^2\sigma^2[v_L] + (2)(1)\sigma[v_L]b\sigma[v_L] \\ &= \sigma^2[v_L](1 + 2b + b^2) \\ &= (1 + b)^2\sigma^2[v_L]\end{aligned}$$

specified distributions and combine them in the model to get one observation on our integrated variable of interest. For instance, if direct material costs are normally distributed and direct labor costs are uniformly distributed, we may draw an observation from each distribution, and add them to get an observation of direct costs. By repeating this procedure we can get more observations on direct costs and build up an empirical probability distribution.

The first step in conducting a simulation is to determine the important variables in the system and their interrelationships. What are the factors that are determined exogenously, such as demand for the product? (In decision theory terms, what are the states of nature?) What are the decision variables in the system, and what are the performance variables (payoffs) that will be used to evaluate alternative decisions? For instance, in a simple cost–volume–profit situation, the decision variables may be the amount produced and the price charged, while the exogenous, random variables are variable cost and demand. The criterion or performance variable could be the probability that the contribution margin exceeds a target that is specified in advance.

$$\begin{array}{ll} \text{Decision variables:} & \text{Price, } p \\ & \text{Production, } x \\ \text{Exogenous variables:} & \text{Demand, } d \\ & \text{Variable cost, } v \\ \text{Contribution:} & C = \begin{cases} pd - vx, & \text{if } d < x \\ (p - v)x, & \text{if } d \geq x \end{cases} \end{array} \tag{5.19}$$

After determining the key variables, the next step is to specify how the random variables are to be generated. Simulation is an integrative technique in that we must specify how the parts vary, and then the simulation puts them together to see how the whole varies. The process of generating random numbers according to specified distributions is an interesting one, but rather technical. Therefore we will just touch on the topic. The basis of most random number generation is a random number distributed uniformly between 0 and 1. Most computer languages include such a function along with logarithms, square roots, and so on, and every time the function is used a new random number is generated. In the absence of a computer to generate random numbers, you could use tables of random numbers such as those in Appendices 5.1 and 5.2 at the end of the chapter. Pick a random starting point in the table, take five digits, put a decimal point in front of them and this will *approximate* a variable R drawn from a $U(0, 1)$ distribution, Knowing that R is distributed uniformly between 0 and 1 [$R \sim U(0, 1)$], we can use it to generate other distributions. For example, by defining $X = \alpha + (\beta - \alpha)R$, we have a random variable X distributed uniformly between α and β. By defining

$$X = \begin{cases} \text{"heads,"} & \text{if } R \leq 0.5 \\ \text{"tails,"} & \text{if } R > 0.5 \end{cases} \tag{5.20}$$

we have a random variable that describes the flip of a fair coin.[6] Simulating the roll of

[6]If the coin is unfair, with the odds of a "heads" being 3 to 1, then this could be simulated as

$$X = \begin{cases} \text{"heads,"} & \text{if } R \leq 0.75 \\ \text{"tails,"} & \text{if } R > 0.75 \end{cases}$$

TABLE 5.1 THREE RANDOM VARIABLE GENERATORS

Uniform

Parameters: α, β

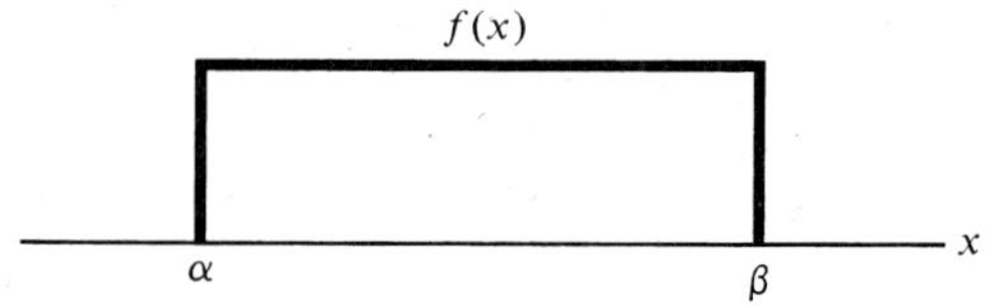

Mean: $\dfrac{\alpha + \beta}{2}$ Variance: $\dfrac{(\beta - \alpha)^2}{12}$

Generator:[a] $x = \alpha + (\beta - \alpha)R$

Triangular

Parameters: α, β, γ

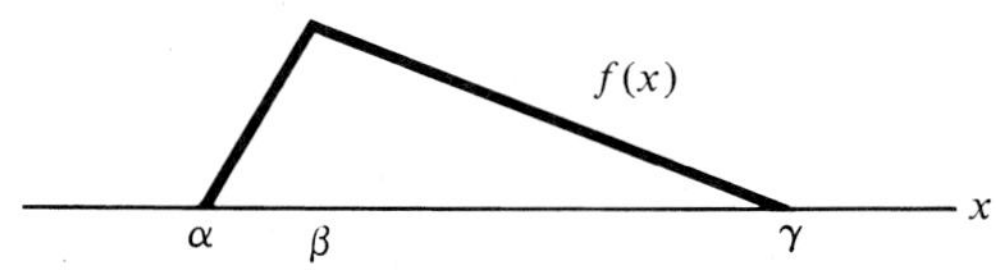

Mean: $\dfrac{\alpha + \beta + \gamma}{3}$ Variance: $\dfrac{\alpha(\alpha - \beta) + \gamma(\gamma - \alpha) + \beta(\beta - \gamma)}{18}$

Generator: $X = \begin{cases} \alpha + [(\beta - \alpha)(\gamma - \alpha)R]^{1/2}, & \text{if } 0 \le R \le (\beta - \alpha)/(\gamma - \alpha) \\ \gamma - [(\gamma - \beta)(\gamma - \alpha)(1 - R)]^{1/2}, & \text{if } (\beta - \alpha)/(\gamma - \alpha) < R \le 1 \end{cases}$

Normal

Parameters: μ, σ^2

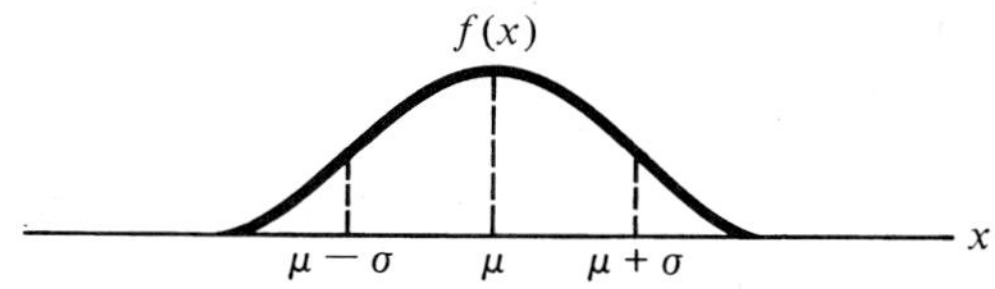

Mean: μ Variance: σ^2

Generator: $X = \mu + \sigma\,(-2 \log_e R_1)^{1/2}[\cos(2\pi R_2)]$

[a]All random number generators here are based on a random variable R, uniformly distributed between zero and one. The generation of a normal variable requires two such variables R_1 and R_2.

a die is done similarly—we just make six divisions instead of two. Techniques for generating three common distributions are described in Table 5.1.

In our example, suppose that variable costs will be \$7 per unit with probability 1/2 or \$8 per unit with probability 1/2. We can simulate this cost behavior with a simple coin flip. If the coin is "heads," then the cost is \$7; if it's "tails," the cost is \$8. Demand will be, in part, dependent on the price charged. For our example, let us say that demand is equal to $(100 - 3p)f$, where f takes the value 0.9 with probability 1/2 and 1.1 with probability 1/2. We can now simulate the product's contribution for a particular price–production combination. We will start with $p = \$20$, $x = 40$ where demand in excess of 40 cannot be satisfied. Coin flip #1 will determine the variable cost (heads → \$7, tails → \$8) and coin flip #2 will determine the demand factor (heads → 0.9, tails → 1.1).

Trial #	#1	#2	Variable cost	Units sales	Contribution
1	Heads	Tails	\$7	40	\$520
2	Tails	Tails	\$8	40	\$480
3	Heads	Heads	\$7	36	\$440
4	Heads	Tails	\$7	40	\$520
.	.	.	.	.	.
.	.	.	.	.	.
.	.	.	.	.	.

This simulation could be repeated and, after a large number of trials, we could determine the percentage of trials where the contribution exceeded a target amount. Of course, this simulation is an extremely simple one since there are only four possible outcomes and each is equally likely, but it shows how the technique is used. The next step would be to consider another decision combination, for example, $p = \$18$, $x = 40$, or $p = \$22$, $x = 35$, and for each of these alternatives, repeat the simulation until a choice can be made.

As with other types of experimentation, we must exercise some care in interpreting the results, since they are subject to sampling variation. Suppose that we have a choice between two alternative courses of action, and that we have simulated n profit observations (independently) for each of them. Let us say that the average profit for alternative 1 is greater than that for alternative 2, but an important question is whether the difference in averages is significant or whether it could have been caused by chance. One statistical test of this question would be a t-test computed as the following

$$t = \frac{\overline{X}_1 - \overline{X}_2}{[(s_1^2 + s_2^2)/n]^{1/2}} \tag{5.21}$$

where $\overline{X}_i$ and s_i^2 are the sample mean and variance of alternative i.[7] This statistic has $2(n - 1)$ degrees of freedom, and we can find the critical value of the test by referring to a table of t-values such as that which appears at the end of Chapter 6. The larger t is, in absolute value, the less chance there is that the difference in means was caused by chance.

5.5 A SERVICE DEPARTMENT SIMULATION EXAMPLE

Before moving on to statistical methods of cost estimation in the next chapter, we will explore an example that combines some of the information issues of service department allocation with a simulation analysis. Suppose that a manager receives proposed job orders which could be processed over the next week. The number of proposals received varies from week to week, but she has only capacity enough for six jobs every week. The manager knows the price less the direct cost for each job (this varies from job to job), but the production process can also use services which are supplied by two non-operating departments, called service departments 1 and 2. In service department 1, the variable cost of a unit of service is \$100, while the variable cost of a unit in service department 2 is \$200. There are no reciprocal service department usages, but different jobs can require different levels of service.

Past experience has enabled the manager to be more precise about some of these uncertainties in Exhibit 5.1. The table of service department usage indicates that, on average, a job uses 2.5 units of service 1 and 2.5 units of service 2, representing an average cost of 2.5(100) + 2.5(200), or \$750 per job. One possible cost allocation scheme would be to simply charge each job \$750 for expected service department usage—

[7]If x_{ij} is the jth outcome observed for alternative i, then

$$\overline{X}_i = \frac{1}{n}\sum_{j=1}^{n} x_{ij} \quad \text{and} \quad s_i^2 = \frac{1}{(n-1)}\sum_{j=1}^{n} (x_{ij} - \overline{X}_i)^2$$

EXHIBIT 5.1
PROBABILITY DISTRIBUTIONS

Job Proposals

Number of job proposals arriving for a week	Probability
10	0.05
11	0.1
12	0.15
13	0.2
14	0.2
15	0.15
16	0.1
17	0.05

Price Less Direct Cost

The price less direct cost for job proposals follows a uniform distribution between \$500 and \$1,000; that is, all dollar values between \$500 and \$1,000 are equally likely

Service Department Usage

Probabilities of different service department usage for each job proposal are shown in the following table.

	Units of service 2 used				
Units of service 1 used	1	2	3	4	Row totals
1	0.04	0.06	0.06	0.04	0.20
2	0.06	0.09	0.09	0.06	0.30
3	0.06	0.09	0.09	0.06	0.30
4	0.04	0.06	0.06	0.04	0.20
Column totals	0.20	0.30	0.30	0.20	1.00

we will call this method *allocation alternative 1,* or AA1. Another possibility would be to find out the amount of service 2 that will be used and allocate at the rate of \$200 per unit. Service 1 costs would be based on the average usage of 2.5 units, or a charge of \$250, per job. This method could be called *allocation alternative 2,* or AA2. Finally, the manager may find out the amounts of both services 1 and 2 to be used by a job, and then allocate the cost of \$100 per unit of service 1 used and \$200 per unit of service 2 used. This last alternative will be called AA3.

As we move from AA1 to AA2 to AA3, the manager receives better information about the resources that will be used by each job, and this should enable her to make a better ranking of the available jobs. But AA3 requires information about the planned service department usage that AA1 does not require. In some businesses, this information may be easily obtained, in others, with more difficulty. For instance, if the job passes through many different operating departments, each of which may utilize services at different stages of production, then it may require some effort (and expense) to tabulate the service usages for each job, each week. At any rate, the main issue is whether a shift from, say, AA1 to AA3, "pays off" in that the profit increase from improved decision making is greater than the increased cost of the information.

Since this is a rather complex situation to analyze, we may use a simulation model to *estimate* the effects of the allocation alternatives on decision making and profits. We will briefly examine how the simulation could be set up, and then discuss some results. We start by examining AA1 and its performance for a simulated week. For this week, we first need to determine how many job proposals arrive, based on the probability distribution in Exhibit 5.1. This is done using a random number uniformly distributed between 0 and 1, as depicted in Exhibit 5.2.[8] Let us begin to simulate a week using the random numbers in Appendix 5.1, starting with the first number at the top left and working across a row and then down to the next. For each five-digit number, we will put a decimal point in front of it to approximate a random number between 0 and 1. The first random event is the number of job proposals, and the first random number R is 0.05341. Exhibit 5.2 indicates that when R is between 0.05 and 0.15, the simulated number of proposals is 11. Now for each of these proposals we must simulate the price less the direct cost *and* the service department usages. The next random number is 0.54008, so we can simulate that job proposal number 1 has a price less the direct cost of 500 + 500 (0.54008) or \$770.04. Under AA1, this job proposal would also be charged \$750 for expected service usage so the remaining profit would be \$20.04. But for comparison purposes, we also want to simulate the actual service department usages. The next random number is 0.32771, and Exhibit 5.2 indicates that if R is between 0.26 and 0.35, then two units of each service are used. The variable cost of this usage is only \$600, so the actual contribution of simulated job proposal 1 is not \$20.04 but \$770.04 − \$600, or \$170.04. Job proposals 2–11 then are simulated in the same way, as shown below.

Week: 1
Job Proposals: 11

Job no.	Price less direct cost	AA1 contribution	Service 1 usage	Service 2 usage	AA3 contribution
1	\$770.04	\$ 20.04	2	2	\$ 170.04
2	929.26	179.26	4	2	129.26
3	817.07	67.07	1	4	(82.93)
4	718.29	(31.71)	1	2	218.29
5	973.55	223.55	3	3	73.55
6	625.76	(124.24)	4	4	(574.24)
7	850.27	100.27	3	2	150.27
8	514.16	(235.84)	4	4	(685.84)
9	775.78	25.78	3	4	(324.22)
10	623.92	(126.08)	2	2	23.92
11	870.82	120.82	2	2	270.82

Best six jobs under AA1: 5, 2, 11, 7, 3, 9
Best six jobs under AA3: 11, 4, 1, 7, 2, 5

The choices of the best six job proposals under AA1 and AA3 have some similarities: the best four jobs under AA1 are included in the best six for AA3. But jobs 3 and

[8]It should be pointed out that there are other ways that these random events might be simulated. There is nothing unique about Exhibit 5.2.

EXHIBIT 5.2
RANDOM EVENT SIMULATION

How Many Job Proposals Arrive?

If R[1] is >	and ≤	Then the simulated number of job proposals is
0.00	0.05	10
0.05	0.15	11
0.15	0.30	12
0.30	0.50	13
0.50	0.70	14
0.70	0.85	15
0.85	0.95	16
0.95	1.00	17

For example, if $R = 0.52224$, then 14 job proposals arrive in the simulated week.

What is a Job Proposal's Price Less Direct Cost?

$$\text{Price less direct cost} = \$500 + (\$1{,}000 - 500)R$$
$$= \$500 + \$500R$$

For example, if $R = 0.34832$, then a simulated job proposal's price less direct cost is $500 + 500(0.34832) = \$674.16$

What is the Amount of Service that Will Be Used?

If R is		Then services used will be	
>	and ≤	in service department 1	in service department 2
0.00	0.04	1	1
0.04	0.10	1	2
0.10	0.16	1	3
0.16	0.20	1	4
0.20	0.26	2	1
0.26	0.35	2	2
0.35	0.44	2	3
0.44	0.50	2	4
0.50	0.56	3	1
0.56	0.65	3	2
0.65	0.74	3	3
0.74	0.80	3	4
0.80	0.84	4	1
0.84	0.90	4	2
0.90	0.96	4	3
0.96	1.00	4	4

[1] R is uniformly distributed between 0 and 1.

9 would be using up more resources than they generate, causing negative contributions. As measured under AA3 (the most accurate measurement), jobs 5, 2, 11, 7, 3, and 9 would generate a contribution of $216.75, while the contribution from jobs 11, 4, 1, 7, 2, and 5 would be $1,012.23. Therefore the opportunity cost of using AA1 *for this simulated week* is $795.48.

The next step in the simulation is to repeat the simulation for more weeks under AA1, and then to repeat the process for AA2 and for AA3. A computer simulation was run for 50 weeks, with the following results.

Allocation method	Average weekly profit (measured using AA3)	Standard deviation of weekly profit
AA1	$ 831.30	521.56
AA2	1,234.49	523.46
AA3	1,346.87	514.46

It appears that the risk (as measured by the standard deviation) does not vary significantly between the different allocation systems. However, there are rather large differences between the average weekly profits. For instance, there was a $515.57 average loss in weekly profits that arose from using AA1 instead of AA3. If we apply the t-test described in the last section, the resulting value of t is close to 5, indicating that there is little chance that the $515.57 difference was caused by random fluctuations. We can also see that AA2 represents a significant improvement over AA1 ($403.19 per week, on average). If the cost of determining each job's usage of service 1 was significant, then it may be that AA2 represents the best choice for this firm. Of course, these results are contingent on the particular situation that was portrayed in the simulation. For instance, a change in the service department costs and usages, or in the number of jobs that could be accepted, or in a variety of other variables, could change the simulation results, and an analysis of the sensitivity of the results should be considered.

5.6 SUMMARY

Throughout this book, we will be looking at the effect of information (usually cost information) on decision making in a variety of situations—short-term planning, cost control, budget setting, and so on. In many of these situations we will examine the effect of better information on the decisions and payoffs that occur. In this chapter, we have briefly examined some of the engineering techniques that may be used to produce the estimates of costs, and have indicated some of the instances where they may be useful in estimating cost behavior.

In most cases, engineering measurement methods are rather expensive ways to examine cost behavior. The detailed analysis of production tasks and the steps necessary to complete them are worthwhile only when a given process is to be repeated many times. Therefore, there may be some costs, for example, supervision costs, which are not amenable to measurement using these methods.

The other estimation methods that were described in this chapter are known as integrative methods. That is, a manager may know the way that costs behave in the individual parts, but not in the greater whole. In using the integrative methods, the manager must provide both the information on the individual parts and on the relationships between the parts. For instance, in the service department allocation, the manager must provide the direct cost information for the service departments and the interdepartmental demands. Then the allocation system can combine these to produce the desired information. A similar situation exists in simulation, where the individual probability

APPENDIX 5.1 TABLE OF RANDOM NUMBERS

05341	54008	32771	85851	87253	63413	19098	43658	06656	94709
67030	25151	99511	70053	64980	02832	98233	55156	74074	24784
30856	74164	33802	17871	98360	49489	14797	62789	87068	08293
63605	43049	72096	80481	73434	39075	08649	96918	50515	33346
52815	88177	00786	05701	61556	85709	32238	36859	91543	21844
49050	09590	97984	26277	59799	05199	38135	31924	68080	03526
67788	69063	81882	86462	42443	68854	07729	35604	19649	63333
50682	32258	54320	83074	16679	57436	04593	58356	13710	93028
24793	22681	47127	18289	71300	05742	21991	16868	02543	39285
46583	68603	71970	54760	26550	54215	37423	82154	67244	57646
55282	54676	74897	56683	81631	01727	57792	34684	71091	55930
20402	73538	82677	48444	69252	52501	70422	10134	09401	54049
91585	71573	50305	58021	01957	65383	95266	47482	58210	21552
51978	04028	16721	70945	25504	06621	32404	46478	22952	37444
63396	79603	51141	78389	65194	99134	15424	11054	94178	39452
22032	15571	05261	28787	78076	72952	56579	99761	89201	66261
03630	84705	60761	74751	02794	13313	01330	80899	10155	16156
14504	65717	81506	27030	08273	09925	73517	75922	87988	95119
42568	92526	59883	02606	44743	10928	31066	13396	37006	60238
08356	09381	74856	72785	95935	70987	13500	79435	01205	80690
11367	11932	30104	18332	23078	00557	89452	64629	06474	76466
84600	03526	16763	71698	22953	13981	08858	17996	10448	78180
42066	45642	51560	76842	69544	86964	55157	92735	50013	71657
26299	04822	38386	31464	70924	95286	90455	97838	95851	46018
64065	03108	06432	37445	14420	75796	11242	50870	98779	49991
12706	68478	71761	55972	21154	70987	90037	24897	39598	38825
11159	87633	76612	54467	90038	75922	36964	97754	83639	21217
27470	51748	47461	53505	53483	95704	39055	04822	23580	13271
12162	08085	41355	83115	26089	91229	14797	88302	36337	88930
49260	10427	96938	29707	52146	28452	66323	45307	27051	25734
00284	68352	83136	81819	55491	30000	25755	79477	87152	59946
61138	00012	52522	89933	95224	23266	06223	51413	33659	32300
06098	76717	84141	06370	08524	95537	51727	27951	68415	40791
43530	78055	42735	41585	65194	37402	88155	30251	23245	88762
61054	38825	23915	12267	16345	96708	73141	88929	10991	37696
77741	00640	01664	90602	43069	27825	44743	87465	76528	51790
95140	60029	84057	55889	10991	39745	71300	18498	46625	56600
44784	22388	59590	42631	11912	48862	05973	29582	76277	78934
41564	47733	47043	93321	21865	28243	28390	73622	05596	04320
27721	01141	46499	05366	49803	58063	02710	61660	02626	23935
29728	07876	92715	81527	82760	71363	23956	10970	20234	86210
04634	93279	95600	82697	40393	11514	67871	91982	37758	44931
92255	46102	02961	76006	23664	74458	40769	85751	20234	09673
59172	54885	37465	82906	64693	65006	31736	26194	62393	97419
59130	68938	58210	34308	75441	43760	60134	54048	38511	80648
72346	41753	02375	12811	02250	75211	25462	69649	56955	37779
62392	82614	40937	10175	71008	84036	61891	73998	05345	04780
24877	09381	23831	76592	37006	98507	81088	28578	03923	23267
33785	94241	32154	62915	39473	04446	27930	99929	51894	88594
97189	15320	30356	80481	47922	90978	28013	10092	83136	07331

25734	74772	20255	03672	96165	89285	03986	77700	00765	97775
01100	11576	22304	60134	41292	13877	40916	28933	58649	90540
37612	63480	81108	46039	94282	18101	42171	88071	92526	49176
71530	24040	12476	13960	02103	57541	36315	68247	64170	96562
44764	68708	88887	46457	18247	70548	08293	14630	40414	31025
52961	05847	89933	05931	54341	28097	49866	50765	42421	85562
01811	23078	51581	86818	24730	78954	10050	35458	00807	74187
49280	40644	13104	64274	02773	06558	39703	06767	00222	39431
64253	57750	72200	46374	67766	73015	51330	34203	30962	09235
68770	08273	35437	21614	55387	73643	61326	67411	41752	38594
90811	03588	60490	08774	05784	84475	41585	90707	86671	67620
17077	89452	13605	09109	17537	12120	71113	65906	74416	65529
36399	92338	20046	55031	93404	45956	84119	86859	23434	81672
99553	66951	06328	58796	95454	03296	23977	30481	05324	00075
57980	54279	57687	64692	88469	86273	86629	03086	97628	82258
22430	22074	67348	00075	96249	27010	78055	93760	38951	24124
09883	21740	81108	20527	46186	38637	55345	21865	66511	01121
92819	34663	53630	65571	24395	65153	87674	88072	81819	19272
50828	25588	95370	03840	22639	32446	97378	24208	85876	67369
17537	86608	21844	85269	88762	99323	11556	43112	41334	65654
35730	96395	06411	94471	74793	01497	16031	90833	12392	14504
01937	59506	28369	92380	93237	09653	03442	90623	22262	45453
20381	66784	21049	74312	59318	74604	20171	02166	01267	73392
51079	34663	28118	16302	44931	79498	21468	62057	32593	40560
61451	66742	45809	26131	30251	84977	16031	41857	09758	73433
73245	93091	79226	89661	50661	87235	21133	89745	77679	30230
16491	28306	86922	28892	46018	62016	08377	88574	92484	48423
74082	15508	36022	43614	15780	16805	58817	02208	63751	98110
40414	82049	50327	64776	62413	38343	05199	25379	07289	28348
60113	83513	56056	07854	47692	48340	89431	32363	96750	22869
89013	59422	41669	15675	36106	45119	10677	32698	10552	45245
36399	79582	95412	15299	51163	61681	71112	12832	83492	87570
20130	92756	67474	62016	21133	13208	32216	91836	58357	28515
11222	82384	09882	96228	33011	41062	60531	71258	30502	73810
87800	11744	35145	85102	75922	73183	76926	83806	05324	10782
87884	74981	56139	81798	99762	65738	11723	43196	42840	60552
51623	49302	49448	67118	56265	57667	49280	91669	09297	23203
75253	38971	90560	04048	57645	17014	81945	55700	27616	31150
63877	34538	17202	88783	18833	96646	56976	93509	26654	97817
78390	54487	69230	94722	12601	77072	28160	43739	90476	66324
83576	99782	44931	30523	18833	22158	05073	72973	12308	64023
03233	03714	47942	82927	71447	25462	05868	36127	39117	47671
67098	77072	38867	73643	12350	64776	00681	11075	24396	54446
57771	66198	83367	02166	39536	46123	71447	63730	78599	55324
68185	96980	04948	00326	56348	57123	50619	88532	17244	00243
46186	25881	31882	82133	24270	18018	80983	60636	14860	71468
44972	90958	48820	91292	07499	29185	59067	86943	48402	31108
75880	61723	49574	54571	30418	22158	90267	55952	54718	76822
54132	88992	78180	29310	22179	11827	34601	86441	73957	81129
52794	55910	92234	52104	65968	41606	57143	80837	03525	52982

APPENDIX 5.2 NORMALLY DISTRIBUTED RANDOM NUMBERS
(Mean = 0; Standard Deviation = 1)

+0.3767	-0.0537	+0.0479	+1.3331	-0.8308	+0.1048	-1.6433	-0.2420
-0.1262	-1.3179	-1.3018	-1.6375	-1.0557	-1.7320	-0.2486	-2.4881
-0.8705	+0.1018	-1.1566	+0.2884	+0.1722	+0.6404	-1.3410	-0.4671
-0.0843	-0.3421	+0.3645	-0.5692	+2.2629	-1.7629	+1.5514	+0.6727
+0.2212	+0.5203	-1.6009	-0.6624	+0.8648	-0.1520	+1.2756	-1.4977
+1.8315	+0.8468	-0.5575	-0.6768	-0.5765	-0.1104	+0.9655	+0.4883
+1.6934	+1.7121	+0.3109	+0.0065	-0.0083	-1.6525	-0.4201	+1.2077
-0.8842	+0.0525	-0.7322	+0.9883	-0.2049	+0.0652	-0.1408	+2.0424
+0.1082	-0.3554	-2.1936	+0.5990	-0.1735	-0.3249	-0.9513	+0.1822
-0.1363	-0.3562	-0.2616	-0.8255	-1.4374	+0.6914	+0.3764	-0.7403
-0.6684	+0.6837	-0.3293	-0.4258	-1.5688	+0.8295	-0.9811	+0.4076
-0.2831	+0.5906	+0.6057	+0.5988	-0.0606	+0.6015	-0.3953	+1.2350
-0.0575	-0.5556	-1.0487	+0.3511	-0.3340	-0.4628	+0.6122	+1.2001
-0.8818	-0.0036	+0.6967	-0.0095	-0.4421	+2.2514	-1.5565	+0.9773
+1.1623	-0.0706	-1.5972	-0.6702	-0.5841	-1.6025	-1.6189	-0.9166
+1.7435	+1.4500	+0.0177	-1.1458	+0.5880	-0.9906	+0.2215	+0.6776
-0.2147	+1.0491	+0.6579	-1.8647	+0.1300	-0.5193	-0.2182	-1.0334
+0.2599	+0.1637	+0.8850	+0.2703	+0.0689	-0.6110	-0.2536	-1.2310
-0.3506	-1.3824	+1.0087	-0.5092	-0.1626	+0.5793	-0.3930	-0.3374
+0.2964	+0.4931	-1.2154	+0.8895	-1.1254	-0.3100	+0.7428	+1.9767
-0.4182	-0.2481	+1.6392	+0.8757	-0.7456	-0.4737	+1.3469	-0.8978
+1.3928	-1.7555	+0.4244	+0.9503	+1.0498	-1.1036	+2.2160	+1.6412
+0.3062	-0.2478	-0.9292	+0.0805	+1.9937	-0.7734	-1.0071	+0.6340
-0.5866	+1.0810	+0.3425	-0.2493	+1.4098	+2.2964	-0.0355	+1.2238
-0.5302	-1.1844	+1.1824	-0.6610	-1.0503	-0.4004	-0.8452	+0.7816
-1.1960	+1.6712	+1.2386	+1.1768	+0.8815	-0.2329	-0.0715	-0.0998
+0.0590	+1.3075	-0.3674	+0.7197	+0.8674	+0.0844	-1.5423	+0.2292
-1.2714	+1.3895	-0.7439	-0.6110	-1.2870	-0.3460	-1.0044	+0.6635
-0.6749	+1.4085	-0.1889	-0.5434	+1.4621	-0.2477	+0.4751	+0.6489
-0.3379	-1.3739	+0.1803	+0.3418	+2.6832	+1.6549	-0.3617	+0.5409
-0.6941	+1.0006	+1.6459	+0.9628	+0.3246	+0.4177	-0.2974	-0.3027
+0.5083	+0.2445	+0.6788	+1.3697	+0.5895	-0.6336	-0.3946	+1.9988
-0.7955	+0.2570	-1.1892	+0.2200	-0.6103	-0.1056	-0.1919	-0.6840
+0.5605	+0.9813	-0.2787	-0.4716	+0.9685	+1.2563	+0.5558	-0.8008
+0.5528	+0.0110	-0.4646	+0.6188	-0.3588	-0.3580	-0.7880	-1.4113
+0.5777	-0.0100	-0.0209	-1.1855	+0.1044	+1.3750	+1.1332	+1.2195
-0.8713	-2.5045	-1.0972	-1.0810	-0.5368	-0.0042	+0.0449	-0.2962
-0.1812	-0.4999	-1.7862	-1.2299	+0.1054	-0.1195	+0.5752	+1.0618
-1.6614	-1.2561	-0.2319	-0.2320	-1.1571	+1.1976	-1.0570	+1.8525
+0.2495	-0.8273	-1.0095	+0.4684	-0.5326	-0.1590	+0.8805	+0.6548
-0.9003	+0.2519	-0.1952	+0.0998	+0.8847	+0.0515	+0.4345	+0.5955
-1.4275	+0.1069	-1.3117	-1.5844	-0.7480	-0.4420	-1.1767	-1.3734
+0.9086	-0.6017	+0.4197	-0.9642	-0.7584	-0.5248	-0.1174	+0.9987
-1.3831	-0.5706	+0.3260	+0.0839	+0.9028	-0.3885	-1.0508	+1.9487
-0.8663	+0.2889	+0.8007	+0.8707	-0.3812	+2.4065	-0.5927	+1.8331
+0.5171	+0.0746	-0.6212	-0.1019	-1.0041	-1.0933	-0.5544	+1.7744
-2.5659	+0.4348	-1.1225	-1.2069	+0.4970	+1.3691	-0.3653	-1.3422
-1.4439	-1.2632	-0.7410	-1.7340	-1.0005	+0.6604	-1.4394	+1.1728
-0.8169	-0.8096	+0.9975	-0.6511	-0.1655	+2.4877	+0.6174	-0.4921
+0.4792	-1.2484	-0.6809	+0.5371	-0.5881	+0.6494	+2.0750	-0.1843

distributions and decision rules are combined to produce information on a variable such as costs or profits. As shown, this information may be used to evaluate alternative courses of action or alternative cost estimation systems.

PROBLEMS

5.1. Identify a relatively simple task that you can observe (scooping ice cream cones, typing business letters, etc.). Identify the steps that are necessary to complete the task, and, if possible, take measurements of the amount of time necessary to complete the task. Compute the mean and standard deviation of the time necessary to complete the task. How might these measurements be used for planning and control?

5.2. A firm has two service departments, S_1 and S_2, which provide service to the two production departments P_1 and P_2, and to each other as shown below. (The program SERVCOST may be helpful in doing this problem.)

	Units of service needed to produce a unit in			
Service from	S_1	S_2	P_1	P_2
S_1	0	0.5	3	0
S_2	0.5	0	0	2

Direct variable costs per unit	
S_1	\$ 6.00
S_2	10.00
P_1	30.00
P_2	40.00

Required

A. Suppose that the total revenue curves for the outputs of P_1 and P_2 were the following:

$$\text{TR}_1 = 100P_1 - (2/3)(P_1)^2 \; [\text{price} = 100 - (2/3)P_1]$$
$$\text{TR}_2 = 200P_2 - (2/3)(P_2)^2 \; [\text{price} = 200 - (2/3)P_2]$$

If the firm's objectives were to maximize total profit, how much of P_1 and P_2 should be produced?

B. An outside firm has offered to supply service S_1 at a cost of \$18.00 per unit. How large would the *fixed avoidable* costs of department S_1 have to be in order to make the order attractive?

C. Suppose that the variable service department costs are subject to uncertainty. What happens to the variable costs of P_1 and P_2 if the unit cost of S_2 increases to \$11.00? If it declines to \$9.00?

5.3. Paul Robertson's business has just received a project proposal from a customer to build a special-purpose machine for use in the customer's production process. The customer is willing to pay \$75,000 for the machine. Robertson has discussed the proposal with his manufacturing supervisor, and they have agreed that the amount of materials and labor may vary depending on the difficulty that they encounter in overcoming some design problems and in testing the machine. After considering a number of different possible outcomes, they arrived at the following estimates.

Type of cost	Expected value	Standard deviation
Materials	$15,000	2,000
Direct labor	$30,000	3,000
Set-up costs	$10,000	0

In addition, variable overhead costs for power, maintenance, etc., amount to one-half of the direct labor costs. In the past, Robertson has had experience with cost overruns, which took away most or all of the profit margin on this type of project.

Required

A. What is the expected profit for the project?

B. What is the standard deviation of the costs of completing the project, assuming that materials and labor costs are not correlated?

C. If costs follow a normal distribution, what is the probability that Robertson will break even on the proposed project?

D. If labor and material costs have a correlation of 0.5, what is the standard deviation of the cost of completing the project?

5.4. (Based on a paper by M. Paliferro). The data processing division of a large bank consists of eight service departments. The Computer Services Department (CSD) is responsible for all hardware functions, running all production and test jobs, and distributing production output, involving the bank's systems. The Systems Management Division (SMD) is divided into seven departments. Six of these departments are responsible for development and maintenance of any computerized systems that service their corresponding profit center. The bank is divided into two kinds of areas—profit centers and service departments. A profit center is defined as an area of the bank with a definable product that produces direct income for the bank. Service departments are all areas that either don't have definable products or produce services to another area of the bank, thereby not producing direct income.

The six departments and the profit centers they service are: SMG1—personal banking department; SMG2—personnel and control departments; SMG3—bond and trust departments; SMG4—commercial banking department; SMG5—international banking department; and ISG—executive department. The seventh department in SMD is the Application Support Group (ASG). This department supplies generalized services to the other six SMD departments as well as some specialized service to CSD.

The profit centers of the bank have a standard cost system, based on a product router. For each product associated with a profit center, a product router is created. A product router is made up of three parts: a list of the sequence of operations needed to produce the product; the processing time required for each product; and the processing cost for each operation and each product. As part of the annual budgeting process, these product routers are reviewed and revised if any of the parameters have changed.

There are three other phases to the budgeting process. A manpower plan must be produced, showing the staff needed to produce a product or service. It also contains the product or service volume at a given level of efficiency.

The next part of the budget is a plan of the direct expenses anticipated for the year. Direct expenses include the following: expense accounts for officers; space rental; repairs and building services; salary; overtime; shift differential; leave, profit sharing; health bene-

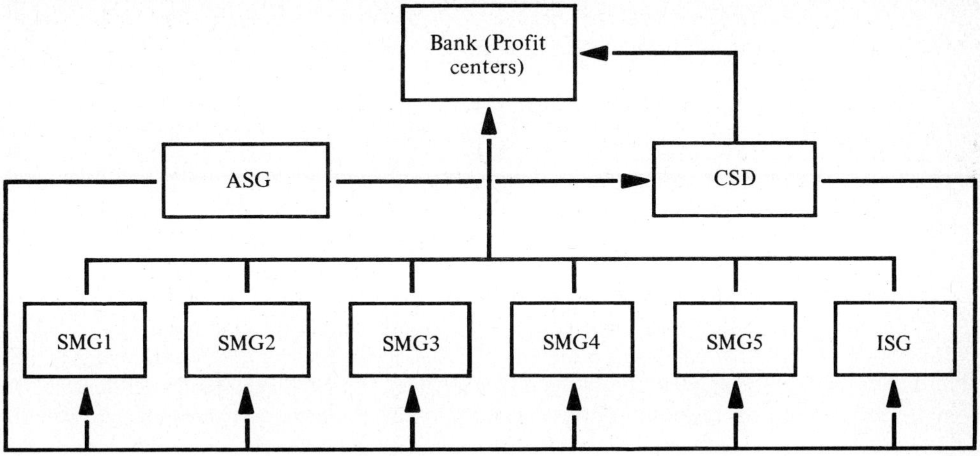

fits; tuition refund; equipment usage and maintenance; postage; stationery; telephone; travel and entertainment; local taxes; and outside services.

The last phase of the budget is the indirect expenses. Indirect expenses are the costs incurred by a department for utilizing products and services of other departments. There are two ways a department can specify their indirect expenses: unit charges and allocation. Unit charges are incurred on the volume of services used. The department receiving the services plans the volume of services it will use. The second method, allocation, is based on a percentage of the allocating department's budget. The allocating department decides on the percentages for all of the departments it services.

All four of the budgeting processes are combined to come up with a service charge rate or product standard cost. Profit centers must complete all four phases, whereas service departments only participate in the last three phases. Currently, the various data processing departments use different methods of charging out their services. The six departments in SMD, excluding ASG, charge the profit centers on a volume basis. Volume of service is equal to the number of hours spent servicing a profit center. ASG, on the other hand, charges the other SMG departments on an allocation basis. Each of the six departments is charged one-sixth of ASG's expenses. This shows up in the budgeting plan as an indirect expense for each of the SMG departments. The services that ASG provides CSD are included in this allocation and get charged directly to SMD, so these charges never enter into the CSD budget. ASG's allocation method would not affect SMD management's decision making if the allocations remained constant, if all the departments used one-sixth of ASG's total services, or if ASG's total expenses did not increase drastically in any single year. However, this is not the case.

In 1981 the SMD service charge rate was \$21.75/hr. Included in this figure was an ASG staff of thirty people. During the year, ASG committed five of its thirty people to work on a special CSD project. The mini-computer support unit, made up of fifteen people, was incorporated into ASG. (Almost all mini-computer applications were in the international banking department.) This accounted for the major portion of the 1982 service charge rate increase to \$32.45/hr. This sharp increase caused some of the SMD departments to lose projects. Many of the profit centers contracted outside services to automate their operations. They were able to find outside services that charged less than \$32.45/hr. Since their goal is to maximize their department's profit, the optimal decision for them was to contract outside.

Required

A. How would you expect the existing allocation system to affect decision making in the bank?

B. What modifications would you suggest?

5.5. Christopher Patrickson operates a small tool-and-die company in a large city. He has been in business for about three years, and currently employs 30 people. The business has prospered to the point where Patrickson receives more orders than he can handle. The firm has a capacity of about 800 direct labor hours per week, and Patrickson would prefer to not expand for the next year or two.

The problem that Patrickson is currently facing is how to price his scarce capacity. "If I just accept the first jobs that have a positive contribution margin, then I may not have sufficient capacity to do a really lucrative job that comes in a little later. On the other hand, if I wait for a really lucrative job, then it may never show up and I would have been better off taking the earlier jobs. I think the best way for me to handle this is to assign a cost to the use of capacity—an opportunity cost. But I don't really see how to come up with an opportunity cost that will maximize my expected contribution margin."

After further conversation, you have the following information. Job proposals arrive randomly each working day (Monday through Friday). If a job is accepted, it is scheduled for the following week. Once the following week's capacity is used up, additional job proposals must be rejected. The following probability information is gathered from past data.

(i)

Number of job proposals arriving in a day	Probability
0	0.20
1	0.30
2	0.30
3	0.20

(ii) Direct labor hours per job proposal is distributed uniformly between 80 hr and 120 hr.

(iii) The contribution margin (revenue less material costs, in this case) per direct labor hour follows a triangular distribution (see Table 5.1) with parameters $\alpha = \$6.00$, $\beta = \$10.00$, $\gamma = \$14.00$.

Required

A. Set up a simulation model that will assist Patrickson in choosing an opportunity cost per direct labor hour that will maximize the expected contribution margin per week. Run a sample simulation for one week.

B. Can you think of other situations where this sort of analysis would be useful?

5.6. One of the important factors in evaluating the desirability of a computer systems project is the length of time that will be required to implement the system. Unfortunately, the amount of systems analyst time, programmer time, and testing time that will be necessary are uncertain. To calculate the probability of the new system recovering its implementation costs within three years, we have to know the probability distribution of the costs necessary for implementation. There are three stages in implementation, and for the project currently under consideration we have the following information.

System Analysis

Analyst time: uniformly distributed between 400 and 550 man-hours
Cost per hour: $13.00

Programming

Programmer time: uniformly distributed between 800 and 1,000 man-hours
Cost per hour: $10.50

Testing

Testing time: uniformly distributed between 300 and 400 man-hours
Cost per hour: $15.00

Required

A. Run a simple simulation to generate ten observations of the total cost of implementing the proposed system.

B. The expected benefits of the proposed system are estimated to be $7,500 per year. Based on your results in A, what is the likelihood that the system would break even in three years?

5.7. You have been retained as a consultant to a plant that produces corrugated fiberboard containers (''cardboard boxes''). These plants are basically job shops where an order for a particular type of box arrives periodically from regular customers.

As orders are received at a plant they are sent to the production scheduler, who takes note of the requested delivery date as well as the order specifications. Then, on the scheduled day, the production order is sent to the production area where four operations occur.

1. The specified types of paper are fed into the corrugating machine, with the desired thickness, width, and length of cardboard coming out the other end.
2. The cardboard ''blanks'' are then taken to the ''printing–slotting'' operation, where any printing on the box is done, and the ''slots'' for folding the top and bottom are cut.
3. Next, the cardboard is folded and glued along the side seam of the box.
4. Finally, the boxes are stacked according to the customer's specifications, wrapped with metal straps and loaded onto a waiting truck. (The plant has very limited space for warehousing finished products, so the production scheduler will try to be able to send the finished product right onto the truck.)

While the operation is a fairly simple one, there are a number of places where the costs are uncertain. For instance, on the corrugator, there is a 90-in-wide capacity, so if a 55-in-wide box is being run, the scheduler will try to match a 35-in box with it, to minimize scrap costs. But obviously, the scrap costs will depend on the other orders available, and certain orders (very wide or very narrow) may be hard to match.

You have been asked to look into a problem that relates to the routing of an order through the plant. The basic operations are listed above, but different machines may do the tasks. Specifically, there are different ways of completing operations 2 and 3. First, (we'll call it Route 1) the order may be processed through the printer–slotter, which does step 2 and then moved to the folder–gluer which does step 3. Alternatively, the flexo-folder–gluer may be used to complete both steps, and we'll call this Route 2. A schematic appears in Exhibit 1, and the costs of a sample of different orders for different routes appears in Exhibit 2. You will notice that almost all orders are completed faster, and at less labor cost on

EXHIBIT 1

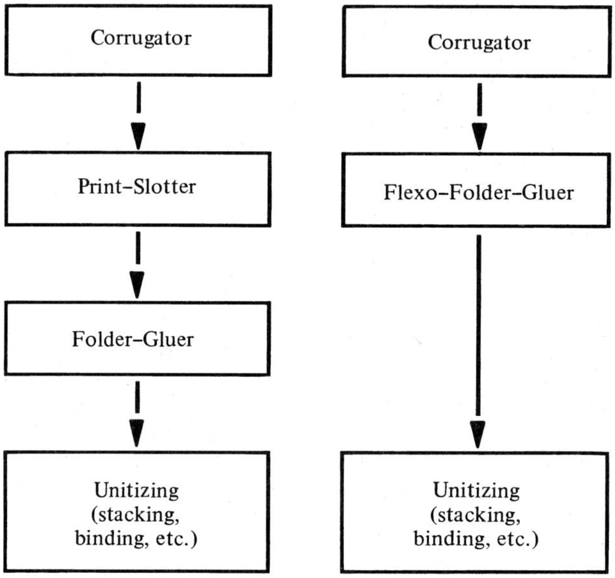

Route 2, since it is a much faster machine. Therefore, whenever he can, the production scheduler uses Route 2, but when there are too many jobs or when the ''flexo'' is broken, the other route is used.

The cost estimation problem is the following. When a bid is made to a customer, it is usually not known with certainty which route will be used to produce the order, although the present cost-estimating system uses the most efficient route to arrive at the estimated

EXHIBIT 2
LABOR HOURS FOR DIFFERENT ROUTES ON JOBS FOR ONE DAY

Order no.	Route 1	Route 2
10246	3.4[a]	2.9
73427	7.5[a]	5.3
66634	8.3	Not possible
45700	2.1	2.0[a]
54076	4.6[a]	4.0
32531	1.5	1.7[a]
34759	7.9[a]	3.8
26979	6.4[a]	5.7
88133	9.7[a]	7.0
96467	6.7	6.0[a]
04325	4.2[a]	4.0
33457	5.6[a]	5.3
66421	5.1	4.7[a]
72349	1.4[a]	1.8
77667	3.9	Not possible

[a]Estimate of cost, since job was run on other route.

cost. The order may, in fact, be run on the "flexo," but it may bump another order to Route 2, increasing total costs. Which order should bear the additional costs? The problem boils down to finding a cost for using the productive facilities. Historical and current replacement costs are available for all machines.

Required How would you approach the problem of assigning a cost to the use of productive facilities? Remember that the goal is to obtain better cost estimates for bidding, so positing a hypothetical order might help you to define the issues you need to address. Be specific as to the analysis you would recommend, including the specific questions you would try to answer and the tools you might use.

5.8. Michael Harrison runs the service department for a company that sells and services microcomputers, printers, and related devices. The company has several retail operations in the Boston area, but the service and repair operation is located at the main branch in the downtown area. There are six employees in the service department, not including Michael Harrison. Three of these employees are responsible for repairs and service in the shop, while the remaining three make service calls, primarily to business customers. In a conversation, Michael relates the following information.

"The company has built a reputation for providing a high level of service to customers, and it's my responsibility to maintain the efficiency that supports that service reputation. As you can imagine, it's not always easy to get the information that would enable me to confidently assess the level of efficiency which we achieve as a department, or as individuals. For instance, when I walk through the shop, everyone is busy at work on their assigned project, but I'm not so naive that I believe that's the way it always is. I can't keep an eye on everyone, since I'm also responsible for the inventory that we need for the service operation. Moreover, I don't want to keep an eye on everyone, since I don't think the service personnel would like that.

"At the same time, I need some approach to assessing the efficiency of the employees, so that I can spot problem areas. As a start, I have been trying to walk through the service area at least once an hour, as close to on the hour as possible, for the last month. I kept track of the type of job each employee was working on, and I also have the total number of jobs completed by each employee for the month. Of course different job types are expected to take different amounts of time. I have the manufacturer's standard service time for each type of service."

The data below is a simplification of that collected by Michael Harrison. For each employee and job type, two numbers are given X/Y. The first is the number of times the employee was observed performing this job type, and the second number is the number of jobs of this type completed by the employee in the month.

Employee number	Job type 1	Job type 2	Job type 3	Job type 4
1	37/36	38/41	23/45	62/30
2	42/28	36/33	33/33	49/20
3	38/40	40/41	28/47	54/31
Manufacturers' standard time	1 hr	1 hr	0.5 hr	2 hr

Required

A. Assuming that each employee worked for 160 hours during the month sampled, use work sampling to estimate the amount of time required for each employee to do each type of service job. Can you identify any potential problem areas that warrant Michael Harrison's attention?

B. What limitations do you see to the above approach? Do you think that one month's observations are sufficient, or is more information required? How would you go about assessing the accuracy of the estimates found in part A?

5.9. The service department reallocation technique described in this chapter uses information at a very detailed level. For example, a_{ij} represents the *units* of service j required to produce *one unit* of service i. While this information is easily obtained for some cases, in others it may be difficult to deal with single units of service.

An alternative approach uses information available from the actual operation of the service departments to allocate costs. For instance, in the situation portrayed in Figure 5.1b, service department 1 produces 160 units of service at a cost of $10 × 160, or $1,600, with 70/160 or 43.75% of this service going to operating department 1. Similarly, service department 2 produces 180 units (140/180 or 77.78% going to operating department 2) at a cost of $2,700. At the end of the period of operation, the service departments will know their costs and the percentages of their service that were supplied to other service departments and to the operating departments. Using this information, we can define some new variables to be used in allocating the service costs.

C_i = cost to be allocated *from* service department i
= cost incurred in service department i *plus* service department i's share of the cost to be allocated from the other service departments

In our example

$$C_1 = \$1{,}600 + (40/180)C_2; \qquad C_2 = \$2{,}700 + (90/160)C_1$$

Required

A. Compute the amounts C_1 and C_2 that satisfy the above relationships.

B. For operating department 1, allocate its share (43.75%) of C_1, the cost to be allocated from service department 1. For this amount, it received 70 units of service, so calculate the cost allocated per unit of service received. How does this compare to the per unit figure of $15.7 found in this chapter? Do the same for operating department 2.

C. Perform the same analysis as in parts A and B for the situation depicted in Figure 5.1c. Service departments 1 and 2 now incur traceable costs of $1,680 and $2,730. How does the cost allocation to operating department 2 change? What is the new cost per unit of service for operating department 1?

5.10. In estimating the administrative costs for her division for the next year, Kelsey Meredith has developed the following information on some of these costs.

	Expected value	Standard deviation
Propery tax	$25,000	$2,000
Casuality insurance	20,000	2,000
Rent on administrative offices	55,000	5,000

Required

A. Assuming that each of the costs is normally distributed and independent of the other two, calculate the expected total cost and the standard deviation of total cost. Meredith has received a preliminary budget of $98,000 for the next year. What is the probability that the costs will exceed the budget?

B. Actually, the rental on administrative offices represents an intracompany charge for space used in the company's corporate headquarters complex. The charge has been $50,000 for the last few years, and there is currently discussion of a proposal to increase the charge by 20% to $60,000. Meredith believes that this charge will be $50,000 or $60,000, each with equal probability. How does this affect your answer in part A?

5.11. "At present I have enough capacity to produce 6,000 units per year, and for the first half of the year I plan to produce equal amounts of three products, A101, B204, and C531. At this point, I'm not sure what the variable cost per unit will be for each of them, so there is some uncertainty about the contribution margin that I will be able to earn for the year. My best estimates are the following:

Product A101: Contribution per unit uniformly distributed between $40 and $50.
Product B204: Contribution per unit uniformly distributed between $35 and $45.
Product C531: Contribution per unit uniformly distributed between $32 and $52.

By the end of six months, we will have produced 1,000 units of each, and the uncertainty about contribution margin will have been resolved. At that point, I will drop the product with the lowest contribution margin and split the productive capacity between the remaining two products. Each product requires the same productive capacity per unit, so that means I'll produce 1,500 units of the two winners for the last half of the year.

"My question is the following. If I follow this strategy, what is the probability that my contribution margin will exceed $270,000? That amount would enable us to pay off the bank loan and implement our plans for expansion."

Required Using simulation, estimate the probability that the contribution margin will exceed $270,000. Would this probability be higher if the manager simply produced equal amounts of products A101 and C531 for the whole year, rather than conducting the experiment for the first half of the year? More generally, what does your simulation tell you about the relative riskiness of these two strategies?

5.12. The general manager of AC Division of the ACME Corporation has been approached by an industrial caterer with a proposal to provide meal service to the employees of the division's plant. At present, the division operates its own cafeteria, and, on average, employees eat one meal in the cafeteria for every eight hours worked at the plant. For the last month, the cafeteria supplied 2,160 meals at a variable cost of $6,479, or about $3.00 per meal. This amount is considerably less than the $5.00 per meal offered by the industrial caterer. There are fixed costs associated with the cafeteria operation, but the division's general manager does not believe that they are avoidable. In an effort to determine whether the caterer's proposal should be accepted, the general manager asked the plant controller to develop the following information.

Last Month's Operation

Department	Service unit	Units produced	Traceable, variable cost
Building services	Hour of service	3,294	$26,351
Cafeteria	Meals served	2,160	6,479
Personnel	Employee-day	2,160	2,160
Accounting	Hour of service	917	13,761
Computer	Hour of service	819	12,289

Interdepartmental Service Usage

Service source	Units needed to produce 1 unit of service in department: Bldg svce	Cafeteria	Personnel	Accounting	Computer
Building services	0.0	0.1	0.02	0.02	0.02
Cafeteria	0.125	0.1	0.03	0.125	0.125
Personnel	0.125	0.1	0.03	0.125	0.125
Accounting	0.01	0.02	0.15	0.01	0.01
Computer	0.0	0.0	0.05	0.25	0.1

Required On the basis of variable cost per meal served, should the caterer's proposal be accepted?

REFERENCES

Capettini, R., and G. Salamon. "Internal versus External Acquisition of Services when Reciprocal Services Exist," *Accounting Review*. July 1977.

Kaplan, R. "Variable and Self-Service Costs in Reciprocal Allocation Models," *Accounting Review*. October 1973.

Kottas, J., and H. Lau. "Direct Simulation in Stochastic C–V–P Analysis," *Accounting Review*. July 1978.

Kottas, J., A. Lau, and H. Lau. "A General Approach to Stochastic Management Planning Models: An Overview," *Accounting Review*. April 1978.

Largay, J., III, and F. Levy. "Using Segment Reporting and Input–Output Analysis for Managerial Planning," *Management Accounting*. November 1978.

Lin, W. "Multiple Objective Budgeting Models: A Simulation," *Accounting Review*. January 1978.

Sundem, G., "Evaluating Simplified Capital Budgeting Models Using a Time-State Preference Metric," *Accounting Review*. April 1974.

Chapter 6

Cost Estimation: Statistical Methods

The cost estimation techniques described in Chapter 5 can be very useful in facilitating managerial decision making, but there are yet other techniques that have a different set of strengths (and weaknesses). For instance, engineering measurement methods are best suited to situations where a well-defined task is to be repeated frequently, but many indirect product costs do not fall into this category. Simulation can help integrate two component distributions, but it cannot tell us what the component distributions are. Subjective estimates of cost behavior are dependent on the abilities and motivation of the estimator.

In this chapter we will explore another major source of information for decision making—the analysis of past data. There are a variety of techniques that can be used to analyze past data, but we will concentrate on a flexible, generally available technique called *regression analysis*. Of course, the past data approach has its own limitations, and we will note many of them in the chapter. But by the end of this chapter, we will have covered a large portion of the ''menu'' of major cost estimation techniques that can be used to address the managerial accounting issues we will examine in future chapters.

6.1 SIMPLE COST STATISTICS

Actually, we have already introduced some basic statistical cost estimates (Chapter 5). Suppose that a clean-up crew comes in after each production run to ready the machines and area for the next run. If we have observations on the number of man-hours for clean-up, then we can develop a forecast for this indirect cost that could be used in production scheduling, product pricing, and so on.

Let C_j denote the clean-up cost of job j, where $C_j = wt_j$. (Wages per hour are w, man-hours of clean-up for job j are t_j.) The following data were gathered by the production foreman (wages are \$6/hr).

Job	Clean-up hours, t_j	Clean-up cost, C_j
1	6	\$36
2	8	48
3	8	48
4	5	30
5	6	36
6	7	42
7	5.5	33

If we want to forecast clean-up costs for Job 8, including an estimate of the forecast's accuracy, how do we use the above data? The answer is to use the sample mean $\overline{C}$, and sample variance s_c^2.

$$\overline{C} = \frac{1}{T}\sum_{j=1}^{T} C_j = \frac{1}{7}(36 + 48 + \cdots + 42 + 33)$$

$$= \frac{\$273}{7} = \$39/\text{job}$$

$$s_c^2 = \frac{1}{T-1}\sum_{j=1}^{T}(C_j - \overline{C})^2 = \frac{1}{6}[(36-39)^2 + (48-39)^2 + \cdots + (33-39)^2] \quad (6.1)$$

$$= \frac{1}{6}(306) = 51$$

$$s_c = (s_c^2)^{1/2} = (51)^{1/2} = 7.14$$

We can interpret these statistics in the following way. The average clean-up cost is $\overline{C}$ or \$39 per job, and unless Job 8 is different in some way from the previous seven, this \$39 is an *unbiased estimate*[1] of the expected clean-up cost for Job 8. In addition, if we assume that the clean-up costs follow a normal distribution, we can make an estimate of the degree of uncertainty associated with the cost forecast. Suppose that we wanted to determine a *confidence interval* such that there was a probability α that the actual cost would fall outside that interval. The items of information needed are (i) the *sample standard deviation* s_c, which we have already calculated; (ii) the *degrees of freedom,* which is one less than the number of observations $(T - 1)$; and (iii) the t-distribution value from Appendix 6.2. The appropriate t-value is found by going down the rows to the appropriate degrees of freedom and then across the columns to the chosen value of α.

In our clean-up cost example, the degrees of freedom would be 6 (= 7 observations − 1), and let us say that we choose an α of 0.10. The t-value from Appendix 6.2 is 1.943, which we use in the following limits.

[1]Usually, we never know how close our estimates are to the true expected cost, because we never get to see the true expected cost. But an estimate is unbiased if, loosely speaking, we have no reason to believe that it will tend to overestimate the expected cost, or that it will tend to underestimate the expected cost.

$$\begin{aligned} \text{Lower limit} &= \overline{C} - s_c t_{T-1;\alpha} \\ &= 39 - (7.14)(1.943) = \$25.13 \\ \text{Upper limit} &= \overline{C} + s_c t_{T-1;\alpha} \\ &= 39 + (7.14)(1.943) = \$52.87 \end{aligned} \tag{6.2}$$

We interpret these limits as follows: the probability that a job's clean-up costs are less than \$25.13 *or* greater than \$52.87 is 0.10. Equivalently, there is a 90% chance that the clean-up costs will fall between \$25.13 and \$52.87.

From this, you can see how past data can be used to forecast future costs, and to estimate the confidence we ought to place in those forecasts. Unfortunately, the data that the managerial accountant has to work with is usually much less detailed than that in the above example. Rather than having indirect labor for each job, we would probably have, say, indirect labor costs for the month and some data on the number of tasks that were done by indirect labor during the month. This more aggregate data leaves us with a problem of estimating a more complex relationship, using one of a variety of techniques.

6.2 SIMPLE LINE-FITTING TECHNIQUES

For planning purposes, we usually want to determine the relationship between two or more variables. If one variable is an outcome, such as cost or profit, while the other variable is a decision, such as output, we can use the relationship in budgeting the effect of decisions on outcomes. For instance, suppose that we have only some very aggregate data: three monthly observations of overhead cost and output. The three data points are graphed in Figure 6.1. How much do overhead costs change when output changes? That is, what is the estimate of variable overhead cost (and a measure of its uncertainty) that would be useful in the CVP models in Chapter 4?

Month	Overhead cost	Output (units)
1	\$155,000	10,000
2	127,000	8,000
3	168,000	12,000

There are a variety of ways to answer that question. One simple method is the high–low technique which fits a line between the highest (output) and lowest (output)

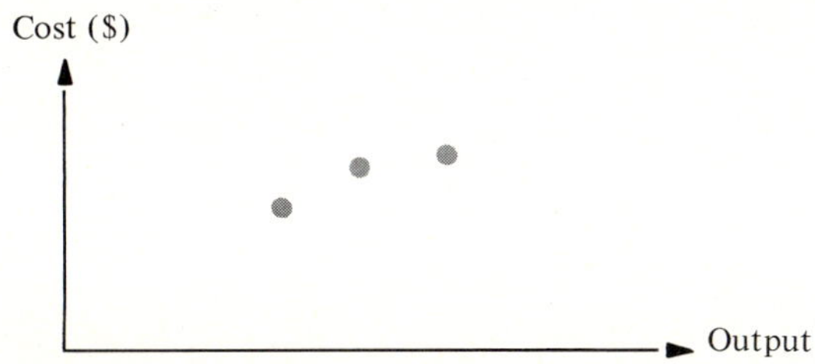

Figure 6.1

observations, and ignores all other observations. In our example, this line would be

$$\text{Slope} = \frac{\$168{,}000 - \$127{,}000}{12{,}000 - 8{,}000\,\text{units}} = \$10.25/\text{unit}$$
$$\text{Intercept} = \$168{,}000 - \$10.25(12{,}000) = \$45{,}000 \tag{6.3}$$

So, if we were planning an output of 11,000 units, the budgeted cost would be \$45,000 + \$10.25(11,000) = \$157,750.

The basic problem with this approach is that it does not utilize all the information available, and as a result, the cost estimate is somewhat arbitrary. For instance, suppose that the actual overhead costs for the fourth month were \$160,000 and output was 11,000. The manufacturing supervisor would be charged with an unfavorable overhead variance of \$2,250, but he could argue that the cost relationship should be estimated using the observations from the first and third months, and this would yield a favorable variance rather than an unfavorable one.[2] Unless the managerial accountant can defend the choice of data points, the unfavorable variance would be regarded as an arbitrary one.

6.3 THE REGRESSION MODEL

Regression is a statistical technique for using data to estimate parameters in a model. If we assume that

$$\text{cost} = F + v(\text{output})$$

we may use regression with data on costs and output to estimate the values of F and v. The use of regression has become much more common with the increasing accessibility of computing power, and the applications of regression are becoming more varied—from the valuation of property for tax purposes to an independent accountant's analytic review of a company's account balances. As a result, managers in many fields are using regression and should be familiar with what regression does and what assumptions are necessary for its proper application. After we review some of the technical aspects of the regression model, we shall discuss its application to cost estimation and point out a number of potential problems.

The basic regression model starts with a set of five assumptions.

A1. $Y_t = \beta_0 + \beta_1 X_{1t} + \cdots + \beta_k X_{kt} + \varepsilon_t$ for each observation $t = 1, \ldots, T$. This model assumption states that for each of our T observations, the value of the dependent variable Y_t is a linear function of the k independent variables (X_{it} is the value of independent variable i for observation t) and an unknown, unobservable factor ε_t, which is called the *disturbance term*. (In essence, ε_t incorporates all the factors that influence Y_t other than $X_{1t}, X_{2t}, \ldots, X_{kt}$.) While this model assumption may seem fairly innocuous at first, it is a very important one, and determines whether our regression analysis tells us much of relevance.

[2]Slope = \$6.5; intercept = \$90,000; estimated cost at output of 11,000 is 90,000 + 6.5(11,000) = 161,500.

A2. $E[\varepsilon_t] = 0$, for all $t = 1, \ldots, T$.

A3. (a) Variance of ε_t is constant for all t, and, in particular, doesn't depend on the independent variables. $\sigma^2[\varepsilon_t] = \sigma^2$; $t = 1, \ldots, T$.
(b) The disturbance in period t is uncorrelated with the disturbance in any other period. Covariance $[\varepsilon_t, \varepsilon_s] = 0$ for all t, s where $t \neq s$.

A4. The values of the independent variables are "fixed in repeated samples." That is, the *classical linear regression* assumes that we are in an experimental setting where the values of these variables can be manipulated.

A5. No independent variable, X_{it}, $t = 1, \ldots, T$, is a linear combination of the remaining independent variables.

Some of these assumptions are less important than others, in that we may violate them without doing serious damage to the regression results. But we shall return to these considerations later. If the assumptions are met and we have enough data ($T \geq k + 1$), then we may use regression to get estimates of the coefficients of the model in A1 using the vector of observed dependent variables **Y**, and the matrix of observations on the independent variables **X**.

$$\mathbf{Y} \equiv \begin{pmatrix} Y_1 \\ Y_2 \\ \cdot \\ \cdot \\ \cdot \\ Y_T \end{pmatrix}; \qquad \mathbf{X} \equiv \begin{pmatrix} 1 & X_{11} & \cdots & X_{k1} \\ 1 & X_{12} & \cdots & X_{k2} \\ \cdot & \cdot & \cdot & \cdot \\ \cdot & \cdot & \cdot & \cdot \\ \cdot & \cdot & \cdot & \cdot \\ 1 & X_{1T} & \cdots & X_{kT} \end{pmatrix} \tag{6.4}$$

The *true* and *estimated* coefficients will be referred to as $\boldsymbol{\beta}$ and $\hat{\boldsymbol{\beta}}$, respectively.[3]

$$\boldsymbol{\beta} = \begin{pmatrix} \beta_0 \\ \beta_1 \\ \cdot \\ \cdot \\ \cdot \\ \beta_k \end{pmatrix}; \qquad \hat{\boldsymbol{\beta}} = \begin{pmatrix} \hat{\beta}_0 \\ \hat{\beta}_1 \\ \cdot \\ \cdot \\ \cdot \\ \hat{\beta}_k \end{pmatrix} = (\mathbf{X}'\mathbf{X})^{-1}\mathbf{X}'\mathbf{Y} \tag{6.5}$$

Example We will take the data on monthly costs and output from Figure 6.1 and use regression to determine how they are related. The data are:

Month	Cost	Output
1	155,000	10,000
2	127,000	8,000
3	168,000	12,000

[3]The derivation of the regression estimate can be found in most statistics books. The regression objective is discussed below.

The model we wish to estimate is $\text{cost}_t = \beta_0 + \beta_1 (\text{Output}_t)$, so β_0 and β_1 are the intercept and slope of the cost line, respectively. From the data we may get estimates $\hat{\beta}_0$ and $\hat{\beta}_1$.

$$\mathbf{Y} = \begin{pmatrix} 155{,}000 \\ 127{,}000 \\ 168{,}000 \end{pmatrix} \qquad \mathbf{X} = \begin{pmatrix} 1 & 10{,}000 \\ 1 & 8{,}000 \\ 1 & 12{,}000 \end{pmatrix}$$

$$\hat{\boldsymbol{\beta}} = \left[\begin{pmatrix} 1 & 1 & 1 \\ 10{,}000 & 8{,}000 & 12{,}000 \end{pmatrix}\begin{pmatrix} 1 & 10{,}000 \\ 1 & 8{,}000 \\ 1 & 12{,}000 \end{pmatrix}\right]^{-1} \begin{pmatrix} 1 & 1 & 1 \\ 10{,}000 & 8{,}000 & 12{,}000 \end{pmatrix}\begin{pmatrix} 155{,}000 \\ 127{,}000 \\ 168{,}000 \end{pmatrix} \tag{6.6}$$

$$= \begin{pmatrix} 47{,}500 \\ 10.25 \end{pmatrix} = \begin{pmatrix} \hat{\beta}_0 \\ \hat{\beta}_1 \end{pmatrix}$$

From the data, the cost relationship is estimated to be $\text{cost}_t = \$47{,}500 + \$10.25(\text{Output}_t)$. With this relationship, the estimated overhead cost of producing 11,000 units would be \$160,250. Of course the computations quickly get unmanageable with more variables and more data, but computer programs are usually available, and many are quite easy to use.

6.4 STATISTICAL PROPERTIES OF REGRESSION

There is a reason for choosing the above estimation procedure from among the many possible procedures. Suppose that we had the four data points (Y_t, X_t), plotted on the graph in Figure 6.2. There are a variety of lines, $Y_t = \beta_0 + \beta_1 X_t$ that could be drawn to fit these data. Two such lines are drawn in Figure 6.3. Which of these lines better fits the data? Or more generally, how do we find the line (i.e., the values of $\hat{\beta}_0$ and $\hat{\beta}_1$) that *best* fits the data? Regression answers this question by choosing a particular error measure and then finding the values $\hat{\beta}_0$ and $\hat{\beta}_1$ that minimize the error measure. For a particular observation (Y_t, X_t), the error is the distance between the actual value of Y_t and the value estimated by the line $\hat{Y}_t = \hat{\beta}_0 + \hat{\beta}_1 X_t$. This error, or residual, is called $\hat{\varepsilon}_t = Y_t - \hat{Y}_t$, and the objective of linear regression is to minimize the sum of the squared errors, which is why it is often called *least-squares regression*.

$$\min_{\hat{\beta}_0, \hat{\beta}_1} \left[\sum_{t=1}^{T} (Y_t - \hat{\beta}_0 - \hat{\beta}_1 X_t)^2\right] \quad \text{or} \quad \min_{\hat{\beta}_0, \hat{\beta}_1} \left(\sum_{t=1}^{T} \hat{\varepsilon}_t^2\right) \tag{6.7}$$

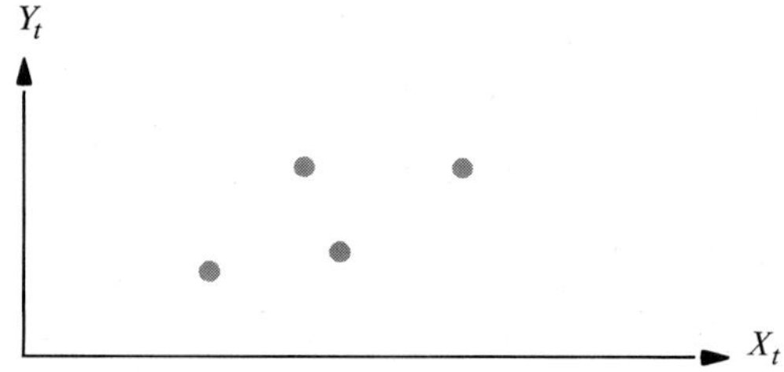

Figure 6.2

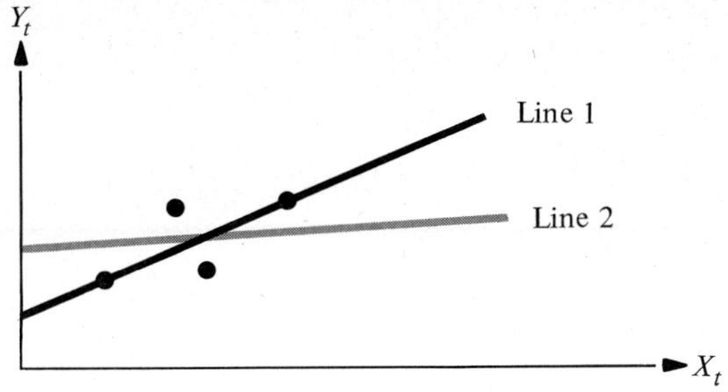

Figure 6.3

Choosing the parameter estimates $\hat{\beta}_0$, $\hat{\beta}_1$ in this way means that these estimates have certain desirable statistical properties. We cannot observe the values of $\boldsymbol{\beta}$ directly, but given some data we get an estimate. With another set of data we would get a somewhat different estimate because the values of ε_t would change. In essence then, when we use regression we are "taking a draw" from a probability distribution of estimates.

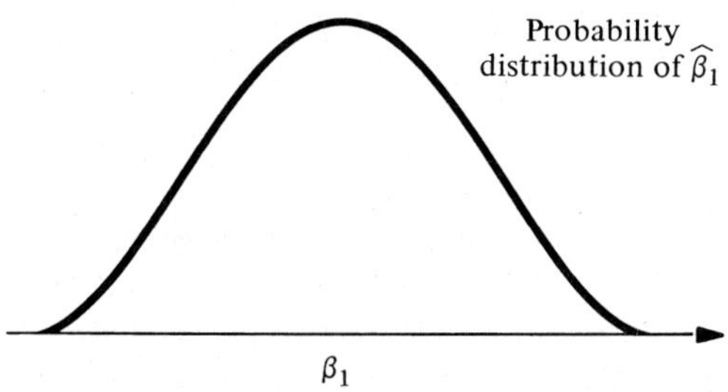

If the regression assumptions are met, then our regression estimates have some notable attributes. They are unbiased in the sense that $E[\hat{\boldsymbol{\beta}}] = \boldsymbol{\beta}$, or in other words the probability distribution of $\hat{\boldsymbol{\beta}}$ is *centered* at the true value $\boldsymbol{\beta}$; and the estimates are *best* in that the expected squared error $E[(\beta_i - \hat{\beta}_i)^2]$ is lower than for any other estimate. As we will discuss later in the chapter, violations of the regression assumptions or various data problems can cause the regression estimates to be biased or no longer best.

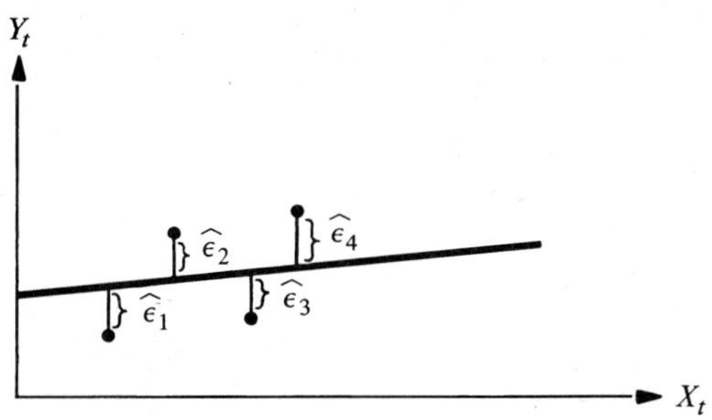

Figure 6.4

A common assumption made in regression is that the disturbances, ε_t, are distributed normally with mean zero and variance σ^2. When that assumption is made, then there are a variety of other statistics that can be used to analyze the strength of the relationships found by the regression.

Along with each estimated coefficient $\hat{\beta}_i$, there is a standard error of the coefficient $S_{\hat{\beta}_i}$ that may be used to determine the confidence of our estimate of β_i. By using a table of t-statistics like Appendix 6.2, we can find a value $t_{T-k-1;\alpha}$, where $T - k - 1$ is the number of degrees of freedom, and α is the probability of a larger absolute value. Then $(1 - \alpha)$ is the probability that the true value β_i is between $(\hat{\beta}_i - S_{\hat{\beta}_i} t_{T-k-1;\alpha})$ and $(\hat{\beta}_i + S_{\hat{\beta}_i} t_{T-k-1;\alpha})$. If $\hat{\beta}_i$ is an estimate of variable overhead, then this confidence interval may give us an idea of the chance that the contribution margin will exceed a given amount. If we are uncertain about whether a variable affects costs, we can see whether the confidence interval includes zero. If not, then there is less than an α chance that the variable has no effect on costs.

In addition, a regression analysis produces a statistic called R^2, or *coefficient of determination,* which is a measure of the percentage of variation in the dependent variable that is explained by changes in the independent variables.

$$R^2 = 1 - \frac{\sum_{t=1}^{T} (Y_t - \hat{Y}_t)^2}{\sum_{t=1}^{T} (Y_t - \bar{Y})^2} = 1 - \frac{\text{Variation in } Y_t \text{ unexplained by regression}}{\text{Total variation in } Y_t \text{ to be explained}} \tag{6.8}$$

The R^2, which may be between 0 and 1, measures the strength of the entire regression relation, not just a single variable.

Finally, the standard error of estimate $S_{\hat{\varepsilon}}^2$ is an estimate of the variance of the disturbances σ^2. As such, it plays a role in determining the values of R^2 and $S_{\hat{\beta}_i}$ above, and also in establishing the level of confidence in forecasts based on the regression equation. If we have estimated $\hat{\boldsymbol{\beta}}$ using regression, and want to forecast the value of Y^* that will occur when the independent variables are $\mathbf{X}_* = [1X_{1*} \cdots X_{k*}]$, this is a relatively simple matter.

$$\hat{Y}_* = \hat{\beta}_0 + \hat{\beta}_1 X_{1*} + \cdots + \hat{\beta}_k X_{k*}$$

$$= [1X_{1*} \cdots X_{k*}] \begin{pmatrix} \hat{\beta}_0 \\ \hat{\beta}_1 \\ \cdot \\ \cdot \\ \cdot \\ \hat{\beta}_k \end{pmatrix} = \mathbf{X}_* \hat{\boldsymbol{\beta}} \tag{6.9}$$

Of course, knowing the forecasted value $\hat{Y}_*$ is only part of the problem, since some idea of the confidence we have in the forecast is usually desirable. For this we define the expected squared prediction error, S_f^2.

$$S_f^2 = E[(Y_* - \hat{Y}_*)^2] = S_\varepsilon^2 + S_\varepsilon^2 \mathbf{X}_*(\mathbf{X}'\mathbf{X})^{-1}\mathbf{X}_*' \tag{6.10}$$

$$\text{where } S_\varepsilon^2 = \frac{\sum_{t=1}^T \hat{\varepsilon}_t^2}{T-k-1} = \frac{\sum_{t=1}^T (Y_t - \hat{Y}_t)^2}{T-k-1}$$

This error measure reflects two sources of prediction error: errors that result from the inherent randomness reflected in the disturbance (ε_*), and errors that occur because we have misestimated $\boldsymbol{\beta}$. The importance of this second type of error depends on how the value of $\mathbf{X}_*$ compares to those used to estimate the regression coefficients. This can be seen if we compute S_f^2 when there is only one independent variable X_t, $t = 1, \ldots, T$.

$$S_f^2 = S_\varepsilon^2\left[1 + \frac{1}{T} + \frac{(X_* - \overline{X})^2}{\sum_{t=1}^T (X_t - \overline{X})^2}\right] \tag{6.11}$$

The further X_* is from the center of our data $\overline{X}$, the higher is the expected squared forecast error. The larger the range of values covered by the data, that is, the larger $\sum_{t=1}^T (X_t - \overline{X})^2$, the lower the expected squared forecast error. Using S_f^2 we can again use a t-value, $t_{T-k-1;\alpha}$, to say that the value of Y^* will fall in the range $\hat{Y}_* \pm S_f t_{T-k-1;\alpha}$ with probability $(1 - \alpha)$.

At first, the proliferation of statistics associated with regression is somewhat confusing, and there are yet more statistics to come. But a meaningful application of regression frequently requires familiarity with these statistics, so we will review an example.

Example The Brown Company has received an order for 50 units of product from a customer who is willing to pay $18 per unit. Before the receipt of the order, the company's forecasted level of activity for the next month was 600 units. In conducting an analysis of the company's costs, the data below was compiled for the last twelve months. Should the order be accepted?

Month	Units of output	Cost
1	545	$ 9,207
2	570	9,544
3	516	8,547
4	571	9,693
5	587	9,774
6	569	9,524
7	507	8,652
8	644	10,614
9	519	8,818
10	521	8,799
11	504	8,674
12	634	10,736

A high–low analysis of the costs using months 11 and 8 yields an estimated variable cost of about $13.86 per unit. This leaves a contribution margin of $18 − 13.86 = $4.14 per unit on the special order, but this analysis ignores any information from the other ten months' data. A regression analysis allows all twelve data points to be used in estimating the variable cost. The results of such a regression analysis are as follows:

COST MODEL:[a] COST = $F + v$ (OUTPUT)

	F	v
Estimated coefficient	\$743.30	\$15.50
Standard error of coefficient	377.34	0.67
t-statistic	1.97	22.97
R^2	0.9814	
Degrees of freedom (number of observations − number of coefficients)	10	

[a]To conform to our cost–volume–profit terminology, the regression variables of Y, β_0, β_1, and X are translated to cost, F, v, and output, respectively.

There are a variety of interpretations that may be gleaned from these statistics. First, the best straight line fitted through the data has a slope of \$15.50, indicating that when we increase output by one unit the estimated costs will increase by \$15.50. But we can also make an estimate of the confidence that we have in that prediction. If we set $\alpha = 0.10$ and find the t-value with 10 degrees of freedom (from Appendix 6.2 it's 1.812), we can say that there is only a 10 percent chance that costs will increase less than \$15.50 − (0.67)(1.812) = \$14.29 per unit or more than \$16.71 per unit. This sort of analysis can be useful in determining the probability of a positive contribution margin on an order such as that in the example. (In this case, the probability is greater than 0.005. If the price per unit on the order were \$16.00 instead of \$18.00, the probability of not breaking even would be greater than 0.20.) We can also make forecasts on a more aggregate basis, and we will come to that in a moment. The R^2 of 0.9814 indicates that the model we have estimated explains over 98 percent of the variations in costs from month to month. Thus, the model is a strong one (this is also indicated by v's t-statistic of 22.97), but we must still exercise some caution in interpreting the relationship between cost and output. Regression does not test causality or guarantee that the estimated relationships will continue into future periods or at levels of output not represented by the data points. These considerations must be evaluated by the manager, who must develop a model that is useful for decision making.

If we wish to forecast total costs for a given production level, say 600 units, we can do so as described above. Estimated costs are $\hat{Y}_* = \hat{F} + \hat{v}X_* = \$743.30 + (15.50)(600) = \$10{,}043.30$. The accuracy of this prediction is not an easy thing to calculate, but some regression programs will calculate the standard error of prediction. In this example, the standard error of prediction, S_f, is \$114.28 when the output is 600 units, so that we can form a confidence interval around \$10,043.30 using this standard error of prediction and the t-values such as the 1.812 used in the confidence intervals above. There is a 90 percent chance that the costs of producing 600 units of output will be between \$9,836.22 and \$10,250.38 [\$10,043.30 ± (114.28)(1.812)]. The same sort of estimate can be made for an output of 650 units (expected cost is \$10,818.3; standard error of forecast, S_f, is 127.07), and the expected profit risk can be compared for the two alternative courses of action as in Chapter 4.

The ability to make these types of estimates has made regression an increasingly used tool in practice. It uses an objective criterion to estimate relationships, and therefore its estimates or budgets are not as soft or arbitrary as those from simpler techniques such as high–low or a visual fit of the data. At the same time, there are a number of assumptions that must be considered for a proper application of regression.

6.5 VIOLATIONS OF ASSUMPTION A1

This model assumption is in many ways the most important of the five assumptions, in that if we do a good job of specifying the model to be estimated and gather appropriate data, many other problems never occur. And, when an analysis of a regression indicates that other assumptions are violated, the usual response is to modify the model to improve the estimations.

There are a number of potential problems that arise when we use cost data that are produced by the accounting system. Some types of accrual (or the lack thereof) make it difficult to estimate the relationship of interest. For instance, in standard costing systems it is common for fixed manufacturing costs (depreciation, property taxes, etc.) to be allocated throughout the year using a measure of activity such as direct labor hours. As depicted in Figure 6.5, this can cause an overestimation of variable cost if the cost of goods completed data are used in a regression with direct labor hours. In fact, any allocation of fixed costs based on actual activity would tend to produce an overestimate of variable costs. This problem could arise in a process–costing situation, where the critical data would be the measures of conversion cost. In general, we would rather have cost-incurred data than cost-allocated data for the dependent variable.

On the other hand, there are cases where an accounting system's *lack* of accruals can make cost estimation difficult. For instance, it can be difficult to determine how an organization's material costs vary with activity if the organization only keeps track of *expenditures,* with no inventory records kept. (This practice is not uncommon among not-for-profit organizations). In this case, the data on expenditures may not be very helpful in estimating cost behavior. (See Figure 6.6). Based on a regression analysis, we could easily conclude that there was no relationship between material costs and activity, and that the person in charge of material usage was doing an inefficient job

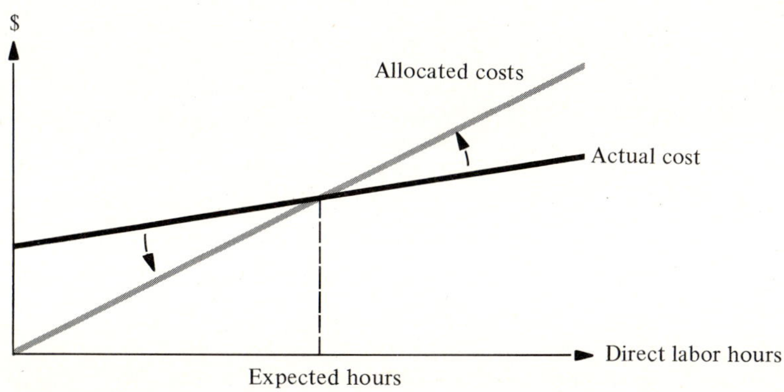

Figure 6.5

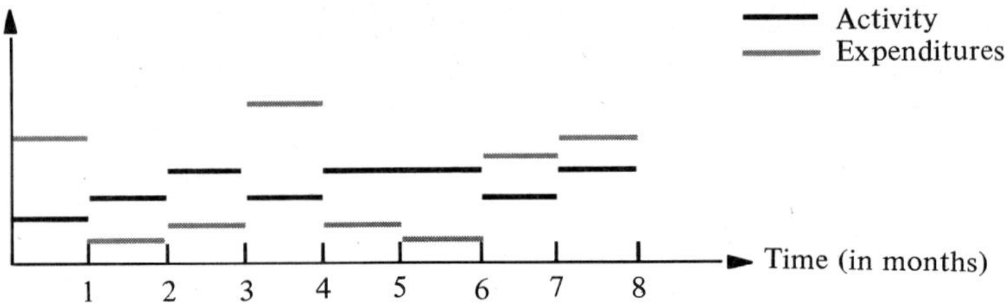

Figure 6.6

when, in fact, we do not have adequate data to make such a conclusion.[4] Usually, the cost model is based on a manager's perceptions of the firm's *economic* relationships, but one has to be cautious in using the numbers produced by the cost accounting system, since they may not match the economic variables in the manager's conceptual model of cost behavior.

In addition to dealing with accounting measurement problems, we may also have to choose the periods over which the data will be measured. That is, how long should each observation period be and how far back in history should data be collected? Do we want the most recent 12 months of data or the most recent 26 weeks, and so on. The shorter each observation period is, the harder it is to do an accurate job of cost accrual so there may be more errors in the data and some sorts of cost relationships may be difficult to estimate. For instance, if maintenance is done on slow production days, using daily data to estimate maintenance costs as a function of activity will produce a negative relationship when, given a longer-term perspective, this is not the case. Of course, shorter time periods usually entail more frequent measurements and therefore more expense in gathering data.

A related problem is caused by the fact that cost relationships change over time due to changes in prices, efficiency, product mix, and so on. For instance, if we estimate overhead $= F + v$(direct labor hours), the value of v will depend on many factors such as the wage rates for indirect labor, costs of utilities, the amount of supplies used per direct labor hour, and so on. A change in any of these factors would change v. If our cost model does not take these changes into account explicitly, then we must decide how far back in history to go in collecting data. The further back we go, the more observations we have and the lower the sampling error, but we also increase the chances that we are using data from a cost process that is not comparable to the one faced today. When these changes are known, they can sometimes be taken into account, either by adjusting variable definitions as described below, or if a major technological change has occurred, simply omitting data prior to the change.

In addition to the problems of gathering data, a critical part of the cost estimation process is the specification of the cost model. That is, which independent variables should be included in the equation to be estimated, and in what form should they be included? Certainly we should include decision variables, since the primary objective of the cost estimation is to estimate how costs are affected by decision alternatives. For instance, in short-term planning situations, such as those described in Chapter 4, the level of

[4]See Kaplan (1974) for an in-depth analysis of such a situation.

activity was the decision variable, and a regression analysis to aid in this decision situation should probably include the level of activity as an independent variable. Usually the measurement of activity involves measuring units produced, but this may not always be the case. For instance, when the production process takes longer than a month, the units completed may not be a good measure of the level of activity during the month. Such errors in measurement of the independent variables can lead to biases in the estimates of variable costs. In addition to planning situations, the results of the regression can be used to set up a flexible budget for evaluating a manager's performance. In these cases, we would want to include uncontrollable variables so that their impact on costs can be washed out in an *ex post* evaluation of the manager. (We will return to these considerations in a later chapter.)

Not only do we have to consider which variables to include, but also the form in which the variables affect costs. As an example, it is seldom the case that costs are an exactly linear function of output. Therefore, we could consider more than one possible relationship, such as those in Models 1, 2, and 3 below and in Figure 6.7.

$$\text{Model 1: } C_t = \beta_0 + \beta_1 X_t + \varepsilon_t$$
$$\text{Model 2: } C_t = \gamma_0 + \gamma_1 X_t + \gamma_2 X_t^2 + \varepsilon_t$$
$$\text{Model 3: } C_t = \alpha_0 + \alpha_1 X_t + \alpha_2 X_t^2 + \alpha_3 X_t^3 + \varepsilon_t$$

We could estimate models 1 and 2 using regression and, noting that the two models are identical if $\gamma_2 = 0$, use a t-statistic to see whether the data suggests that γ_2 is indeed equal to zero. If not, then the data indicate that model 2 is more descriptive of the way costs behave than model 1, and after making a similar comparison to model 3, we can use it for cost estimating. For instance, the data in the Brown Co. example above was used to estimate a quadratic model (model 2) with the following results (t-statistics in parentheses).

$$\begin{aligned} C_t &= 2308.50 + 9.982X_t + 0.0048X_t^2 \\ &\quad (0.420) \qquad (0.516) \qquad (0.285) \\ R^2 &= 0.9816 \end{aligned} \tag{6.12}$$

We can see that the R^2 is improved by only 0.0002 over the linear model, and the t-statistic for the X_t^2 coefficient is not significantly different from zero. Therefore, the linear model appears to be an adequate one.

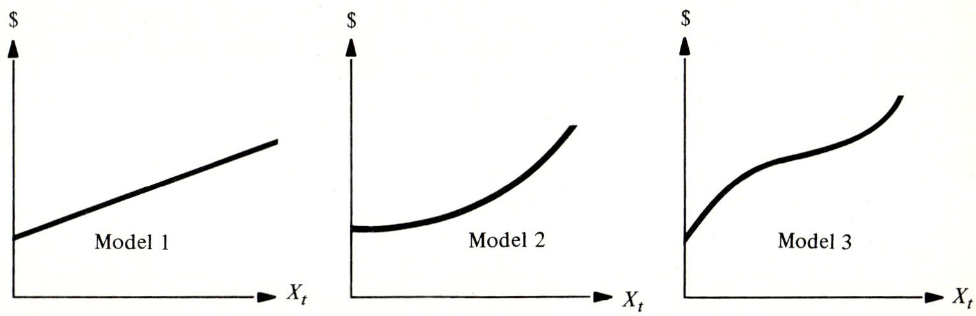

Figure 6.7

While the regression statistics can help in choosing a model from a given set, the choice of what models to include in the set is a matter of judgment. In essence, this decision is an information decision, and we might want to explicitly consider the effect of a model choice on estimates, decisions, and ultimately, on payoffs. That is, if $\gamma_2 \neq 0$, what is the expected cost of using a simplified model such as model 1? This analysis could follow along the lines of the section on nonlinear cost behavior in Chapter 4.

In addition to the functional form aspects of assumption A1, it is also assumed that the coefficients are stable across all data points. When the data encompass long periods of time, this assumption can be rather troublesome. For instance, if β_1 = (variable overhead cost/direct labor hour)(direct labor hour/unit of output), then either a change in the unit costs of variable overhead items or a change in efficiency could change β_1 from one period to the next. Seasonal heating and cooling costs might cause β_0 to take on different values in different periods. Changes in prices may be taken into account in one of two ways. First, an index of indirect cost could be calculated for each data period, and then all the cost data could be deflated by these indices to put them on a common basis. That is, if time period 1 is the base period, then $I_1 = 1$ and the indices for successive periods will be I_t = (price level in period t)/(price level in period 1). The new cost model would be

$$\frac{C_t}{I_t} = \beta_0' + \beta_1' X_t + \varepsilon_t' \tag{6.13}$$

In essence, the cost relationship is estimated in terms of year 1 dollars. Then a forecast can be made in the following way: If the expected activity is X_*, then $\hat{\beta}_0' + \hat{\beta}_1' X_*$ is the forecasted cost in terms of year 1 dollars. To bring this up to the forecast year's dollars requires a forecast of that year's price level I_*.

$$\hat{C}_* = I_*(\hat{\beta}_0' + \hat{\beta}_1' X_*) \tag{6.14}$$

However, if different types of indirect costs experience different inflation rates, a composite index may be difficult to construct. An alternative for some types of indirect costs would be to use units (e.g., kilowatt-hours, indirect labor hours) as the dependent variable instead of costs. Yet one other common cause of instability in the cost parameters is learning, where average costs decrease as cumulative output increases. This phenomenon, and its cost estimation implications, will be discussed in the next chapter.

6.6 VIOLATIONS OF ASSUMPTION A3(a)

There are three other assumptions we will deal with in some detail—A3(a), A3(b), and A5. Assumption A3(a) states that the variance of the disturbance term ε_t is not affected by the values of the independent variables. For example, the riskiness or unpredictability of costs is not affected by the level of output. Figure 6.8 depicts this assumption and its violation.

Nonconstant variance can result from the fact that larger or busier organizations are inherently more difficult to control, and therefore the factors that are included in ε (such as efficiency) can take on a wider range of values. Or, alternatively, if we are

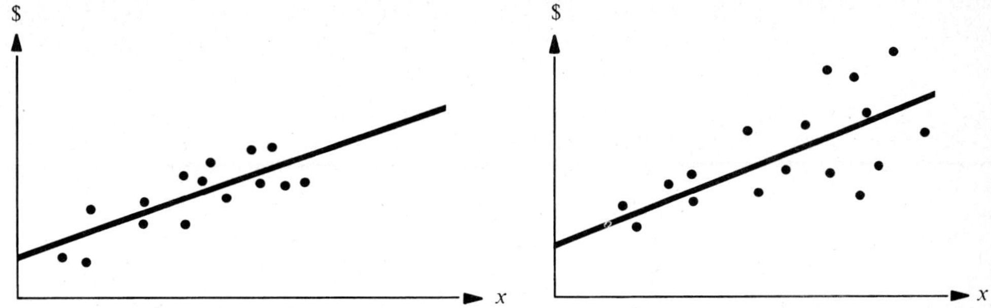

Constant variance or "homoskedasticity"

Nonconstant variance or "heteroskedasticity"

Figure 6.8

using cross-sectional data[5] on cost and output to estimate a long-run cost curve, larger operating units may be subject to greater fluctuations in activity (and costs). But there are three critical questions about nonconstant variance. How do we know if it exists? What effect does it have on our estimates? How do we deal with it?

Of course, nonconstant variance is most likely to be a problem when there is a large range in values for the independent variable (e.g., output). A simple, informal analysis would involve graphing the data points and the regression line as in Figure 6.8 and trying to discern whether the estimated residuals $\hat{\varepsilon}_t$ are larger (in absolute value) for larger values of the independent variable. A more formal analysis would be to (i) split the data into two subsamples, one with small values of X_t and the other with large values; (ii) estimate a regression for each subsample; and (iii) take the standard error of estimate S_ε^2 from each subsample and compare them. If $S_\varepsilon^2(1)$ is the larger of the subsample standard error of estimates and $S_\varepsilon^2(2)$ the smaller, then the ratio $S_\varepsilon^2(1)/S_\varepsilon^2(2)$ has an F-distribution, and the significance of the difference can be tested using a table like Appendix 6.3. If $S_\varepsilon^2(1)$ is based on a subsample of T_1 observations, then its degrees of freedom would be $T_1 - k - 1$. Likewise, $S_\varepsilon^2(2)$ would have $T_2 - k - 1$ degrees of freedom.

As an example, the Brown Co. data could be checked for nonconstant variance by dividing the twelve observations into those with output less than 550 and those with output greater than 550, and running regressions for each subsample (this is shown at the top of p. 124).

Since the standard error of estimate is higher for the high-output subsample, our statistic is 14189.3/13506.7, or 1.051. Appendix 6.3 indicates that the critical value for 4,4 degrees of freedom and an α of 0.05 is 9.6, so there is no evidence that the variance depends on the level of output.

If the disturbances do have nonconstant variance, with higher variance for larger values of X_t, then the regression estimates are affected. The estimated coefficient $\hat{\beta}_i$ is still unbiased but not best, because another estimate will be more accurate, as we will see in a moment. The misestimation occurs with the coefficients' standard errors, which are *under*estimated so that the t-statistics are *over*estimated. In addition, the standard

[5]That is, instead of measuring costs and output for one operation over time, we gather the data from many operations at a single point in time.

Low output subsample		High output subsample	
Output	Cost	Output	Cost
545	\$9,207	570	\$ 9,544
516	8,547	571	9,693
507	8,652	587	9,774
519	8,818	569	9,524
521	8,799	644	10,614
504	8,674	634	10,736

Low output subsample	High output subsample	
$\hat{F} = 1439.1; \hat{v} = 14.159$	$\hat{F} = 641.1; \hat{v} = 15.675$	
$R^2 = 0.7969$	$R^2 = 0.9621$	(6.15)
$S^2_\varepsilon = 13506.7$	$S^2_\varepsilon = 14189.3$	
Degrees of freedom = 4	Degrees of freedom = 4	

error of any forecasts will be underestimated, particularly for large values of X_*, the planned level of activity.

These estimation problems can be remedied by *deflating* the equation to be estimated. For instance, if the original equation was

$$Y_t = \beta_0 + \beta_1 X_t + \varepsilon_t \tag{6.16}$$

But it was found that $\sigma^2[\varepsilon_t] = \sigma^2 X_t^2$, the model could be deflated by dividing by X_t.[6] Then the following equation would give better estimates of β_0 and β_1.

$$\frac{Y_t}{X_t} = \beta_0\left(\frac{1}{X_t}\right) + \beta_1 + \frac{\varepsilon_t}{X_t} \tag{6.17}$$

That is, the dependent variable is now average cost, and the independent variable is the reciprocal of output. The new regression estimates could then be used to estimate the cost budgets for alternative levels of output by first estimating the cost per unit $(Y/X)_* = \hat{\beta}_0(1/X_*) + \hat{\beta}_1$ and then multiplying $(Y/X)_*$ by X_* to obtain the estimated total cost.

6.7 VIOLATIONS OF ASSUMPTION A3(b)

Assumption A3(b) states that one period's random disburbance is not correlated with the disturbance from any other period, that is, $\text{cov}[\varepsilon_t, \varepsilon_s] = 0$ for all $t, s, t \neq s$. The violation of this assumption is called *serial correlation,* and can result from a variety of factors. Perhaps the most common cause of serial correlation is the possibility that the factors that make up the random disturbances can last for more than one measurement period. Of course this is most likely to occur when the measurement periods are short (e.g., one week), but seasonal influences can produce serial correlation even with monthly data. Or, if we are using cross-sectional data (e.g., from 30 plants around the country), they may all be affected by general economic conditions, causing their random disturbances to be correlated.

[6]If $\sigma^2[\varepsilon_t] = \sigma^2 X_t$, then the appropriate change would be to deflate by $(X_t)^{1/2}$. The deflated error term $\varepsilon_t/(X_t)^{1/2}$ would have a variance equal to σ^2, a constant.

If serial correlation exists, its effects on the estimated coefficients are much the same as those of nonconstant variance. The estimated coefficients are not biased, but they are no longer the best estimates. If there is positive serial correlation ($\text{cov}[\varepsilon_t, \varepsilon_{t-1}] > 0$), then the t-statistics will be overestimated, and the standard error of forecast will be underestimated. Negative serial correlation reverses the directions of the misestimations. The signals of serial correlation are the correlations among the regression residuals, and many regression packages incorporate automatic checks of residuals that will alert the user to possible serial correlation. The Durbin–Watson d statistic[7] is an estimate of $2(1 - \rho)$, where ρ is the correlation between ε_t and ε_{t-1}. If the statistic is close to 2, there is no evidence of serial correlation, but as d moves toward 0 (4) there is increasing indication of positive (negative) serial correlation. The Durbin–Watson statistic for the Brown Co.'s twelve months of data is 1.9582, indicating no significant autocorrelation.

The existence of serial correlation means that some adjustment to the accounting model is in order, but the adjustment will depend on what factors are causing the problem. (A more detailed explanation of time-series models appears in Appendix 6.1.) For instance, we may incorporate seasonality into the model by adding dummy variables that take on values of either zero or one, depending on the time of year.

$$C_t = \beta_0 + \beta_1 X_t + \beta_2 S_t + \beta_3 F_t + \beta_3 W_t \tag{6.18}$$

where $C_t \equiv$ cost in month t

$X_t \equiv$ activity in month t

$$S_t \equiv \begin{cases} 1, & \text{if } t \text{ is a Summer month} \\ 0, & \text{otherwise} \end{cases}$$

$$F_t \equiv \begin{cases} 1, & \text{if } t \text{ is a Fall month} \\ 0, & \text{otherwise} \end{cases}$$

$$W_t \equiv \begin{cases} 1, & \text{if } t \text{ is a Winter month} \\ 0, & \text{otherwise} \end{cases}$$

Another cause of serial correlation is the phenomenon known as *cost-stickiness,* where costs, once increased, are difficult to reduce even when activity is reduced. (See Figure 6.9, where the cost/output combinations are numbered chronologically.) As activity increases, costs increase, but as output decreases (in periods 4 and 7), costs do not decrease along the same line. This behavior could be modeled by adding a dummy variable that has the value 1 when output decreases, and 0 otherwise. But it might be more useful to determine which economic factors cause the stickiness. For instance, in an operation that expects to grow, but which experiences fluctuations in activity, there may be a reluctance to lay off skilled employees for a short time period. To do so might make rehiring difficult and increase training costs. But it is the *labor hours* that are

[7] $d = \dfrac{\sum_{t=2}^{T} (\hat{\varepsilon}_t - \hat{\varepsilon}_{t-1})^2}{\sum_{t=1}^{T} \hat{\varepsilon}_t}$

A table of critical values of the Durbin–Watson statistic appears in Appendix 6.4.

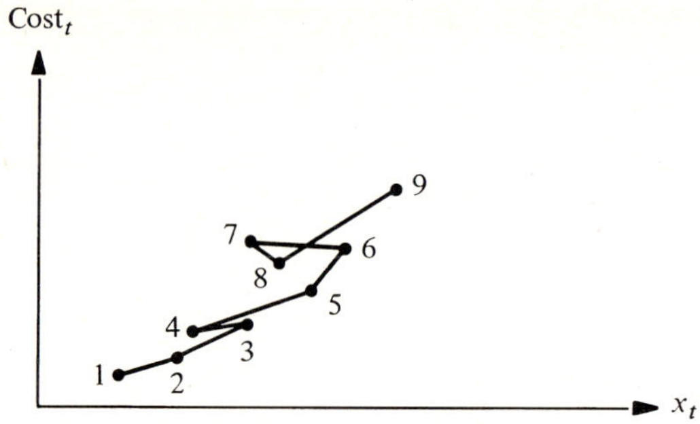

Figure 6.9

sticky, and we can estimate a more meaningful cost relationship by changing the model to something like the following

$$\text{Cost}_t = \beta_0 + \beta_1 (\text{labor hours})_t + \beta_2 (\text{machine hours})_t + \varepsilon_t \tag{6.19}$$

In forecasting costs for future periods, it is necessary first to forecast the output, and then to consider how that will combine with the firm's labor policies, to determine the labor hours and machine hours. The estimated relationship can then account for stickiness in forecasting costs for various output alternatives.

6.8 VIOLATIONS OF ASSUMPTION A5

An out-and-out violation of assumption A5 makes regression impossible because we've noted that the estimates are $\hat{\boldsymbol{\beta}} = (\mathbf{X}'\mathbf{X})^{-1}\mathbf{X}'\mathbf{Y}$, and violation of A5 implies that $(\mathbf{X}'\mathbf{X})^{-1}$ does not exist. But there are also situations where A5 is bent rather than broken, and these situations can produce regressions that are difficult to interpret. We can see the problem with the following monthly data on costs, direct labor hours, and machine hours.

Month	Cost	Direct labor hours	Machine hours
1	$18,000	1,000	800
2	19,600	1,100	880
3	16,400	900	720
4	17,200	950	760

Suppose we want to estimate a cost model of the form $C_t = F + v_1\text{DLH}_t + v_2\text{MH}_t$ from this data. Unfortunately, there is not just one model that fits the data, but an infinite number of models.

$$C_t = \$2{,}000 + 16\text{DLH}_t + 0\text{MH}_t$$

or

$$C_t = \$2{,}000 + 0\text{DLH}_t + 20\text{MH}_t \tag{6.20}$$

or

$$C_t = \$2{,}000 + 8\text{DLH}_t + 10\text{MH}_t, \qquad \text{etc.}$$

The problem is not that there isn't a strong relationship between the dependent variable (cost) and the independent variables (labor and machine hours). Any of the

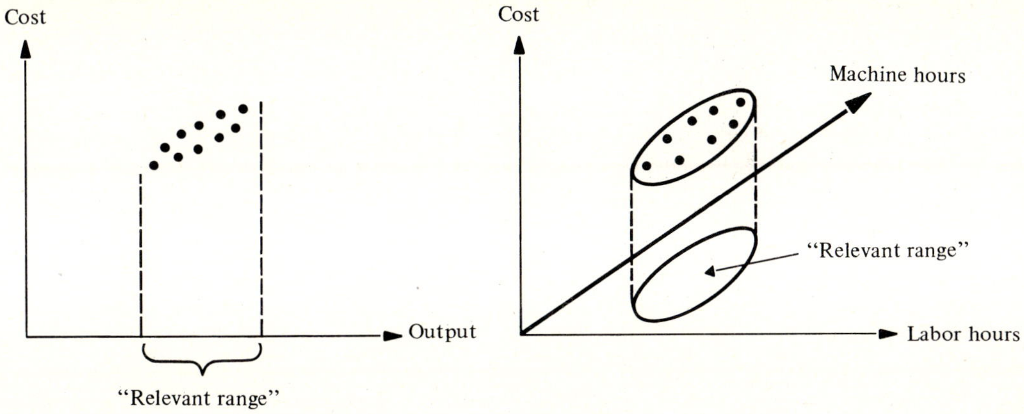

Figure 6.10

above models predict cost behavior perfectly. The problem is that the independent variables move together (are correlated), and so it is difficult for us to discern each activity measure's contribution to costs. In fact, the signals of multicollinearity are reflective of this—high R^2 and low t-statistics. We know there is a relationship, but we cannot be very confident about each variable's estimated coefficient.

Is this a serious problem? Not necessarily. If our objective is to forecast costs in a period where the independent variables maintain their previous relationship to each other, than we can have some confidence in the forecasts. In effect, the relevant range takes on a two-dimensional meaning, and labor hour/machine hour combinations that do not conform to the previous behavior will produce cost forecasts with a lower level of confidence (see Figure 6.10).

For instance, if the activity for month 5 was forecasted to be 1,050 direct labor hours and 840 machine hours, we might forecast costs of $18,800 with some confidence. However if the forecasted activity was 1,100 direct labor hours and 720 machine hours, then the level of confidence in a prediction would be much lower. In these cases, the best alternative may be to further analyze the cost data and to split the costs included in C_t into those we expect to depend on labor hours C_{Lt}, and those expected to vary with machine hours, C_{Mt}. Then we could estimate each relationship separately, and the future costs would be estimated separately.

$$C_{Lt} = F_L + v_L \text{DLH}_t + \varepsilon_{Lt} \qquad (6.21)$$
$$C_{Mt} = F_M + v_M \text{MH}_t + \varepsilon_{Mt}$$

6.9 SUMMARY

At this point, we have covered the basic types of cost estimation techniques available to a managerial accountant. Statistical cost estimation is a method that is becoming increasingly available and increasingly used in management. The information it provides can answer a number of questions that arise in planning and in performance evaluation.

TABLE 6.1 REGRESSION PROBLEMS
$Y_t = \beta_0 + \beta_1 X_t + \varepsilon_t$

Problem	Common causes	Effect on regression estimates	Diagnosis	Possible solutions
Nonconstant variance [violates A3(a)]	Larger volume operations are inherently more difficult to control. Therefore $\sigma^2[\varepsilon_t]$ is influenced by the value of X_t.	The estimated coefficients are still unbiased, but *t*-statistics will be overstated, and standard error of prediction will be understated for large values of X_t.	An informal look at the regression residuals *or* Bartlett's test to see if $\sigma^2[\varepsilon_t]$ is the same for large and small values of X_t.	If $\sigma^2[\varepsilon] = kX_t^2$, then *deflate* the model by X_t, i.e., estimate $Y_t/X_t = \beta_0(1/X_t) + \beta_1 + \varepsilon_t/X_t$. If $\sigma^2[\varepsilon_t] = kX_t$, deflate by $X_t^{1/2}$.
Serial correlation [violates A3(b)]	Seasonality Poor accrual Time-series changes in the cost process that are not incorporated into the model. Cost stickiness	The estimated coefficients are still unbiased, but if there is positive serial correlation the *t*-statistics are overstated, and S_f^2 is understated. Negative serial correlation causes the opposite effects.	Durbin–Watson statistic $d = \frac{\Sigma(\varepsilon_t - \varepsilon_{t-1})^2}{\Sigma\varepsilon_t^2}$ is an estimate of $2(1 - \rho)$, where ρ is the correlation between ε_t and ε_{t-1}.	Change the model to incorporate sources of serial correlation, e.g., a dummy variable for seasonality, or a model of learning, or the cause of stickiness, etc.
Errors in measuring X_t (violates A4)	Errors in the accounting data Available accounting measures don't match the "economic" measure of activity.	The estimated slope coefficient $\hat{\beta}_1$ is *biased* toward zero.	No statistical diagnosis.	Improve measurement techniques. Estimate amount of bias and compensate for it.
Correlated independent variables ("bends" A5)	Different measures of activity are correlated with one another	Makes it difficult to determine which variable is causing what effect. Doesn't bias the estimates, but $S_{\hat{\beta}_i}^2$ will be large.	Usual symptoms are significant R^2, but low *t*-statistics. Estimate correlation of X_{it} and X_{jt}.	If only want to use the relationship to predict, then there's no real problem. Otherwise, could split into two relationships. For example, instead of overhead as a function of direct labor and machine hours, estimate two equations, one for OH related to labor and one for OH related to machines.

But regression must be used with caution as well. It is a neutral technique that will estimate useless relationships between irrelevant or badly measured variables. A number of statistical problems (summarized in Table 6.1) can affect the regression results and interpretations. The choices of model and evaluation of data are the most important parts of regression analysis, and the managerial accountant must be familiar with the decision situations and the accounting system's characteristics to do this job effectively.

APPENDIXES

APPENDIX 6.1: A TIME-SERIES MODEL

One of the assumptions of regression analysis discussed in this chapter was that each observation was independent of the others. That is, the month's costs C_t depended on that month's activity X_t, and the other factors in the disturbance ε_t, and furthermore ε_t was not correlated with the disturbances in other months. The effects of violations of this assumption are discussed in the chapter, along with some remedies. But in this Appendix we will look at a time-series model that could be used to deal with situations where observations are correlated through time.

A6.1 First-Order Autoregressive Error Model

As in the chapter, the costs of a period are determined as $C_t = F + vX_t + \varepsilon_t$. However, instead of being independent of other disturbances, ε_t is determined in the following way

$$\varepsilon_t = \rho\varepsilon_{t-1} + \mu_t \qquad \text{(A6.1)}$$

where $-1 < \rho < 1$,[8] and μ_t has an expected value of zero, standard deviation of σ_μ, and is independent of all μ_s, $s \neq t$. The disturbances ε_t have the following properties

$$\begin{aligned}\varepsilon_t &= \rho\varepsilon_{t-1} + \mu_t \\ &= \rho^2\varepsilon_{t-2} + \rho\mu_{t-1} + \mu_t \\ &= \rho^3\varepsilon_{t-3} + \rho^2\mu_{t-2} + \rho\mu_{t-1} + \mu_t \\ &= \sum_{j=0}^{\infty} \rho^j\mu_{t-j}\end{aligned} \qquad \text{(A6.2)}$$

$$E[\varepsilon_t] = \sum_{j=0}^{\infty} \rho^j E[\mu_{t-j}] = 0$$

$$\begin{aligned}\sigma^2[\varepsilon_t] &= \sum_{j=0}^{\infty} (\rho^j)^2\sigma_\mu^2 \\ \text{cov}[\varepsilon_t, \varepsilon_{t-j}] &= \rho^j\sigma^2[\varepsilon_t]\end{aligned} \qquad \text{(A6.3)}$$

[8]If $\rho < 0$, then the disturbances are negatively correlated. For instance, accrual problems may assign costs that belong in period t to period $t - 1$ or $t + 1$, so that positive (negative) disturbances will tend to be followed by negative (positive) ones.

If $\rho > 0$, a disturbance will tend to be followed by a disturbance of the same sign, a phenomenon that is caused by variables which are excluded from the regression and whose effects last for more than one measurement period.

TABLE A6.1 COST DATA WITH SERIAL CORRELATION

Month, t	Cost, C_t	Units produced, X_t
1	$153,971	716
2	158,033	700
3	154,015	608
4	149,549	539
5	173,167	735
6	148,443	595
7	146,578	576
8	167,880	744
9	158,275	688
10	165,595	771
11	149,684	620
12	144,011	540
13	161,418	687
14	169,948	759
15	149,524	621
16	142,670	531
17	141,139	563
18	141,571	544

The correlation[9] between ε_t and ε_{t-j} is equal to ρ^j and it is this correlation that shows up in the Durbin–Watson statistic and alerts us to the problem of serial correlation. As described in the chapter, a positive serial correlation ($\rho > 0$) leads to an overestimation of the t-statistics, and the regression estimates of F and v no longer have the lowest expected error.

The solution to this problem is a modification of the regression model as shown in (A6.4) below. The new dependent variable is $C_t - \rho C_{t-1}$ and the new independent variable is $X_t - \rho X_{t-1}$. The disturbances μ_t are independent of each other, so the serial correlation has disappeared, and the estimates of $\hat{F} = (1 - \rho)F$ and v will be best, and can be used in forecasts for future periods.

$$\begin{aligned} &C_t = F + vX_t + \varepsilon_t = F + vX_t + \rho\varepsilon_{t-1} + \mu_t \\ &C_{t-1} = F + vX_{t-1} + \varepsilon_{t-1} \\ &\rightarrow C_t - \rho C_{t-1} = (1 - \rho)F + v(X_t - \rho X_{t-1}) + \mu_t \end{aligned} \tag{A6.4}$$

The careful reader will have noted that the above modification is not easily made, for we have no way of knowing the value of the serial correlation ρ that is used to modify the dependent and independent variables. However, the estimated serial correlation can be used to improve the estimates of the coefficients in the following way. To illustrate the steps, the data in Table A6.1 will be used.

The first step is to use a simple regression analysis to estimate the parameters, and to check whether a serial correlation problem exists. The data in Table A6.1 produced the following results:

[9]The correlation between two variables X and Y is defined as $\rho_{xy} = \text{cov}(X,Y)/(\sigma[X]\sigma[Y])$. In this case

$$\rho_{\varepsilon_t,\varepsilon_{t-j}} = \frac{\rho^j\sigma^2[\varepsilon_t]}{\sigma[\varepsilon_t]\sigma[\varepsilon_{t-j}]} = \rho^j$$

Since $|\rho| < 1$, the correlation decreases (in absolute value) as j increases.

$$
\begin{aligned}
C_t &= 83{,}605 + 110.13X_t \\
&\quad (10.865) \quad (9.248) \qquad (t\text{-statistics}) \\
R^2 &= 0.8424 \\
S_\varepsilon &= 4128.2 \\
&\text{Durbin–Watson, } d = 1.011 \\
&\text{Serial correlation between } \hat{\varepsilon}_t \text{ and } \hat{\varepsilon}_{t-1},\ \hat{\rho} = 0.418
\end{aligned}
\tag{A6.5}
$$

While the relationship between cost and output appears to be a strong one, there is some evidence of a positive correlation between the residuals. The next step is to consider whether this positive correlation is statistically significant. To test whether $\rho > 0$, the Durbin–Watson statistic d can be compared with the critical values, such as those found in Appendix 6.4. For the number of observations n and the number of independent variables (k), there are two critical values in Appendix 6.4. If $d < d_L$, then the probability that $\rho \leq 0$ (the null hypothesis) is less than the stated level of significance, 0.05. As a result, we would accept the hypothesis that a significant positive serial correlation exists. If $d > d_U$, then the null hypothesis (no positive serial correlation) is accepted. If $d_L < d < d_U$, then the test is inconclusive. In our case, $n = 18$ and $k = 1$, so the critical value $d_L = 1.16$, and the estimated value $d = 1.011$ indicates that a positive serial correlation most likely exists.[10,11]

The next step is to estimate a revised autoregressive model based on the results above. The new dependent variable is $C_t - \hat{\rho}C_{t-1}$ or $C_t - 0.418C_{t-1}$, and the independent variable is revised in the same way. The results of this estimation are the following.

$$
\begin{aligned}
C_t - 0.418C_{t-1} &= 45{,}855 + 119.02\,(X_t - 0.418X_{t-1}) \\
&\quad (13.225) \quad (12.899) \qquad t\text{-statistics} \\
R^2 &= 0.9173 \\
S_\varepsilon &= 3200.1^{12} \\
&\text{Durbin–Watson, } d = 1.6863 \\
&\text{Serial correlation between } \hat{\varepsilon}_t \text{ and } \hat{\varepsilon}_{t-1},\ \hat{\rho} = 0.157
\end{aligned}
\tag{A6.6}
$$

The coefficients estimated in this model are $(1 - \hat{\rho})F$ for the intercept and v for the slope, so the estimates of fixed and variable costs would be the following:

$$
\begin{aligned}
F &= \frac{45{,}855}{1 - 0.418} = 78{,}788.7 \\
v &= 119.02
\end{aligned}
\tag{A6.7}
$$

These differ rather substantially from the estimates of the original regression. The Durbin–Watson $d = 1.6863$ indicates that there is no significant positive serial correlation remaining in the model, so the estimation process may stop at this point.

One shortcoming of this process is that we are operating with an estimate $\hat{\rho}$ that may not be terribly close to the actual value of ρ. If that is the case, then the estimated autoregressive model will also show some serial correlation. If this occurs, the values of F and v from the autoregressive model can be used to compute $\hat{\varepsilon}_t$'s and a new estimate of the serial correlation, say $\hat{\hat{\rho}}$. This new estimate of ρ is then used to estimate a new autoregressive model, which is then checked for serial correlation. This iterative process can continue until no significant serial correlation remains in the autoregressive model, as depicted in Figure A6.1.

[10] Tables for other levels of statistical significance may be found in some statistics books.

[11] To test for negative autocorrelation, the statistic d is replaced by the quantity $4 - d$, and used in the test procedures outlined above.

[12] This is really an estimate of σ_μ.

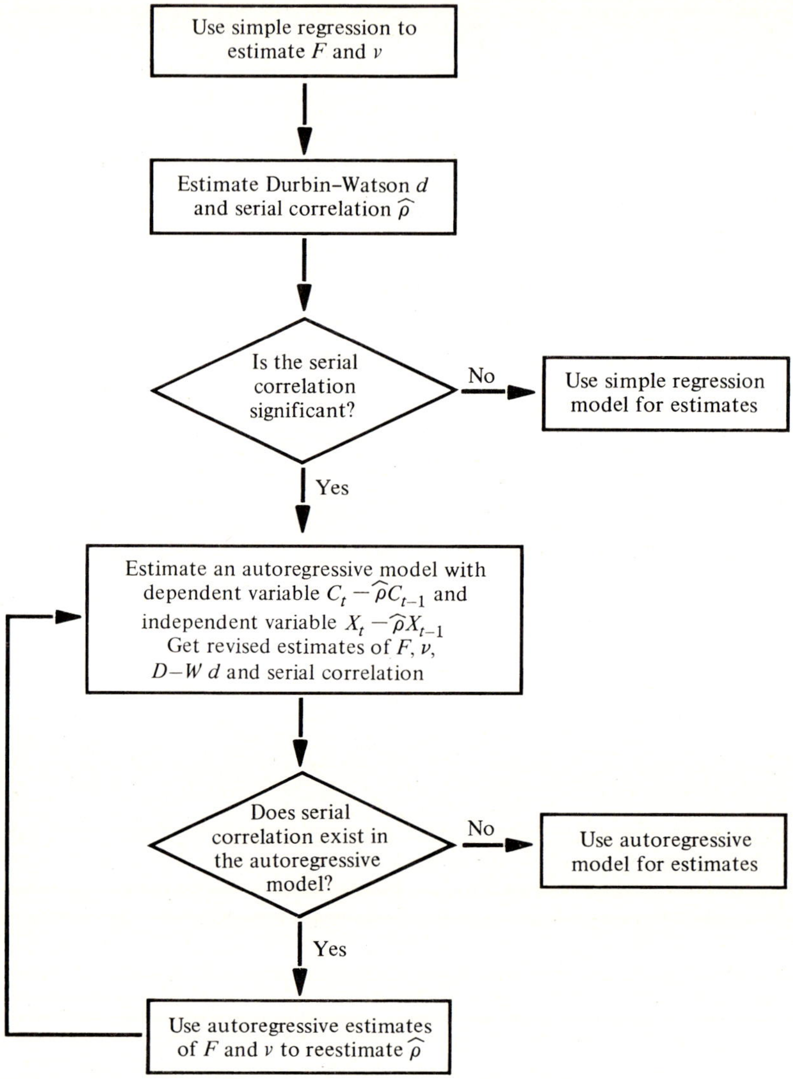

Figure A6.1

A6.2 Other Time-Series Models

There are many other approaches to estimating the time-series behavior of a sequence of observations. Some approaches are simpler than the one outlined above, and many are much more complex. Given our objectives, we will not explore these further, but the interested reader may wish to explore these topics in a text such as that by Nelson.[13]

[13]Charles Nelson. *Applied Time Series Analysis*. San Francisco: Holden-Day 1973.

APPENDIX 6.2 THE DISTRIBUTION OF t^* (TWO-TAILED TESTS)

Degrees of freedom	Probability of a Larger Value, Sign Ignored				
	0.40	0.25	0.10	0.05	0.01
2	1.061	1.604	2.920	4.303	9.926
3	0.978	1.423	2.353	3.182	5.841
4	0.941	1.344	2.132	2.776	4.604
5	0.920	1.301	2.015	2.571	4.032
6	0.906	1.273	1.943	2.447	3.707
7	0.896	1.254	1.895	2.365	3.499
8	0.889	1.240	1.860	2.306	3.355
9	0.883	1.230	1.833	2.262	3.250
10	0.879	1.221	1.812	2.228	3.169
11	0.876	1.214	1.796	2.201	3.106
12	0.873	1.209	1.782	2.179	3.054
13	0.870	1.204	1.771	2.160	3.012
14	0.868	1.200	1.761	2.145	2.977
15	0.866	1.197	1.753	2.131	2.947
16	0.865	1.194	1.746	2.120	2.921
17	0.863	1.191	1.740	2.110	2.898
18	0.862	1.189	1.734	2.101	2.878
19	0.861	1.187	1.729	2.093	2.861
20	0.860	1.185	1.725	2.086	2.845
21	0.859	1.183	1.721	2.080	2.831
22	0.858	1.182	1.717	2.074	2.819
23	0.858	1.180	1.714	2.069	2.807
24	0.857	1.179	1.711	2.064	2.797
25	0.856	1.178	1.708	2.060	2.787
26	0.856	1.177	1.706	2.056	2.779
27	0.855	1.176	1.703	2.052	2.771
28	0.855	1.175	1.701	2.048	2.763
29	0.854	1.174	1.699	2.045	2.756
30	0.854	1.173	1.697	2.042	2.750
35	0.852	1.170	1.690	2.030	2.724
40	0.851	1.167	1.684	2.021	2.704
45	0.850	1.165	1.679	2.014	2.689
50	0.849	1.164	1.676	2.009	2.678

APPENDIX 6.3 5% DISTRIBUTION OF F (TWO-TAILED TESTS)

Degrees of freedom for smaller mean square	Degrees of freedom for larger mean square							
	4	6	8	10	15	20	25	30
4	9.60	9.20	8.98	8.84	8.66	8.56	8.50	8.46
6	6.23	5.82	5.60	5.46	5.27	5.17	5.11	5.07
8	5.05	4.65	4.43	4.30	4.10	4.00	3.94	3.89
10	4.47	4.07	3.85	3.72	3.52	3.42	3.35	3.31
15	3.80	3.41	3.20	3.06	2.86	2.76	2.69	2.64
20	3.51	3.13	2.91	2.77	2.57	2.46	2.40	2.35
25	3.35	2.97	2.75	2.61	2.41	2.30	2.23	2.18
30	3.25	2.87	2.65	2.51	2.31	2.20	2.12	2.07

APPENDIX 6.4 DURBIN–WATSON TEST BOUNDS

	Level of significance $\alpha = 0.05$									
	$k = 1$		$k = 2$		$k = 3$		$k = 4$		$k = 5$	
n	d_L	d_U	d_L	d_U	d_L	d_U	d_L	d_U	d_L	d_U
15	1.08	1.36	0.95	1.54	0.82	1.75	0.69	1.97	0.56	2.21
16	1.10	1.37	0.98	1.54	0.86	1.73	0.74	1.93	0.62	2.15
17	1.13	1.38	1.02	1.54	0.90	1.71	0.78	1.90	0.67	2.10
18	1.16	1.39	1.05	1.53	0.93	1.69	0.82	1.87	0.71	2.06
19	1.18	1.40	1.08	1.53	0.97	1.68	0.86	1.85	0.75	2.02
20	1.20	1.41	1.10	1.54	1.00	1.68	0.90	1.83	0.79	1.99
21	1.22	1.42	1.13	1.54	1.03	1.67	0.93	1.81	0.83	1.96
22	1.24	1.43	1.15	1.54	1.05	1.66	0.96	1.80	0.86	1.94
23	1.26	1.44	1.17	1.54	1.08	1.66	0.99	1.79	0.90	1.92
24	1.27	1.45	1.19	1.55	1.10	1.66	1.01	1.78	0.93	1.90
25	1.29	1.45	1.21	1.55	1.12	1.66	1.04	1.77	0.95	1.89
26	1.30	1.46	1.22	1.55	1.14	1.65	1.06	1.76	0.98	1.88
27	1.32	1.47	1.24	1.56	1.16	1.65	1.08	1.76	1.01	1.86
28	1.33	1.48	1.26	1.56	1.18	1.65	1.10	1.75	1.03	1.85
29	1.34	1.48	1.27	1.56	1.20	1.65	1.12	1.74	1.05	1.84
30	1.35	1.49	1.28	1.57	1.21	1.65	1.14	1.74	1.07	1.83
31	1.36	1.50	1.30	1.57	1.23	1.65	1.16	1.74	1.09	1.83
32	1.37	1.50	1.31	1.57	1.24	1.65	1.18	1.73	1.11	1.82
33	1.38	1.51	1.32	1.58	1.26	1.65	1.19	1.73	1.13	1.81
34	1.39	1.51	1.33	1.58	1.27	1.65	1.21	1.73	1.15	1.81
35	1.40	1.52	1.34	1.58	1.28	1.65	1.22	1.73	1.16	1.80
36	1.41	1.52	1.35	1.59	1.29	1.65	1.24	1.73	1.18	1.80
37	1.42	1.53	1.36	1.59	1.31	1.66	1.25	1.72	1.19	1.80
38	1.43	1.54	1.37	1.59	1.32	1.66	1.26	1.72	1.21	1.79
39	1.43	1.54	1.38	1.60	1.33	1.66	1.27	1.72	1.22	1.79
40	1.44	1.54	1.39	1.60	1.34	1.66	1.29	1.72	1.23	1.79
45	1.48	1.57	1.43	1.62	1.38	1.67	1.34	1.72	1.29	1.78
50	1.50	1.59	1.46	1.63	1.42	1.67	1.38	1.72	1.34	1.77
55	1.53	1.60	1.49	1.64	1.45	1.68	1.41	1.72	1.38	1.77
60	1.55	1.62	1.51	1.65	1.48	1.69	1.44	1.73	1.41	1.77
65	1.57	1.63	1.54	1.66	1.50	1.70	1.47	1.73	1.44	1.77
70	1.58	1.64	1.55	1.67	1.52	1.70	1.49	1.74	1.46	1.77
75	1.60	1.65	1.57	1.68	1.54	1.71	1.51	1.74	1.49	1.77
80	1.61	1.66	1.59	1.69	1.56	1.72	1.53	1.74	1.51	1.77
85	1.62	1.67	1.60	1.70	1.57	1.72	1.55	1.75	1.52	1.77
90	1.63	1.68	1.61	1.70	1.59	1.73	1.57	1.75	1.54	1.78
95	1.64	1.69	1.62	1.71	1.60	1.73	1.58	1.75	1.56	1.78
100	1.65	1.69	1.63	1.72	1.61	1.74	1.59	1.76	1.57	1.78

Source: J. Durbin and G. S. Watson. "Testing for Serial Correlation in Least Squares Regression II," *Biometrika*. **38:**159–178. 1951. Used with permission.

PROBLEMS

6.1. (CMA). The Alpha Company, which produces several different products, is making plans for the introduction of a new product that it will sell for \$6 a unit. The following estimates have been made for manufacturing costs on 100,000 units to be produced the first year.

Direct materials	\$50,000	
Direct labor	\$40,000	(The labor rate is \$4/hr.)

Overhead costs have not yet been estimated for the new product, but monthly data on total production and overhead cost for the past 24 months have been analyzed using simple linear regression. The following results were derived from the simple regression and will provide the basis for overhead cost estimates for the new product.

Simple Regression Analysis Results ($y = a + bx$)

Dependent variable (y) – factory overhead costs
Independent variable (x) – direct labor hours
Computed variables:

y-intercept	\$40,000
Coefficient of independent variable	\$2.10
Coefficient of correlation	0.953
Standard error of estimate	\$2,840
Standard error of regression coefficient	0.42
Mean value of independent variable	\$18,000
Coefficient of determination	0.908

A. What percentage of the variation in overhead costs is explained by the independent variable?
(a) 90.8%
(b) 42%
(c) 48.8%
(d) 95.3%
(e) some other amount.

B. To determine a confidence interval for the parameter estimated by b in the regression computation, an appropriate t value should be selected from a table of values from the Student's t distribution corresponding to the desired level of confidence and having
(a) 0 degrees of freedom.
(b) 2 degrees of freedom.
(c) 10 degrees of freedom.
(d) 22 degrees of freedom.
(e) 24 degrees of freedom.

C. Assuming that the appropriate t value is 2.07, a 95% confidence interval for the b values would be
(a) (1.23, 2.97)
(b) (0.10, 4.10)
(c) (2.1, 2.97)
(d) (0.22, 3.97)
(e) some other amount.

D. The total overhead cost for an estimated activity level of 20,000 direct labor hours would be
(a) \$42,000
(b) \$82,000
(c) \$122,000
(d) \$222,000
(e) some other amount.

E. The expected contribution margin per unit to be earned during the first year on 100,000 units of the new product would be

(a) \$4.49
(b) \$4.89
(c) \$0.30
(d) \$5.10
(e) some other amount.

6.2. (CMA, adapted). The controller of the Connecticut Electronics Company believes that the identification of the variable and fixed components of the firm's costs will enable the firm to make better planning and control decisions. Among the costs the controller is concerned about is the behavior of indirect supplies expense. He believes there is some correlation between the machine hours worked and the amount of indirect supplies used.

A member of the controller's staff has suggested that a simple linear regression model be used to determine the cost behavior of the indirect supplies. The regression equation shown below was developed from 40 pairs of observations using the least-squares method of regression. The regression equation and related measures are as follows:

$$S = \$200 + \$4\text{H}$$

where

S = total monthly costs of indirect supplies
H = machine hours per month

Standard error of estimate: $S_e = 100$
Coefficient of determination: $R^2 = 0.76$

Required

A. When a simple linear regression model is used to make inferences about a population relationship from sample data, what assumptions must be made before the inferences can be accepted as valid?

B. Assume the assumptions identified in requirement A are satisfied for the indirect supplies expense of Connecticut Electronics Company.

(a) Explain the meaning of 200 and 4 in the regression equation, $S = \$200 + \$4\text{H}$.
(b) Calculate the estimated cost of indirect supplies if 900 machine hours are to be used during a month.
(c) In addition to the estimate for the cost of indirect supplies, the controller would like the range of values for the estimate if a 95 percent confidence interval is specified. He would use this range to judge whether the estimated costs indicated by the regression analysis was good enough for planning purposes. Calculate, for 900 machine hours, the range of the estimate for the cost of indirect supplies with a 95 percent confidence interval.

6.3. (CMA). Brown Company employs twenty salesmen to market its products in well-defined sales territories. The company has analyzed the weekly sales order-getting costs for the past year using regression analysis. The following was derived from the regression analysis:

$$C = \$6{,}000 + \$.50M + \$6.00S$$

where C = weekly sales order-getting costs
M = number of miles driven per week by the sales force
S = number of sales calls completed per week
Standard error of the estimate for C given the values for M and S = 400

Required

A. The sales department has estimated that the sales force will drive 10,000 miles and make 500 calls during the first week in July.

(a) Calculate the estimated sales order-getting costs for the week.

(b) What criteria should be met before Brown's sales department relies on the estimate derived in A.1. above?

B. What does the value for the standard error of the estimate for $C(400)$ mean, and how might it be used in cost estimation?

6.4. Paul Roberts has set up a small business to print slogans onto pins to be worn during election campaigns (''Vote Early, Vote Often''), ethnic holidays (''It's So Easy Being Green''), etc. The company buys the pins already made, and when a customer places an order, the printing die is made, and then the slogan is stamped on the pins and covered with a lacquer finish. The pins are counted, put in boxes, and shipped. There are usually no repeats on orders, so the printing dies are discarded when the order is complete. Roberts uses a job cost system with overhead being applied on the basis of number of pins produced using an annual rate.

Roberts has decided to find out more about the behavior of costs for his business, and has accumulated the following data for the last three months.

Month	Total cost	Number of jobs	Number of pins
1	$122,500	50	1,000,000
2	126,000	40	1,200,000
3	121,000	60	900,000

A. If Roberts uses the number of pins as an activity measure, and if the selling price per pin is two times the variable cost per pin, how many pins would Roberts have to sell to break even? (Your answer may be left in fraction form.)

B. Roberts has received two separate orders. Using the analysis in A, what is the incremental cost and price charged for each job?

Job #1: 3,000 pins
Job #2: 18,000 pins

C. Estimate the variable cost per job. Why doesn't this number make sense? Estimate a *more complete* cost function using the data available.

6.5. The following data are available for one month's operation in the ABC Company. This company has two production departments, X and Y, and one service department S, which provides services to both X and Y. The measure of production activity is *direct labor hours* in both X and Y, and this measure is used for cost allocation purposes. Items produced are sold immediately upon completion.

	S	*X*	*Y*
Beginning raw material inventory		$100,000	$ 75,000
Raw material purchases		185,000	525,000
Ending raw material inventory		125,000	50,000
Direct labor costs incurred		640,000	550,000
Direct labor hours incurred		80,000	110,000
Overhead costs incurred	$480,000	360,000	410,000
Annualized overhead allocation rate (includes S's costs)		6.50	6.50
Beginning work in process		0	0
Ending work in process		0	0

A. For production department *X*, what is the cost of goods sold? Use accounting procedures required for financial reporting, including an annualized application of overhead costs.

B. (Optional) For the firm as a whole, what is the over- or underapplication of overhead for this month? What are two alternative methods of accounting for these over- or underapplications?

C. The manager of department *X* would like to know how much she would have to produce (as measured in direct labor hours) to meet a monthly target net income of $50,000. Net sales revenue on finished goods usually averages about $19 per direct labor hour spent on the item. To help *X*'s manager, you have assembled data from another month's operation.

	S	*X*	*Y*
Overhead costs incurred	$500,000	$400,000	$400,000
Direct labor hours		100,000	100,000

If the overhead costs in *S* depend on the level of total firm activity, while overhead costs in *X* and *Y* depend only on the activity in their own departments, estimate cost behavior in *S* and in *X*.

D. If a "dual-rate" allocation of *S*'s costs is used, with *S*'s fixed costs being equally divided between *X* and *Y*, how many direct labor hours in *X* would produce a target income of $50,000 for department *X*?

6.6. The Acme Soap Company produces a type of liquid dishwashing detergent that is sold in bulk to chain stores who then bottle it and sell it under the store brand. The productive process is a fairly simple one, with almost all of the basic materials being added at the beginning of the process. The mixture then goes through a variety of processing steps until, two-thirds of the way through production, some rather expensive scents, emollients, etc., are added to the product. While these frill ingredients add no appreciable volume to the mixture, their cost is a significant one. Then processing continues until completion. Acme uses a process-costing system with a FIFO cost flow assumption for financial reporting purposes. You have been supplied with the following information for the first and second months of 1986.

	January	February
Beginning inventory		
Gallons	20,000	10,000
Basic material cost	$50,000	?
Frill material cost	0	?
Conversion cost	$20,000	?
Stage of completion	1/2	1/2
Gallons begun	100,000	80,000
Costs incurred		
Basic material	$200,000	$160,000
Frill material	110,000	70,000
Conversion	205,000	175,000
Ending inventory		
Gallons	10,000	20,000
State of completion	1/2	1/2

A. What is the value of *cost of goods completed and transferred out* for the month of January?

B. What is the value of *ending work in process* on January 31?

C. Assume that completed product is sold at $6 per gallon immediately upon completion. How many gallons must Acme produce and sell for a month in order to achieve a monthly profit of $10,000?

6.7. "Well, I guess I was wrong about overhead depending on direct labor and machine hours. I used twelve months of data and a regression program to estimate the way overhead behaves. The results looked something like this:

$$\begin{array}{lcccc} \text{Overhead} & = \$140{,}000 + & \$9\text{DLH} + & \$1\text{MH} \\ (t\text{-statistics}) & (17.1) & (1.2) & (0.7) \\ & R^2 = 0.83 & & \end{array}$$

"The t-statistics are a little low, but the R^2 is pretty good, so I think I can just use a direct labor rate to allocate overhead."

A. Do you agree with this assessment? If so, state why. If not, state why, and suggest a specific alternative approach to the cost estimation problem.

B. Seasonal heating and cooling costs are becoming more significant in most operations. Suppose that activity is also seasonal, with heavy production in Spring and Fall. How would these facts combine to affect the estimates of variable costs in a regression? (That is, would the variable cost estimates be overestimated, underestimated or unaffected?) Why? If the estimates are affected, how would you overcome this problem?

6.8. The Green Products Company is considering two offers to produce additional units. Both offers are for $50 per unit, but the first offer is for 10 units, while the second offer is for 50 units. The currently budgeted level of production is 325 units.

To aid you in making your recommendation, the controller of Green Products has acquired the following information on costs and output for the last twelve months.

Month	Output (units)	Cost ($)
1	295	14,345
2	234	11,577
3	301	14,460
4	252	12,310
5	230	11,618
6	284	13,767
7	295	14,398
8	284	13,587
9	271	13,380
10	240	11,913
11	268	13,125
12	347	16,831

Required If the company has sufficient capacity to accept either or both jobs, what would you recommend?

6.9. Your consulting firm has been retained by the Bully Manufacturing Company to evaluate their costing system and to recommend changes that improve the system's decision facilitating features. Bully's controller wants to be able to get realistic flexible budgets, but wants to keep the system as simple as possible. That is, he would prefer a plantwide variable overhead rate to departmental rates, and single-department rates to dual rates.

You are evaluating the cost relationships for two departments that produce one of Bully's new electronic products. In department 1, the body of the product is produced with plastic injection equipment, and in department 2 the electronic components are put in place and connected. Product testing also takes place in department 2. The most recent eight weeks' overhead costs for the two departments are given below, as well as the direct labor and machine hours.

	Department 1			Department 2		
Month	Overhead	Direct labor hours	Machine hours	Overhead	Direct labor hours	Machine hours
1	$54,000	960	980	$94,180	520	260
2	49,280	980	980	71,360	420	230
3	46,320	840	780	90,620	600	230
4	41,520	820	820	86,400	580	210
5	42,120	900	860	84,880	460	290
6	50,780	960	920	85,520	580	240
7	53,360	1000	980	82,620	600	230
8	56,400	900	900	76,680	580	280

Required Use regression analysis to consider whether departments 1 and 2 could use a common variable overhead cost rate. If not, do the departments need to have separate rates for direct labor and machine hours?

6.10. Sarah Larcker was explaining the goal-setting process in her company. "We try to set performance targets that are not way out of line, but that managers have to work to achieve. But that's not always an easy thing to judge. As an illustration, look at the cost data from one of our manufacturing departments below. It's evident that the department's costs depend on the level of activity, but this level is not controlled by the department manager. Also, high levels of activity mean that when things go well, they go really well and when things go badly, they go very badly. Next month's activity is scheduled to be 195 units, and I would like to set a cost budget so that the department manager has a 20% chance of achieving costs below the budget. What do you think next month's budget should be?"

Month	Costs	Units processed
1	$331,319	114
2	479,545	168
3	397,736	144
4	417,270	156
5	373,566	133
6	419,763	189
7	309,192	114
8	410,910	166
9	373,769	136
10	414,988	196
11	318,174	108
12	470,269	150
13	345,755	132
14	385,161	134
15	441,565	176
16	490,223	183

6.11. The Harrison Company has received a special order from one of its customers for 500 units of output. The price which the customer said he is willing to pay is somewhat lower than Harrison's usual price. As a result, there has been a great deal of discussion about the order, and a fairly extensive study of the direct labor and materials that the order would require. Due to the current excess capacity, Harrison's management decided that if the variable overhead costs were less than $180 per unit, then the order's contribution margin was large enough to warrant acceptance.

The Company had been planning to do an extensive study of its overhead costs for some time, but the study was barely begun, and the customer was pressing Harrison for a decision. The only records that were readily available were the overhead costs and production levels for the last 24 months. The general manager indicated that she would be willing to accept the order if a thorough analysis of the data indicated that the variable overhead cost would be less than $180. (She emphasized "thorough.")

Month	Overhead cost	Units produced
1	$ 915,880	3227
2	831,766	2962
3	870,836	2964
4	836,206	2792
5	894,915	3000
6	946,725	3265
7	958,881	3386
8	929,287	3120
9	861,418	2619
10	884,345	2642
11	1,044,453	3476
12	911,853	2974
13	942,413	3292
14	926,071	3362
15	794,245	2568
16	825,984	2567
17	937,228	3052
18	806,693	2548
19	881,630	3056
20	879,221	2920
21	842,471	2636
22	909,587	2773
23	902,304	2804
24	890,370	2829

Required Write a one-page report to Harrison's general manager, summarizing your findings and recommending a course of action.

6.12. "In the past, sales and production of our two products have depended on general market conditions," remarked David Michaelson, "but the marketing group really wants to push product *X* in the coming quarters. As assistant controller of the manufacturing division, I've been asked to do a preliminary analysis of the variable overhead costs to see how they will be affected by this plan. The data below will be the starting point for my analysis."

Quarter	Variable overhead	Units of product X	Units of product Y
1	$299,440	3643	6909
2	257,050	3482	6439
3	174,676	2277	4159
4	193,629	2357	4388
5	183,632	2421	5107
6	123,202	1886	4159
7	304,647	3674	6859
8	214,592	2537	4912
9	144,509	1969	4203
10	269,958	3333	6954
11	155,102	2316	4357
12	215,379	2481	4979

Required

A. A ''normal'' production plan for the next quarter might call for 3,000 units of product X and 6,000 units of product Y. What variable overhead would you forecast for this production plan?

B. The marketing group would like to increase production of product X to 4,000 units while dropping production of Y to 4,000 units. What variable overhead would you forecast for this production plan?

C. Compare the confidence that you place in your forecasts in A and B. Be as specific as you can.

6.13. (Based on a paper by William Murray). The purpose of this case is to describe a product-costing decision model for a large international manufacturer of hospital and medical supplies. The growth of this company (and the industry in general) has been astounding. A compound rate of yearly sales increase in excess of 20% has been realized over the past 20 years. Much of this growth has stemmed from a continual infusion of new products and product lines. However, as financially rewarding as this increasing growth has been, certain functions of the firm have had to suffer the consequences of making allowances in accuracy to keep up with their work load. This problem centers on the inaccuracies associated with the current method of product standard cost determination, and then proposes a decision model for determining more accurately the standard costs of the most worthy new product proposals.

Current Method of Standard Cost Determination. Product standard costs are calculated by the manufacturing engineering department's cost estimation group. These estimates are determined on a dollar per thousand basis, which are then broken into subcategories of raw material, scrap, mold amortization, direct labor, direct overhead, and variable overhead. No problems are encountered in accurately determining the raw material, scrap, and direct labor components, since these costs are readily available from current usage, or, in the case of new product proposals, from historic data of similar processes. Also, mold amortization does not present a problem since all mold tooling is amortized over a three-year production period. Once the marketing group has calculated a three-year sales projection, the mold amortization component can be easily calculated given the cost of the mold tooling. However, because of the number of cost estimates that must be made by the cost estimation group (two full-time employees) the calculations of the direct and variable overhead components have been simplified, thus inaccurately reflecting the true overhead associated with many products.

The current method of overhead determination is to calculate standard direct and variable overhead rates for each production facility (similar to the direct labor rate). The total yearly direct and variable overhead for each plant are divided by the total yearly labor hours available to calculate these rates. These rates are then multiplied by the standard hours of production to determine the overhead costs assignable to the product. Typical rates are shown below:

Direct labor	= \$6.50/standard hour
Direct overhead	= \$7.40/standard hour
Variable overhead	= \$6.35/standard hour

The problem with this method of overhead allocation is that wide variations in overhead usage are found across the products manufactured. Some products require special component machinery, filling line equipment, and sterilization equipment. These are typically large-scale projects requiring as much as 10% of total plant facilities for molding, filling, assembly, packing, staging, and warehousing. Also, these product lines are normally automated to minimize direct labor input. However, a large portion of plant management's time must be spent on the products to keep them operating smoothly (e.g., an I.V. solution container line). On the other hand, there are many other products that require no new capital investment. They normally involve the manual assembly of component parts on standard assembly lines which only require one room. These products, if sterilized, are usually done in the standard plant gas sterilizers. Production is routine, so little staff management supervisory time is required. Also the products are typically smaller and lighter than the previously described product type, so much less warehouse space is required (e.g., I.V. solution administration sets).

When the current overhead cost allocation system is used, the smaller-scale, labor-intensive products are forced to bear plant overhead, which is actually being caused by the larger-scale, capital-intensive, automated products. This results in inaccurate product costing, which can detrimentally affect decisions regarding the desirability of producing new products.

Proposed Method for Standard Cost Determination. A method that would be more desirable to use for the evaluation of new product proposals is an attributable cost concept.[14] Using this method, raw material, scrap, mold amortization, and direct labor components would continue to be estimated in the present manner, however overhead costs would be assigned on a basis of those costs which could be avoided, on the average, if a product were discontinued entirely without changing the supporting organization. In other words, only those overhead costs attributable to the production of the new product would be included in the total standard cost calculation. Because of the present established condition of the company and its manufacturing facilities, it is obvious that they will continue regardless of whether any new product proposals are implemented or not. Under these conditions the attributable cost concept most correctly answers the question of how to best utilize the existing organization and common facilities.

Using this method of new product costing, each of the overhead categories would be analyzed to determine the expected increases associated with production of the product, and

[14]The attributable cost concept was proposed by Shillinglaw (1963).

would form the basis for the overhead cost of the product. A partial listing of those categories is listed below:

Variable overhead	Fixed overhead
Direct labor fringes	Plant manager's staff
Production supplies	Supervision
Maintenance	Insurance
Downtime and changeover	Depreciation
Utilities	Utilities
Uniform and Laundry	Taxes
Quality contol check and inspection	Quality control administration
Inventory shrinkage	

Since plant space is a scarce resource at the production facilities, most of the fixed overhead categories would be included but only in relation to the amount actually consumed. The depreciation of equipment would be found to vary the most between products.

Recently, William Murray was involved in conducting an attributable cost analysis on a proposed new product. The product consisted of simple injection-molded parts assembled on an 11-person production line. Using the current costing method a standard cost of $.6449 was calculated. This was considered unacceptable by marketing since the unit would have to be sold at a price of $.95–$1.05 to be competitive. However, of this total cost, $.2581 was composed of overhead of which 74.6% was allocated to the product because of the standard labor hours of final assembly and packing. This cost seemed highly suspect because the assembly was conducted in a single medium-sized room (600 ft^2) and required no special equipment. The new product proposal was recosted on an attributable cost basis. These results determined the actual cost to the company of producing this product to be only $.5329 (a decrease of 17.4%), which was well within the predetermined allowable cost range, and the decision was made to produce the product. Marketing now feels that this product will open up a new important product area for the company.

Murray remarked, ''If an attributable costing method of new-product-proposal standard-cost estimating were implemented, fewer worthy new products would be rejected due to a biased costing method. Based on the results of my experience, it definitely appears to be worthwhile.''

Proposed Decision Rule. As previously stated, the members of the cost estimation group are unable to perform this type of costing for all new-product proposals because of their current work loads and the amount of time involved in conducting each attributable cost determination. Discussing the problem with the members of the cost estimation group, it was learned that their time is spent on both the estimation of new-product-proposal standard costs (averaging 60–80 per year), and on the continual cost updating of all currently produced products (in excess of 500). Historically, an average of only 10 to 12 product proposals, for which cost estimations are conducted, are implemented into production each year. The others are rejected due to cost considerations. The group members further predicted, given the extra time involved in conducting a detailed attributable cost analysis, that 10 to 15 such analyses could probably be performed per year.

Required

A. How should the company use the 10 to 15 attributable cost studies that are available every year?

B. What other cost estimation alternatives are available for Murray to consider? How do they compare to the attributable cost studies?

6.14. "Modern management techniques, my foot! All I want to know is how our overhead costs vary when we change output, and this regression stuff gives me nonsense. If our variable overhead costs are $32 per unit, I'll eat my tie! We've been growing at a respectable rate, and inflation may have been 10% a year, but I know this business too well to believe that $32 number. And negative fixed costs! It's beyond belief.

"Here's the data and the regression output (below). I don't care if you use regression, Hi–Lo, or whatever. Just get me the information I want—our variable overhead per unit in 19X6!"

Year	Output, X	Overhead cost, C
19×1	100,000	$1,500,000
19×2	110,000	1,760,000
19×3	125,000	2,117,500
19×4	130,000	2,395,800
19×5	140,000	2,781,790
19×6	160,000	3,382,071

Regression results

$$C = -\$1{,}764{,}700 + \$32.06X$$
$$(-8.65) \qquad (20.3)$$
$$R^2 = 0.99$$

Required "Just get him the information he wants." Include a brief discussion of the shortcomings of the approach used above, and your approach to overcoming those problems.

REFERENCES

Benston, G. "Multiple Regression Analysis of Cost Behavior," *Accounting Review*. October 1966.

Dyckman, T., and L. J. Thomas. *Fundamental Statistics for Business and Economics*. Englewood Cliffs, NJ: Prentice-Hall. 1977.

Geurts, M., and T. Buchman. "Accounting for 'Shocks' in Forecasts," *Management Accounting*. April 1981.

Jensen, R. "Multiple Regression Analysis for Cost Control—Assumptions and Limitations," *Accounting Review*. April 1967.

Johnston, J. *Statistical Cost Analysis*. New York: McGraw-Hill. 1960.

Johnston, J. *Econometric Methods*. 2nd ed. New York: McGraw-Hill. 1972.

Kaplan, R. S. "Management Accounting in Hospitals: A Case Study," in J. Livingston and R. Gunn, Eds., *Accounting for Social Goals*. New York: Harper & Row. 1974.

Nelson, C. *Applied Time-Series Analysis*. San Francisco: Holden-Day. 1973.

Oliver, F. R. "A Cross-Section Study of Marginal Cost," *Applied Statistics*. June 1962.

Shillinglaw, G. "The Concept of Attributable Cost," *Journal of Accounting Research*. Spring 1963.

Chapter 7

Short-Term Planning Revisited

Learning Curves and Multiple Products

In Chapter 4 we explored the situation where a manager had to make a decision about the level of activity to be achieved in the short term. By "short-term," we mean a period of time over which no significant changes in capacity and fixed costs can be achieved. Therefore, CVP analysis focuses on the costs that will be affected by these short-term activity decisions, and we have explored methods of estimating these costs in Chapters 5 and 6.

The decision setting in Chapter 4 was deliberately chosen to be a simple one, so that issues such as risk analysis and cost estimation could be more easily introduced. But there are a variety of ways in which the CVP model can be expanded to more realistic and more complex situations. In this chapter, we will explore the impacts of learning and of multiple products on the decision situation and on the estimation of cost behavior.

7.1 THE EFFECTS OF LEARNING

One of the basic issues in short-term planning is the identification of those costs that vary when activity (production) varies. In most cases, we assume that these variable costs have the same value for each unit of production, but there are a variety of reasons why this may not be so. For instance, the cost per unit of input may change, causing later units to cost a different amount than those produced earlier. Or, it may be that there are economies and/or diseconomies of scale in production, as depicted in Figures 7.1a and 7.1b. During a given period of time, the cost of one additional unit may vary depending on the number of units that are already being produced. However, the cost of a unit does not depend on the amount produced in any previous period. (Nor will this period's production affect the costs in later time periods.)

There are many situations where the cost of an additional unit *does* depend on how many units have been produced up to this point in time, because efficiency improves as

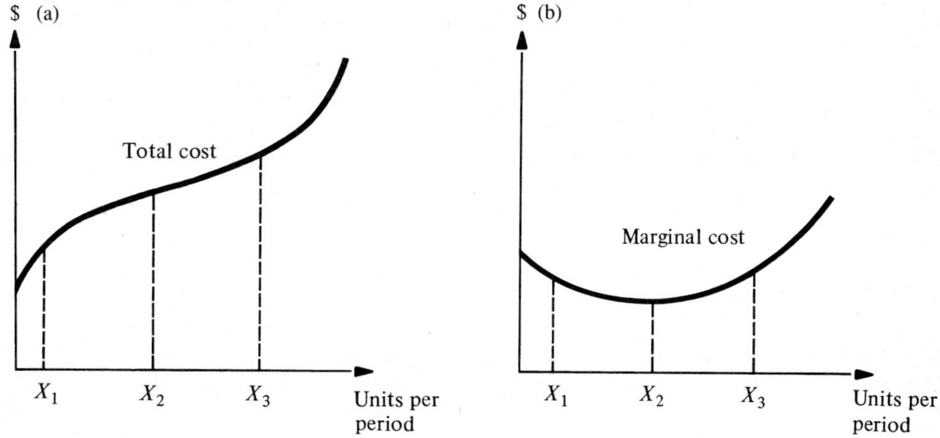

Figure 7.1

more units are produced. This phenomenon is called *learning,* of course, and we have only to look around us to see examples. A six-year-old working a jigsaw puzzle over and over will, up to a point, require less time each time the puzzle is put together. Typing or computer programming are also examples where more experience usually creates more efficiency. These efficiencies may result from an employee becoming quicker at the assigned task, or from making fewer mistakes, or from requiring less raw material or other inputs. These learning effects occur in varying degrees in business. Some of the most visible examples in the recent past have occurred in the electronics industry, where product innovation and the learning phenomenon have lowered costs (and prices) dramatically. However, these phenomena occur in many industries, whenever a new product or a new process is instituted.[1]

Graphically, the learning curve may look like one of those in Figure 7.2. A key difference between this figure and Figure 7.1 is that the horizontal axis is cumulative output rather than output per period. In addition, the curves here are average cost curves, or cumulative costs divided by cumulative output, while Figure 7.1 portrays the total and marginal cost curves. An algebraic representation of a learning curve could be the following.

$$\overline{Y}_t = v_0 + \alpha \overline{X}_t^{\beta} \tag{7.1}$$

where $\overline{Y}_t \equiv$ cumulative average cost through period t

$\overline{X}_t \equiv$ cumulative production through period t

$v_0 \equiv$ average cost once the learning effect is completed; $v_0 > 0$

$\alpha \equiv$ additional cost (over v_0) of the first unit completed; $\alpha > 0$

$\beta \equiv$ a parameter that controls the speed of the learning process; $\beta < 0$; as β gets further away from 0, the learning effect occurs more quickly

[1]For a discussion and some examples, see Baloff and Kennelly (1967).

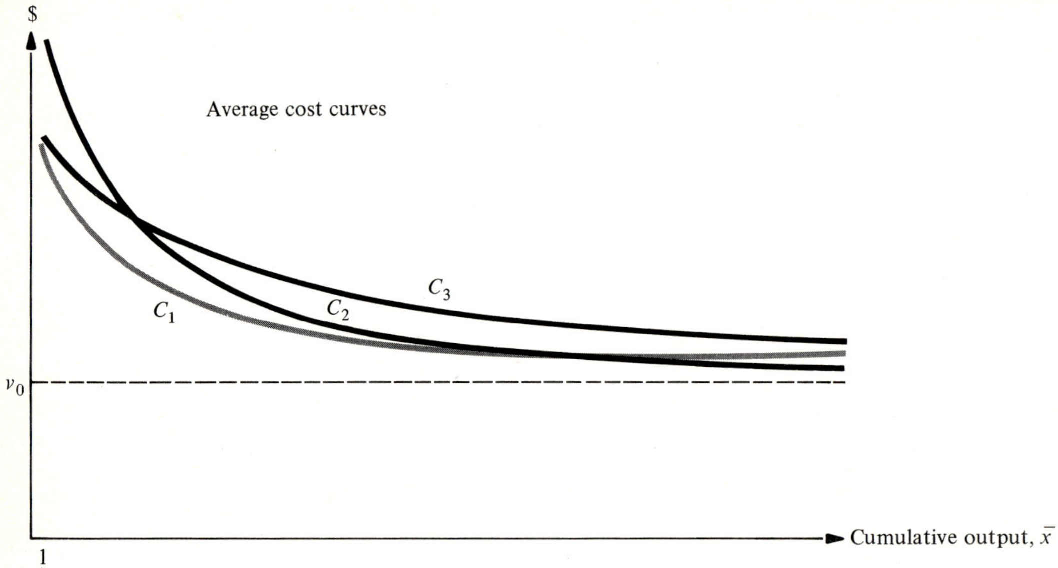

Figure 7.2 Average cost curves.

The *total cost* through period t is

$$C_t = \bar{Y}_t\bar{X}_t = v_0\bar{X}_t + \alpha\bar{X}_t^{\beta+1} \tag{7.2}$$

The *marginal cost* at a cumulative production of $\bar{X}_t$ is

$$\text{MC}_t = \frac{dC_t}{d\bar{X}_t} = v_0 + \alpha(\beta + 1)\bar{X}_t^{\beta} \tag{7.3}$$

The *average cost* as $\bar{X}_t$ gets very large is

$$\lim_{\bar{X}_t \to \infty} \bar{Y}_t = v_0 \tag{7.4}$$

The relationship between the total cost, average cost, and marginal cost can be seen in Figure 7.3. We can also compare the parameters of the three different curves in Figure 7.2. The height of the curves at a cumulative output of 1 is $v_0 + \alpha$, the cost of the first unit. Therefore, the value of α is highest for C_2 and lowest for C_1, with C_3 falling in between. The speed of the learning effect is greater for C_2 than for C_3, so the value of β will be lower[2] for C_2 than for C_3.

To get a better feeling for the effect of the learning parameters, some sample cost figures are presented in Table 7.1. In each case examined, the average and marginal costs decrease as the cumulative output increases. But when $\beta = -0.3$, the decrease is much slower than when $\beta = -0.7$. If $\alpha = 200$ and $\beta = -0.3$, the average cost of the first ten units is \$200.2, but if $\beta = -0.7$, these ten units have an average cost of \$139.9. (The marginal costs also reflect the learning parameter.)

[2]Since β is less than zero, $|\beta|$ will be greater for C_2 than for C_3

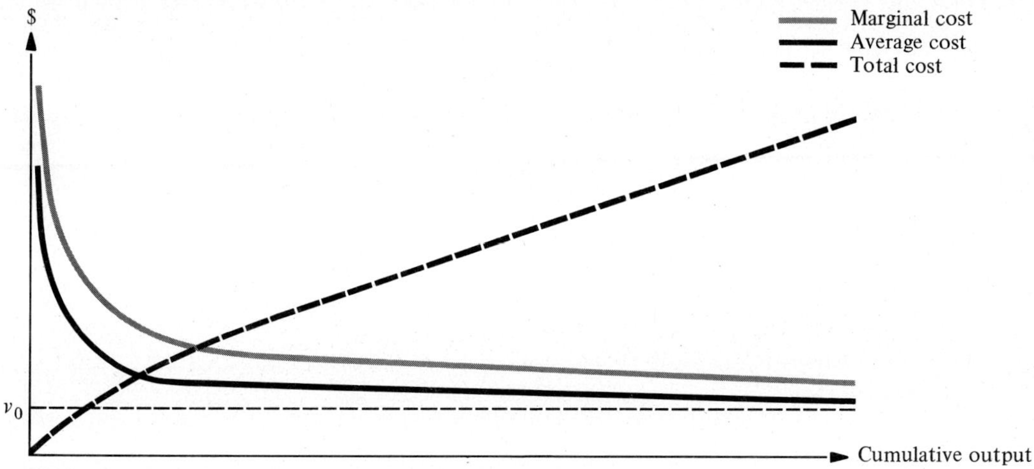

Figure 7.3

There are a variety of ways in which the learning phenomenon can affect decision making within an organization. Suppose that we have just completed 10 units, and a customer has approached us about an order for an additional 40 units. As we enter into price negotiations, it would be useful to know what the expected cost of those additional 40 units might be. And if we are successful in obtaining the order, it is usually desirable

TABLE 7.1 LEARNING CURVE COSTS (v_0 = 100)

α	β	$\bar{X}_t$	Total cost of $\bar{X}_t$ units	Average cost of $\bar{X}_t$ units	Marginal cost at $\bar{X}_t$ units
		10	$ 1,501	$150.1	$135.1
	−0.3	50	6,546	130.9	121.6
		100	12,512	125.1	117.6
		10	$ 1,316	$131.6	$115.8
100	−0.5	50	5,707	114.1	107.1
		100	11,000	110.0	105.0
		10	$ 1,200	$120.0	$106.0
	−0.7	50	$ 5,323	106.5	101.9
		100	10,398	104.0	101.2
		10	$ 2,002	$200.2	$170.2
	−0.3	50	8,092	161.8	143.3
		100	15,024	150.2	135.2
		10	$ 1,632	$163.2	$131.6
200	−0.5	50	6,414	128.3	114.1
		100	12,000	120.0	110.0
		10	$ 1,399	$139.9	$112.0
	−0.7	50	5,647	112.9	103.9
		100	10,796	108.0	102.4

to have a realistic cost estimate for the evaluation of the production manager. (This subject will be discussed more in later chapters.)

Example A company has just completed the first 10 units of a new product at a total cost of approximately $1,500. It is generally agreed that efficiency has been increasing as the work crews gain more experience, but no records have been kept on the individual units. Engineering studies have indicated that the variable cost per unit should approach $100 when the learning is completed. But the company has just been asked to bid on a contract to supply 40 units to one of its customers. The sales department has analyzed the situation with the customer, and made the following estimates.

Bid price for 40 units	Probability customer will accept bid
$4,500	1.0
5,000	0.7
5,500	0.2
6,000	0.0

With this information on the demand side, the manager then needs cost estimates to determine which bid will achieve the firm's financial objectives. Unfortunately, there exist more than one possible cost curve, given the information available. Let us say that there are two possible states, s_1 and s_2, which are equally likely.

	s_1	s_2
v_0	100	100
α	250	100
β	−0.7	−0.3

Both of these states would produce costs of about $1,500 for the first 10 units and a long-term marginal cost of $100. But the cost of the next 40 units would be about $4,310 for s_1 and about $5,045 for s_2. (From Table 7.1, we can see that the cost of producing the first 50 units under s_2 would be $6,546, while the cost of producing the first 10 units is 1501. Therefore the estimated incremental cost of the next 40 units would be $6,546 − $1,501, or $5,045.) This situation is summarized in the upper part of Table 7.2, and indicates that the firm should bid $5,000 in its current situation if its objective is to maximize its expected profit. If the company were able to resolve this uncertainty regarding its cost, it could increase its expected payoff by $61.25, as shown in the lower part of Table 7.2.

Of course, there are many other examples of the effect of the learning phenomenon on managerial decision making. Many firms are "pricing out on the learning curve," where initial prices do not cover the production costs of the early units. However, the lower price is meant to achieve a higher cumulative volume for the product. Therefore, more units will be produced after the learning effect is complete, and the profit on these units will more than offset the losses in the early stages of the product's life.

TABLE 7.2 TABLE OF PAYOFFS AND PROBABILITIES

Action	Customer accepts bid s_1	Customer accepts bid s_2	Customer rejects bid	Expected payoffs
Bid $4,500	190	(545)	0	($177.5)
(probabilities)	(0.5)	(0.5)	(0.0)	
Bid $5,000	690	(45)	0	$225.75
(probabilities)	(0.35)	(0.35)	(0.3)	
Bid $5,500	1,190	455	0	$164.5
(probabilities)	(0.1)	(0.1)	(0.8)	
Bid $6,000	1,690	955	0	$0
(probabilities)	(0.0)	(0.0)	(1.0)	

Expected payoff with perfect information:

(1) State	(2) Probability of state	(3) Best action	(4) Expected payoff	(2) × (4)
s_1	0.5	Bid $5,000	(690)(0.7) = 483	241.5
s_2	0.5	Bid $5,500	(455)(0.2) = 91	45.5
				$287.0

EVPI = $287.0 − $225.75 = $61.25

7.2 ESTIMATION OF THE LEARNING EFFECT

Having discussed the usefulness of information about the learning effect, we now turn to the estimation techniques that can be used to generate such information. In Chapters 5 and 6, we discussed some of the estimation techniques that are available to a manager, and with some modification these techniques can be used here.

Suppose that we have already produced six units of a new product, and that cost data were kept for each unit. The average costs and a plot appear in Table 7.3. How can we use this data to estimate the cost of the seventh unit or the tenth unit or the fortieth unit? To do so, we need estimates of the parameters v_0, α, and β, and it seems natural[3] to use the data on the first six units to estimate these parameters.

Can we use the regression techniques described in Chapter 6? Not easily, for regression is designed for cases where the unknown variables are additive constants and/or multipliers of the independent variables. But the learning curve also has a parameter β, which is an exponent of the independent variable.

$$\overline{Y}_t = v_0 + \alpha \overline{X}_t^{\beta} + \varepsilon_t \tag{7.5}$$

As a result, normal regression will not work except in a couple of special cases which follow.

[3]If there is reason to believe that the past data is *not* relevant for forecasting the future, then we must look elsewhere for the estimates.

TABLE 7.3 CUMULATIVE AVERAGE COST AND OUTPUT

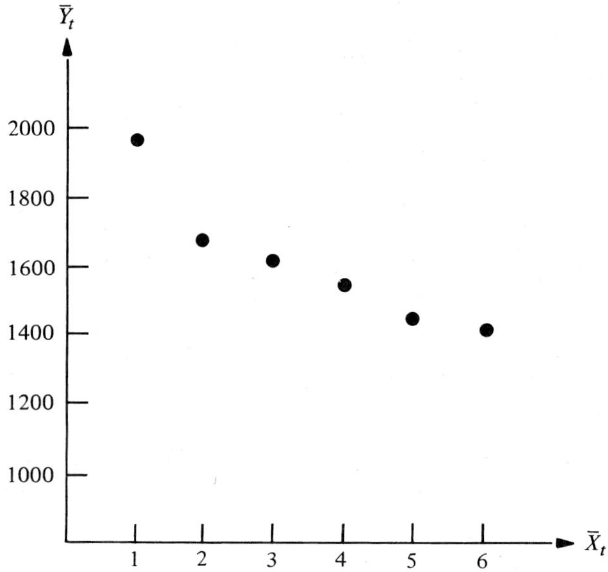

Cumulative average cost, $\overline{Y}_t$	Cumulative output, $\overline{X}_t$
$1,977	1
1,673	2
1,617	3
1,548	4
1,465	5
1,434	6

7.2.1 Case 1: β is Known

The parameter β reflects the speed with which the learning effect occurs, and would most likely be influenced by factors such as the complexity of the task, the employees' abilities and skill levels, the degree of managerial effort devoted to efficiency improvement, and so on. If the current task is similar to another task where the learning process is complete, then the learning parameter β might be estimated from the data on the other product.

Of course, the parameter β is a little hard to deal with intuitively. Table 7.4 may help somewhat by describing what happens to the learning term $\alpha\overline{X}^{\beta}$ when the production is doubled. In Figure 7.4, this learning term is L_1 for production of $\overline{X}_1$, and L_2 when production is doubled to $\overline{X}_2 = 2\overline{X}_1$. The right-hand column in Table 7.4 is L_2/L_1, so if $L_2/L_1 = 0.66$, a learning parameter $\beta = -0.6$ would be indicated.

Once β is known from other sources, normal regression can be used to estimate v_0 and α. The new independent variable would be $\overline{\overline{X}}_t = \overline{X}_t^{\beta}$. In the case of our data in Table 7.3, suppose that we had concluded that doubling output would reduce the learning

TABLE 7.4 EFFECT OF DOUBLING OUTPUT ON THE LEARNING TERM, $\alpha\bar{X}^{\beta}$

β	Learning term after doubling output ÷ learning term before doubling output[a]
0.0	1.000
−0.1	0.933
−0.2	0.871
−0.3	0.812
−0.4	0.758
−0.5	0.707
−0.6	0.660
−0.7	0.616
−0.8	0.574
−0.9	0.536
−1.0	0.500

[a]The values in this column are simply 2^{β}, because $\alpha(2x)^{\beta}/\alpha x^{\beta} = 2^{\beta}$.

term to 59–60% of its current value, indicating a β of about -0.75 from Table 7.4. Regression results would be

$$\bar{Y}_t = 1{,}271 + 708(\bar{X}_t^{-0.75}) \tag{7.6}$$

That is, the regression estimate for v_0 is 1,271 and for α is 708, and these values could be used to estimate the cost of future production.

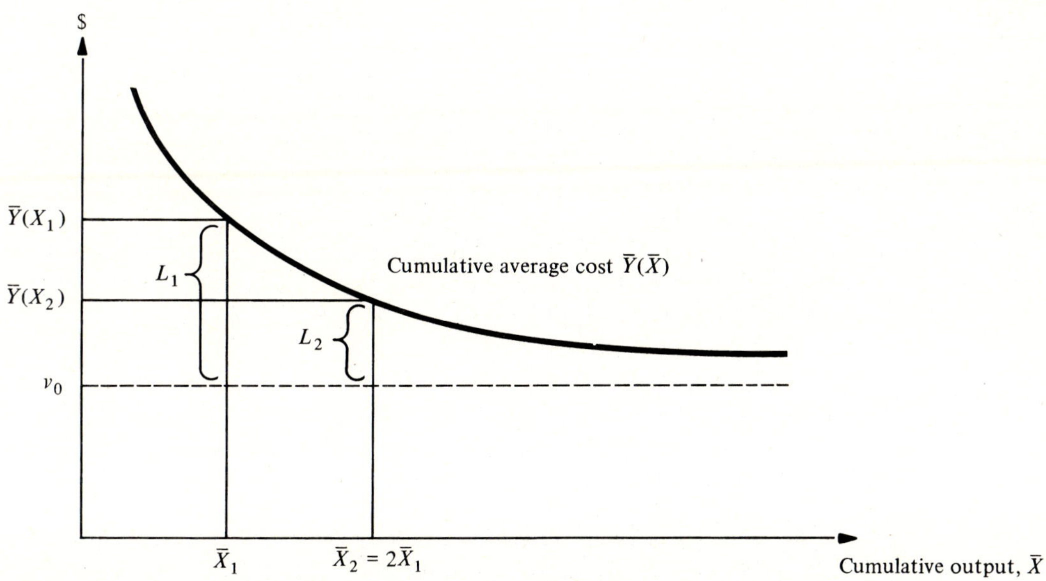

Figure 7.4

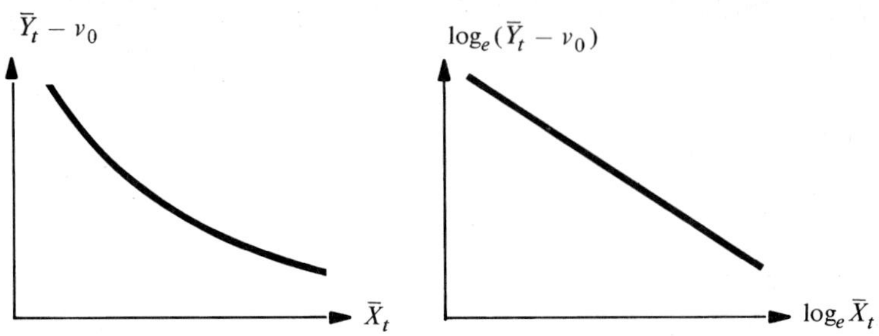

Figure 7.5

7.2.2 Case 2: v_0 is Known

An alternative estimation procedure can be used if v_0 is known, while α and β are not. Suppose that a new production process has been installed to reduce raw material usage by 15% and energy consumption by 30%. The equipment manufacturer has provided specifications indicating the amount of materials, labor, energy, etc. that are necessary to produce a given level of output, once the process has all the bugs worked out. Inquiries to the equipment manufacturer's other customers have confirmed that the specifications are realistic. Knowing v_0 allows us to transform the learning curve in the following way

$$\begin{aligned} \overline{Y}_t &= v_0 + \alpha \overline{X}_t^{\beta} \\ \rightarrow \overline{Y}_t - v_0 &= \alpha \overline{X}_t^{\beta} \end{aligned} \tag{7.7}$$

If we think of v_0 as being the *standard cost,* the new dependent variable $(\overline{Y}_t - v_0)$ could be thought of as the *average variance* from producing the first $\overline{X}_t$ units. This formulation is still not linear, but it can be made linear by using logarithms.[4]

$$\begin{aligned} \log_e(\overline{Y}_t - v_0) &= \log_e(\alpha \overline{X}_t^{\beta}) \\ &= \log_e \alpha + \log_e(\overline{X}_t^{\beta}) \\ &= \log_e \alpha + \beta \log_e \overline{X}_t \end{aligned} \tag{7.8}$$

By transforming the variables to logarithms, we transform a nonlinear equation to a linear equation. (See Figure 7.5.) And a regression analysis can be done with dependent variable $\log_e(\overline{Y}_t - v_0)$ and independent variable $\log_e(\overline{X}_t)$.

In the sample data in Table 7.3, suppose that the value of v_0 is believed to be \$1,200. (That is, after the learning effect is complete, each unit will cost \$1,200.) The regression results are the following.

$$\log_e(\overline{Y}_t - 1{,}200) = 6.665 - 0.64673 \log_e(\overline{X}_t) \tag{7.9}$$

That is, the estimate of β is -0.64673, and the estimate of $\log_e(\alpha)$ is 6.665, so the estimate of α is $e^{6.665}$, or 764.5.[5] The cost of producing additional units can be estimated using the following equation

$$\overline{Y}_t = 1{,}200 + 764.5(\overline{X}_t^{-0.64673}) \tag{7.10}$$

[4] $\log_e(XY) = \log_e(X) + \log_e(Y)$; $\log_e(X^Y) = Y \log_e(X)$.

[5] Recall that the definition of $\log_e(\alpha)$ is the power to which e must be raised so as to equal α. That is, $e^{\log_e \alpha} = \alpha$.

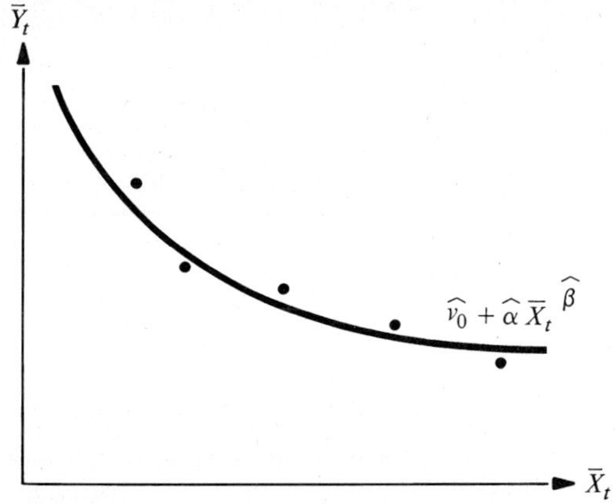

Figure 7.6

7.2.3 An Alternative Estimation Method

We have now seen that the estimation methods of Chapter 6 only work in a learning situation where either the learning speed β *or* the ultimate variable cost v_0 is known. If all we have are the data, and no reliable estimates of v_0 and β, then we must utilize an alternative estimation method. If we have data points such as those in Figure 7.6, we can measure how well a line fits the data points by computing the residuals $\hat{\varepsilon}_t$, and then, as in regression, looking for the parameter values $\hat{v}_0$, $\hat{\alpha}$, $\hat{\beta}$, which minimize the sum of the squared residuals.

$$\min_{\hat{v}_0,\hat{\alpha},\hat{\beta}} (\Sigma\hat{\varepsilon}_t^2) \leftrightarrow \min_{\hat{v}_0,\hat{\alpha},\hat{\beta}} [\Sigma(\bar{Y}_t - \hat{v}_0 - \hat{\alpha}\bar{X}_t^{\hat{\beta}})^2] \quad (7.11)$$

There are computer programs which search for the values of $\hat{v}_0$, $\hat{\alpha}$ and $\hat{\beta}$, that provide the best fit with the data. The techniques, called *nonlinear estimation,* are quite complex and we will not discuss them in detail here.[6] Essentially, the manager provides his or her best estimates of the parameters, and the computer program refines these estimations to reduce the sum of the squared residuals $\Sigma\hat{\varepsilon}_t^2$. A program that does this form of estimation appears at the end of the book and was used on the data in Table 7.3, resulting in the following estimation.

$$\bar{Y}_t = 1{,}122.4 + 848.3(\bar{X}_t^{-0.5402}) \quad (7.12)$$

Starting from original guesses of $\hat{v}_0 = 1{,}000$, $\hat{\alpha} = 1{,}000$, $\hat{\beta} = -0.5$, the program found values which improved the fit with the six data points. The long-run cost v_0 is estimated to be 1,122.4, while the final values of α and β are 848.3 and -0.5402, respectively. These values can then be used to estimate the costs of further production.

7.2.4 Summary

When a new product or a new process is introduced, there is normally a period of learning, where employees are mastering new tasks and/or new equipment. In cases

[6]For an explanation see Draper and Smith (1966), Chapter 10.

where the task is simple and frequently repeated, the duration of the learning effect may be short and its impact on costs insignificant. In the case of large, complex tasks, for example, the construction of technologically complex machinery (airplanes, gas turbines), the learning effect may be significant in both size and duration. In these situations, the estimation of the learning effect can have a significant influence on management's decisions in pricing, performance evaluation, and so on.

The estimation of the *learning curve* represents a more complex problem than those encountered in Chapters 5 and 6. Engineering measurement methods may be most effective in finding the value of v_0 which represents the level of efficiency that should ultimately be achieved. Past experience with similar employees and processes may provide estimates of the speed with which learning will occur, and this speed can be translated into an estimate of β. Finally, if independent estimates of v_0 or β are not available, a nonlinear curve-fitting technique can be used to simultaneously estimate the parameters of the learning curve.

7.3 MULTIPLE PRODUCTS

Up to this point in the text, we have been dealing with decision situations that were of a short-term nature, involving a single product. In this section, we will retain the short-term decision horizon, but recognize the problems that occur when dealing with multiple products.

How does the analysis change when we have many products instead of just one? Certainly there is a scale change. If an item of information is worth \$10 in an accept/reject decision, then facing multiple accept/reject decisions would increase the information's value.[7] But there are some new considerations that arise when dealing with multiple products. For example, different products may be competing for scarce common resources, so information concerning each product's need for these resources becomes valuable. In addition, there is a significant change in the risk analysis when there are multiple products, and in the type of information that may be valuable to the decision maker.

7.4 RISK ANALYSIS WITH MULTIPLE PRODUCTS

In Chapter 4 we considered the effect of volume decisions on the probability distribution of profits when the variable cost per unit v was uncertain.

$$\begin{aligned} \pi &= (p - v)x - F \\ E[\pi] &= (p - E[v]) \cdot x - F \\ \sigma^2[\pi] &= \sigma^2[v]x^2;\ \sigma[\pi] = \sigma[v]x \end{aligned} \tag{7.13}$$

Now suppose that there are two products that can be produced by the available facilities (i.e., no change in F). Each has its own unit price (p_1 and p_2) and its own random variable cost (v_1 and v_2). Now the activity level decision is two-dimensional, since the

[7]If there are n such decisions, all independent, the value would be \$10n.

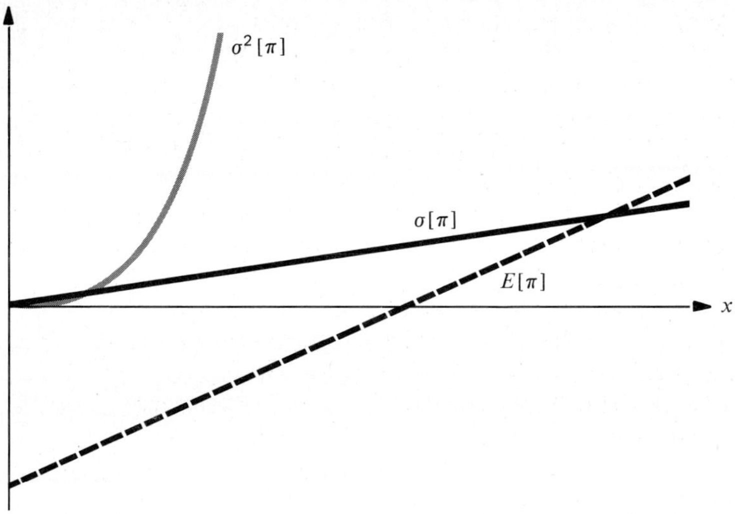

Figure 7.7

manager chooses both x_1 and x_2. The effect on the expected profit is straightforward, but the variance of the firm's profits depends on the *covariance* between v_1 and v_2.[8] (See Figure 7.7.)

$$\begin{aligned} \pi &= (p_1 - v_1)x_1 + (p_2 - v_2)x_2 - F \\ E[\pi] &= (p_1 - E[v_1])x_1 + (p_2 - E[v_2])x_2 - F \qquad (7.14) \\ \sigma^2[\pi] &= x_1^2\sigma^2[v_1] + x_2^2\sigma^2[v_2] + 2x_1x_2\,\text{cov}[v_1, v_2] \end{aligned}$$

The covariance term depends on the way in which movements in v_1 and v_2 are related to each other. For instance, suppose that the uncertainty in variable costs is caused by uncertain raw material prices, and products 1 and 2 use the same raw materials. Then the two variable costs will tend to vary directly (high v_1 means v_2 will likely be high), and the cov[v_1, v_2] will be positive. If the products use no common raw materials, then it may be that cov[v_1, v_2] = 0. It is more difficult to think of situations where the covariance may be negative, but one such case could occur in the multicollinearity situation described at the end of Chapter 6. We know that a cost has been incurred in the past by either product 1 or product 2, but we don't know which one. In this case, values of v_1 in excess of $E[v_1]$ would tend to occur when v_2 was less than $E[v_2]$, and vice versa, producing a covariance less than zero.

7.5 A SIMPLE EXAMPLE OF COVARIANCE

The concept of two variables tending to vary directly or inversely is familiar to all of us, but the measurements that are used are not necessarily familiar. So a simple example will be used to illustrate them.

[8] $\text{Cov}[v_1, v_2] = E[(v_1 - E[v_1])(v_2 - E[v_2])] = E[v_1v_2] - E[v_1]E[v_2] = \rho_{v_1v_2}\sigma[v_1]\sigma[v_2]$, where $\rho_{v_1v_2}$ is the correlation coefficient between v_1 and v_2.

Consider a simple bet: a coin is flipped, and depending on the outcome, you get \$0 or \$100. This bet has the following expected value and variance:

$$\begin{aligned} z &= \text{the amount you receive} \\ E[z] &= (1/2)0 + (1/2)100 = \$50 \\ \sigma^2[z] &= (1/2)(0-50)^2 + (1/2)(100-50)^2 = \$2{,}500 \\ \sigma[z] &= 50 \end{aligned} \tag{7.15}$$

You are going to engage in this type of bet with two friends, and you have the choice of the following arrangements.

Bet 1: Flip one coin. If "heads," both friends must pay. If "tails," neither pays.

Bet 2: Flip two coins. If coin 1 is "heads," friend 1 pays, but if coin 1 is "tails," friend 1 pays nothing. Same for coin 2 and friend 2.

Bet 3: Flip one coin. If "heads," friend 1 pays, and friend 2 does not. If "tails," friend 2 pays, and friend 1 does not.

We feel that bet 1 is the riskiest, while bet 3 is the least risky, and this intuition is confirmed when the variances are computed.

	Probability of payoff, $z_1 + z_2$					
	0	100	200	$E[z_1 + z_2]$	$\sigma^2[z_1 + z_2]$	$\sigma[z_1 + z_2]$
Bet 1	1/2	0	1/2	\$100	10,000	100
Bet 2	1/4	1/2	1/4	\$100	5,000	71
Bet 3	0	1	0	\$100	0	0

The variances for the different bets reflect the correlations between z_1 and z_2. For bet 1, they are perfectly *directly* correlated, so $\rho = 1$. For bet 2, they are independent, so $\rho = 0$. For bet 3, z_1 and z_2 are perfectly *inversely* correlated, so $\rho = -1$.

7.6 EFFECT ON PRODUCT MIX DECISIONS

In Chapter 4, we discussed how the manager's feelings about risk could affect the short-term activity decision. The same is true with multiple products, and the relationships *between* the products will influence the risk level. Of course, we have focused on uncertainties in the variable costs, but there are also uncertainties in the demand for the products produced. If the manager chooses to produce x_i of product i, then the revenue received per unit p_i may also be uncertain. For instance, when a toy manufacturer decides how many units to produce for the Christmas season, he or she does not know how many will be left over in January and will have to be sold at substantial discounts. While each product faces some risk, there are also interrelationships between the products' risks. The manufacturer of a video game system knows that sales of the preprogrammed cartridges are tied to the sales of the basic console, since they are complementary products.

Other products may have differing degrees of correlation. Products that are substitutes for each other would tend to have lower correlation than products that are complements of each other, but general economic factors (such as inflation, unemployment, etc.) would tend to affect all products and produce positive correlations.

In making product mix decisions, the manager must manage these risks, so that the appropriate levels of production are chosen. The effect of product mix on risk can be seen in Table 7.5, where two products with equal contribution margin variance may be produced in any proportion, but total production must not exceed 10 units. If the manager were risk neutral, then he or she would ignore the risk and choose the product with the higher expected contribution margin. Likewise, if the two products' contribution margins are perfectly correlated ($\rho = 1$), the product mix does not affect the risk, and he or she should choose the product with the higher expected contribution margin. However, if there is less than perfect correlation between the two products, then the product mix affects the risk and the manager could be willing to diversify to a product with a lower expected contribution margin in order to reduce his or her risk. For instance, if the two contribution margins are uncorrelated ($\rho = 0$), then Table 7.5 indicates that a product mix of $x_1 = x_2 = 5$ has a contribution margin variance of half the variance of a single product alternative such as $x_1 = 10$, $x_2 = 0$. The joint effects of product mix and correlation are depicted in Figure 7.8.

Example Sam Eubank runs a small plant that manufactures women's dresses. Almost all of the company's business comes from a large, national, clothing company that contracts with Eubank's firm (and others) to supply its products. For the coming season,

TABLE 7.5 EFFECT OF PRODUCT MIX ON CONTRIBUTION MARGIN RISK

$$\pi = (p_1 - v_1)x_1 + (p_2 - v_2)x_2 - F$$
$$\sigma^2[p_1 - v_1] = \sigma^2[p_2 - v_2] = \sigma^2$$
$$\sigma^2[\pi] = \sigma^2 M$$

where M is a factor that depends on the product mix and the correlation between the contribution margins.

Product mix		Variance multiplier M when correlation between $(p_1 - v_1)$ and $(p_2 - v_2)$ is				
x_1	x_2	$\rho = -1$	$\rho = -0.5$	$\rho = 0$	$\rho = 0.5$	$\rho = 1$
0	10	100	100	100	100	100
1	9	64	73	82	91	100
2	8	36	52	68	84	100
3	7	16	37	58	79	100
4	6	4	28	52	76	100
5	5	0	25	50	75	100
6	4	4	28	52	76	100
7	3	16	37	58	79	100
8	2	36	52	68	84	100
9	1	64	73	82	91	100
10	0	100	100	100	100	100

Eubank has already agreed to produce 10,000 units of model A, and he has enough capacity to produce an additional 10,000 units. The clothing company has offered Eubank a choice between model B and model C to utilize the excess capacity. The prices offered, and Eubank's estimates of the unit variable costs are as follows.

Model	Unit price	Expected variable cost per unit	Standard deviation of variable cost
A	40	20	3
B	35	20	3
C	35	21	4

Eubank comments on this situation. ''It looks as though model B is the best choice—higher profit and lower risk. But that's not the whole story. I won't know exactly how much the variable costs are until the decision is made and the production is under way. But the potential production problems for A and B are similar since they are similar styles. If A turns out to cost more than \$20, then I'm pretty sure B will also cost more than \$20. On the other hand, the potential problems with C are of a completely different nature, so the risks are unrelated to those in model A.''

If we assume that the correlations between variable costs are 0.75 for models A and B, and 0 for models A and C, the expected contribution margins and standard deviations can be computed as follows.

a_1: Produce models A and B

$$\begin{aligned}
E[\text{contribution margin}] &= (40 - 20)(10{,}000) + (35 - 20)(10{,}000) \\
&= \$350{,}000 \\
\sigma^2[\text{contribution margin}] &= (3)^2(10{,}000)^2 + (3)^2(10{,}000)^2 + 2(10{,}000)^2(0.75)(3)^2 \\
&= 3{,}150{,}000{,}000 \\
\sigma[\text{contribution margin}] &= 56{,}125
\end{aligned} \tag{7.16}$$

a_2: Produce models A and C

$$\begin{aligned}
E[\text{contribution margin}] &= (40 - 20)(10{,}000) + (35 - 21)(10{,}000) \\
&= \$340{,}000 \\
\sigma^2[\text{contribution margin}] &= (3)^2(10{,}000)^2 + (4)^2(10{,}000)^2 + 2(10{,}000)^2(0)(3)(4) \\
&= 2{,}500{,}000{,}000 \\
\sigma[\text{contribution margin}] &= 50{,}000
\end{aligned}$$

This analysis indicates that producing model B will yield a higher expected profit, but there is also a somewhat higher risk involved, as measured by the standard deviation of the contribution margin. Which action is preferred will depend on the manager's preferences for trading off risk and expected return.[9]

[9]If the normal distribution is assumed and the fixed cost is known, the probability of breaking even can be calculated as in Chapter 4. If $F = \$300{,}000$, action a_1 has a higher probability of breaking even, while if $F = \$240{,}000$, action a_2 has a higher probability of breaking even.

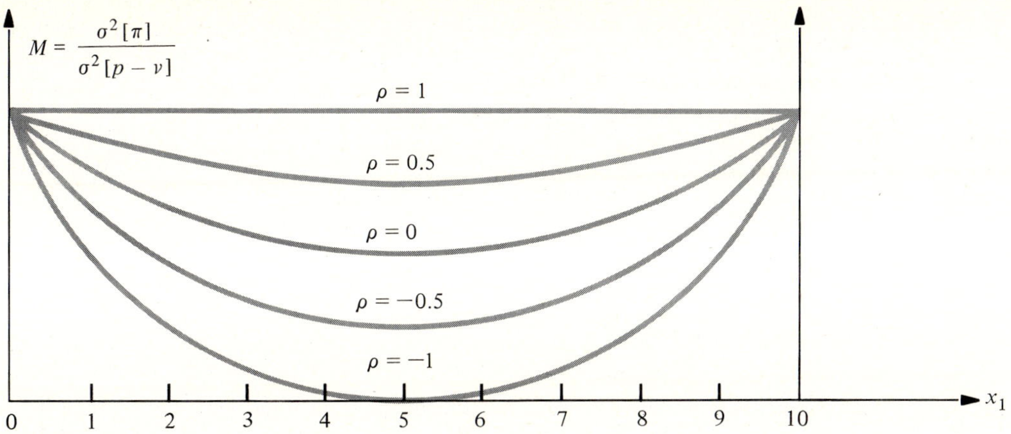

Figure 7.8

7.7 THE IMPORTANCE OF COVARIANCE INFORMATION

As the last two sections have shown, the estimates of covariance between products can have a significant impact on the risk analysis of different product mixes. In the preceding example, the standard deviation for product B was lower than that of model C, but its relationship to the existing product caused a greater total risk when it was combined with model A. Clearly, this risk analysis is sensitive to the estimates of correlation between the two products. If the correlation between the variable costs of A and C were 0.3 instead of 0, then alternative a_1 would have a lower risk than a_2. Or, if the correlation between A and B were below 0.4 instead of 0.75, the risk of a_1 would be lower than a_2.

If the manager is unsure of the levels of covariance among the firm's products, then there is the possibility that it would be valuable for the accountant to provide information on those covariances. It is possible for us to put together an example to demonstrate this fact, but it would have to be a rather complex example, so we will forego it and simply note that covariance information may influence the manager's product mix decisions. (A more complex analysis of the product mix decision appears in Appendix 7.1.)

7.8 ESTIMATES OF COST COVARIANCE

There are a variety of factors that influence the correlation between the variable costs of two products, but the principal cause is the usage of common factors of production. For instance, both products may be influenced by labor productivity in a particular department. Or, they may both use a raw material which can be supplied by only one company. If there are service departments (Chapter 5), then both products' costs will depend on the levels of efficiency in the service departments.

We will briefly describe two approaches to estimating the covariance between product costs—one analytic and one statistical. The analytic approach is an extension of those introduced in Chapter 5, and it makes use of the following facts about covariance.

$$\begin{aligned}
&\text{cov}[x,y] = E[xy] - E[x]E[y] \\
&\text{cov}[ax, by] = ab\,\text{cov}[x,y], \qquad \text{where } a \text{ and } b \text{ are constants} \\
&\text{cov}[x, y + z] = \text{cov}[x, y] + \text{cov}[x, z] \\
&\text{cov}[x, x] = E[x^2] - E[x]^2 = \sigma^2[x]
\end{aligned} \tag{7.17}$$

If we have a list of all the n factors of production, and for each of these we know the expected cost per unit $\bar{f}_i$, $i = 1, \ldots, n$, and the variance of the cost per unit $\sigma^2[f_i]$, $i = 1, \ldots, n$, then we may be able to estimate the covariance between two products that use these factors. We need a list of the amount of each factor used by each product, so let a_i and b_i represent the number of units of factor i needed by product 1 and product 2, respectively. Then the relationships between the two costs, v_1 for product 1 and v_2 for product 2, will be the following.

$$\begin{aligned}
E[v_1] &= a_1\bar{f}_1 + a_2\bar{f}_2 + \cdots + a_n\bar{f}_n \equiv \sum_{i=1}^{n} a_i\bar{f}_i \\
E[v_2] &= \sum_{i=1}^{n} b_i\bar{f}_i \\
\sigma^2[v_1] &= a_1^2\sigma^2[f_1] + a_2^2\sigma^2[f_2] + \cdots + a_n^2\sigma^2[f_n] \\
&= \sum_{i=1}^{n} a_i^2\sigma^2[f_i] \\
\sigma^2[v_2] &= \sum_{i=1}^{n} b_i^2\sigma^2[f_i] \\
\text{cov}[v_1, v_2] &= a_1b_1\sigma^2[f_1] + \cdots + a_nb_n\sigma^2[f_n] \\
&= \sum_{i=1}^{n} a_ib_i\sigma^2[f_i]
\end{aligned} \tag{7.18}$$

In the expression for covariance, we can see that if either a_i or b_i are zero, then the term $a_ib_i\sigma^2[f_i]$ is zero. Therefore, if products 1 and 2 use no common factors (i.e., a_ib_i is always 0), then the cost covariance will be equal to zero.[10] On the other hand, if

[10]These relationships assume that the costs of the factors f_i, are not correlated with each other. For example, material prices do not vary together. *If* $\text{cov}[f_i, f_j]$ is not zero, then the expressions for variance and covariance change to the following.

$$\begin{aligned}
\sigma^2[v_1] &= \sum_{i=1}^{n} a_i^2\sigma^2[f_i] + \sum_{i=1}^{n}\sum_{\substack{j=1\\ j\neq 1}}^{n} a_ia_j\,\text{cov}[f_i, f_j] \\
\sigma^2[v_2] &= \sum b_i^2\sigma^2[f_i] + \sum_{i=1}^{n}\sum_{\substack{j=1\\ j\neq 1}}^{n} b_ib_j\,\text{cov}[f_i, f_j] \\
\text{cov}[v_1, v_2] &= \sum_{i=1}^{n}\sum_{j=1}^{n} a_ib_j\,\text{cov}[f_i, f_j] \\
&= \sum_{i=1}^{n} a_ib_i\sigma^2[f_i] + \sum_{i=1}^{n}\sum_{\substack{j=1\\ j\neq i}}^{n} a_ib_j\,\text{cov}[f_i, f_j]
\end{aligned}$$

both products are heavy users of a factor that has considerable risk (i.e., a_i, b_i, and $\sigma^2[f_i]$ are all large), then the covariance between v_1 and v_2 will be large.

Example A department produces two products which use the same materials and labor, but in differing proportions. The expected factor costs, standard deviations of factor costs, and the factor usages are as follows.

Factor	Expected cost per factor unit	Standard deviation of unit factor cost	Amount needed to produce	
			Product 1	Product 2
Material A	20	1	3	4
Material B	15	2	6	2
Labor	8	0	2	3
Variable overhead	4	0.5	2	3

If we assume that the fluctuations in the material costs, labor costs, and the overhead costs are independent, we can derive the following statistics for the variable costs of products 1 and 2.

$$E[v_1] = 3(20) + 6(15) + 2(8) + 2(4) = 174$$
$$E[v_2] = 4(20) + 2(15) + 3(8) + 3(4) = 146$$

$$\begin{aligned}
\sigma^2[v_1] &= 3^2(1)^2 + 6^2(2)^2 + 2^2(0)^2 + 2^2(0.5)^2 = 154 \\
\sigma[v_1] &= (154)^{1/2} = 12.41 \\
\sigma^2[v_2] &= 4^2(1)^2 + 2^2(2)^2 + 3^2(0)^2 + 3^2(0.5)^2 = 34.25 \\
\sigma[v_2] &= (34.25)^{1/2} = 5.85
\end{aligned} \tag{7.19}$$

$$\begin{aligned}
\text{cov}[v_1, v_2] &= (3)(4)(1)^2 + (6)(2)(2)^2 + (2)(3)(0)^2 \\
&\quad + (2)(3)(0.5)^2 = 61.50
\end{aligned}$$

$$\rho_{v_1,v_2} = \frac{61.50}{(12.41)(5.85)} = 0.847$$

From these calculations, we can see that the costs of products 1 and 2 are quite closely correlated, and this information can be used in making product mix decisions as shown above and in Appendix 7.1.

It should be pointed out that the data requirements of the analytic approach represent a potentially severe problem. If there are n factors and m products, we need mn usages (i.e., a_i's, b_i's, . . . , etc.), n expected costs $\bar{f}_i$, and n variances $\sigma^2[f_i]$. If the factor costs f_i are also correlated, then there are $(n - 1)n/2$ covariances that will need to be estimated. If $n = 20$ and $m = 10$, this represents a total of 430 parameters to be input for the analytic model.

An alternative to the analytic approach would be a statistical approach, which is an extension of the techniques discussed in Chapter 6. If we have data on variable costs from the past, then an estimate of the covariance can be calculated.

$$\begin{aligned}
v_{1t} &\equiv \text{variable cost of a unit of product 1 in period } t,\ t = 1, \ldots, T \\
v_{2t} &\equiv \text{variable cost of a unit of product 2 in period } t,\ t = 1, \ldots, T
\end{aligned} \tag{7.20}$$

$$\widehat{\text{cov}}(v_1, v_2) = \frac{\sum_{t=1}^{T} (v_{1t} - \bar{v}_1)(v_{2t} - \bar{v}_2)}{T - 2}$$

where $\bar{v}_1 = (1/T)\ \Sigma_{t=1}^{T}\ v_{1t}$ and $\bar{v}_2 = (1/T)\ \Sigma_{t=1}^{T}\ v_{2t}$ are the sample means.

The correlation between v_1 and v_2, ρ_{v_1,v_2}, can also be estimated from the data.

$$\hat{\rho}_{v_1,v_2} = \frac{\Sigma_{t=1}^{T}(v_{1t} - \bar{v}_1)(v_{2t} - \bar{v}_2)}{[(\Sigma_{t=1}^{T}(v_{1t} - \bar{v}_1)^2)(\Sigma_{t=1}^{T}(v_{2t} - \bar{v}_2)^2)]^{1/2}} \tag{7.21}$$

Example Suppose we have four quarters of data on the direct costs of two product lines, 1 and 2. Find the sample covariance and correlation coefficients for the two variable costs.

	Direct cost per unit	
Quarter	Product 1	Product 2
1	\$20	\$29
2	18	27
3	22	31
4	25	33

$$\bar{v}_1 = (20 + 18 + 22 + 25)/4 = 21.25$$
$$\bar{v}_2 = (29 + 27 + 31 + 33)/4 = 30 \tag{7.22}$$

Quarter	$v_{1t} - \bar{v}_1$	$(v_{1t} - \bar{v}_1)^2$	$v_{2t} - \bar{v}_2$	$(v_{2t} - \bar{v}_2)^2$	$(v_{1t} - \bar{v}_1)(v_{2t} - \bar{v}_2)$
1	−1.25	1.5625	−1	1	1.25
2	−3.25	10.5625	−3	9	9.75
3	0.75	0.5625	1	1	.75
4	3.75	14.0625	3	9	11.25
Total	0	26.75	0	20	23

$$\hat{\text{cov}}(v_1, v_2) = \frac{\Sigma_{t=1}^{4}(v_{1t} - \bar{v}_1)(v_{2t} - \bar{v}_2)}{4 - 2} = \frac{23}{2} = 11.5$$
$$\rho_{v_1,v_2} = \frac{23}{[(26.75)(20)]^{1/2}} = \frac{23}{23.13} = 0.9944 \tag{7.23}$$

These estimates could then be used in choosing the optimal production plan for products 1 and 2.

7.9 MULTIPLE PRODUCTS AND LIMITED RESOURCES

To this point, we have discussed the choice of product mix as a form of risk management. That is, management's objective was to choose a portfolio of products in accordance with the preferred trade-offs between risk and return. Yet another aspect of product mix management is the effective utilization of the organization's scarce resources.[11] For instance, suppose that there are two production departments, each having a capacity of 1,000 labor hours per week. A unit of product 1 requires 2 labor hours in department A

[11] A model dealing with both risk management and limited resources appears in Appendix 7.1.

and 1 labor hour in department B, so we could produce 500 units of product 1. But that would leave department B 50% idle, so we might search for a product that used only department B. Suppose we found product 2 that required 1 labor hour in department A and 2 labor hours in department B. Then we could produce 333 units each of products 1 and 2. Is this desirable? It would depend on whether the increased contribution on 333 units of product 2 exceeded the lost contribution on 500 − 333 = 167 units of product 1.

While an example with two products and two resource limitations (called *constraints*) is rather easy to analyze, increasing the number of products and constraints can make a solution difficult to find. However, there are a number of management-science techniques which are able to search efficiently through the possible product mixes to find the one that maximizes the organization's objectives. The most common of these techniques is called *linear programming,* which may be used when both the objective *and* the constraints can be expressed as linear functions of the decision variables (i.e., the product mix). For instance, suppose that there are four products and three departments. Department j has b_j units of capacity and a unit of product i uses a_{ij} units of department j's resources. If management's objective is to maximize the expected contribution margin, a linear programming formulation would take the following form,

$$\max_{x_1,x_2,x_3,x_4} \; [(p_1 - \bar{v}_1)x_1 + (p_2 - \bar{v}_2)x_2 + (p_3 - \bar{v}_3)x_3 + (p_4 - \bar{v}_4)x_4] \tag{7.24}$$

subject to

$$\begin{aligned} a_{11}x_1 + a_{21}x_2 + a_{31}x_3 + a_{41}x_4 &\le b_1 \\ a_{12}x_1 + a_{22}x_2 + a_{32}x_3 + a_{42}x_4 &\le b_2 \\ a_{13}x_1 + a_{23}x_2 + a_{33}x_3 + a_{43}x_4 &\le b_3 \\ x_1 \ge 0, \quad x_2 \ge 0, \quad x_3 \ge 0, \quad x_4 &\ge 0 \end{aligned} \tag{7.25}$$

In this form, the product mix problem can be solved by standard linear programming packages. These would provide the user with the best product mix, that is, the values of x_1, x_2, x_3, and x_4 that maximize expected contribution margin but do not exceed the resource capacities. In addition, the linear program can provide a *sensitivity analysis* to see whether changes in the parameters (the contribution margins, the resource utilization, etc.) would have a significant effect on the product mix.[12]

There may be a variety of reasons why the linear programming formulation does not match the decision problem faced by the manager. For instance, it may be that the values of $x_1, \ldots, x_4$ are required to be integers. (The contribution margin for producing half a sailboat is probably not half the contribution margin of a completed sailboat.) Or, the manager may wish to take risk into account as measured by the variance of the contribution margin. But as we have seen, the variance is not a linear function of $x_1, \ldots, x_4$. The seriousness of these difficulties may vary from case to case, but there are formulations (integer programming, nonlinear programming) that can accommodate more complex situations than the linear one.

[12]For more information, see Rappaport (1967).

7.10 SUMMARY

In earlier chapters we examined the problem of choosing an activity level for a single product, including the effects of nonlinear costs, uncertain demand, and so on. These complications can also occur with multiple products, and we could handle them in much the same way as in Chapter 4. However, there may be a temptation to deal with each product individually, ignoring the interrelationships between products. In this chapter, we have seen that these interrelationships can be quite important, particularly in analyzing the risks of different product mixes, but also when different products must compete for common resources. Much of the covariability between products will result from the revenue side as general economic conditions, consumer tastes, and other factors affect demand for all products in the company's portfolio. But there are also covariances on the cost side, and the managerial accountant may be asked for information on these risks.

APPENDIX 7.1: Product Portfolio Decisions and Resource Constraints

In this chapter we explored the effect of the covariance between two products on the risks of different product mixes (Figure 7.8.) But in this appendix, we assume a particular risk-return preference on the part of the decision maker, and examine the decisions made in: (i) a single-product situation; (ii) a multiproduct situation; and (iii) a multiproduct situation with a constrained resource.

A7.1 SINGLE-PRODUCT CASE

Let's begin with a description of a single-product problem with uncertain variable costs v. Then profits will be $\pi = (p - v)x - F$ with

$$E[\pi] = px - E[v]x - F \quad \text{and} \quad \sigma^2[\pi] = x^2\sigma^2[v] \tag{A7.1}$$

If we introduce a risk-averse decision maker whose objective is to maximize $E[\pi] - w\sigma^2[\pi]$,[13] the choice of activity level may be analyzed in the following way.

$$\max_x \{E[\pi] - w\sigma^2[\pi]\} \leftrightarrow \max_x \{px - E[v]x - F - wx^2\sigma^2[v]\}$$

$$\frac{\partial}{\partial x}\{px - E[v]x - F - wx^2\sigma^2[v]\} = p - E[v] - 2wx\sigma^2[v] = 0 \tag{A7.2}$$

$$\rightarrow x^* = \frac{p - E[v]}{2w\sigma^2[v]}$$

That is, the level of production is affected by the expected contribution margin, by the cost uncertainty, and by the risk preferences of the decision maker.

[13]The parameter w incorporates the decision maker's expected return–risk tradeoffs. That is, increasing values of w reflect increasing risk-aversion. The term $E[\pi] - w\sigma^2[\pi]$ may be thought of as a *certainty equivalent value* of an uncertain profit outcome.

A7.2 MULTIPRODUCT CASE

When we move to the multiproduct case, a new factor arises. Suppose we have two products x_1 and x_2, each with uncertain variable costs, v_1 and v_2. Then our decision problem becomes the following.

$$\begin{aligned}\pi &= (p_1 - v_1)x_1 + (p_2 - v_2)x_2 - F \\ E[\pi] &= (p_1 - E[v_1])x_1 + (p_2 - E[v_2])x_2 - F \\ \sigma^2[\pi] &= x_1^2\sigma^2[v_1] + x_2^2\sigma^2[v_2] + 2x_1x_2\,\text{cov}[v_1, v_2]\end{aligned} \quad \text{(A7.3)}$$

The new factor in this analysis is the last term in the expression for the variance of profit, the *covariance* between v_1 and v_2. The lower the covariance, the lower the risk, all things being equal, and the better off our decision maker will be. But the level of covariance can also affect the output decisions in the model at the beginning of this section.

$$\max_{x_1, x_2}\{E[\pi] - w\sigma^2[\pi]\} \rightarrow x_1^* = \frac{(p_1 - E[v_1]) - (p_2 - E[v_2])\text{cov}[v_1, v_2]/\sigma^2[v_2]}{2w(\sigma^2[v_1] - \text{cov}[v_1, v_2]^2/\sigma^2[v_2])} \quad \text{(A7.4)}$$

(The expression for x_2^* can be found by interchanging subscripts.)

Obviously, the information that is supplied to this decision maker about covariances will affect the amount of output planned. If the covariance between v_1 and v_2 is zero, then the level of production is the same as in the single-product case. But if the covariance is greater (less) than zero, the optimal production will be less (greater) than the single-product production level. This can be seen in the following example.

$$\begin{aligned} p_1 = p_2 &= 30 = p \\ E[v_1] = E[v_2] &= 15 = \bar{v} \\ \sigma^2[v_1] = \sigma^2[v_2] &= 30 = \sigma^2 \\ w &= 0.0005 \end{aligned} \quad \text{(A7.5)}$$

$$x_i^* = \frac{(p - \bar{v})(1 - \rho)}{2w\sigma^2(1 - \rho^2)} = 500\frac{1 - \rho}{1 - \rho^2}$$

$\text{cov}(v_1, v_2)$	$\rho_{v1,v2}$	x_1^*	x_2^*
− 7.5	−0.25	667	667
0	0	500	500
7.5	0.25	400	400
15.0	0.50	333	333

As $\rho_{v1,v2}$ increases from zero, the *joint risk* of x_1 and x_2 increases, and the optimal level of production decreases. As $\rho_{v1,v2}$ decreases from zero, the level of production increases because the negative correlation provides the risk-averse manager with some insurance.

A7.3 MULTIPLE PRODUCTS WITH RESOURCE CONSTRAINTS

One of the issues that we have not yet addressed is the problem that arises when we have some constraints on the amount of production. For example, in the short run, the supply of labor with the necessary skills may be fixed, or the amount of machine time may be limited by the number of machines available. We will deal with the case where there is one constraining factor.

Suppose that the available amount of the constrained factor is b, and every time we produce a unit of x_i, we use a_i of this factor. Then our *feasible set* of product mixes will be all values of x_1, x_2 such that $a_1x_1 + a_2x_2 \leq b$, and our manager's decision problem becomes the following.

$$\max_{x_1, x_2} \{E[\pi] - w\sigma^2[\pi]\} \tag{A7.6}$$

subject to $a_1x_1 + a_2x_2 \leq b$ and $x_1 \geq 0$, $x_2 \geq 0$. As a first step, we might solve the decision problem, ignoring the constraints as we did above, and if the optimal production from the analysis x_1^*, x_2^* is feasible, that is $a_1x_1^* + a_2x_2^* \leq b$, then there is no need to go further.

However, if $a_1x_1^* + a_2x_2^* > b$, then we need to include the constraint that $a_1x_1 + a_2x_2 - b = 0$. We can do this by forming a Lagrangian $\mathcal{L}$ and maximizing it with respect to x_1, x_2 and the multiplier λ.

$$\begin{aligned}\mathcal{L} &= E[\pi] - w\sigma^2[\pi] - \lambda(a_1x_1 + a_2x_2 - b) \\ &= (p_1 - E[v_1])x_1 + (p_2 - E[v_2])x_2 - w(x_1^2\sigma^2[v_1] + x_2^2\sigma^2[v_2] \\ &\quad + 2x_1x_2\,\mathrm{cov}[v_1, v_2]) - \lambda(a_1x_1 + a_2x_2 - b)\end{aligned} \tag{A7.7}$$

The solution to this problem is a new production plan, x_1^{**} and x_2^{**}.

$$\begin{aligned}x_1^{**} &= \frac{(p_1 - E[v_1]) - (a_1/a_2)(p_2 - E[v_2]) - 2w(b/a_2)(\mathrm{cov}[v_1, v_2] - (a_1/a_2)\sigma^2[v_2])}{2w\{\sigma^2[v_1] - 2(a_1/a_2)\mathrm{cov}[v_1, v_2] + (a_1/a_2)^2\sigma^2[v_2]\}} \\ x_2^{**} &= \frac{b - a_1x_1^{**}}{a_2}\end{aligned} \tag{A7.8}$$

In Section A7.2 we derived the solution to a problem with no production constraint, where $p_1 = p_2 = 30$, $E[v_1] = E[v_2] = 15$, $\sigma^2[v_1] = \sigma^2[v_2] = 30$, $w = 0.0005$, and $\rho = 0.25$. The optimal solution was to produce at $x_1^* = x_2^* = 400$. Suppose that we now augment this example by assuming that we have a capacity of 1,000 direct labor hours, and product 1 requires 2 direct labor hours per unit, while product 2 requires only 1 direct labor hour per unit. That is, to our original example we have added the constraint that $2x_1 + x_2 \leq 1{,}000$. Our original optimal production plan is no longer feasible, since $2(400) + 400 = 1{,}200 > 1{,}000$. However, we *can* find the optimal feasible production plan using the above formulas.

$$\begin{aligned}x_1^{**} &= \frac{(15) - 2(15) - 2(0.0005)(1{,}000)[7.5 - 2(30)]}{2(0.0005)[30 - 2(2)(7.5) + (2)^2(30)]} \\ &= 312.5 \\ x_2^{**} &= \frac{1{,}000 - 2(312.5)}{1} = 375\end{aligned} \tag{A7.9}$$

We find that $x_2^{**} > x_1^{**}$ because product 2 requires less of the scarce resource than product 1. However, rather than produce just product 2, risk considerations cause product 1 to be produced. That is, product 2 is emphasized, but product 1 is not excluded. Going beyond the single constraint to multiple constraints would make the analysis considerably more complicated, requiring a non-linear program approach. (Unless $w = 0$, in which case a linear programming analysis may be sufficient.)

PROBLEMS

7.1. Using the cost and output data below, estimate the learning curve relationship

$$\text{Cumulative average cost} = v + \alpha(\text{cumulative output})^{\beta}$$

End of period	Cumulative average cost	Cumulative output
2	\$75.00	64
3	\$70.00	100

Required

A. Assume that the value of v is \$50, and determine the values of α and β. Estimate the cost of the next 69 units.

B. Assume that the value of β is -0.5, and determine the values of v and α. Estimate the cost of the next 69 units.

7.2. The personnel department of a large bank has developed a proposal to reduce employee turnover in a major service department within the bank. For the last few years, the average length of employment in the department has steadily declined to the point where a typical employee stays for only one year. It takes approximately four months for an employee to become fully trained in all aspects of the service department, and this start-up must be incurred whenever an existing employee leaves and is replaced by a new employee. The units of service that the department must supply is essentially fixed by the operating departments, so the *cost* of learning is reflected in increased employee costs rather than in reduced service levels. The average cost per unit of service provided by an employee is reflected in the following relationship.

$$\text{Cumulative average cost} = \$100 + \$250(\text{cumulative service units})^{-0.15}$$

Required If the personnel department's proposal would increase the average tenure of an employee from one year to two years, and thereby increase the cumulative units of an employee from 100 units to about 215 units, what would be the average amount (per unit of service) saved by the plan?

7.3. Choose a relatively well-defined activity (e.g., putting a puzzle together, completing a given type of accounting problem, etc.) and complete that activity at least three times. Record the amount of time it takes to complete each repetition of the activity.

Required

A. Estimate the following form of the learning curve:

$$\text{Cumulative average time} = v + \alpha(\text{cumulative number of repetitions})^{\beta}$$

B. Estimate the amount of time it would take to complete ten repetitions of the task.

7.4. The Toasti-Buns Company has developed a new electronic, programmable toaster that it is planning to market to consumers. The product has a number of innovative features, including the capability of letting each family member set values for a variety of toasting variables. The toaster then remembers the settings when the person enters their identification code. (A voice-recognition model is under development.) Currently, the company's management is trying to set a selling price for the product, which has been dubbed "Compu-Toast." If the price is set at \$50 per unit, the marketing department forecasts sales of 400,000 units, while a reduction to \$40 per unit would probably lead to sales of 700,000 units. The head of the marketing department is recommending the \$40 price because it would let the company get further down the learning curve, and thereby increase the payoff.

The production department has studied the costs of producing the new toaster, although there is still some uncertainty about the effects of learning on the costs. For simplicity, you may assume that there are two possible learning patterns as described below.

Possibility 1: Cumulative average cost = $\$30 + \$70(\text{cumulative output})^{-0.2}$
Possibility 2: Cumulative average cost = $\$25 + \$80(\text{cumulative output})^{-0.3}$

Required

A. Plot each of the cost behavior possibilities on a piece of graph paper. At which level of cumulative output does possibility 2 begin to have a lower average cost than possibility 1?

B. If each cost possibility is regarded as equally likely, and if the objective is to set the price so as to maximize the expected profit to the company, what is the expected value of perfect information about the cost behavior?

7.5. "One of the hardest parts of setting performance targets is incorporating the effects of learning that occurs with increased production," said Cory Johnson. "If you base the targets on past performance, they become easier to achieve due to learning. On the other hand, targets based on long-run expectations may not be attainable in the short-run, leading to reduced motivation. The whole problem is compounded by the fact that the effects of learning are uncertain."

"Here's a problem that will give you an idea of the difficulties encountered in this type of situation. We have a new product start-up scheduled for next month in one of our departments, and I'd like to set a tentative target for the department's manager. We expect to produce 100 units in that time. If he's doing a good job of cost control, there should be a significant probability (say, 0.8) that he will make the target and we won't waste our time with post-mortems. On the other hand, if the cost control is not good, I want a significant probability (say, 0.8) that costs will exceed the target and we can identify the problem. Unfortunately, I'm not certain what the rate of learning will be over the first month. In the cost relationships below, the value of β could be anywhere between -0.25 and -0.75. I'd say that all the values in that range are equally likely."

Good control: Cumulative average cost = $500 + 2{,}000(\text{cumulative output})^{\beta}$
Poor control: Cumulative average cost = $500 + 3{,}200(\text{cumulative output})^{\beta}$

Required

A. Can you find a cost target that meets the conditions that Cory Johnson wants?

B. Can you find a target such that there is a 0.6 probability of costs being below target if control is good and a 0.6 probability of costs exceeding the target if cost control is poor?

7.6. "We must decide whether to enter a market that has a limited expected life. The present product will, in all probability, be obsolete in two years' time due to technological advances in computer software and communications. The market is already fairly competitive, so we don't have much discretion in pricing the product. The basic question is whether we will get down the learning curve fast enough to make a profit in the next two years. The answer depends on the rate at which learning will occur, and that is uncertain at this time. The cost of production will follow the pattern below:

$$\text{Cumulative average cost} = \$350 + \$1{,}500(\text{cumulative output})^{\beta}$$

where β may take on the values $(-0.1, -0.2, -0.3, -0.4)$ with equal probability. "Over the two years, we would expect to produce 10,000 units, and the revenues from the sale of these units would be \$6 million. Alternatively, we could simply pass the opportunity by, with little long-term effect on our other business."

Required

A. If the objective is to maximize expected profits, should the company enter the market for two years? What would be the expected value of perfect information about the rate of learning?

B. How would your answers in part A change if the manager making the decision was risk-averse, with the following preference function for profits from the product:

$$U(\text{profit}) = (5{,}000{,}000 + \text{profit})^{0.5}$$

7.7. "We've been producing these electronic control devices for almost two months now, and I'm beginning to get concerned about the production costs. We have a contract to supply 400 of these units to a producer of automated assembly lines, and I'm not sure how profitable it's going to be. The customer is paying us a flat fee of $100,000 and then reimbursing our variable costs up to $600,000. If it costs more than $600,000, the customer will reimburse only 50% of the costs over $600,000. Our profit on the order looks like the following.

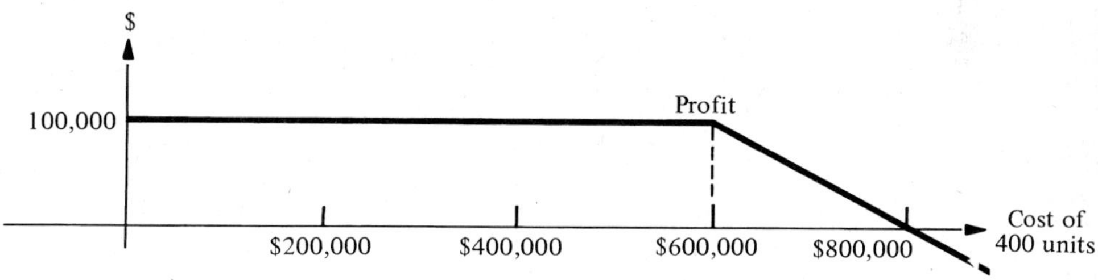

"It should take us another five months or so to finish the order, but the president wants me to make an estimate of the profit that we'll make. Below are the data on our experience to date. There has been a learning effect on labor time, since production has increased while labor costs have remained pretty constant. But it's hard for me to figure out what's going on with material costs and variable overhead. There should be some learning effects here too, but it's hard to sort out the learning from the volume changes."

"Anyway, what I would like is an estimate of the costs of completing the order. Don't put any slack or cushion in the estimate—I can do that myself. Just give me your best estimate. The only additional information I can give you is that the engineering studies estimated the material costs to be $950 per unit, but that's based on minimal scrap and waste. Also, our experience with this type of project in the past has been that a doubling of output causes the cumulative average labor cost to go down by 16–20%. I can't help you much on the overhead costs."

Week	Output	Direct labor cost	Direct material cost	Variable overhead
1	12	$ 8,363	$ 12,797	$ 4,056
2	15	8,761	15,096	4,512
3	15	8,325	14,712	3,789
4	16	8,264	15,719	4,455
5	16	8,138	15,487	4,294
6	16	8,616	15,778	4,339
7	17	8,769	16,371	4,575
Totals	107	$59,236	$105,960	$27,844

Required Provide the requested estimate.

7.8. Your division has been producing a single product *X*, and is considering expansion into one of two additional product lines, *Y* or *Z*. No additional plant capacity would be needed, and marketing research indicates that you could sell 10,000 units per month of either *Y* or *Z* at a price of $100 per unit. (Product *X* currently sells for $88 per unit, and recent sales levels of 20,000 units per month are expected to continue.)

The following list of direct cost components have been compiled with an engineering study.

	Input quantity per unit of output		
	X	*Y*	*Z*
Material *A* (lb)	3	4	3
Material *B* (lb)	2	3	4
Direct labor (hr)	3	2	2

Materials must be purchased monthly in markets where prices fluctuate. Past analysis indicates that material *A* has an average price of $10/lb with a standard deviation of 1. Material *B* also has an average price of $10/lb and a standard deviation of 1, but fluctuations in material *B* prices are independent of those in material *A*'s prices. Labor rates are fixed by union contract at $8/hr.

Required

A. On the basis of the available data, which product combination has the higher expected monthly contribution margin, *X* and *Y*, or *X* and *Z*?

B. On the basis of the available data, which product combination has the higher variance of monthly contribution margin, *X* and *Y*, or *X* and *Z*?

C. If the material costs are assumed to be normally distributed, which product combination has the higher probability of achieving a monthly contribution margin in excess of the monthly fixed overhead costs of $400,000?

7.9. The productive activities necessary to manufacture products *F* and *G* are too complex to be amenable to an analytic examination of the covariance of their costs. However, the following data from the past six months has been compiled by the cost accounting system.

	Variable cost per unit	
Month	*F*	*G*
4	$6	$18
5	$5	$20
6	$6	$19
7	$7	$17
8	$5	$19
9	$7	$15

Required

A. Estimate the variance and standard deviation of the variable cost of product *F*. Do the same for product *G*.

B. Estimate the covariance and the correlation coefficient between the variable costs of products F and G.

7.10. "I know that most people think my attitude is a little crass, but I want to take my compensation into account in making decisions about which products to push," said Wats N.T. Furmi, the district sales manager for a distributor of personal copier machines. "I figure that the top management of the company set up the bonus system expecting people to react that way, so by acting this way, I'm really doing what they want. If there's a difference between what I'm doing and what they want me to do, then the fault lies with the bonus compensation system, not with me.

"Anyway, I have to decide which product combination to work with over the next six months. My performance is evaluated on the basis of the contribution margin of products sold in my area, and if I exceed the six-month target of \$475,000, I'll get a bonus of \$15,000. If I don't meet the target, I don't get anything. Up to this point, we've been selling two products—the basic model, which has a standard contribution margin of \$200 per unit, and the deluxe model with a standard contribution margin of \$300 per unit. Now we have a new model, the super-deluxe, which has a standard contribution margin of \$325 per unit. Of course, the standards don't mean too much if the competition heats up and we have to give the dealers discounts. I'll come back to this issue a little later.

"My original order for the next six months was 1,000 units each of the basic model and the deluxe model. Now I have to put in a new order taking the super-deluxe into account. I have the choice of sticking with my original order of 1,000 basic and 1,000 deluxe or changing it to 1,000 basic, 500 deluxe and 500 super-deluxe. (I can reduce the units of the other two as long as I'm ordering the new model.) The thing I'm not sure of is whether there will be any cannibalism between the deluxe and super-deluxe models. If the super-deluxe takes off, it could be at the expense of the deluxe model. Then, I'd have to really discount the deluxe model to move it. On the other hand, if the customers view the super-deluxe as being too much for a personal copier, the deluxe will stay strong, and I'll have to discount the super-deluxe. Of course, the demand for all models will depend on the market in general, and on our competitors' actions in particular.

"Some of the basic data are reported below. As I said, I'm unsure as to whether there will be any cannibalism between the two products, so I've given you two sets of correlations. At this point, it's anyone's guess how it will turn out, so I suppose you could say that the two possibilities are equally likely."

	Basic	Deluxe	Super-deluxe
Expected unit contribution margin	\$ 200	\$ 300	\$ 325
Standard deviation of unit contribution margin	15	20	25
Correlations with no cannibalism			
Basic	1.00	0.25	0.25
Deluxe	0.25	1.00	0.25
Super-deluxe	0.25	0.25	1.00
Correlations with cannibalism			
Basic	1.00	0.25	0.25
Deluxe	0.25	1.00	−0.25
Super-deluxe	0.25	−0.25	1.00

Required

A. Compute the expected contribution margin and the standard deviation of the contribution margin for each decision alternative under
(a) no product cannibalism;
(b) product cannibalism.

B. If you assume that the contribution margins are normally distributed, which product alternative provides the highest expected bonus compensation to Furmi under
(a) no product cannibalism;
(b) product cannibalism.

C. What is the expected value to Furmi of perfect information about the existence of product cannibalism between the deluxe and super-deluxe models?

7.11. When statistical regression is used to estimate cost relationships, we often use the estimated coefficients of that relationship to make decisions. For instance, the relationship below produces estimates of the variable costs of producing a unit of product 1 and a unit of product 2, and these estimates can be used in a short-term planning analysis such as CVP.

$$\text{Production cost} = F + v_1(\text{units of product 1}) + v_2(\text{units of product 2}) + \varepsilon$$

In addition, the regression provides estimates of the accuracy of the estimates in the standard error for each coefficient. The use of this information was illustrated in Chapter 6.

However, it is not usually the case that the estimates are independent of each other. That is, if there is a negative correlation between the estimates, it means that if we *over*-estimated v_1, we have probably *under*estimated v_2. For this reason, it is important to assess the riskiness of different product combinations by considering *both* products at the same time.

Required

A. Using the data below and a regression program that reports the correlations or covariances between the regression estimates, make estimates of the cost relationships. Estimate the correlation between the variable costs per unit of product 1 and product 2.

Cost ($)	Units of product 1	Units of product 2
195,000	10,000	5,000
218,000	11,000	5,400
180,000	9,000	4,400
158,000	8,000	4,100

7.12. Suppose a firm produces two products with the following characteristics.

	Product 1	Product 2
Unit selling price, p	$20	$30
Variable cost per unit		
Mean $E[\tilde{v}]$	$12	$22
Variance $\sigma^2[\tilde{v}]$	20	20

Firm objective: max $\{E[\pi] - 0.0004\sigma^2[\pi]\}$

Required

A. If $\rho_{v1,v2} = 0$, what is the optimal production of x_1 and x_2?

B. If $\rho_{v1,v2} = 0.25$, what is the optimal production of x_1 and x_2?

C. Suppose that each product requires 1 direct labor hour to produce and the production capacity is 800 direct labor hours. What happens to the optimal production plans in A and B? (No computations should be necessary.)

D. With the production constraint in C, suppose it is equally likely that $\rho_{v1,v2}$ is 0 or 0.25. What would be the value of information on $\rho_{v1,v2}$?

REFERENCES

Baloff, N., and J. Kennelly. ''Accounting Implications of Product and Process Start-ups,'' *Journal of Accounting Research*. Autumn 1967.

Draper, N. R., and H. Smith. *Applied Regression Analysis*. New York: Wiley. 1966.

Grinnell, D. ''Product Mix Decisions: Direct Costing vs. Absorption Costing,'' *Management Accounting*. August 1976.

Jackson, B., and B. Shapiro. ''New Way to Make Product Line Decisions,'' *Harvard Business Review*. May–June 1979.

Jensen, R. ''Sensitivity Analysis and Integer Linear Programming,'' *Accounting Review*. July 1968.

Johnson, G., and S. Simik II. ''Multiproduct C–V–P Analysis under Uncertainty,'' *Journal of Accounting Research*. Autumn 1971.

Johnson, G., And S. Simik II. ''The Use of Probability Inequalities in Multiproduct C–V–P Analysis under Uncertainty,'' *Journal of Accounting Research*. Spring 1974.

LeBrone, H. ''The Learning Curve: A Case Study,'' *Management Accounting*. February 1978.

Magee, R. ''Cost–Volume–Profit Analysis, Uncertainty, and Capital Market Equilibrium,'' *Journal of Accounting Research*. Autumn 1975.

McIntyre, E. V. ''Cost–Volume–Profit Analysis Adjusted for Learning,'' *Management Science*. October 1977.

Morse, W., ''Reporting Production Costs That Follow the Learning Curve Phenomenon,'' *Accounting Review*. October 1972.

Rappaport, A. ''Sensitivity Analysis in Decision Making,'' *Accounting Review*. July 1967.

Chapter 8

Planning, Competition, and Cost Information

There are a variety of factors that influence the importance of cost accounting information. In fact, the information analysis of Chapters 2 and 3 is a situation-specific analysis: the value of information depends on the action choices, uncertainties, and preferences. At the same time, it is useful to look for general tendencies that can help us to predict the effects of various factors on the value of cost information. For instance, as the decision maker's uncertainty about cost increases, will the value of information about costs increase? Usually, the answer is yes, but not always, as we will see in this chapter. Most of our attention in this chapter will be focused on the effects of competition (in the product market) on the value of cost information. In general, we will find that greater competition gives a manager less margin for error, and this results in an increase in the value of cost information. However, there are competitive situations in which the acquisition of cost information can make the manager (or the firm) worse off.

8.1 ACCEPT/REJECT DECISIONS

The simplest decision setting we have examined is the case where the decision maker is approached by a potential customer who is willing to pay an amount p for a special order. The value of p will be influenced (positively) by the value of the order to the customer, and (negatively) by the number of competing firms (and/or competing products) that the customer can go to if the order is rejected. For the manager of the supplying firm, the cost of fulfilling the order may be uncertain if the product has not been made before, or if current conditions differ from those when the product was last manufactured. For a start, we will assume that the order's costs may be $\bar{v} - \Delta v$, $\bar{v}$, or $\bar{v} + \Delta v$, with equal probability (1/3 each). The expected cost is $\bar{v}$, and a risk-neutral manager (with excess production capacity) would accept the order if p was greater than the expected cost $\bar{v}$. How much would it be worth to resolve the uncertainty over costs? We can

TABLE 8.1 INCREMENTAL PAYOFFS

	Cost of order		
Action	$\bar{v} - \Delta v$	$\bar{v}$	$\bar{v} + \Delta v$
Accept	$p - \bar{v} + \Delta v$	$p - \bar{v}$	$p - \bar{v} - \Delta v$
Reject	0	0	0
Probability	1/3	1/3	1/3

explore that question by looking at the incremental profits in Table 8.1. If p is greater than $\bar{v} + \Delta v$, then regardless of the cost outcome, the firm is better off if the order is accepted, so the value of cost information will be zero. The same is true if p is less than $\bar{v} - \Delta v$, since the order should be rejected regardless of the result of a cost study. If p is equal to $\bar{v}$, then the acceptance of the order would have an expected profit of zero, but there is a 1/3 probability that the order will cost $\bar{v} + \Delta v$, resulting in a loss of Δv. Therefore perfect information on the costs before the decision would enable the manager to avoid an expected opportunity loss of $(1/3)\Delta v$ by rejecting the order if costs will be $\bar{v} + \Delta v$. What happens if p is between $\bar{v}$ and $\bar{v} + \Delta v$? In the absence of further information, the order would be accepted, but there would still be a 1/3 probability of a negative profit of $p - \bar{v} - \Delta v$. The effect of p on the expected opportunity loss EOL (which is equivalent to the EVPI) can be seen in Figure 8.1.

We can see that as the customer price decreases from $\bar{v} + \Delta v$ to $\bar{v}$, the cost information becomes more valuable. If p is related to the level of competition, increased competition increases the value of the cost information. In a way, this result is paradoxical since as the firm's expected profit declines, the price it would be willing to pay for information on its costs increases. We can also see that an increase in the *spread* of cost outcomes, that is, an increase in Δv, would result in higher values of the EVPI around $\bar{v}$.

Does this phenomenon depend on the type of probability distribution that we have assumed for the order cost? No, although the exact shape of the EVPI curve will depend on how costs are distributed. For instance, if the order's costs are distributed uniformly between $\bar{v} - \Delta v$ and $\bar{v} + \Delta v$,[1] the EVPI is as depicted in Figure 8.2.[2] Again, higher

[1]That is, all costs between $\bar{v} - \Delta v$ and $\bar{v} + \Delta v$ are equally likely.

[2]If $p \geq \bar{v}$, the EVPI $= (1/4\Delta v)[v + \Delta\bar{v} - p]^2$. If $p \leq \bar{v}$, the EPVI $= (1/4\Delta v)[p - \bar{v} + \Delta v]^2$.

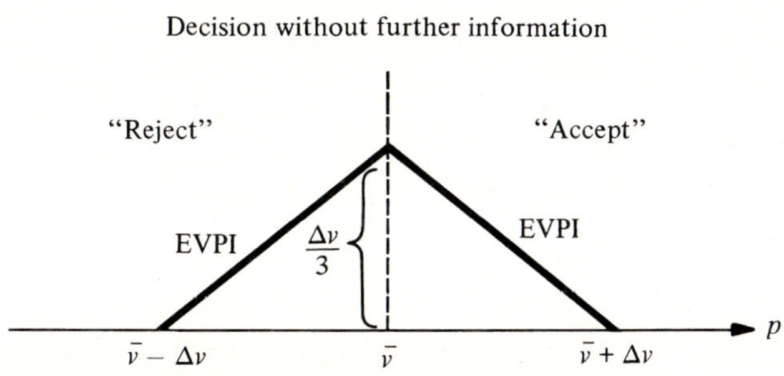

Figure 8.1 Decision without further information.

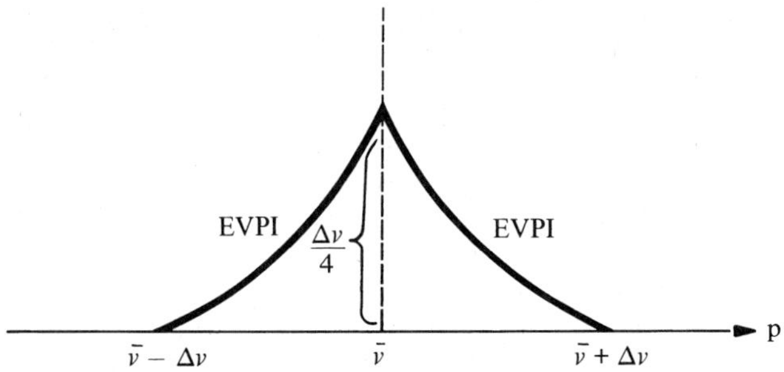

Figure 8.2 EVPI for uniformly distributed costs.

values of Δv (i.e., more uncertainty concerning costs) result in higher values of EVPI for a given p and $\bar{v}$. That is, the less the decision maker knows about costs, the higher the value of information about those costs. These general tendencies might be used to allocate resources to the gathering of cost information if management decides not to undertake a value-of-information analysis for each order that arrives.

8.2 PRICING AND ACTIVITY DECISIONS

In Chapter 4, we examined the situation where a manager set a price for the product, and that price determined the demand for the product. In that example, the unit price was $100 - 2.5x$, and revenue was $100x - 2.5x^2$, but in this chapter we will use the parameters A and B instead of the values 100 and 2.5 (see Figure 8.3.) At a price of A, no units will be sold, and a price decrease of B will always sell one additional unit. As in the previous section, we will assume that costs are uncertain. In particular, the variable costs per unit may take on values of $\bar{v} - \Delta v$, $\bar{v}$, or $\bar{v} + \Delta v$, with probabilities ϕ, θ, ϕ, respectively.[3] The manager is assumed to want to choose the price–quantity combination that will maximize the expected profit. The level of production that maximizes the expected profit, x^*, can be found by taking the derivative of the expected profit and setting it equal to zero as in (8.1). In words, the optimal output depends on the factors

[3] $E[v] = \bar{v}$, $\sigma^2[v] = 2\phi(\Delta v)^2$. Of course, $\phi + \theta + \phi = 1$.

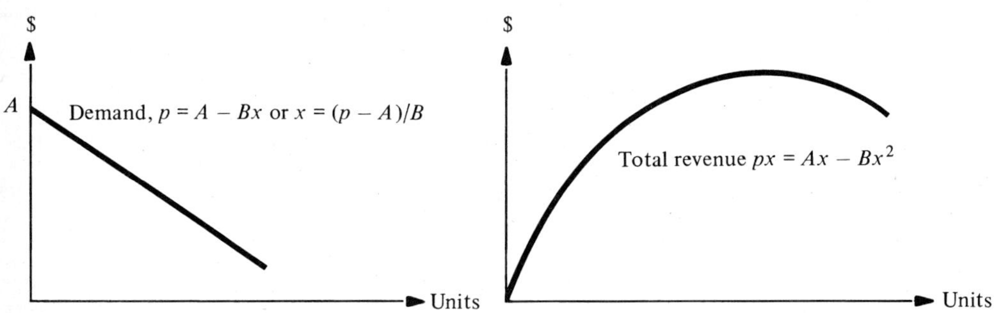

Figure 8.3

$A - E[v]$, and on B, the speed with which the demand curve slopes downward. The price p^* will be set at $A - Bx^*$ or $(A + E[v])/2$.

$$\begin{aligned} \pi(x) &= Ax - Bx^2 - vx - F \\ E[\pi(x)] &= (A - E[v])x - Bx^2 - F \\ \frac{d}{dx}E[\pi(x)] &= (A - E[v]) - 2Bx = 0 \\ x^* &= \frac{A - E[v])}{2B} = \frac{A - \bar{v}}{2B} \end{aligned} \tag{8.1}$$

Of course, the demand curve faced by the firm is dependent on the characteristics of the market for its products. Specifically, the demand depends on the consumers' tastes and preferences which determine the total market demand, and on the amount of competition between the companies that make the product. As competition increases, the demand for an individual firm's product becomes increasingly sensitive to the price it charges. For a monopolist, the demand curve is the market demand curve. Under perfect competition, the firm's demand curve is a flat line, with $B = 0$. (See Figure 8.4.) Therefore, increasing competition would be reflected by a decrease in B and, probably, a decrease in A. (For our example, we will assume that the market does not reach perfect competition so that B does not equal zero.)

But in a given market situation, the manager will maximize the expected profits by producing $x^* = (A - \bar{v})/2B$ and charging a price of $p^* = (A + \bar{v})/2$. The expected profit from this decision would be the following.

$$\begin{aligned} E[\pi(x^*)] &= (A - \bar{v})x^* - Bx^{*2} - F \\ &= \frac{(A - \bar{v})^2}{4B} - F \end{aligned} \tag{8.2}$$

If the variable cost turns out to be equal $\bar{v}$, then the decision that maximized *expected* profits will also maximize *actual* profits. That is, there would be no opportunity loss from not knowing the variable cost. But if the variable cost turns out to be $\bar{v} - \Delta v$, then the firm would have maximized profits by choosing a lower price p^{**} and a higher output

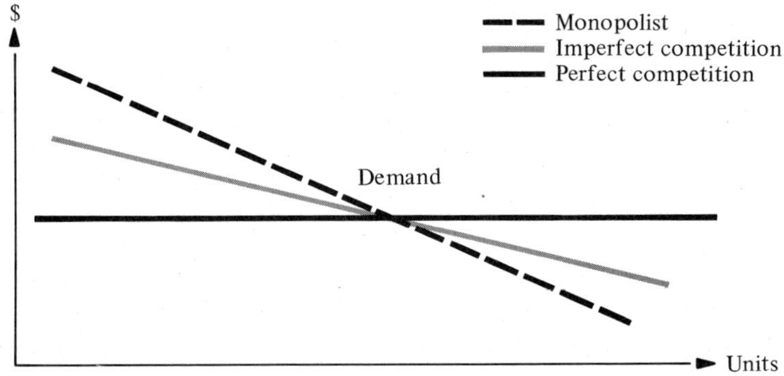

Figure 8.4

x^{**}, as seen below.

$$\pi_L(x) = [A - (v - \Delta v)]x - Bx^2 - F$$

$$x^{**} = \frac{A - v + \Delta v}{2B} > x^* \tag{8.3}$$

$$p^{**} = \frac{A + \bar{v} - \Delta v}{2} < p^*$$

In the absence of information that the variable costs would be $\bar{v} - \Delta v$, the manager would choose x^* and p^* to maximize the expected profit. The opportunity loss is the difference between $\pi_L(x^{**})$ and $\pi_L(x^*)$, when $v = v - \Delta v$.

$$\begin{aligned} \text{OL}_1 = \pi_L(x^{**}) - \pi_L(x^*) &= (A - v + \Delta v)x^{**} - Bx^{**2} - F \\ &\quad - [(A - \bar{v} + \Delta v)x^* - Bx^{*2} - F] \\ &= \frac{(\Delta v)^2}{4B} \end{aligned} \tag{8.4}$$

The same analysis can be carried out to determine the opportunity loss if the variable costs turn out to be $\bar{v} + \Delta v$. The optimal quantity x^{***} will be lower than x^*, and the optimal price p^{***} will be higher than p^*.

$$\begin{aligned} x^{***} &= \frac{A - v - \Delta v}{2B} < x^* \\ p^{***} &= \frac{A + v + \Delta v}{2} > p^* \end{aligned} \tag{8.5}$$

Again, the opportunity loss from not knowing that $v = \bar{v} + \Delta v$ can be computed, and will have the same value as OL_1.

$$\text{OL}_2 = \pi_H(x^{***}) - \pi_H(x^*) = \frac{(\Delta v)^2}{4B} \tag{8.6}$$

Now we are in a position to discover the expected opportunity loss from not knowing the variable cost with certainty. This number is important from an informational viewpoint because it is also the EVPI about the variable costs.

$$\begin{aligned} \text{EOL} &= \phi\text{OL}_1 + \theta 0 + \phi\text{OL}_2 \\ &= (2\phi)\frac{(\Delta v)^2}{4B} = \text{EVPI} \end{aligned} \tag{8.7}$$

As in the previous section, we can see which parameters affect the value of information on variable costs. As B decreases (i.e., as the product market becomes more competitive), the information on costs becomes more valuable. The value of A relative to $E[v]$ plays no part in determining the expected value of the cost information. The probability distribution of variable costs influences the EVPI through the size of Δv and the probability of $\bar{v} + \Delta v$ and $\bar{v} - \Delta v$. In fact, there is a direct relationship between $\sigma^2[v]$ and the EVPI in this situation.

$$\text{EVPI} = \frac{\sigma^2[v]}{4B} \tag{8.8}$$

TABLE 8.2 THE EFFECT OF VARIOUS PARAMETERS ON EVPI

	Parameters						Decisions			
Case #	A	B	$\bar{v}$	Δv	ϕ	θ	x^*	x^{**}	x^{***}	EVPI
1	100	1	50	10	1/4	1/2	25	30	20	12.50
2	100	2	50	10	1/4	1/2	12.5	15	10	6.25
3	100	0.5	50	10	1/4	1/2	50	60	40	25.00
4	200	1	50	10	1/4	1/2	75	80	70	12.50
5	200	2	50	10	1/4	1/2	37.5	40	35	6.25
6	200	0.5	50	10	1/4	1/2	150	160	140	25.00
7	100	1	50	15	1/4	1/2	25	32.5	17.5	28.125
8	100	1	50	20	1/4	1/2	25	35	15	50.00

Regardless of the probability distribution of v, the EVPI increases as $\sigma^2[v]$ increases in the problem described above.

These effects can be seen in a series of examples in Table 8.2. The values of A, B, and Δv are allowed to change. We can see that a more steeply sloping demand curve (higher B) results in a lower value being attached to the cost information. When the value of A changes, the decisions change (increases in A cause increased production), but the EVPI remains unchanged as can be seen when cases 1 and 4, 2 and 5, or 3 and 6, are compared. Finally, when cases 1, 7, and 8 are compared, we can see that the effect of increasing Δv is to increase the EVPI. Therefore, the cases with the highest EVPI will be those where the product market is very competitive and the cost uncertainty ($\sigma^2[v]$) is high.

8.3 A COMPETITIVE BIDDING SITUATION

Another type of decision situation in which price and activity are determined occurs when a manager must enter into a bidding process in order to be awarded a contract to supply a good or service. This practice is quite common if the potential customer is a governmental agency, but it is not unusual for companies to request bids on, say, major construction projects, information systems projects, and so on.

From the point of view of the customer, there are a number of issues that need to be addressed in designing the bidding process and the contract form. Generally, the customer will try to obtain the lowest possible price while maintaining some form of quality control. The simplest system might be a sealed-bid auction where each competing company places a secret, fixed-price bid, and the customer chooses the lowest bidder to supply the good or service. We will analyze this system in some detail, but there are others which might be used. For instance, if the project is a large one with numerous engineering obstacles to overcome, the contract may be a cost plus fixed fee arrangement, or some other alternative that allows the customer and supplier to share the risks of cost of production.

The bidding system we will analyze is one where the competing suppliers place secret, fixed-price bids, and the customer chooses the supplier who made the lowest bid. From the supplier's standpoint, the higher the bid he or she places, the higher the expected profit if the contract is awarded. But, higher bids also mean that the probability of being awarded the contract decreases.

One way to analyze the bidding problem would be to formulate the probability that a bid of p will be accepted by the customer. In general, we would expect that this probability $\phi(p)$ would not increase as p increased, and that the function might look like that in Figure 8.5. In this situation, the manager who wishes to maximize expected profits must make a tradeoff between the probability of the order being accepted and the contribution margin if it is accepted. The point at which the product of these two factors

$$\text{Expected profit, } E[\pi] = \phi(p)(p - E[v])$$

is maximized is the optimal bid. The cost estimate does play a role in determining the best bid, and information on costs may be valuable, as seen in the following example.

Price bid, p	Probability of acceptance, $\phi(p)$	Cost of supplying good or service	Probability
$100,000	0.9	$85,000	0.3
105,000	0.6	90,000	0.35
110,000	0.3	95,000	0.35

A payoff table can be constructed with each entry being the value of $\phi(p)(p - v)$. Then this quantity can be used to calculate the expected payoff for each possible bid.

Price bid	Cost outcome $85,000	$90,000	$95,000	$E[\pi]$
$100,000	(0.9)(100,000 − 85,000) = $13,500	$9,000	$4,500	$8,775
$105,000	$12,000	$9,000	$6,000	$8,850
$110,000	$7,500	$6,000	$4,500	$5,925

Based on the manager's current assessment of the situation, the expected profits are highest if the bid of $105,000 is placed. However, there is a 0.3 probability that the

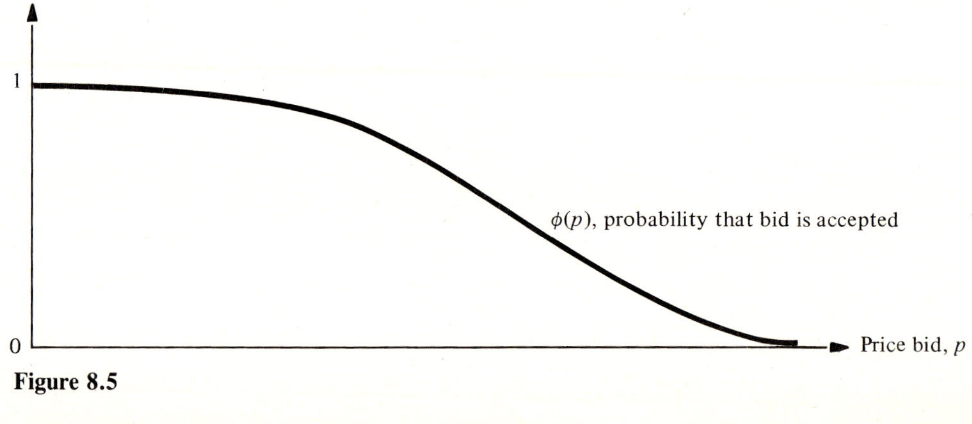

Figure 8.5

cost of supplying the good or service will be $85,000, and the manager could have increased the expected profit by $1,500 if he decreased the bid to $100,000. Therefore, knowing the costs would enable the manager to avoid an opportunity loss of $1,500 with probability 0.3, and the expected value of perfect cost information would be $450.

8.4 ESTIMATES OF COST AND EXPECTED MARGIN

One limitation of the bidding analysis in the last section is that it assumes that the probability of winning the contract is independent of the cost outcome probabilities. But if each potential supplier is making his or her own estimate of the cost, then the contract will tend to be awarded to the bidder who underestimated the costs by the largest amount. In the context of the previous section's example, a bid of $105,000 that wins may mean that other competitors assess the probabilities of costs of $95,000 (or more) as higher than the winning bidder. This phenomenon, called the *winner's paradox,* means that the winner's expected profit will be less than the price he or she bid minus the cost estimate.

To illustrate, suppose that the actual cost of supplying the good or service is v for all firms, but that each firm i gets an estimate $v_i = v\varepsilon_i$, where ε_i represents the effects of estimation errors. For our example, we will assume that ε_i has the following probability distribution.

ε_i	Probability
0.8	0.15
0.9	0.20
1.0	0.30
1.1	0.20
1.2	0.15

That is, there is a 0.15 probability that the cost estimate will be 80% of the actual cost, and so on. If two firms are each estimating costs and then adding the same margin to arrive at the bid price, then the winning firm will be the one with the lower estimate of costs, $v_{\min} = \min[v_1, v_2]$. What is the probability distribution of the minimum cost estimate, or equivalently, what is the probability distribution of the minimum value of ε_i?

If there are two bidders, the probability that $\varepsilon_{\min}$ is 0.8 is the probability that $\varepsilon_1 = 0.8$ *or* $\varepsilon_2 = 0.8$. The probability that $\varepsilon_{\min}$ is 1.2 is the probability that $\varepsilon_1 = 1.2$ *and* $\varepsilon_2 = 1.2$. The probability distributions for $\varepsilon_{\min}$ with one bidder, two bidders, and three bidders appear in Table 8.3. It is evident that as the number of bidders increases, the probability distribution of the winning cost estimate shifts toward underestimation. The probability of a 20% underestimation ($\varepsilon_{\min} = 0.8$) for the winning bid changes from 0.15 to about 0.28 to about 0.38 as the number of bidders increases. At the same time, the probability the winning bid will have a 20% overestimation drops from 0.15 to less than 0.01. The effects of this "winner's paradox" on profit margins should be clear. If a firm's bid is, say, 110% of its cost estimate, then its expected margin (if it wins the contract) is not 10%, but less. If there are two bidders, the expected winning cost estimate is 92.9% of the actual cost.

TABLE 8.3 PROBABILITY DISTRIBUTION OF MINIMUM COST ESTIMATES

	ε_{min} value					
	0.8	0.9	1.0	1.1	1.2	$E[\varepsilon_{min}]$
One bidder	0.15	0.2	0.3	0.2	0.15	1.0
Two bidders	0.2775	0.3	0.3	0.1	0.0225	0.929
Three bidders	0.385875	0.3395	0.23175	0.0395	0.003375	0.8935

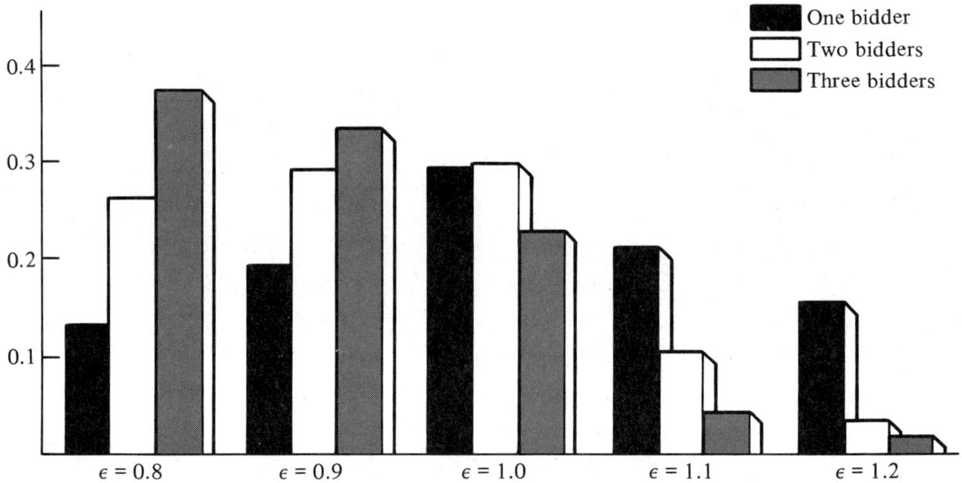

$$\begin{aligned} &E[v_i \mid \text{firm } i \text{ wins}] = 0.929v \\ &\text{Price bid, } p_i = 1.1v_i \\ &E[\text{margin} \mid \text{firm } i \text{ wins}] \\ &\quad = p_i - v = (1.1)(0.929v) - v \\ &\quad = 0.0219v \end{aligned} \tag{8.9}$$

The actual expected margin is just a little over 2% of the project cost, not the 10% planned by the firm. If there are three bidders, the firm would actually expect to make a loss if its bid was 110% of its cost estimate. The firm would have to bid about 112% of its cost estimate just to expect to break even.[4]

What influences the size of the margin that must be used simply to expect to break even? Certainly the number of bidders plays a role, as seen in Table 8.3. As the number of competing firms increases, the expected underestimation of the winning bid is increased. Therefore, both the competitive situation and the cost estimation system affect the usefulness of different bidding strategies that the firm might use.

[4]Breakeven $\rightarrow p - v = 0 \rightarrow (1 + m)E[v_1] - v = 0 \rightarrow (1 + m)(0.8935v) - v = 0 \rightarrow m = 0.1192$.

8.5 BIDDING WITH COST ESTIMATION BIASES

In fact, the situation may be even more complex, if the bidding firms use different simplifications in their cost estimations. In this case, the estimation systems can drive the firm into a particular market segment. To illustrate, suppose that there are two firms operating in a given market where customers present job proposals, and the two firms make bids to see who gets the job. Let us suppose that the actual cost of job i would be the following.

$$C_i = 200 + 10M_i + 20L_i \tag{8.10}$$

where M_i is the amount of material required and L_i is the amount of labor required.

While this cost is the same for firms 1 and 2, the managers of these two firms have chosen different cost estimation systems. The average job in this industry uses 20 units of material and 10 units of labor, yielding an average cost of \$600 for the job. Firm 1's manager says, "The average job cost is \$600 with material usage of 20, so I will estimate a job's cost to be \$30 times the amount of material required." Firm 2's manager uses the same type of reasoning, but bases his cost estimates on labor, at the rate of \$60 per unit of labor. If each manager decides to bid \$50 over the estimated cost, what happens when they face the job proposals in Table 8.4?

TABLE 8.4 EFFECTS OF COST ESTIMATION BIASES ON BIDDING

Job	M_i	L_i	Actual cost
1	21	8	200 + 210 + 160 = \$570
2	24	11	200 + 240 + 220 = 660
3	18	10	200 + 180 + 200 = 580
4	22	9	200 + 220 + 180 = 600
5	16	12	200 + 160 + 240 = 600
6	19	10	200 + 190 + 200 = 590
Total	120	60	\$3,600

	Firm 1		Firm 2		
Job	Cost estimate	Price bid	Cost estimate	Price bid	Winning firm
1	\$630	\$680	\$480	\$530	2
2	720	770	660	710	2
3	540	590	600	650	1
4	660	710	540	590	2
5	480	530	720	770	1
6	570	620	600	650	1

	Anticipated income	Actual income
Firm 1	(590 − 540) + (530 − 480) + (620 − 570) = \$150	(590 − 580) + (530 − 600) + (620 − 590) = −\$30
Firm 2	(530 − 480) + (710 − 660) + (590 − 540) = \$150	(530 − 570) + (710 − 660) + (590 − 600) = \$0

The phenomenon that occurs in the example is that firm 1 gets all the jobs where the ratio of M_i to L_i is less than 2:1, and Firm 2 gets the jobs where the ratio is greater than 2:1. In no case does a firm overestimate the job cost and then win the bidding competition. As a result, the actual profits turn out to be significantly lower than the $50 per job anticipated by the firms.

Is this a problem that will correct itself over time? Not as long as firm 1 sticks to its materials-based estimation, and firm 2 sticks to its labor-based estimation. Based on its experience above, firm 1 would find a new rate per unit of material required ($33.4 instead of $30), but it would still get the labor-intensive jobs, while the material-intensive jobs would go to firm 2. The cost estimation techniques, combined with the bidding strategies, effectively push the firms into different market segments.

Of course, it is simple for us to suggest that the firms use a cost estimation of $200 for set-up, $10 per unit of material, and $20 per unit of labor, and in this simple example, we would expect that the firms would adopt this approach. But for many products and services, the number of factors that influence cost is quite large. It is unlikely that any one firm's costing system will take all factors into account, so it is possible that the cost estimation systems will influence which companies get which types of jobs.

8.6 INFORMATION ANALYSIS

In bidding situations such as those discussed above, should the manager use resources to get better information about the cost of fulfilling the contract? In situations we have analyzed before, the EVPI has always been non-negative. That is, at worst an item of (costless) information did no harm. *But* these results occurred when the acquisition of information did not affect the underlying probabilities of costs or of a competitor's behavior. In a competitive bidding situation, the competitor may know that we acquired additional information, and his or her bidding strategy may be affected even without seeing the contents of the additional cost report. In this situation, it is *possible* that the EVPI can be negative![5]

Before we turn to an example, let us consider the situation from the competitor's point of view. Suppose that the government was opening up a new tract of offshore property for oil exploration, and two oil firms were going to bid on the lease. Each firm has conducted its own geological surveys and has arrived at an estimate (probability distribution) of the value of the recoverable oil. As one of the firms, we have arrived at a price that we will bid, which is some percentage of the estimated value. Then we find out that the other firm has been operating wells in a tract adjacent to the one being bid on. As a result, the other firm has much better information about the value of the tract we are bidding on. Would we change our bidding strategy? The answer is probably yes, because of the winner's paradox. If the other firm knows the value of the tract exactly, then we can *only* win the bid if we overestimate the value.

Let's explore these issues with an example. Suppose that we are operating an electronics firm that is bidding to supply a component to a customer. There is one other firm that is bidding to supply the part, and since both firms are equally capable of

[5]For a further analysis of such situations, see Baiman (1975) and Wilson (1969).

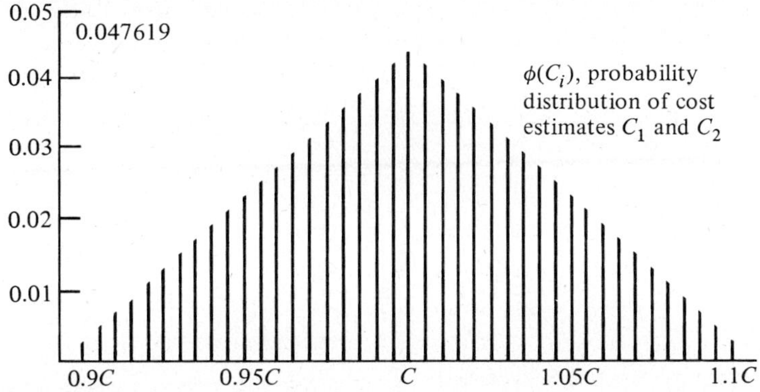

Figure 8.6

supplying the component, the customer will choose the supplier with the lower bid. We have conducted a fairly thorough engineering study of the component, and this study has provided a cost estimate C_1 to produce the components required by the customer. Our competitor has gone through a similar process, and has an estimate C_2, but we don't know the value of C_2. Both C_1 and C_2 are only estimates of the actual cost C of supplying the components. For this example, we will assume that the cost estimates are drawn from the *discrete triangular* probability distribution depicted in Figure 8.6. The most likely occurrence is that $C_i = C$, but there is less than 0.05 chance of this happening. The worst underestimate is 90% of C, and the worst overestimate is 110% of C.

Our bidding strategy involves choosing a mark-up percentage m_1 to be applied to our cost estimate. That is, the price that we will bid is $(1 + m_1)C_1$, and since the competitor is doing the same analysis their bid will be $(1 + m_2)C_2$. We will win the bid if $(1 + m_1)C_1$ is less than $(1 + m_2)C_2$, and the profit we make will be $(1 + m_1)C_1 - C$. For each combination of margins, m_1 and m_2, we can calculate the expected profit for firm 1

$$E[\pi_1 \mid m_1, m_2] = \sum_{C_1} \sum_{C_2} [(1 + m_1)C_1 - C]\theta_1(C_1, m_1, C_2, m_2)\phi(C_1)\phi(C_2) \quad (8.11)$$

where $\theta_1(C_1, m_1, C_1, m_2)$ is the probability that firm 1 will win the bid, given the cost estimates and the mark-ups.

$$\theta_1(C_1, m_1, C_2, m_2) \equiv \begin{cases} 1, & \text{if } (1 + m_1)C_1 < (1 + m_2)C_2 \\ 1/2, & \text{if } (1 + m_1)C_1 = (1 + m_2)C_2 \\ 0, & \text{if } (1 + m_1)C_1 > (1 + m_2)C_2 \end{cases} \quad (8.12)$$

The same sort of expected payoff function can be calculated for the competitor. A compilation of $E[\pi_1 \mid m_1, m_2]$ and $E[\pi_2 \mid m_1, m_2]$ appears in Table 8.5. (The numbers in the table are measured as a proportion of C, so if C is \$1 million and $m_1 = m_2 = 0.11$, each of the firms has an expected profit of \$41,420 or 4.142% of C.)

What are we looking for in Table 8.5? There are various bidding strategies, and we can see that our expected payoff depends both on our own m_1 *and* on the competitor's m_2. It would be best for *us* to have $m_1 = 0.09$ and $m_2 = 0.11$, because our expected

TABLE 8.5 EXPECTED PAYOFFS[a] TO TWO COMPETING FIRMS AFTER ENGINEERING STUDIES

Our firm's margin, m_1	Competitor's margin, m_2 0.06	0.07	0.08	0.09	0.10	0.11
0.06	0.01704 (0.01704)	0.02010 (0.01855)	0.02419 (0.01844)	0.02844 (0.01763)	0.03270 (0.01628)	0.03670 (0.01472)
0.07	0.01855 (0.02010)	0.02191 (0.02191)	0.02538 (0.02302)	0.03012 (0.02227)	0.03499 (0.02085)	0.03980 (0.01898)
0.08	0.01844 (0.02419)	0.02302 (0.02538)	0.02679 (0.02679)	0.03070 (0.02746)	0.03608 (0.02608)	0.04157 (0.02405)
0.09	0.01763 (0.02844)	0.02227 (0.03012)	0.02746 (0.03070)	0.03167 (0.03167)	0.03604 (0.03188)	0.04206 (0.02987)
0.10	0.01628 (0.03270)	0.02085 (0.03499)	0.02608 (0.03608)	0.03188 (0.03604)	0.03655 (0.03655)	0.04139 (0.03628)
0.11	0.01472 (0.03670)	0.01898 (0.03980)	0.02405 (0.04157)	0.02987 (0.04206)	0.03628 (0.04139)	0.04142 (0.04142)

[a]All numbers in the table are measured as a proportion of the true cost C. The first number is $E[\pi_1 \mid m_1, m_2]$, and the number below, in parentheses, is $E[\pi_2 \mid m_1, m_2]$.

payoff would be 0.04206, the highest in the table. But we cannot expect this to happen because the competitor can raise his or her expected payoff from 0.02987 to 0.03188 by reducing m_2 from 0.11 to 0.10. That is, $m_1 = 0.09$ and $m_2 = 0.11$ is not an *equilibrium*. Is there any combination of m_1 and m_2 where neither party can unilaterally make itself better off?[6] Yes, the combination of $m_1 = m_2 = 0.10$ is the only one that satisfies these conditions, and at this equilibrium both firms have an expected profit margin of 0.03655 of C.

But now suppose that our firm has the opportunity to produce a prototype of the electronic component before we make a bid. To keep the example simple, suppose that producing the prototype would enable our firm to discern the cost of fulfilling the order C. The situation changes, because we no longer have to worry about the winner's paradox, but it becomes a more serious problem for the competitor. Our firm's expected payoff can again be calculated.

$$E[\pi_1 \mid m_1, m_2] = \sum_{C_2} (m_1 C)\theta_1(C, m_1, C_2, m_2)\phi(C_2) \tag{8.13}$$

$$\text{where} \quad \theta_1(C, m_1, C_2, m_2) = \begin{cases} 1, & \text{if } (1 + m_1)C < (1 + m_2)C_2 \\ 1/2, & \text{if } (1 + m_1)C = (1 + m_2)C_2 \\ 0, & \text{if } (1 + m_1)C > (1 + m_2)C_2 \end{cases}$$

From the definition of $\theta_1(\cdot)$, we can see that if $m_1 = m_2$, we will lose those jobs ($\theta_1 = 0$) where $C > C_2$, that is, where the competitor underestimated the cost. A compilation of expected payoffs appears in Table 8.6.

[6]Such a combination is called a *Nash equilibrium*. See Davis (1973).

TABLE 8.6 EXPECTED PAYOFFS[a] TO TWO COMPETING FIRMS AFTER PROTOTYPE IS BUILT

Our firm's margin, m_1	Competitor's margin, m_2 0.06	0.07	0.08	0.09	0.10	0.11
.06	0.03000 (0.01149)	0.03415 (0.01172)	0.03918 (0.01027)	0.04367 (0.00867)	0.04762 (0.00702)	0.05102 (0.00539)
.07	0.03016 (0.01588)	0.03500 (0.01632)	0.03984 (0.01585)	0.04571 (0.01358)	0.05095 (0.01125)	0.05556 (0.00896)
.08	0.02776 (0.02202)	0.03447 (0.02140)	0.04000 (0.02114)	0.04553 (0.01999)	0.05224 (0.01688)	0.05823 (0.01382)
.09	0.02449 (0.02829)	0.03122 (0.02839)	0.03878 (0.02692)	0.04500 (0.02597)	0.05122 (0.02413)	0.05878 (0.02019)
.10	0.02063 (0.03450)	0.02721 (0.03542)	0.03469 (0.03476)	0.04304 (0.03244)	0.05000 (0.03079)	0.05692 (0.02826)
.11	0.01646 (0.04044)	0.02270 (0.04231)	0.02993 (0.04256)	0.03816 (0.04113)	0.04739 (0.03796)	0.05500 (0.03562)

[a]As in Table 8.5, all numbers are measured as a proportion of C. The first number is $E[\pi_1 \mid m_1, m_2]$, and the number below, in parentheses, is $E[\pi_2 \mid m_1, m_2]$.

When only the engineering studies were done, the two firms' equilibrium mark-ups were 10% over estimated cost. *If* those mark-ups are maintained after our firm builds the prototype, then the information gained causes our expected profit to rise from 3.655% to 5% of C. At the same time, the competitor's expected payoff drops from 3.655% to 3.079% of C. But we can also see that $m_1 = m_2 = 0.10$ is no longer an equilibrium. If we can hide the fact that we built a prototype, and the competitor continues with $m_2 = 0.10$, then we can improve our expected payoff still further by reducing our margin to $m_2 = 0.08$. This is because our competitor thinks we're playing the bidding game in Table 8.5, while we know we're playing the game in Table 8.6.

If we cannot build the prototype without the competitor knowing about it, then we must look for an equilibrium in Table 8.6. The only equilibrium point is at $m_1 = m_2 = 0.07$; that is, each firm uses a 7% mark-up over its cost estimate. And our firm would have an expected payoff of 3.5% of C, *less* then the equilibrium payoff before we built the prototype! Therefore, building the prototype and finding C makes our firm worse off, even before we count the costs of the prototype. Why does this happen? Because we are no longer subject to the winner's paradox, it is to our advantage to reduce our markup, since it increases the probability of our winning the bid enough to offset the decline in mark-up.[7] But this increases the competitive pressure on the other firm's manager, and causes him or her to reduce margin m_2 also. The result is that the equilibrium is at $m_1 = m_2 = 0.07$, and we are worse off than before we built the prototype.

[7]If $m_2 = 0.1$, and we reduce m_1 from 0.1 to 0.08, the probability of our winning the bid increases from 0.5 to about 0.653. Therefore, the expected profit goes from $0.1 \times 0.5 = 0.05$ to $0.08 \times 0.653 = 0.05224$.

8.7 SUMMARY

We have tried in this chapter to analyze the effect that competition has on the importance of the cost information system. In the first sections we found that the expected margin affected the value of cost information in accept/reject decisions, and the demand curve's slope affected the value of cost information in activity level decisions. In general, greater competition increased the value of information about costs.

In competitive bidding situations, there is a phenomenon called the *winner's paradox,* where the firm that submits the winning bid is the one that has most likely underestimated the cost of fulfilling the contract. The degree of expected underestimation increases as the number of competitors increases, and is greater as the level of cost uncertainty is greater. As a result, a firm must add a margin to its cost estimate in order to expect to breakeven. Differences in accounting allocations may compound this problem and inhibit its correction.

Analyzing the usefulness of cost information in these settings can be quite difficult. If our acquisition of information has no effect on the behavior of our competitors, then the information analysis can proceed as in Chapter 3. This condition might hold if there are many competitors, or if the quality of cost information could be kept secret. But if there are few competitors, and each is aware of the quality of information received by the others, then information analysis becomes much more difficult, and it is even possible that improved information may make the decision maker worse off.

PROBLEMS

8.1. Jeffrey Allen has the responsibility of determining the pricing and production of his company's major product. A substantial amount of market research as already been conducted to estimate the consumer response to the product, so one period's demand curve is believed to be reflected in the following relationships.

$$\text{Demand} = (8{,}000 - 1{,}000 \times \text{Price}) \text{ units}$$
$$\text{Revenue} = 8 \times (\text{units sold}) - 0.001 \times (\text{units sold})^2$$

The production cost behavior is less certain, since the variable cost per unit is not known. For simplicity, assume that there are three possible cost relationships, each equally likely.

$$\text{Possibility 1: Cost} = 1.00 \times (\text{units produced})$$
$$\text{Possibility 2: Cost} = 1.05 \times (\text{units produced})$$
$$\text{Possibility 3: Cost} = 1.10 \times (\text{units produced})$$

Required

A. For *each* of the above cost possibilities, determine the optimal price, output, and profit, assuming that all units produced are sold.

B. Given the current level of uncertainty and an objective of maximizing expected profit, what is the best price/output combination? What is the expected profit?

C. What is the expected value of perfect information about the variable cost per unit, assuming an objective of maximizing expected profit?

D. How would your answers to the above questions change if the revenue curve were changed to the following?
(a) Revenue $= 8 \times$ (units sold) $- 0.002 \times$ (units sold)^2.
(b) Revenue $= 8 \times$ (units sold) $- 0.005 \times$ (units sold)^2.

8.2. Software Consultants is in the business of customizing computer programs for small businesses in the Los Angeles area. For the most part, this customization is based on existing data base and spreadsheet programs, with Software Consultants setting up the accounts and functions to suit the client.

The operations manager has just received an offer from one of the company's clients to design some customized software from scratch. The client is willing to pay \$20,000 for the program, but the costs of producing the program are quite a bit more uncertain than the company's normal business. The costs could be \$12,000 or \$16,000, each with probability 1/4 or \$14,000, with probability 1/2. The same resources could be used to produce a margin of \$5,000 with certainty in the company's normal business.

Required

A. If the operating manager wishes to maximize the expected value of the profit that can be earned with the resources, what would be the expected value of perfect information (EVPI) about the cost of producing the software?

B. How would your answer in part A change if the possible cost outcomes were \$11,000 or \$14,000 or \$17,000, all with equal probability?

C. How would your answer in part A change if the margin that could be earned on normal business was \$3,000? If it were \$9,000?

8.3. Refer to the original information in Problem 8.2. However, suppose that the operations manager is risk-averse, and would accept the special project if the expected utility that it produces is greater than that which can be achieved by using the same resources to complete a normal project. The operations manager's utility for incremental profit is reflected in the following function:

$$U[\text{incremental profit}] = (-2{,}000 + \text{incremental profit})^{1/2}$$

Required

A. What is the maximum amount that the operations manager would be willing to pay for perfect information about the cost of producing the software?

B. How would your answer to part A change if the three cost outcomes were all equally likely?

8.4. The Biltrite Company produces two products which are similar in many respects. They both require the same amount of capacity to produce a unit, and they have identical demand curves. The only difference is that the variable costs for product 1 are known, while the variable costs for product 2 are uncertain.

	Product 1	Product 2
Number of units	X_1	X_2
Total revenue curve	$50X_1 - 0.005(X_1)^2$	$50X_2 - 0.005(X_2)^2$
Total variable cost	$30X_1$	$\begin{Bmatrix} 25X_2 \text{ with probability } 1/2 \\ 35X_2 \text{ with probability } 1/2 \end{Bmatrix}$

Required

A. If there are no capacity constraints and management's objective is to attain the highest expected contribution margin, how much of each product should be produced based on the existing information? What is the expected value of perfect information about product 2's variable cost?

B. Suppose that the company only has enough capacity to produce 3,000 units in total. How much of each unit should be produced based on the existing information? What is the expected value of perfect information about product 2's variable cost?

C. Suppose that product 1's revenue curve were changed to

$$60X_1 - 0.005(X_1)^2$$

How would the EVPI be affected in parts A and B above?

8.5. "We've analyzed our competition pretty closely on this project. Of course, we don't know exactly what they're going to bid, but we have a pretty good feeling for the parameters. This customer always seems to choose the lowest bid when it lets out projects like this one. If we bid less than \$200,000, we'll get the project for sure, and if we bid more than \$300,000, we don't stand a chance. In between those two extremes, I guess you can extrapolate—if we bid \$250,000 there's a 50–50 chance we'll get the job, if we bid \$225,000 there's a 75% chance, and so on."

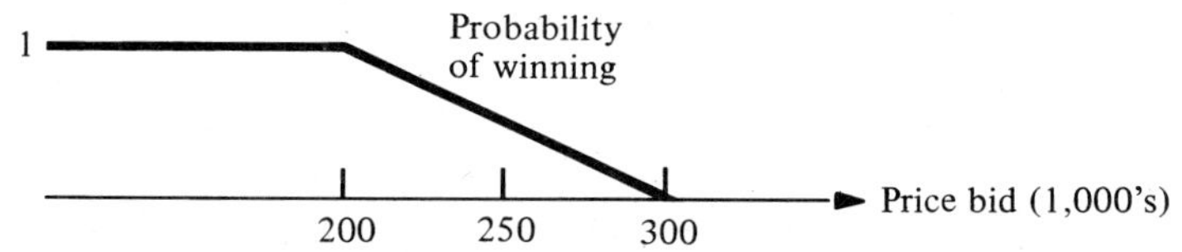

Required

A. If the project cost will be \$220,000, and if the management's objective is to maximize the expected contribution on the project, what is the optimal bid?

B. If the costs are not known with certainty, but can be \$200,000 or \$240,000 (each with probability 1/2), what is the optimal bid?

C. How much would it be worth to resolve the cost uncertainty in B above?

8.6. Patton Electronics is planning to submit a bid for a government contract to supply electronic components on a defense project. There are a number of technical difficulties to be overcome, so there is some uncertainty about the cost of supplying the components. Therefore, the contract will be a cost plus fixed fee arrangement, but with an upper limit on the government's payment. At this point, Patton's engineers have estimated that the costs of fulfilling the contract will be between \$15 million and \$19 million. The company is trying to decide between two contract possibilities. There is one other company that will be bidding on the contract.

Bid alternative	Fixed fee	Limit on total government payment	Probability of winning the contract
1	\$1,000,000	\$19,000,000	2/3
2	1,500,000	19,000,000	1/2

A. If the company wanted to maximize its expected profit, what bid alternative should it submit?

B. Which of the bidding alternatives is riskier?

C. Patton's engineers have proposed an experimental prototype that should provide some information on the project's cost. The company's bid must be submitted within the next two months, so the prototype would require a crash program costing \$300,000. Should the company go ahead with this program?

8.7. A large regional bank decided that it will no longer provide its own maintenance services, but will contract with an outside supplier of these services. The bank has about twenty-five branches in the area, and it has developed a list of services and service standards which it expects the supplier to provide. The bank has provided the list to all qualified maintenance service organizations in the area, and has requested a bid for one year's service. The bank intends to accept the lowest bid.

Each potential supplier must make an estimate of the cost of providing service to the bank for one year, and then determine a bid based on that information. Of course, it is impossible to determine the cost exactly, so each potential supplier gets an estimate with the following characteristics:

Estimate as a percent of actual cost	Probability
90	1/3
100	1/3
110	1/3

That is, there is an equal probability that the cost estimate will be 90% of the actual costs, exactly equal to the actual costs, or 110% of actual costs.

Assume that each potential supplier will add a 15% margin to the estimated cost in arriving at the price to be bid on the contract.

Required

A. If there is only one company bidding on the contract, what is the expected profit (as a percent of costs)?

B. If there are two companies bidding on the contract, what is the expected profit (as a percent of costs) for the company that wins the contract? If there are three companies?

C. Suppose that, for some reason, there was one bidder that had perfect information about the cost of providing service to the bank, while you have estimates with the characteristics above. Would it make sense to go ahead with a bid for the contract? Would the bid be different than in the case where all firms have information of the same quality?

8.8. The Crown Company was a small, family-run manufacturer until it was purchased by a group of investors led by Sally Graff. The investors had known that the company was in dire need of modern management techniques, including a new information system, but they had not anticipated the lack of even basic information for decision making. "The family ran the business to meet their needs, and operated out of their hip pockets," explained Sally Graff. "Since they had been in business for a long time, they did pretty well just by intuition. At the moment, we're just trying to keep things on an even keel while we develop the information systems that we need. If I can just keep a positive contribution margin for the next couple of months, I'll be satisfied."

"For instance, we have almost no information about the costs of individual jobs. We have to bid for orders with our customers, based on their specifications for the product, but the old management only kept cost data at the most aggregate level. For instance, we know the total number of jobs done in the last two months, and we know the labor costs for the period, but there is no direct tracing of the labor costs to the jobs handled. The data we have are shown below. I don't want to include older data, since there were some changes that make that information less relevant."

"We have some jobs (shown below) that I'd like to bid on, but I need to get an estimate of the cost before I'll know what price to bid. As I'm getting to know the market, I plan to add a 40% mark-up over the estimated variable costs of producing the job."

Month	Variable production cost	No. of Jobs	Units completed
1	$140,000	200	300,000
2	164,000	250	320,000

Proposed job	Number of units
1	4,000
2	2,000
3	500
4	1,000

Required

A. If the cost estimates are based only on the number of jobs done and not on the number of units, what will be the amount estimated and bid for each of the proposed jobs?

B. If the cost estimates are based only on the number of units and not on the number of jobs done, what will be the amount estimated and bid for each of the proposed jobs?

C. If the cost estimates are based on the number of jobs done *and* on the number of units, what will be the amount estimated and bid for each of the proposed jobs.

D. Suppose that Sally Graff uses the estimates and bids in part A, while one of her competitors uses the estimates and bids from part B. Which jobs will her company get? What is the expected profit on those jobs?

8.9. For this exercise you will be a member of the management team of an electronics company that is growing rapidly. The balance sheet and income statement for the last year appear below. A large part of the firm's original equity was provided by a venture capital company, and many of the employees own significant numbers of shares.

In the last six weeks, the company has been approached by four potential customers who are interested in having your firm develop and produce components for use in their products. They will reimburse the costs of development, but they want you to bid a fixed price for the production of a contracted number of components. You will receive estimates of the incremental production cost of each product, but you know that these estimates are not necessarily very precise since each of these products has unique features that you have not dealt with before. In addition, you have enough capacity to handle two of the orders with no trouble, but if you manage to get three or four orders, you will have to quickly get the additional people and production facilities to meet the contract schedules. If you get three orders, the costs of producing them will go up 10%. If you get all four, the increase is 20%.

You will be bidding against two competitors. These firms are very similar to your own, and each has the engineering capability to complete the orders. Therefore, the customers will probably choose the firm that submits the lowest bid. The costs of fulfilling each contract would be the same for each firm, unless a firm gets three or more of the contracts.

For each contract, you will be given an estimate of the costs of fulfilling the contract, and a measure of the accuracy of the cost estimate—its standard deviation. For example, if your cost estimate is $700,000 with a standard deviation of 50,000, you can assume that the actual cost is normally distributed with about 67% chance of being between $650,000 and $750,000. Your competitors have estimates of *similar quality,* although they are not the same estimates.

During class you will be given the cost estimates, and you will have the opportunity to purchase more cost information that will cut the standard deviation in half. This information will come from special engineering studies that will cost $15,000 each. If you decide to conduct these studies, you will receive the updated cost estimates. Then each firm must submit a sealed bid on each contract. The contracts will be awarded to the lowest bidder. After the profitability of each firm has been determined, another four projects will be proposed for a second operating period.

Balance sheet (000)

Cash	$ 3,138	Accounts payable	1,512
Accounts receivable	4,145	Accrued liabilities	1,078
Inventories		Current maturities	
Raw materials and parts	1,545	Long-term debt	472
Work in progress	2,007	Capital lease obligations	102
Finished goods	1,654	Total current liabilities	$ 3,164
Prepaid expenses	161		
Total current assets	$12,650	Long-term debt	$ 4,164
		Capital lease obligations	708
Property, plant, and equipment, at cost		Deferred income taxes	33
Land and property	$ 2,596	Total liabilities	$ 8,069
Machinery and equipment	3,901		
Furniture and fixtures	603	Common stock at par	611
Tools, dies, jigs, and fixtures	399		
	$ 7,499	Additional paid-in-capital	2,226
Less accumulated depreciation	3,945	Retained earnings	5,849
Property, plant, and equipment, net	3,554	Less stock held in Treasury	120
Other assets and deferred charges	431	Total owner's equity	$ 8,566
Total assets	$16,635	Total equity	$16,635

Income statement (000)

Net sales revenue	$14,976
Cost of goods sold	9,072
Gross earnings	$ 5,904
Selling, general, and administrative expenses	$ 3,542
Earnings from operations	$ 2,362
Interest earned	$ 271
Interest charges on debt	527
Other charges	35
Earnings before income tax	$ 2,071
Provision for income tax	787
Net income	$ 1,284

REFERENCES

Baiman, S. ''The Evaluation and Choice of Internal Information Systems within a Multi-person World,'' *Journal of Accounting Research*. Spring 1975.

Brown, K. ''A Note on Optimal Fixed-Price Bidding with Uncertain Production Costs,'' *Bell Journal of Economics*. Autumn 1975.

Davis, M., *Game Theory: A Nontechnical Introduction*. New York: Basic Books. 1973.

Hilton, R. ''The Determinants of Cost Information Value: An Illustrative Analysis,'' *Journal of Accounting Research*. Autumn 1979.

Wilson R. ''Competitive Bidding with Disparate Information,'' *Management Science*. March 1969.

Chapter 9

Cost Variances and Control

At this point in our study of managerial accounting issues, we begin to look at new ways in which accounting reports may be used. Up to this point, our attention has been focused on the use of accounting information in the planning process. In the planning process there was a single decision point, and the decision maker was left with no recourse to alter the decision later on. While there are some decisions like this, such as strategic product line decisions or diversification decisions, a significant part of management decision making concerns ongoing operations.

Much of the decision making for ongoing operations is of the *control* type. For instance, most organizations go through a yearly planning/budgeting process in which courses of action are planned for the year and expectations about external (uncontrollable) states of nature are formed. These plans and expectations are combined to form a set of budgeted costs and profits for the various responsibility centers or subunits in the organization. As time passes and operations proceed, there may be a variety of reasons why the reported costs and profits differ from those that were budgeted. The purpose of control actions is, on the receipt of an accounting report of cost or profit, to ascertain whether the agreed-upon actions were the ones taken, whether the actual states of nature differed from the expectations, and, finally, whether some corrective or adaptive action is appropriate.

While there are some differences between one-time planning decisions and ongoing control decisions, our approach to information planning is still based on the effects of information on decision making. In this chapter, we will explore ways to make the best use of a given cost variance system. Once that groundwork has been established, we can explore the effects of changes in the variance system (e.g., frequency, level of aggregation) in Chapter 10.

9.1 THE THEORY BEHIND COST VARIANCES

The outcomes of economic activity are the result of many factors and many people's decisions. For instance, the contribution margin on a sale depends on decisions made by the sales personnel, the customer, the production personnel (including production scheduler, supervisors, assembly-line employees, etc.), purchasing personnel, suppliers, as well as on events that are controlled by nature (weather, technological breakthroughs, etc.). At the initial planning stage, a manager may make assessments of those factors that are beyond his or her control, and then choose a course of action that leads to the most preferred probability distribution of outcomes (as in Chapter 2). At the control stage, a period of operation is complete, and the usual objective is to determine, as well as possible, the factors which caused the economic outcomes that were achieved. Then corrections, modifications, and adjustments can be made to improve the next period's outcome probabilities. We could look at the control process as one of sequential acquisition of information. The initial set of variances is used to determine which areas need to be investigated further, until the corrections and adjustments are completed.

The objective of variances is to facilitate the search and correction process by disaggregating the economic outcomes. If an aggregate outcome (e.g., cost), is the result of more than one action and state, then a set of variances divides this aggregate outcome in a way that facilitates the control process. Suppose that cost x depends on two actions a^1 and a^2, and on two states of nature s^1 and s^2. If the agreed-upon actions are $\bar{a}^1$ and $\bar{a}^2$, and the forecasted states are $\bar{s}^1$ and $\bar{s}^2$, then actual costs will be $x(a^1, a^2, s^1, s^2)$, and the cost budget will be $x(\bar{a}^1, \bar{a}^2, \bar{s}^1, \bar{s}^2)$. The total cost variance V will be the following.

$$V = x - \bar{x} = x(a^1, a^2, s^1, s^2) - x(\bar{a}^1, \bar{a}^2, \bar{s}^1, \bar{s}^2) \tag{9.1}$$

Of course, there are a variety of reasons why V may be positive (unfavorable) or negative (favorable), and if the manager wants to determine the cause of a variance, he or she must check four possible sources (both actions and both states). However, a set of variances could divide the total variance. For instance, if $x(a^1, a^2, s^1, s^2) = y_1(a^1) + y_2(a^2) + z_1(s^1) + z_2(s^2)$, then V can be divided as follows.

$$\begin{aligned} V &= x - \bar{x} \\ &= [y_1(a^1) - y_1(\bar{a}^1)] + [y_2(a^2) - y_2(\bar{a}^2)] \\ &\quad + [z_1(s^1) - z_1(\bar{s}^1)] + [z_2(s^2) - z_2(\bar{s}^2)] \\ &= V_1 + V_2 + V_3 + V_4 \end{aligned} \tag{9.2}$$

If a system of variances can succeed in this division, the job of making control decisions is made much simpler. If we want to know the effect of action a^1 on the total cost variance, we look at V_1. There are no other factors cluttering up the picture. In other words, we have a measure that depends on the specific action, with no uncontrollable factors to make evaluation difficult. Of course, it is usually difficult (i.e., very costly) to define and report a set of variances that are completely successful in accomplishing this objective, and, moreover, it would not be keeping with the sequential information aspect of the control process. More likely, the first round of variance reports might try to separate the effects of a^1 and s^1 from those of a^2 and s^2, leaving the manager to decide which areas to investigate further.

To illustrate, take the case of a set of variances for a direct cost, such as labor or materials.[1] The actual amount of this direct cost is

$$A = (AP)(AU)(AX) \tag{9.3}$$

where $AP \equiv$ the *actual* price paid per unit of input
$AU \equiv$ the *actual* number of units of input used per unit of output
$AX \equiv$ the *actual* number of units of output produced.

The budgeted direct cost B, is equal to $(BP)(BU)(BX)$, where BP, BU, and BX are defined similarly to AP, AU, and AX, except that the term "actual" is replaced by "budgeted." The *budget variance* is equal to the difference between actual costs and budgeted costs, and it is easy to see that this variance may be caused by actual prices, usages and/or output not being equal to the budgeted amount. As seen below, a set of variances can be defined that attempt to separate these effects.

$$\begin{aligned}
\text{Budget variance} &= A - B = (AP)(AU)(AX) - (BP)(BU)(BX) \\
&= \{(AP)(AU)(AX) - (BP)(BU)(AX)\} + \{(BP)(BU)(AX - BX)\} \\
&= \text{flexible budget variance} + \text{budget adjustment variance} \qquad (9.4) \\
&= \{(AP - BP)(AU)(AX)\} + \{(BP)(AU - BU)(AX)\} + \{(BP)(BU)(AX - BX)\} \\
&= \text{price variance} + \text{usage variance} + \text{budget adjustment variance}
\end{aligned}$$

The objective of these variances (which may be applied to direct materials or labor) is to separate the effects of price, usage, and activity on costs. The first two variances might be used to evaluate the purchasing and production activities, respectively, while the third variance removes the (perhaps uncontrollable) effect of output fluctuations. Unfortunately, there may be a number of reasons why the variances may not completely attain their objective.

For instance, let us look at the price variance. If $AP = BP$, then the variance is zero, regardless of the values of AU and AX. However, if $AP > BP$ (an unfavorable price variance), then the *size* of the variance depends on the usage and output, neither of which are a part of the purchasing function. Of course, we can further divide the price variance as

$$\begin{aligned}
\text{Price variance} &= (AP - BP)(AU)(AX) \\
&= (AP - BP)(BU)(AX) + (AP - BP)(AU - BU)(AX) \qquad (9.5) \\
&= \text{pure price variance} + \text{joint price–quantity variance}
\end{aligned}$$

but to which function (purchasing or production or both or neither) is the joint price–quantity variance to be ascribed? That is, if it is unfavorable, where should we look for the cause?

There are a variety of other reasons why interpretation of variances may be difficult, for example, the variances may be "noisy" indicators of the underlying decisions and events. Suppose that purchasing could decrease input price by buying lower quality input, resulting in higher material input levels. In this case, $AP < BP$ leads to $AU > BU$, and the unfavorable usage variances are not indicative of the source of the problem. Or alternatively, it may be that the flexible budget assumption of linear costs is not exactly true, so that the level of activity can affect the flexible budget variance. If the budgeting system is incorrect or incomplete, this can make variance interpretation much more

[1] A listing of standard variances appears in Appendix 9.1.

difficult. We will return to this issue in Chapter 10. Further, there are many other factors that affect a variance that are not controllable by the manager responsible for the variance, and the effect of these factors on decision making will be examined in Chapter 11.

This leads to the information issues concerning variances. How many variances should be computed? We could develop a set for each department, or each product line, or each type of input (material and labor), or each machine, and so on. In other words, how far are we willing to disaggregate? Aggregation means that we lose information, but it requires less detail in record keeping. In essence, we face the same issues we did in accounting for planning decisions. For example, the plantwide overhead allocation rate that makes planning difficult also makes it difficult to discern whether an overhead variance is caused by inefficiency or by the fact that the allocation rate does not describe the way costs behave.

Before we can address these information questions, we must find out what will be done with these cost variances. That is, how do the cost variances affect the investigation decisions and, ultimately, the costs incurred by the organization? We shall address this question in the sections that follow.

9.2 COST VARIANCE INVESTIGATIONS

When a manager receives a cost variance report, what should he or she do? Let's say that the variance is an unfavorable material price variance. There are a variety of events (or states of nature) that could have caused that variance. It could have resulted from an uncontrollable, random event that will not affect future costs at all, for example, temporary price fluctuations or a higher price paid for a special rush order. Or it may be that the variance was caused by an uncontrollable factor that is expected to continue, for example, a permanent change in the raw material price. Finally, the variance may have resulted from some inefficiencies in the material purchasing operation that will continue until corrected, for example, not taking advantage of quantity discounts. There are other possibilities (e.g., an accounting cost estimation error that causes a variance), but these three basic causes will be our primary concern.

Corresponding to these three causes of cost variance we have three actions that the manager could take *if* he or she knew the cause of the cost variance. If the variance is a random fluctuation, the best action would be to take no action, that is, leave things as they are. If the variance is the result of some permanent change in cost behavior, the manager cannot change the costs but he or she can adapt to them. For example, the manager cannot change the price charged by a raw material supplier, but he or she can adapt by using substitute raw materials or by shifting the product mix to use less of the now expensive input. Finally, if the variance is caused by some correctible inefficiency, then the best managerial response is usually some form of correction that will result in the resumption of efficient operation.

While we've enumerated the possible causes and appropriate actions, the manager's problem is more complicated, since the only information he or she has is a cost variance which could have been caused by a number of things. The cost variance may be a red flag that says "something could be wrong here," but that's about all. In order to determine just what caused the cost variance, the manager must conduct an *investigation,* that

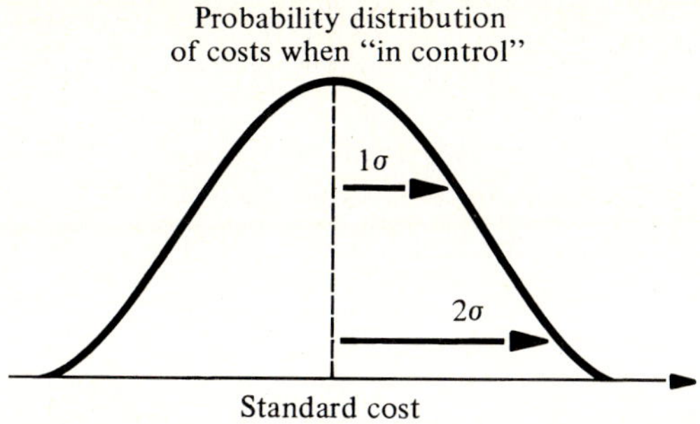

Figure 9.1

is, a search through the (detailed) records of the period's costs to determine what caused the cost variance.[2] For instance, an investigation of a material usage variance could entail an examination of the job tickets for the previous month to find a cause for the additional costs. Was it related to a particular product, foreman, machine, etc.? Knowing the cause, an appropriate action may be taken. In essence, the problem amounts to deciding when to conduct a cost variance investigation. Since cost investigations require resources (labor, computer time, etc.) we only want to conduct such an investigation when the benefits are expected to outweigh the costs.

When shall a manager investigate a cost variance? Obviously not always, since investigating a favorable variance may seem to be a waste of resources. But perhaps all unfavorable variances could be investigated. Or those that exceed budgeted costs by more than 5%, or 10%, or 15%. While these investigation rules are rather easy to implement, they don't explicitly consider the amount of random fluctuation in the costs under consideration. For instance it may not be unusual for a material price variance to exceed 10%, but very unusual for a material usage variance to exceed 2%.

Using the cost estimation techniques that were described in Chapters 5 and 6, we could form a probability distribution of costs when there are no inefficiencies, as in Figure 9.1. (For the time being we will leave out the possibility of permanent, uncontrollable changes in costs. These will be included in a later section.) With this probability distribution we could use a rule like, "Investigate if costs exceed the standard by more than one standard deviation (a 1σ rule)" or ". . . by more than two standard deviations (a 2σ rule)." These rules, which are called *control chart rules,* have some appeal because they are relatively simple to apply and attempt to keep the manager from investigating many variances that are caused by random fluctuations. But they still do not incorporate the costs and benefits of different investigation rules, so we don't know whether to use a 1σ rule, a 3σ rule, 1.5σ rule, and so on.

9.3 A MODEL OF COST BEHAVIOR

There are a variety of methods that may be used to determine an optimal rule for investigating cost variances. Most of the models are based on a common set of assump-

[2]See Demski (1970) for an analysis of the investigation process.

tions about the way that inefficiencies occur and their effect on costs. These assumptions are obvious simplifications of the real world, but they serve as a starting point and can be relaxed later on.

We assume that there are two *states of control:* "in control," θ_1, and "out of control," θ_2. When costs are in control there may be some variances, but these are caused by short-term fluctuations, and there are no controllable inefficiencies that will continue unless corrected. The probability distribution of costs in state θ_1 is depicted by $f_1(x)$ in Figure 9.2. When there are no controllable inefficiencies, the average cost is μ_1, and the standard deviation of costs is σ_1. When there are controllable inefficiencies that will continue until corrected, costs are considered to be out of control with distribution $f_2(x)$ (see Figure 9.2.) If the two distributions don't overlap, then the investigation rule is simple, since the cost reports will give us perfect information about the state of efficiency. If $\bar{x}$ were the highest possible cost when operations were in control, the rule would be "investigate if the costs exceed $\bar{x}$."

In addition to describing how costs behave in each state of control, we must model how inefficiencies develop. As we come into an accounting measurement period, the process generating costs may be either in control or out of control. If there are no inefficiencies at that point, there is a probability, say g, that none will develop, and we will operate in state θ_1 until the start of the next period. On the other hand, there is a probability of $(1 - g)$ that an inefficiency will develop at the start of the accounting period, and we will operate in θ_2 for the period. If the cost process comes into the accounting period in an out-of-control state, then it will stay that way for the entire period. (That is, we assume there is no chance of the process self-correcting. This assumption is easily relaxed and is discussed again at a later point in the chapter.) This transition process is depicted in Figure 9.3.

Before proceeding to an analysis of variance investigations using the model of cost behavior, we should note some of its limitations. In particular, the model assumes that the parameters of the cost process are not affected by the investigation strategy. That is, the values of g, μ_1, μ_2, σ_1, and σ_2 are the same whether we always investigate or never investigate. This lack of response is probably more descriptive of a mechanical system than a human system. That is, a machine's tendency to go out of adjustment is not affected by the frequency with which its output is examined.

On the other hand, we would expect that those aspects of the cost process that are

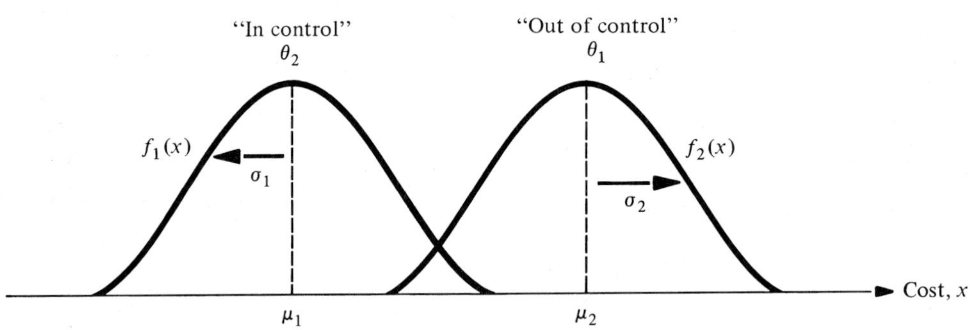

Figure 9.2

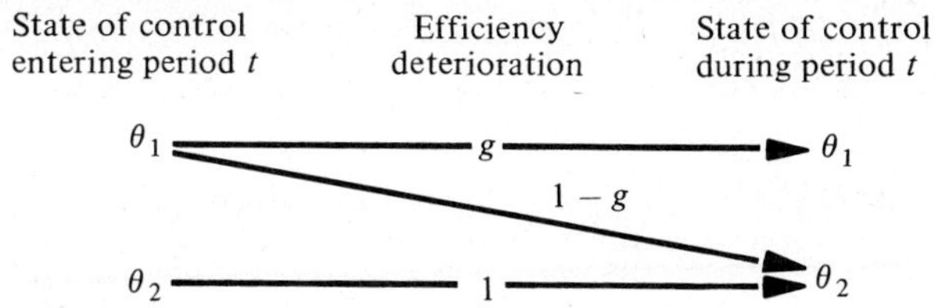

Figure 9.3

controlled by people might very well change as the investigation strategy changes. For instance, suppose that in control means that the person worked as hard (expended as much effort) as he or she was supposed to. If the person doesn't work very hard, the costs tend to increase, and follow the out-of-control distribution. Finding a variance investigation strategy can be rather difficult in this situation. First, we would have to know how the employee was being compensated—straight salary, output incentive, etc. In particular, how do the results of any investigation affect the employee's performance evaluation? If the employee is punished for not working hard, and if we always investigate, the person will know that his or her actions will always be checked, so the probability of slipping to θ_2 is equal to zero. Therefore, it would appear that there is never any need to conduct an investigation. However, if there is never any investigation, the employee's actions will never be checked, and therefore, we would always be operating in θ_2 (assuming that the employee prefers to shirk).

The whole matter of budgeting and variance investigation becomes more difficult when we deal with human systems. Behavioral researchers have found that more well-defined objectives and more frequent and timely feedback influence people's motivation to achieve the objectives. Therefore, a change in the variance reporting system might affect the cost process independently of the investigation strategy. The motivational aspects of performance measurement, budgeting, and investigations will be addressed in the last four chapters of the book. For the rest of this chapter and the next, we will utilize the mechanistic cost process to formulate investigation strategies and to evaluate different variance reporting alternatives.

9.4 AN INVESTIGATION MODEL

The model described in the previous section is a common one in the development of investigation rules. The effect of the investigation is to reverse the deterioration of control depicted in Figure 9.3; that is, to increase the chances of efficient operations. While there are a variety of investigation models[3] to choose from, we will explore one which will be both efficient and easily implemented in most cases. Dittman and Prakash [1978] have developed a control chart approach to variance investigation that weighs the various costs involved so that, in essence, we can decide where to place the control limit, at 1σ or 2σ or wherever.

Basically, a control chart approach involves the choice of a critical value $\overline{X}$, such that whenever costs exceed $\overline{X}$, an investigation is undertaken, incurring a cost of K. The

[3]See Kaplan (1975) and Magee (1976) for reviews and evaluations of variance investigation models.

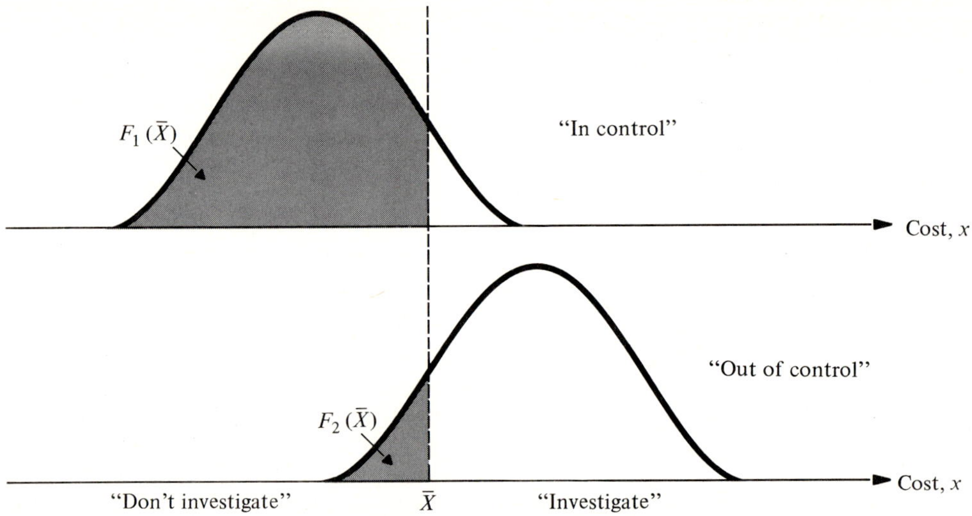

Figure 9.4

effect of such a rule can be seen in Figure 9.4. If costs are in control, then the probability of not investigating is the probability that costs are less than $\bar{X}$. This probability is the shaded area under the $f_1(x)$ curve to the *left* of $\bar{X}$, called $F_1(\bar{X}) \equiv \text{Prob}\ (x < \bar{X}|\theta_1)$. The probability of investigating when the process is in control (and wasting resources) is the area to the right of $\bar{X}$, which is $1 - F_1(\bar{X})$. As we move $\bar{X}$ to the left (right), the probability of this type of mistake increases (decreases). Of course, if we look at the effects of $\bar{X}$ when costs are out of control, the implications are reversed. The mistake occurs where an out-of-control process is not investigated, and the probability of this occurring is the shaded area $F_2(\bar{X})$ in Figure 9.4. The probability of investigating (and correcting) an out of control situation is $1 - F_2(\bar{X})$.

This last amount can be used to depict a complete control cycle by adding the investigation probabilities to Figure 9.3. The complete cycle is shown in Figure 9.5. After an efficiency deterioration, there is a probability of $F_2(\bar{X})$ that the investigation rule will fail to catch the inefficiency and the process will enter period $t + 1$ in state θ_2. If the cost exceeds $\bar{X}$, then the process will be brought back under control entering period $t + 1$.

Of course, this process is repeated, period after period, but the percentage of time that is spent in control will depend on the value of $\bar{X}$ chosen. Define $\pi_1(\bar{X})$ and $\pi_2(\bar{X})$

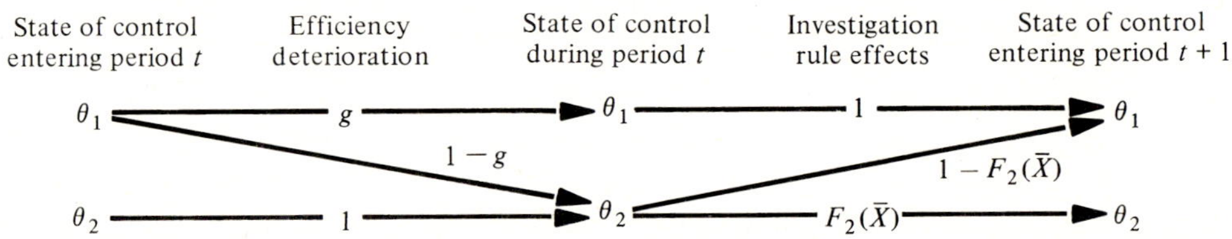

Figure 9.5

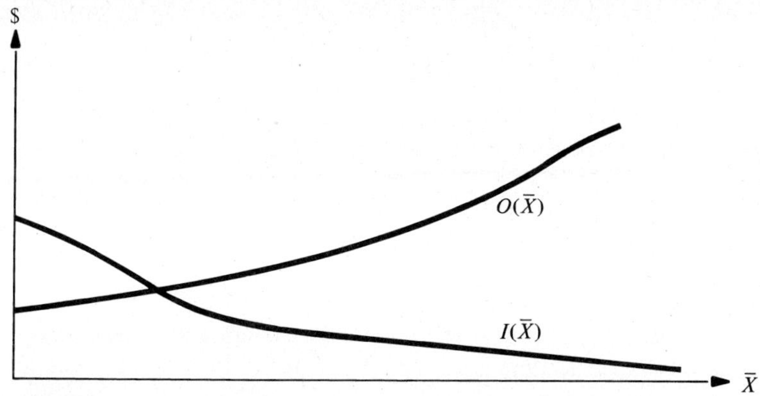

Figure 9.6

to be the long-run probabilities of being in states θ_1 and θ_2, respectively, *during* the accounting period. Obviously, these are important numbers if we are to evaluate different investigation rules. For instance, the expected operating cost per period will be $[\pi_1(\bar{X})\mu_1 + \pi_2(\bar{X})\mu_2]$ if an $\bar{X}$ investigation rule is followed. What are the values of $\pi_1(\bar{X})$ and $\pi_2(\bar{X})$? The derivation of the answer to this question is given in Appendix 9.2, but the answers are the following.

$$\pi_1(\bar{X}) = \frac{g[1 - F_2(\bar{X})]}{1 - gF_2(\bar{X})}$$
$$\pi_2(\bar{X}) = \frac{1 - g}{1 - gF_2(\bar{X})} \tag{9.6}$$

How are these probabilities affected by our choice of $\bar{X}$? As we set $\bar{X}$ higher and higher, the value of $F_2(\bar{X})$ approaches 1, and that would make $\pi_1(\bar{X})$ approach 0, and $\pi_2(\bar{X})$ approach 1. That is, if we never investigate the process, the probability of operating efficiently is zero in the long run. On the other hand, if we set $\bar{X}$ very low so that $F_2(\bar{X})$ approaches 0, then $\pi_1(\bar{X})$ approaches g, and $\pi_2(\bar{X})$ approaches $1 - g$. As we have noted before, there are two types of costs that must be balanced in an effective investigation rule: operating costs and investigation costs. These can be expressed as follows, and are depicted in Figure 9.6.

$$\begin{aligned} O(\bar{X}) &\equiv \text{expected operating cost per period} \\ &= \mu_1(\text{probability in } \theta_1) + \mu_2(\text{probability in } \theta_2) \\ &= \mu_1\pi_1(\bar{X}) + \mu_2\pi_2(\bar{X}) \\ I(\bar{X}) &\equiv \text{expected investigation cost per period} \\ &= K(\text{probability of an investigation}) \\ &= K\{\pi_1(\bar{X})[1 - F_1(\bar{X})] + \pi_2(\bar{X})[1 - F_2(\bar{X})]\} \end{aligned} \tag{9.7}$$

The objective of our choice of a control limit is to minimize the *total* expected cost per period, $O(\bar{X}) + I(\bar{X})$.[4] Unfortunately, this value of $\bar{X}$ may not be easily found. Neither

[4]An alternative objective might be to minimize the expected present value of operating and investigation costs. See Kaplan (1969; 1975).

$O(\overline{X})$ nor $I(\overline{X})$ are easily differentiated, and finding the $\overline{X}$ such that $O'(\overline{X}) + I'(\overline{X}) = 0$ and $0''(\overline{X}) + I''(\overline{X}) > 0$ will not be easy without the use of a computer.

Example The monthly material costs for a particular operation can vary due to temporary price fluctuations or because the purchasing policies are not being followed. When material purchases are in control, they have a monthly average cost of \$10,000 with a standard deviation (estimated from past data) of 500. When there are inefficiencies in purchasing, the average costs increase to \$10,750 per month, and there is more variability so the standard deviation is estimated to be 600. Investigation of a material price variance usually requires an hour of managerial time and some computer time to search through past records, costing a total of \$125. After discovering the inefficiency (if one exists), correction is simply accomplished with a memo, costing a negligible amount. Past experience indicates that the probability of the purchasing process slipping into inefficient operation from one month to the next is 0.15. From this description we can get the estimates necessary to use the cost variance model.

$$\begin{gathered} f_1(X): \text{normal with } \mu_1 = 10{,}000, \sigma_1 = 500 \\ f_2(X): \text{normal with } \mu_2 = 10{,}750, \sigma_2 = 600 \\ g = 0.85; (1 - g) = 0.15 \\ K = 125 \end{gathered} \tag{9.8}$$

We will work through one calculation to see how it is done, but in general it is much easier to let the computer do the work. We will try a value of $\overline{X}$ = \$10,750, which represents a policy of investigating all costs that exceed the average cost when out of control. The value of \$10,750 is 1.5 standard deviations σ_1 to the right of μ_1, so $F_1(10{,}750) = 0.9332$ (see Appendix 4.1.) Since μ_2 = \$10,750, the probability of an out-of-control cost being less than \$10,750 is one-half, so $F_2(10{,}750) = 0.5$. The long-run probabilities can be calculated as follows.

$$\begin{aligned} \pi_1(10{,}750) &= \frac{g[1 - F_2(10{,}750)]}{1 - gF_2(10{,}750)} = \frac{0.85(0.5)}{1 - 0.85(0.5)} = 0.739 \\ \pi_2(10{,}750) &= \frac{1 - g}{1 - gF_2(10{,}750)} = \frac{0.15}{1 - 0.85(0.5)} = 0.261 \end{aligned} \tag{9.9}$$

That is, if $\overline{X} = 10{,}750$, the long-run probability of operating in control during a period is 0.739. From these probabilities we can determine the expected operating and investigation costs per period.

$$\begin{aligned} O(10{,}750) &= 10{,}000\pi_1(10{,}750) + 10{,}750\pi_2(10{,}750) \\ &= 10{,}000(0.739) + 10{,}750(0.261) \\ &= \$10{,}195.75 \\ I(10{,}750) &= 125\{\pi_1(10{,}750)[1 - F_1(10{,}750)] + \pi_2(10{,}750)[1 - F_2(10{,}750)]\} \\ &= 125[(0.739)(0.0668) + (0.261)(0.5)] \\ &= \$22.48 \end{aligned} \tag{9.10}$$

So the expected cost per period from a policy of $\overline{X} = 10{,}750$ is the sum of the operating and investigation costs, or \$10,218.23.

The same computations can be made for other values of $\overline{X}$, but that clearly is a tedious process. A computer program, called INVRUL that will compute $O(\overline{X}) + I(\overline{X})$ appears at the end of the book. A sample run using the numbers in our example indicates that a value of $\overline{X}$ = $10,299 minimizes the expected costs at a value of $10,185.21 per period.

9.5 EFFECTS OF DIFFERENT PARAMETERS

The investigation strategy can be tailored to the parameters of each situation, but it is interesting to see how increases in different parameters affect the strategy. If the cost of investigation K increases, then the mistake of investigating an in-control process becomes more costly. Since the investigation strategy is designed to balance the operating and investigation costs, we would expect an increase in K to result in an increased value of $\overline{X}$. We will spend a greater proportion of time in θ_2, but this is necessary to keep the investigation costs from being too high. If we change the previous section's example by setting K = 250, the best $\overline{X}$ is $10,485, and the expected cost is $10,224 per period.

If the mean of the out-of-control cost distribution increases, then there are two effects. First, when we are in state θ_2 it costs us more (on an expected basis), because the effects of inefficiencies are more serious. But at the same time, the increased separation between the two distributions makes it easier to discern whether there is an inefficiency and to control the process. As a result, we spend less time in state θ_2, but when in θ_2 it costs us more. If the example in the previous section is changed by letting μ_2 = $11,250, then the best $\overline{X}$ increases to $10,475, and the expected cost is $10,241 per period.

If the standard deviations of the costs increase, then the process becomes more difficult to control, because for a normal $\overline{X}$ (between μ_1 and μ_2), the probability of investigating an in-control process $[1 - F_1(\overline{X})]$ and the probability of not investigating an out-of-control process $[F_2(\overline{X})]$ both increase. The effect of increases in σ_1 and σ_2 are difficult to predict. Increasing σ_1 alone would tend to increase $\overline{X}$, while increasing σ_2 would have the opposite effect. If the example in the previous section is altered by increasing σ_1 and σ_2 by 50% (to 750 and 900, respectively), then $\overline{X}$ decreases to $10,181, and the expected cost per period increases to $10,204.

As we would expect, the parameters of the cost control problem may have a significant impact on the investigation decision. In fact, there may be some cases where it does not pay to investigate at all. If K is high and g and $(\mu_2 - \mu_1)$ are low, then it may be better to let the process run without investigating. In essence, this outcome would mean that the financial control system (budgets, variances, etc.) is not able to control the operation, and management might look for new means of operational control (supervision, etc.) to keep the costs lower.

9.6 ESTIMATION OF PARAMETERS

If the parameters of a cost variance investigation problem influence its solution, then we need to examine the ways that these parameters can be estimated. Some of these factors, such as the expected cost when in control, or the expected cost of investigation, are fairly easy to estimate using techniques such as those in Chapters 5 and 6. Given some past data and standard costs, μ_1 and K can be found. Knowing the extent to which random factors affect costs, plus some past data, may help to get estimates of σ_1. But the estimation of other factors may be more difficult.

One of the more difficult estimation problems involves finding the probability distribution of out-of-control costs. In part, this difficulty may be attributed to the fact that costs jumping to an inefficient state is not usually the way that we think of the deterioration of cost control. (Other models are briefly discussed in section 9.8.) The use of past data to estimate $f_2(x)$ is complicated by the fact that for many past cost reports we may be uncertain as to whether a report was caused by an in-control process or an out-of-control process. Of course, we could wait until we conducted an investigation, and then if an inefficiency were found, that cost report could be put with the out-of-control data to estimate $f_2(x)$.

Unfortunately, the data would be affected by our investigation rule, since we would never have any observations for $f_2(x)$ where $x < \bar{X}$, and this would bias our estimation of $f_2(x)$. If the manager believes that $\bar{\bar{X}}$ is the lowest possible cost when there is an inefficiency, then he or she could temporarily alter the investigation strategy. By investigating all costs in excess of $\bar{\bar{X}}$, he or she would identify all costs that were drawn from $f_2(x)$, and estimates of μ_2 and σ_2 could be calculated. But if g is fairly high it may take a number of periods before enough observations are recorded to estimate μ_2 and σ_2 with some confidence. If K is large, and $[1 - F_1(\bar{\bar{X}})]$ is significant, then there will be a large cost in unnecessary investigations. In such circumstances, the manager may consider other methods of estimation (e.g., some form of engineering estimates). In addition, if the costs of all such estimates are large, the manager may conduct a value of information analysis to determine whether the improved parameter estimates would be worth their cost.

Before turning to the EVPI analysis, however, we must also consider estimates of the value of g, the probability that an in-control cost process will stay in control next period. Again, the manager's subjective estimates or an engineering analysis can be used. But there is also an estimate that may be derived from past data if the company has followed a consistent investigation policy, if the number of investigations made is known, and if the cost distributions $F_1(x)$ and $F_2(x)$ are known. Let's say that for the past n periods, the manager has investigated all costs in excess of $\bar{X}_0$, and there were k investigations actually conducted. From the earlier part of the chapter, we know that the probability of an investigation, ϕ_0, and the probabilities of being in θ_1 and θ_2 are the following.

$$\begin{aligned} \phi_0 &= \pi_1(\bar{X}_0)[1 - F_1(\bar{X}_0)] + \pi_2(\bar{X}_0)[1 - F_2(\bar{X}_0)] \\ \pi_1(\bar{X}_0) &= \frac{g[1 - F_2(\bar{X}_0)]}{1 - gF_2(\bar{X}_0)} \\ \pi_2(\bar{X}_0) &= 1 - \pi_1(\bar{X}_0) \end{aligned} \tag{9.11}$$

From these expressions, an expression for g can be derived.

$$g = \frac{1 - F_2(\bar{X}_0) - \phi_0}{F_1(\bar{X}_0) - F_1(\bar{X}_0)F_2(\bar{X}_0) - \phi_0 F_2(\bar{X}_0)} \tag{9.12}$$

If $\overline{X}_0$ is known for the past n periods, and $F_1(\overline{X}_0)$ and $F_2(\overline{X}_0)$ can be found, it only remains to find an estimate of ϕ_0. But if k investigations were conducted over the last n periods, then k/n is an estimate of ϕ_0, and can be used to calculate $\hat{g}$.

$$\hat{g} = \frac{1 - F_2(\overline{X}_0) - (k/n)}{F_1(\overline{X}_0) - F_1(\overline{X}_0)F_2(\overline{X}_0) - (k/n)F_2(\overline{X}_0)} \tag{9.13}$$

The accuracy of $\hat{g}$ will depend on whether k/n is an accurate estimate of ϕ_0. If n is large (e.g., a year of weekly observations), then the estimate will be more accurate than if it is derived from a small number of observations (e.g., six monthly observations). In any case, the estimate should be interpreted in light of the manager's subjective estimate of g.

When there is uncertainty about some of the parameters of the cost variance investigation model, it is probably appropriate for the manager to evaluate the expected effect of parameter misestimations on the investigation rules and expected costs. For instance, if we are unsure as to whether the mean of the out-of-control cost distribution is μ_2 or μ_2', we could run INVRUL twice (once using μ_2 and once using μ_2'). Then we could evaluate different cost investigation rules to see which gives the best expected results given the probabilities of μ_2 and μ_2'. This would give us an optimum $\overline{X}$ and an expected payoff, given our present uncertainty about the mean of the out-of-control costs. The EPVI about μ_2 and μ_2' could easily be computed using the same two runs of INVRUL. If the EVPI is large, then a special study of the causes of inefficiencies and their costs may be in order.

Example Suppose that the manager in charge of controlling the variances of a particular operation has provided the following parameter estimates for the investigation rule model.

$$\begin{aligned} \mu_1 &= 0, \sigma_1 = 20 \\ K &= 15 \\ \sigma_2 &= 20 \\ \mu_2 &= \begin{cases} 30, & \text{with probability } 0.5 \\ 40, & \text{with probability } 0.5 \end{cases} \\ g &= \begin{cases} 0.85, & \text{with probability } 0.6 \\ 0.7, & \text{with probability } 0.4 \end{cases} \end{aligned} \tag{9.14}$$

The manager wants the answers to two questions. Given the manager's present knowledge, what is the best investigation rule? What is the EVPI on μ_2 and g?

We can fill in the following table of expected costs per period using INVRUL.

Investigation rules	States of nature: $\mu_2 = 30$, $g = 0.85$	$\mu_2 = 40$, $g = 0.85$	$\mu_2 = 30$, $g = 0.7$	$\mu_2 = 40$, $g = 0.7$	Expected cost per period
$\overline{X} = 10$	11.2	12.5	17.5	20.2	14.63
$\overline{X} = 20$	10.1	11.1	16.9	19.3	13.61
$\overline{X} = 30$	10.5	11.0	17.8	19.9	14.02
$\overline{X} = 40$	12.8	12.6	20.3	22.1	16.11
$\phi(s)$	0.3	0.3	0.2	0.2	

Given the strategies considered, and the current information, the optimal strategy is to use an $\bar{X}$ of 20, with expected variance per period of \$13.60. The only state where this policy is less than optimal is when $\mu_2 = 40$, $g = 0.85$, where an $\bar{X} = 30$ would reduce costs by \$.10. The probability of this state is 0.3, so the EVPI on μ_2 and g is only (\$.10)(0.3) = \$.03 per period.

Of course, we cannot make general statements about the value of knowing the parameters of the cost variance model. In the above example, the value was very small, but in another situation, the added payoff might warrant a study of the sources, effects, and magnitudes of inefficiencies that might develop. An EVPI analysis such as that in the example can help the manager identify those situations where the investment in improved estimates is expected to pay off.

9.7 SELF-CORRECTING SITUATION

To this point, we've taken the description of the cost process pretty much for granted. That is, we've assumed two distinct states (in control and out of control), a probabilistic transition between them, and so on. There may be situations that match these assumptions, but there are a variety of ways in which the cost process may be more complex. We can develop investigation rules for these more complex situations, but adding these bells and whistles can complicate the model and make it more difficult to solve. In this section and the next we will explore a couple of the simpler extensions and discuss some other possibilities.

One of the assumptions we've made is that the out-of-control cost process can be corrected only with an investigation. Suppose there is a probability h that an out-of-control process will correct itself without managerial investigation. This situation is easily modeled by modifying the diagram in Appendix 9.2 to that in Figure 9.7.

As one would expect, this modification affects the long-run probability of being in control, because there is a chance that the process will correct itself if the manager does not investigate. For a given investigation strategy $\bar{X}$, we would expect the probability of being in control $\pi_1(\bar{X})$ to increase. The probabilities can be derived in the same manner as shown in Appendix 9.2, and would be

$$\pi_1(\bar{X}) = \frac{[1 - F_2(\bar{X})]g + F_2(\bar{X})h}{1 - g + [1 - F_2(\bar{X})]g + F_2(\bar{X})h}$$
$$\pi_2(\bar{X}) = \frac{1 - g}{1 - g + [1 - F_2(\bar{X})]g + F_2(\bar{X})h} \tag{9.15}$$

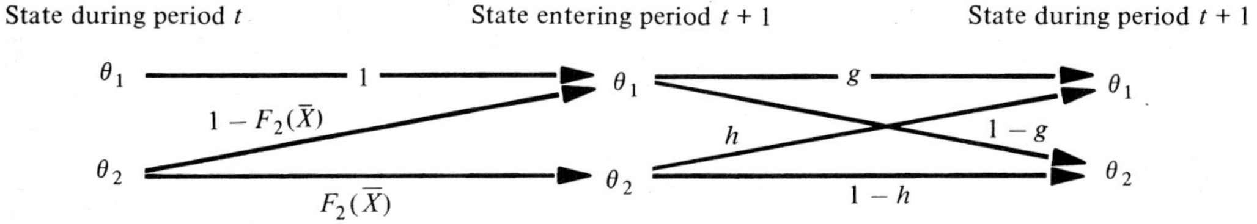

Figure 9.7

We can see that if $h = 0$, the long-run probabilities are the same as those developed earlier in this chapter (Eq. 9.6). But when $h > 0$, these probabilities can be used to find the expected operating and investigation costs per period for a given $\bar{X}$.

Earlier in the chapter, we calculated the probabilities and costs for an example with $\mu_1 = 10{,}000$, $\sigma_1 = 500$, $\mu_2 = 10{,}750$, $\sigma_2 = 600$, $g = 0.85$, and $K = 125$. If $\bar{X} = 10{,}750$, we found that π_1 was 0.739 (Eq. 9.9). What happens if we let $h = 0.30$ in this example? We know that $F_2(10{,}750) = 0.5$, so the probabilities would be the following.

$$\pi_1(10{,}750) = \frac{(0.5)(0.85) + (0.5)(0.3)}{1 - 0.85 + (0.5)(0.85) + (0.5)(0.3)} = 0.793 \tag{9.16}$$

Therefore, the self-correcting characteristic of the cost variances has caused the long-run probability of being in θ_1 to increase from 0.739 to 0.793. This change would result in decreases in both the expected operating costs per period $O(\bar{X})$ and the expected investigation costs per period $I(\bar{X})$. With these new probabilities, the manager can then try different levels of $\bar{X}$ to find the most desirable.

9.8 MULTIPLE OUT-OF-CONTROL DISTRIBUTIONS

Another assumption we've made is that there is only one state of inefficiency θ_2. In fact, there may be multiple causes of inefficiencies, with differing effects on the costs of operation. It is not even necessary that all out-of-control situations result in unfavorable variances in the short run. If favorable variances can be caused by decreasing product quality, then there can be an out-of-control distribution "to the left" of $f_1(x)$, as depicted in Figure 9.8. Such a situation could result in increased long-term costs through rework, product liability, etc., although these costs would not be evident in the period's variance reports.

We can address this situation by defining a more general investigation rule: "investigate all variances *less* than $\bar{X}_L$ or *greater* than $\bar{X}_H$." Again, we can find the long-run probabilities of being in each of the states, although the calculations will be more complicated. If the state of control is θ_2, the probability of an investigation is equal to the probability that costs will be in excess of $\bar{X}_H$, $1 - F_2(\bar{X}_H)$, plus the probability that

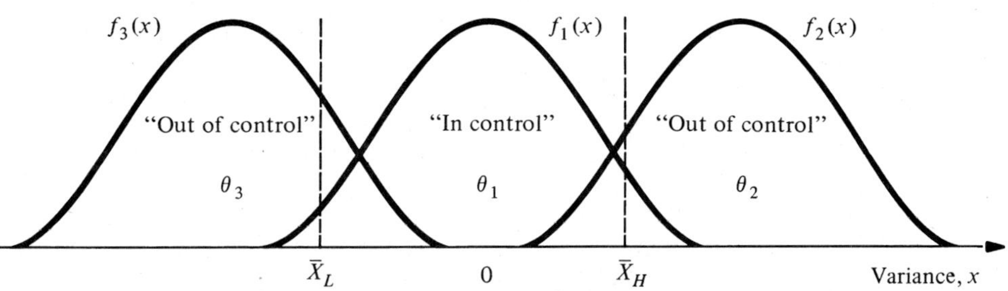

Figure 9.8

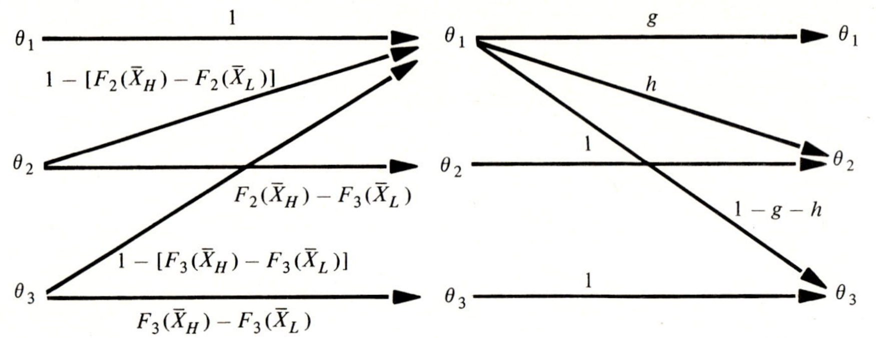

Figure 9.9

costs will be less than $\overline{X}_L$, $F_2(\overline{X}_L)$.[5] Therefore, the probability of a transition from θ_2 to θ_1 because of investigation is $1 - [F_2(\overline{X}_H) - F_2(\overline{X}_L)]$. The transition probabilities are depicted in Figure 9.9, where h is the probability of a θ_2 inefficiency developing and $1 - g - h$ is the probability of a θ_3 inefficiency developing.

Although it is more complex, we can derive the long-run probabilities of being in states θ_1, θ_2, and θ_3. These probabilities will depend on both $\overline{X}_L$ and $\overline{X}_H$, and can be used to calculate the expected operating cost and the expected investigation cost.[6] If μ_1, μ_2, and μ_3 represent the *long-run* cost of operating in states θ_1, θ_2, and θ_3, the expression for the expected operating costs $O(\overline{X}_L, \overline{X}_H)$ and investigation costs $I(\overline{X}_L, \overline{X}_H)$ will be the following.

$$\begin{aligned} O(\overline{X}_L,\overline{X}_H) &= \mu_1\pi_1(\overline{X}_L,\overline{X}_H) + \mu_2\pi_2(\overline{X}_L,\overline{X}_H) + \mu_3\pi_3(\overline{X}_L,\overline{X}_H) \\ I(\overline{X}_L,\overline{X}_H) &= K\{\pi_1(\overline{X}_L,\overline{X}_H)[1 - F_1(\overline{X}_H) + F_1(\overline{X}_L)] \\ &\quad + \pi_2(\overline{X}_L,\overline{X}_H)[1 - F_2(\overline{X}_H) + F_2(\overline{X}_L)] \\ &\quad + \pi_3(\overline{X}_L,\overline{X}_H)[1 - F_3(\overline{X}_H) + F_3(\overline{X}_L)]\} \end{aligned} \tag{9.17}$$

[5]For most values of $\overline{X}_L$ and $\overline{X}_H$, we would expect $F_2(\overline{X}_L)$ and $[1 - F_3(X_H)]$ to be quite small.

[6]The same methods as in Appendix 9.2 can be used to determine the probabilities.

$$\pi_1(\overline{X}_L,\overline{X}_H) = \frac{g}{g + \dfrac{h}{1 - F_2(\overline{X}_H) + F_2(\overline{X}_L)} + \dfrac{1 - g - h}{1 - F_3(\overline{X}_H) + F_3(\overline{X}_L)}}$$

$$\pi_2(\overline{X}_L,\overline{X}_H) = \frac{\dfrac{h}{1 - F_2(\overline{X}_H) + F_2(\overline{X}_L)}}{g + \dfrac{h}{1 - F_2(\overline{X}_H) + F_2(\overline{X}_L)} + \dfrac{1 - g - h}{1 - F_3(\overline{X}_H) + F_3(\overline{X}_L)}}$$

$$\pi_3(\overline{X}_L,\overline{X}_H) = \frac{\dfrac{(1 - g - h)}{1 - F_3(\overline{X}_H) + F_3(\overline{X}_L)}}{g + \dfrac{h}{1 - F_2(\overline{X}_H) + F_2(\overline{X}_L)} + \dfrac{1 - g - h}{1 - F_3(\overline{X}_H) + F_3(\overline{X}_L)}}$$

Searching for a satisfactory control policy will be more complex, since both $\overline{X}_L$ and $\overline{X}_H$ can be controlled. But again, a computerized search can make the job manageable by scanning over the combinations of interest.

While these extensions of the basic cost variance investigation model are instructive, they by no means exhaust the potential modifications. For instance, we could allow for another state in which an innovation has occurred, which will reduce operating costs. Discovery of such an innovation, coupled with the possibility of implementation actions, could allow the decision maker to use the innovation in other, similar operations as well as in controlling costs in the innovating operation. Another possibility might involve the evaluation of two or more cost variances simultaneously. That is, considering a material price variance and a material usage variance together might tell us more about the state of efficiency than dealing with each one separately.

We can usually modify our model of cost behavior to incorporate a great number of real-world phenomena. To do so is not always easy, however, involving increased modeling effort as well as increased computer time to determine the investigation rule. Therefore, where possible, we may want to evaluate how much additional benefit we may expect from this increasing sophistication to see if (or when) they exceed the additional costs. Simulation (as discussed in Chapter 5) may be a useful technique for making this type of evaluation. The complex, realistic environment can be simulated, and different investigation rules can be compared in the simulated environment.[7]

9.9 PERMANENT COST CHANGES

The cost investigation models in the previous sections only dealt with two sources of variances: random fluctuations and inefficiencies. There is also the possibility that a permanent, uncontrollable cost change could cause the variance. In this case, there is no corrective action possible. In fact, if the firm can make no adjustments in its operations, the only appropriate action would be to change the cost standards to reflect the new cost. In our investigation model we could define a new state to represent the occurrence of a permanent change. An investigation may discover this state and correct it by changing the standards. Alternatively, we could adjust the in-control cost distribution to reflect the possibility of permanent cost changes. In any case, if the problem appears to be an important one, we could incorporate it into our investigation rule.

However, if the firm may *adapt* its operations to the new cost, then an investigation may have added value over that from discovering inefficiencies. For instance, if a change in an input's cost is permanent, the firm may change inputs, change its final product mix, change its price, and so on.

As an example, suppose a firm had a budgeted marginal revenue curve of $\$(100 - x)$, where x is output and a budgeted variable cost of \$20 per unit of output. (Total revenue, TR $= 100x - \frac{1}{2}x^2$; total variable cost, TC $= 20x$.) Using the analysis from Chapter 4, the optimal budgeted output is $x = 80$, with a budgeted profit of $\$100(80) - \frac{1}{2}(80)^2 - 20(80) = \$3{,}200$. Last period, the actual variable cost was \$25 per unit, but the manager is uncertain of the cause of the \$5 variance. There is a 0.4 probability

[7]For an example of this type of approach, see Magee (1976).

it was a *random* fluctuation that will not occur next period, a 0.3 probability it was caused by an *inefficiency* that will continue until corrected, and a 0.3 probability that the cost increase was a *permanent* change. If it is permanent, then the optimal action would be to adapt to the increased cost by decreasing output to $x = 75$ with an expected profit of $\$100(75) - \frac{1}{2}(75)^2 - 25(75) = \$2{,}812.5$.

Without an investigation the manager must simply choose $x = 75$ or $x = 80$ as reflected in the following payoff matrix.

	States			
	Random	Inefficiency	Permanent	E[Profit]
$x = 75$	3187.5	2812.5	2812.5	2962.5
$x = 80$	3200.0	2800.0	2800.0	2960.0
$\phi(s)$	0.4	0.3	0.3	

In this situation, the optimal action is to reduce output to 75 with an expected profit of \$2,962.50. But if we conduct an investigation to determine the cause of the cost variance, we can *correct* the inefficiency, if it exists, or adapt output if the variance turns out to be a permanent one.

Investigation report	Optimal action	Payoff
Random	$x = 80$	3200
Inefficiency	Correct, then $x = 80$	3200
Permanent	$x = 75$	2812.5

The $E[\text{payoff}|\text{investigation}] = 0.4(3{,}200) + 0.3(3{,}200) + 0.3(2{,}812.5) = \$3{,}083.75$, and the expected value of the investigation is $\$3{,}083.75 - 2{,}962.5 = \$121.25$. Part of this value is due to the investigation's discovery and correction of possible inefficiencies, but another part is due to the investigation's aid in deciding on the appropriate adaptive action.

9.10 SUMMARY

The objective of a variance reporting system is to help the manager identify those areas of operation that are most likely to benefit from some attention. "Management by exception" requires a reporting system that enables the exceptions to be identified. But the investigation of exceptions requires resources, and if a variance is caused by normal variations in operating conditions, those resources produce no benefit. Therefore, a manager should decide on a variance investigation strategy that weighs both the operating and investigation costs. The models presented in this chapter are representative of those that can aid the manager in identifying a satisfactory investigation strategy.

There are yet a number of information issues that should be addressed. When we design a set of variances, there are a number of choices to be made. For instance, how accurate should the budgets be that are compared with the actual results in computing the variances? How disaggregated should the variances be? How often should variances and other feedback information be reported? Now that we have developed a cost variance investigation model, these information problems are addressed in the next chapter.

APPENDIX 9.1: Basic Variances for a Standard, Direct Cost System

Any set of variances must be developed to match the system of revenue and expense recognition that is being used in the operation. In this appendix, we examine a set of variances for a *standard, direct cost* system. These qualifiers imply that inventory is carried at its standard variable cost, while fixed production cost and any variable production cost variances are recognized (in income) in the period in which they occur.

To begin, let us assume that this company sells n products, and that it has developed the following standards. (If a variable has a caret over it, it represents a standard, while a variable with no caret represents the actual outcome.)[8]

	Standard	Actual
Fixed production costs	$\hat{F}_p$	F_p
Fixed selling and administrative costs	$\hat{F}_s$	F_s
For each product, $i = 1$ to n:		
Revenue per unit	$\hat{R}_i$	R_i
Material cost per unit	$\hat{M}_i$	M_i
Labor cost per unit	$\hat{L}_i$	L_i
Variable production overhead per unit	$\hat{V}_i$	V_i
Variable selling cost per unit	$\hat{S}_i$	S_i
Unit contribution margin	$\widehat{UCM}_i = (\hat{R}_i - \hat{M}_i - \hat{L}_i - \hat{V}_i - \hat{S}_i)$	$UCM_i = (R_i - \hat{M}_i - \hat{L}_i - \hat{V}_i - S_i)$
Number of units sold	$\hat{X}_i$	X_i

As a unit is produced and placed in inventory, it is assigned a cost of $(\hat{M}_i + \hat{L}_i + \hat{V}_i)$, and any production variances are assigned to the income statement. When the unit is sold, this standard cost is matched against the revenue achieved. The budgeted income statement and the actual income statements would look like the following.

	Standard	Actual
Revenue	$\sum_{i=1}^{n} \hat{R}_i\hat{X}_i$	$\sum_{i=1}^{n} R_iX_i$
Variable production costs of goods sold	$\sum_{i=1}^{n} (\hat{M}_i + \hat{L}_i + \hat{V}_i)\hat{X}_i$	$\sum_{i=1}^{n} (\hat{M}_i + \hat{L}_i + \hat{V}_i)X_i$
Variable selling costs	$\sum_{i=1}^{n} \hat{S}_i\hat{X}_i$	$\sum_{i=1}^{n} S_iX_i$
Contribution margin	$\sum_{i=1}^{n} \widehat{UCM}_i\hat{X}_i$	$\sum_{i=1}^{n} UCM_iX_i$
Fixed production costs	$\hat{F}_p$	F_p
Fixed selling and administrative costs	$\hat{F}_s$	F_s
	Budgeted income	Actual income before production variances
		− Variable production cost variances
		Actual income

[8]The term "actual" is used here in the context of the accounting measurement system.

It should be clear from looking at these two statements that there are a large number of reasons why the actual income may differ from the budgeted income. A simple set of variances designed to help identify the individual causes of the differences are presented below. They are split into three basic sets—contribution margin variances, fixed cost variances, and variable production cost variances.

A9.1 CONTRIBUTION MARGIN VARIANCES

These variances are designed to explain the differences between the contribution margins in the budgeted and actual income statements, that is,

$$\Sigma\, UCM_i X_i - \Sigma\, \widehat{UCM}_i \hat{X}_i.$$

	Product *i*	Total
Contribution margin variance	$UCM_i X_i - \widehat{UCM}_i \hat{X}_i$	$\Sigma\, UCM_i X_i - \Sigma\, \widehat{UCM}_i \hat{X}_i$
Physical volume variance	$\widehat{UCM}_i (X_i - \hat{X}_i)$	$\Sigma\, \widehat{UCM}_i (X_i - \hat{X}_i)$
Unit contribution margin variance	$(UCM_i - \widehat{UCM}_i) X_i$	$\Sigma(\widehat{UCM}_i - UCM_i) X_i$
Unit revenue variance	$(R_i - \hat{R}_i) X_i$	$\Sigma(R_i - \hat{R}_i) X_i$
Variable selling cost variance	$(S_i - \hat{S}_i) X_i$	$\Sigma(S_i - \hat{S}_i) X_i$

Of course, these variances are related to one another. The contribution margin variance equals the sum of the physical volume variance and the unit contribution margin variance. In turn, the unit contribution margin variance equals the unit revenue variance minus the variable selling cost variance. In turn, we might be able to break down some of these variances yet further. For instance, if the standard variable selling cost is based upon (i) a standard cost per call that a salesperson makes and (ii) a standard number of units sold per call, we could break down the variable selling cost variance into a part reflecting the cost per call and a part reflecting the number of units sold per call. In addition, physical volume variances could be computed by geographic region as well as by product.

A9.2 FIXED COST VARIANCES

Because we are using a direct costing system, the computation of variances for fixed costs is quite easy.

$$\begin{aligned} \text{Fixed production cost budget variance} &= F_p - \hat{F}_p \\ \text{Fixed selling and administrative cost budget variance} &= F_s - \hat{F}_s \end{aligned} \qquad \text{(A9.1.1)}$$

The refinements in these variances can be of two types. First, the costs and budgets can be disaggregated to provide better information about the causes of any variances. For instance, the fixed production costs could be split into depreciation, heating, supervision, etc. Second, these costs are fixed with respect to output and sales, but they may be variable with respect to other (perhaps uncontrollable) factors. Therefore, it may be possible to use these factors to arrive at flexible budgets and more meaningful variances. For instance, heating costs are not affected by output, but they can be influenced by the degree-days for the accounting period. We could develop heating budgets that flex with respect to degree-days and thereby remove an uncontrollable factor from the heating cost variance.

A9.3 VARIABLE PRODUCTION COST VARIANCES

The variable production cost variances include those for direct materials, direct labor, and variable production overhead. For the direct costs $\hat{M}_i$ and $\hat{L}_i$, the standards are based on two factors—the standard cost per unit of input and the standard amount of input per unit of output.

$$\hat{M}_i = \hat{P}_{mi}\hat{U}_{mi} \qquad \text{(A9.1.2)}$$
$$\hat{L}_i = \hat{P}_{li}\hat{U}_{li}$$

where $\hat{P}_{mi}, \hat{P}_{li} \equiv$ standard cost per unit of direct material and direct labor, respectively
$\hat{U}_{mi}, \hat{U}_{li} \equiv$ standard amount of direct material and direct labor, respectively, per unit of product i

We will also define Y_i as the amount of product i produced, and Z_{mi} as the number of units of product i's material input purchased during the accounting period.[9]

	Product i	Total
Labor variances		
Labor rate variance	$(P_{li} - \hat{P}_{li})U_{li}Y_i$	$\Sigma(P_{li} - \hat{P}_{li})U_{li}Y_i$
Labor efficiency variance	$\hat{P}_{li}(U_{li} - \hat{U}_{li})Y_i$	$\Sigma\hat{P}_{li}(U_{li} - \hat{U}_{li})Y_i$
Material variances		
Material price variance[10]	$(P_{mi} - \hat{P}_{mi})Z_{mi}$	$\Sigma(P_{mi} - \hat{P}_{mi})Z_{mi}$
Material usage variance	$\hat{P}_{mi}(U_{mi} - \hat{U}_{mi})Y_i$	$\Sigma \hat{P}_{mi}(U_{mi} - \hat{U}_{mi})Y_i$

As with other variances, these may be disaggregated to provide greater detail. If there are different types of labor or different departments involved, the labor variances could be calculated for each. Likewise, material variances could be calculated for each type of material.

The variable overhead variances depend on how the variable overhead is applied to products. By the nature of indirect costs, these cannot be directly traced to units of output. Yet to construct a set of variances, we need to have a flexible budget for variable overhead. A simple approach to this problem would be to estimate the following (perhaps using regression).

$$\text{Variable overhead} = \hat{V}_1Y_1 + \hat{V}_2Y_2 + \cdots + \hat{V}_nY_n \qquad \text{(A9.1.3)}$$

Then production of Y_1 units yields a flexible budget of $\hat{V}_1Y_1$ and the variance would be the following.

	Product i	Total
Variable overhead flexible budget variance	$(V_i - \hat{V}_i)Y_i$	$\Sigma(V_i - \hat{V}_i)Y_i$

If the variable overhead can be disaggregated further (power costs, supplies, maintenance, etc.), then such variances could be computed on a disaggregated basis.[11]

[9]In keeping with the notation we've been using, the absence of a caret means "actual." For example, P_{mi} is the actual cost per unit of direct material for product i.

[10]Based on units of inputs purchased.

[11]An alternative approach might be used if variable overhead was closely related to the level of direct labor hours (e.g., $\hat{V} = V_l \cdot$ labor hours). In this case, $\hat{V}_i$ can be defined as $\hat{V}_l\hat{U}_{li}$, and the variable overhead variance can be caused by over (under)-spending and/or labor efficiency. In this situation, the variable overhead variance above can be broken down into two components.

	Product i	Total
Variable overhead spending variance	$(V_i - \hat{V}_lU_{li})Y_i$	$\Sigma(V_i - \hat{V}_lU_{li})Y_i$
Variable overhead efficiency variance	$\hat{V}_l(U_{li} - \hat{U}_{li})Y_i$	$\Sigma\hat{V}_l(U_{li} - \hat{U}_{li})Y_i$

For all of these variable production cost variances, positive (negative) variances are unfavorable (favorable) in the sense that they decrease (increase) the current period's income. The labor variances, material variances, and the variable overhead flexible budget variance may be added together and subtracted in the income statement to determine the actual income.

APPENDIX 9.2: Long Run Probabilities

In this appendix we describe how the long-run probabilities are derived in the cost variance investigation model described in the chapter. Suppose that π_1^t and π_2^t are the probabilities of being in states θ_1 and θ_2 during period t. We can figure out the values of π_1^{t+1} and π_2^{t+1} for the next period, using the following diagram of the paths and probabilities between t and $t + 1$.

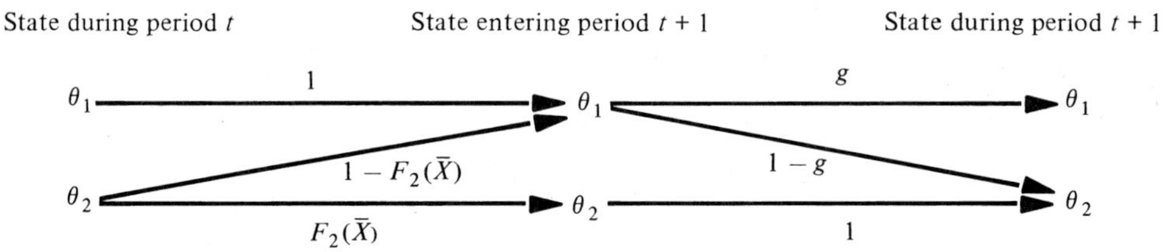

The probability of being in θ_1 during $t + 1$ is the probability of being in θ_1 during t *and* staying in control, *plus* the probability of being in θ_2 during t *and* being corrected *and* staying in control. The probability of being in θ_2 during $t + 1$ can be found the same way.

$$\begin{aligned} \pi_1^{t+1} &= \pi_1^t g + \pi_2^t[1 - F_2(\bar{X})]g \\ \pi_2^{t+1} &= \pi_1^t(1 - g) + \pi_2^t\{F_2(\bar{X}) + (1 - g)[1 - F_2(\bar{X})]\} \end{aligned} \tag{A9.2.1}$$

Suppose that $g = 0.80$ and that $\bar{X}$ has been set so that the probability of not investigating an out-of-control process $F_2(\bar{X})$, is 0.1. Then we have

$$\begin{aligned} \pi_1^{t+1} &= \pi_1^t 0.8 + \pi_2^t 0.72 \\ \pi_2^{t+1} &= \pi_1^t 0.2 + \pi_2^t[0.1 + (0.2)(0.9)] \\ &= \pi_1^t 0.2 + \pi_2^t 0.28 \end{aligned} \tag{A9.2.2}$$

Now, the process of finding the long-run probabilities simply involves the fact that, as we look ahead to the long run, the probabilities ought to be the same for periods t and $t + 1$. That is, $\pi_1^t = \pi_1^{t+1} = \pi_1$ and $\pi_2^t = \pi_2^{t+1} = \pi_2$. So we can solve the above equations for values of π_1 and π_2 that sum to 1.

$$\begin{aligned} \pi_1 &= \pi_1 g + \pi_2[1 - F_2(\bar{X})]g \\ \pi_2 &= \pi_1(1 - g) + \pi_1\{F_2(\bar{X}) + (1 - g)[1 - F_1(\bar{X})]\} \\ \pi_1 + \pi_2 &= 1 \quad \text{or} \quad \pi_2 = 1 - \pi_1 \end{aligned} \tag{A9.2.3}$$

The long-run probabilities in Eq. 9.6 satisfy these three relationships. In the numerical example

$$\begin{aligned} \pi_1 &= \pi_1 0.8 + \pi_2 0.72 \quad \text{and} \quad \pi_2 = 1 - \pi_1 \\ \rightarrow \pi_1 &= \pi_1 0.8 + (1 - \pi_1)0.72 \\ &= 0.08\pi_1 + 0.72 \end{aligned} \tag{A9.2.4}$$

$$\rightarrow 0.92\pi_1 = 0.72 \rightarrow \pi_1 = \frac{0.72}{0.92} \approx 0.78$$

The long-run probability of being in θ_1 is about 0.78, while the probability of being in θ_2 is about 0.22.

PROBLEMS

9.1. Mr. B. Lunder is the manager of the lawn sprinkler division of the Evergro Lawn Products Company. Lunder's division is primarily concerned with the assembly of the company's lawn sprinkler. The company uses standards based on a forecasted, or expected, level of efficiency. The forecasted activity level for the month of February was 10,000 sprinklers. The budgets and actual outcomes appear in the table below:

	Budget	Actual
Parts, materials	$20,000	$18,000
Labor	30,000	28,000
Variable overhead	10,000	9,000
Fixed overhead	11,000	12,000
Total	$71,000	$67,000
Sprinklers Produced	10,000	8,000

Lunder's attached comment was "as is seen by the figures, while we did not manage to attain the production forecast, the actual figures (with the exception of a slight unfavorable fixed overhead budget variance) indicate that the sprinkler division did do better than the budget."

In an attempt to analyze the factors underlying the sprinkler division's performance, you find the standards for the following:

Standard wage/hour:	$6.00
Standard hours/sprinkler:	1/2
Standard VOH/hour:	$2.00
Actual direct labor hours:	5,000

Required Using the forecasted standards, find the labor rate variance, labor efficiency variance, and variable overhead spending variance. Indicate *U* (unfavorable) or *F* (favorable).

9.2. Abbie Baker has recently been put in charge of the control and evaluation function in the controller's department. In this position she is responsible for the periodic reporting of variances and other performance measures. Abbie also has the responsibility to recommend changes in the measurement and reporting system which will improve motivation and coordination.

The firm is a large manufacturer, with corporate headquarters in Chicago, and eighteen production facilities geographically dispersed throughout the country. Each of the eighteen plants operates in its own market, and the plant managers are given considerable autonomy and profit responsibility. Each quarter an income statement and balance sheet are produced for each plant and augmented by variances and ratios. The most important factor in the plant manager's performance evaluation is the return on investment (ROI) ratio.

Among the variances calculated for each plant are those for fixed and variable overhead. The standards for these variances are found by using a regression cost estimate, a sophisticated management application of which Abbie is rather proud. Every year, the most recent three years' data are used to estimate F and v in the following relationship.

$$\text{Overhead} = F + v\,(\text{direct labor hours})$$

The most recent estimate for plant #6 are \$150,000/fiscal quarter for F and \$3/DLH for v. Last quarter's results for plant #6 are included in the following.

Actual direct labor hours:	9,500
Standard direct labor hours:	9,000
Budgeted direct labor hours:	\$10,000
Actual fixed overhead:	\$160,000
Actual variable overhead:	\$25,000

Required

A. Compute and label as ''favorable'' or ''unfavorable'' the following.
   1. Variable overhead spending variance.
   2. Variable overhead efficiency variance.
   3. Fixed overhead spending variance.

B. Describe, *briefly but clearly,* two potential problems with the overhead standards as they are currently set (i.e., leading to improper motivation, inappropriate interpretations, etc).

9.3. The purchasing manager's responsibility is to balance two types of costs: (i) the costs incurred and payable to suppliers for materials, and (ii) inventory holding costs. We will refer to these as *purchasing costs PC* and *holding costs HC*. Purchasing costs consist of a cost per order S, and a cost per unit V. The holding costs are I per unit held per period.

$$\begin{aligned} PC &= S(\#\text{ of orders}) + V(\#\text{ of units}) \\ &= S(D/X) + VD \\ HC &= I(\text{avg. }\#\text{ of units held}) = I(X/2) \end{aligned}$$

where D = total material demanded (in units)
X = units per order.

This is a simple inventory ordering problem that is solved by an EOQ (economic order quantity) model which minimizes total cost TC.

$$\begin{aligned} TC &= PC + HC \\ &= S(D/X) + VD + I(X/2) \end{aligned}$$

$$X^* = \frac{2SD}{(I)^{1/2}} \quad \text{is the economic order quantity.}$$

A. Suppose that estimates of demand and holding costs (D and I) are provided to the purchasing manager, what would be the budget for TC, the total material cost?

B. Design a set of variances that would separate the effects of (i) inaccurate estimates of D and I and (ii) the purchasing manager's performance.

9.4. Suppose that a material usage variance follows the random behavior described in this chapter and in Appendix 9.1. The probability of an inefficiency developing at the start of a week is 0.1, and if it develops, it will continue for the remainder of the week. If the material usage is out of control, the variances will follow the probability distribution below:

Variance, x	Probability, $f_2(x)$	Cumulative probability, $F_2(x)$
$ 0	0	0
500	0.1	0.1
1,000	0.4	0.5
1,500	0.3	0.8
2,000	0.2	1.0

A. Draw a graph such as that in Appendix 9.1, and fill in the probabilities if the investigation rule is ''investigate all variances exceeding $1,200.''

B. For *each* of the values π_1^t and π_2^t, calculate the probability of being in control next week, π_1^{t+1} (see Appendix 9.1).

(a) $\pi_1^t = 1, \pi_2^t = 0$

(b) $\pi_1^t = 0, \pi_2^t = 1$

(c) $\pi_1^t = 9/11, \pi_2^t = 2/11$

C. Is *B*(c) ''steady state?'' How do you know? If it is, what is the expected cost variance per period? (Assume that when costs are in control the expected variance is 0.)

9.5. Refer to the information given in problem 9.4. Suppose that there is also a probability of 0.2 that the cost process will self-correct if it is out of control. The probability of developing an inefficiency and the probabilities of cost variances if an inefficiency exists are unaffected.

Required

A. Draw a graph such as that in Figure 9.7, and fill in the probabilities if the investigation rule is ''investigate all variances exceeding $1,200.''

B. Calculate the steady-state probabilities of being in the in-control and out-of-control states. What is the expected cost variance per period?

C. Repeat parts A and B if the investigation rule is ''investigate all variances exceeding $800.'' How does the expected cost variance per period change?

9.6. Matthew Eubank is in charge of manufacturing control for a small company in the southeastern United States. Every week, he receives a variance report which enables him to review the past week's operations. Based on this report, he can conduct investigations into various aspects of the plant's operations. ''One problem is that the manufacturing costs depend both on the level of cost control that is achieved in the plant and on the attention to quality control. That is, it is possible for a favorable cost variance to be caused by poor quality control. Of course, such a situation costs us more in the long run, but it doesn't show up on the weekly reports. Therefore, I should investigate favorable variances, as well as unfavorable variances, although my boss feels I shouldn't waste time investigating situations where there are no cost overruns.''

To analyze this type of situation, suppose that at the beginning of each week there is a 0.7 probability that an in control process will stay that way, a 0.2 probability that a cost control inefficiency will develop and remain until corrected, and a 0.1 probability that a quality control inefficiency will develop and continue until corrected. (You may assume that it is not possible for there to be *both* a cost control inefficiency and a quality control inefficiency at the same time.) The probability distributions of the weekly cost variances are given below for each of the possible states of control.

Cost variance, x($)	Probability if in-control, $f_1(x)$	Probability if out-of-control (costs), $f_2(x)$	Probability if out-of-control (quality), $f_3(x)$
−2,000	0.00	0.00	0.10
−1,500	0.00	0.00	0.20
−1,000	0.10	0.00	0.40
−500	0.20	0.00	0.20
0	0.40	0.10	0.10
500	0.20	0.20	0.00
1,000	0.10	0.40	0.00
1,500	0.00	0.20	0.00
2,000	0.00	0.10	0.00

Required

A. If the investigation strategy is to investigate all unfavorable variances, what is the probability of an out-of-control (quality) situation being corrected? What are the steady-state probabilities of being in each of the three states? (You shouldn't have to do any calculations.)

B. Suppose that the investigation strategy is to "investigate if the absolute value of the variance exceeds $800." That is, a variance of $1,000 would be investigated regardless of whether it was favorable or unfavorable.

(a) Set up a graph such as that in Figure 9.9, and fill in all the probabilities.

(b) Determine the steady-state probabilities of being in each of the three states. What is the long-run probability of investigating when the cost process is in control?

C. If it were possible for there to be both cost control and quality control inefficiencies at the same time, how would the analysis above be affected? Do you think it would have a significant impact on the investigation strategy?

9.7. Assume that the random process presented in this chapter is descriptive of a labor efficiency variance. The probability of staying in control g is 0.7, the cost of investigation is $500, and the variance probabilities are the following.

	In-control probabilities		Out-of-control probabilities	
Variance, x	$f_1(x)$	$F_1(x)$	$f_2(x)$	$F_2(x)$
1,000 *F*	0.1	0.1	0	0
500 *F*	0.2	0.3	0	0
0	0.4	0.7	0.1	0.1
500 *U*	0.2	0.9	0.2	0.3
1,000 *U*	0.1	1.0	0.4	0.7
1,500 *U*	0	1.0	0.2	0.9
2,000 *U*	0	1.0	0.1	1.0

Required

A. Design a simple situation, for example, using a deck of playing cards, that would enable you to evaluate different investigation rules. Choose an investigation rule and simulate the variances and decisions for three periods.

B. Which simplifying assumption about the cost process bothers you the most? Try to relax it in your simulation model.

9.8. Michael Bitner has responsibility for control of two manufacturing processes. Every week he receives a cost variance report for each of the two processes, broken down by labor costs, materials costs, and so on. One of the two processes, which we'll call process *A*, involves a stable easily controlled production process with a little fluctuation in variances. Process *B* involves more random events: the equipment is more sensitive and prone to breakdown, the raw material prices fluctuate more, and so on.

"It seems like I'm spending more of my time with process *B* than with process *A*," says Michael Bitner. "Yet I know that the probability of an inefficiency developing and the expected costs of inefficiencies are the same for the two processes. It's just the magnitude of random fluctuations that differ between the two, as you can see in the information below.

"At present, I investigate variances if they exceed $2,500, regardless of whether it was process *A* or *B*. I suspect that such a policy is not the most efficient. I should probably set a higher limit for process *B*."

	Process *A*	Process *B*
Expected variance: in control	$ 0	$ 0
Standard deviation of variance: in control	5,000	10,000
Expected variance: out of control	$7,500	$ 7,500
Standard deviation of variance: out of control	5,000	10,000
Expected cost of investigation	$2,500	$ 2,500
Probability of an in-control process remaining in that state next period	0.75	0.75

Required

A. Why is it that Michael Bitner spends more time investigating variances from process *B* than from process *A*?

B. Using the program INVRUL, determine the optimal investigation policy for processes *A* and *B*. Do the optimal policies confirm his intuition that the investigation limit should be higher for process *B* than for process *A*? Why?

9.9. About five months ago, Peter Campbell was given responsibility for cost control of a small service department located in the plant that he managed. Prior to this the department had been controlled by the company's main office, located in another state. Since he was unfamiliar with the department operations, Campbell chose to investigate all unfavorable variances for the past twenty weeks. The variances and investigation results are presented below, including the cost of staff time used in investigating the variances.

At this point Campbell is afraid that he is wasting time and resources with the present investigation policy, and he has asked you to recommend an alternative.

Week	Operating variance	Investigation?	Correction needed?	Investigation cost
1	560 F	No		
2	1,472 U	Yes	Yes	848
3	477 F	No		
4	3,238 U	Yes	Yes	893
5	470 U	Yes	Yes	862
6	1,128 U	Yes	No	776
7	1,711 F	No		
8	4 U	Yes	No	829
9	1,644 F	No		

Week	Operating variance	Investigation?	Correction needed?	Investigation cost
10	4,028 U	Yes	Yes	796
11	4,665 U	Yes	Yes	765
12	365 U	Yes	No	827
13	294 F	No		
14	90 U	Yes	No	795
15	898 F	No		
16	1,649 U	Yes	No	739
17	370 U	Yes	Yes	811
18	500 F	No		
19	758 U	Yes	No	814
20	437 U	Yes	Yes	823

Required

A. Estimate the following parameters from the data provided.

(a) μ_1 and σ_1.

(b) μ_2 and σ_2.

(c) K.

(d) g.

B. Is a change in investigation policy desirable? Why?

C. Use the program INVRUL to determine a better investigation policy.

9.10. "I can see the need to look at the costs and benefits of different cost variance investigation strategies," said Clair Brown, "but I don't particularly like the assumption that the strategy will not affect the likelihood of an inefficiency developing. I'm responsible for the operations of a number of service departments within the bank, and there aren't too many machines in these departments that can go out of control. It's the people who work in the departments that determine the level of efficiency, and if I don't check up on costs often, then it's more likely that inefficiencies will develop. On the other hand, if I check all unfavorable variances, then I'll probably never see any inefficiencies. I feel like the efficient policeman who sees no problems on his rounds because everyone knows he's there."

An example of this sort of situation is given below.

Expected variance: in control	$ 0
Standard deviation of variance: in control	5,000
Expected variance: out of control	$7,500
Standard deviation of variance: out of control	5,000
Expected cost of investigation	$2,500

Strategy: "Investigate if variance exceeds X"	Probability of an in-control process remaining in that state next period
$500 < X < $2,500	0.80
$2,500 < X < $4,500	0.70
$4,500 < X	0.60

Required

A. For each of the following investigation strategies, find the expected cost per period using the INVRUL program. Which yields the most favorable results?

(a) Investigate if the variance exceeds \$2,000.
(b) Investigate if the variance exceeds \$3,000.
(c) Investigate if the variance exceeds \$4,000.
(d) Investigate if the variance exceeds \$5,000.

B. What other parameters might change if the investigation strategy were to change?

9.11. Timber Products, Inc. (TPI) is an integrated producer of paper products, including fiberboard containers (also known as cardboard boxes) for sale to other businesses. The container business is very competitive, with many small, independent producers and a number of large corporations such as TPI. There has been chronic overcapacity in recent years, and there has been commensurate pressure on profit margins. Therefore, TPI has been stressing the need for efficient operation in its 24 container plants around the company.

One of the important steps in the production of a fiberboard container is the printing and slotting operation. A blank, rectangular piece of cardboard (cut to the required size) is fed into a printer–slotter, which imprints the customer's logo and other information on the blank and also cuts away the parts of the blank that are not needed for the final box. Following this operation, the cardboard is folded and glued and packed for shipment to the customer.

Each customer order is unique in the printing and cutting that must be done—some jobs are relatively simple (standard size box, no printing), while others are more difficult (multiple colors, unusual size and cuts). As each piece leaves the printer–slotter it is visually inspected by an employee. Unusable units are set aside, or if they are not caught by the employee, the customer may return defective boxes for a refund. There are some natural, uncontrollable variations in the production yield, but if the production manager believes that the machine is out of adjustment, it is stopped and readjusted.

The percentage of usable containers from those produced is a vital factor in the profitability of TPI's container plants. For instance, one of the major customers of TPI's Chicago plant is the Azimuth Electronics Corporation, which produces a range of consumer electronics products. The container for Azimuth's most popular television requires two-color printing on all four sides, plus one-color printing on the top and bottom. The container has a selling price of \$1.25, and the variable cost of producing a container (whether it is usable or not) is \$1.00. Therefore, if 90% of the boxes are usable, TPI makes about \$.15 per box, but if the yield falls below 80%, TPI's contribution margin is negative.

The target yield on this type of box is 90%, and if there are no serious problems with the raw materials, the equipment, or the employees' procedures, the yields fluctuate from 85% to 95% with an average of 90%. However, there is a 10% chance each hour of an equipment or material problem occurring, and if this happens the yields tend to fall by 5 to 6%. Past experience indicates that once such problems occur, they continue until corrected. Based on hourly reports, the production manager may halt production to determine the cause of the yield variance and to correct any problems found. On average, it takes 1 hr (out of a 16-hour work day) to find and correct a problem. The average production run for this type of container is 50,000 units, and the maximum rate of production on the printer–slotter is 1,000 units per hour.

The current procedure is to stop the machine and investigate whenever the hourly yield rate drops below 90% (the target yield), but the production manager believes that there might be a better strategy.

Required Evaluate the investigation strategy used by TPI's plant manager. Can you find a strategy that will be more efficient?

REFERENCES

Demski, J., "Optimizing the Search for Cost Deviation Sources," *Management Science*. April 1970.

Dittman, D., and P. Prakash. "Cost Variance Investigation: Markovian Control of Markov Processes," *Journal of Accounting Research*. Spring 1978.

Dittman, D., and P. Prakash. "Cost Variance Investigation: Markovian versus Optimal Control," *Accounting Review*. April 1979.

Dyckman, T. "The Investigation of Cost Variances," *Journal of Accounting Research*. Autumn 1969.

Jacobs, F. "An Evaluation of the Effectiveness of Some Cost Variance Investigation Models," *Journal of Accounting Research*. Spring 1978.

Kaplan, R. "Optimal Investigation Strategies with Imperfect Information," *Journal of Accounting Research*. Spring 1969.

Kaplan, R. "The Significance and Investigation of Cost Variances: Survey and Extensions," *Journal of Accounting Research*. Autumn 1975.

Magee, R. "A Simulation Analysis of Alternative Cost Variance Investigation Models," *Accounting Review*. July 1976.

Magee, R. "Cost Control with Imperfect Parameter Knowledge," *Accounting Review*. January 1977.

Chapter 10

Evaluating Cost Variance Information and the Timing of Feedback Information

The major continuing theme of this book is that managerial accounting alternatives cannot be evaluated without reference to a decision making situation. For instance, if we must decide on the level of aggregation in cost variance reports or on the number and type of uncontrollable factors to incorporate in the *ex post* flexible budgets, it is useful to know how the reports will be used in control decisions. In Chapter 9 we presented some models of the cost variance investigation process, and we can now use that model to address feedback/control information issues. First, we will examine the effects of more accurate/less aggregated variance reports, and then we will address the problems of information timing. For most of this chapter we will use the simplest model in Chapter 9, although the more complex models in Chapter 9 could also be used here.

10.1 WHAT ARE "BETTER VARIANCES?"

In the context of cost variance investigations, the objective of the feedback reports from the accounting process is to enable the manager to assess whether there is an inefficiency that requires some corrective action. Loosely speaking, a *better* set of variances means that the manager will make fewer investigation mistakes. That is, he or she will investigate fewer in-control situations and more out-of-control situations. In addition, where there are many possible sources of inefficiencies, the manager will tend to investigate the inefficient ones first.

Of course, the usual set of variances exemplifies the desire to separate costs into variances that are more interpretable. If production volume is beyond the control of the operating manager, then the budget adjustment variance is designed to extract the fluctuations in costs that do not reflect the level of operating efficiency. The next step in calculating variances is to separate price and usage effects to facilitate the search for any inefficiencies. We will look at these information issues in the next two sections.

10.2 ELIMINATING "UNCONTROLLABLES"

We can look at a variance as a difference between an actual cost number and a standard, or flexible, budget. Essentially, the information problem is how much "flex" to put in a flexible budget. Suppose that the actual cost C depends on the level of control (θ_1 is in-control; θ_2 is out-of-control) and two other, uncontrollable factors, ε_1 and ε_2. For instance, if C is factory power costs, then θ could depend on whether energy conservation procedures were being followed, ε_1 could represent the level of production activity, and ε_2 could represent the weather effect (e.g., degree-days).

There are four budgets that could be used to determine a variance: (i) a static budget $\hat{C}_1$, which does not depend on ε_1 or ε_2; (ii) a flexible budget $\hat{C}_2(\varepsilon_1)$, which incorporates the influence of ε_1 on costs; (iii) a flexible budget $\hat{C}_3(\varepsilon_2)$, which incorporates ε_2; and (iv) a flexible budget $C_4(\varepsilon_1, \varepsilon_2)$, which incorporates the effects of both ε_1 and ε_2. With these four budgets, we would get four different variances.

$$
\begin{aligned}
V_1(\theta, \varepsilon_1, \varepsilon_2) &= C(\theta, \varepsilon_1, \varepsilon_2) - \hat{C}_1 \\
V_2(\theta, \varepsilon_2) &= C(\theta, \varepsilon_1, \varepsilon_2) - \hat{C}_2(\varepsilon_1) \\
V_3(\theta, \varepsilon_1) &= C(\theta, \varepsilon_1, \varepsilon_2) - \hat{C}_3(\varepsilon_2) \\
V_4(\theta) &= C(\theta, \varepsilon_1, \varepsilon_2) - \hat{C}_4(\varepsilon_1, \varepsilon_2)
\end{aligned}
\tag{10.1}
$$

A variance such as V_1 is more difficult to interpret because unfavorable/favorable variances can be caused by uncontrollable factors ε_1 and ε_2. That is, it is likely that more investigation errors will be made with this variance than with the others. The last variance V_4 is the easiest to interpret since the effects of the uncontrollable factors have been washed out by the flexible budgeting process. But the demands on the flexible budgeting process are the greatest, since the values of ε_1 and ε_2 must be recorded by the accounting system, *and* their effects on costs must be known.

In fact, the flexible budgeting process is a cost estimation problem, with the techniques described in Chapters 5 and 6 as our tools. For instance, in a regression context, the choice of independent variables to include can be viewed as a flexible budgeting choice. In the above flexible budgets and variances $\hat{C}_2(\varepsilon_1)$ could be the result of a regression of past costs on past values of ε_1. For example, the factory power costs might be regressed on the level of production activity. The regression's R^2 would represent the amount of variability in costs that can be washed out by the flexible budget, and $1 - R^2$ would be the percentage of variability in costs that will remain in the cost variance. Adding more (statistically significant) independent variables to the regression[1] would increase the flexible budget's ability to explain cost behavior, and make the interpretation of cost variances somewhat easier.

How would a set of better variances affect the investigation decision and, ultimately, the costs of the organization? We can answer that question in the context of the investigation rule (and the model of cost behavior) that we developed in Chapter 9. There are a variety of uncontrollable factors that influence a cost variance. For instance, a labor efficiency variance may be influenced by employee illness, input material quality, effi-

[1]This would include any variables such as $(\text{output})^2$ that would let the flexible budget reflect nonlinear cost behavior.

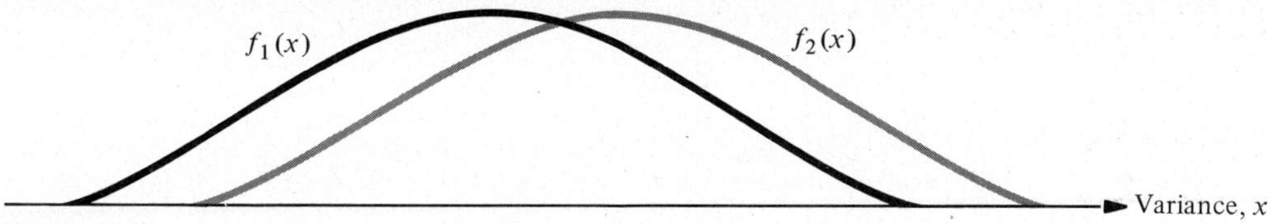

Figure 10.1

ciency in other departments, and many other things that are beyond the control of the production supervisor who has been given responsibility for the labor costs.

We would expect that a well-developed cost standard would reflect the average impact of these factors, but period-to-period fluctuations would affect the cost variances by increasing the likelihood of random, nonrecurring variances. Let's say that this situation is reflected in Figure 10.1. Given these conditions we could find the optimal investigation rule $\bar{X}$, and the expected cost per period associated with this rule $C(\bar{X})$, using a program like INVRUL described in Chapter 9.

But now suppose that a more detailed information system would enable us to eliminate some of these uncontrollable factors from the set of variances. For instance, we may take account of material input quality, the speed with which the maintenance department returns equipment to production, or a variety of other factors. How do these changes affect the above situation? To begin, a source of random, uncontrollable variances has been removed so the new cost distributions may look like those in Figure 10.2.

There is less overlap between the in-control and out-of-control cost distributions, and this means that when we receive a cost variance report there will tend to be less ambiguity about the state of cost control. Another benefit may be a reduction in the expected cost of investigation. If there are fewer factors to sort out in discovering the causes of the cost variance, then it should cost less to discover those causes. With these new parameters, we could again solve for the optimal investigation strategy $\bar{\bar{X}}$ and the expected cost per period given the new parameters, called $\bar{C}(\bar{\bar{X}})$. Then the expected savings per period due to the improvement in the cost variance system is $C(\bar{X}) - \bar{C}(\bar{\bar{X}})$, and this saving (plus savings from other investigation decisions) can be compared to the costs of gathering and processing the data necessary to change the cost variance system.

As an example, suppose that variable overhead depends on the level of cost control, the number of labor hours, the number of machine hours, and the number of production runs, in the following way.

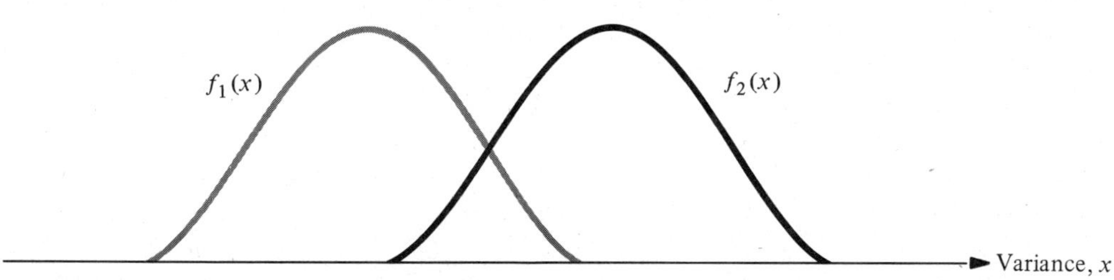

Figure 10.2

$$\text{VOH} = 400\,\theta + \$8\,LH + \$6\,MH + \$50\,\text{runs} \tag{10.2}$$

where $\theta = \begin{cases} 0, & \text{if costs are in-control} \\ 1, & \text{if costs are out-of-control} \end{cases}$

Machine hours and production runs are, in part, related to the number of labor hours. Let's say that on average there is one machine hour and one-twentieth of a production run for every labor hour.

$$\begin{aligned} MH &= LH + \nu; \qquad E[\nu] = 0; \qquad \sigma^2[\nu] = \sigma_\nu^2 \\ \text{Runs} &= (LH/20) + \varepsilon; \qquad E[\varepsilon] = 0; \qquad \sigma^2[\varepsilon] = \sigma_\varepsilon^2 \end{aligned} \tag{10.3}$$

If we develop a flexible budget based on labor hours, it would be [\$8 + \$6 + \$50(1/20)] = \$16.50 per labor hour. But the accuracy of this flexible budget depends on how closely MH and Runs are correlated with LH (i.e., on how big σ_ν^2 and σ_ε^2 are).

$$\begin{aligned} \text{Variable overhead spending variance} &= \text{VOSV} = \text{VOH} - \text{flexible budget} \\ &= (400\,\theta + 8\,LH + 6\,MH + 50\,\text{Runs}) - (16.50\,LH) \\ &= 400\,\theta + 6\,(MH - LH) + 50(\text{Runs} - LH/20) \\ &= 400\,\theta + 6\,\nu + 50\,\varepsilon \end{aligned} \tag{10.4}$$

How much of the VOSV's variability is due to the inaccuracy of the flexible budget? The standard deviation of the uncontrollable factors in VOSV will be $\sigma[6\nu + 50\varepsilon] = (36\sigma_\nu^2 + 2{,}500\sigma_\varepsilon^2)^{1/2}$ and this variability is due to the limited nature of the flexible budget. The information issue here involves an improvement in the flexible budget (e.g., by making it dependent on both labor hours and production runs).

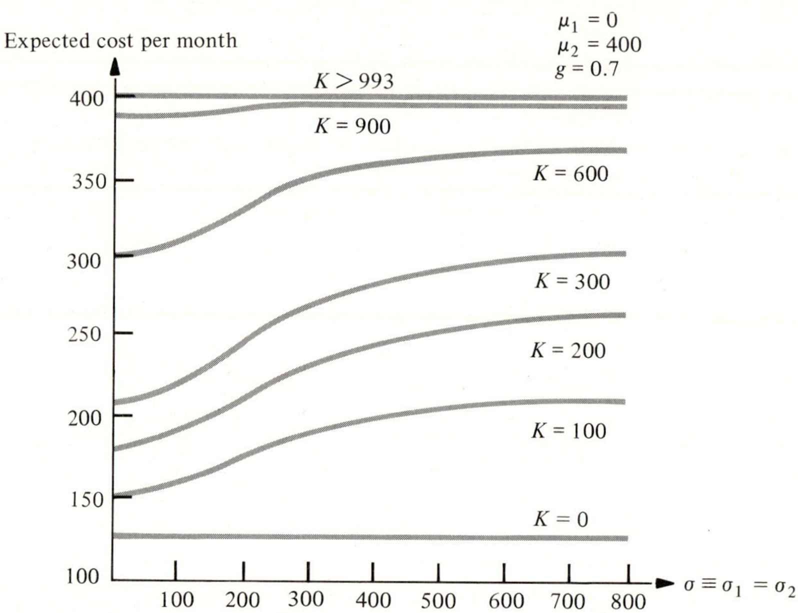

Figure 10.3

$$\begin{aligned} \text{VOSV} &= \text{VOH} - \text{flexible budget} \\ &= \{400\theta + 8LH + 6MH + 50\text{Runs}\} - \{14LH + 50\text{Runs}\} \qquad (10.5) \\ &= 400\theta + 6(MH - LH) = 400\theta + 6\nu \end{aligned}$$

Now the standard deviation of VOSV is reduced to $6\sigma_\nu$. With a little more information, we can explicitly value this information change. We know that $E[\nu] = E[\varepsilon] = 0$, so the expected variance when costs are in control (μ_1) is 0, and the expected variance when costs are out of control (μ_2) is 400. We will assume that the probability of an in-control situation staying that way next period is $g = 0.7$. For our example, assume that $\sigma_\nu = 20$ and $\sigma_\varepsilon = 3$, so that when the flexible budget is based on labor hours only, the standard deviation of the uncontrollable factors will be $[(36)(400) + (2{,}500)(9)]^{1/2} = 192$. The cost of an investigation is \$100. If the flexible budget is based on both labor hours *and* production runs, then the cost of investigation decreases to \$50, and the standard deviation of the VOSV declines to $(6)(20) = 120$. Now these two sets of parameters can be used in the INVRUL program.

	Flexible budget based on	
	Labor hours	Labor hours and production runs
INVRUL parameters:		
μ_1	0	0
μ_2	400	400
σ_1	192	120
σ_2	192	120
K	100	50
g	0.7	0.7
INVRUL results:		
Best strategy	$\overline{X} = \$177$	$\overline{\overline{X}} = \$169$
Cost per period	\$172.05	\$139.96

This analysis indicates that the improved variance would decrease expected costs by \$172.05 − 139.96 or \$32.09 per month. This amount could then be compared to the cost of keeping track of the number of production runs and determining their effect on the variable overhead costs.

The exact amount of savings from more accurate variances will depend on a variety of factors, including the cost of investigation K. For instance, if K is very low, then we would almost always investigate, but it wouldn't cost very much. Therefore, better information wouldn't be very valuable. On the other hand, if K is so high that it never pays to investigate, there will be no benefits from better information on variances. The graphs in Figure 10.3 show how changes in K and $\sigma_1 = \sigma_2 = \sigma$ affect the example above. Each curve shows how the expected monthly costs are affected by increasing the "noise" in the cost variances from $\sigma = 0$ to $\sigma = 800$. The increase in costs as σ increases can be thought of as the loss from increasing the noise in the cost variances. As we compare different curves, we can see that the cost of investigation K influences both the level of costs *and* the loss due to less accurate cost variances. As K becomes small or as K approaches the level where investigations are no longer desirable ($K > 993$ in this example), the potential gain from increasing the accuracy of the variances becomes small. In these cases, the benefits from better information will probably be less than the incremental costs.

While the example above is a simple one, it illustrates how we might address issues of information accuracy in a cost variance situation. In some situations, greater accuracy in variances is achieved by exercising more care in measuring the costs incurred, while in others it may be achieved through more complete flexible budgeting. In either situation, additional resources must be devoted to the cost variance system, and the analysis above would help to determine whether the payoff in improved control exceeds the costs of improved variances.[2]

10.3 SPLITTING THE SOURCES OF INEFFICIENCIES

In the previous section, we considered a situation in which there was one source of possible inefficiency, and a variety of controllable, random factors that made it more difficult to interpret the variances. In this section we tackle a more difficult question. Suppose that a particular operation runs two shifts, and we are trying to evaluate a labor efficiency variance that encompasses *both* shifts. Obviously, it is possible that neither, one, or both, shifts are operating inefficiently. What is the best variance investigation policy in this situation, and, further, how much would it be worth to get separate variances for the two shifts? More generally, how do we value variance systems that provide differing levels of aggregation in their reports? More disaggregate systems will make it easier to discern inefficiencies, but will be more costly to implement.

To address these issues a more complex cost variance investigation model is needed, and we will briefly describe how we might develop one. Instead of two states of control, θ_1 and θ_2, there must be four states of control to describe a situation with two sources of possible inefficiencies. We will call these states θ_{11}, θ_{12}, θ_{21}, and θ_{22}, and define them as in Figure 10.4, where the probability distributions of total costs are also depicted. We can use the same sort of investigation rule as in Chapter 9, where we investigate whenever costs exceed a critical amount $\bar{X}$. (An investigation would check *both* sources.) If we incorporate the probabilities of inefficiencies occurring [$(1 - g_1)$ for source 1 and $(1 - g_2)$ for source 2], we can describe the transitions in a diagram somewhat like that in Appendix 9.1, but more complex (see Figure 10.5).

Even in this more complex situation, we can find the long-run probabilities of being in each of the states as a function of the investigation strategy: $\pi_{11}(\bar{X})$, $\pi_{12}(\bar{X})$, $\pi_{21}(\bar{X})$, and $\pi_{22}(\bar{X})$. These probabilities can be used to find the expected operating cost per period $O(\bar{X})$ and the expected investigation cost per period $I(\bar{X})$.

$$
\begin{aligned}
O(\bar{X}) &= \mu_{11}\pi_{11}(\bar{X}) + \mu_{12}\pi_{12}(\bar{X}) + \mu_{21}\pi_{21}(\bar{X}) + \mu_{22}\pi_{22}(\bar{X}) \\
I(\bar{X}) &= K\{\pi_{11}(\bar{X})[1 - F_{11}(\bar{X})] + \pi_{12}(\bar{X})[1 - F_{12}(\bar{X})] \\
&\quad + \pi_{21}(\bar{X})[1 - F_{21}(\bar{X})] + \pi_{22}(\bar{X})[1 - F_{22}(\bar{X})]\}
\end{aligned} \tag{10.6}
$$

We can now evaluate different investigation rules to discover the most efficient way to use a cost variance that aggregates two sources of possible inefficiencies, and we can estimate the aggregate average cost per period $\bar{C}_A = O(\bar{X}^*) + I(\bar{X}^*)$.

[2]In more complex situations, a simulation analysis may also prove helpful.

θ_{11}: Both sources of inefficiencies (e.g., both shifts) are in control.
θ_{12}: Only Source 2 is out of control.
θ_{21}: Only Source 1 is out of control
θ_{22}: Both Source 1 and Source 2 are out of control.

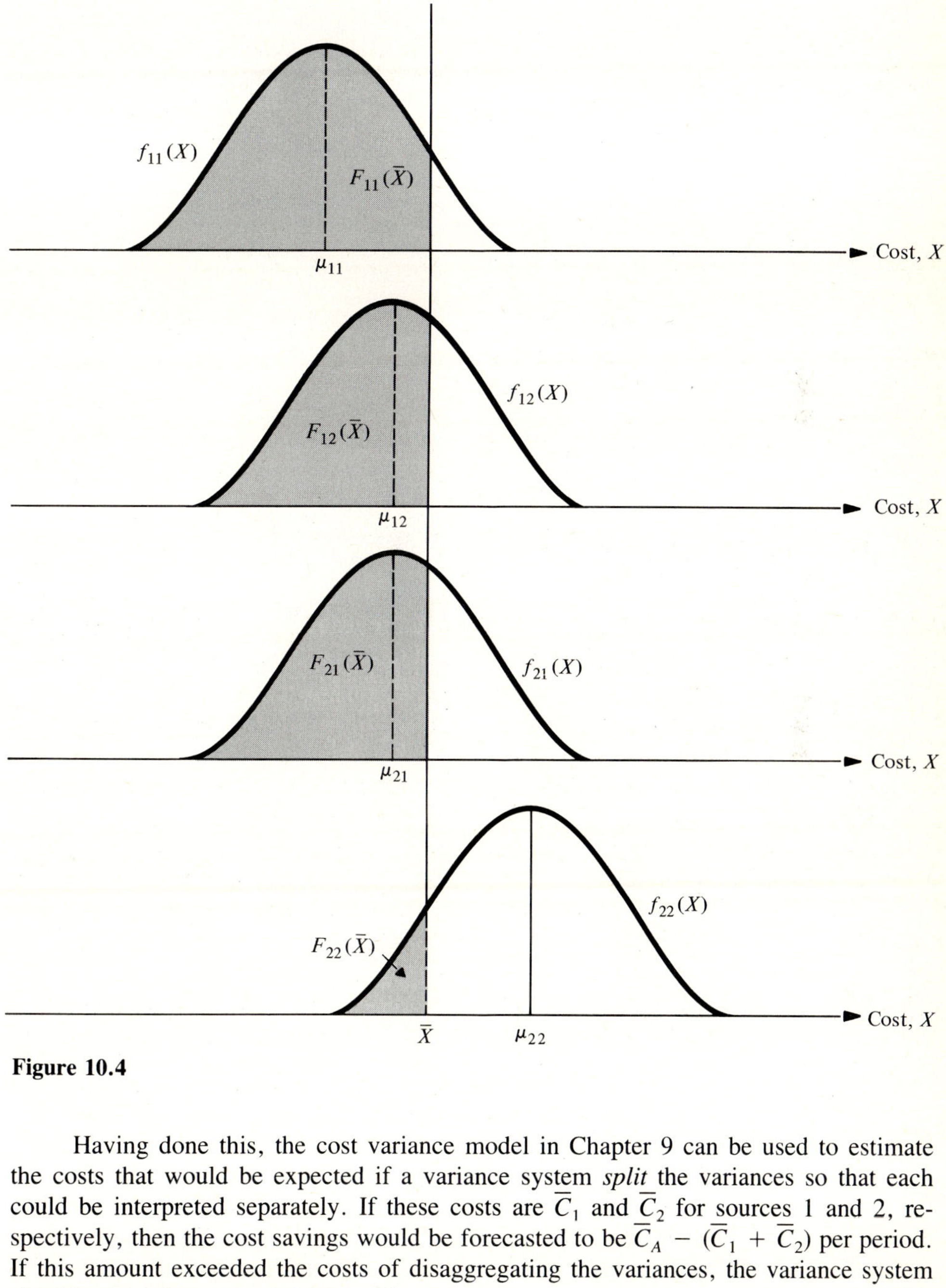

Figure 10.4

Having done this, the cost variance model in Chapter 9 can be used to estimate the costs that would be expected if a variance system *split* the variances so that each could be interpreted separately. If these costs are $\bar{C}_1$ and $\bar{C}_2$ for sources 1 and 2, respectively, then the cost savings would be forecasted to be $\bar{C}_A - (\bar{C}_1 + \bar{C}_2)$ per period. If this amount exceeded the costs of disaggregating the variances, the variance system should report the variances separately.

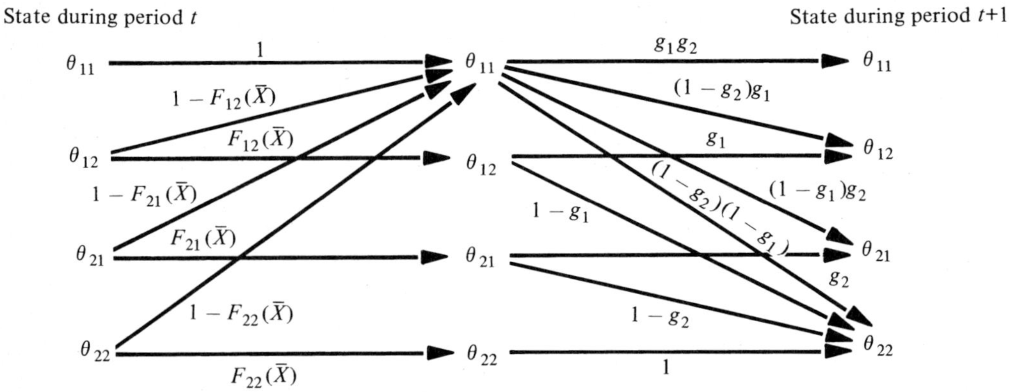

Figure 10.5

Clearly, this information analysis is a very complicated one, and it would be very difficult to implement it on a comprehensive basis. (A simple example is done in Appendix 10.1.) However, the rigorous analysis does provide some pointers that can be useful in conducting a less formal information analysis, because it highlights the key variables to be considered. First, it is necessary to identify the possible sources of inefficiencies that will continue until corrected. Which of these are combined in the current variance reporting system? What is the cost of investigating the combined variance? (If this is low, then there will be little gain to separating the variances.) How would separating the variances affect the costs of reporting, the costs of investigating, and the likelihood of investigating? If these considerations are incorporated in analyzing the alternative variance aggregations, it is more likely that the decisions will make a proper tradeoff between the costs and benefits of improved information.

10.4 THE FREQUENCY OF VARIANCE REPORTS

In setting up a variance reporting system, there are a number of information decisions that need to be made. Ideally, these decisions should be made to maximize the net benefits to the organization. In the last two sections we have taken this approach in determining how many factors to incorporate in the flexible budgets and in deciding which variances to aggregate in the reports. The major remaining issue to be addressed is the frequency with which the variance reports will be received. That is, should reports be received daily, weekly, monthly, or quarterly? Again, we will try to examine this issue by considering the benefits of more timely information (through more effective decision making) and comparing these benefits to the costs.

The costs of a more timely system would most likely arise from the necessary information processing and transmitting capacity and from the data entry activities. For instance, if employees turn in their time records every two weeks, it would require a system change to get labor variance reports on a weekly basis. Or, if the cost of materials is determined by a periodic (monthly) inventory system, it will not be possible to get weekly material cost variances unless a perpetual system is adopted or inventory counts are more frequently made.

While the costs of changing the timing of variance reports are not too difficult to measure, the benefits of more timely information are more difficult to estimate. Suppose we are considering the benefits of getting a variance every week versus every two weeks. Clearly, the benefit of weekly variances is that there is a possibility that costs could get out of control in a given week and we would have the chance to correct that situation right away rather than waiting another week. But *measuring* the benefits of more timely decision making is not easy, as we shall see below.

There is also a potential benefit to waiting an additional week if the weekly variances are noisy. If the weekly means and standard deviations are μ_1 and σ for in-control and μ_2 and σ for out-of-control, and if σ is large relative to $\mu_2 - \mu_1$, there will be a significant overlap in the two distributions. If the variances of two independent weeks are added together, the means go up by a factor of 2 (to $2\mu_1$ and $2\mu_2$) but the standard deviations go up by a factor of $(2)^{1/2} = 1.414$. Therefore the degree of overlap between these two distributions decreases. As a result, biweekly variance reports might reduce the expected number of inappropriate investigations.

If we have the parameters of the weekly cost process ($\mu_1, \sigma_1, \mu_2, \sigma_2, K$, and g), we can use a program like INVRUL to determine the best weekly investigation strategy $\overline{X}_w^*$ and the expected cost per week C_w. But in order to evaluate the benefits of weekly variances versus biweekly variances, we need to have a two-week model of the cost process. To begin, if we assume that an inefficiency can develop (with probability $1 - g$) at the start of each week, then there are three possible states for the two-week process. The process could be in control for both weeks (state θ_{11}), out of control for both weeks (state θ_{22}), or in control for the first week but out of control for the second (state θ_{12}). For each of these states, there would be a probability distribution for the two-week cost, as depicted in Figure 10.6.

As in previous models, the investigation policy could be to investigate if the biweekly cost exceeds a critical value $\overline{X}$, and the probabilities of investigating would be $1 - F_{11}(\overline{X})$ for θ_{11}, $1 - F_{12}(\overline{X})$ for θ_{12}, and $1 - F_{22}(\overline{X})$ for θ_{22}. With these probabilities we can develop the probabilities of transitions between the various states. If a process is in states θ_{12} or θ_{22} at the start of a two-week period, then it will be in θ_{22} for the period, since we have assumed that the process cannot correct itself. If it begins in θ_{11}, there is a $(1 - g)$ probability that it will go out of control immediately (to θ_{22}), a $gg = g^2$ probability of remaining in control throughout the two-week period (θ_{11}), and a $g(1 - g)$ probability of staying in control for the first week and slipping out of control the second. These transition probabilities are depicted in Figure 10.7.

In order to compare the weekly system with the biweekly system, we need to determine the best biweekly investigation policy and the expected biweekly cost. As in previous problems, the key to this analysis is finding the long-run probabilities of being in each of the three states [$\pi_{11}(\overline{X})$, $\pi_{12}(\overline{X})$ and $\pi_{22}(\overline{X})$] as a function of the investigation parameter $\overline{X}$. Although the transitions are more complex, we can utilize the technique described in Appendix 9.2 and set the probabilities before transition equal to the probabilities after transition. (It is also necessary that the three probabilities sum to 1.)

θ_{11}: In control for both weeks.
θ_{12}: In control for the first week, out of control for the second.
θ_{22}: Out of control for both weeks.

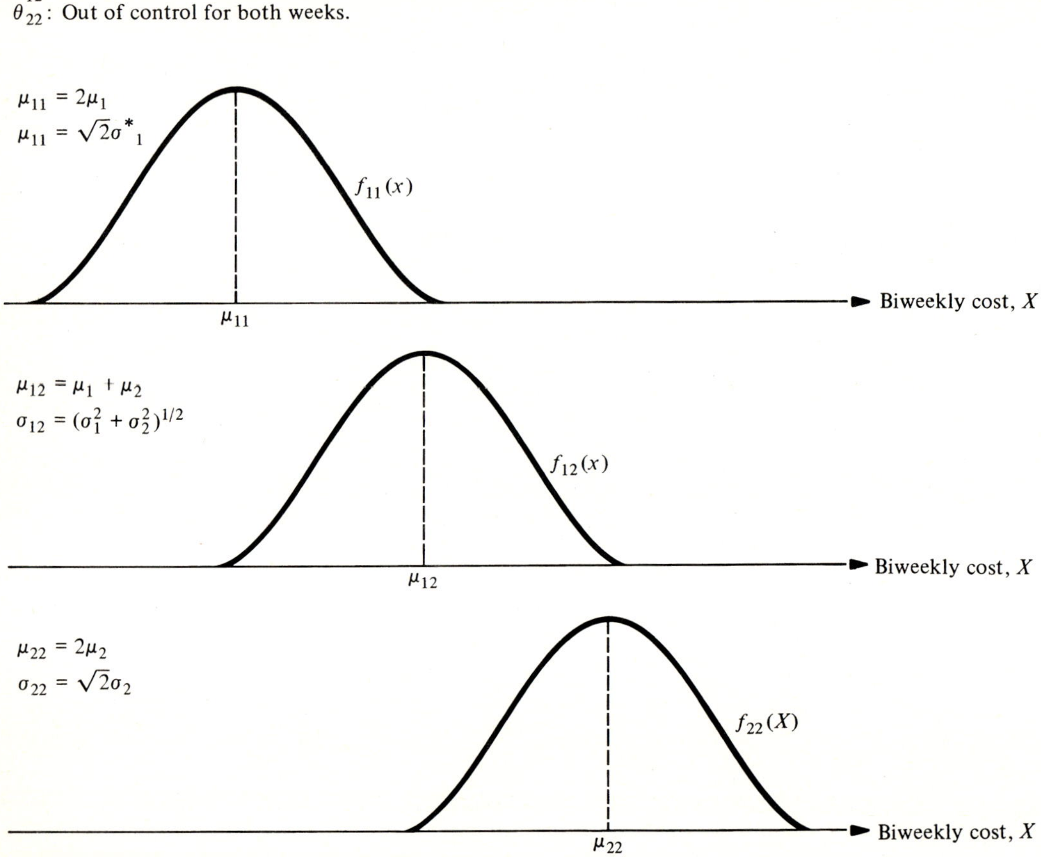

Figure 10.6

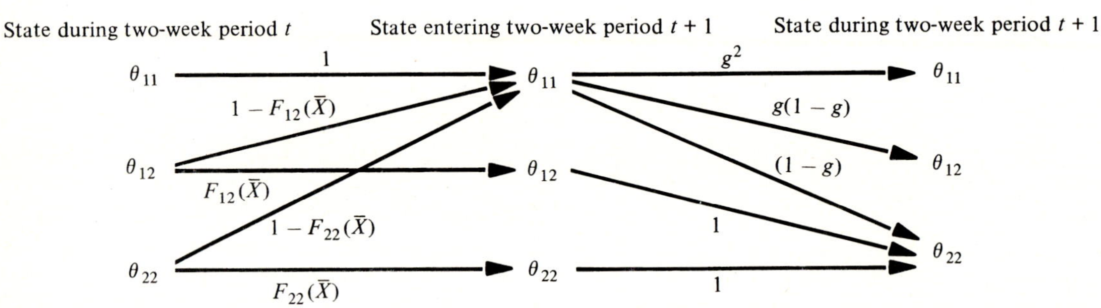

Figure 10.7

Probabilities before transition		Probabilities after transition
$\pi_{11}(\bar{X})$	=	$g^2\pi_{11}(\bar{X}) + g^2[1 - F_{12}(\bar{X})]\,\pi_{12}(\bar{X}) + g^2[1 - F_{22}(\bar{X})]\,\pi_{22}(\bar{X})$
$\pi_{12}(\bar{X})$	=	$g(1 - g)\,\pi_{11}(\bar{X}) + g(1 - g)[1 - F_{12}(\bar{X})]\,\pi_{12}(\bar{X})$ $+ g(1 - g)[1 - F_{22}(\bar{X})]\,\pi_{22}(\bar{X})$
$\pi_{22}(\bar{X})$	=	$(1 - g)\,\pi_{11}(\bar{X}) + \{(1 - g)[1 - F_{12}(\bar{X})] + F_{12}(\bar{X})\}\,\pi_{12}(\bar{X})$ $+ \{(1 - g)[1 - F_{22}(\bar{X})] + F_{22}(\bar{X})\}\,\pi_{22}(\bar{X})$

Given these relationships it is possible to determine the values of $\pi_{11}(\bar{X})$, $\pi_{12}(\bar{X})$, and $\pi_{22}(\bar{X})$ that satisfy them,[3] and to use these probabilities to determine the expected biweekly costs of operation and investigation.

Expected operating cost:

$$O_B(\bar{X}) = \pi_{11}(\bar{X})\mu_{11} + \pi_{12}(\bar{X})\mu_{12} + \pi_{22}(\bar{X})\mu_{22} \tag{10.7}$$

Expected investigation cost:

$$I_B(\bar{X}) = K\{\pi_{11}(\bar{X})[1 - F_{11}(\bar{X})] + \pi_{12}(\bar{X})[1 - F_{12}(\bar{X})] + \pi_{22}(\bar{X})[1 - F_{22}(\bar{X})]\} \tag{10.8}$$

The expected cost per investigation K may or may not change from the weekly system. For instance, if an investigation consists of an examination of the most recent day's operations, then it is likely that the cost per investigation will not differ between the two systems.

Different values of $\bar{X}$ can be examined until the one which yields the lowest value of $O_B(\bar{X}) + I_B(\bar{X})$ is found. We'll call this investigation parameter $\bar{X}_B^*$ and its expected biweekly cost C_B. We would now be in a position to compare the benefits of the weekly and biweekly variance reporting systems. The net savings from the more timely information would be $\frac{1}{2}C_B - C_W$ per week, and this saving could be compared to the additional cost of collecting, processing, and reporting the variances weekly instead of biweekly.

As an example, suppose the weekly cost process had the following parameters.

$$\mu_1 = 0; \quad \sigma_1 = 200; \quad \mu_2 = 400; \quad \sigma_2 = 300; \quad K = 150; \quad g = 0.8 \tag{10.9}$$

Putting these parameters into the INVRUL program yields an investigation strategy of $\bar{X}_w = 240$, and an expected weekly cost of $C_w = \$145.32$. If we were to only get cost variances every two weeks, and if the random cost factors are uncorrelated from week to week, we would get the following parameters.

[3]The values can be found using the following relationships:

$$\pi_{11}(\bar{X}) = \frac{1}{1 + \dfrac{1-g}{g} + \dfrac{(1-g)[1 + gF_{12}(\bar{X})]}{g^2[1 - F_{22}(\bar{X})]}}$$

$$\pi_{12}(\bar{X}) = \frac{1-g}{g}\,\pi_{11}(\bar{X})$$

$$\pi_{22}(\bar{X}) = \frac{(1-g)[1 + gF_{12}(\bar{X})]}{g^2[1 - F_{22}(\bar{X})]}\,\pi_{11}(\bar{X})$$

$$
\begin{aligned}
\mu_{11} &= 0 + 0 = 0 & \sigma_{11} &= (200^2 + 200^2)^{1/2} = 283 \\
\mu_{12} &= 0 + 400 = 400 & \sigma_{12} &= (200^2 + 300^2)^{1/2} = 361 \\
\mu_{22} &= 400 + 400 = 800 & \sigma_{22} &= (300^2 + 300^2)^{1/2} = 424 \\
K &= 150 & g &= 0.8
\end{aligned}
\tag{10.10}
$$

The following table shows the effect of different values of $\overline{X}_B$ on the probabilities and costs. Increasing $\overline{X}_B$ increases the expected operating cost $O_B(\overline{X})$, but decreases the expected investigation cost $I_B(\overline{X})$. The lowest expected biweekly cost of $C_B = 332.51$ occurs at $\overline{X}_B = 200$.[4]

$\overline{X}_B$	$\pi_{11}(\overline{X}_B)$	$\pi_{12}(\overline{X}_B)$	$\pi_{22}(\overline{X}_B)$	$O_B(\overline{X}_B)$	$I_B(\overline{X}_B)$	C_B
0	0.6225	0.1556	0.2219	$239.78	$99.21	$338.99
100	0.6127	0.1532	0.2341	248.56	84.96	333.52
200	0.5996	0.1499	0.2505	260.34	72.17	332.51
300	0.5829	0.1457	0.2714	275.43	61.82	337.25
400	0.5622	0.1405	0.2973	294.05	54.08	348.13

This amount may be divided by 2 and compared to C_w to determine the expected gain from more frequent information. In this case, $\frac{1}{2}C_B - C_w = 166.25 - 145.32 =$ $20.93 per week. If weekly variances could be produced at an incremental cost of less than $20.93 per week, then the more timely information is worth its cost.

The cost savings from more timely information will depend on a number of factors. As the cost of investigation decreases we would expect these savings to increase, since the cost of making a large number of weekly investigations would also decrease. Also, if there were little overlap between the weekly in-control and out-of-control cost distributions, there would be little chance of conducting an unnecessary investigation. In such cases there would be a larger gain from changing from biweekly cost variances to weekly variances.

There are a variety of embellishments that might be made to the model of biweekly variances above. For instance, we might allow the cost process to correct itself with probability h (as in Chapter 9), or we could expand the model to consider a monthly (four-week) variance reporting system. There would have to be five states of nature, and the transition probabilities would be more complex, but the essentials of the analysis would remain unchanged. (At some point it might be easier to analyze the information choices using simulation.)

10.5 TIMING OF INFORMATION: ANOTHER ANALYSIS

Timing is one of the basic attributes of information we discussed in Chapter 1, and in the previous section we analyzed how one might make decisions about the timing (frequency) of variance reports. Naturally, issues of information timing occur in a variety of other situations, and we can attempt to determine the effects of different information timing on decision making and on the payoffs to the organization. In order to do this we

[4] We might look a little further (e.g., $\overline{X}_B = 175$ or 225) to see if yet lower costs could be achieved.

need to have a clear understanding of the *periodic* decision making of the manager and of the ways in which the decision environment can *change* over time. It is the interaction between these two that gives rise to issues in the timing of information, as we saw in the last section. On a very simple basis, the information analysis in Chapter 3 could be viewed as an information timing analysis. The EVPI is a measure of the (expected) value of changing the timing of information about the state of nature from *after* the decision to *before* the decision.

To illustrate a more complex analysis of information timing, suppose that a manager is responsible for setting the price on a product weekly. There are many suppliers of this product, and the customers are other businesses themselves, rather than final consumers. The market for this product has experienced price fluctuations in recent years. The manager knows that the demand for the product depends on the price charged, so the demand and total revenue for week t are the following.

$$\begin{aligned} \text{Demand } x_t &= (A - P_t)/B \\ \text{Revenue}_t &= Ax_t - Bx_t^2 \end{aligned} \tag{10.11}$$

where $x_t \equiv$ the amount sold in week t
$P_t \equiv$ the price charged in week t

The primary reason for price fluctuations is the instability in the price of raw materials used to produce the manager's product. The result of this instability is that the variable cost of producing the product varies from week to week. If v_t is the variable cost per unit in week t, then the relationship between weekly variable costs is the following.

$$v_t = v_{t-1} + \varepsilon_t \tag{10.12}$$

where $\varepsilon_t \equiv$ a random change in the weekly cost

We will assume that ε_t has a mean of zero and a variance of σ_ε^2. If the manager knows v_t at the time he or she sets the price, then he or she will choose to sell the amount x_t that maximizes the contribution margin π_t.

$$\begin{aligned} &\max_{x_t} [Ax_t - Bx_t^2 - v_t x_t] \\ &\rightarrow x_t^* = \frac{A - v_t}{2B}; \quad P_t^* = \frac{A + v_t}{2}; \quad \pi_t^* = \frac{(A - v_t)^2}{4B} \end{aligned} \tag{10.13}$$

We can see from this that the manager's price will be affected by the variable cost, and that he or she would try to pass along half the increases and decreases in the variable costs.

However, it may be difficult for the manager to know v_t at the time he or she sets a price. For instance, the manager may only know v_{t-1}, the variable cost for the week before. In fact, depending on the *timing* of the accounting reports, the manager may only know the variable cost from two weeks ago v_{t-2}, or last month's variable cost. How much does this information delay cost the company? In order to answer this question we need to determine the forecasts, decisions, and payoffs that would occur under different systems, as illustrated below.

		One-week delay	Two-week delay
(a)	Best estimate of v_t	$E[v_t \mid v_{t-1}] = v_{t-1}$	$E[v_t \mid v_{t-2}] = v_{t-2}$
(b)	Expected squared forecasting error	$E(v_t - v_{t-1})^2 = \sigma_\varepsilon^2$	$E(v_t - v_{t-2})^2 = \sigma_\varepsilon^2 + \sigma_\varepsilon^2 = 2\sigma_\varepsilon^2$
(c)	Output that maximizes expected contribution margin	$\dfrac{A - v_{t-1}}{2B}$	$\dfrac{A - v_{t-2}}{2B}$
(d)	Actual profit	$\dfrac{(A - v_t)(A - v_{t-1})}{2B} + \dfrac{(A - v_{t-1})^2}{4B}$	$\dfrac{(A - v_t)(A - v_{t-2})}{2B} + \dfrac{(A - v_{t-2})^2}{4B}$
(e)	Lost profit from not knowing v_t: π_t^* minus the amount in (d)	$\dfrac{(v_{t-1} - v_t)^2}{4B}$	$\dfrac{(v_{t-2} - v_t)^2}{4B}$
(f)	Expected lost profit from information delay	$E\left[\dfrac{(v_{t-1} - v_t)^2}{4B}\right] = \dfrac{\sigma_\varepsilon^2}{4B}$	$E\left[\dfrac{(v_{t-2} - v_t)^2}{4B}\right] = \dfrac{2\sigma_\varepsilon^2}{4B}$

The expected opportunity loss from the information delay increases as the delay increases, and the magnitude of the loss depends on the responsiveness of output and price decisions to changes in costs (reflected in B) and on the degree to which the costs change over time (reflected in σ_ε^2). In the example above, a delay of n time periods means an expected lost profit of $n(\sigma_\varepsilon^2/4B)$. On the other hand, we might expect the cost of providing the information to be a declining function of n. These two factors might be

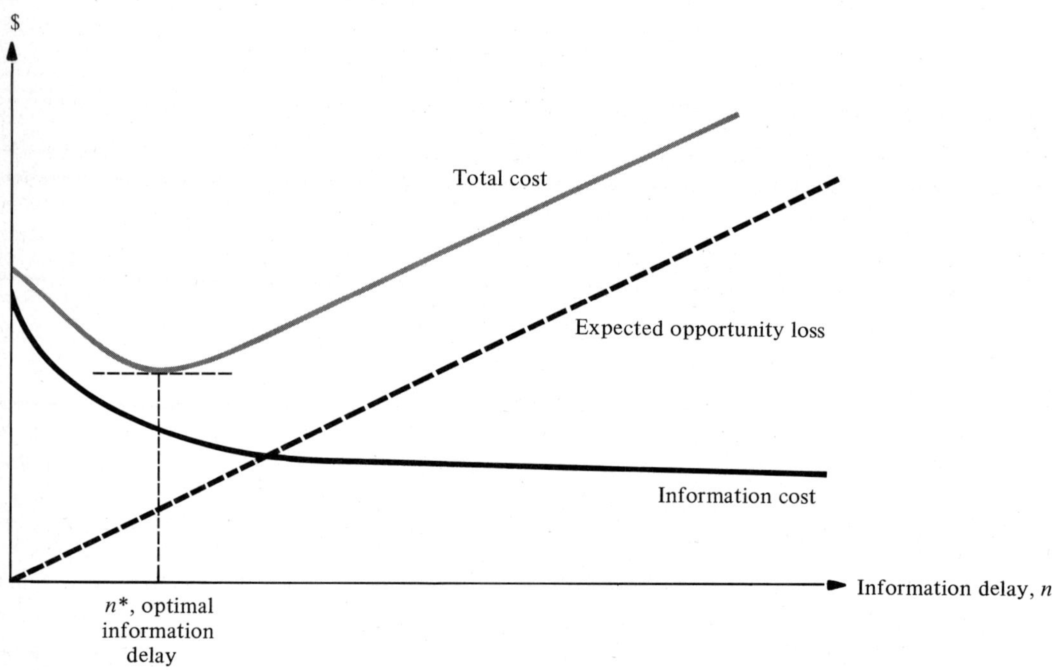

Figure 10.8

depicted as in Figure 10.8, where the optimal time delay would be that which minimized the sum of the two costs.

In addition to the standard variances listed in the appendix to Chapter 9, it is possible to define nonstandard variances that might help to ascertain the contributions of different factors to costs and/or profits. For instance, suppose that a manager earned a contribution margin π_t when the variable cost of production was v_t. One possible variance calculation would be to compare π_t to $\pi_t^* = (A - v_t)^2/4B$, but this calculation would also include any loss due to the fact that the manager's decision was made before v_t was known. If the manager knew v_{t-1}, then he or she should have produced $\hat{x} = (A - v_{t-1})/2B$ units. Therefore, the profit variance $\pi_t - \pi_t^*$ can be broken down into a *flexible profit variance* and an *information delay variance*.

$$\pi_t - \pi_t^* = \underbrace{\{\pi_t - [(A - v_t)\hat{x} - B\hat{x}^2]\}}_{\text{Flexible profit variance}} + \underbrace{\{[(A - v_t)\hat{x} - B\hat{x}^2] - \pi_t^*\}}_{\text{Information delay variance}} \tag{10.14}$$

If the operating manager does not have control over the information delay, then it might make sense to remove the information delay variance before deciding whether to investigate for possible inefficiencies in the operation.

10.6 SUMMARY

As the decision making environment becomes more complex, it becomes more and more difficult to analyze the benefits of different accounting information systems. In looking at multiperiod control decisions, it is first necessary to determine how best to use a given information system and to forecast the costs or profits that will result. The analysis in Chapter 9 demonstrated one approach to this task. In this chapter we have expanded that approach to consider how different information alternatives affected decision making and the periodic costs of the organization. In particular, we tried to find approaches that would let us put a value on a variance reporting system that was more accurate or less aggregated or more timely. It is true that these approaches are complex, and it would probably not be appropriate to utilize them for making all variance reporting decisions. Nevertheless, it is important to understand how one might apply an *information economics* perspective in these situations, since it highlights the critical variables and their impact on the information system choice. (For example, Figure 10.3 illustrates the effect of investigation cost on the value of more accurate variances.)

There is one aspect of the models in Chapters 9 and 10 that represents a limitation that should be recognized. These models assume that the manager's investigation policy (e.g., $\overline{X}$) has no effect on the parameters of the cost process (g, u_2, σ_2, etc.) That is, there is no motivation effect to the investigation strategy. While there are situations in which this assumption is realistic, there are undoubtedly other situations in which it is not. An alternative approach would be to specifically consider the effects of the management control system on the decision making within the organization. In the remaining chapters of the book, we will consider the role that managerial accounting plays in organizations' performance evaluation systems.

APPENDIX 10.1: Estimating the Savings from Disaggregating Variances

The process of estimating how much would be saved by splitting the sources of inefficiencies was described in the chapter. In this appendix, we do a simple numerical example to illustrate that process.

Suppose we had two identical operations that could be reported separately or together. Each process may be in-control or out-of-control, and each is independent of the other. If a process is in-control, its cost variances are normally distributed with mean \$0 and standard deviation 283. If an inefficiency occurs, the mean increases to \$400. The probability of an inefficiency developing at the beginning of a period is 0.2, and it costs \$100 to investigate a variance. If the investigation rule is to check all variances in excess of \$200, then it is a simple matter to find the expected cost per period $\overline{C}_1$ using INVRUL.

$$\begin{aligned} &u_1 = 0; \quad \sigma_1 = 283 \\ &u_2 = 400; \quad \sigma_2 = 283 \\ &K = 100; \quad g = 1 - 0.2 = 0.8 \\ &\overline{X} = 200 \text{ yields } \overline{C}_1 = \$136 \end{aligned} \tag{A10.1}$$

Since we have two identical independent operations, we know that the expected cost per period will be $\overline{C}_1 + \overline{C}_2 = 2\overline{C}_1 = \$272$, *if* the variances are reported separately.

If the variances are reported in total, then the analysis becomes more complex because there are four states instead of two. (See Figure 10.4). The means and standard deviations of the cost variances will be the following.

State	Expected variance	Standard deviation of variance
θ_{11}	0 + 0 = \$ 0	$(283^2 + 283^2)^{1/2} = 400$
θ_{12}	0 + 400 = \$400	400
θ_{21}	400 + 0 = \$400	400
θ_{22}	400 + 400 = \$800	400

That is, if operation 1 is in control and operation 2 is out of control, the aggregated cost variance will have a normal distribution with mean \$400 and standard deviation of 400.

For this example we assume that an investigation will take place if the aggregate variance exceeds $\overline{X} = 400$ and the investigation of the combined process costs \$200. In order to determine the steady-state probabilities, we need to determine $F_{ij}(\overline{X})$, the probability of no investigation if the state is θ_{ij}. (See Figure 10.4). If $\overline{X} = 400$, the approximate values will be the following (based on the normal distribution).

$$\begin{aligned} F_{11}(400) &= 0.84 \\ F_{12}(400) &= 0.50 \\ F_{21}(400) &= 0.50 \\ F_{22}(400) &= 0.16 \end{aligned} \tag{A10.2}$$

We also know that $g_1 = g_2 = 0.8$, so the next step is to determine the steady-state probabilities $\pi_{11}(\overline{X})$, etc. This must be done by using the transition probabilities in Figure 10.5 and the technique described in Appendix 9.2. (The calculations are more complex, but the logic remains the same). The following probabilities result. (You can check to see whether these are steady-state probabilities.)

$$\begin{aligned}\pi_{11}(400) &= 0.49828\\ \pi_{12}(400) &= 0.20761\\ \pi_{21}(400) &= 0.20761\\ \pi_{22}(400) &= 0.08650\end{aligned} \tag{A10.3}$$

From these probabilities we can calculate the expected operating cost and the expected investigation cost using the equations in the chapter.

$$\begin{aligned}O(400) &= (\$0)(0.49828) + (\$400)(0.207613) + (\$400)(0.207613)\\ &\quad + (\$800)(0.086506)\\ &= \$235\\ I(400) &= \$200[(0.49828)(0.16) + (0.207613)(0.5) + (0.207613)(0.5)\\ &\quad + (0.086506)(0.84)]\\ &= \$72\\ \overline{C}_A &= O(400) + I(400) = \$307\end{aligned} \tag{A10.4}$$

We can see that the expected cost per period is \$307 or \$35 per period *more* than when the variances were reported separately. Therefore, if the disaggregation of the variances costs less than \$35 per period, it would be beneficial to do so. (However, we should check other policies for the aggregated process before arriving at a final decision.)

PROBLEMS

10.1. The ABC Company is considering a change in its accounting system that would give it more accurate information about the direct labor usage costs in their chain of automobile transmission repair shops. Use the program INVRUL to determine the effect that the proposed system would have on the investigation policy for the monthly direct labor costs of a typical shop shown below.

	Current	Proposed
Expected cost (in control)	\$14,000	\$14,000
Standard deviation (in control)	\$ 1,500	\$ 900
Expected cost (out of control)	\$16,000	\$16,000
Standard deviation (out of control)	\$ 2,000	\$ 1,000
Expected cost of investigation	\$ 600	\$ 400
Probability of inefficiency developing	0.2	0.2

Required

A. Use INVRUL to determine the optimal investigation policy and the expected cost per period for (i) the current system and (ii) the proposed system.

B. How should the analysis in A be used in evaluating the proposed system?

10.2. "The sales representative from the computer company says that their new cost accounting package would make our management-by-exception system easier to implement. Apparently, the input data is stored in more detail, so it makes it a lot easier to investigate the cause of a cost variance. But of course there's no such thing as a free lunch; it's going to cost us something to get this new capability.

"To get an idea as to whether it's worth it, I want you to look at one of our labor variances. The standard cost is \$50,000, but there are always some random, uncontrollable factors that influence costs. Historically, these factors mean that there is a standard deviation of $4,000 around the standard, even when there is no correctable inefficiency. When there is a problem that requires correction, the expected cost increases by about 12%, but the random fluctuations are not affected. If things are OK in a given month, I think there's about an 80% chance that they'll be OK the next month too.

"Now, we've been investigating all the unfavorable variances that have occurred. That's about 60% of the months in the past couple of years. An investigation costs about $2,500 on average, and the new system should cut that in half. That means a monthly expected savings of 0.6(2,500 − 1,250) = $750, which is pretty impressive. It looks to me like we ought to go ahead with the new system. What do you think?"

Required Below are the results of two runs of the program INVRUL. Write a brief (but specific) memo about the benefits of the proposed system change.

INVRUL results

$\mu_1 = 50{,}000$; $\sigma_1 = 4{,}000$

$\mu_2 = 56{,}000$; $\sigma_2 = 4{,}000$

$g = 0.8$

$\bar{X}$	Expected monthly cost if K = 2,500	Expected monthly cost if K = 1,250
$50,000	$52,747	$52,007
50,500	52,662	51,975
51,000	52,583	51,947
51,500	52,512	51,926
52,000	52,451	51,913
52,500	52,402	51,909
53,000	52,366	51,916
53,500	52,346	51,935
54,000	52,344	51,968
54,500	52,359	52,017
55,000	52,395	52,081
55,500	52,451	52,163
56,000	52,528	52,264

10.3. For simplicity, assume that the probability distributions of weekly costs are as below.

	In control		Out of control	
Costs, x	$f_1(x)$	$F_1(x)$	$f_2(x)$	$F_2(x)$
$1,000	0.5	0.5	0.0	0.0
1,500	0.5	1.0	0.5	0.5
2,000	0.0	1.0	0.5	1.0

The probability of an inefficiency developing during a week (if none existed the week before) is 0.2, and the expected cost of an investigation is $400. As a cost-cutting measure, the company is considering reporting these costs only every two weeks.

Required

A. If the weekly cost variance investigation policy is to investigate whenever costs exceed

$1,600, what are the long-run probabilities of being in control and out of control? What are the long-run expected costs per period? (You will need to refer to Chapter 9 to answer this question.)

B. If costs are only reported biweekly, what is the distribution of cost reports? What are the long-run probabilities if the policy is to investigate all reports exceeding $3,200? What are the long-run expected costs per period?

10.4. At present, the ABC Company calculates its overhead cost variance based on a static budget of $200,000 per month. That is, the variance is calculated as follows:

$$\text{Overhead variance} = \text{actual monthly overhead} - \$200{,}000$$

An analysis of overhead cost behavior has found that some of these costs vary with the level of activity, while others do not. The result of this result is the cost model below.

$$\text{Monthly overhead} = \$100{,}000 + \$10\text{DLH} + \text{other factors}$$

The direct labor hours (*DLH*) fluctuate from month to month, and are expected to follow a normal probability distribution with mean of 10,000 and standard deviation of 400. The other factors represent the effects of month to month fluctuations, and you may assume that they follow a normal distribution with a mean of $0 and standard deviation of $5,000.

When an inefficiency develops in the overhead costs, the fixed portion increases by $15,000, and this will continue until an investigation (costing $3,000, on average) is conducted to determine the cause of the problem. If no inefficiency exists in a given month, the probability of one not developing the next month is 0.85.

Required

A. Determine the cost variance investigation parameters for the existing variance calculations.

B. Determine the cost variance investigation parameters for a variance based on a flexible budget of $100,000 + $10DLH.

C. Using INVRUL, determine the effects of the change in variance calculation on the optimal investigation policy and on the expected cost per period.

10.5. Refer to the data given in problem 9.9. Based on the information given there, consider the possibility that the variances might be reported only every other week? If Peter Campbell had followed the same strategy of investigating all unfavorable variances, how would the cost process have been affected? That is, look for instances where unnecessary investigation costs might have been avoided, or where an out-of-control cost process might have gone uncorrected.

Required

A. Based on your analysis of the actual cost over the twenty weeks, would you recommend that variances only be reported biweekly? (Assume that the cost of investigation is unchanged.)

B. Using the parameter estimates you developed in problem 9.9, evaluate a biweekly investigation strategy besides the one proposed above.

10.6. Rebecca Chandler has the responsibility of determining the pricing and production of her company's major product for the next *two periods*. A substantial amount of market research has already been conducted to estimate the consumer response to the product so *each period's demand curve* is believed to be reflected in the following relationships.

$$\text{Demand} = (8{,}000 - 1{,}000 \times \text{Price}) \text{ units}$$
$$\text{Revenue} = 8 \times (\text{units sold}) - 0.001 \times (\text{units sold})^2$$

The production cost behavior is less certain. The period's fixed costs will be $10,000, but the variable cost per unit is not known. For simplicity, assume that there are two possible cost relationships, each equally likely.

$$\text{Possibility 1: Cost} = 10{,}000 + 1.00 \times (\text{units produced})$$
$$\text{Possibility 2: Cost} = 10{,}000 + 1.10 \times (\text{units produced})$$

Required

A. Assuming that Rebecca Chandler must operate for both periods with the cost information given above, what is the best level of production for each of the two periods? What is the expected profit for this period of time?

B. Suppose that Rebecca Chandler could get a special cost report that would let her know which cost possibility was true before choosing the level of production for the first period. What would be the expected value of the information contained in that report?

C. If the report in part B were delayed until the end of the first period of operation, what would be the expected cost of this delay?

D. In general, what factors influence the cost of information delay?

10.7. Katie Lambert is in charge of manufacturing control for a small company in the southwestern United States. Every week, she receives a variance report that enables her to review the past week's operations. Based on this report, she can conduct investigations into various aspects of the plant's operations. "One problem is that the manufacturing costs depend both on the level of cost control that is achieved in the plant and on the attention to quality control. That is, it is possible for a favorable cost variance to be caused by poor quality control. Of course, such a situation costs us more in the long run, but it doesn't show up on the weekly reports. Therefore, I should investigate favorable as well as unfavorable variances.

To analyze this type of situation, suppose that at the beginning of each week there is a 0.2 probability that a cost control inefficiency will develop and remain until corrected, and a 0.2 probability that a quality control inefficiency will develop and continue until corrected. (You may assume that the occurrence of a cost control inefficiency is independent of the occurrence of a quality control inefficiency. That is, it is possible for both to occur at the same time, for a cost process with a cost control inefficiency to develop a quality control inefficiency, and so on.)

The possible states of control and the probability distributions of the weekly cost variances are given below.

State no.	Description
1	No inefficiencies
2	Cost control inefficiency only
3	Quality control inefficiency only
4	Cost control *and* quality control inefficiencies

Cost variance, x($)	Probability if in control, $f_1(x)$	Probability if out of control (costs), $f_2(x)$	Probability if out of control (quality), $f_3(x)$	Probability if out of control (cost and quality), $f_4(x)$
−2,000	0.00	0.00	0.10	0.00
−1,500	0.00	0.00	0.20	0.00
−1,000	0.10	0.00	0.40	0.10
− 500	0.20	0.00	0.20	0.20
0	0.40	0.10	0.10	0.40
500	0.20	0.20	0.00	0.20
1,000	0.10	0.40	0.00	0.10
1,500	0.00	0.20	0.00	0.00
2,000	0.00	0.10	0.00	0.00

Required

A. Suppose that the strategy is to investigate all variances that are more than $1,200 favorable *or* unfavorable. What are the steady-state probabilities for the four states? (You shouldn't have to do extensive calculations.)

B. Construct a diagram that describes the transition probabilities among the four states from one period of operation to the next. Fill in the probabilities if the strategy is to investigate all variances that exceed $800 favorable or unfavorable. Can you determine the steady-state probabilities?

C. The production standards department has proposed a system which would provide quality control information on a continuing basis. In effect, it would give Katie Lambert a report every week as to whether a quality control inefficiency existed. How would such information influence the investigation problem above? In particular, would it help to control the cost inefficiencies?

10.8. The behavior of weekly costs for the repair and maintenance department of the Hapless Manufacturing Company is described by the parameters below.

In control:	
Expected cost per week	$15,000
Standard deviation	2,000
Out of control:	
Expected cost per week	$17,000
Standard deviation	2,000
Expected cost of conducting an investigation	$ 500
Probability that an in-control situation will remain in control the next week	0.8

Required

A. The plant manager has responsibility for controlling the costs of the repair and maintenance department. He receives a cost report every week, and decides whether to investigate the last week's activities. If the weekly investigation strategy is to investigate if costs exceed $16,000, what is the expected cost per week?

B. Suppose that the manager were to receive reports on total costs every two weeks instead of every week. How many states of control are there? What is the probability distribution of costs for each state of control? (Assume that the uncontrollable factors are independent from week to week.)

C. If the strategy is to investigate if the two-week costs exceed $32,000, determine the steady-state probabilities of being in each state. What is the expected cost of operation? Of investigation? How do these costs compare to those found in part A?

10.9. "I have responsibility for cost control at two different operations servicing the northeastern United States," said Josh Andersen. "I get reports every month about the revenues, production levels, and costs for the previous month. One difficulty that I have is trying to base my decisions on the information from both operations rather than on the results from a single operation. For instance, in energy costs, both operations face common uncertainties—utility rate changes, weather conditions, and so on. Therefore, I should probably make my investigation decisions on how the two operations fared. If they both went over budget, it's probably because of common uncontrollable factors, while if one is over budget and the other is not, it's much more likely that the first was operating inefficiently.

The information given below reflects the cost behavior of the monthly heating costs at the two operations. Each operation has a probability of 0.2 of an inefficiency developing in the month following a month of efficient operation. The cost of investigation is $1,000.

$$\text{Cost of process } 1 = 10{,}000 + 1{,}000\theta_1 + \mu_1$$
$$\text{Cost of process } 2 = 10{,}000 + 1{,}000\theta_2 + \mu_2$$

where $\theta_i = 0$ if process i is in control and 1 if process i is out of control. The following table shows the joint probabilities of the random cost fluctuations μ_1 and μ_2.

	μ_2		
μ_1	−1,000	0	+1,000
−1,000	0.2	0.1	0.0
0	0.1	0.2	0.1
+1,000	0.0	0.1	0.2

Required

A. Calculate the correlation between the random disturbances μ_1 and μ_2.

B. Using simulation, estimate the expected cost per period if the rule is to investigate all unfavorable variances for either cost process.

C. Do you think you might be able to improve on the cost variance investigations in part B by considering both variances simultaneously? What sort of investigation strategy would you want to consider? Use simulation to determine the expected cost per period for your strategy.

10.10. (CMA). Pearsons, a successful regional chain of moderate-priced-menu restaurants, each with a carryout delicatessen department, is planning to expand to a nationwide operation. As the chain gets larger and the territory covered becomes wider, managerial control and reporting techniques become more important.

The company management believes that a budget program for the entire company as well as each restaurant–deli unit is needed. The budget presented below was prepared for a typical unit in the chain. A new unit, once it is in operation, is expected to perform in accordance with the budget.

TYPICAL PEARSONS RESTAURANT-DELI
BUDGETED INCOME STATEMENT FOR THE YEAR
ENDING DECEMBER 31
(000 omitted)

	Delicatessen	Restaurant	Total
Gross sales	$1,000	$2,500	$3,500
Purchases	$ 600	$1,000	$1,600
Hourly wages	50	875	925
Franchise fee	30	75	105
Advertising	100	200	300
Utilities	70	125	195
Depreciation	50	75	125
Lease expense	30	50	80
Salaries	30	50	80
Total	$ 960	$2,450	$3,410
Net income before income taxes	$ 40	$ 50	$ 90

All units are approximately the same size, with the amount of space devoted to the carryout delicatessen similar in each unit. The style of the facilities and the equipment used are uniform in all units. The unit operators are expected to carry out the advertising program recommended by the corporation. The corporation charges a franchise fee which is a percentage of gross sales for the use of the company name, the building and facilities design, and the advertising advice.

The Akron, Ohio unit was selected to test the budget program. The Akron, Ohio restaurant–deli performance for the year ended December 31, 1985 compared to the typical budget is presented below. A careful review of the report and a discussion of its meaning was carried out by the company management. One conclusion was that a more meaningful comparison would result if a flexible budget analysis for each of the two lines was performed, rather than just a single budget comparison as in the test case.

PEARSONS RESTAURANT–DELI
AKRON, OHIO
NET INCOME FOR THE YEAR ENDED DECEMBER 31, 1985

	Actual results				
	Delicatessen	Restaurant	Total	Budget	(Under) budget
Gross sales	$1,200	$2,000	$3,200	$3,500	$(300)
Purchases	$ 780	$ 800	$1,580	$1,600	$(20)
Hourly wages	60	700	760	925	(165)
Franchise fee	36	60	96	105	(9)
Advertising	100	200	300	300	
Utilities	76	100	176	195	(19)
Depreciation	50	75	125	125	
Lease expense	30	50	80	80	
Salaries	30	50	80	80	
Total	$1,162	$2,035	$3,197	$3,410	$(213)
Net income before income taxes	$ 38	$ (35)	$ 3	$ 90	(87)

Required

A. Prepare a schedule that compares a flexible budget for the deli line of the Akron restaurant–deli to its actual performance.

B. Would a complete report, comparing a flexible budget to the performance of each of the two operations, make the problems of the Akron operation easier to identify? Explain, using an example from the problem and your answer to requirement A.

C. Should a flexible budget comparison to actual performance become part of the regular reporting system

1. for the annual review?

2. for a monthly review?

Explain your answer. If you believe more information is needed before making a recommendation, describe that information and how you would obtain it.

10.11. (CMA). The Justin Company has recently installed a standard cost system to simplify its factory bookkeeping and to aid in cost control. The company makes standard items for inventory, but because of the many products in its line, each is manufactured periodically under a production order. Prior to the installation of the system, job order cost sheets were maintained for each production order. Since the introduction of the standard cost system, however, they have not been kept.

The fabricating department is managed by a general supervisor who has overall responsibility for scheduling, performance, and cost control. The department consists of four machine/work centers. Each work center is manned by a four-person work group or team and the centers are aided by a twelve-person support group. Departmental practice is to assign a job to one team and expect the team to perform most of the work necessary to complete the job, including acquisition of materials and supplies from the stores department and machining and assembling. This has been practical and satisfactory in the past and is readily accepted by the employees. Information regarding production cost standards, products produced, and actual costs for the fabricating department in March is presented below.

UNIT STANDARD COSTS

	Part		
	A7A	C6D	C7A
Material	$2.00	$ 3.00	$1.50
Direct labor	1.50	2.00	1.00
Overhead (per direct labor dollar)[a]			
Variable	3.00	4.00	2.00
Fixed	.75	1.00	.50
	$7.25	$10.00	$5.00

[a]The departmental standard overhead rates are applied to the products as a percentage of direct labor dollars. The labor base was chosen because nearly all the variable overhead costs are caused by labor activity. The departmental overhead rates were calculated at the beginning of the year as follows:

	Variable (including indirect labor)	Fixed
Estimated annual cost	$360,000	$ 90,000
Estimated annual department direct labor dollars	$180,000	$180,000
Overhead rate	200%	50%

ANALYSIS OF THE FABRICATING COMPANY
ACCOUNT FOR MARCH

Charges		
Materials		
Job No. 307-11	$ 5,200	
Job No. 307-12	2,900	
Job No. 307-14	9,400	$17,500
Labor charges		
Job No. 307-11	$ 4,000	
Job No. 307-12	2,100	
Job No. 307-14	6,200	
Indirect labor	12,200	24,500
Variable overhead costs (e.g., supplies, electricity, etc.)		18,800
Fixed overhead costs (e.g., supervisor's salary, depreciation, property tax, insurance, etc.)		7,000
Total charges to department for March		$67,800
Credits		
Completed jobs		
Job No. 307-11: 2,000 units part A7A @ 7.25	$14,500	
Job No. 307-12: 1,000 units part C6D @ 10.00	10,000	
Job No. 307-14: 6,000 units part C7A @ 5.00	30,000	$54,500
Variances transferred to the factory variance account		
Materials[a]	$ 1,500	
Direct labor[b]	1,300	
Variable overhead	9,000	
Fixed overhead	1,500	13,300
Total credits		$67,800

[a]Material price variances are isolated at acquisition and charged to the stores department.
[b]All direct labor was paid at the standard wage rate during March.

Required

A. Justin Company assumes that its efforts to control costs in the fabricating department would be aided if variances were calculated by jobs. Management intends to add this analysis next month. Calculate all the variances by job that might contribute to cost control under this assumption.

B. Do you agree with the company's plan to initiate the calculation of job variances in addition to the currently calculated departmental variances? Explain your answer.

REFERENCES

Demski, J. ''An Accounting System Structured on a Linear Programming Model,'' *Accounting Review*. October 1967.

Hicks, J. ''The Application of Exponential Smoothing to Standard Cost Systems,'' *Management Accounting*. September 1978.

Hughes, J. ''Optimal Timing of Cost Information,'' *Journal of Accounting Research*. Autumn 1975.

Ijiri, Y., and H. Itami. ''Quadratic Cost–Volume Relationship and Timing of Demand Information,'' *Accounting Review*. October 1973.

Itami, H. *Adaptive Behavior: Management Control and Information Analysis*. Sarasota, FL: AAA. 1977.

Magee, R. ''The Usefulness of Commonality Information in Cost Control Decisions,'' *Accounting Review*. October 1977.

Magee, R., and J. Dickhaut. ''Effects of Compensation Plans on Heuristics in Cost Variance Investigations,'' *Journal of Accounting Research*. Autumn 1978.

Rockness, H., J. Bazley, and L. Nikolai. ''Variance Analysis for Pollution Control,'' *Management Accounting*. January 1977.

Ronen, J. ''Nonaggregation versus Disaggregation of Variances,'' *Accounting Review*. January 1974.

Chapter 11

Performance Evaluation

In the mid-1970s an article in the financial press described the new executive compensation plan at a large manufacturing concern. Under the new plan, executives could buy shares of stock at book value per share,[1] receive regular dividends, and, eventually, sell the stock back to the company at the then-prevailing book value per share. An executive's return would be dividends plus the change in the book value per share, or, simply, net income per share, as measured by the accounting system. However, the article also described an adverse reaction on the part of shareholders to this plan.

The modern corporation is not only characterized by a separation of ownership and control, but control is often dispersed through the organization by decentralization. This separation produces a set of problems that we have not yet addressed in this book, namely, those problems that involve the conflicting objectives of shareholders and managers, or of central management and decentralized managers. In the article described above, accounting measures are used to reward top-level managers—a practice that is common at many levels of many organizations. But at least some of the shareholders do not perceive that these plans are in their best interest, and the financial press frequently reports disagreements between shareholders and management over the latter's compensation.

In this chapter, we examine performance evaluation and performance measurement issues in a general way, and develop a framework that can be used to address these issues. Questions of motivation, risk aversion, and information must be considered in determining the role that accounting plays in measuring performance.

The chapters that follow examine specific managerial accounting issues in more detail. Chapter 12 examines the target setting or budget setting process, and explores the difficulties that occur when the decentralized manager has better information than the central management. Chapters 13 and 14 are devoted to the effects of accounting allo-

[1]Book value per share equals assets minus liabilities divided by the number of shares.

cations on performance measurement and managerial decision making. Chapter 13 examines allocations across activities such as service department allocations, responsibility accounting, and transfer pricing. Allocations over time, such as revenue recognition and depreciation, are explored in Chapter 14.

11.1 THE AGENCY RELATIONSHIP AND SOME KEY QUESTIONS

Examples of the relationship between a *principal* and an *agent* surround us in modern society. A principal delegates decision making authority to an agent, and then must provide appropriate incentives or controls to influence those decisions. Examples of this relationship include those between the government and the governed, between the owners and the board of directors, between the chief executive officer (CEO) and his or her division managers, and so on. For the most part, we will be dealing with principal–agent relationships *within* a decentralized organization, since the accounting issues that arise in this situation are most readily classified as managerial accounting issues. The vast majority of large U.S. corporations have incentive plans or bonus plans for their management that are based on results measured by an accounting system.

There are a number of reasons why the agent's choice of action may not conform to the principal's preferred action. For instance, the department manager may be more risk-averse than top management, causing him or her to choose a conservative product mix. Top management may have a ten-year decision horizon, while the department manager only expects to be in the current job for two more years. As a result, there may be a difference of opinion about the desirability of an eight-year investment project. There are a variety of other sources of conflict between the principal and the agent who has been given decision making authority, and we shall consider additional causes in a later section. But an important determinant in the solution of these problems is the amount and types of information available to the agent and the principal, and in a large, decentralized organization, this information is largely influenced by the planning, budgeting, and accounting process.

Basically, there are three key questions that must be answered if the performance evaluation system is to be effective: (1) From the organization's point of view, what is the desired decision making behavior by the decentralized manager? (2) Given the current performance evaluation system, what decision making behavior is being encouraged? If the answers to (1) and (2) differ, then there is the possibility that we may be able to improve the performance evaluation system. However, such improvements may not be easy to find, requiring a careful orchestration of both the organization's and the decentralized manager's objectives and opportunities. The organization cannot continue to improve its position at the expense of the manager—he or she will seek opportunities elsewhere. Therefore, if the answers to questions (1) and (2) differ, we may ask (3) whether there are modifications of the accounting (performance measurement) system and/or bonus calculations and/or organizational structure that might improve the welfare of the organization without making the manager worse off. The remainder of the book will be aimed at developing a framework for answering these three questions.

11.2 THE ECONOMIC EFFECTS OF PERFORMANCE EVALUATION

The objective of the performance evaluation system (or incentive system) is to accomplish two related goals. (We could call these *sub*goals because the overall goal of the system is assumed to be the maximization of the benefits accruing to the principal.) These two goals are *motivation* and *evaluation of abilities*. In most cases, the principal's payoff is a function of the decisions of the agent as well as the agent's abilities (acquired or innate). A performance evaluation system affects the agent's decisions by affecting the payoffs that accrue to the agent under different circumstances. For example, if an accounting measure of profit is used as the only performance measure, say, in a profit-sharing system, the entries in the agent's payoff matrix will be dependent on the accounting measure and the profit-sharing parameters. By altering these two factors, the principal can alter the agent's *motivation* to take various courses of action. Roughly, we can see that the *direction* of the agent's efforts and the *amount* of effort could be altered. (For "effort," we could substitute the term "resource allocation.") For example, a manager's propensity to accept an investment project will depend on the accounting performance measure (profit, ROI, residual income, etc.) on which his or her bonus is based.

In addition to motivating the agent to make more desirable decisions, the performance evaluation system can provide feedback on managerial abilities. Of course, definition of the term "abilities" is not necessarily an easy job. Perhaps managerial abilities could be defined as all the managerial factors that influence performance which are not the result of management decisions. This distinction is not a completely satisfactory one, since an individual may, in the long run, affect his or her skill level. However, it may only be possible to affect abilities within certain limits, and therefore we could redefine "abilities" as these limits and the ease with which they can be reached.

In any case, there are a variety of methods for assessing an agent's abilities. Prior to employment, a battery of tests may be used to determine if the agent's skills match those needed for the job. After employment, on-the-job evaluation provides additional information. The source of this information may be a supervisor's observation, or it may be an accounting report, depending on the agent's position in the organization. This information can then be used for personnel decisions, such as hiring, dismissing, job assignment, career planning, and so on, all with the object of matching jobs and skills to obtain a higher level of organizational benefit. Of course, this sort of system will also affect motivation, if effort can be substituted for abilities by the employee, and we shall have to consider this in evaluating abilities. That is, we may prefer a hard-working employee over a talented employee, depending on the relative returns to (and costs of) effort and abilities.

The problem of choosing an accounting performance measure and an incentive system is really composed of two related problems: the agent's problem and the principal's problem. If the principal is to make an informed choice between performance evaluation systems, he or she must be able to form a budget, or a forecast, of the way that each of the alternatives will affect the agent's decisions and the organization's performance. The next section describes an approach to forming such budgets.

11.3 EVALUATING AN EVALUATION SYSTEM

The types of decisions that have to be made about the performance evaluation system are: what variables shall we measure, and how does the bonus plan (or other rewards and penalties) depend on these variables? For the most part, we use the accounting system as a primary source of observable variables. While this assumption is a simplification, in most large, decentralized organizations it is close to the truth, particularly at levels below top management. Many of the accounting issues we have raised in previous situations also apply here. What forms of cost allocation should be used in evaluating performance? How accurate should the overhead allocation process be? How many uncontrollable factors should be *factored out* in deriving the performance evaluation measure? At the same time, we must recognize that there are different forms of incentive functions, for example, profit-sharing plans and budget-based plans. (A budget-based plan is one where incentive pay is determined by a comparison of actual results to a pre-set target.) In addition, there may be cases where the incentive is based on sequential information acquisition, as in the case where a cost report that exceeds a budget by a prespecified amount causes an investigation to determine whether the unfavorable variance was controllable. If it was, then this information adversely affects the agent's performance evaluation. (We will look more closely at these types of performance evaluation functions in the next chapter.)

In Chapter 2 we discussed a decision-theoretic model of decision making, where action alternatives, uncertainties, payoffs, and preferences were combined to arrive at a desirable course of action. The situation faced by an agent (let's use the term *decentralized manager* for concreteness) is basically the same. He or she has been delegated certain choices (actions) and faces various sources of uncertainty, including some sources from within the organization. However, the *payoff function* faced by the decentralized manager depends on the incentive function $I(\cdot)$, *and* on the performance measure $r(a, s)$. One example might be that $r(a,s)$ is a cost variance measure that depends on the manager's cost control efforts a and uncontrollable cost factors s. Then the incentive function would translate the performance measure into a bonus or salary increase or increased probability of promotion or some other payoff to the manager. For instance, the manager might get a fixed bonus if the cost variance was favorable. Alternatively, $r(a,s)$ could be a measure of profit, and $I(\cdot)$ could be a profit-sharing plan. At any rate, the decision matrix shown in equation (2.4) could be replaced by that in Figure 11.1. (Of course, a utility function for the manager that describes risk aversion, an aver-

		States of Nature			
		s_1	s_2	$\cdots$	s_m
	a_1	$I(r(a_1, s_1))$	$I(r(a_1, s_2))$	$\cdots$	$I(r(a_1, s_m))$
	a_2	$I(r(a_2, s_1))$	$I(r(a_2, s_2))$	$\cdots$	$I(r(a_2, s_m))$
Actions	$\vdots$	$\vdots$	$\vdots$		$\vdots$
	a_n	$I(r(a_n, s_1))$	$I(r(a_n, s_2))$	$\cdots$	$I(r(a_n, s_m))$

Figure 11.1 Payoff table for decentralized manager.

States of Nature

		s_1	s_2	$\cdots$	s_m
Actions	a_1	$x(a_1, s_1) - I(r(a_1, s_1))$	$x(a_1, s_2) - I(r(a_1, s_2))$	$\cdots$	$x(a_1, s_m) - I(r(a_1, s_m))$
	a_2	$x(a_2, s_1) - I(r(a_2, s_1))$	$x(a_2, s_2) - I(r(a_2, s_2))$	$\cdots$	$x(a_2, s_m) - I(r(a_2, s_m))$
		.	.		.
		.	.		.
		.	.		.
	a_n	$x(a_n, s_1) - I(r(a_n, s_1))$	$x(a_n, s_2) - I(r(a_n, s_2))$	$\cdots$	$x(a_n, s_m) - I(r(a_n, s_m))$

Figure 11.2 Payoff table for central management.

sion to expending effort, etc., can be incorporated into the decision table by replacing $I(r(a_i, s_j))$ with $U[I(r(a_i, s_j)), a_i]$.)

The result of this decision process is a chosen course of action that depends on the incentive system and the accounting measure of performance. If the delegated decision is to choose a level of investment, the action chosen could very well depend on whether $r(\cdot)$ was based on historical cost or current replacement value and on whether $I(\cdot)$ was based on return on assets or residual income. At this point, we have modified the decision theory framework to address the second key question: how will a manager behave (make decisions) under the existing performance evaluation system.

The answer to the first key question requires that we determine how the principal (whom we will refer to as *central management*) would like the decentralized manager to behave in making decisions. In a sense, this is easily done by a simple alteration in Figure 11.1. Instead of the entries being the decentralized manager's payoff $I(r(a, s))$, we substitute the centralized management's payoff $x(a, s) - I(r(a, s))$.[2] From Figure 11.2, we can determine the action preferred by the central management.

Comparing the decision matrices in Figures 11.1 and 11.2 lets us be very specific about some of the expressions frequently heard in discussions of performance evaluation systems. For instance, *goal congruence* means that the decentralized manager and the central management will agree on the action to be taken. That is, the optimal decision from Figure 11.1 will match that from Figure 11.2. In addition, the two figures make it clear that a number of factors could make the chosen actions different. If a cost is not allocated to the decentralized manager, it will not enter his or her decision analysis, but it will be present in the organization's payoff table. The decentralized manager may measure payoffs over a two-year horizon, while the central management's payoffs could be measured over ten years. If the decentralized manager's performance measurement does not incorporate the future period effects of his or her decisions, it is unlikely that goal congruence will result. Before examining an illustration of this relationship, there are three areas that need to be examined in more detail—the characteristics of (i) the manager; (ii) the evaluation system; and (iii) the delegated decisions.

[2]This payoff is the total proceeds $x(a, s)$, less what has to be paid to the manager $I(r(a, s))$. At some organizational levels, the latter factor will be much smaller than the former, and might be omitted for simplicity. Risk aversion of the principal could be incorporated by replacing the net payoff $x(\cdot) - I(\cdot)$ with the utility of that payoff $G[x(\cdot) - I(\cdot)]$.

11.4 MANAGER CHARACTERISTICS

Ultimately, our objective is to be able to choose performance evaluation systems that will fulfill the organization's objectives. However, a necessary step in achieving this objective is being able to project the effects of different evaluation systems on a manager's decision making. In turn, this means that we must have some idea about the manager's goals, likes, dislikes, and so on. For instance, one behavioral model might posit that managers are essentially self-oriented, preferring more income to less income and less effort to more effort. In the absence of explicit incentives, no productive actions will be chosen. An alternative behavioral model might depict managers as organization-oriented, deriving an innate satisfaction in working to achieve organizational goals. Obviously, a performance evaluation system designed for an organization-oriented manager would not work very well if applied to a self-oriented manager, and vice versa. We cannot evaluate a performance measurement system without reference to a behavioral model of the decentralized manager. This model should probably include the manager's attitudes about factors such as income, risk, effort, time horizon, as well as cultural influences.

Actually, it is the interrelationships among these factors that are important. For instance, in considering whether to accept or reject a special order, the manager will weigh the additional expected income from the order against the riskiness of the order's profitability. If we expect a decentralized manager to be more risk-averse than central management, then the performance evaluation system might attempt to overcome this difference in risk preferences. At the same time, however, we must be aware of the manager's other characteristics as well. For instance, how does the manager feel about expending effort toward organizational goals? We will usually assume that the manager will not expend effort toward those activities which result in a decrease in personal payoff. That is, if there is no incremental payoff to the manager, he or she will expend no incremental effort. This is an obvious simplification, since many of us enjoy our work. But there may be some aspects of a job that are more enjoyable than others, and usually we do the ''others'' because we are encouraged to do so by the incentive structure. We will try to keep our model of the manager's behavior as simple as possible, but making alterations in that model is relatively easy, in principle.

One of the interesting, and frustrating, aspects of working in this area is that it is difficult to patch up one problem without creating another. For instance, in the context of the previous paragraph, suppose that a risk-averse, effort-averse manager is considering an accept/reject decision on a special order with uncertain costs. The manager has responsibility for this type of decision and for controlling costs. One way to reduce the project's riskiness would be to use *standard* costs instead of actual costs in evaluating the manager's profitability. While this change would reduce risk and lead to more accepted orders, the manager would then have little incentive to control costs, since there would be no impact on the profitability measure.

In addition to tradeoffs between factors such as effort and income, the manager's time horizon is also important in assessing the effects of performance measurement. This is especially true when the manager has been delegated decisions which will impact the organization far into the future such as investment, research and development, employee relations, and so on. Suppose a division manager receives a bonus of 2% of the division's profits. Current year profits are at $500,000, and the manager has the opportunity to spend $50,000 on a project that will reduce costs by $100,000 next year. However, the $50,000 will be charged against this year's income, and the manager does not expect to remain in this job past this year. The payoff tables for the manager and organization are as follows.

Action	Manager's bonus	Organizational profits (before bonus)
Accept project	$ 9,000	$450,000 + 600,000
Reject project	$10,000	$500,000 + 500,000

This difference in time horizons can lead to an underinvestment in projects with long-run payoffs unless the performance evaluation system can overcome this tendency. We return to this topic in greater detail in Chapter 14.

The choices of both the decentralized manager and central management are limited by the existence of a labor market for managers. Central management must limit its choices of $I(\cdot)$ to those which meet the decentralized manager's opportunity value in the market. Otherwise, the firm will not be able to attract or retain managers. In addition, the decentralized manager's actions may affect his or her reputation in the marketplace. The services of a manager who has left three jobs in the last three years will probably have a lower ''price'' than the services of a manager who has achieved good results at one position over the same time period. Thus, there is some *market discipline* that influences the choices of both the decentralized manager and central management.

Finally, there are cultural differences between employees in different countries that affect the types of evaluation systems that will be effective. For instance, employees in Japan threatened a work stoppage when a U.S. firm proposed piece-rate incentives. These differences can sometimes be translated into differences in attitude toward risk or effort, etc., but an incentive scheme that is appropriate in one culture will not necessarily be effective in another.

11.5 EVALUATION SYSTEM CHARACTERISTICS

In effect, these characteristics are the choices that are available to central management in setting up a performance system. We can divide the characteristics into two basic categories, since the central management must choose both a performance measure $r(\cdot)$ and an incentive scheme $I(\cdot)$, which translates the performance measure into dollars of bonus, likelihood of promotion, and so on.

In large, decentralized organizations, the primary source of performance measures is the accounting system, as reflected in terms such as *cost center* and *profit center*. Of course, this means that we have a wide range of accounting issues to decide in choosing a performance system. What costs will be allocated to responsibility centers? What allocation method should be used? Which costs benefit future periods and could be capitalized, and subsequently amortized? Should investments in inventories be measured by current replacement cost or historical cost? What measure of revenue should be used? Which factors are controllable and which are not? In addition, there may be some question as to whether we can create a *single* financial performance measure, or whether *multiple* measures are necessary. In many cases, a firm might come up with a variety of measures

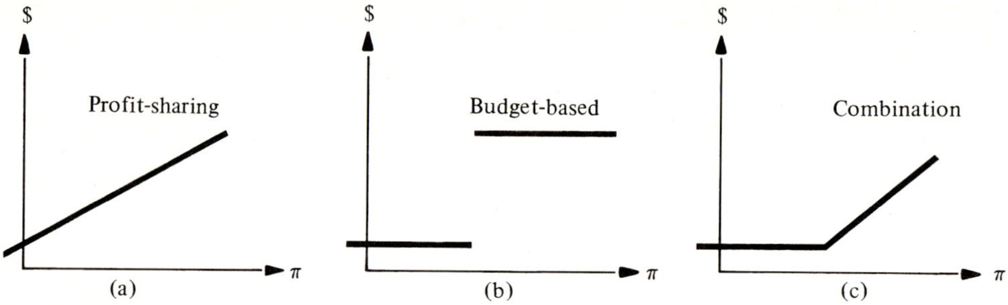

Figure 11.3 Accounting-based incentives.

to overcome the limitations of individual performance measures. (This issue is explored further in Appendix 11.2.)

While we will be concerned primarily with accounting-based performance measures, there are a couple of alternatives that must be mentioned. When the accounting-based measures do an inadequate job of motivating managers, then these alternatives should be considered. First, central management might choose to observe the manager's action directly, rather than rely on the accounting reports. This shift from an output measure to an input measure probably only makes sense if the central management has enough information to determine the most-preferred action; for example, the best product mix, the best R&D budget, etc. Then the performance evaluation is based on an "instructionlike" contract, where the decentralized manager is merely the implementer of central management decisions. If instructions are carried out, then the manager is compensated, if they are not, then he or she is punished. This system (which really isn't very decentralized) will only work well if the manager's actions are observable without great cost, and if the central management has sufficient information to make the decisions. At the level of a division manager, these conditions are less likely to hold than at lower levels of the organization where tasks are more well-defined.

Yet another measure of performance is the return on the firm's shares in the marketplace. There is a considerable body of literature in finance and accounting to support the notion that the securities markets are efficient, that is, that stock prices reflect all publicly available information in a timely and unbiased fashion. Since the shareholders' concern is with share returns, there may be advantages to basing the manager's compensation on share returns.[3] The disadvantage of stock-based incentives is the limited

[3]This could be done by granting the manager stock or stock options, or other schemes which are based on changes in share prices such as stock appreciation rights.

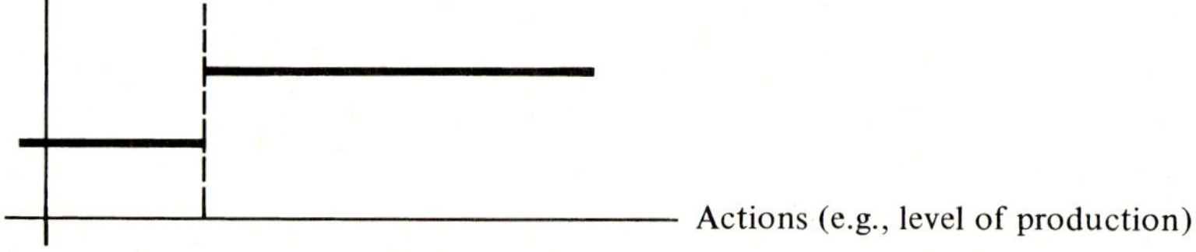

Figure 11.4 Action-based incentives.

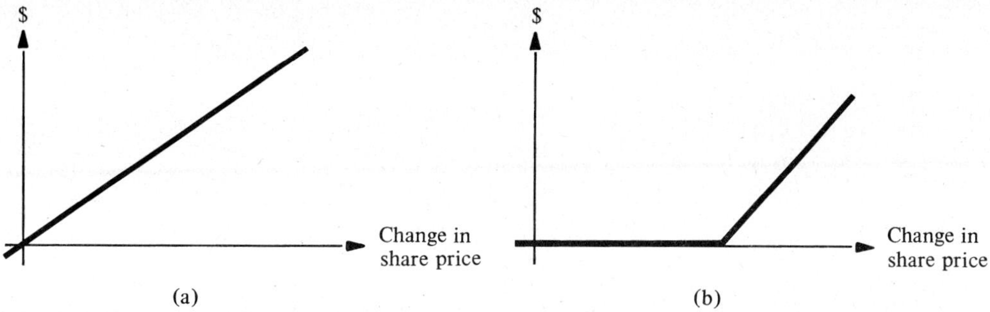

Figure 11.5 Share price-based incentives.

controllability that managers have over the determinants of share prices. For example, managers have no control over government fiscal policy, changes in the money supply, supplier cartels, etc., but all these factors influence share prices. Often, this lack of controllability can have an adverse influence on managerial incentives. Moreover, at the division manager level, there is even less controllability, since the share prices will also reflect the results of other divisions which cannot be affected by his or her decisions.

In addition to defining the measure(s) of performance, central management will determine how these measures are translated into dollars of bonus, probability of promotion, etc. One simple system based on accounting numbers would be a profit-sharing arrangement (see Figure 11.3a). This arrangement has the advantage of providing incentive to increase profits regardless of the current profit level, but it also may subject the manager to an inordinate amount of risk. (The risk might still be lower than a stock option plan.) The budget-based system depicted in Figure 11.3b reduces the manager's downside risk, but it also limits the incentives over some range of profits.[4] In fact, once a manager has exceeded the budget, there may be an incentive to hold back on further profit increases by saving them for the next period. Finally, there are combinations of these two basic systems, which attempt to retain the strengths of each.

If performance measures other than accounting-based ones are used, central management must still decide how these measures translate into a bonus or other incentives. If the evaluation is based on action, then a form like that in Figure 11.4 might be used. If the performance measure is share-price, then the compensation would look like Figure 11.5a for a grant of shares and 11.5b for a stock option.

11.6 DELEGATED DECISIONS

Finally, we must be clear about the decisions that have been delegated to the decentralized manager. Some of these decisions will have been explicitly delegated by central management, while others are taken for granted or have built up through tradition. In any case, we cannot design a performance measurement system without considering the full range of decisions made and their impact on the organization.

[4]In general, the incentive function should be increasing in the performance measure as long as higher performance measures are indicative of higher managerial efforts.

Of course, we cannot develop an exhaustive list of decisions that may be delegated within an organization, but examples of the more common ones follow:

- level of production
- product mix
- allocation of resources in generating sales
- level of risk-reducing activities
- usage of centralized service departments
- level of search for profitable investments
- allocation of resources to investments
- accuracy of forecasts used in budgeting
- level of attention paid to cost control
- level of effort devoted toward organizational goals

We could make this list more detailed, for instance in the allocation of resources in generating sales. The manager may determine (i) how many customers to call on, (ii) how many miles to travel, (iii) which products to provide as free samples, etc. And when we consider a specific performance evaluation problem, we will have to go into greater detail concerning the decisions that the manager makes. If we focus on one *decision* and provide proper incentives for that decision, we can encourage dysfunctional behavior on another aspect of the decision maker's responsibility.

11.7 THE PRINCIPAL'S PROBLEM

These last three sections have detailed some of the factors involved in setting up a system for performance evaluation. The principal's problem is to choose the system that does the best job of meeting the organization's goals. In order to do this we must be able to forecast the effects of different performance measures and incentive functions on managers' decisions and organizational payoffs. It is possible to formulate this problem mathematically (as in Appendix 11.1), but we will do it in a descriptive fashion.

$$\max_{I(\cdot),r(\cdot)} \text{(expected organization payoff)} \tag{11.1}$$

subject to the following constraints:

1. Manager's expected utility meets that available in the labor market for managers.
2. Manager chooses the delegated decisions so as to maximize his or her expected utility.

Having set up the problem in words, we now turn to an illustration.

Example For an example, assume that we have a situation where central management has delegated an activity level decision to a decentralized manager. In essence, this manager is faced with a cost–volume–profit situation with uncertain variable costs like those described in Chapter 4. The manager must decide how many units x to produce, where the level of production influences the expected profits as well as the variance (risk) of profits. (See Chapters 4 and 8.)

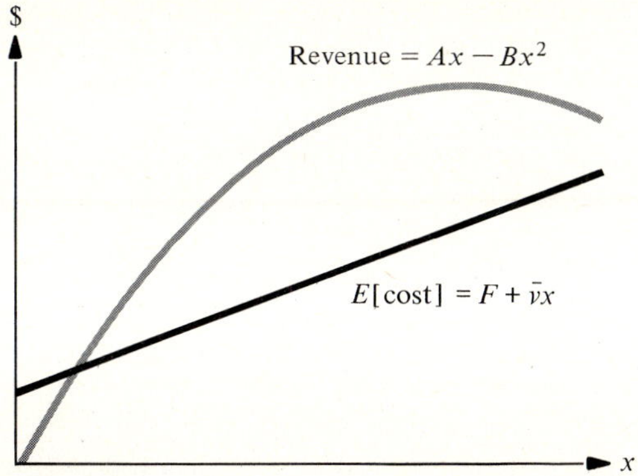

Figure 11.6

$$\begin{aligned} \pi &= Ax - Bx^2 - F - vx \\ E[\pi] &= Ax - Bx^2 - F - \bar{v}x \\ \sigma^2[\pi] &= x^2\sigma^2[v] \end{aligned} \tag{11.2}$$

If the manager's bonus is a proportion $l(0 < l < 1)$ of the unit's profits, how many units will the manager choose to produce? How many would the central management want produced? As we indicated in Chapter 4, the optimal output depends on risk preferences. If central management has many such decentralized units, they will be essentially risk-neutral with regard to different production levels in this unit. In other words, the central management will want to maximize expected profits, and x_c^* will be the optimal output[5] from central management's point of view.

$$x_c^* = \frac{A - \bar{v}}{2B} \tag{11.3}$$

But if the manager is not also risk-neutral, there may be a conflict in the desired levels of output. For instance, suppose the manager says, "I will measure risk as a constant δ times the variance of my profit share, and I will increase output as long as the increase in my expected compensation is greater than the increase in my risk." The result of this decision rule would be

$$\begin{aligned} \bar{I} \equiv E[I(\cdot)] &= lE[\pi] = l[(A - \bar{v})x - Bx^2 - F] \\ \text{Risk} &= \delta\sigma^2[I(\cdot)] = \delta\sigma^2[lxv] = \delta l^2x^2\sigma^2[v] \end{aligned} \tag{11.4}$$

where $I(\pi)$ is the manager's profit share. Changes with respect to output x would be

$$\begin{aligned} \frac{d}{dx}\bar{I} &= l[(A - v) - 2Bx] \\ \frac{d}{dx}(\text{risk}) &= 2\delta l^2 x\sigma^2[v] \end{aligned} \tag{11.5}$$

[5]x^* is the point where both increases or decreases in output will decrease expected profits. It can be found by taking the first derivative of expected profits with respect to output, and setting it equal to zero. See Chapter 4.

The manager's decision rule is to increase x as long as $dI/dx > d\,(\text{risk})/dx$, so the level of production would be

$$x_m^* = \frac{A - \bar{v}}{2(B + l\delta\sigma^2[v])} \tag{11.6}$$

Unless l or δ or $\sigma^2[v]$ is equal to zero, the value of x_m^* will be less than x_c^*. That is, the risk-averse manager will choose a level of output that is lower and a price that is higher than that desired by the central management. The greater the risk aversion (the larger δ), the greater this difference will be.

How can the central management deal with this situation? Their expected payoff would be increased by increasing output beyond that which the manager will choose, but how can they encourage the manager to choose a higher output? There is not just one answer to this question, but several. For instance, the central management could do away with the profit-sharing and impose an output quota on the manager. The manager would receive a good evaluation only if production met x_c^*. This alteration in the performance evaluation system is ideal in that the manager will choose x_c^*, *and* bear no risk as long as x_c^* is chosen. However, a much greater burden has been placed on central management and on the accounting system. Central management must know all of the factors that are necessary to determine optimal output, and this information requirement may put a heavier burden on the accounting system. In addition, the accounting system will have to report on the decentralized manager's actions, rather than on the financial results of those actions. Finally, we should recognize that this represents a change in the nature of decentralization in the organization; a manager who was a decision maker has now become an implementer of central management's decisions.

Are there other ways to encourage the manager to increase production and still maintain the basic decentralized nature of the situation? Two come to mind readily. The manager's profit-sharing percentage is l, and as l gets smaller we can see that the *risk adjustment* term in the denominator of (11.6) gets smaller, and x_m^* gets closer to x_c^*. Decreases in l would probably have to be accompanied by increases in salary, so that this employment remains attractive to the manager. Alternatively, suppose that central management could set a *standard cost* $\hat{v}$ equal to the expected variable cost per unit $\bar{v}$. Then the decentralized manager could receive a share of standard profit (revenue less standard cost). Since there is no cost risk, the best output would be set at

$$\hat{x}_m = \frac{A - \hat{v}}{2B} \tag{11.7}$$

and this is equal to x_c^* if $\hat{v}$ is equal to $\bar{v}$.

Both of these alternatives will increase output toward x_c^*, but both have the potential to create other problems *if* the manager makes decisions in addition to the level of output. For instance, suppose that the decentralized manager also decides how much effort to allocate to cost control. If we base this evaluation on standard cost, with no penalty when costs exceed standard, then we can expect that the manager will devote little time to cost control. Similar problems can occur if l is decreased: the manager has less of a stake in the actual performance of the decentralized unit.

Let's look at a couple of these alternatives in a little more detail. Suppose that the decentralized manager chooses the level of output *and* the level of attention to cost control. If the attention to cost control is high, v has expected value $\bar{v}_H$; if the attention is low, v's expected value is $\bar{v}_L(\bar{v}_L > \bar{v}_H)$. In either case, the variance of v is $\sigma^2[v]$. Under the profit-share performance plan, what decisions will the manager make? If there is low cost control effort, then the optimal output is x_m^L, and a similar expression can be found for high cost control output x_m^H.

$$x_m^L = \frac{A - \bar{v}_L}{2(B + l\delta\sigma^2[v])} \qquad (11.8)$$
$$x_m^H = \frac{A - \bar{v}_H}{2(B + l\delta\sigma^2[v])}$$

So the decentralized manager has two basic choices: (i) pay a high degree of attention to cost control and produce x_m^H; or (ii) pay less attention to cost control and produce a lesser level of output x_m^L. Exactly which of these is chosen will depend on the manager's attitudes concerning cost control. If he doesn't mind it, he will probably choose (i); otherwise there will be little cost control and lesser output. At any rate, we must make an assessment of these attitudes, and then we can forecast the manager's actions when faced with this performance evaluation system. For the sake of this discussion, let's say that the manager would exert a high degree of cost control and produce x_m^H.

In contrast, what would the manager do under the standard cost system, where the manager gets a share of standard profit $Ax - Bx^2 - F - \hat{v}x$? We have already indicated that the manager would have no incentive to control costs, and would produce $\hat{x}_m = (A - \bar{v}_L)/2B$, since $\hat{v}$ would be set at $\bar{v}_L$.

Now, which performance reporting system would central management prefer? If *actual profits* are used, the manager chooses high cost control and x_m^H. If *standard profits* are used, the manager chooses low cost control and $\hat{x}_m$. Which is better? Well, if the organizational objective is to maximize the expected profits, we can answer this question with the following computations.

$$E(\text{profit}|\text{actual profits system}) = \bar{\pi}_{AP} = Ax_m^H - B(x_m^H)^2 - F - \bar{v}_H x_m^H \qquad (11.9)$$
$$E(\text{profit}|\text{standard profits system}) = \bar{\pi}_{SP} = A\hat{x}_m - B(\hat{x}_m)^2 - F - \bar{v}_L\hat{x}_m$$

If $\bar{\pi}_{AP}$ is greater than $\bar{\pi}_{SP}$ after considering the manager's expected compensation, the central management should prefer the actual profit system. There are two basic factors that will determine this comparison: the manager's risk aversion and the difference between $\bar{v}_L$ and $\bar{v}_H$. If the manager's risk aversion is great (δ large), then a move to a standard profit system will create benefits (through increased output) that will outweigh the costs (of increased variable costs). On the other hand, if $\bar{v}_L$ is considerably larger than $\bar{v}_H$, and if δ is small, then it may turn out that x_m^H is even larger than $\hat{x}_m$. In this case, a move to a standard profit performance measure could both increase costs *and* decrease output, and the central management would certainly prefer to measure performance using actual profits.

In fact, this example portrays a very common problem in performance measurement. It is generally agreed that it is better to evaluate managers on their *controllable* performance, and to filter out the uncontrollable factors. In practice, it may be impossible to completely segregate the controllable and uncontrollable aspects of an outcome such as costs or revenues. Such is the case with the variable costs in the above example: they are neither completely controllable nor uncontrollable by the decentralized manager. Therefore, we face a dilemma in determining the measure of performance. Including uncontrollable factors (i.e., using actual costs) subjects the manager to risk that may distort his or her decision making from that preferred by central management. Excluding the uncontrollable factors (i.e., using standard costs) also excludes some controllable factors, and this can also result in a distortion of the manager's decisions. Therefore, we are left with a choice between two imperfect solutions, and we must determine which creates the least costly problems. We did such an analysis in the previous paragraph. The importance of the controllable and uncontrollable factors can be seen by comparing $\bar{v}_L - \bar{v}_H$ (the controllable part) and $\sigma^2(v)$ (the uncontrollable part). For example, if the controllable part is much larger than the uncontrollable part, then performance based on actual profits will be preferred. Two approaches to reducing the effects of uncontrollable factors are introduced in Appendix 11.2.

What we have done in this example is a rather thorough analysis of the effects of different performance measurements, albeit in a simple decision setting.[6] The objective was to be very specific about the factors that must be considered in this type of analysis, but do we need to be quite so rigorous and as thorough in evaluating such problems? The answer is a mixed one. It is *not* necessary to use decision theory, calculus, or other quantitative tools explicitly. It *is* necessary that the three key questions listed earlier be answered, or we cannot make a reasoned choice among performance evaluation alternatives.

It may be that past operating data will provide some clues as to the effects of different performance systems. If identical operations are subjected to different performance measures, the operation which performs best[7] would appear to have the best performance system. But this sort of experimentation can be rather costly to the organization, and the advantage of approaches such as decision theory or simulation is that they allow us to experiment "on paper" without disrupting the organization.

11.8 A POSTSCRIPT ON PERFORMANCE MEASURE CHARACTERISTICS

When information is fulfilling a decision facilitating role, its purpose is to provide a decision maker with reports that can alter his or her beliefs about the uncertain state of nature. In performance evaluation situations, information plays a decision influencing role by providing reports that central management can use to infer which course of action was taken by the decentralized manager. That is, the performance measure must be *informative* about the manager's actions (how hard he or she worked, how much he or she invested, etc.)

In order for the performance measure to be informative about the manager's actions, it must be the case that different courses of action produce different probabilities for the performance measure outcomes. That is, it may be possible to achieve a good or a bad

[6]An even more structured analysis appears in Appendix 11.1.

[7]We must be careful here. The "performs best" criterion must be evaluated using a consistent performance measure, not the operations' own measures.

performance measure outcome whether or not the manager works hard, but the *probabilities* of the performance outcomes must change (e.g., increased effort by the manager could increase the probability of a good outcome and decrease the probability of a bad outcome.) An example of this situation appears in Figure 11.7, where the performance measure is partially controllable by the manager. By choosing one course of action (high effort), the manager shifts the probabilities toward more favorable performance outcomes, and therefore the performance measure is informative about the course of action chosen by the manager. In fact, we refer to higher performance outcomes as being more favorable because they are indicative of a more preferred course of action being chosen by the decentralized manager.

At the extreme, the performance report could inform the central management of the exact actions chosen by the decentralized manager. This situation is one in which the performance measure is completely controllable by the decentralized manager, and the centralized management can encourage whatever decisions it wishes as long as it is willing to compensate the decentralized manager for any disutility (e.g., loss of leisure time) associated with the course of action. As discussed earlier in the chapter, such completely controllable performance measures depend on the observability of the decentralized manager's action *and* on the centralized management's ability to determine the optimal course of action.

Performance evaluation problems can frequently be traced to undesirable characteristics of the performance measures being used. For instance, a manager is usually delegated more than one decision, with a single performance measure being used to evaluate the performance on all decisions. Such a situation may be efficient when the desired actions all tend to increase the performance measure, but there are many cases where the desired courses of action have offsetting effects on the performance measure. The most common example is a manager who makes decisions which influence the short-term *and* long-term performance of the company, and whose performance is evaluated on the basis of current profitability. Efforts devoted to short-term operations (action 1 in Figure 11.8) tend to shift the performance outcome probabilities to the right, but many long-term efforts, such as investments in facilities, employee training, and research and development, tend to shift the performance outcome probabilities to the left (action 2 in Figure 11.8). Therefore, a manager who devotes significant effort to both the short-term and long-term will find his or her performance measures lower than a manager who

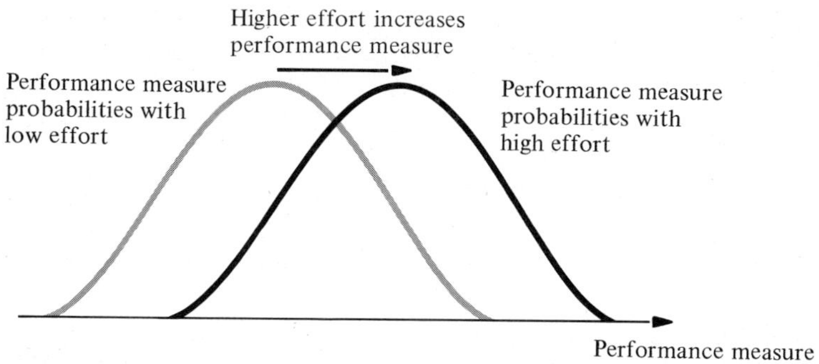

Figure 11.7

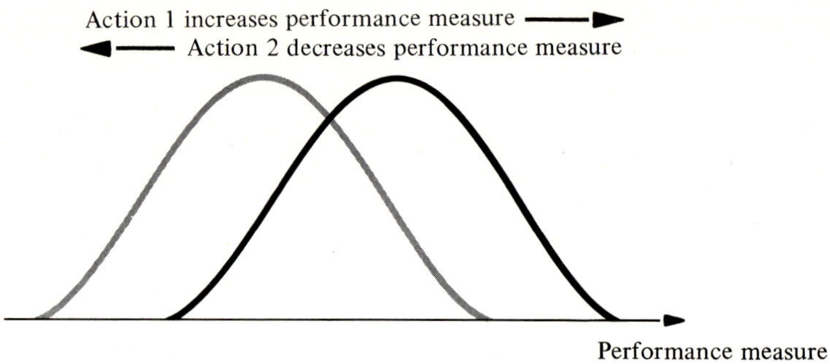

Figure 11.8

devotes all effort to short-term operations. In these situations, it is extremely difficult (impossible?) for the centralized management to develop an incentive function that promotes action 2, because the performance measure is not informative enough about the two types of decisions made by the decentralized manager. We will return to this type of situation in Chapter 14.

Controllability is another performance measure characteristic that can cause some difficulties in the performance evaluation system. Figures 11.9a and 11.9b depict two performance measures where the first is less controllable than the second. The Figure 11.9a performance measure is *less informative* about the decentralized manager's effort choice than the more controllable performance measure in Figure 11.9b. While it is possible to encourage the decentralized manager to choose a high level of effort in either

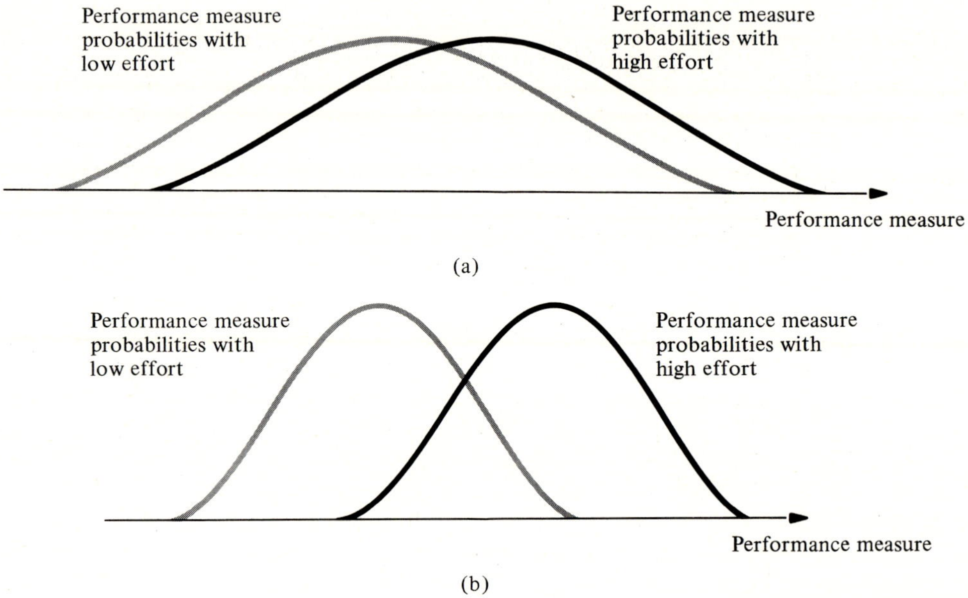

Figure 11.9 (a) A less controllable performance measure. (b) A more controllable performance measure.

case, it is clearly more difficult to do so with a less controllable measure of performance, because it is more difficult for the decentralized manager to influence the odds of getting a good performance evaluation. For any performance target, the probability of achieving the target is represented by the area under the probability curve to the right of the target, and the incentive to choose the higher effort level is dependent on the *increase* in the probability of target achievement that accompanies the higher effort choice. That probability increase is lower for the less controllable performance measure, and therefore a larger bonus will be required to encourage the decentralized manager to choose the higher effort level. At the extreme, where the performance measure is completely uncontrollable, the manager cannot influence the probability distribution of the outcomes, and it will provide no incentives for choosing the higher effort level. In this case the performance measure is not informative about the decentralized manager's decisions, and there is nothing to be gained by using it to evaluate his or her performance.

The concept of informativeness is a useful one, because it makes us focus on the connections between the decisions made by the decentralized manager and the measurement of performance. It is often the case that *dysfunctional decision making* in an organization can be traced to the use of a performance measure that is not informative about the range of decisions that have been delegated to the manager, and we will utilize this concept in dealing with more specific accounting issues in the following chapters.

11.9 SUMMARY

In this chapter we have tried to outline a framework for assessing the desirability of alternative performance evaluation schemes. There are a wide range of choices from instructions to accounting-based and stock price-based systems, and each system has its benefits and drawbacks. In order to make reasoned choices, we must know some of the managers' characteristics and the way that decision making authority is delegated.[8]

In the section 11.7 example, we had to know just what decisions had been delegated, the manager's risk preferences, and how much the central management knew about the decentralized unit's profit opportunities, cost control opportunities, and so on. Does the same manager have responsibility for choosing output levels *and* cost control, or are these responsibilities divided among managers? Can central management choose the output (or price) and do as effective a job as a decentralized manager?

In the chapters that follow, we will be looking at some more specific managerial accounting issues, namely, budgeting and cost allocations. We will use the framework set up in this chapter, for the most part, and an important question raised here will be raised again: How much information does central management have about the opportunities and problems faced by the decentralized manager and about the decisions which he or she makes? We expect that there will be some *information differential;* otherwise there is little need for a decentralized organization. But in general, the less information that central management has, the greater the reliance on the financial control system. Since we know that accounting measurement is a limited science, there will be room for

[8]For the most part, the organizational structure will be taken as a given. But if an organizational design creates or accentuates performance measurement difficulties, then it may be appropriate to consider alternative ways of delegating responsibility and authority in the organization.

dysfunctional decision making. However, this situation is not necessarily an inefficient one, since the costs of overcoming the information differential may exceed the costs of the dysfunctional decisions. In the first part of this book, we often found that acquiring perfect information was not an efficient choice, and we may expect the same sort of phenomenon in performance evaluation systems.

APPENDIX 11.1: Factors that Influence the Optimal Profit Share

It is very common in U.S. businesses for a manager's compensation to depend on the profitability of his or her operation. Most corporations have bonus pools that are functions of profits or of some profitability measure such as residual income. We might even think of franchising arrangements as profit-sharing arrangements, where the profit-share parameter is close to 1 for the franchisee, and a fixed franchise fee he or she pays may be thought of as a negative salary. In this appendix, we extend the output example in the text and try to determine which factors influence the choice of a profit-sharing parameter.

Central management must set a salary level k and profit-sharing parameter l so that the decentralized manager's compensation will be $I = k + l\pi$. These parameters should be set so as to maximize the expected payoff to the organization, after the payment to the manager. There are two constraints to this problem: the manager gets to choose the level of output, and the manager's expected utility must meet what he or she could get in alternative employment. The firm's profits are influenced by output in the following way:

$$\bar{\pi}[x] = E[\pi|x] = (A - \bar{v})x - Bx^2 - F \qquad \text{(A11.1.1)}$$
$$\sigma^2[\pi(x)] = x^2\sigma^2[v]$$

The decentralized manager's choice of output is influenced by three factors. As in section 11.7, we assume that the manager likes expected profit share and dislikes risk, as measured through the variance of the profit share. Here we also recognize that increased levels of output will require increased effort by the manager, and we assume that the manager incurs a "disutility" from expending effort. For the purposes of our example, the manager is assumed to choose output to maximize the following expected utility function.

$$EU_m \equiv \underbrace{k}_{\text{Salary}} + \underbrace{l\bar{\pi}(x)}_{\text{Expected profit share}} - \underbrace{\delta l^2\sigma^2[\pi(x)]}_{\text{Risk adjustment}} - \underbrace{ax^2}_{\text{Effort adjustment}} \qquad \text{(A11.1.2)}$$

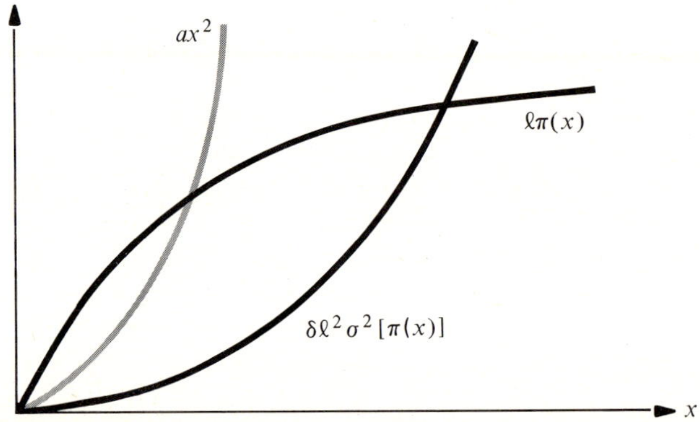

Figure A11.1

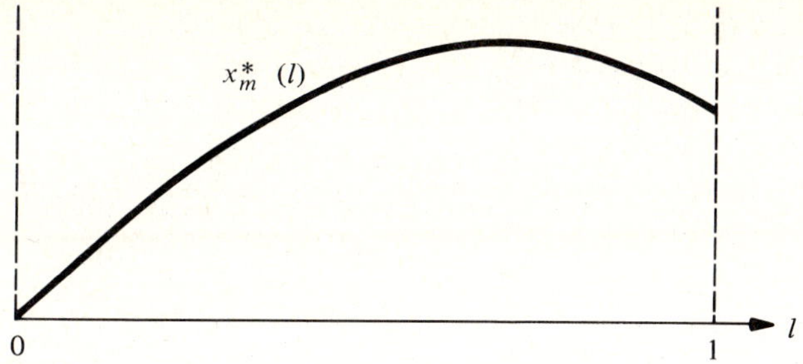

Figure A11.2

The level of output that will maximize this function depends on the profit share l, and is the following.

$$x_m^*(l) = \frac{l(A - v)}{2(lB + \delta l^2\sigma^2[v] + a)} \tag{A11.1.3}$$

As shown earlier in the chapter, we can see that risk aversion decreases the level of output from that which maximizes expected profit. In the expression above, we can also see that effort aversion decreases output through the parameter a.

What effect does the profit-sharing parameter have on the level of output? There is no clear-cut answer because increasing l increases both the expected profit share and its risk. We can say that as l moves from zero to one, $x_m^*(l)$ increases for a while, but then decreases as the risk effects become more important. (See Figure 11.A2.)

The above expression incorporates the constraint that the manager choose the level of output, but we still need to insure that the manager will accept employment. For a given l the salary k must be set so as to make sure that the manager's expected utility is equal to $\underline{U}$, the amount the manager could get in alternative employment. This value of k will depend on the particular l chosen.

$$k + l\overline{\pi}[x_m^*(l)] - \delta l^2\sigma^2[v][x_m^*(l)]^2 - a[x_m^*(l)]^2 = \underline{U}$$

$$\text{or } k(l) = \underbrace{\underline{U}}_{\text{Opportunity value}} + \underbrace{\delta l^2\sigma^2[v][x_m^*(l)]^2}_{\text{Risk premium}} + \underbrace{a[x_m^*(l)]^2}_{\text{Effort premium}} - \underbrace{l\overline{\pi}[x_m^*(l)]}_{\text{Expected profit share}} \tag{A11.1.4}$$

We can see that there are four factors that influence the value of $k(l)$. The manager's salary must compensate for his or her opportunity value $\underline{U}$, for the level of risk that he or she has to bear $\delta l^2\sigma^2[v][x_m^*(l)]^2$, and for the personal cost of the effort he or she expends $a[x_m^*(l)]^2$. However, this compensation may be reduced by the expected profit share $l\overline{\pi}[x_m^*(l)]$, so it might even be possible for $k(l)$ to be negative, reflecting a franchise fee.

For every value of l chosen by the central management, we now know the level of output and the amount of salary that must be paid. We can now turn to the central management's problem of choosing the best profit-sharing arrangement. We will assume that the objective is to maximize the expected profit that is left after compensating the manager. This problem can be expressed as the following.

$$\max_l \{(1 - l)\overline{\pi}[x_m^*(l)] - k(l)\} \tag{A11.1.5}$$

The values of $x_m^*(l)$ and $k(l)$ we have found above can be substituted into this expression, and in doing so we incorporate the constraints that (i) the manager must be paid enough to meet the market and (ii) the choice of output is left to the manager. The conditions for the best value of l, say l^*, are quite complex, and we will not present them here. There is no simple equation of $l^* = \{\ \}$ unless we go to a specific numerical example or make some more specific assumptions.[9] But there are some interesting insights into the forces which influence l^*.

Basically, there are two conflicting forces at work in determining l^*. The larger l is, the more risk is given to the manager, and he or she must be compensated for this. Therefore, the manager's risk aversion, reflected in δ, and the riskiness of the situation, reflected in $\sigma^2[v]$, "push" l^* toward smaller values. That is, if $\delta\sigma^2[v]$ increases and all other factors are held constant, l^* decreases toward zero. The other factor, which influences l^* in the opposite direction, is the manager's aversion to effort. As the effort aversion parameter a increases, the value of l^* increases toward 1, because this additional incentive is needed to prevent output from decreasing too much. Therefore, we can see that these two factors, risk aversion and effort aversion, push the value of l^* in opposite directions. If the agent has no effort aversion ($a = 0$), then $l^* = 0$; and if the agent has no risk aversion ($\delta = 0$), then $l^* = 1$. So we may see different profit-sharing arrangements (including those such as franchising) as reflecting the different factors incorporated into our model of the principal/agent relationship.

APPENDIX 11.2: Reducing Risk in Performance Measures

In this appendix we explore two of the more difficult areas in performance evaluation—the use of multiple performance measures and relative performance evaluation. In Appendix 11.1 we explored the effect of risk in performance evaluation. Since the central headquarters can be assumed to be less risk-averse than the decentralized manager, it makes (economic) sense for most risk to be borne by the central headquarters. However, if the risky outcome (e.g., profit) is affected by the manager's decision making, it is desirable that the manager bear some of the risk. Otherwise, he or she is in an incentiveless position.

If there are ways to motivate the manager while subjecting him or her to less risk, then the performance evaluation system becomes more efficient, and the central management (principal) benefits. In this appendix we consider two ways of improving the performance evaluation system. The first involves the disaggregation of performance measure into multiple measures, while the second uses a peer group's performance as a "moving benchmark" to evaluate a manager.

A11.2.1 Disaggregated Performance Measures

When a manager of a responsibility center can affect both revenues and costs, it is common to classify the center as a *profit center,* and to base the manager's evaluation on profits (revenues less costs). Yet this aggregation of revenues less costs may not be the most efficient way of evaluating performance. Perhaps one measure is less risky than another, and therefore provides a less risky indicator of the manager's action. For instance, in Appendix 11.1 revenues were a

[9]If we assume that $B = 0$ in the revenue function, then the optimum profit-sharing parameter is the following.

$$l^* = \begin{cases} 1, & \text{if } \delta = 0 \\ 0, & \text{if } a = 0 \\ \dfrac{-a + \{a^2 + 4a\delta\sigma^2[v]\}^{1/2}}{2\delta\sigma^2[v]}, & \text{if } \delta > 0, a > 0 \end{cases}$$

Try different values of a, δ, and $\sigma^2[v]$ to see what effect they have on l^*.

noiseless function of the agent's action x. Therefore, we could have based the agent's evaluation on revenues alone, and the principle would have benefitted.

For this section, assume that the manager makes a decision x that affects both revenues and costs in the following way.

$$\begin{aligned} R &= rx + \varepsilon_r; \qquad r > 0, E[\varepsilon_r] = 0, \sigma^2[\varepsilon_r] = \sigma_r^2 \\ C &= cx + \epsilon_c; \qquad r > c > 0, E[\varepsilon_c] = 0, \sigma^2[\varepsilon_c] = \sigma_c^2 \\ \text{Profit: } \pi &= R - C \end{aligned} \tag{A11.2.1}$$

As in Appendix 11.1, we assume that the central management is risk-neutral and chooses the bonus function so as to maximize the expected payoff to the central headquarters. The decentralized manager chooses the action x so as to maximize the following expected utility function.

$$EU_m = E[\text{compensation}] - \delta\sigma^2[\text{compensation}] - ax^2 \tag{A11.2.2}$$

We will briefly examine two incentive alternatives, one based on profits π, and one based on the separate measures of revenues R and costs C.

Profit Bonus Compensation, $I = k + l_\pi \pi$

$$\begin{aligned} EU_m &= k + l_\pi E[\pi|x] - \delta l^2(\sigma_r^2 + \sigma_c^2) - ax^2 \\ x^* &= \frac{l_\pi(r - c)}{2a} \\ l_\pi^* &= \frac{(r - c)^2}{(r - c)^2 + 4a\,\delta(\sigma_r^2 + \sigma_c^2)} \end{aligned} \tag{A11.2.3}$$

This result is similar to the one in Appendix 11.1, but not exactly identical because there is a slight difference in the models. (The profit risk does not increase with production.) The term for l_π^* represents the optimum profit-sharing parameter: as risk or risk aversion increases l_π^* decreases, and as the expected return to effort $(r - c)$ increases l_π^* increases.

However, it is possible that restricting the bonus to be a function of profits is not efficient. For instance, we might separate the revenues and costs in the bonus calculation. Would this separation be beneficial? The answer is "yes," in general.

Revenue/Expense Bonus Compensation, $I = k + l_r R - l_c C$

$$\begin{aligned} EU_m &= k + l_r E[R|x] - l_c E[C|x] - \delta[l_r^2\sigma_r^2 + l_c^2\sigma_c^2] - ax^2 \\ x^* &= \frac{l_r r - l_c c}{2a} \\ l_r^* &= \frac{4r(r - c)a\delta\sigma_c^2}{(r^2 + 4a\delta\sigma_r^2)(c^2 + 4a\delta\sigma_c^2) - r^2c^2} \\ l_c^* &= \frac{-4c(r - c)a\delta\sigma_r^2}{(r^2 + 4a\delta\sigma_r^2)(c^2 + 4a\delta\sigma_c^2) - r^2c^2} \end{aligned} \tag{A11.2.4}$$

There are some interesting aspects of this bonus system. First, it is not true that $l_r^* = l_c^*$, so the revenue/expense bonus system does not "collapse" into a profit bonus and central management is better off with the disaggregation. Surprisingly, l_r^* and l_c^* are of opposite sign, with l_c^* negative. This implies that higher costs mean a higher bonus! This result seems nonsensical until we remember that higher costs are indicative of higher effort levels, and therefore should be rewarded.

Of course, the model we are using is a simplified one, and if we recognized that the manager might exert cost control effort to reduce c, we might find $l_c^* > 0$. Nevertheless, we should recognize the possibility that an incentive system based on multiple measures may be more efficient than one based on an aggregate measure.

A11.2.2 Relative Performance Evaluation

In the models we have examined, profit was composed of a part the manager could control and a part that was uncontrollable. The uncertainty created by the uncontrollable factors makes performance evaluation more difficult because bonuses that provide more motivation also subject the manager to more risk. One approach to reducing the risk is to look outside the manager's operation, or even outside the firm, to obtain information on the uncontrollable factors. For instance, rather than evaluating a sales manager by comparing sales growth to a fixed target, we might compare the sales growth to the average sales growth for similar firms. If the other firms' sales are subject to many of the same uncontrollable factors, then their average sales growth represents a moving target that is adjusted for common uncontrollable factors. If the manager achieved 10% sales growth, that might be very good if everyone else had 5% growth, or not so good if everyone else achieved 15%. The basic principle is similar to an instructor assigning grades on a curve, thereby removing a source of uncertainty common to all students—the difficulty of the examination. Contests among salesforce personnel are also examples of relative performance evaluation, as are executive incentive plans such as the one described in problem 11.9.

To analyze these plans, we will use a model similar to that in the earlier part of this appendix, except that we will not consider breaking profits π down into revenues and costs, and we introduce an *industry index* π_0, which is correlated with the uncontrollable factors affecting π. Again, assume that the risk-neutral central manager chooses a linear bonus function to motivate a risk-averse and effort-averse decentralized manager.

$$\begin{aligned}&\text{Firm profits: } \pi = (r - c)x + \varepsilon_\pi;\ E[\varepsilon_\pi] = 0,\ \sigma^2[\varepsilon_\pi] = \sigma_\pi^2\\ &\text{Industry index: } \pi_0 = \bar{\pi}_0 + \varepsilon_0;\ E[\varepsilon_0] = 0,\ \sigma^2[\varepsilon_0] = \sigma_0^2\\ &\rho = \text{correlation between } \varepsilon_\pi \text{ and } \varepsilon_0\end{aligned} \tag{A11.2.5}$$

Relative Performance Bonus

$$\begin{aligned}\text{Compensation, } I &= k + l_\pi \pi + l_0 \pi_0\\ &= k + \underbrace{(l_\pi + l_0)\pi}_{\text{Absolute performance evaluation}} \underbrace{- l_0(\pi - \pi_0)}_{\text{Relative performance evaluation}}\end{aligned}$$

$$EU_m = k + l_\pi E[\pi|x] + l_0 E[\pi_0] - \delta(l_\pi^2\sigma_\pi^2 + l_0^2\sigma_0^2 + 2\rho l_\pi l_0 \sigma_\pi \sigma_0) - ax^2$$

$$x^* = \frac{l_\pi(r - c)}{2a} \tag{A11.2.6}$$

$$l_\pi^* = \frac{(r - c)^2}{(r - c)^2 + 4a\delta\sigma_\pi^2(1 - \rho^2)}$$

$$l_0^* = \frac{-\rho\sigma_\pi}{\sigma_0} l_\pi^*$$

To see the effect that relative performance evaluation has, compare the l_π^* here to that found in equation (A11.2.3) in the first section of this appendix. The term $(\sigma_r^2 + \sigma_c^2)$ is represented by σ_π^2, but there is an additional term $(1 - \rho^2)$. As ρ, the correlation between firm profits and the industry index, increases, the term $(1 - \rho^2)$ decreases, and the optimal l_π^* increases, approaching 1.0. As long as ρ is positive, l_0^* will be negative, thereby "washing out" the uncontrollable factors common to the firm and the industry. The effect can be seen by looking at the variance of the manager's compensation.

$$\sigma^2[I] = l_\pi^2\sigma_\pi^2 + l_0^2\sigma_0^2 + 2\rho l_\pi l_0 \sigma_\pi \sigma_0 = l_\pi^2\sigma_\pi^2(1 - \rho^2) \rightarrow 0, \text{ as } \rho \rightarrow 1 \qquad \text{(A11.2.7)}$$

As ρ approaches 1 (perfect correlation), the relative performance evaluation system is able to reduce the manager's risk to zero.

The ability to reduce risk has made relative performance evaluation an increasingly popular approach to motivating managers. However, there are some important issues that have not been completely resolved. For instance, if investment decisions have been delegated to the manager, relative performance evaluation may cause him or her to bias decisions in favor of investments that increase ρ. Such a bias is not necessarily in the best interests of the shareholders or central management. As always, a performance system can only be evaluated with reference to the decisions that have been delegated to the manager.

PROBLEMS

11.1. In October of 1985, the Turner Toy Company found that its new doll, Lotta Luvin, was going to be the hit of the holiday buying season. "We can sell every doll that we can make between now and December 1st," said the president, "so we're really putting a lot of pressure on the production people. We want them to expend as much effort as possible to keep production up for the next month-and-a-half, but we want them to pay attention to quality control as well. It won't help the company in the long run if the dolls are not made to our quality specifications. How do I set a production quota for the next month-and-a-half that will encourage the production people to keep production *and* quality up? Let's say that the production characteristics look like the following."

Course of action			
Production effort	Quality effort	Expected production	Standard deviation of production
Low	Low	250,000	10,000
Low	High	240,000	10,000
High	Low	260,000	10,000
High	High	250,000	10,000

Required

A. If you assume that the production personnel's objectives are to do what's best for the organization, what production quota should you set? What bonus should be paid if the production quota is met?

B. If the production personnel will expend increased effort only if they expect an increase in compensation or some other recognition of their performance, what production quota should you set?

C. Why is it difficult to set up the production quota in part B? Discuss the "informativeness" of production. How would the situation change if

(a) there was a separate report on the quality of products produced?; or

(b) the effect of high effort in production was to increase expected production by 50,000 units instead of 10,000 units?

11.2. At present, the manager of the specialty products division expects his division to earn income of $500,000 for the coming year, with average assets of $2,500,000 over the year.

A customer has approached the manager with an order for a specialized machine that would take a little less than a year to construct. For that year, the division manager's average assets would increase by about \$100,000 due to the work-in-process on the machine. There are few uncertainties about the work: it is simply a big project with an estimated contribution margin of \$18,000. The customer would pay for the machine at the end of the year. (Ignore the effects of taxes.)

Required

A. For each of the following bonus schemes, determined the amount of bonus the manager would receive if he accepted the order and if he rejected the order.

(a) Four percent of the division's income.

(b) One-thousand dollars times the division's percent return on average assets.

(c) Sixteen percent of the division's residual income (income less 15% times the average assets).

B. If the company wanted the manager to accept a project like this only if it had a discounted rate of return of 15% or more, which performance measure would be most likely to produce the desired results?

C. Suppose that the special machine would not be delivered until the next year, and revenue and income would be recognized at that time. If the manager expects to be in this job for only one more year, which of the bonus schemes in part A would encourage him to accept the order? Evaluate the *informativeness* of the different performance measures.

11.3. The manager of a small operating division has the capacity to manufacture 100 units of output. The output may be any combination of two products X and Y, although we will limit our consideration in the problem to three possibilities:

Action 1: Produce 100 units of product X
Action 2: Produce 50 units of each of products X and Y
Action 3: Produce 100 units of product Y

Revenue for each product will be \$100 per unit, and the costs of producing Y will be \$90 per unit. The costs of producing X are uncertain, and the manager believes that the costs could be \$85 per unit (with probability 0.6) or \$95 per unit (with probability 0.4). The manager receives a bonus of 10% of the profits of his division.

Required

A. The central headquarters of the company receives 90% of the division's profits, less the fixed salary paid to the division manager. If the central management is viewed as being risk-neutral, which product mix would they prefer?

B. Suppose that the manager is risk-averse, and his preferences for bonus payments are reflected in the following function.

$$U[\text{bonus}] = \log_e(\text{bonus})$$

Which product mix will the division manager choose?

C. What approaches might be taken by central management to reconcile this difference in risk attitudes.

11.4. One of the more controversial components of recent managerial compensation packages is the *golden parachute*. A golden parachute provides a very lucrative severance package for an executive in the event that the company he works for is taken over by another firm.

For instance, the 1982 proxy statement of Celanese Corporation states that if an executive is terminated, following a change in control of the company, he will receive:

> . . . the sum of his annual base salary at that time and his most recent bonus, multiplied by the lesser of four or the difference between his age at that time and 65; (plus) the equivalent of his benefits under the Executive Pension Plan as it existed prior to . . . the change of control.

There are many different examples of golden parachutes, with many different provisions, but they all become effective when a change of control occurs and when the executive's employment is terminated. The number of executives covered by the parachute is usually less than ten, and the size of the payments can, in some cases, be as large as 10% of the market value of the firm's common stock, so the amounts received by the executives can be in the millions of dollars.

Required

A. Analyze the motivational implications of golden parachutes. How might the existence of a golden parachute affect management's attitude toward a merger proposal? If management is against a merger proposal, what actions might they take? As a shareholder, what actions would you like them to take?

B. At this time, shareholders vote on the adoption of golden parachutes for a company's management (although the vote is not binding on the board of directors). If you were a shareholder, under what conditions would you vote in favor of such a proposal?

11.5. The Quick Chick Corporation operates fast-food restaurants in the southeastern United States, with a concentration on fried chicken. (A barbequed ribs product is being test-marketed in selected areas.) The company has built its reputation on the consistency of its product quality, and its advertising is based on the assurance of high-quality food at a moderate price. The company goes to considerable lengths to insure that its suppliers are reliable, its employees are properly trained, and that the managers of the individual restaurants maintain their operations so as to foster customer satisfaction. Product decisions and pricing policies (including special promotions) are set by the central headquarters in Atlanta.

As a part of its quality assurance program, Quick Chick has established an Operational Assessment Department operating out of its corporate headquarters. The department has teams of two inspectors each who travel to the company's restaurants and make an inspection of various aspects of the operation. They test product quality and assess the level of service provided by the employees. The physical plant is inspected to insure that the customer areas are kept clean and attractive, paper products are kept well stocked, followed by an inspection of the food preparation area. The storeroom is inspected for proper levels of stock and for storage procedures. Finally, the recent financial and employee records are reviewed with the restaurant manager. The results of the inspection are recorded on a standard form—one copy is kept by the restaurant manager, one copy is kept for his or her personnel file, and a third copy goes to the regional manager. Given the company's quality objectives, a heavy weight is placed on inspection results in evaluating the performance of restaurant and regional managers, and in determining promotions and salary adjustments.

The Operational Assessment Department has been growing significantly in recent years, and the corporate controller has expressed concern about the department's efficiency. The department's budget is set annually, and the company president has usually accepted the increases requested by the department's manager. At its present rate of growth, the operational assessment costs will reach 15% of corporate administration costs within the next year or two.

Required

A. Prepare an analysis of the above situation for the corporate controller. What are the decisions that are most likely made in the Operational Assessment Department? What are their current incentives in making those decisions? Can you think of performance measures that might be used to assess the department's efficiency? What problems might such measures cause?

B. What other situations pose similar difficulties in measuring output and efficiency? How is control achieved in those situations?

11.6. You have been asked to set up a bonus function for a sales representative. The sales representative will decide on one of two possible actions—to "work hard" or to "not work hard." This decision will impact on the probability distribution of the contribution margin earned by the firm. For simplicity, assume that there are only two possible outcomes for the contribution margin ($40,000 and $60,000), with the following probabilities:

	Contribution margin probabilities	
	$40,000	$60,000
Sales representative "works hard"	1/3	2/3
Sales representative "does not work hard"	2/3	1/3

As you can see, the effect of the sales representative's effort is to shift the probability distribution up toward the more favorable outcome of $60,000. You may assume that the sales representative is risk-averse, and that his utility for compensation is reflected by the square-root function. That is, an income of $\$x$ produces a utility of $(x)^{1/2}$. The sales representative is also effort-averse, with the action "work hard" creating a disutility of 10 "utils" more than the action "not work hard." Finally, the sales representative must be paid enough to keep him from moving to another job. Assume that he could earn a fixed salary of $16,900 by working hard in another job.

Required

A. Find a compensation function for the sales representative that will induce him to choose the action "work hard" and will keep him from moving to another job. (*Hint:* Although this problem is not very realistic, it does allow you to set up a bonus function in a simple situation. The same principles apply in a more complex setting, although the computations can become burdensome. Your objective is to find two amounts: s_1 and s_2 are the compensations paid to the sales representative when the contribution margin is $40,000 and $60,000, respectively. One interpretation is that s_1 is the salary paid to the sales representative and s_2 is salary plus a bonus for achieving the higher contribution margin. The expected utility of working hard is $(1/3)(s_1)^{1/2} + (2/3)(s_2)^{1/2} - 10$, the expected utility of not working hard is $(2/3)(s_1)^{1/2} + (1/3)(s_2)^{1/2} - 0$, and the expected utility of the alternative employment opportunity is $(16{,}900)^{1/2} - 10$. The objective is to find values of s_1 and s_2 that will make the action "work hard" more attractive than "not work hard" and that will meet the *market utility* for the sales representative.)

B. If it is available, use the program INCNTV to solve the incentive problem posed in A.

C. How does the expected compensation in A compare with the $16,900 that would have to be paid if we could directly observe the sales representative's effort level.

D. Choose another set of probabilities for the actions and outcomes. See how the bonus is affected by the new probabilities.

11.7. Refer to the situation in problem 11.6. One possibility for influencing the action choice of an agent is the use of conditional investigations of the type described in Chapters 9 and 10.

Required

A. Suppose that in setting up the sales representative's bonus scheme, you could choose to investigate the representative's actions when the contribution margin turns out to be $40,000 (i.e., an unfavorable outcome). The investigation would determine, with certainty, whether the sales representative had chosen the "work hard" alternative or not. Can you design a bonus/penalty scheme that would induce the sales representative to choose the "work hard" alternative?

B. What is the expected compensation to be paid in the scheme in part A? If you completed problem 11.6, what is the maximum amount that you would be willing to pay for the option of conducting a conditional investigation?

C. How would your answer in part A change if the investigation were "noisy," that is, if it would not give a *perfect* signal about the representative's action?

11.8. In a *Harvard Business Review* article,[10] two authors describe an incentive/performance evaluation system for state-run colleges and universities in Tennessee. Past budgets for these institutions were based on enrollments, so that increasing resources could be achieved only by increasing the size of the student body, with no consideration of the quality of the program. To alleviate this situation, a policy was adopted that allows a college or university to increase its budget by up to 2% based on its performance. The following five areas of performance were identified:

1. Number of academic programs accredited (law, engineering, etc.).
2. Performance of graduates on a measure of outcomes in general education (ability to communicate, analyze, evaluate, etc.).
3. Performance of graduates in tests in their major fields (nursing, engineering, etc.).
4. Evaluation of programs and services by enrolled students, recent alumni, and community-employer representatives, primarily through follow-up questionnaires.
5. Evaluation of institutional programs by peers (colleagues from similar institutions).

Each of the colleges and universities can receive a maximum of 20 points in each of the five areas, so a total score of 100 is the maximum. In 1981, the authors report that the scores achieved ranged from a low of 13 to a high of 88. The median score was 60, so the median institution received an additional budget amount of 2% × (60/100), or 1.2% of its budget based on enrollment. (The largest institution in the system had a 1979 budget of approximately $50 million.)

[10]Bogue and Brown (1982)

Required Based on your experience in educational institutions, evaluate the strengths and weaknesses of the system described above. Consider the problems of measuring performance, setting targets for a variety of institutions, and the effect of incentives on decision making in the colleges and universities. What effect might it have on the relationships between institutions? Do you think a maximum budget increase of 2% is sufficient, or should it be larger? Can you suggest improvements to the system?

11.9. In a recent proxy statement, Consolidated Foods Corporation describes its long-term incentive plan for executive, senior, and group vice-presidents. The bonuses in this plan are based on the four-year growth rate in earnings-per-share (EPS), and on the executive's salary. There are two criteria on which performance is judged. The first of these is the comparison of the four-year EPS growth rate against the targets set by the company.

Criterion 1

Four-year EPS growth rate	Percent of base salary paid as bonus
14% or more	37.5%
13%	30.8%
.	.
.	.
.	.
7%	4.9%
6%	2.3%
less than 6%	0.0%

In addition to this criterion, a second part of the bonus calculation is based on the comparison of Consolidated Foods' EPS growth rate with a set of 24 ''peer companies,'' including Beatrice Foods, Dart & Kraft, General Foods, Quaker Oats, and others. If Consolidated Foods ranks highly, the executives receive a larger bonus, regardless of the performance on the first criterion.

Criterion 2

EPS growth rank among peer group	Percentage of base salary paid as bonus
1, 2, or 3	37.5%
4	34.6%
5	31.8%
6	29.2%
.	.
.	.
.	.
15	4.9%
16	3.2%
17	1.6%
18 or higher	0.0%

Required

A. Which of the two performance criteria do you believe will be more effective in motivating Consolidated Foods' management?

B. What is the objective of the second, peer group part of the bonus calculation? As companies become more diversified, it becomes more difficult to identify firms that are in precisely the same businesses. What criteria would you use in establishing such a peer group? (How big should it be? Which firms should be included?)

C. What effects do you think peer group performance might have on decision making in the organization, particularly on diversification decisions?

11.10. One trend in compensation systems is the increasing use of *relative performance measurement,* in which the performance target is defined by the actual performance of a peer group of firms or responsibility centers. The objective of this technique is to reduce the riskiness of performance evaluation by controlling for economic events which affect all firms within the peer group. In essence, the peer group's actual performance represents a flexible budget. If our firm's profits declined, that's not bad if the peer's group's profits declined by more.

The data below provide information on the performance of two large banks and on a peer group (the median for other large banks).

	Changes in return on equity		
Year	Citibank	Chase Manhattan	Industry median
1962	−0.1	−0.2	−0.4
1963	−0.2	0.4	0.0
1964	0.9	0.4	0.6
1965	0.6	0.7	0.3
1966	0.9	0.4	0.6
1967	−1.0	−0.6	0.2
1968	−1.4	0.9	0.7
1969	2.1	−0.8	0.1
1970	0.2	−0.2	−0.2
1971	1.3	1.2	0.2
1972	0.3	−0.2	−0.2
1973	1.0	0.3	0.4
1974	1.2	0.4	0.6
1975	−0.3	−1.8	−0.4
1976	0.3	−3.7	−0.4
1977	−2.0	−0.1	0.1
1978	1.6	2.4	1.6
1979	0.3	5.7	1.0
1980	1.5	−0.3	0.0

Required

A. Which of these two firms has a higher correlation with the peer group? What are some possible reasons for this?

B. Which company would get the most benefit from evaluating its management based on relative performance? Why is the relative performance measurement *more informative?*

C. The median change in ROE was −0.1 in 1981. What flexible budget would you set for each of these firms? What confidence do you have in the target?

D. What are some potential problems that might result from the use of relative performance evaluations?

11.11. The Mohawk Office Products Company is a distributor of a wide variety of furniture and equipment in the midwestern United States, with a 1982 sales of around $25 million. The company has a salesforce of 20 people, with territories divided geographically for the most part. In the last three years, Mohawk has expanded its traditional products (desks, filing cabinets, etc.) to include more electronic products such as copiers, printing equipment, and a microcomputer system designed for business use. In planning this expansion, Mohawk hoped to capitalize on its existing customer relationships and on its established distribution system. However, sales of the newer products have not met expectations. Paul Roberts, the Vice-President for Sales, has speculated on possible reasons behind the rather disappointing performance.

"Of course, competition in the area of office electronics has been a lot stiffer than we had anticipated, but I don't think that's the whole problem. We have a very effective salesforce, but like most people, it takes them a while to adjust to change. In order to be successful in selling the new products, they have to invest a good deal of effort in learning the products' characteristics, which products can help which customers, and so on. Moreover, it may require a change in the types of customers they approach. Our traditional lines were purchased by new or expanding businesses, but the new electronic equipment can be used by a wider variety of potential customers.

"The salesforce receives a commission on its sales revenue in addition to the salaries that we pay. The salaries vary according to length of service, and we also try to take the type of territory into account. We don't want to punish a salesman who happens to be assigned to an area with little growth. Up to this point, the commission has been 1% of the total sales revenue earned in a territory, but I'm not sure that this has provided enough incentive for the salesmen to push the new product line. Maybe we should split the sales revenue into two parts—one for the older, established products, and one for the new electronic products. Then we could have different commission rates on the two lines. Another problem area that we ought to consider is the expense incurred by the salesforce for travel, entertainment, and so on. At present, we review the expense reports submitted, and if it looks like someone is getting a little extravagant, we talk with him or her about it. Maybe we should subtract selling expenses from sales revenue in calculating the commission."

Required You have been hired as a compensation consultant to help Mohawk evaluate its salesforce commission system. Your assignment for this problem is to prepare a list of questions and issues that you wish to discuss in your first meeting with Roberts. (You can assume that the question of your own compensation has already been settled.) You should have a clear idea of the reason that each issue is important for the solution of the problem that Roberts has posed. What data might you need to collect from other sources?

11.12. In recent years, the cost of health care in the United States has steadily increased at a rate exceeding the general inflation rate. There are a number of possible reasons for such increases, including the creation of new, more expensive technology. However, a continuing concern is the possibility that some of the increase could be attributed to inefficiencies in the health care delivery systems. As a result, institutions such as the U.S. government (which administers the Medicare system) and health insurance companies have begun to explore ways to motivate hospitals to keep tighter control of costs.

For many years, these institutions (called *third-party payers*) reimbursed the hospitals for the cost of providing health care to the patients they covered. That is, the hospital would determine the cost of providing service to all patients covered by Blue Cross, and then Blue Cross would reimburse the hospital for these costs plus a small additional amount. The current trend is away from such *cost reimbursement,* and toward different forms of *prospective payment* by the third-party payers. A principle form of prospective payment has been adopted by Medicare, in which Medicare will pay the hospital a fixed amount for designated medical problems. For instance, if a patient enters the hospital for an appendectomy, Medicare will pay the hospital a fixed amount (determined by surveying costs in other hospitals in the same region). If the hospital can provide treatment for a cost below the fixed payment, it gets to keep the difference. But if treatment costs more, Medicare will pay no more and the hospital loses the difference.

Required

A. How does the shift from cost reimbursement to prospective payment affect the allocation of the risks of health care cost?

B. Hospital administrators must make a number of decisions that affect both the level of health care service and the level of health care costs. (For example, staffing of nurses, purchases of equipment, etc.) Evaluate the incentives for an administrator who makes such decisions under a cost reimbursement system.

C. How will the decisions in B be affected by a change to a prospective payment system such as described in the problem above?

11.13. Problem 8.9 describes a competitive bidding situation, where the manager uses existing cost information, decides whether to acquire more information, and then submits a bid to a potential customer. For this problem, assume that these decisions are delegated to a divisional manager. A survey of local businesses indicates that a manager with comparable abilities and responsibilities earns an average of $70,000, although the exact amounts range from $45,000 to $95,000. The company's policy is to pay their managers average compensation for satisfactory performance, and above average amounts when the manager has achieved a significant benefit for the company. As stated in the original problem, most of the management team members are shareholders, and this particular division manager owns $50,000 worth of stock (although the stock is not actively traded on any exchanges).

Required Design a performance evaluation system for the division manager who has been put in charge of the bidding decisions. You should consider the issues of performance measure(s) and incentive function in developing a competitive compensation plan for the division manager. For example, you should consider whether to pay the manager a fixed salary or to pay some form of bonus based on the various performance measures available—profits, revenue, capacity utilization, number of successful bids, and so on. If the latter, what form should the bonus take, and how much should be paid as fixed salary?

REFERENCES

Anthony R., J. Dearden, and N. Bedford. *Management Control Systems,* 5th Ed. Homewood, IL: R. D. Irwin. 1984.

Arrow, K. ''Control in Large Organizations,'' *Management Science*. April 1964.

Baiman, S. ''Agency Research in Managerial Accounting: A Survey,'' *Journal of Accounting Literature*. Spring 1983.

Bogue, E. G., and W. Brown. ''Performance Incentives for State Colleges,'' *Harvard Business Review*. November–December 1982.

Chow, C., and W. Waller, ''Management Accounting and Organizational Control,'' *Management Accounting*. April 1982.

Holmström, B. ''Moral Hazard and Observability,'' *Bell Journal of Economics*. Spring 1979.

Jennergren, L. P. ''On the Design of Incentives in Business Firms—A Survey of Some Research,'' *Management Science*. February 1980.

Lambert, R., and D. Larcker. ''Golden Parachutes: Executive Decision Making and Shareholder Wealth,'' *Journal of Accounting and Economics*. April 1985.

Lessard, D., and P. Lorange. ''Currency Changes and Management Control: Resolving the Centralization/Decentralization Dilemma,'' *Accounting Review*. July 1977.

Magee, R. ''An Evaluation of Prospective Payment Plans for Hospitals,'' *Journal of Business*. October 1977.

Reece, J., and W. Cool. ''Measuring Investment Center Performance,'' *Harvard Business Review*. May–June 1978.

Salter, M. ''Tailor Incentive Compensation to Strategy,'' *Harvard Business Review*. March–April 1973.

Sasser, W. E., and S. Pettway. ''Case of Big Mac's Pay Plans,'' *Harvard Business Review*. July–August 1974.

Young, D., and R. Saltman. ''Preventive Medicine for Hospital Costs,'' *Harvard Business Review*. January–February 1983.

Chapter 12

Budgets and Participation

The basic idea underlying managerial incentives is that shareholders or central management can be made better off by tieing the decentralized manager's income (present or future) to a measure of performance. However, there are a variety of performance measures and many ways in which a measure may be used to determine the manager's income. For instance, the granting of stock or stock options would tie the manager's financial well-being directly to the shareholders' well-being, and we would expect a considerable degree of *goal congruence* to result. But a manager's income would be affected by many factors beyond his or her control, for example, government fiscal policy, actions by supplier cartels, the Federal Reserve's monetary policies, and so on. As we demonstrated in the previous chapter, this riskiness can cause motivational problems if the manager perceives that his or her actions have only minimal impact on the evaluation of performance. The *book value stock plan* described at the start of Chapter 11 is a response to this problem that uses a less risky measure of performance, so that managers have a profit-sharing scheme that is *less volatile* than traditional stock options. As we found in Chapter 11, many performance measurement choices involve such a tradeoff between incentives and risk, and in the 1970s and early 1980s many firms made their incentive plans more dependent on accounting results and less dependent on security returns.

In the last chapter, we described a framework for performance evaluation problems, and focused on the performance measure $r(\cdot)$ and its effect on decision making. In this chapter, we will concentrate more on the incentive function $I(\cdot)$, which translates the performance measures into dollars of compensation. For instance, with a strict profit-sharing or commission plan, it is possible for a manager to lose money if the organization (or responsibility center) makes a loss for the year. That is, the manager might have to pay back some of his or her salary. To avoid such situations, many firms use *budget-based* performance evaluation systems which serve to limit the manager's *downside risk*. These incentives can take a number of forms, as seen in Figure 12.1, and they can also

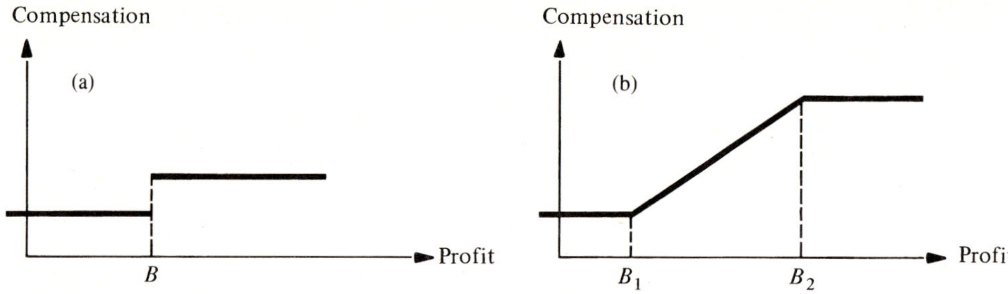

Figure 12.1

create new decision problems. How will the budget be set? Will managers participate in setting their own budgets? What types of dysfunctional behavior can these budget-based incentives create? We address these issues in this chapter.

12.1 BUDGET SETTING

How should a manager's budget be set? We cannot answer this question without first determining how the budget is going to be used. In performance evaluation, the term budget usually refers to a *target* level of sales, costs, or profits.[1] The manager's performance is judged relative to the budget, for example, a bonus or other favorable performance evaluation is received if the budgeted level of profits is met or exceeded. This situation could be graphed in Figure 12.2a, where *k* is the manager's salary, *l* is the bonus, and *B* is the budgeted profits. (Figure 12.2b shows the same sort of system for costs.) Central management can control the budget and the size of the bonus, but before asking, "where should the budget be set?," we first need to determine how the budget will influence the manager's decision making.

Different decentralized managers can influence their performance measures in a variety of ways. A sales manager may decide which prices to set, how many calls to make, and how many samples to give away, and all these will influence the level of sales and whether budgeted sales will be exceeded. An operating manager may decide how much effort to expend to control costs, and this will influence whether costs will be lower than the budgeted target. We can look at this latter example in a little more detail. Suppose that the operating manager can expend either a "high" or a "low" degree of effort toward controlling costs, and that if everything else is held constant, the manager would prefer to direct attention elsewhere and exert low effort toward cost control. Specifically, let's assume exerting a high level of cost control effort would have to increase the manager's expected income by $1,500 in order to be deemed worthwhile. As central management, we could set a budget that would be extremely difficult to achieve even with a high degree of cost control effort (a *tight* budget), a budget that is easily achieved with a low degree of effort (a *loose* budget), or a budget somewhere between

[1]In some situations (e.g., governmental units), the budget represents an authorized level of spending. This authorized level could also be thought of as a target, with severe penalties if it is exceeded.

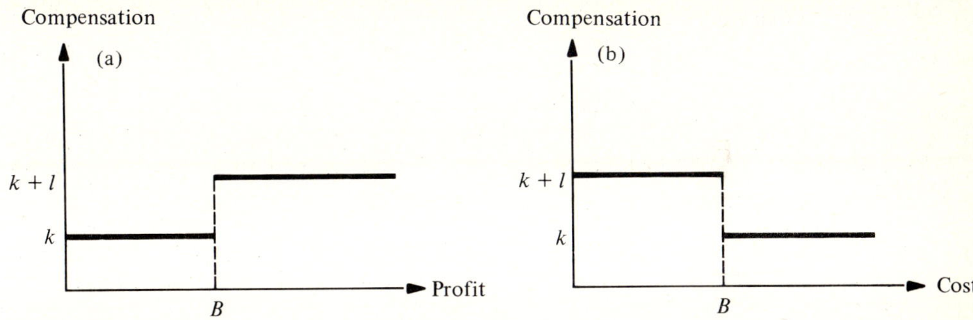

Figure 12.2

these two extremes. The manager's chances of doing better than the budget might be summarized in a table like the following.

	Probability of costs less than budget		
	Loose budget	Medium budget	Tight budget
High effort	0.9	0.6	0.3
Low effort	0.6	0.4	0.25

If the manager's bonus for meeting the budget is \$10,000, which budgets will elicit a high degree of effort directed toward cost control? As things stand, the probability of making the budget would have to increase by at least 0.15 to make the effort worthwhile. This occurs with the medium budget *and* the loose budget, and the central management might prefer the medium budget because it produces the same decision with a lower expected compensation (\$6,000 versus \$9,000 for the loose budget). If the budget is set too tightly, the incremental probability of getting a bonus is too low to induce high effort from the manager.

The problem of setting a budget for a manager is essentially the same as setting a standard for any employee that receives a bonus if the standard is exceeded. In some cases, the standard may be set using engineering estimation techniques such as those discussed in Chapter 5, or the statistical techniques that are presented in Chapter 6. As a manager's responsibilities increase, the standard setting becomes more complex because there are a variety of factors beyond the manager's control that can affect costs or profits, and these uncontrollable factors affect whether a budget is tight or loose in a given period. The following model illustrates which variables are important in a budget setting situation.

12.2 A BUDGET SETTING MODEL

Suppose we have a manager (agent) who must choose how much effort to devote to an operation. For simplicity, we will assume that this manager only cares about his or her

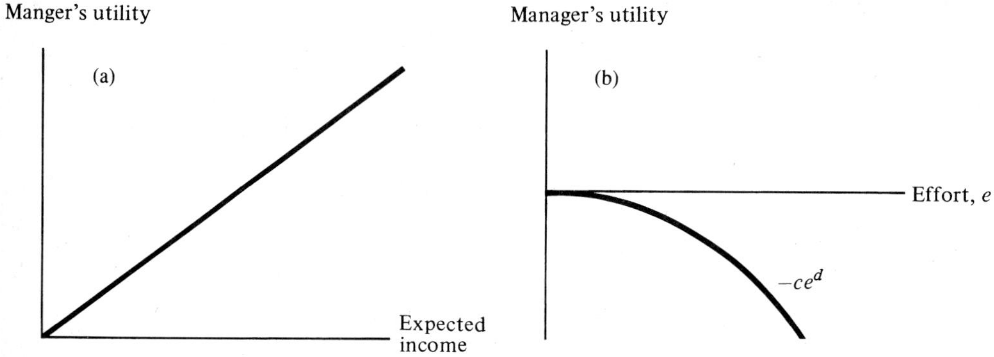

Figure 12.3

expected income $E[I|e]$, and the amount of effort that he or she must expend e. (The manager likes income, and dislikes effort. See Figure 12.3.)

$$E[U|e] = E[I|e] - ce^d; \qquad c > 0, d > 1 \tag{12.1}$$

In essence, these assumptions imply that in order for the manager to increase his or her effort from e to $e + \Delta e$, the accompanying increase in expected income must be at least $c(e + \Delta e)^d - ce^d$.

The profits that accrue to the manager's operation are assumed to be influenced by effort and by some uncontrollable factors. In the model we will analyze, assume that profits $\pi = ae^b + \mu$, where the parameters $a > 0$, $0 < b < 1$ determine the impact of the manager's efforts on profits. The uncontrollable factors are incorporated in μ, which is assumed to be uniformly distributed between μ_L and μ_H. The range of profits as a function of effort is depicted in Figure 12.4.

If the manager chooses an effort level of e, the lowest possible profit is $\pi_L = ae^b + \mu_L$, and the highest possible profit is $\pi_H = ae^b + \mu_H$. The income received by the manager consists of a fixed salary k plus a fixed bonus l which is paid when the operation's profits exceed a preset budget B. (This *step* incentive function is illustrated in Figure 12.2a.)

$$I(\pi, B) = \begin{cases} k, & \text{if } \pi < B \\ k + l, & \text{if } \pi \geq B \end{cases} \tag{12.2}$$

In this situation, the central management's decision problem is to set the budget B and the bonus l so as to influence the decentralized manager's decisions in a way that leads to the best outcome for the firm. On the other hand, the decentralized manager's problem is to decide on a level of effort given the bonus, the budget, and so on.

From the discussions above, we have some expectations about a manager's budget-oriented behavior. If the target is set too tight, the manager will view it as unattainable,[2] and will not work to achieve it. On the other hand, if the standards are too loose, the bonus can be obtained with relatively little effort, and there is no incentive to work

[2]More precisely, the rewards from meeting the target do not warrant the effort necessary to achieve the target.

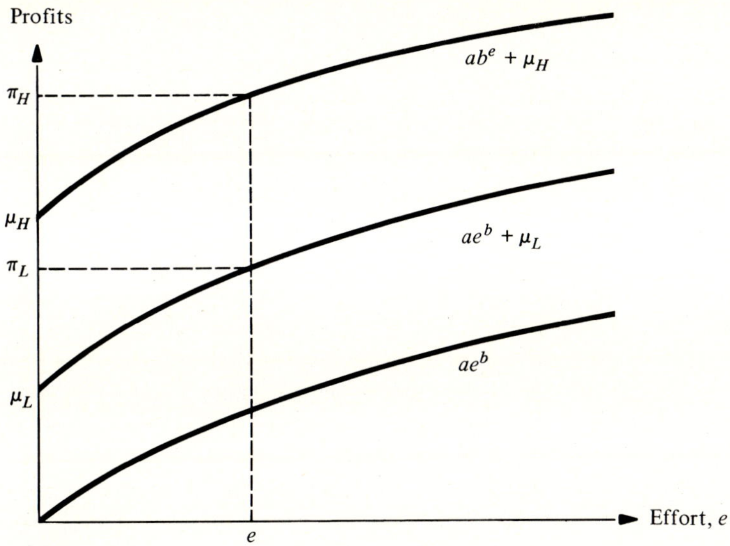

Figure 12.4

harder. The model we've described above has these properties. For instance, if $B < \mu_L$, then even zero effort will ensure a bonus. (See Figure 12.4.) There will be different regions of budget-oriented behavior, but we can start by determining the maximum amount of effort the manager will expend.

$$\max_e \{E[I|e] - ce^d\} \leftrightarrow \max_e \{k + l\,\text{Prob}[\pi \geq B|e] - ce^d\}$$

$$\leftrightarrow \max_e \left[k + l\left(1 - \frac{B - ae^b - \mu_L}{\mu_H - \mu_L}\right) - ce^d\right] \tag{12.3}$$

$$\rightarrow \hat{e} = \left(\frac{ab}{cd}\frac{l}{\mu_H - \mu_L}\right)^{1/d-b}$$

We can see that the maximum amount of effort is affected positively by the profit parameters a and b and negatively by the effort disutility parameters c and d. Also, higher bonuses l produce higher effort, while greater uncertainty $(\mu_H - \mu_L)$ reduces effort. That is, if we had two identical managers in identical situations, but we gave one a higher bonus, we would predict a higher level of effort from this manager. Or, if the two managers faced identical situations, but one was more averse to effort (higher c and/or d), then we would predict that this manager would exert a lower level of effort. If it is found that different managers have differing levels of motivation, then the variables that determine $\hat{e}$ may help to explain some of the difference. If the budget is set too tight, that is, $B > a\hat{e}^b + \mu_H$, then the manager will have no chance to make the bonus, and he or she will expend minimal effort. Also, if $B < a\hat{e}^b + \mu_L$, then the manager can achieve the bonus with an effort level less than $\hat{e}$. The complete effort function and a graph (in Figure 12.5) appear below.

$$\text{Optimal effort, } e^* = \begin{cases} 0, & \text{if } B > a\hat{e}^b + \mu_H \\ \hat{e}, & \text{if } a\hat{e}^b + \mu_H \geq B \geq a\hat{e}^b + \mu_L \\ \left(\dfrac{B - \mu_L}{a}\right)^{1/b}, & \text{if } \mu_L < B < a\hat{e}^b + \mu_L \\ 0, & \text{if } B \leq \mu_L \end{cases} \tag{12.4}$$

For low budgets, there is little (or no) effort exerted. Then the budget elicits increasing effort until it reaches $\hat{e}$, and it stays there until the bonus is viewed as unattainable or not worth the effort. At this point the level of effort returns to zero. There are some other facets of this graph that should be recognized. First, the level of maximum effort $\hat{e}$ depends on the bonus parameter l as we noted above. Increasing the value of l will increase $\hat{e}$. In addition, the values of B_L and B_H will increase (i.e., move to the right on the graph). So the total amount of *budget pressure* the manager can cope with could be an increasing function of l, the bonus. Also, the distance between B_L and B_H is equal to $(\mu_H - \mu_L)$, and this uncertainty impacts negatively on the amount of effort $\hat{e}$ that the manager is willing to expend.

Having set up a model of the manager's response to different budgets, we can evaluate the expected net payoff to the central management with the different budgets. For budgets below μ_L, the manager will exert zero effort, and the expected payoff to the owner is $\frac{1}{2}(\mu_L + \mu_H) - k - l$. Similarly, if B is greater than B_H, no effort is exerted with expected central management payoff of $\frac{1}{2}(\mu_L + \mu_H) - k$. Between μ_L and B_L, the owner receives increased effort from an increased budget, and from B_L to B_U the effort remains constant, but the probability of paying a bonus decreases. This expected payoff function is graphed in Figure 12.6.

It appears that the best thing for the central management to do (given the values of k and l) is to set the budget close to B_H to obtain maximum effort at a minimum cost. Since $B_H = a\hat{e}^b + \mu_H$, this means that we determine how much effort can be elicited at maximum $\hat{e}$, translate that to expect profit $a\hat{e}^b$, and then add on an optimistic assessment of uncontrollable factors μ_H. This process would maximize the manager's effort while minimizing the expected bonus payment.

In practice, there are a variety of factors that may prevent central management

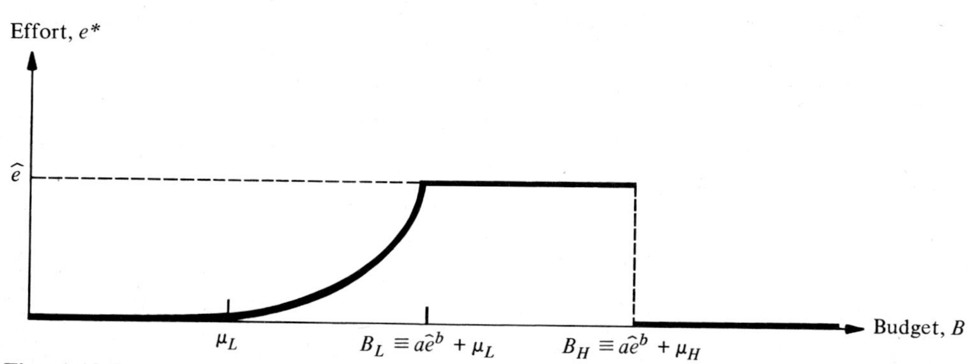

Figure 12.5

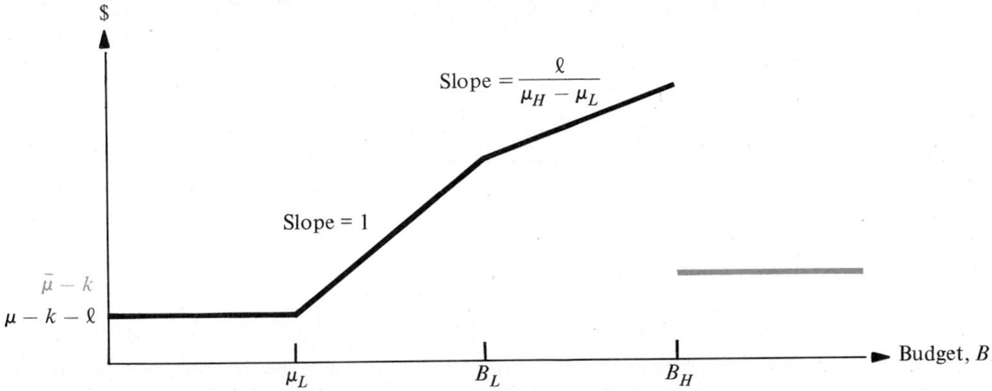

Figure 12.6 Expected payoff to the owner with fixed salary and bonus.

from setting the budget at the maximum B_H. For instance, it is very possible that the manager has better information about the uncontrollable factors in μ, and setting the budget at B_H may mean a high risk of zero effort. We will return to this issue later in the chapter. Yet another problem is that if the budget is set at (or very close to) B_H, the manager expends effort of $\hat{e}$, but there is essentially zero probability of achieving the bonus. Unless the fixed salary k is enough to compensate for the effort disutility, the manager will not want to stay in this job, and he or she may take other, more attractive opportunities. Central management could overcome this problem by increasing k *or* by decreasing the budget level so that the combination of salary and expected bonus was sufficient to keep the manager satisfied. For instance, if the budget was set at $a\hat{e}^b + (\mu_L + \mu_H)/2$, the manager would have a 1/2 probability of achieving the bonus and an expected income of $k + \frac{1}{2}l$. The budget (and the salary) may be decreased without affecting the owner's payoff as long as the budget is not reduced below B_L, because then it would begin to affect the manager's decisions.

Another approach to this budget setting problem would be to set an expected level of effort, say $\bar{e}$, and then determine the minimum profit that could occur if the manager chooses $\bar{e}$. That profit level would be $a\bar{e}^b + \mu_L$ in our model, and central management might set an extreme penalty if profits are below this minimum. If the penalty is large enough, then this *forcing contract* will cause the manager to choose $\bar{e}$. This rather extreme arrangement only works if the minimum profit outcome moves upward as effort is increased, as in the model above. (Under these circumstances, the manager can avoid the possibility of a penalty by choosing $\bar{e}$.) If the minimum does not increase with effort, then this type of contract places a significant amount of risk on the manager, and would not be very efficient. In addition, there are frequently institutional restrictions that prevent central management from imposing the risk of large penalties on employees.

Of course, there are other budget-based contract types (see Figure 12.1), and these budget setting problems can be evaluated in much the same way. In fact, we would probably want to include the manager's risk aversion in the process, since that is one of the primary reasons for budget-based incentives. By doing this, we could evaluate the effects of different budgets on the manager's behavior and the resulting effect on the organization. The effects of bonus size could also be explored.

However, there are a variety of problems that can arise in budget-based systems. As the budget becomes a primary factor in performance evaluation, managers may become interested in side-stepping, influencing, or even manipulating the system. There are a variety of ways that this may be accomplished, and the next two sections will detail some of the resulting problems.

12.3 INFLUENCING THE TIMING OF COSTS

From time to time, articles appear in the financial press describing management practices that manipulate performance measures in a firm. Frequently, managers who have ensured themselves of a bonus in the current period try to increase the probabilities of future bonuses by *banking* income. The reason for doing this can be seen in the following example. Suppose a manager receives a bonus of $15,000 if his or her division's net income exceeds $500,000 for the year. If income for 19X8 was $550,000, and 19X9 income was projected to be $480,000, the manager could be tempted, at the end of 19X8 to defer $35,000 of income to 19X9. This would ensure bonuses for each year, rather than for 19X8 only. This smoothing effect would be even more desirable if 19X9's budget were based on 19X8's income. In this case, the manager will wish to ensure a steady growth in income.

How can income be deferred by a manager? That is, how can the manager affect the timing of revenues and expenses? In some cases, managers made prepayments and advances to suppliers and (inappropriately) recognized these payments as expenses. Then next year, the suppliers would deliver goods or services at no charge. Of course, there are a number of other ways to accomplish the same result. A sales representative, having met 19X2's sales goal, may not enter some of the late December orders until January, 19X3. And there are usually discretionary expenditures such as research and development, maintenance, continuing education, and so on that can be reduced, or delayed, in order to make a budget. At the extreme, managers can even provide inaccurate reports. For instance, reserve inventories may be built up by a manager during good months, so that when a bad month comes along, production quotas can be met and costs kept below budget.

We would expect that central management would be watching the expenditure reports to try to discourage the types of behavior described above. This control can be implemented through *operations audits* that determine whether discretionary expenditures are appropriate. Or, central management can simply track the time series of discretionary expenditures to see whether they are being used to smooth out the cost or income behavior. If the variability of total costs is less than that of nondiscretionary costs, then it may be that discretionary costs are being used to smooth costs. (See Figure 12.7.)

Yet another problem is that budget-based incentives can discourage innovative activity. If a manager tries something new, he or she may lose this period's bonus, and next period's bonus will not be any higher, even if the venture is successful. Or, if the bonus is "already lost" this period, the manager may increase the costs this period to increase the likelihood of a bonus in the future.

The problem of setting budgets in a multiperiod situation is a very difficult one, particularly when the incentive function is a single step at the budget (Figure 12.2). The

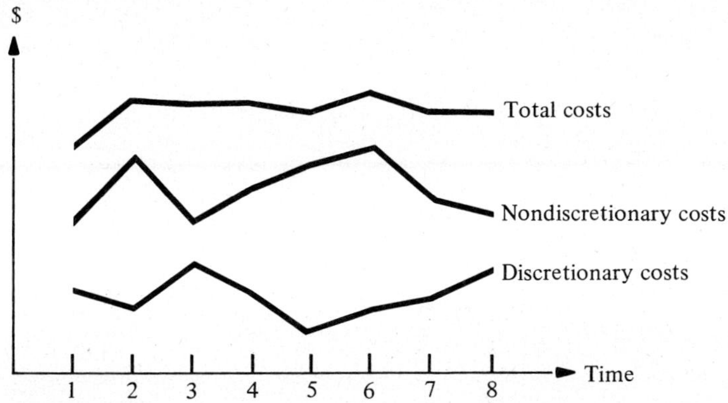

Figure 12.7

incentive function is flat over most of the possible outcomes, so that there are no incentives to increase profits or decrease costs except in the region right around the step. And in this region, the incentives are very substantial. Therefore, a policy of, say, setting this year's budget equal to last year's actual would lead the decentralized manager to always try to be just on the acceptable side of the budget. To do more would only produce a more difficult target next year. Innovation would only have an effect for a single period; after that the innovation's effect would be incorporated in the budget. The resulting multiperiod budget games are difficult to control.

Two approaches to this problem may provide some benefits. First, a combination of budget-based and profit-sharing incentives might change the manager's decision making. We will discuss this type of incentive in the next section. In addition, the budget-setting process should not fixate on past results. There is no doubt that past results contain useful information, but they should be used with care. The central management must make a careful assessment of the manager's current environment, problems, and opportunities, and then set a budget that provides the most beneficial motivation.

12.4 OPTIONLIKE INCENTIVES

In addition to the step incentives, there are also budget-based incentives which set a minimum outcome, and then incorporate a profit-share for outcomes better than the minimum. (See Figure 12.8.) This type of function is very common in setting a corporation's bonus pool where B is defined to be a percentage of shareholder's equity or of the assets employed. Unlike the step incentive, the optionlike incentive does provide motivation for the manager to increase profits beyond the budgeted level while also providing assurance of a minimum compensation if profits fall below the budget.

A potential difficulty with this incentive is that it may distort the risk-taking behavior of the manager. For instance, suppose that the bonus will be 10% of divisional profits in excess of \$500,000, and that if the manager doesn't accept a new investment project, divisional profits will be \$520,000 with certainty. This would lead to a bonus of 10% (520,000 − 500,000) = \$2,000. But an investment project is available that

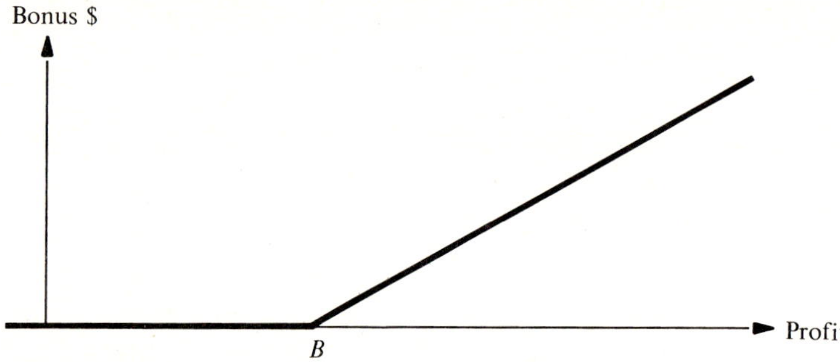

Figure 12.8

could change divisional profits to \$400,000 or \$600,000, each with probability 1/2. From the firm's point of view, the investment would decrease expected profit and increase risk. But the expected bonus to the manager increases to 1/2(0) + 1/2(10%)(600,000 − 500,000) = \$5,000. Therefore, this type of incentive can encourage risk-taking behavior, depending on the placement of the budget *B*, although we should recognize that such encouragement can benefit an organization is some cases. It can also encourage managers to influence the timing of income, as discussed in the last section. However, with optionlike incentives the manager may wish to accentuate variations in income rather than to smooth out the variations. A recent study by Healy (1983) found evidence that managers did try to increase their incentive payments by affecting the accounting measures.

12.5 PARTICIPATION

In the budget setting analysis above, the centralized management and the decentralized manager both had the same amount of information concerning the uncontrollable factors μ. But this assumption is not totally realistic, since one of the reasons for adopting a decentralized organizational structure is that the decentralized managers are "closer to the action," and therefore have better information. For instance, we would expect that a sales representative in the field would have better information about customers' financial condition, personnel changes, and production plans, than central management. A production manager would know more about the state of repair of equipment, real capacity (if different from that claimed by the manufacturer), the levels and types of training available among the current employees, and so on.

This *information differential* can cause some difficulties in the process of setting the budget at central headquarters. In the budget setting model we analyzed earlier, both the central management and the decentralized manager knew μ was uniformly distributed between μ_L and μ_H. But suppose that the manager was able to tell whether μ was going to be in the lower, middle, or upper third of $[\mu_L, \mu_H]$. We might think of this as the manager being able to discern whether the conditions were going to be unfavorable, neutral, or favorable. In Figure 12.9, the central management's information about μ is reflected in (*a*), but the central management does not know whether the decentralized manager is facing the probability distribution in (b), (c), or (d). The decentralized man-

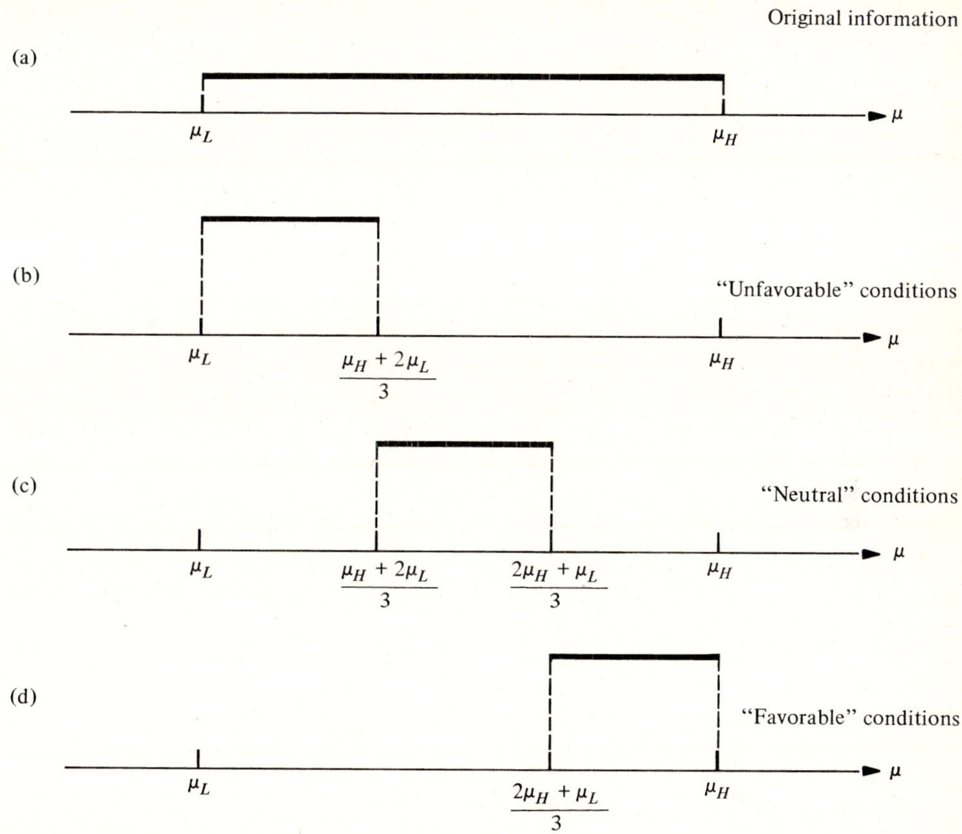

Figure 12.9

ager faces less uncertainty than he did with the original information, so he will be willing to exert more effort *if* the budget is not set too tight or too loose. Unfortunately, when the manager has superior information, there is a greater chance of setting a budget that produces little motivation. The relationships between effort and budget can be seen in Figure 12.10. Under the original information, a budget close to B_H would elicit the maximum effort, but if the manager has better information, a budget of B_H produces effort only under favorable conditions. Thus, there is a 2/3 chance that minimal effort will result. To avoid this possibility, central management would have to know as much about the decentralized environment as the decentralized manager does, since that would enable the budgets to be set to maximize the organization's performance.

But where can central management get this information? We would probably need a very extensive (and expensive) system to duplicate the information that the decentralized managers have. In effect, we would need to do a preoperations audit, and that would not be an easy task to accomplish. It would also alter greatly the nature of decentralization in the organization.

A natural alternative might be to ask the decentralized manager what his or her environment will be like over the next accounting period and then use his or her report

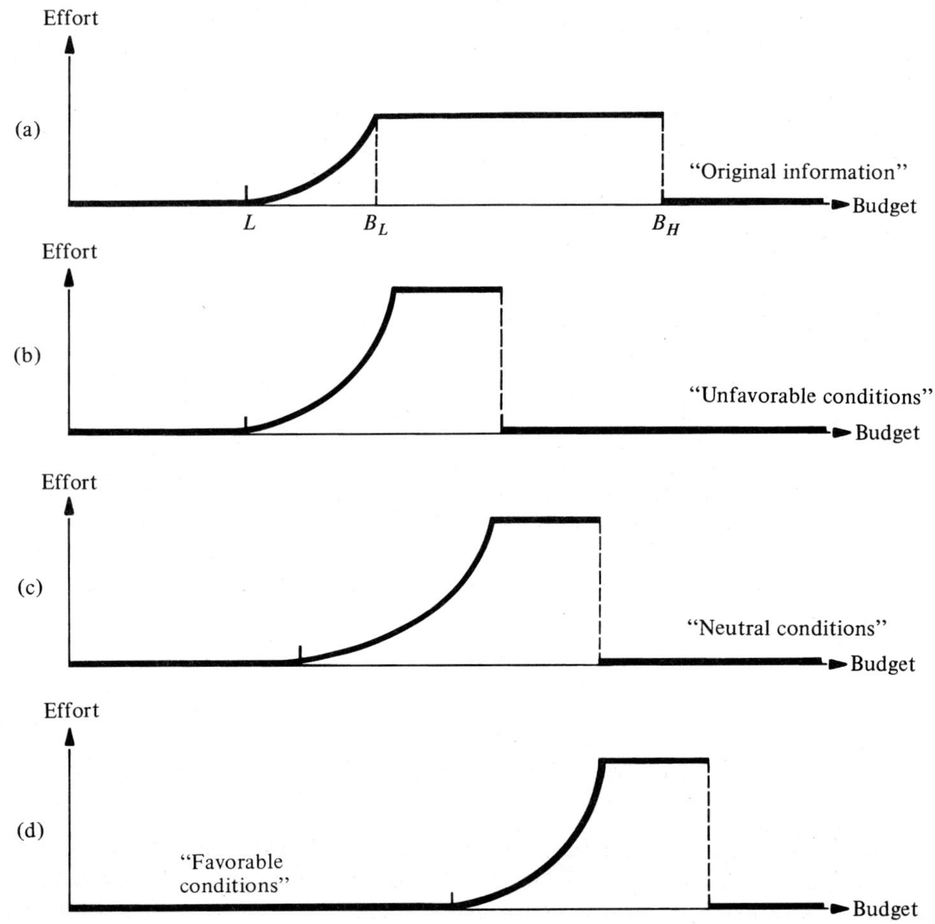

Figure 12.10

in setting the budget. That is, the manager *participates* in the goal setting process, and, ideally, this should increase the likelihood of a meaningful budget being chosen. However, there is a fundamental problem which must be overcome in order for participation to be useful. Participation allows a manager to influence his or her performance evaluation through the goal setting process. There may be many cases where managers provide accurate estimates and then expend the effort necessary to achieve the resulting budget. But there is also the possibility that the manager will try to pad the budget by giving pessimistic or conservative estimates of revenues and costs. From the budget setting analysis above, we can graph the manager's expected utility as a function of the budget (Figure 12.11). Not surprisingly, the manager is never better off when the budget increases, and therefore we might expect that the manager will attempt to pad the budget by reporting unfavorable conditions when the conditions are actually neutral or favorable.

The owner (or central administration) is now faced with a dilemma. A centrally specified budget (i.e., *top-down* budget) runs the risk of being perceived as unattainable

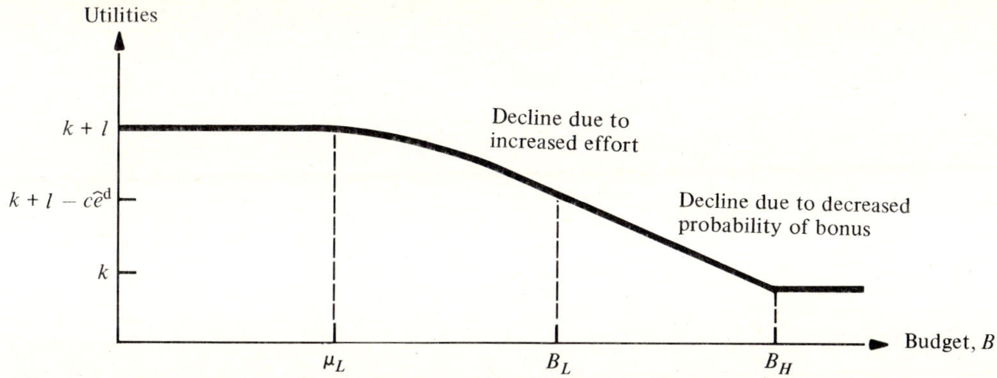

Figure 12.11 Expected utility of manager.

by the manager, resulting in lower effort. A manager-specified budget (i.e., *bottom-up* budget) is not likely to result in a maximum amount of effort, either. How are we to weigh information provided by a manager whose performance evaluation depends upon that information? If we make an across-the-board cut to eliminate padding, a manager who provided unpadded estimates will be inordinately penalized. This problem is not limited to budget-based incentive plans, but occurs whenever there is an information differential between the central management and the manager.

12.6 CONTROL OF THE PARTICIPATION PROCESS

There are a few ways in which central management might try to deal with the budget participation problem. The first two methods involve the production of information by central management, but only *sometimes*. The next three methods deal with the participation problem by incorporating incentives for the manager to report honestly. While we will discuss these techniques in the context of a budgeting problem, they may be applied in other differential information situations, as well.

12.6.1 Random Verification of Forecasts

While it may be too expensive for central management to duplicate the decentralized manager's information system, it may be possible to close the information gap on a random or spot-check basis. For instance, central management may ask to see the data and analysis that led to a pessimistic forecast. This may be done informally at a budget meeting, or it may involve the internal audit staff. The effectiveness of this approach will depend on the costs that the manager bears if he or she is found to be padding the budget. The manager will then have to choose between (i) setting a realistic budget and expending effort to achieve it, or (ii) setting a padded budget that is more easily achieved, but with a probability that the padding will be discovered and result in loss of bonus, promotion opportunities, etc. If the probability of discovery and/or the potential costs are high enough, the manager will refrain from very much budget padding. On the other hand, it may often be difficult (expensive) to verify a manager's forecasts, and it may be more efficient to utilize one of the other participation controls.

12.6.2 Conditional Variance Investigations

There is some evidence that a step-function (budget) bonus system is not the most effective form of managerial incentive. In essence, it tells the manager, "If costs exceed budget, that's bad, whatever the reason. If costs are below budget, that's good, whatever the reason." Such an attitude can have dysfunctional results, as we've outlined above, such as manipulation of discretionary expenditures and discouraging innovation. If there are factors that are beyond the manager's control (e.g., economic conditions, cost allocations from the other departments), then this usage of budgets will be a source of frustration, perhaps causing the manager to look for other employment.

Given the shortcomings of top-down budgeting (and accounting data), it is more appropriate to interpret an unfavorable variance as a signal that something *may* be wrong. Therefore, an alternative approach to the budgeting problem would be to set the budget at central headquarters, and then to investigate unfavorable variances to determine whether the manager could have controlled the problem. If $\hat{e}$ is the agreed-upon level of effort (or some other decision), then the incentive function might take the following form.

$$I(\pi, B) = \begin{cases} k + l, & \text{if } \pi \geq B \\ k + l, & \text{if } \pi < B \text{ and investigation reveals } e \geq \hat{e} \\ k, & \text{if } \pi < B \text{ and investigation reveals } e < \hat{e} \end{cases} \tag{12.5}$$

The advantage of this approach to using budgets and variances is that the manager is still under pressure to exert effort toward the organization's goals, but he or she will not lose a bonus due to factors beyond his or her control. Or, if the manager is trying out some new production techniques that increase costs now, but will reduce costs in the future, such innovation will not cause a loss of bonus. Of course, these *conditional investigation* incentives place a greater burden on central management, since an unfavorable variance results in a costly investigation. These costs should not be too great for a central management that keeps in close contact with the decentralized division, since it ought to be reasonably easy to determine whether the manager's decisions were appropriate ones. However, there are cases where an investigation would be quite costly, and where the decentralized manager has considerable latitude to affect the timing of costs and revenues. In such cases, a budget-based incentive system is not likely to be as efficient as one which slopes upward over a range of performance.

12.6.3 A Budget/Bonus Menu

The two participation controls discussed above are based on central management's acquisition of information, either about the manager's forecasts or about the manager's decisions. This possibility provides a check on the manager who might want to pad the budget. In this section and in the two that follow, the central management's participation control is based on rewarding a manager who accepts a more difficult target.

One approach to the participation problem is to let the manager choose his or her own budget, but to increase the bonus with the budget. In the budget setting model above, the central management set a single budget B with bonus l. An alternative would be to give the manager a choice of one of three bonus/budget pairs—(B_1, l_1), (B_2, l_2), (B_3, l_3)—where $B_1 < B_2 < B_3$ and $l_1 < l_2 < l_3$. If these bonuses and budgets are carefully set, the manager will choose (B_1, l_1) under unfavorable conditions, (B_2, l_2) under neutral conditions, and (B_3, l_3) under favorable conditions. Generally, the difficulty is not in having the manager choose overly ambitious targets [e.g., (B_2, l_2) under unfavorable conditions], but in setting l_2 and l_3 high enough to encourage honest reporting under neutral and favorable conditions.

For instance, consider the case where the manager knows that there will be neutral conditions. The maximum effort level is $\hat{e}$, which depends on l_2 as follows.

$$\hat{e} = \left[\frac{ab}{cd}\,\frac{l_2}{(1/3)(\mu_H - \mu_L)}\right]^{1/(d-b)} \tag{12.6}$$

The total effort curve is depicted in Figure 12.12. We will assume that B_2 is set at $a\hat{e}^b + \mu_L + (\mu_H - \mu_L)/3$, so that under neutral conditions the manager can guarantee a bonus l_2 by exerting effort $\hat{e}$. On the other hand, the manager can guarantee a bonus l_1 by exerting a lesser amount of effort $\hat{\hat{e}}$ to achieve bonus B_1. In order for the *menu* of bonuses to reveal the manager's knowledge, we must have the following condition. Given neutral conditions, the manager's expected utility is greater with (B_2, l_2) than it is with (B_1, l_1), or

$$k + l_2 - c\hat{e}^d > k + l_1 - c\hat{\hat{e}}^d \tag{12.7}$$
$$\text{or } l_2 > l_1 + c(\hat{e}^d - \hat{\hat{e}}^d)$$

In other words, l_2 must be set high enough over l_1 to compensate the manager for the increased effort. Similar conditions would have to be found for l_3.

In a sense, this menu approach to budget setting has some aspects of a profit-sharing scheme: higher performance is rewarded by higher bonus. One aspect that should be pointed out is that this menu of budgets may not be seen as being equitable by all managers. A manager who happens to have favorable conditions will get a larger bonus than a manager with unfavorable conditions. Central management may try to alleviate that problem by setting up different menus for different managers. If it is still viewed as a serious problem, one of the controls described in the two previous sections may be more attractive.

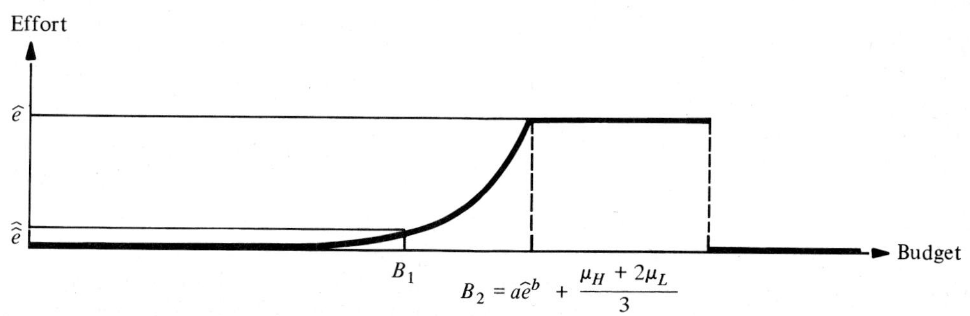

Figure 12.12

12.6.4 The New Soviet Incentive Scheme

The problems faced by central management in setting performance targets for managers have a lot in common with those faced by any centralized decision making group. In a planned economy, it is important for the central planning agency to have estimates of output from "firms," and to provide incentives for increasing that output. Having experienced padded budgets and lower output in the past, the Soviet Union instituted a new incentive plan in the 1970s.

After an initial budget is set by the central planning office, a manager is allowed to modify his or her budget, but the higher the budgeted output $\overline{O}$, the higher the budgeted bonus (see Figure 12.13a). Once the budgeted output is set, there is a penalty for not attaining it, and, in a sense, even for exceeding it. If we combine the profit-sharing function and the forecasting loss function in Figure 12-13b, we get a bonus function of the form in Figure 12.14.

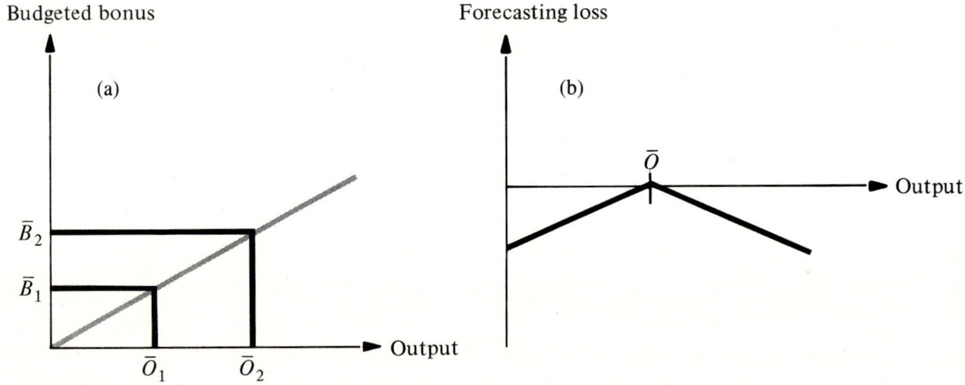

Figure 12.13

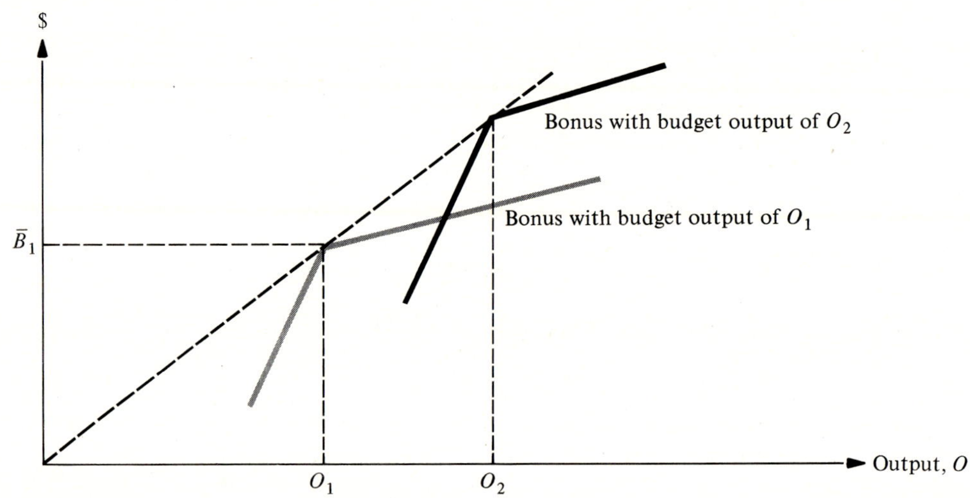

Figure 12.14

If the manager has forecasted output to be O_1, and if actual output equals this, the budgeted bonus B_1 is received. However, if the manager has found opportunities to increase output beyond O_1, he or she has incentive to do so. If output increases to O_2, compensation increases, but it is not as high as it would have been for a forecasted output of O_2. At the same time, there is a significant loss if output falls below O_1, so the manager has an incentive to achieve the output he or she has budgeted. However, you should give some thought as to when this system will be effective as a participation control. Some problems still remain, particularly if the manager can influence timing of costs and revenues.

Finally, we should recognize that the Soviet incentive plan is not limited to centralized, planned economies. A 1978 article in the *Harvard Business Review*[3] describes essentially the same approach to establishing salesmen's bonuses and indicates that such a plan is being used in a Latin American subsidiary of a large U.S. computer manufacturer. The problem of participation control occurs in all decentralized organizations, and the alternatives outlined above can provide a basis for such control.

12.6.5 Internal Competition

In some situations, central management must set performance targets for several managers who are performing similar functions in similar environments. In such cases, it may be beneficial to set *relative* performance targets rather than absolute performance targets, as we explored in the appendix to Chapter 11. For instance, central management may award a bonus to managers in the top quartile, or award a different size bonus according to the manager's ranking. If the decentralized managers know that they face similar environments, then there is no need for the central management to try to overcome the information differential. The managers will know that they must exert a significant level of effort in order to hope to obtain a bonus. The exact formulation should depend on the degree of similarity in the managers' environments. If they are all identical (an unlikely situation), then ranking by outcomes also ranks by effort. As the situations managers face become more diverse, we might expect the number of managers who receive bonuses to increase, and the differential bonuses between managers to decrease.

As in all comparative performance evaluation systems, one must be aware of the possibility of collusion among managers. That is, the managers may decide among themselves to restrict effort and to take turns obtaining the bonus. The more managers that participate in the plan and the fewer the number that receive bonuses, the less likely it is that such collusion would persist.

12.7 SUMMARY

The design of a performance evaluation system requires both the choice of the measures of performance and the choice of an incentive function which translates the measures into some type of evaluation or payoff (bonus, likelihood of promotion, etc.). In many cases, the incentive function is *budget-based* and reduces the amount of risk borne by the decentralized manager. In most cases, we can think of the budget as a threshold

[3]Gonik (1978).

between rewardable performance and unrewardable performance. As such, the budget can play a large role in determining the equity and efficiency of the performance evaluation system. If one sales territory is more favorable than another, then giving an average sales quota to each of the sales representatives will not be seen as equitable, nor will it induce much motivation. The same is true whenever managers' performance is heavily influenced by uncontrollable factors which continue over many performance periods.

While the goal setting process is a very important factor in the success of a performance evaluation system, there are a number of potential difficulties which are not easily overcome. First, it will frequently be the case that the decentralized manager knows more about the local environment than the central management knows. This situation makes the setting of budgets both important and difficult, as we saw in the chapter. There are a variety of ways in which central management may try to deal with this problem (developing better information, rewarding more ambitious budgets, conducting variance investigations, etc.).

Yet another difficulty may occur if the decentralized manager has control over the timing of revenues and/or expenses. In such cases, a *step* incentive may cause the manager to smooth income (or costs) and to inhibit innovation and reduce efforts to increase profits beyond the budget. An *optionlike* incentive may cause the manager to accentuate variations in income and to take on projects whose risk-return characteristics are not desirable for the organization. If these problems become too severe, then we would expect the organization to not use a budget-based performance evaluation system, but to find some other solution.[4]

In this chapter and the preceding one, we have examined performance evaluation issues at a rather general level. The next two chapters deal with accounting issues in the context of performance evaluation. In Chapter 13 we examine the accounting allocations across activities that are necessary for responsibility accounting, while in Chapter 14 we consider the effect of the recognition of revenues and costs on management's incentives for investment.

PROBLEMS

12.1. "The competition in this industry is really getting fierce," said Mary Jo Crihfield, "and if we don't change our ways, we'll be joining the growing list of companies that have succumbed to complacency. I'm particularly concerned with the manufacturing part of the business. We need to expend every possible effort looking for ways to become more efficient, and if we do that, we should be able to reduce our manufacturing costs by 15%. But the only way to shake up those people in the plant is to hit them in the bonus! If they continue on a 'business as usual' basis, I project that the yearly manufacturing costs will be about $4,000,000. That's just an estimate, so let's say that the expected value of the costs is $4,000,000 with a standard deviation of $200,000, *if* they continue as they have been. If they go all out to achieve efficiency, then the costs should be reduced by, say, 15%.

"I want to give them a real message in the budget and bonus. If they continue on as they have there should be almost no chance of their making the bonus. But if they achieve a significant improvement in cost efficiency, they should have a good chance of making a bonus."

[4] In some cases, a change in organization design may be necessary to achieve effective control.

Required

A. Where would you recommend that the cost budget be set?

B. What are the potential dangers in setting a target such as that in part A? What other information would you like to have before setting the target?

12.2. The User-Friendly Software Corporation has two sales representatives responsible for the Gotham City area. Rather than dividing the sales territory geographically, it was decided that each sales representative would concentrate on a defined set of potential customers. The two representatives, Bill North and George West, were believed to be equally competent, and their assignments within Gotham City were determined more by chance than by seniority or differential abilities.

The Regional Sales Director must set sales targets for each sales representative, and she wants to set these targets so as to encourage extra effort by the sales personnel. A major problem is caused by the fact that the company is pretty confident about its sales forecasts for the group of potential customers that are Bill North's responsibility, but it has much less experience with the customer group that George West will call on. The Regional Sales Director wants to set up equitable targets for the two men, using the following information. More specifically, the Regional Sales Director believes that a representative will choose the extra effort action only if it increases his expected bonus by at least $4,000.

	North's customers	West's customers
Normal effort:		
Expected sales	$200,000	$200,000
Standard deviation	10,000	20,000
Extra effort:		
Expected sales	$220,000	$220,000
Standard deviation	10,000	20,000

Required

A. If the budget is set equal to $210,000 for Bill North, how high does the bonus have to be to encourage him to choose to expend extra effort? What is the expected bonus payment for North if he chooses the extra effort action?

B. Suppose the bonus you found in part A was used for George West. Which action would he take? What would be his expected bonus payment? Is this equitable?

C. Try to find a budget/bonus combination for George West that will encourage him to expend extra effort *and* gives him the same expected bonus payment as Bill North got in part A.

12.3. It is often the case that the benchmark or budget that is used to evaluate performance is the last year's costs or profits. Suppose that a manager has purchased a machine with an acquisition cost of $18,000 and a two-year life. The exact benefits in each year are uncertain. (See the table below.) The manager receives a bonus if the profits (benefits less depreciation) meet or exceed the budget. The budget for the first year is $6,000 for this machine, and the second year's budget will be set at the first year's profit.

Yearly benefits (income before depreciation)	Probability
$12,000	0.3
$15,000	0.4
$18,000	0.3

Required

A. What is the probability of achieving a bonus in year 1? In year 2?
  1. under straight-line depreciation?
  2. under sum-of-years-digits depreciation?

B. What other accounting allocations could produce the steady growth that will increase the likelihood of receiving future bonuses?

12.4. Suppose that the manager of a responsibility center is scheduled to receive a bonus of \$15,000 if the level of profits reported for his center exceeds \$400,000. With nine months to go, the manager estimates that profits will have an expected value of \$425,000 and a standard deviation of \$25,000. (Assume a normal distribution.) The production department has proposed a change in the manufacturing procedures that should reduce costs over the long run, but there is considerable uncertainty as to whether these benefits will have begun to materialize by the end of the current year. As a result, the manager estimates that accepting the project would increase expected profits to \$430,000 but it would also increase the standard deviation of profits to \$50,000.

Required

A. What effect does the project have on the manager's expected bonus? Do you think the manager will accept the project?

B. Suppose that the budget were set at \$450,000 instead of \$400,000. How would your answer to part A change?

C. Suppose the manager received 2% of the center's income in excess of \$425,000. Would the proposed project increase the size of his expected bonus?

12.5. In a *Harvard Business Review* article,[5] an author addressed the problem of motivating employees to be good forecasters when the forecasts are used in their performance evaluation. In the system he proposed, the salesman would forecast sales F, and the bonus would depend on the forecast and the actual sales A, in something like the way depicted below.

In this system, the author concluded, the salesman would always have incentive to increase sales, regardless of the forecast. At the same time, a salesman could maximize compensation by being an accurate forecaster (i.e., if he knows sales will be F', he does better by forecasting F'.)

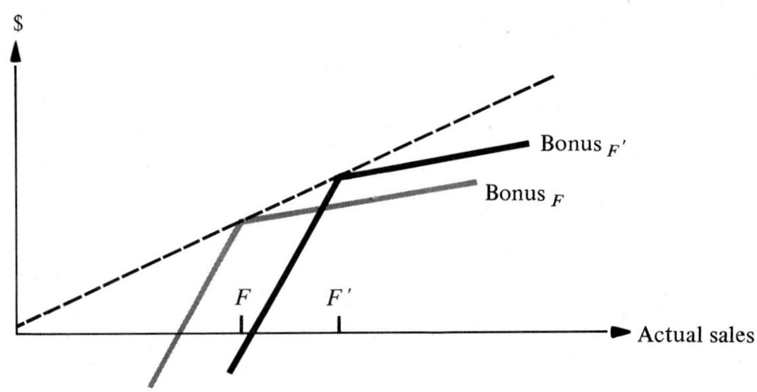

[5]Gonik (1978).

Required

A. The system described is for salesmen. Develop an equivalent system for a manager in charge of a cost center.

B. Suppose that this system were used for the monthly bonuses of a cost center manager. Is the system as beneficial as its author purports, or can you find some dysfunctional behavior that might result?

C. This system is, in essence, a *participation control* system. What other controls are possible, and what factors will influence their desirability?

12.6. As a part of the annual budget process, Paul Robertson is reviewing the last twelve quarters' sales for the company's four regions. Each region is assigned to a regional sales director (RSD), who is in charge of a sales staff, makes promotional decisions, etc. Although prices are set at central headquarters, each RSD provides input to those decisions. There are a number of factors that affect a region's sales besides the RSD's decisions, such as local economic conditions. The company is well established, so a base level of orders would come in (at least in the short run) even if the RSD was not doing an effective job. Robertson's assessment is that the RSD's decisions can have about a ±5–7% influence on a quarter's sales, and short-term economic conditions can have a slightly larger effect.

		Sales region			
Year	Quarter	Northeast	Midwest	South	West
19X1	1	$ 955,870	$512,855	$582,930	$ 825,767
	2	978,330	514,020	517,436	719,384
	3	887,230	802,290	479,267	678,266
	4	886,430	452,490	607,695	851,361
19X2	1	974,060	550,000	632,850	897,667
	2	860,980	561,504	497,664	699,777
	3	876,040	781,088	559,461	777,564
	4	1,025,730	500,505	687,922	954,892
19X3	1	1,127,390	545,085	613,839	866,878
	2	1,179,250	581,754	662,688	928,441
	3	1,034,530	702,968	716,892	1,007,600
	4	1,020,150	520,268	716,134	1,017,740

Required

A. Suppose that Robertson must set budgets for each of the regions for each of the next two quarters. The budgets will be used in a step bonus of $7,500 per quarter. That is, a bonus of $7,500 is paid to an RSD if his quarterly sales exceed the budget. Based on the information you have, where would you set the budgets?

B. Suppose that instead of using a step bonus, as in A, the company uses a conditional investigation system. If sales do not meet the budget, an investigation is conducted into the cause of the shortfall. Depending on the results of the investigation, the RSD may receive no bonus or a partial bonus, or, in exceptional cases, a full bonus. Based on the information you have, where would you set the budgets for this system?

C. What are some of the shortcomings of using past performance to establish budgets? In a situation such as that described above, what alternative approaches would you explore?

12.7. "Up until a year ago, we had no formal cost control evaluation for the production managers. At that time, we instituted a budgetary control system where each production manager had a specific cost budget for each month. When the manager makes the budget (and fulfills the output quota), he or she receives a set number of performance points which play a large part in determining the bonus at the end of the year. It's hard to put an exact value on a favorable variance, but it's worth roughly $3,000 to make the budget in a month.

"There's no question that the change has had an effect on operations, but I'm not sure that all the effects are beneficial. The production managers cannot control the timing of expenses for labor, direct materials, or utilities, but they can affect purchasing policy for supplies, repair and maintenance schedules, and some other types of costs. I'm afraid that they're using this discretion to affect their budget performance, without really improving their cost control performance.

"Below are the costs for one of our production units for the last year before the budgetary system and the first year under the system. The budget for this operation was $500,000 per month, and you can see that this target was met more often after the system was instituted. I have made a rough split between those costs whose timing cannot be influenced by the manager and those whose timing can be influenced (i.e., speeded-up a month, or delayed a month)."

Costs (in $1,000s)

	Year 19X6 (before system)			Year 19X7 (after system)		
Month	Nondiscretionary	Discretionary	Total	Nondiscretionary	Discretionary	Total
January	400	106	506	382	110	492
February	404	99	503	409	91	500
March	399	95	494	393	98	491
April	403	106	509	411	93	504
May	402	100	502	388	101	489
June	392	94	486	399	101	500
July	399	94	493	391	99	490
August	397	95	492	407	95	502
September	411	97	508	408	90	498
October	403	100	503	414	93	507
November	396	102	498	400	98	498
December	403	104	507	393	101	494

Required

A. Analyze the information above to see whether it appears that the production manager is using the discretionary expenses to influence budget performance.

B. Budget behavior like that described in the problem is not unusual. When is such behavior detrimental to the organization? What controls could be instituted to reduce this behavior?

12.8. (This problem is a modifiction of problem 11.6). You have been asked to set up a bonus function for a sales representative. The sales representative will decide on one of two possible actions—to "work hard" or to "not work hard." This decision will impact on the probability distribution for the contribution margin earned by the firm. However, the impact of the representative's effort is not certain. If the conditions are favorable, then higher effort means a higher probability of more favorable contribution margins. However, there is also a chance that the environmental conditions are unfavorable, in which case the representative's efforts have no effect on the contribution margin probabilities. The sales representative knows the conditions under which he will be operating, but you do not. However, you have developed the following information about the effects of effort on contribution margins.

	Contribution margin probabilities	
	C.M. = $40,000	C.M. = $60,000
Favorable conditions:		
Sales representative ''works hard''	1/3	2/3
Sales representative ''doesn't work hard''	2/3	1/3
Unfavorable conditions:		
Sales representative ''works hard''	2/3	1/3
Sales representative ''doesn't work hard''	2/3	1/3

You may assume that the sales representative is risk-averse and that his utility for compensation is reflected by the square-root function. That is, compensation of $\$x$ produces a utility of $x^{1/2}$. The sales representative is also effort-averse, with the action ''work hard'' creating a disutility of 10 ''utils'' more than the action ''not work hard.'' Finally, the sales manager must be paid enough to keep him from moving to another job. Assume that he could earn a fixed salary of $16,900 by working hard in another job.

Required

A. Assuming favorable conditions, find a compensation function for the sales representative that will induce him to choose the action ''work hard'' and will keep him from moving to another job. (Use the INCNTV program at the end of the book, if it is available.)

B. Suppose that the sales representative knows that conditions will be unfavorable. What effort will the incentive function in A produce? What will be the best incentive function under unfavorable conditions? (Assuming that the sales representative *must* be employed, even under unfavorable conditions.)

C. Develop a menu of contracts such that the manager will choose one contract and ''work hard'' under favorable conditions, while under unfavorable conditions he will choose the other contract and the action ''not work hard.''

12.9. One difficult problem that is often faced in business (and personal) situations is the control of an agent who has better information about the situation than you do. For instance, when you take your car to the repair shop and it is inspected, the mechanic usually knows more about the car's condition and his or her ability to improve that condition than you do. It may be that the car is ''healthy,'' and the likelihood of breakdown is very low, regardless of any service provided by the mechanic. Or, if the car is ''hopeless,'' the likelihood of breakdown may be very high, regardless of any service provided by the mechanic. Finally, if the car is ''treatable,'' the mechanic can significantly decrease the likelihood of breakdown by servicing the car.

Unfortunately (for control purposes), the mechanic's training enables him or her to form a superior judgment about the car's condition, but as customers, we cannot observe that judgment. All we can observe is the amount of service provided (parts and labor) and whether the car breaks down in a period following inspection. For a concrete example, use the following numbers:

	Probability of breakdown	Probability of no breakdown
Situation 1: "Hopeless"		
Mechanic's action:		
Service	0.8	0.2
Don't Service	0.8	0.2
Situation 2: "Treatable"		
Mechanic's Action		
Service	0.2	0.8
Don't Service	0.8	0.2
Situation 3: "Healthy"		
Mechanic's Action		
Service	0.2	0.8
Don't Service	0.2	0.8

Required

A. Suppose that the mechanic would expect to receive compensation of \$100 for the length of time it would take to service your car. In addition there are no guarantees with his or her service if the car breaks down in the following period. What behavior would you expect if:
   1. The mechanic would receive \$150 to service your car?
   2. The mechanic would receive \$75 to service your car?

B. Ideally, we would like for the mechanic to service the car only when it is "treatable," and to leave it alone when it is either of the other two conditions. Can you find a set of compensation outcomes that will encourage the mechanic to behave this way? (If you need more information to solve this problem, make some reasonable assumptions.)

C. What role does the possibility of repeat business play? That is, would you expect this control situation to be less of a problem with your local, regular mechanic than with a mechanic at a garage when you're on vacation a thousand miles away from home? Why?

D. Does this same sort of problem occur with other "experts" who are trained to diagnose and treat problems? How are incentives handled for these people?

12.10. You have been given responsibility for establishing the budget and bonus for a manager who controls a profit center in your company. Your objective in setting these amounts is to encourage the manager to expend the level of effort that is most beneficial to the corporation, but which also takes into account her own preferences and characteristics.

The manager's performance is judged on the basis of the contribution margin earned by her responsibility center, and the probability distribution of the contribution margin depends on her actions in the following ways.

	Outcome probabilities		
Manager's decision	C.M. = \$50,000	C.M. = \$75,000	C.M. = \$100,000
Action 1: Don't work hard	0.50	0.30	0.20
Action 2: Work hard	0.25	0.50	0.25
Action 3: Work *very* hard	0.20	0.30	0.50

The manager is risk-averse, and her utility for money is reflected in the square-root function, that is, $U[\text{compensation}] = (\text{compensation})^{1/2}$. In addition, the manager is averse to effort, and the expected utility of compensation from working hard must exceed that from not working hard by 5 in order for the manager to believe that the extra effort is worthwhile. The manager will choose to work *very* hard only if the expected utility from compensation is 6 greater than that from working hard and 11 greater than from not working hard. Finally, the manager could earn $32,400 by working hard for another company where she would be paid a salary.

Required

A. Determine a budget and bonus that would encourage the manager to choose action 2 (work hard). Is there more than one such combination? If so, which seems most efficient for your company? (Since there are only three outcomes in this simple example, the budget partitions the outcomes, so that those below this amount receive one compensation and those above this amount receive a larger compensation, that is, an additional "bonus." For instance, a "low budget" would pay a salary if the contribution margin is $50,000 and a salary plus bonus if the contribution margin is $75,000 or more.)

B. Determine a budget and bonus that would encourage the manager to choose action 3 (work *very* hard). Is the expected net payoff to the company higher under part A?

12.11. You have been given responsibility for establishing the budget and bonus for a manager who controls a profit center in your company. Your objective in setting these amounts is to encourage the manager to expend the level of effort that is most beneficial to the corporation, but which also takes into account his own preferences and characteristics.

The manager's performance is judged on the basis of the contribution margin earned by his responsibility center, and the probability distribution of the contribution margin depends on his actions *and* on the conditions which he faces in the following ways. That is, the manager may face an unfavorable environment in which his efforts will produce an expected profit which is lower than that which his efforts would produce in a favorable environment. While the manager cannot control the environment which he faces, he does observe whether the conditions are favorable or not *before* he makes his choice of action.

The probabilities of various contribution margins with different conditions and courses of action are given below:

Manager's decision	C.M. = $50,000	C.M. = $75,000	C.M. = $100,000
Under unfavorable conditions:			
Action 1: Don't work hard	0.50	0.30	0.20
Action 2: Work hard	0.25	0.50	0.25
Under favorable conditions:			
Action 1: Don't work hard	0.25	0.50	0.25
Action 2: Work hard	0.20	0.30	0.50

Assume that the manager is risk-averse, and his utility for money is reflected in the natural logarithm function, that is, $U[\text{compensation}] = \ln(\text{compensation})$. In addition, the manager is averse to effort, and the expected utility of compensation from working hard must exceed that from not working hard by 0.10 in order for the manager to believe that the extra effort is worthwhile. In addition, the manager could earn $33,000 by working hard for another company where he would be paid a salary.

The favorable and unfavorable situations are regarded as equally likely. The *manager* will observe the favorability of the situation prior to choosing his course of action, but you will not.

Required

A. Try to design a budget/bonus combination that will cause the manager to choose the "work hard" option, regardless of the situation he faces. What is the expected payoff to the organization, net of the manager's compensation?

B. Suppose that after observing the contribution margin, you could conduct a conditional investigation to determine the course of action chosen by the manager. The investigation costs $1,000. How could you use this investigation possibility to improve the control over the manager's decisions?

C. Suppose that there is not one such manager, but many who will all face identical conditions. That is, you do not know whether they will all face favorable or unfavorable conditions, but you know that each will face the same as all the others. How would this influence the type of incentive arrangement you set up? How would the existence of many managers facing identical situations improve the expected payoff to the organization?

12.12. The Outland Steel Company is a large, integrated producer of a diverse line of steel and related products. Within the company's organization, there are approximately 65 operating cost centers, each headed by a manager who has been given responsibility for the costs he or she controls. These costs include labor costs, materials costs, and repairs and maintenance costs. (The cost center managers do not make major capital investment decisions, so depreciation is not considered to be within their control.) Production quotas are set by division management, and the cost center managers are expected to meet these quotas.

Since the cost center managers do not make production quantity decisions, their cost performance is judged relative to a flexible budget which increases as the level of production increases. This was true for repairs and maintenance as well as for direct labor and materials. Ideally, repairs and maintenance should take place when production was low, since this would minimize machine down-time.

As the manager of a cost center, Michael Harrison's performance is evaluated by his division manager based on the monthly cost variances. The division manager places a great emphasis on the ability to meet the budget on a continuing basis. In fact, he almost never gives a favorable performance evaluation when costs exceed budget, regardless of other considerations.

Required

A. In the above situation, how would you make repair and maintenance decisions, if you were Michael Harrison? How would these decisions be reflected in the cost data that would be reported?

B. How would you change the situation to improve the scheduling of repairs and maintenance?

12.13. (Based on a paper by W. Assmus). O.C.C.D. is a large transportation engineering consulting firm specializing in the planning and design of highway, railroad, and rail rapid-transit facilities. No tangible products are directly produced other than drawings, reports, and related documents. Most of the firm's clients are governmental agencies.

Management accounting is based on designating a *job number* for each assignment; direct costs are then recorded using a job order costing system. Reimbursement on most contracts is based on cost-plus-a-fixed-fee for profit, with total compensation not to exceed a fixed amount. Reimbursement for employee fringe benefits and all other overhead items is made by applying a predetermined multiplier factor to direct labor costs. This multiplier is generally fixed for the duration of the contract.

The 15 years between 1955 and 1970 were very good business years for most transportation engineering consulting firms. The Interstate Highway Program followed by increased focus on public transit planning resulted in generally profitable conditions for O.C.C.D. and no special emphasis was given to cost accounting and cost management. Since 1970, however, economic and general environmental factors have resulted in two major changes:

1. A decline in the work load with only limited reductions possible in fixed overhead and human resources.
2. An increase in uncertainty as to project duration and work scope because of new legislative and more complex governmental review procedures.

As a result of these changes, there was increased uncertainty about the amount and timing of cash inflows.

Cash Management Developments

In an effort to maximize profits under these dynamic influences, O.C.C.D. began to give more attention to formal management information systems and the elements of sound business administration. About two years ago, O.C.C.D. established the position of financial officer and filled the post by hiring an accountant from W.R.T., the parent company of O.C.C.D. One of the financial officer's first actions was to establish a cash management program, since in the recent past O.C.C.D. was frequently required to obtain relatively expensive, short-term loans to cover shortages created by erratic cash inflows.

The new financial officer's approach to cash management was based on shifting, where possible, the timing of cash outflows to better coincide with expected cash inflows. Cash inflow information on each project was to be obtained from estimates by the project manager of each assignment (see the table below). Midway in a quarter the project manager would be asked to predict billings for each of the three (or four[6]) four-week periods in the next quarter and then estimate billings by quarters thereafter for the balance of the calendar year. This was to be done by all project managers, in all 13 regional offices, regardless of the size (average billings) of an assignment.

In order to assure that the project managers gave some thought to the billing estimates, the financial officer convinced the president that the evaluation of a project manager's performance was, in part, to be based on how well his projected and actual billings coincided. Approximately a month after the close of the next quarter, the financial officer compared the actual billings for each period against the amounts predicted approximately 5½ months before. Whenever the period's actual billing was less than 90% of the subjective estimate, the project manager was required to submit a written explanation for the variance. The president received a copy of the written reply. Favorable variances (actual billings greater than estimated) were never questioned.

[6]For accounting purposes O.C.C.D. divides the year into 13 four-week periods; each quarter is three periods long, except the fourth quarter, which covers four periods.

Cash inflow forecasts

Office: Chicago	Officer in charge: Galloway
Job No.: 2600-01	Description: A.D.O.T. 95th St. Studies
Total fee: $470,000	Date: November 30, 19x6
Project manager: Spencer	

Total billing to date		$205,000
Projected billings:		
Next quarter: Quarter No. 1		
Period 1	$10,000	
Period 2	$18,000	
Period 3	$ 5,000	
Period ___	$	
	$33,000	
Following quarter: Quarter No. 2		$45,000
Remaining quarters in year No. 3		$20,000
No. 4		$30,000
No. ___		$
Estimated total billings to end of 19x7		$333,000
Remaining billing:		$137,000

Implementation Problems

When the forecasting system went into effect, no explanation was given to project managers (PMs) as to the need for the information. Each was given a brief memo asking that the attached form (shown above) be filled out and returned to the financial officer. About three months later, the same request was made for the head of each project to predict billings for the next three periods. Most PMs were surprised when they got a memo entitled "Request for Explanation of Cash Inflow Variances," with a copy of the response to be sent to the president. The memo showed their projected billings and actual billings for the past three periods, and noted where under-billings were more than ten percent.

The first problem for most project heads was to figure out what a cash inflow variance was and what constituted an unacceptable variance. The next issue was how their response should be structured and in what detail. Care was required since the president would review the responses. Some PMs wrote four- and five-page explanations; one senior PM responded simply, "I apologize for my lack of clairvoyance." The longer responses described lack of adequate staff, interdepartmental problems, etc.

Another shortcoming in the initial request for forecasts was inadequate definition of the information that was requested. For example, the PM considered his first period billing to be the *total* amount the client was billed for on the invoice that went out at the start of the second period for services in the previous period. PMs did not take into account retainages held by the client until project completion. The information the financial officer really wanted to know was "the size of the checks your client will send us in the next three periods," although the form used asked for "billings." Therefore, even if a PM had forecasted *billings* accurately, delays in payment or retainages could cause the unfavorable variances reported by the financial officer.

When this problem was discovered after the first variance analysis, the financial officer issued a brief memo explaining more precisely the information he was requesting. However, by this time the second set of projections from the PMs had already been submitted and analyzed, and a lot of time had been wasted by relatively high-priced personnel with little useful information resulting.

PM Performance Evaluation

The primary measure of a PM's performance on a job was the *comparative factor*. This figure was calculated for each period as well as for the job to date.

CF	comparative factor
G	gross billings to client (without reductions for retainage)
L	direct payroll costs
m	multiplier factor to cover overhead costs (factor fixed by contractural agreement)
P	profit allotment for completion of a specific work task
OC	other direct nonpayroll costs for which O.C.C.D. was reimbursed (printing, travel, etc.)

Then, generally

$$CF = \frac{G - OC}{L}$$

where $G = mL + OC + P$. Therefore

$$CF = \frac{mL + P}{L} = m + (P/L)$$

or, since m is generally constant for a particular assignment

$$CF = \text{function of } (P/L)$$

Thus the comparative factor indirectly measures how much profit was earned per dollar-of-labor expended.

As an example, assume that a 10% retainage contract was negotiated in 19x3, with a total budgeted cost to the client of the following

Direct payroll	\$10,000
Overhead, etc.	11,000
Nonpayroll costs	3,000
Profit allowance	4,000
TOTAL	\$28,000

The target CF is then 2.50 (\$28,000 less \$3,000, divided by \$10,000). Note that overhead is applied at 110% of payroll, indicating the contract multiplier m to be 2.1. Also, the \$4,000 profit allowance is for completing the task; it does not vary with amounts expended. Now, assuming that the actual nonpayroll costs turn out to be exactly \$3,000, what would be the effect if the work were done very efficiently and direct payroll costs turned out to be \$8,500, \$8,000, or \$7,500?

Budgeted expenditure	Estimate of cash inflow	Actual labor cost	Comparative factor	Actual cash inflow	Variance in cash flow estimate
$28,000	$25,200	$10,000	2.50	$25,200	
28,000	25,200	8,500	2.57	22,365	−11%
28,000	25,200	8,000	2.60	21,420	−15%
28,000	25,200	7,500	2.63	20,475	−19%

From the viewpoint of evaluating the PM's performance to generate profit by using labor, if only $7,500 were expended in payrolls, a comparative factor of 2.63 would indicate a very good return (53¢ on each dollar of labor invested). However, as an estimator of cash inflows, the PM would receive a very poor rating because he fell 19% short of his target. Thus, the total performance evaluation system shows a lack of *goal congruence*—that is, the prime objective of the PM conflicts with the cash-management objectives of the financial officer.

Additional Issues

Value of Explanatory Memos. Most PMs explained variances as being due either to inadequate staff on the project or to delays caused by a client falling behind on his commitments. Many times drawings or reports would be sent in for review and, although the mutually established study schedule allowed a certain time for the review process, the client would take much more time. Sometimes the client is not directly at fault since Federal law might require that documents be reviewed by other government agencies who in no way are committed to the study schedule.

Internally, the O.C.C.D. financial officer had no power to rectify staff inadequacies. Thus, although much effort and expense was invested in getting information on variances, this feedback had no control function. The president had too little time to read all the explanatory memos (about 100 memos coming two months after the close of each quarter) and the PM's believed that the financial officer neither understood their problems nor had the power to effect corrective action.

Quarter Versus Period Estimates. The PM's made projections by period for the next three (or four) periods. On some assignments a PM could accurately estimate his total cash inflows for a quarter, but not by period. For example:

	Cash inflows	
	Estimate	Actual
Period 1	$ 5,000	$ 2,000
Period 2	10,000	7,000
Period 3	5,000	11,000
1st Quarter	$20,000	$20,000

Although the PM had supplied a perfect forecast of the quarter total, in two out of three periods he was evaluated as having unsatisfactory variances. When this was pointed out to the financial officer, he explained that for his cash management purposes it was periodic estimates that counted not the quarterly total. The period fluctuations were exactly the information he needed to elicit from the PMs, not quarterly totals.

Cash Inflow Estimates and Manpower Needs. The financial officer observed that for the company as a whole the total actual cash inflows generally varied from 75 to 105% of the total projection for each period. After the cash flow estimation system had been in use for $1\frac{1}{2}$ years, an interesting fact came to light. In certain larger offices there are special department's whose services were required on different projects. For example, O.C.C.D.'s Chicago office has only six electrical engineers. However, by eliciting estimates of cash flow by project, it was possible for this to occur:

Job	Estimated work by Chicago electrical department in period 2 (man-month)
A	1
B	3
C	1
D	2
E	2
TOTAL	9

Thus, although the five individual PMs projected that about nine electrical engineers would be active on production in period 2, this was literally impossible, since only six engineers were available. Thus, without any hiring or advance coordination, the period 3 cash inflows would be based on 50% more electrical engineering than available. The same situation occurred with other smaller departments. Variances were unavoidable under these conditions.

This problem did not occur in the smaller O.C.C.D. offices, since these offices had no department structure. To prepare the subjective estimates of cash inflows, the PMs in the smaller offices would meet, establish who would be working on what project in which period, and then calculate their cash inflow projections by job. This approach eliminated the possibility of overcommitting the services of any one staff member.

Required You have been called in as a special consultant by the financial officer. Evaluate the current system and its likely impact on the PM's cash flow forecasts. What changes would you recommend in the cash budgeting procedures?

REFERENCES

Argyris, C. *The Impact of Budgets on People*. New York: The Controllers Foundation. 1952.

Baiman, S., and J. Demski. "Economically Optimal Performance Evaluation and Control Systems," *Journal of Accounting Research*. Supplement. 1980.

Barrett, M. E., and L. Fraser III. "Conflicting Roles in Budgeting for Operations," *Harvard Business Review*. July–August 1977.

Brownell, P. "Participation in the Budgeting Process—When It Works and When It Doesn't," *Journal of Accounting Literature*. Spring 1982.

Chow, C. "The Effects of Job Standard Tightness and Compensation Scheme on Performance: An Exploration of Linkages," *Accounting Review*. October 1983.

Demski, J., and G. Feltham. "Economic Incentives in Budgetary Control Systems," *Accounting Review*. April 1978.

Demski, J., J. Patell, and M. Wolfson, ''Decentralized Choice of Monitoring Systems,'' *Accounting Review*. January 1984.

Gonik, J. ''Tie Salesmen's Bonuses to Their Forecasts,'' *Harvard Business Review*. May–June 1978.

Healy, P. ''The Effect of Bonus Schemes on Accounting Decisions, *Journal of Accounting and Economics*. April 1985.

Hopwood, A. *Accounting and Human Behavior*. London: Haymarket. 1974.

Magee, R. ''Equilibria in Budget Participation,'' *Journal of Accounting Research*. Autumn 1980.

Ronen, J., and J. L. Livingstone. ''An Expectancy Theory Approach to the Motivational Impacts of Budgets,'' *Accounting Review*. October 1975.

Schiff, M., and A. Lewin. ''The Impact of People on Budgets,'' *Accounting Review*. April 1970.

Swieringa, R., and R. Moncur. *Some Effects of Participative Budgeting on Managerial Behavior*. New York: NAA. 1975.

Weitzman, M. ''The New Soviet Incentive Scheme,'' *Bell Journal of Economics*. Spring 1976.

Zimmerman, J. ''Budget Uncertainty and the Allocation Decision in a Nonprofit Organization,'' *Journal of Accounting Research*. Autumn 1976.

Chapter 13

Responsibility Accounting

Allocations Among Activities

In the previous two chapters, we examined some of the general issues in evaluating performance measurement systems. As in previous chapters, the decision maker's behavior plays an important part in the analysis. When comparing performance measures, we must be able to evaluate their effects on the manager's decisions. We have examined some general issues (controllability, budgets, participation), but in this chapter and in the next we direct our attention toward more specific accounting issues. In this chapter, we focus on accounting allocations to responsibility units within an organization. For instance, what happens if central administration costs are allocated to the decentralized units? What happens if responsibility and authority don't match? How do various transfer pricing systems allocate profits to divisions? We examine the effects of different allocations on the incentives of decentralized managers. In Chapter 14, we look at another set of accounting issues that are just as important: the allocation of costs and benefits over time (e.g., asset and liability recognition).

13.1 RESPONSIBILITY ACCOUNTING AND ORGANIZATION DESIGN

As a simple example, suppose we have a business that has three products and three functional areas—material acquisition, production, and selling. If we also employ three managers, how do we divide their responsibilities? We could give each manager responsibility for a product line from start to finish, or we could divide responsibilities along functional lines with one manager in charge of materials acquisition for all three products, one in charge of production, and the last in charge of selling. In part, the answer depends on the *economies of effort* in the functional areas. In other words, if three managers are trying to ensure efficient production of their individual products, would their collective effort and the return to that effort be greater than if one person were to ensure efficient production of all three products?

These issues of task allocation are important ones for organizational design, but there are also some important performance measurement/responsibility accounting issues that influence the success of an organizational design. If the managers' respective influences on profits (or organizational performance) are independent of one another, then central management may deal with each independently. However, when the decision makers jointly affect the payoffs to the organization, then we may encounter some difficulty in providing incentives for each while at the same time maintaining a reasonable level of controllability. For example, the additional costs of processing rush orders is affected by the inventory decisions of the production manager and by the actions of the sales manager in accepting (encouraging) such rush orders. If we attribute these additional costs to one of these decision makers, he or she will be evaluated, in part, on performance that he or she cannot control. Further, we have placed the other manager in an incentiveless position, thereby biasing the decisions he or she might make.

13.2 INTERDEPENDENT RESPONSIBILITY CENTERS

When decisions made in one responsibility center affect the results of other responsibility centers, a number of questions arise. First, there are organizational issues. Should interdependent units be consolidated into a single responsibility center? Should central administration adopt a *laissez-faire* approach, or should some decisions not be delegated to the responsibility centers? In addition to these organizational issues, some informational questions arise. Since it is not always desirable to organize a firm into totally independent units, can we develop a set of performance measures that provide the information necessary to motivate the decentralized managers?

Let's suppose that the payoff to the firm depends on the payoffs (or results) for two responsibility centers, called RC1 and RC2. If $x(\cdot)$ is the total firm payoff, then

$$x(a_1, a_2, \varepsilon_1, \varepsilon_2) = x_1(a_1, a_2, \varepsilon_1) + x_2(a_1, a_2, \varepsilon_2) \qquad (13.1)$$

where x_i is the payoff for RCi; a_i is the decision made in RCi; and ε_i reflects random, uncontrollable events in RCi.

For instance, $x_1(\cdot)$ may represent sales revenue, and $x_2(\cdot)$ may represent (minus) production costs—both dependent on actions chosen by the sales manager and the production manager. What happens if we use $x_1(\cdot)$ to evaluate the manager of RC1 and $x_2(\cdot)$ to evaluate the manager of RC2? From an informational point of view, this is inefficient because the outcome of $x_2(\cdot)$ has some information about RC1's action a_1 and $x_1(\cdot)$ conveys information about a_2. For instance, high sales volume conveys positive information about the production manager's efforts, if we can't sell what we haven't produced. Therefore, the performance evaluation of RC1 should depend on $x_1(\cdot)$ and $x_2(\cdot)$, and RC2's evaluation should depend on $x_2(\cdot)$ and $x_1(\cdot)$.[1] However, both measures of performance are dependent on factors that are outside the manager's control. The only way

[1]The arguments here are similar to those reviewed in Appendix 11.2.

to change this situation is to alter the measurement system which has produced $x_1(\cdot)$ and $x_2(\cdot)$. For instance, we might try to separate x into the following measures.

$$x(a_1, a_2, \varepsilon_1, \varepsilon_2) = \hat{x}_1(a_1, \varepsilon_1) + \hat{x}_2(a_2, \varepsilon_2) \tag{13.2}$$

If this separation can be achieved, then we can use $\hat{x}_i$ alone to evaluate RCi.[2]

Evaluating RC1 on the basis of $x_1(a_1, a_2, \varepsilon_1)$ alone is not only inefficient in its use of information, but it can also lead to some incentive problems since RC1 is not bearing the full consequences of its action a_1. For instance, if we make the assumption that the manager of RC1 will choose a_1 so as to maximize the expected value of $x_1(\cdot)$, this decision will not coincide with that which maximizes the total expected firm payoff. For instance, if $x_1(\cdot)$ is sales revenue, $x_2(\cdot)$ is (minus) production costs, and a_1 is the number of rush orders, the sales manager (RC1) may choose to maximize expected sales revenue without regard to the effect on production costs.

Situations in which such interdependencies occur are usually those in which services or products are transferred between responsibility centers. Methods of allocating service department costs and transfer pricing are designed to move toward responsibility accounting measures which achieve the separation of $\hat{x}_1$ and $\hat{x}_2$ above. When the *division of responsibility* and *division of controllability* don't quite mesh in an organization, there is the possibility that one manager's decisions affect another manager's performance. When these effects are substantial, then a revision in the performance measurement system can avoid dysfunctional decision making (and frustration on the part of the manager whose performance is affected by others). In the sections that follow, we apply these responsibility accounting concepts to the problems of cost allocation and transfer pricing.

13.3 CENTRAL COST ALLOCATIONS

The question of whether services should be acquired by individual responsibility centers or provided centrally depends on two factors: the degree of control that central management wishes to exert over the function and the costs of providing the service. For instance, central management may wish to ensure that the performance measurement system is consistently applied across units, so this function is centralized to facilitate independence. Or, central management may wish to ensure that advertising plans are fully coordinated, rather than having each unit run its own campaigns.

A more frequent reason for centralizing certain functions is their cost structure. If a function's cost is influenced by *economies of scale*, then a central department can serve the needs of the decentralized units more efficiently. In Figure 13.1, the economies of scale mean that if two decentralized units, each needing X units of service, produced this service individually, their costs would be $2C(X)$. If the service for both were produced centrally, the cost would only be $C(2X)$. For these reasons, functions such as data

[2]If a partial separation can be achieved, such as the following, $x(a_1, a_2, \varepsilon_1, \varepsilon_2) = \hat{x}_1(a_1, \varepsilon_1) + \hat{x}_2(a_1, a_2, \varepsilon_2)$, then it would still be beneficial to use both $\hat{x}_1(\cdot)$ and $\hat{x}_2(\cdot)$ to evaluate RC1 and RC2.

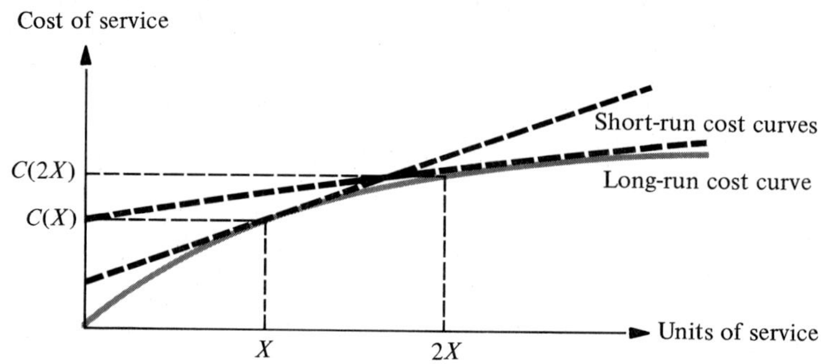

Figure 13.1

processing, engineering consulting, legal services, and so on, are often provided by central service departments.

Of course, this organizational arrangement produces an accounting/motivation problem: how should the costs of these services be allocated to the decentralized units? Should they be allocated at all? As we know from the previous two chapters, we cannot answer these questions without being more specific about the decisions that have been delegated to the decentralized manager, his goals and preferences, and so on.

In the context of responsibility accounting discussed in the previous section, suppose that the quantity of service used a_1, is determined by the decentralized manager in charge of RC1, and $x_1(\cdot)$ is the operating profit earned in RC1. The term $x_2(\cdot)$ represents (minus) costs incurred in RC2, the service department. These costs are affected by a_1 and the service department's cost control decision a_2.

$$x(a_1, a_2, \varepsilon_1, \varepsilon_2) = x_1(a_1, \varepsilon_1) + x_2(a_1, a_2, \varepsilon_2) \tag{13.3}$$

It's clear that both $x_1(\cdot)$ and $x_2(\cdot)$ should be taken into account in evaluating RC1. In fact, we might develop a cost allocation of $\bar{x}_2(a_1, a_2^*)$, where a_2^* is a standard action for RC2. Then we would have a system that is closer to responsibility accounting with two measures which separate profit into a factor that depends on a_1 (and ε_1) and one that depends on a_2 (and ε_2) as in equation (13.4).[3] Of course, as the number of operating departments increases, the choice of a cost allocation becomes more difficult.

$$x(\cdot) = [x_1(a_1, \varepsilon_1) + \bar{x}_2(a_1, a_2^*)] + [x_2(a_1, a_2, \varepsilon_2) - \bar{x}_2(a_1, a_2^*)] \tag{13.4}$$

As a simple illustration, suppose that there is one central department which provides service to ten identical operating departments (see Figure 13.2). The central department has fixed costs of $30,000 per month plus variable costs of $1,000 per unit of service provided. The operating departments must decide how much service to use, and each faces the schedule in Table 13.1. For the moment, we'll ignore the additional problems posed by risk aversion or the effort needed for (or reduced by) utilization of the service. These issues will be discussed below.

[3]If there were multiple service departments and reciprocal service usages, an approach like that in Section 5.2 of Chapter 5 might be used.

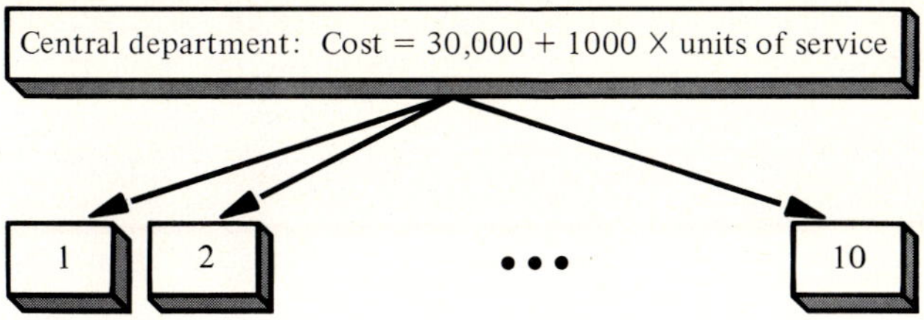

Figure 13.2

From the perspective of the overall organization, the optimal service usage would be where the expected operating department benefit less the variable service cost is maximized. In Table 13.1, this occurs at 4 units of service per month per operating department, creating $7,800 in operating department benefits and $4,000 in variable service costs. The $3,800 net benefit, multiplied by 10 departments, more than covers the fixed service department costs of $30,000.

But will the operating managers choose to use 4 units apiece? The answer depends on the cost allocation system. Suppose no service department costs are allocated to the operating department and the operating managers maximize the expected department payoff. Then the service becomes a *free good,* and the operating department managers will demand as much service as they can, as long as the incremental operating department benefit is positive. In Table 13.1, the manager would demand 6 units, more than the optimum from the organization's point of view. This result is obvious, you might think, since not allocating costs would always lead to overusage (and unwarranted growth in service department costs). But the same phenomenon can occur even if *all* service department costs are allocated to the operating departments. Suppose that, since the operating departments are all identical, the total service cost is split ten ways, each receiving one-tenth of the cost. If this is the case, what is the incremental service cost allocated to operating department 1 when its manager increases service usage by 1? The answer is one-tenth of $1,000 or $100, and this would also lead to the choice of 6 units of service and overusage.

If no allocation leads to overutilization, what happens if a *full-cost* measure is used to allocate costs? At the organizational optimum, 40 units of service would be used and their full cost would be $1,000 + $30,000/40 = $1,750 per unit of service. But if the

TABLE 13.1

Units of service	Operating department expected benefit: Total	Operating department expected benefit: Incremental	Variable service cost	Organizational net benefit
1	$3,000	$3,000	$1,000	$2,000
2	5,200	2,200	2,000	3,200
3	6,700	1,500	3,000	3,700
4	7,800	1,100	4,000	3,800
5	8,600	800	5,000	3,600
6	9,100	500	6,000	3,100

operating manager is charged \$1,750 per unit, the optimal usage is only 2 units, since the third has an incremental benefit of \$1,500 to the department. Therefore, the service department will be *underutilized,* and the total organizational benefit will be 10 × \$3,200 − \$30,000 = \$2,000. But the \$1,750 full cost was based on usage of 40, and only 20 units of usage have materialized. What happens if the full cost is adjusted to the new activity level? The new cost is \$1,000 + \$30,000/20 = \$2,500, and this would cause the operating departments to curtail their usage even further. More adjustments to full cost could eliminate service usage altogether, making it clear that while covering fixed service costs may be a worthwhile objective, using a full-cost approach may not be the way to accomplish it.

In this situation the way to ensure that the operating departments will use the appropriate amount of service is to charge the variable costs based on actual service used.[4] Then the operating department's benefits will be maximized at the same place as the organization's benefits (i.e., at four units). But we must keep in mind that this solution is unique to the setting we've assumed, and there are a number of reasons why *variable costing* of central services might not lead to optimal decisions by the operating department. We will discuss three possibilities, but others are possible.

First, the service department may have capacity constraints that preclude it from meeting all demands from operating departments. For instance, the service department might be able to produce only 30 units of service per month. If the operating departments are only charged \$1,000 per unit, then there will be 10 units of demand that cannot be satisfied. We could use a "first-come, first-served" procedure, but this form of rationing services will not work as well as raising the price so that each operating department will demand only 3 units. From Table 13.1, we can see that a service price greater than \$1,100 and less than \$1,500 would produce the desired reduction in demand. In effect, we have made a simple move from *cost allocation* to *transfer pricing,* by including an opportunity cost for the limited service capacity. This opportunity cost might be approximated by a full-cost allocation of fixed costs, but this would be a coincidence. We will return to fixed-cost allocations in a later section.

There may be other cases where one operating department's usage of the central service actually benefits another operating department. As an example, suppose the components division enlists the aid of a central engineering consulting group in designing and manufacturing an item that will then be transferred to the systems division. If a better part is produced more efficiently and with fewer delays, then *both* operating divisions can benefit from the component division's use of the central service. If this is the case, will the component division use enough service, from the organization's point of view? In our example of Table 13.1, suppose that each unit of service used *also* produces benefits of \$250 for the other divisions (see Table 13.2). The organization would prefer that 5 units of service be demanded, since organizational benefits are maximized at this level of service. But a variable-cost service allocation would cause the operating department manager to choose 4 units of service, because the external benefits to other departments are not reflected in his or her performance evaluation. If central management can estimate the benefits to other departments, then it could *subsidize* the service cost allocation by letting

[4]This doesn't mean that fixed costs should not be allocated, just that they shouldn't be allocated based on actual usage.

TABLE 13.2

Units of service	Operating department benefit		Benefit to other departments		Variable service cost	Organizational net benefit
	Total	Incremental	Total	Incremental		
1	$3,000	$3,000	$ 250	$250	$1,000	$2,250
2	5,200	2,200	500	250	2,000	3,700
3	6,700	1,500	750	250	3,000	4,450
4	7,800	1,100	1,000	250	4,000	4,800
5	8,600	800	1,250	250	5,000	4,850
6	9,100	500	1,500	250	6,000	4,600

$$\text{Cost allocated} = \text{variable cost} - \text{estimate of external benefits}$$

However, these estimates may be quite subjective, and if we allow the operating manager to participate in their estimation, he or she could try to influence (increase) the estimated external benefits.

Finally, there is also the possibility that the operating manager may hesitate to use central services because to do so will require some additional effort on his or her part or because the benefits of the service are uncertain. For instance, suppose a manager could use central computer services to facilitate planning and control. But to do so would require that he or she become more familiar with the computer and its capabilities and limitations, and this would require time and effort that might be used elsewhere. In addition, the amount of service needed and the ultimate benefits may be uncertain. In this case, a service charge of variable cost could again lead to underutilization that can only be overcome by a reduction in the allocated cost. For instance, central management may decide not to allocate the costs of a central legal department so as to encourage operating managers to use the legal services. This attitude could result if the service department costs were essentially fixed, or if operating managers need to be encouraged to expend the additional effort to utilize the central services.

There are other reasons why a departure from variable-cost allocations may make the organization better off, but we will not deal with any more at this time. At the very least, we have underscored the necessity of having a *model* of a manager's decision making and the impact that those decisions have on the organization and its payoffs as measured by the accounting system. Without these, there is no basis on which to evaluate different cost allocation procedures. Once we have such models, the analyses in Chapters 11 and 12 can help us determine the cost allocations that will achieve the goals of the overall organization. (A more complete model appears in Appendix 13.1.)

13.4 HOW MANY COST POOLS?

If there is a service department/cost center whose costs are allocated to production centers, it is sufficient to have just one cost pool (and one allocation base) per cost center? Or are there differing types of service that can be provided by one department that should each have their own cost pool and be allocated separately to the production centers? For instance, a central computer department provides various services—processing time, data storage, user services, and so on. Can all of these costs be thrown together and allocated simultaneously (e.g., on CPU time)? Or, should we keep track of the costs and the usages of the subservices individually, and then allocate them separately?

Basically, the answer to these questions depends on the ability of the operating/production managers to vary their usages of the individual subservices, and on the costs of doing the separate allocations. For the latter, the computation costs are probably not large, but the data entry costs could be significant, since actual usages must be recorded for each cost pool. Perhaps a more significant problem is the possibility that a single-cost pool allocation can cause a ''warping'' of the subservice usages. As an example, if a manager were only charged on the basis of CPU time, he or she could utilize extensive storage and consulting to minimize the CPU time and the resulting allocation, probably resulting in higher total service cost. Or, if an operating manager has an application that utilizes almost no storage and no user consulting services, the allocated cost may be too expensive since it includes a charge for the average storage and consulting services used with CPU time.

In large measure, these issues are cost estimation issues such as those we have discussed in Chapters 5 and 6. Regression could be used to see which activity measures are correlated with costs. If two activity measures are highly correlated, then the nature of the service may be such that operating managers are required to use both subservices in constant proportion, and a single cost pool would not distort usage.

13.5 FIXED COST ALLOCATIONS

The previous two sections have dealt primarily with the allocations of variable central overhead costs to operating units. But it is frequently the case that a large portion of such costs is fixed with respect to decisions made by the operating units. Therefore, allocations of these costs provide no information about the decentralized manager's short-term decisions. If this is the case, then allocating fixed costs must be done with some care, in order that the resulting operating decisions are not dysfunctional. For instance, in Table 13.1, allocating fixed service costs based on usage caused the operating managers to underutilize the central service. If we were to allocate such costs based on some other factor, such as sales revenue, we would be ''taxing'' sales revenue and reducing the payoff to a manager that attempts to increase sales revenue. (Allocation based on profitability or ability to bear would have the same effect: managers' incentives to increase profitability are reduced.)

Why allocate fixed, central overhead costs? If decentralized managers exercise no influence over these costs, what is the purpose of the allocation? A response often heard is that the allocations ''make decentralized managers aware of the *total* costs of doing business. These costs must be covered before the firm makes a profit.'' In other words, managers are expected to behave differently if central overhead costs are allocated. One possibility would be that these allocations are a part of the *budget pressure* or *incentive pressure* systems that are used to motivate managers, but the same effect could be achieved by adjusting the budget target rather than allocating costs over which managers have no influence.

An alternative explanation for fixed (capacity)-cost allocation is that managers' decisions do not just affect the current operating period through variable costs, but also have an influence on future needs for capacity. For example, if the operating departments demand a great deal of a central service (e.g., computing services), to the point where the demands cannot be met internally, then central management may consider increasing the service department's capacity (and fixed costs) in the future. In effect, there are two decision processes that may be related to each other: operating departments are determining their short-term service usage, and service departments are planning for their future capacity requirements. Allocating costs in a way to facilitate both short-term efficiency and long-term efficiency is not an easy problem to solve. We have already seen that allocating fixed costs on a per-unit-of-service basis can lead to underutilization of the service department in the short term. But are there other allocations that avoid these difficulties?

Suppose that the service department based its capacity decisions on past usage by the operating departments, and then allocated the fixed costs based on those past usages. There are two difficulties with this approach to cost allocations. First, an operating manager knows that increasing current usage will increase future allocations of fixed cost, and this could distort the short-term service usage. Additionally, an operating manager who has planned a substantial increase or decrease in future service usage ought to be able to communicate that planned change to the central service department. (For example, if the central department arranged financing for decentralized investment centers, plans for major acquisitions and dispositions of assets would probably be valuable information for the central department.) But if central service capacity is based on projections by the operating departments, then we must consider whether the cost allocation system could lead to biases in the projections. In effect, the problem is similar to the *budget participation* problems that were discussed in the previous chapter, and most of the approaches described there could be applied here.

Suppose that the central service department can choose between two cost curves that represent two operating plans. Plan 1 has a low fixed cost of \$10 and a variable cost of \$2 per unit of service. Plan 2 has a higher fixed cost of \$20 and a lower variable cost of \$1 per unit of service. (See Figure 13.3.) The breakeven point between these two plans is at 10 units of service, and the service department requests service usage projec-

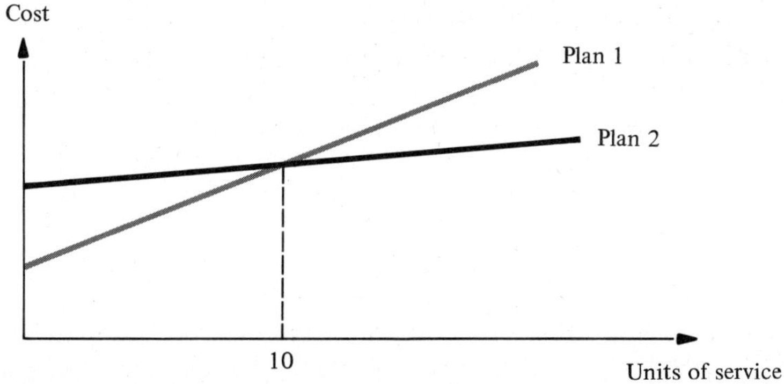

Figure 13.3

tions from two operating departments, A and B. If the total projected usage exceeds 10, then plan 2 will be adopted, otherwise plan 1 will be chosen.

One approach to this allocation problem is based on the notion, from cooperative game theory, that a department should not be made worse off by using central services instead of acquiring the services on its own. That is, if there are economies of scale in producing the service, the service department costs allocated to the operating department should be less than the amount that the operating department would have to pay to acquire the services on its own. More than one allocation meets this criterion, but one which does (the Shapley value) is based on the idea that the operating departments could arrive randomly at the service department and are assigned the expected incremental cost of providing their service. If $C(A)$, $C(B)$, and $C(AB)$ are the costs of providing service to A alone, B alone, and both A and B, respectively, then the allocated costs would be the following.[5]

$$\begin{aligned} C_A &= \text{cost allocated to operating Department } A \\ &= (1/2)[C(A)] + (1/2)[C(AB) - C(B)] \\ C_B &= (1/2)[C(B)] + (1/2)[C(AB) - C(A)] \end{aligned} \tag{13.5}$$

In our example above, suppose that both A and B want to use 6 units of service. The cost of providing service to either A or B alone would be $\$10 + (2)(6) = \$22$. If both A and B were provided service, the service department would switch to plan 2, and the total service cost would be $\$20 + (1)(12) = \$32$. Therefore, the cost allocated to A would be $(1/2)(22) + (1/2)(32 - 22) = \$16$. This is less than the \$22 it would cost A to acquire service on its own. In the case where the different cost curves are linear as in Figure 13.3 and the operating departments are of equal size, the allocations can be computed by splitting the fixed service cost equally among the operating departments, and then basing the variable allocation on actual usage. For example,

$$\begin{aligned} C_A &= \frac{\text{fixed service cost}}{\text{no. of operating departments}} + (\text{variable unit cost})(A\text{'s actual usage}) \\ &= \begin{cases} \$\ 5 + 2(A\text{'s actual usage}) \text{ under plan 1} \\ \$10 + 1(A\text{'s actual usage}) \text{ under plan 2} \end{cases} \end{aligned} \tag{13.6}$$

The allocation of cost to operating department B is similarly defined.

This allocation method is an appealing one, since it uses the service usages to develop allocations that are lower than the operating departments could achieve on their own. However, it is likely that the service department will have to choose its operating plan based on forecasts of the operating departments' usages rather than on the usages themselves. Will the cost allocation above provide an incentive for the operating departments to forecast accurately?[6]

The answer to this question depends on the relative sizes of operating departments A and B. For the moment, suppose that A and B each expect that their service usage will

[5] If there were three operating departments, A, B and D, the cost allocated to A would be:

$$C_A = (1/3)[C(A)] + (1/6)[C(AB) - C(B)] + (1/6)[C(AD) - C(D)] + (1/3)[C(ABD) - C(BD)]$$

[6] Since only variable costs are being allocated based on actual usage, we assume that the operating departments will make appropriate short-term usage decisions.

be 6 units in the future. If they both report projected usages of 6 and actually use 6 units, plan 2 will be adopted, and their allocations will be

$$\begin{aligned} C_A &= (1/2)(20) + 1(6) = \$16 \\ C_B &= (1/2)(20) + 1(6) = \$16 \end{aligned} \tag{13.7}$$

If operating department A decides to underestimate its projected usage by 3, but still uses 6 units, then plan 1 will be chosen, and the cost allocations will be

$$\begin{aligned} C_A &= (1/2)(10) + 2(6) = \$17 \\ C_B &= (1/2)(10) + 2(6) = \$17 \end{aligned} \tag{13.8}$$

Therefore, we can see that if the actual usages are to be the same size, an operating department cannot improve its performance measure by biasing its forecasts. Therefore this allocation scheme could lead to both short-term and long-term efficiency, *if* the operating departments have the same service needs.

However, what happens if each operating department is charged half of the fixed service cost when operating department A expects to use 4 units of service, while department B expects to use 8 units? If they each report accurate projections, plan 2 will be chosen with the following allocated costs.

$$\begin{aligned} C_A &= (1/2)(20) + (1)(4) = \$14 \\ C_B &= (1/2)(20) + (1)(8) = \$18 \end{aligned} \tag{13.9}$$

But, if operating department A chooses to underestimate its usage, say by 3 units, the total projected usage will be 1 + 8 = 9 units, and plan 1 will be chosen. If A still uses 4 units, the cost allocations will be

$$\begin{aligned} C_A &= (1/2)(10) + 2(4) = \$13 \\ C_B &= (1/2)(10) + 2(8) = \$21 \end{aligned} \tag{13.10}$$

Operating department A is better off by underestimating the projected usage, since the allocated cost has been reduced from \$14 to \$13. Therefore, this allocation procedure can encourage the smaller user departments to underestimate their usage. The reverse is also true—large departments can improve their cost allocations by overestimating their usage. [What happens in equation (13.10) above if B estimates usage of 10 instead of 8?]

There are ways in which we might attempt to eliminate (or at least control) these estimation/participation problems. First, we could examine other procedures for allocating costs to see if another approach could lead to accurate projections. There are allocation methods that encourage truthful reporting, but they are not commonly used in practice.[7] One alternative would be some form of investigation policy by central management, where large and/or continuing discrepancies between projected usage and actual usage will be examined for deliberate misestimation. Such a policy would have to take into account the amount of uncertainty facing a manager at the time projections were made *and* the costs of determining the causes of the forecast errors. Yet another alter-

[7]One such allocation would be the following:

C_A = fixed cost + (variable cost)(A's actual usage + B's projected usage)
C_B = fixed cost + (variable cost)(B's actual usage + A's projected usage).

native might be to adapt the New Soviet Incentive Scheme described in Chapter 12 from a profit situation to a cost situation by ''flipping it over'' as shown in Figure 13.4. In essence, the operating department pays one variable cost v_1 up to its forecasted usage $\hat{X}$, and a higher variable cost v_2 for usage in excess of $\hat{X}$. The shortcoming of this approach is that it can distort short-term usage decisions. For instance, if the operating department manager receives new information about possible orders, he or she may be discouraged from pursuing them because of the higher price that must be paid for additional service.

If the central service department has very good information about the future service needs of the operating departments, then it may not rely on forecasts from the operating departments. The service department cost configuration could be chosen based on the service department's projections, and no fixed-cost allocations are necessary. However, if the central service department has some (but not perfect) information about the operating departments' demands for service, it can sometimes develop allocations that will lead to accurate reporting using the budget/bonus menu approach described in Chapter 12. Returning to our example where the service department must choose between plans 1 and 2, let's assume that each of the operating departments may face one of two situations which determine the amount of their service demand. (The situation faced by one department is assumed to be independent of the situation faced by the other department.)

Operating department	Situation 1		Situation 2	
	Service demand	Probability	Service demand	Probability
A	1	1/3	4	2/3
B	8	1/2	10	1/2

The probabilities are known by all operating departments and the service department, but each operating department knows its own situation or type with certainty. If each operating department manager tries to minimize the expected service costs allocated, can the service department find an allocation rule that will encourage accurate reporting?

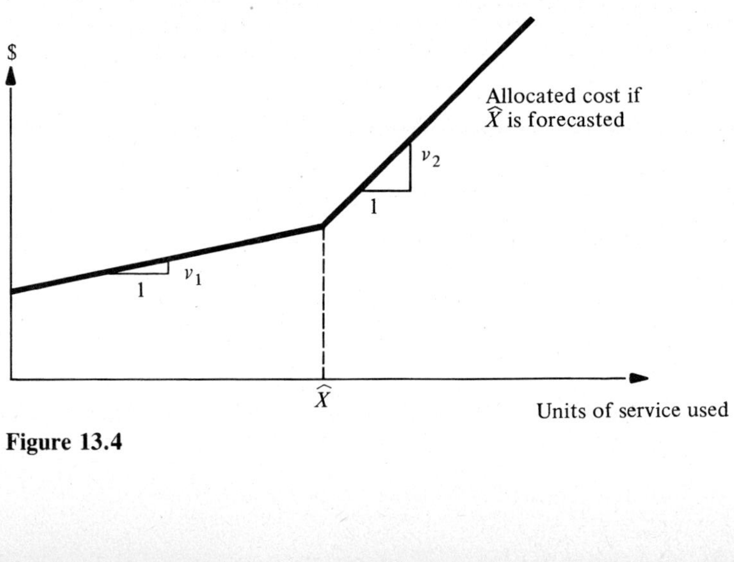

Figure 13.4

The answer is "yes," and the allocation can be found by first determining the service department's response to different reports by the operating department. Define $F(i,j)$ and $V(i,j)$ to be the fixed and variable service department costs if operating department A reports that it faces situation i while B's reported situation is j.

Reported situation A	Reported situation B	Service department plan chosen	$F(i,j)$	$V(i,j)$
1	1	1	10	2/unit
1	2	2	20	1/unit
2	1	2	20	1/unit
2	2	2	20	1/unit

The service department can use a cost allocation of the following form:

$$\begin{aligned} C_A &= \text{cost allocated to operating department } A \\ &= \Phi_A F(i,j) + V(i,j)X_A \end{aligned} \tag{13.11}$$

where Φ_A is the fraction of service department fixed costs assigned to A, and X_A is A's actual service usage.

Similarly, Φ_B is the fraction of fixed service costs assigned to operating department B. In this setting, we can find the values of Φ_A and Φ_B that encourage accurate reporting by looking at four "truth-telling" constraints. That is, for each situation faced by each operating department, the expected service cost should be lower if it reports accurately than if it does not. For instance, if operating department A faces situation 1, the constraint would look like the following.

$$\begin{aligned} &E[A\text{'s allocated cost if report situation } 1|A \text{ faces situation } 1] \\ &\qquad < E[A\text{'s allocated cost if report situation } 2|A \text{ faces situation } 1] \\ &\text{or } (1/2)[\Phi_A F(1,1) + V(1,1)1] + (1/2)[\Phi_A F(1,2) + V(1,2)1] \\ &\qquad < (1/2)[\Phi_A F(2,1) + V(2,1)1] + (1/2)[\Phi_A F(2,2) + V(2,2)1] \\ &\text{or } (1/2)[(\Phi_A)(10) + (2)(1)] + (1/2)[(\Phi_A)(20) + (1)(1)] \\ &\qquad < (1/2)[(\Phi_A)(20) + (1)(1)] + (1/2)[(\Phi_A)(20) + (1)(1)] \rightarrow \Phi_A > 0.1 \end{aligned} \tag{13.12}$$

This result implies that operating department A must be assigned at least 10% of the fixed service cost to encourage truthful reporting when it faces situation 1. A similar analysis can be done for situation 2.

$$\begin{aligned} &E[A\text{'s allocated cost if report situation } 2|A \text{ faces situation } 2] \\ &\qquad < E[A\text{'s allocated cost if report situation } 1|A \text{ faces situation } 2] \\ &\text{or } (1/2)[(\Phi_A)(20) + (1)(4)] + (1/2)[(\Phi_A)(20) + (1)(4)] \\ &\qquad < (1/2)[\Phi_A(10) + (2)(4)] + (1/2)[(\Phi_A)(20) + (1)(4)] \rightarrow \Phi_A < 0.4 \end{aligned} \tag{13.13}$$

From this, we can see that Φ_A must be set between 10% and 40% to induce truthful reporting by operating department A. However, you should note that the analysis above assumed that operating department B was reporting truthfully about its situation. We could do the same sort of analysis for B, and we would find that values of Φ_B between 0.8 and 1.0 encourage truthful reporting.

If we desire to set fixed cost allocations that encourage *both* A and B to report accurately, we must choose Φ_A and Φ_B from the shaded area in Figure 13.5. And, if we want the allocations to add to 100% of fixed cost, they must be on the line between the points $\Phi_A = 0$, $\Phi_B = 1$, and $\Phi_A = 1$, $\Phi_B = 0$. Therefore, we could choose allocations on the line inside the shaded area, and have *full allocation* of the costs and encourage truthful reporting. The allocation $\Phi_A = 0.15$ and $\Phi_B = 0.85$ would be one such point; $\Phi_A = 0.18$ and $\Phi_B = 0.82$ would be another.

While this analysis was successful in finding the type of allocation we were looking for, there are some shortcomings that ought to be pointed out. First, with two operating departments and two possible situations each, there were four constraints to be analyzed. If there are n departments with m situations for each, then the number of constraints is $nm(m - 1)$, and the analysis quickly gets cumbersome; we may wish to let a computer do the computations. We have also assumed that the operating department's objective was to minimize its expected allocated costs, and in many situations this would be an oversimplification. A more general analysis would utilize the principal/agent model described in Chapter 11, but to the constraints that the agent's market price be met and that the agent chooses the action, we would add truth-telling constraints similar to the ones developed above. The form of these constraints would be that the agent's expected utility must be greater if he reports accurately than if he does not.

Finally, there are some situations where the truth-telling allocation may not appear fair or equitable. For instance, if operating departments A and B face situations 2 and 1, respectively, B's service department usage (8 units) will be twice that of A's (4 units). But if $\Phi_A = 0.15$, $\Phi_B = 0.85$, department B will be bearing almost six times the fixed cost that department A bears. This situation may cause some friction within the organization, but a reallocation of the fixed costs would probably upset the accurate forecasting that was encouraged by $\Phi_A = 0.15$, $\Phi_B = 0.85$. As a result, the reallocation might

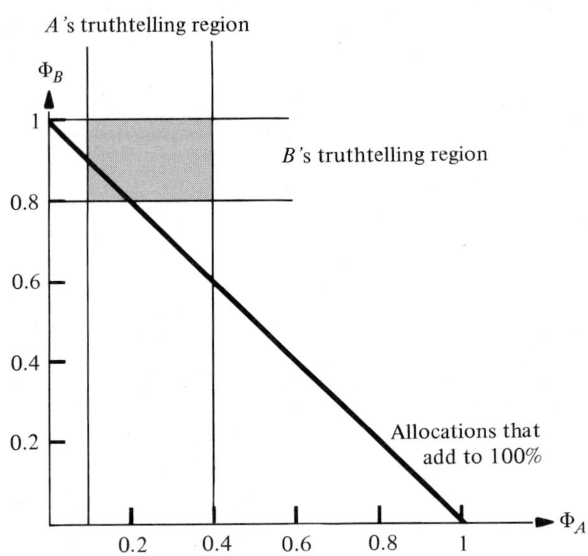

Figure 13.5

result in an inefficient plan being chosen by the service department. Central management may have to make a choice between equity and efficiency in designing the cost allocations.

13.6 SUMMARY ON COST ALLOCATIONS

The preceding sections on cost allocations have served as illustrations of *responsibility accounting,* where the objective is to encourage those decisions that are in the organization's best interests. This congruence is best achieved, not through coercion, but by a careful study of the decentralized decision maker's objectives and needs and of the possible situations he or she may face. Then the cost allocation system can be designed to minimize conflicts between the decentralized decision maker's welfare and that of the organization. In the sections above, we found such cost allocations when the decentralized manager made decisions on service department usage and on forecasting that usage. But the conclusions we reached were specific to the situations we analyzed, so it is the *process* of analysis that is most important. How are costs allocated, and what decisions are delegated? How are the allocations supposed to affect decision making? How do the allocations affect decision making? Are there other allocations (including no allocation) that would encourage decisions that are preferred by the organization? This process of analysis can be applied in other allocation situations, and in the following section we turn to the allocation of profit across activities by transfer pricing.

13.7 TRANSFER PRICING

There are many different types of interdependencies that exist within an organization, so it is difficult to go into detail about all of them. One of the more common forms of interdependence involves the transfer of goods and services between responsibility centers, but these transfers may occur under a variety of settings. In essence, the transfer price between the internal seller and the internal buyer determines the allocation of profit between the two responsibility centers. If the transfer is made at cost (as was done in examples in previous sections), most of the profit is allocated to the internal buyer. If the transfer price reflects the value of the good or service to the internal buyer, then most of the profit will be allocated to the internal producer. The objective of most transfer price systems is to allocate profits in such a way as to encourage decisions which increase the total profits, or, more generally, lead to a more favorable probability distribution of organizational performance.

One of the most important factors in evaluating a transfer pricing system is the delegation of the transfer decision. There are several possibilities. Central management may decide on the amounts of goods and services to be transferred, or the decision may be delegated to the internal buyer or to the internal seller. It is not uncommon for the decision to be delegated to both divisions so that the amount transferred is the amount that the internal seller is willing to sell *and* that the internal buyer is willing to purchase. There are also a number of different transfer prices found in practice:

- market price of the transferred good;
- the internal seller's full cost (or standard full cost) of production (sometimes with an added profit margin);
- the internal seller's variable cost (or standard variable cost) plus the opportunity cost of making the transfer; and
- the internal buyer's net benefit (final product revenue, less the variable costs of readying the transferred good for final sale).

It is important to consider *both* the delegation of the transfer decision *and* the transfer price simultaneously, because there are some combinations that will not work well. For instance, if the internal seller makes the transfer decision and the transfer price is set at standard variable cost, he or she has little to gain by making the transfer. We might analyze this situation using the responsibility accounting framework described earlier, with an additional decision variable representing the amount transferred.

$$x(a_0, a_1, a_2, \varepsilon_1, \varepsilon_2) = x_1(a_0, a_1, \varepsilon_1) - x_2(a_0, a_2, \varepsilon_2) \tag{13.14}$$

where $x(\cdot)$ = the firm's profits
$x_1(\cdot)$ = sales revenue
$x_2(\cdot)$ = production cost
a_0 = number of units transferred from production to selling
a_1 = the sales manager's effort directed toward increasing revenue per unit
a_2 = the production manager's effort directed toward decreasing production cost per unit
$\varepsilon_1, \varepsilon_2$ = uncontrollable factors in sales (ε_1) and production (ε_2)

For this situation, central management must choose which responsibility center will decide on a_0 and also provide a transfer price rule that will determine the performance measures, r_1 and r_2, for each of the responsibility centers. The different transfer price systems could be evaluated by projecting their impact on the effort decisions and on the quantity transferred. A few of the alternatives are described in Table 13.3, along with their shortcomings.

We can look at this problem in the context of the agency model described in Chapter 11. If the central administration knows as much about the revenue and cost functions as the decentralized managers, then there is no need to delegate the transfer decision. The central manager can determine the optimum amount to be transferred a_0^* along with the performance evaluation schemes for the two managers. The sales manager will be evaluated on the basis of the revenue achieved, taking the effects of a_0^* into account. Similarly, the production manager's evaluation will be based on production costs, taking the effects of a_0^* into account. However, it is more likely that the decentralized managers will possess more information about their operations than the central management. If this is the case, then it is very difficult to use a transfer price based on *opportunity costs,* because the opportunities are only known by the decentralized managers. Central management might ask for estimates, but the decentralized managers might be reluctant to report accurately. Again, a budget/bonus menu approach might be used, but the next section describes an alternative transfer price system which attempts to overcome this problem.

TABLE 13.3 TRANSFER PRICE ALTERNATIVES

Transfer price	Sales department's performance measure[a]	Production department's performance measure[a]	Who decides on transfer?	Shortcomings
1. 0	$r_1 = x_1(a_0, a_1)$	$r_2 = -x_2(a_0, a_2)$	Sales	Sales manager has incentive to increase transfers without considering cost. Low efforts are likely.
2. Actual production cost	$r_1 = x_1(a_0, a_1) - x_2(a_0, a_2)$	$r_2 = 0$	Sales	Production manager has no incentive to expend effort and reduce cost
3. Standard production cost (based on standard effort $\bar{a}_2$)	$r_1 = x_1(a_0, a_1) - x_2(a_0, \bar{a}_2)$	$r_2 = x_2(a_0, \bar{a}_2) - x_2(a_0, a_2)$ (a cost variance)	Sales	Both have incentives to expend effort, but more involvement by central management in standard setting
4. Standard revenue (based on standard effort $\bar{a}_1$)	$r_1 = x_1(a_0, a_1) - x_1(a_0, \bar{a}_1)$ (a revenue variance)	$r_2 = x_1(a_0, \bar{a}_1) - x_2(a_0, a_2)$	Production	Both have incentives to expend effort, but more involvement by central management in standard setting

[a]The uncontrollable factors ϵ_1 and ϵ_2 are left out for simplicity, although different transfer prices allocate these risks in different ways.

13.8 A DUAL-PRICE SYSTEM WITH LIMITED DECENTRALIZATION

In the transfer price systems discussed above, the transfer price paid by the buying division was the same as the transfer price received by the selling division. This *single-price* system has a sort of "additivity" in that if we add the two divisions' profit measures together, we obtain the profits of the firm. Under a *dual-price* system, where the price paid by the buyer is not equal to the price received by the seller, this additivity would not result. When the central manager has less information about the conditions in the decentralized units, he or she will have to rely on reports from the decentralized managers in making the transfer decision, and there is a dual-price system that is designed to encourage the decentralized managers to make accurate reports.

The internal buying division's expected revenues will be $x_1(a_0)$, where a_0 is the amount of product transferred. But suppose that only the manager of this division knows this revenue function. Likewise only the internal selling division manager knows the expected production cost function, $x_2(a_0)$. The central manager asks the decentralized managers to report on the effects of transfers on their divisions. The buying division transmits a *reported* revenue function $\hat{x}_1(a_0)$, and the selling division sends its *reported* cost function $\hat{x}_2(a_0)$. Then the central manager derives the reported marginal revenue and marginal cost curves, and sets the quantity to be transferred at a_0^*, where $\hat{x}_1'(a_0^*) = \hat{x}_2'(a_0^*)$. Then the profit measures for the two divisions are the following.

$$\begin{aligned} \text{Internal buyer's profit measure} &= x_1(a_0^*, a_1, \varepsilon_1) - \hat{x}_2(a_0^*) \\ \text{Internal seller's profit measure} &= \hat{x}_1(a_0^*) - x_2(a_0^*, a_2, \varepsilon_2) \end{aligned} \tag{13.15}$$

This transfer price system differs from those in Table 13.3 because it is a dual-price system. The transfer price paid by the buyer is $\hat{x}_2(a_0^*)$, while the transfer price received by the seller is $\hat{x}_1(a_0^*)$. If each tells the truth in his or her report, the expected profit for each division will equal the expected profit for the total firm. This means that our accounting system will have to be augmented to keep track of the reports or projections made by the divisions, and that we will have to forego the "additivity" we discussed earlier. In addition, the quantity transferred is determined centrally, instead of by the divisions, reducing decentralization. An alternative would be to require the revenue and cost reports to be filed and let the divisions find where $\hat{x}_1'(a_0^*) = \hat{x}_2'(a_0^*)$. Periodic, random checks or audits that revealed a departure from this procedure could result in penalties for the division managers.

To see why this control is important, we should first realize that the primary advantage of this system is that truth-telling is a dominant strategy for both the buying and selling divisions. As long as a division tries to maximize its profit measure, then *regardless* of whether the other division has reported truthfully, the best a division can do is to report accurately. As a result, we know that $\hat{x}_1(\cdot) = x_1(\cdot)$, $\hat{x}_2(\cdot) = x_2(\cdot)$, and a_0^* is, in fact, the optimal quantity to transfer from the firm's viewpoint. If we allow the division managers to choose a_0, then truth-telling is no longer guaranteed, as can be seen in Figure 13.6. If the true marginal curves are $x_1'(a_0)$ and $x_2'(a_0)$, the optimal transferred quantity is a_0^* with firm profits equal to the area in OAB (before fixed costs). However, if the buying division overstates $x_1'(\cdot)$ to $\hat{x}_1'(\cdot)$ and the selling division understates $x_2'(a_0)$ to $\hat{x}_2'(a)_0$, then they could agree to produce $\hat{a}_0$, and the seller would get $OAB + ACB$, the buyer would get $OAB + OBD$, and the total firm profits would be $OAB - BCD$.

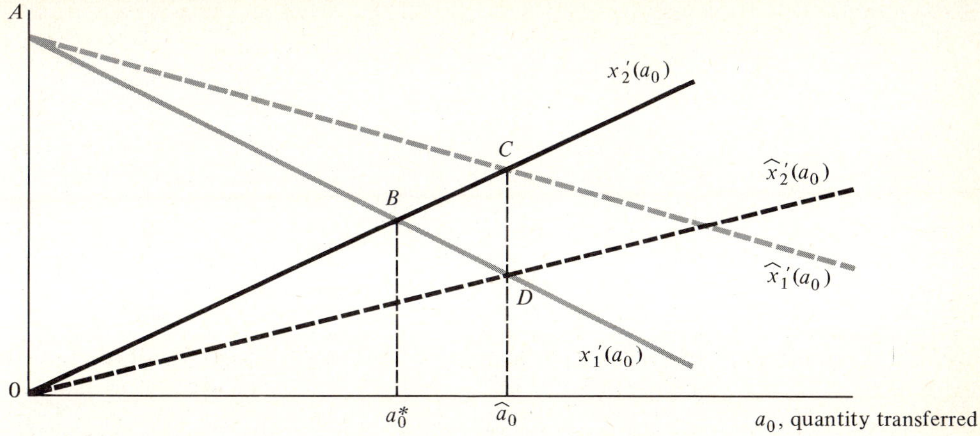

Figure 13.6

Unless the central administration can check and find that $\hat{a}_0$ is not where the reported marginal revenue equalled the reported marginal cost, the truth-telling no longer appears.

Yet another advantage of this transfer pricing scheme is that it retains some notion of *controllability*. The internal selling division's profit depends on actual costs, so the incentives to control costs remain. A similar situation occurs for the internal buying division. However, we have assumed that each of the parties involved in this problem is risk-neutral and only cares about maximizing the expected reported profit measure. In a more complex environment, this transfer pricing system might not work very well, and a more thorough examination of the incentives and information would be in order. For instance, the dual-price system might reduce the manager's incentives to search for suppliers and customers outside the firm.

13.9 TRANSFER PRICING AND RISK SHARING

There are some situations where decentralized units must agree on a transfer pricing arrangement when there is substantial uncertainty about the costs or benefits of the transfer. If this is the case, there may be some disadvantage to establishing a set transfer price before the uncertainty is resolved.

As an example, suppose that a firm has received an offer of \$260 to supply a part to a customer. The part would have to be processed first by department 1, and then transferred to department 2 for completion and delivery to the customer. Each department faces certain technical problems in processing the part, so the cost is uncertain at this time. The possible outcomes and their probabilities are as follows:

Department No.	Probability that departmental costs will be \$100	\$150		Expected cost
1	1/2	1/2		\$125
2	1/2	1/2		\$125
			TOTAL	\$250

If the firm's objective is to maximize expected profit, then the offer should be accepted. (We'll assume that the departmental costs include an opportunity cost for the use of productive resources.) However, if the department managers are risk-averse, their willingness to accept the order will depend on the transfer price structure. For our example, we assume that department i's manager has a preference function $(25 + \pi_i)^{1/2}$, where π_i is the profit allocated to department i. The manager will choose the decision that maximizes the expected value of the preference function.

If we set the transfer price at \$130, will the manager of department 1 agree to the transfer, or will he or she prefer to reject the order and receive zero incremental profit with certainty?

$$\begin{aligned} &\text{Reject: } (25 + 0)^{1/2} = 5 \\ &\text{Accept: } 1/2[25 + (130 - 100)]^{1/2} + 1/2[25 + (130 - 150)]^{1/2} = 4.826 \end{aligned} \tag{13.16}$$

The manager's expected preference is higher if the order is rejected. The same is true for the manager of department 2. Therefore there appears to be a conflict between the managers' decisions and the objective of the firm.

One approach to this problem would be to use a transfer pricing scheme that lets the department managers *share the risk* of their production cost. They can do this by forming a syndicate or partnership where they each receive a share of the total outcome. For our example, we might consider a 50–50 split of the total profit.

Total cost	Probability	Firm profits	Departmental share
\$200	1/4	\$60	\$30
\$250	1/2	\$10	\$ 5
\$300	1/4	(\$40)	(\$20)

Will the department managers be willing to accept the order? We can again calculate the expected preference.

$$\begin{aligned} &\text{Reject: } (25 + 0)^{1/2} = 5 \\ &\text{Accept: } 1/4(25 + 30)^{1/2} + 1/2(25 + 5)^{1/2} + 1/4(25 - 20)^{1/2} = 5.15 \end{aligned} \tag{13.17}$$

By sharing the risk between departments, the project becomes desirable, and would be accepted, leading to a higher expected profit for the firm.

When one department would bear a significant risk in making a transfer, it is sometimes valuable to develop a shedule of transfer prices so that the risk may be spread among more departments. Or, when two or more departments face risks, allowing them to share each other's risks creates a form of diversification. In effect, the departments are entering into a joint-venture arrangement. These risk-sharing arrangements can encourage profitable transfers (i.e., those expected to be profitable) that might otherwise not be made.

One potential problem in such an arrangement is the reduction in motivation for the managers to improve performance within their individual departments. In our example above, suppose the manager of department 1 could decrease costs by \$5 if he or she devoted extra effort to control costs. If the transfer price is set at \$130, then he or she would receive the full benefit of the cost reduction. But if the two departments share the total profit, the manager will only receive a $2.50 increase in profits, and this may not be enough to make it worth the effort. There may be many situations in which the risk-sharing and motivational aspects of transfer prices are at odds with each other. In designing the transfer price system, we need to consider the risks, opportunities, and motivations of the managers who will be making the transfer decisions.

13.10 SUMMARY

Our modern economy is characterized by many organizations of such size and diversity that delegation of decision making is essential for efficient operation. But responsibility must be delegated along with authority to ensure that managers' decisions are consistent with the overall organization's goals. Therefore, when we develop an organizational design of *authority centers,* we must also develop a *responsibility accounting system* that makes the manager aware of the effect of his or her decisions on the organization, and provides central management with information to evaluate the decentralized managers' performance.

There are a variety of accounting practices that impact on the responsibility accounting system: allocations of fixed and variable central overhead, development of flexible budgets, and transfer pricing. In general, we can expect some dysfunctional decision making when the accounting allocations cause one decision maker's performance measure to be significantly influenced by another's decision. The first decision maker's evaluation is influenced by uncontrollables, and the second decision maker is not made aware of his or her effect on the organization.

When these problems become severe and the dysfunctional decisions are costly, there are two courses of action that central management may consider. First, a reorganization of decision making authority could alleviate the problem. Or, alternatively, the responsibility accounting system can be enhanced or realigned to reduce the conflicts between managers' performance measurement and the organization's goals.

APPENDIX 13.1: Allocation of Service Costs

In this appendix, we utilize a model similar to those in the appendixes to Chapter 11, but with some differences. The manager is still assumed to be averse to risk and effort, but in addition to deciding how much effort to expend, the manager also determines the amount of service to be used. Both effort and service increase the payoff to the manager's responsibility center, while service increases costs in the service department.

Decision Variables

$$x_1 \equiv \text{effort of responsibility center manager} \qquad \text{(A13.1)}$$
$$x_2 \equiv \text{amount of service used}$$

Responsibility Center Payoff

$$R = r(x_1 + x_2) + \varepsilon_1; \qquad r > 0,\ E[\varepsilon_1] = 0,\ \sigma^2[\varepsilon_1] = \sigma_1^2 \qquad \text{(A13.2)}$$

Service Department Cost

$$C = cx_2^2 + \varepsilon_2; \qquad c > 0,\ E[\varepsilon_2] = 0,\ \sigma^2[\varepsilon_2^2] = \sigma_2^2 \tag{A13.3}$$

Responsibility Center Manager's Compensation

$$I = k + l_1 R - l_2 C = k + l_1\left(R - \frac{l_2}{l_1}C\right) \tag{A13.4}$$

Responsibility Center Manager's Expected Utility

$$\begin{aligned} EU_m &= E[I] - \delta\sigma^2[I] - ax_1^2 \\ &= k + l_1 r(x_1 + x_2) - l_2 c x_2^2 - \delta(l_1^2\sigma_1^2 + l_2^2\sigma_2^2) - ax_1^2 \end{aligned} \tag{A13.5}$$

$$x_1^* = \frac{l_1 r}{2a};\ x_2^* = \frac{l_1 r}{2l_2 c}$$

The expression for the optimal effort is similar to the ones developed in Appendixes 11.1 and 11.2. Higher profit-sharing (l_1), higher return to effort (r), and lower effort aversion (a), all lead to increased effort. The expression for the amount of service utilized x_2^*, also depends on l_2, the percentage of service costs assigned to the manager. As l_2 gets close to zero, the utilization of the free good gets very large.

Central management's decision problem is to choose the parameters k, l_1, and l_2 so as to maximize its expected payoff. Our particular interest here is in the relationship between l_1 and l_2. If $l_1 = l_2 = l$, then the compensation function becomes $k + l(R - C)$, and a full allocation of C gives us a single performance measure $(R - C)$. If $l_2 < l_1$, then the compensation becomes $k + l_1[R - (l_2/l_1)C]$, and a less than full allocation would be used in the performance measure. The solution to central management's problem is too complicated to present here, but the optimal l_2 depends on the uncertainty in service department costs, as measured by σ_2^2.

$$\begin{aligned} l_2^* &= l_1^*, \qquad \text{if } \sigma_2^2 = 0 \\ l_2^* &< l_1^*, \qquad \text{if } \sigma_2^2 > 0 \end{aligned} \tag{A13.6}$$

Therefore, if the service costs depend only on x_2, a full allocation of those costs to the operating responsibility center would not cause any problems in using the resulting performance measure. However, if there are other, uncontrollable factors which influence the service cost, it would be better to only allocate a fraction l_2/l_1 of these costs in measuring performance. As σ_2^2 or δ gets larger, the fraction decreases, signifying that less of the service department cost should be allocated.

PROBLEMS

13.1. Charles Roberts is the general manager of the Commercial Products Division of the Sharp Optics Company, which sells optical products to other companies. Products intended for final consumers are the responsibility of the Consumer Products Division. Roberts has just received a major order from a customer that, if accepted, would increase his monthly sales from 1,000 units and \$200,000 to 1,500 units and \$268,500. Costs incurred within the Commercial Products Division are expected to continue at their present level of \$78 per unit for both existing units and the proposed additional units. Production of components for both divisions is done at a central plant, and this part of the operations is treated as a cost center. That is, all production costs are allocated monthly to the Commercial Products and Consumer Products Divisions on the basis of the number of units produced. The volume of production influences the central plant's monthly costs in the following way:

$$\text{Cost} = \$50{,}000 + \$50(\text{number of units produced})$$

The production needs of the Consumer Products Division fluctuate from month-to-month. For simplicity in doing the calculations, assume that the production needs of this division will be either 500 units or 1,500 units, with equal probability. (One component unit is needed for each finished unit of the Commercial Products Division. You can ignore any costs besides those described above.)

Required

A. If Charles Roberts's objective is to maximize the expected monthly profit assigned to his division, should he accept the special order?

B. If Charles Roberts receives a bonus in each month that his profits are above \$39,000, would he be likely to accept the special order?

C. What modifications would you recommend in the cost allocation method? (Be specific.)

13.2. Michael Davidson is the manager of the computing services department of a medium-sized manufacturing firm. Davidson's principal responsibility is maintaining the efficient operation of the central computing facility, so that the operating departments get the "best service at the lowest price." Ten months ago, a new computing system was installed that is large enough and flexible enough to meet the future needs of a growing company. It took a couple of months to get the bugs out, but the system has been operating pretty well for the last eight months, except for one concern that Davidson has expressed to you.

"As you know, we provide two basic services—computing time and storage. When we evaluated our needs two years ago, we looked at past usage and potential future applications in estimating the computing and storage requirement for the new system. But the actual usage of the new system has been weighted more heavily toward storage usage than we had projected, and the trend appears to be in the same direction. It looks like we should have purchased a different configuration, but I don't really feel that way."

In addition, Davidson has provided you with some operating data from the past four months and with some information about how costs are allocated to user departments. A variable-cost rate per CPU (computing hour) is developed and charged based on actual usage. Fixed costs are allocated separately, since the department has excess capacity at present.

Month	Variable cost	CPU time (hr)	Storage activity (units)
January	\$102,000	500	2,000
February	108,000	425	2,200
March	110,000	450	2,150
April	109,000	400	2,300
TOTALS	\$429,000	1,775	8,650

Required

A. Based on the data, develop a variable overhead rate per CPU hour.

B. Based on the data, develop a dual-rate variable overhead allocation using CPU hours and storage units (use regression or high-low).

C. Operating department 1 has an application that requires virtually no storage, and would produce benefits (cost savings) of approximately \$180 per CPU hour. Would this application be desirable under the rate in A? Under the rates in B?

D. Operating department 2 is considering a financial forecasting application that can be accomplished in two ways. Plan 1 would save only the basic data in storage and would recompute key statistics and relationships each time the program was used. Plan 2 would save most of the statistics and estimates in storage, so they would not have to be computed each time the program was used. Estimated usage of the application is such that CPU and storage would be 3 hr and 6 units under plan 1 and 2 hr and 12 units under plan 2. Which is the lower cost plan under the allocation in A? Under the allocation in B?

E. Based on your analysis in A–D, write a recommendation to Davidson.

13.3. Department *A* provides services to operating departments *X* and *Y*. The costs incurred in department *A* are allocated to *X* and *Y* based on the actual usages every month. Eight months of recent data are given below.

	Units of service used				
Month	*X*	*Y*	Department *A*'s cost	*X*'s cost allocation	*Y*'s cost allocation
1	189	232	$70,156	$31,563	$38,593
2	159	245	72,749	28,626	44,124
3	183	247	74,851	21,828	43,023
4	164	233	68,774	28,463	40,311
5	177	240	74,234	31,492	42,742
6	221	247	79,959	37,799	42,160
7	222	230	73,527	36,080	37,448
8	197	249	77,210	34,114	43,097

Required Using regression, answer the following questions.

A. How do department *A*'s costs depend on *X*'s and *Y*'s usage?
B. How does *X*'s cost allocation depend on its usage?
C. How does *Y*'s cost allocation depend on its usage?
D. If *X* plans 225 units of usage and *Y* plans 250 units of usage, what are the *expected costs* and their *standard error of forecast*
  a. based on *A*'s cost relationship in part *A*.
  b. based on *X*'s cost allocation relationship in part *B*.
  c. based on *Y*'s cost allocation relationship in part *C*.

13.4. The management of TUV, Inc. prides itself on using the most advanced management accounting techniques. For instance, the costs of service departments are split into fixed and variable costs, and each type of cost is allocated separately. Variable costs are allocated on the basis of actual service usage, while fixed costs are allocated based on forecasts of long-term usage. TUV is highly decentralized, and the production departments are given a great deal of autonomy. They are encouraged to provide input to the planning process at central headquarters, including the planning for central service departments.

While the management of TUV has been generally pleased with the results of the decentralization and the responsibility accounting system, the assistant controller, Margaret Chandler, has noted that the actual usage of central services has exceeded the forecasted usage by a considerable margin. This is disturbing because the service departments could have chosen a larger capacity and provided the service at a lower total cost to the firm.

Of course, the production departments are not expected to make perfect estimates of their service usages, but the underestimation has become common enough that Ms. Chandler has begun to suspect the cost allocation system. She poses the following problem to you.

"Suppose that service department X can choose one of two operating plans. Plan 1 would have costs of \$25,000 per month and \$20 per unit of service. Plan 2 would increase fixed costs to \$50,000 per month, but would decrease variable costs to \$10 per service unit. The manager of department X will choose the plan that minimizes the expected costs based on the forecasted usage from operating departments Y and Z. These forecasted usages will be used to allocate the fixed service costs, while variable costs are allocated based on actual usage."

Required

A. The manager of each of the operating departments (Y and Z) believes that his service usage will be 2,000 units per month. If they each report forecasted usage of 2,000 per month, what will be the service costs allocated to Y and Z? (Assume actual usage of 2,000 units each.)

B. Suppose the manager of Y underestimated his usage by forecasting usage of 1,000 units per month, but the actual usage remained at 2,000. What would be the costs allocated to each department? Is Y better off by underestimating?

C. Of course, two can play at this game. Suppose that Z also underestimates usage by 1,000 units, but actual demand remains at 2,000. Are total service costs the same as in part A above? Is Z better off than in part B?

D. Is the cost allocation method the culprit here? Could you change it to eliminate (or reduce) the underestimation problem?

13.5. "We've been growing at a pretty good rate over the last five years," says Peter Campbell, "and it's time for us to begin thinking about providing our own services rather than buying them from the outside. For instance, we have purchased legal services from a couple of local law firms, and I'm sure that we will continue to purchase some services from them. But a lot of our need for legal services is in contract review and negotiation of contracts, and it probably makes sense for us to consider hiring a full-time lawyer to handle these things. At present, we charge the divisions for the cost of legal services which they actually use, about \$100 an hour on average. I expect that it would cost us a fixed amount, about \$100,000 per year, to hire a lawyer and a secretary, and to get things set up to handle our in-house business. I'm not sure how to allocate the costs of the internal legal department to our two operating divisions. Based on past information, it's not clear how much of their services could have been handled by our internal legal department, and besides, we expect to continue to grow so the past is not a very good indicator of the future. Let's say that the possibilities for expected usage might be the following.

	400 hr	500 hr	600 hr
Division *A*	1/2	1/2	0
Division *B*	0	1/2	1/2

"Each division manager knows what his expected usage is, although they don't have any better information about each other than I do. I want to use an allocation that will encourage the division manager to give me accurate estimates, because there's a chance that it would cost us less to continue purchasing services outside. Also, I don't want to discourage them from using the legal department if we set it up."

Required

A. Suppose the legal department costs were not allocated to the divisions. What forecasting behavior would be encouraged?

B. Suppose that the fixed costs of the legal department would be allocated based on the forecasts of expected usage. What forecasting behavior would be encouraged?

C. Find an allocation method that would encourage the division managers to forecast accurately.

D. Would your analysis of the cost allocation change if the decision to set up the legal department was made at corporate headquarters, with no input from the division managers?

13.6. Refer to the information given in problem 11.6 for the sales representative. Suppose that there are two such representatives working in the same territory as a team. As a result, you cannot observe the contribution margin earned by each, but only the total contribution margin for both.

	C.M. = \$80,000	C.M. = \$100,000	C.M. = \$120,000
Both sales reps "work hard"	1/9	4/9	4/9
Only one sales rep "works hard"	2/9	5/9	2/9
Neither sales rep "works hard"	4/9	4/9	1/9

The information in problem 11.6, which describes the preferences and opportunities of the sales representative, is true for each of the representatives in this problem.

Required

A. Find a compensation function for each sales representative, based on their team output, that will induce each of them to choose the action "work hard" and will keep them from moving to another job.

B. How does the expected compensation in part A compare to the \$16,900 that would have to be paid if we could directly observe the sales representatives' efforts?

C. How does the expected compensation in part A compare to the expected compensation when we could observe each representative's contribution margin individually, as in part A of problem 11.6? What does this difference tell you about the value of responsibility accounting in this situation?

13.7. (Based on a paper by Delmar Davis.) NSC is one of the largest producers of steel plate in the world. Steel plate varies widely in size and composition depending on its intended use. It may range from 3/16 in. to 16 in. thick, from 36 in. to 150 in. wide, and from 96 in. to 1,500 in. long. Various alloying elements can be added to the molten steel to meet strength and metallurgic properties required by the customer. Plates are produced by heating a thicker intermediate product called a slab, and then passing it back and forth between a set of steel rolls until the desired gauge and size are achieved. Depending on its thickness, the plate is either mechanically sheared to the ordered width, or burned with a gas torch. The major measure of production activity is tons produced, and this causes some problems for the operations department. As gauge decreases toward its lower limit, productivity also decreases, since it takes as long to roll a 3/16-in. plate as a thicker one, but it weighs less and fewer tons can be produced in the same period. In addition, in-process damage increases and the rejection rate increases with the lower gauge plates. The lighter gauges have never been the favorite of the operations department, which has responsibility for production at the three U.S. rolling mills.

NSC's product sales group is responsible for setting prices on all products. A price book is published for salesmen, and any special orders or price quotations are referred to the product sales group. In addition, the product sales group provides a liaison between the operations department and the district sales offices, seeking to resolve customer and mill problems and to expedite the prompt delivery of products.

In making pricing decisions, the product sales group monitors competitors' prices, as well as the costs reported by the accounting department. They monitor the margins on all products, and seek to make adjustments whenever the market will bear it. When quoting new products or accounts, they sometimes make use of special accounting studies that estimate costs for plates of an exact size and chemistry. However, these studies are costly, and it takes up to two weeks to complete such a study.

The normal cost accounting system is based on a process cost system. Slabs are "purchased" from other NSC divisions. Plate mill operating costs are accumulated in cost pools, and the cost is applied to final products on a monthly basis. There are approximately 30 product accounts, based on the chemical composition of the steel involved. Size and gauge are not considered in the allocation of costs to the product accounts.

This latter point of costs has been the source of some conflict between the operating department and the product sales group. The operations department feels that the cost information does not reflect a key factor, namely, the size and gauge of the product. Therefore, the costs reported by the accounting department reflect the average of some rather diverse product costs.

Required

A. In NSC, the operations department is held responsible for the profitability of the plate mills. What difficulties can you identify in the current situation? As an organization, how is NSC affected by these difficulties?

B. One possibility would be to improve the cost system to consider more of the differences among products. How would this improved information system affect the organizational problems you described in A?

C. What other changes would you recommend to NSC?

13.8. The Finestkind China Company (FCC) is a medium-sized producer of ceramic china dinnerware products. The company's headquarters and only plant is located in southern Maine, and most of the company's $40 million in sales is in the northeastern United States. FCC's stock is closely held by members of the founding family, and Jeffrey Allen, the founder's great-grandson, holds the position of chairman of the board of directors. However, he does not take an active part in the day-to-day operations of the company.

Until last year, the company had been organized along functional lines, with a director in charge of each of the areas of sales, production, product development, and finance and administration. At that time, the company president, Kevin Bond, convinced the board that a more product-oriented organization was necessary, so the company adopted a matrix form of organization. The positions of the functional directors remained, but two new product-line directors were appointed. One of these managers was given responsibility for the fine china products, while the other was responsible for the remaining products, including the new European design dinnerware and the less expensive lines. Each of these managers would be held responsible for the profitability of their product lines. A product-line director could plan for the mix of products within his assigned lines, and could set pricing policy. However, these plans and policies had to be coordinated with the functional directors who would be responsible for implementing them.

The functional directors retained much of the control in their areas. The sales personnel, organized geographically, continued to sell both products and still reported to the sales director. The production director retained responsibility for the operations of the company's one plant, where both product lines required some of the same equipment and employees. A standard cost system had been developed to facilitate control of the production process, and would be used to allocate costs to the two product lines. Finance and administration costs are allocated to product lines based on sales volume, while product development costs are allocated on the basis of actual projects requested by the product-line directors.

The budgeting process for the past year was rather confused as a result of the organizational change. Kevin Bond had set some overall objectives for the company, but the development of plans and budgets to meet these objectives took considerable time and effort. The product-line directors set their own plans and budgets to meet the objectives, but these were not well received by the functional managers who had to carry them out. For instance, when the product-line directors' plans were consolidated, they called for production at 125% of capacity in some months and at 80% other months. The sales director thought that some of their projections were overly optimistic, and wanted them decreased. On the other side, the product development director found that they had only planned to use about 60% of the resources that he had available. Bond said, ''I think we arrived at a budget that everyone was satisfied with, but it sure took a long time. In a way, this increased tension is what we wanted when we changed to the matrix organization. We just have to be careful to keep the tension creative rather than destructive. Of course, we haven't finished the year yet, so it remains to be seen whether we're going to have an inordinate amount of 'finger-pointing' at the end of the year. For instance, if the profits of the fine china line fall short of budget because sales are below budget and production costs are above, who should be held responsible? At that point, what's past is past, but I don't want to create problems in the future.''

Required

A. One possibility would be for Bond to use a ''team performance'' approach to this problem, by basing all the directors' bonuses on the profits of the whole company. What would be the advantages and disadvantages of this approach?

B. As an alternative, try to develop a set of measures which divide the firm's profits into parts for which an individual manager can be held responsible. (The parts may overlap, if that will facilitate the evaluation of directors' performance.) What are the advantages and disadvantages of this approach?

C. Do you believe that the shift to a matrix organization has made it easier or more difficult to control FCC? Would you recommend a different organizational design?

13.9. The Freight Trailer Corp. (FTC) owns a fleet of trucks and trailers which it leases to companies who want to deliver their own products but who prefer to lease equipment rather than purchase it. Freight Trailer is responsible for the equipment maintenance, and if the equipment breaks down, they provide back-up equipment for the customer. Jonathan Hartman is fleet manager for the Midwest region, with responsibility for sales, customer relations, and equipment maintenance. ''One of my biggest headaches right now is the cost of maintenance and repair,'' he said. ''Up until five years ago, we contracted to have our work done by independent shops, but there were some areas in the region where it was difficult to find shops that could provide timely, competent service on a regular basis. As a result, corporate management decided to establish a repair and maintenance division (RMD) and set up a couple of repair facilities in areas where we do a lot of business. At first, it was a great convenience and solved a lot of headaches. More recently, it seems to be causing more headaches than anything else. The percentage of our repair business done at these in-house facilities has grown from 0% five years ago to 40% today, and it could well be 60% next year. The problem is that RMD is viewed as a profit center in the company, and its prices have risen to be significantly above those charged by competent independent shops. If you add to that the fact that I am required to use RMD on all repairs and maintenance done in its geographic area (which has grown) and that my maintenance cost budget has not been increased accordingly, it means my performance has not been highly rated for the last couple of years. I guess there's not much I can do about it.''

Required Write a memo to the corporate management of FTC on the above issue, including a specific recommendation for any changes you believe desirable.

13.10.

To: Suzanne Robbins, General Manager—Electronics Group
From: Jeffrey Allen, Manager—Consumer Electronics Division
Subject: Pricing of Proposed Transfer from Components Division

Within the next month, the Consumer Electronics Division (CED) must make a sourcing decision on the components for our new line of coffee makers. In keeping with corporate policy, we have requested bids on those components from our own Components Division (CompDiv) and from outside suppliers. There is a significant disparity in these bids, creating a situation which may not be beneficial to the Electronics Group.

As described in the most recent business plan, we have designed a coffeemaker that uses state-of-the-art electronic controls. These include a built-in clock, a variety of programmable controls, and a voice-synthesizer. Our market research indicates that the consumer is ready for such an appliance, and it should place us at the forefront in the application of new electronic technology to consumer products.

These controls were designed in coordination with the CompDiv product development personnel, and we expected that CompDiv would be the source of the components once production began. However, the CompDiv bid on the control was $18 per unit, significantly higher than any other bid which we received from outside suppliers. From among the dependable outside suppliers, the best price is $14 per unit. With a projected volume of 200,000 units per year, this differential has a significant impact on the profitability of CED. We inquired as to how CompDiv had arrived at its price, and they gave us the following breakdown.

Parts and materials	$ 6.00
Direct labor	6.00
Overhead	2.00
Normal profit margin	4.00
TOTAL	$18.00

Of the $18, a total of $6 represents either an allocation of overhead (which is largely fixed) or a profit on internal sales. It is common knowledge that CompDiv is currently operating at less than full capacity, so the actual cost of the components to the corporation is only $12 if they are produced by CompDiv, compared to $14 if we purchase them outside.

Our corporate policy of decentralized operations and profit responsibility gives us the freedom to choose the sources of our components, but it appears that CompDiv's pricing inhibits us from buying from them. There are benefits to purchasing from

CompDiv, but they are not worth an extra $4 per unit to CED. We would be willing to pay up to $15 per unit to CompDiv, but not more. Since this situation is an unusual one and has significant implications for the profitability of the electronics group, I believed it should be brought to your attention.

After receving the above memo, Suzanne Robbins asked you to look into the situation at the Components Division. It is true that the division has excess capacity at the present time, but the general manager pointed out that the business plan forecasted an increase in activity over the next year or two. He said, "I don't want to take on long-term business with a price that reflects the short-term availability of capacity. Any business, internal or external, ought to take into account the long-term picture."

The company has a policy of decentralization, with each division having the authority to make a wide range of decisions and being held responsible for profit performance. Therefore, the CED manager will most likely purchase the components from the outside supplier unless instructed to buy inside by the Electronics Group. Upon further investigation, you discovered that this component will play a large part in determining whether the two divisions achieve their profit targets for the year. If the price is over $15, the CED will not make its profit target, and unless its level of activity increases, the CompDiv will not make its profit target if the price is below $16.

Required

A. Write a memo to Suzanne Robbins analyzing the present situation and making a recommendation as to how to handle it.

B. Describe the current transfer price system in the Electronics Group (à la Table 13.3). What changes in the system would you recommend, if any?

13.11. Divisions *A* and *B* are trying to agree to a transfer pricing arrangement on a government contract that would produce revenues of $23,000,000. Division *A* would produce some of the components, while division *B* would be responsible for other components, assembly, and testing. There are a number of technological problems faced in both divisions, so the costs of completing the contract are not known with certainty. Without the contract, each division would have profits of $500,000. For simplicity, assume that *each* division faces the following cost possibilities:

	Probabilities of incremental costs in each division[a]		
	$0	$10,000,000	$12,000,000
Reject the contract	1	0	0
Accept contract, direct effort to cost control	0	0.50	0.50
Accept contract, do not direct effort to cost control	0	0.45	0.55

[a]Includes the opportunity cost of the productive resources required by the contract.

Assume that each division manager is risk-averse, with a preference for divisional profits reflected in the following functions: U[divisional profit] = (divisional profit)$^{1/2}$. In addition, the division managers would prefer to direct their efforts to other aspects of their operations, so that an expected utility increase of 70 is necessary to encourage them to direct efforts to cost control.

Required

A. Suppose that each division will receive one-half of the revenue, or $11,500,000. Which course of action will the division manager take?

B. Suppose that the divisions decide to treat the contract as a joint venture, with each of them taking half of the profits (or bearing half of the loss) on the contract. Which course of action will each division manager take?

REFERENCES

Abdel-Khalik, A. R., and E. Lusk. ''Transfer Pricing—A Synthesis,'' *Accounting Review*. January 1974.

Dittman, D. ''Transfer Pricing and Decentralization,'' *Management Accounting*. November 1972.

Eccles, R. ''Control with Fairness in Transfer Pricing,'' *Harvard Business Review*. November–December 1983.

Groves, T., and M. Loeb. ''Incentives and Public Inputs,'' *Journal of Public Economics*. August 1975.

Hamlen S., W. Hamlen, and J. Tschirhardt. ''The Use of Core Theory in Evaluating Joint Cost Allocation Schemes,'' *Accounting Review*. July 1977.

Hirshleifer, J. ''On the Economics of Transfer Pricing,'' *Journal of Business*, July 1956.

Jackson, B. ''Manage Risk in Industrial Pricing,'' *Harvard Business Review*. July–August 1980.

Kanodia, C. ''Risk Sharing and Transfer Price Systems Under Uncertainty,'' *Journal of Accounting Research*. Spring 1979.

Lococo, L. ''Selecting the Right Transfer Pricing Model,'' *Management Accounting*. March 1983.

Ronen, J., and G. McKinney III. ''Transfer Pricing for Divisional Autonomy,'' *Journal of Accounting Research*. Spring 1970.

Solomons, D. *Divisional Performance Measurement and Control*. Homewood, IL: Richard D. Irwin. 1968.

Vancil, R. *Decentralization: Management Ambiguity by Design*. Homewood, IL: Dow Jones-Irwin. 1975.

Verrecchia, R. ''An Analysis of Two Cost Allocation Cases,'' *Accounting Review*. July 1982.

Zimmerman, J. ''The Costs and Benefits of Cost Allocation,'' *Accounting Review*. July 1979.

Chapter 14

Allocations Over Time

There are two basic types of accounting measurement issues: allocations across activities (cost *objects*), which were discussed in Chapter 13, and allocations over time, which we explore in this chapter. *Intertemporal allocation* issues, as they are called, arise because we try to provide *timely* information about an organization's performance. If a firm raises capital on January 1, acquires resources, produces and sells goods, and then liquidates on December 31, there are no allocations needed to measure the year's performance. The owners know the amount of cash they paid in on January 1 and the amount they received on December 31, and they can assess whether the enterprise was a success. No intertemporal allocation issues arise in such a situation, for the life of the firm coincides with the performance reporting period.

Of course, few organizations are so short-lived. In fact, a fundamental tenet of financial accounting is the ''going concern'' assumption that firms should be viewed as having an infinite life, unless there is pressing evidence to the contrary. If we are to make assessments of managers' performance in a *subperiod,* then we have to arrive at some rules concerning the measurement of costs and benefits in a subperiod. In many respects, these issues are the same as those faced by policy bodies like the Financial Accounting Standards Board. How should revenue be recognized? How should depreciation be measured? Should financial reports be based on historical cost valuation or replacement cost? The distinction is that we are examining these accounting issues for *internal* decision making and performance evaluation, rather than in the context of general-purpose financial statements.

The basic difficulty in intertemporal allocations is the assignment of costs and benefits to *the period in which they occur,* and therefore to the manager who was responsible for them instead of to his or her successor(s). If we are unsuccessful in designing proper allocations over time, two types of performance evaluation problems occur. First, managers' performance will be affected by past events and decisions, increasing the uncontrollability in their performance. Second, when the costs or benefits are recognized in some future period, there is the potential for some dysfunctional decisions if the manager *discounts* these future effects differently than central management.

14.1 A MULTIPERIOD PRINCIPAL–AGENT FRAMEWORK

In previous chapters, we dealt with the single-period situation where central management has chosen a performance evaluation system (a performance measure and an incentive function) for a decentralized manager. When more than one period must be considered, there are a number of modifications that must be included. Each period's payoff outcome can depend on that period's actions and uncontrollable events as well as on those from previous periods. For instance, let $x(\cdot)$ be the two-period organizational payoff, and $x^i(\cdot)$ be the payoff in period i.

$$x(a^1, s^1, a^2, s^2) = x^1(a^1, s^1) + x^2(a^1, s^1, a^2, s^2) \tag{14.1}$$

In the start-up period, the payoff $x^1(\cdot)$ depends only on the actions and events occurring in that period, a^1 and s^1. However, the second period payoff $x^2(\cdot)$ can depend on the historical actions and events as well as on those occurring in period 2.

The central management must choose an incentive function and a performance measure for each period, thereby influencing the manager's choice of a^1 and a^2. The central management's objective in this choice would be to maximize its two-period expected payoff (less the manager's compensation), subject to the constraints that the manager choose the actions and the compensation plan be sufficient to ''meet the market'' for the manager's services.

The structure of this problem depends greatly on whether there will be the same decentralized manager for both periods. If so, then the manager's choice of a^1 will be made with recognition that it may affect the second period's performance evaluation, and the performance system can make use of this fact. However, if the manager who chooses a^1 leaves and is replaced by a manager who chooses a^2, this poses some different problems. How should the replacement manager be evaluated to encourage the second-period decisions desired by the organization? As we see in the next section, changes in the incentive function and/or the performance measure may be desirable. A second problem involves the evaluation of the original manager who chooses a^1. Basing the evaluation on $x^1(\cdot)$ alone may make it difficult to motivate the desired first-period action. We examine approaches to this problem later in the chapter.

14.2 EFFECTS OF PAST DECISIONS AND EVENTS

Suppose a manager takes over a division that has complete responsibility for a major product line. There are many ways in which the division's profitability may be influenced by decisions made by the division's previous manager. For instance, resources devoted to customer development are expensed as they are used, so the previous manager bore the costs of such development (or lack of it), and the current manager will receive some part of the benefits (or lack of them). The same holds true for product development, employee relations, maintenance, and so on—the benefits occur (at least in part) in accounting periods after the decisions were made and the costs incurred. This is a form of uncontrollability that can cause problems in trying to evaluate managers and in providing proper motivation. External events in past and present periods can influence measures of profitability. One common influence in the recent past has been inflation which, when combined with historical cost accounting, makes it difficult to evaluate the performance of managers.

In this situation, the objective of the central management is to motivate a decision a^2 that produces the most favorable set of outcomes for the organization. Using the actual outcome $x^2(a^1, s^1, a^2, s^2)$ to evaluate the manager may pose some difficulties. As we've discovered in previous chapters, better information about the manager's action produces better expected payoffs for the organization. Therefore, since a^1 and s^1 are not controllable by the manager, the performance evaluation system should try to adjust for them, perhaps based on the prior period outcome $x^1(\cdot)$. For instance, suppose that the payoff functions are

$$x^1(a^1, s^1) = a^1 + s^1 \qquad x^2(a^1, s^1, a^2, s^2) = a^1 + s^1 + a^2 + s^2 \tag{14.2}$$

Should the evaluation system take the first-period outcome into account in evaluating second-period performance by the replacement manager? The answer is clearly "yes," because it allows us to get a better idea of the second-period manager's performance. For instance, we might define the performance measure to be the change in outcomes.

$$r(a^2, s^2) = x^2(\cdot) - x^1(\cdot) = a^2 + s^2 \tag{14.3}$$

This change in performance measure leads to improved information about the action a^2.[1] Alternatively, central management could change the incentive function to take account of the information in $x^1(\cdot)$. For example, if $x^1(\cdot)$ turns out to be favorable, the second-period performance target (budget) may be increased.

Of course, the situation is seldom this simple, with $x^1(\cdot)$ providing perfect information about the effects of first-period actions and events. A more complex setting would be the following.

$$x^1(a^1, s^1) = g(a^1, s^1) \qquad x^2(a^1, s^1, a^2, s^2) = h^1(a^1, s^1) + h^2(a^2, s^2) \tag{14.4}$$

In this case, we cannot simply subtract $x^1(\cdot)$ from $x^2(\cdot)$. However, the principles described above still hold. We still want to wash out the effects of a^1 and s^1 in evaluating the replacement manager's performance, and we might do that by forming the best estimate of $h^1(a^1, s^1)$ based on $x^1(\cdot)$, and adjusting the performance evaluation by this estimate.

As an example, suppose that there are two managers who have taken over responsibility of divisions *A* and *B*. The two divisions are identical except for the fact that the previous manager in division *A* purchased its equipment, while division *B*'s previous manager rented its equipment on a year-to-year basis. Recent years have been characterized by significant levels of inflation and both equipment rentals and used equipment prices have increased significantly. Based on historical cost accounting, the new managers face the following alternatives.

[1]Would this be the case if $x^2(\cdot) = a^2 + s^2$? You should see that there is no need to take $x^1(\cdot)$ into account in evaluating the replacement manager's performance.

	Division *A*		Division *B*	
	Average effort	Extra effort	Average effort	Extra effort
Expected contribution margin	\$400,000	\$450,000	\$400,000	\$450,000
Equipment costs	125,000	125,000	200,000	200,000
Gross margin	\$275,000	\$325,000	\$200,000	\$250,000

Clearly, it is difficult to compare these managers on the basis of gross margins because of the differences in equipment costs (which are the result of past decisions and events). If a relative performance plan were used here (say, the division manager with the higher gross margin were to receive a bonus), it is unlikely that either manager would expend extra effort. Comparison of the gross margins is confounded by factors that neither manager can control.

This difficulty can be reduced in a variety of ways. First, the incentive function may be modified to take account of the individual manager's situations. For example, the performance targets might be set at \$300,000 for division *A* and \$225,000 for division *B*. Alternatively, the performance measure might be changed. One possibility would be to ignore equipment costs in evaluating the managers,[2] while another would be to use inflation-adjusted accounting reports in which equipment costs are placed on a more comparable basis. That is, if division *B*'s equipment costs reflect the current cost of acquiring the necessary machinery, etc., then using current cost in computing *A*'s gross margin could produce numbers that are more comparable. There was a gain to having purchased the equipment prior to the price increases, but there is no advantage to incorporating part of that gain into the performance evaluation of the new manager.[3]

Before turning to the evaluation of the first-period manager, there is one more case to be considered in the evaluation of a second-period, replacement manager. Up to this point, we have been considering the prior period actions and events as uncontrollables that ought to be eliminated from the replacement manager's evaluation. That view is correct when there are no interactions between a^1, s^1, and a^2 in determining the probabilities of second-period payoffs, as in the following.

$$x^2(a^1, s^1, a^2, s^2) = h^1(a^1, s^1) + h^2(a^2, s^2) \tag{14.5}$$

However, if the effects of a^2 are influenced by what happened in the first period, then the best second-period action should depend on the first-period outcomes. An example might be

$$x^2(a^1, s^1, a^2, s^2) = h^1(a^1, s^1)h^2(a^2, s^2) \tag{14.6}$$

For instance, a^1 may reflect efforts to build consumer recognition, while a^2 may reflect effort devoted to production. If the first stage is successful, then a higher value of a^2 may be preferred. Therefore, in choosing a performance evaluation system for the replacement manager, the first-period outcome should be considered. If a high level of

[2] This alternative may pose some problems if the managers control the types and amounts of equipment. They might increase the contribution margins by becoming overly capital-intensive.

[3] If divisions are not in the same line of business, then it may be easier to measure the replacement cost of some division's assets than others. If the measurement error is greater in some divisions, this "risk" should be considered in determining how the information will be used.

consumer recognition is achieved, then a large bonus might be placed on high levels of production, sales, and profits. That plan would probably have to be modified if the first-period efforts resulted in little consumer recognition. In those cases where the second-period action should be adapted to the first-period outcomes, the performance evaluation system should also be adapted to reflect the past outcomes.

14.3 INVESTMENTS AND PERFORMANCE MEASURES

The term *investment* usually refers to a firm's purchases of inventory, property, plant, and equipment, or its holding of the shares of affiliated companies. However, we use the term here in a broader context: a manager makes investment (or *disinvestment*) decisions when the decisions affect the cash flows in future accounting periods. Of course, the above-mentioned assets represent investments, but there are a variety of investments that a manager can make that do not appear as assets in conventional accounting statements. As a result, when a manager incurs a cost during the current accounting period, it may be expensed (charged against income) immediately, even though it is expected to produce benefits in the future. Examples include research and development, customer development, employee goodwill, etc.

In the two-period agency situation analyzed in the previous section, we concentrated on the performance evaluation system for a second-period, replacement manager. A different, and more difficult, problem is developing a performance evaluation system for the first-period manager whose action affects both the first-period and second-period outcomes. In order to understand some of the difficulties involved with using accounting measures to motivate investment activity, we'll first look at the effects of investment on accounting-based performance measures.

Suppose that division 1 is an ''investment center'' which has responsibility for profitability and authority to make investment as well as short-term operating decisions. The division currently projects an income of \$150,000 per year for the next three years with an asset base of \$1,000,000. The division manager has two alternative investment options—first, to invest in a self-constructed machine that will require expenditures of \$50,000 in years 1 and 2, and will produce a benefit of \$200,000 in period 3; or, to invest in a research and development project that will require expenditures of \$50,000 in years 1 and 2 and will produce a benefit of \$200,000 (with probability 1/2) or \$300,000 (with probability 1/2) in year 3. These different alternatives might be compared by computing their net present values (NPV) using the division's required rate of return (assumed to be 10%). These values are shown below.

Alternative 1—No Investment No incremental cash flows, so NPV = 0.

Alternative 2—Invest in Machine

$$\text{NPV} = \frac{-50{,}000}{1 + 0.1} + \frac{-50{,}000}{(1 + 0.1)^2} + \frac{200{,}000}{(1 + 0.1)^3}$$
$$= \$63{,}486$$

Alternative 3—Invest in R&D

Case 1: Benefits of $200,000.

$$\text{NPV} = \frac{-50{,}000}{1 + 0.1} + \frac{-50{,}000}{(1 + 0.1)^2} + \frac{200{,}000}{(1 + 0.1)^3}$$
$$= \$63{,}486$$

Case 2: Benefits of $300,000.

$$\text{NPV} = \frac{-50{,}000}{1 + 0.1} + \frac{-50{,}000}{(1 + 0.1)^2} + \frac{300{,}000}{(1 + 0.1)^3}$$
$$= \$138{,}618$$

These NPVs indicate that the rates of return on both the machine and the R&D are in excess of 10%. If 10% represents the opportunity cost of the funds that would be tied up in these investments, then these projects should be preferred by the firm, and, in general, we should want to create incentives for the manager to accept positive NPV projects such as the machine and the R&D.

The manager's preferences for the three investment alternatives will depend on two important factors. First, what measure of profitability is being used to evaluate his or her performance? Three measures are computed in Table 14.1: net income, return on assets (ROA; net income divided by beginning assets), and residual income (RI; net income, less rate of return times beginning assets). We can see that investing in the *tangible* asset has a slightly depressing effect on the ROA and RI in year 2 due to the larger asset base, but year 3's results are much better than those with no investment. (The ROA increases from 15% to 22.7%.) Investing in an *intangible* asset (R&D) causes

TABLE 14.1 EFFECTS OF INVESTMENT ALTERNATIVES ON PERFORMANCE

	Year 1	Year 2	Year 3
No investment			
Net income	$ 150,000	$ 150,000	$ 150,000
Asset base[a]	$1,000,000	$1,000,000	$1,000,000
Return on assets	15%	15%	15%
Residual income @ 10%[b]	$ 50,000	$ 50,000	$ 50,000
Investment in machine			
Net income	$ 150,000	$ 150,000	$ 250,000
Asset base	$1,000,000	$1,050,000	$1,100,000
Return on assets	15%	14.3%	22.7%
Residual income @ 10%	$ 50,000	$ 45,000	$ 140,000
Invest in R&D			
Expected net income	$ 100,000	$ 100,000	$ 400,000
Asset base	$1,000,000	$1,000,000	$1,000,000
Expected return on assets	10%	10%	40%
Expected residual income @ 10%	$ 0	$ 0	$ 300,000

[a]Asset base at the beginning of the year.

[b]Net income—10% asset base.

a decline in performance measures for the first two years as the ROA drops to 10% and the RI drops to 0. Financial accounting standards require that research and development costs be expensed as incurred, so the profitability measures decline until the benefits are realized in year 3. (If net income is used as a performance measure, the manager would prefer investing in the machine to the status quo, since there is no charge for the investment except through depreciation in year 3.)

All the other comparisons require some tradeoffs between profitability now and profitability later. As we discussed briefly in Chapter 11, a manager may have a different time horizon than the firm or the central management, and the ability to provide incentives for investment is greatly influenced by the time horizon of the manager. In the next sections, we will analyze the investment incentives problem in the two-period agency situation described above.

14.4 INCENTIVES FOR INVESTMENT

Investments require current outlays to obtain future benefits, and as we saw in the last section almost all accounting-based performance measures follow the same pattern. Investment lowers current performance measures and increases future measures. In this section, we will analyze a simple example to gain some insights into the problem of providing incentives for investment.

Suppose that a decentralized manager has three possible courses of action: (1) to exert no effort; (2) to exert effort to achieve short-term results; and (3) to exert effort to achieve short-term results *plus* to find and implement a desirable investment project. Each of these actions influences the probabilities of payoff outcomes over the next two periods. For simplicity, suppose that there are only two possible outcomes in each of the two periods, "good" and "poor." The probabilities are as follows.

	Outcome probabilities			
	Period 1		Period 2	
Action	Poor	Good	Poor	Good
1 No effort	2/3	1/3	2/3	1/3
2 Short-term effort	1/3	2/3	1/3	2/3
3 Short-term *and* long-term effort	1/2	1/2	1/12	11/12

The effect of short-term effort is to increase the probabilities of good outcomes in each period. The addition of long-term effort decreases the probability of a good outcome in the first period, but increases it in the second period. It's pretty easy to see that we would motivate action 2 over action 1 by providing a short-term bonus in each period, that is, by paying higher compensation for good outcomes to make it worth the additional effort. The compensation plan would be the same each period. (see the shaded bars in Figure 14.1.)

Motivating action 3 is more complicated, even if the manager will be there for both periods. If the manager expends both short-term and long-term efforts, then the

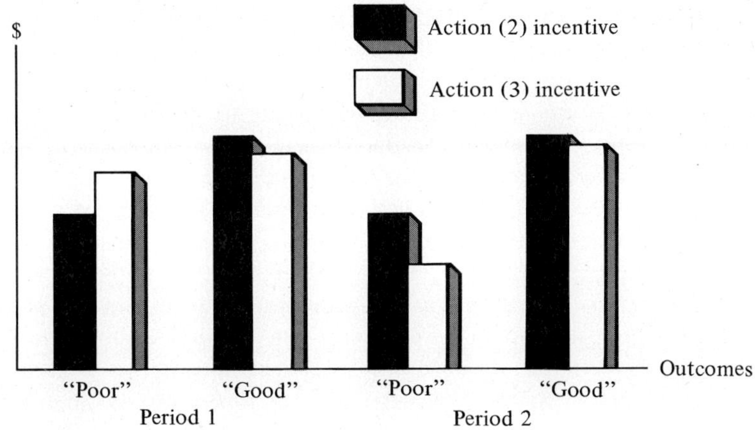

Figure 14.1

first-period results suffer and the second-period results are enhanced. This action can be motivated by placing less emphasis on the first-period results (i.e., by "flattening" the incentive function) and greater emphasis on the second-period results (i.e., by using a steeper incentive function). This incentive function is also depicted in Figure 14.1. (A numerical example appears in Appendix 14.1.)

Another approach to encouraging investment is for central management to require the investment and then not include its cost in the performance measure. For example, central management might budget $1 million for a division's research and development, and require that it be spent. Unfortunately, there may be cases where the division does not have enough good projects to use all the resources. In the example above, suppose that there is a possibility that the action 3 probabilities are the following.

	Outcome probabilities			
	Period 1		Period 2	
Action	Poor	Good	Poor	Good
3 Short-term *and* long-term effort	1/2	1/2	1/3	2/3

In this case, the central management would prefer that action 2 be taken, since the investment opportunities are not attractive. If the manager knows whether the investment opportunities are favorable or not, we might offer the manager a "menu of contracts" as discussed in Chapter 12. In the above example, we might offer the manager a choice of action 2 incentive or action 3 incentive, as depicted in Figure 14.1. If investment conditions are favorable, the manager will choose the action 3 incentive, and if the conditions are unfavorable, the action 2 incentive will be chosen.

Investment incentives become difficult if the manager will only stay for period 1. In fact, if the manager must expend more effort for action 3 than for action 2 or 1, there is no way to motivate action 3 based on period-one outcomes. If we reward "good" more than "bad," the manager will choose action 2, and if we reward "bad" more than "good" the manager will choose action 1. Under special conditions, we may be able to motivate effort toward short-term and long-term goals, but usually we will encounter the fundamental informativeness problem depicted in Figure 11.8. Short-term efforts tend to increase current performance measures, while long-term efforts tend to decrease those measures. Therefore, a manager can duplicate the high short-term/high long-term outcome probabilities by expending less effort in *both* areas.

There are three basic approaches to alleviating this type of problem. First, we might attempt to encourage managers to stay "on the job" for longer periods of time. Long-term incentive plans are one way to make it more attractive for a manager to stay with a firm rather than accepting a new position in another firm. For instance, an executive's bonus may depend on the aggregate rate of compound growth in earnings over the next five years. If the manager has been making progress toward the goal, it is unlikely that he or she will bail out after three or four years, for then he or she would lose the return on the past years' efforts. If we can expect the manager to stay with the firm for an extended period of time, then many of the problems we have discussed become less severe.

Since the early 1970s, a number of firms have adopted long-term performance plans for their executives. These plans are distinguished from short-term bonuses by the length of the evaluation period (3 to 6 years) and by the lack of "vesting." If the executive leaves before the end of the award period, he or she receives no payment under the plan. The plans usually set goals based on accounting measures, and the maximum award is determined in terms of *performance shares* or *performance units*. In a performance share plan, the award will be the number of performance shares earned times the share price at the time of the award. A performance unit plan is similar, except that the value of a unit is predetermined and not influenced by the share price. An example of a long-term plan appears in Table 14.2. If Emerson Electric achieved 12% growth in earnings per share (EPS) over the five years from 1976 to 1981, the executives received 100% of the performance shares. If the growth was less than 11%, they received none. In addition, if an executive left the firm in 1980, he or she would receive no award under the plan, even if the EPS growth had been far in excess of 12%.

The objective of these plans is to encourage the managers to adopt a longer time horizon in making decisions, but there are also some shortcomings. First, the nonvesting

TABLE 14.2 EMERSON ELECTRIC (1977 FISCAL YEAR ADOPTION)

Type of plan:	Performance share
Award period:	5 years
Performance measure:	Earnings per share (EPS)

	EPS 1981	Percentage of shares "earned out"
(1976 EPS = $2.05)	> $3.60	100
	< $3.60, but ≥ $3.55	70
	< $3.55, but ≥ $3.48	50
	< $3.48	0
Form of payment	20 percent cash and 80 percent common stock	

provision limits the manager's mobility, and this may produce some costs for the firm. In addition, the plans do not provide any incentives for investments (such as R&D) which may pay off in 10 or 15 years. Also, as one approaches the end of a plan period, the long-term plan begins to look like a short-term plan. To alleviate this problem, new long-term plans are usually introduced periodically. A recent study[4] compared firms adopting long-term performance plans to similar firms with no such plans and found that the adopting firms experienced significantly higher investment growth and security return around the time of adoption.

A second alternative would be to base more of the manager's compensation on the performance of the firm's share price. There is considerable evidence that the firm's security price reflects all publicly available information quickly and without bias. In other words, the securities markets are not fooled by accounting reports, and a manager who underinvests to increase accounting profitability will find the firm's share price (and his or her compensation) declining.[5] On the other hand, if the market knows that the manager has accepted an investment with a net present value of $1 million, the stock price should reflect this action. There are some shortcomings to this approach, since the share price will also reflect events which are beyond management's control, and a division manager may perceive that there is little relationship between his or her decisions and the stock price, particularly if there are many divisions.

As a result, it may be appropriate to use stock-based incentives heavily for only the top management of the firm. To reduce the risk associated with stock incentives, a relative performance measurement plan might be used. If R_t is the firm's stock return in period t and M_t is the market return over the same period, the following model is an often-used description of the behavior of security prices.

$$R_t = \alpha + \beta M_t + \varepsilon_t \tag{14.7}$$

The βM_t term reflects the *common factors* which influence this firm and others in the market. The residual ε_t reflects all other factors, including management performance. Using data from previous periods, we might estimate $\hat{\alpha}$ and $\hat{\beta}$ and use the following performance statistic.

$$\hat{\varepsilon}_t = R_t - \hat{\alpha} - \hat{\beta} M_t \tag{14.8}$$

The variance of $\hat{\varepsilon}_t$ will be less than that of R_t, thereby reducing the risk faced by the manager in much the same way as described in Appendix 11.2.

There are some potential problems with this approach. For instance, the estimate of $\hat{\alpha}$ will incorporate the manager's effectiveness in prior periods, so we may end up setting continually more difficult targets. Or, this type of plan might encourage the manager to change his or her investment strategies. By diversifying and becoming "like the market," the manager can reduce the risk of $\hat{\varepsilon}_t$. But the shareholders might prefer a different risk–return strategy (e.g., a high risk–high expected return project that is not at all correlated with the market).

Finally, the accounting system may look to some external, objective source to get estimates of economic value. That is, there are other alternatives besides historical cost

[4]Larcker (1983).

[5]Fama (1970); Dyckman, Downes, and Magee (1975).

and using the manager's cash flow estimates. For instance, if there is a market for the used assets, the price ought to reflect that market's assessments of the future benefits that come from owning the asset. The change in price could be used as an estimate of the depreciation over a period of time, and this estimate could be used in conjunction with the other measures that we have discussed. One shortcoming of this approach is that the change in price of a used asset will reflect the service potential used up *and* any changes in the price level. It may be desirable to try to separate these two factors in assessing the manager's performance, as we discussed in a previous section.

14.5 OTHER CONTROLS

There are other controls that limit the degree of underinvestment or overinvestment a manager attempts. First, unfavorable reports affect a manager's reputation and his or her "human capital." If a manager leaves firms immediately prior to poor performance, boards of directors or central managements are likely to infer that the manager is responsible for poor subsequent performance. Therefore, a manager who is concerned with reputation, and the opportunities that will be affected by it, ought to be less likely to engage in the short-run maximizing that we have described.

Finally, central management can take a more active role in long-term planning for its decentralized units.[6] By requiring that long-term plans be submitted, then evaluating them for feasibility and desirability, and monitoring the progress toward achieving the plan, central management can encourage decentralized managers to exercise care in planning for the firm's future. This would constitute a more limited decentralization, with greater central management involvement in the operations of decentralized units, but it may be an effective way to overcome the difficulties in measuring the future period effects of managers' decisions. A critical factor in the success of this approach is a separation of operating results from investment results. Without this separation, a manager might be motivated to reduce investment so as to improve his or her overall performance. In addition to the separate accounting reports, the manager's investment performance must be evaluated by comparing actual results to *benchmarks* that have been set up. This requires that the planning process result in a *timetable* of critical events or outputs of the investment process.

14.6 SUMMARY

There are many accounting conventions that determine the allocation of income to different periods—revenue recognition, matching, conservatism, historical cost, and so on. For external reporting, these choices are made so as to provide useful information to investors and creditors. But within the firm, there are many managers whose decisions are affected by these accounting conventions. In this chapter, we have explored two different cases where these allocations produce performance evaluation problems

[6]Of course, care must be taken to insure that central management has the appropriate long-term incentives.

When a manager takes over responsibility for an existing operation, the accounting-based performance measures will be affected by decisions and events from previous periods. While it may be desirable for the manager to adapt his or her decision making to the situation created by these past occurrences, in general they represent a source of *uncontrollable factors* that should have little impact on the replacement manager's performance evaluation. The effect of prior periods can be reduced by altering the incentive function (e.g., basing it on the *change* in performance) or by changing the performance measure (e.g., using replacement cost accounting).

Accounting conventions can also cause a disincentive for investment, since investment causes most accounting-based performance measures to decline in the short-run. If the manager expects to remain in the same position for the life of the investment, then investment can be encouraged by placing less emphasis (e.g., bonus) on short-term results, and greater emphasis on long-term results. However, if the manager only expects to be in the position for the short-term and he or she cannot be held accountable for future results, it can be very difficult to encourage investment. In this chapter, we have looked at some of the methods that might be used to encourage such managers to make investments which are beneficial to the organization. Essentially, these methods can be broken into three classifications. Some techniques try to defer recognition of the investment cost until the benefits occur, while others speed up the recognition of benefits so that it coincides with the costs (e.g., through stock-based incentives). A third approach is to use long-term incentives to encourage the manager to remain with the firm for a longer period of time. All of these attempts to achieve better matching of costs and benefits—by deferring costs or by speeding up the recognition of benefits or by lengthening the measurement period. If this matching is successful, then the controllability and incentive problems described above can be reduced.

APPENDIX 14.1: A Long-Term Incentive Example

The purpose of this appendix is to further explore the investment incentive example depicted in the chapter. The outcome probabilities remain the same, but we add the assumptions that the central management is risk-neutral and that the decentralized manager is risk-averse and effort-averse. More specifically, we'll assume that the manager's utility for compensation and effort is the following.

$$\begin{aligned} U_m &= (\text{Compensation})^{1/2} - \text{effort aversion} \\ &= (C)^{1/2} - V \end{aligned}$$

If V_i is the effort disutility for action i, and if s_j^k is the compensation for outcome j in period k, then we can motivate action 3 if the following relationships hold.

$$1/2(s_1^1)^{1/2} + 1/2(s_2^1)^{1/2} + 1/12(s_1^2)^{1/2} + 11/12(s_2^2)^{1/2} - V_3 \geq 2/3(s_1^1)^{1/2} + 1/3(s_2^1)^{1/2} + 2/3(s_1^2)^{1/2} + 1/3(s_2^2)^{1/2} - V_1 \quad \text{(A14.1)}$$

$$1/2(s_1^1)^{1/2} + 1/2(s_2^1)^{1/2} + 1/12(s_1^2)^{1/2} + 11/12(s_2^2)^{1/2} - V_3 \geq 1/3(s_1^1)^{1/2} + 2/3(s_2^1)^{1/2} + 1/3(s_1^2)^{1/2} + 2/3(s_2^2)^{1/2} - V_2 \quad \text{(A14.2)}$$

$$1/2(s_1^1)^{1/2} + 1/2(s_2^1)^{1/2} + 1/12(s_1^2)^{1/2} + 11/12(s_2^2)^{1/2} - V_3 \geq \underline{U} \quad \text{(A14.3)}$$

Equation (A14.1) states that action 3 will be preferred to action 1 and equation (A14.2) states that action 3 will be preferred to action 2. Finally, equation (A14.3) states that the expected utility of action 3 will meet the manager's minimum expected utility. If we set $V_1 = 0$, $V_2 = 2$, $V_3 = 3$, and $\underline{U} = 10$, we can find a compensation schedule, (s_1^1, s_2^1, s_1^2, and s_2^2) that will satisfy these constraints and at the same time minimize the expected compensation that central management must pay. The same procedure can be followed to find a compensation plan that will motivate action 2—short-term effort only. As depicted in Figure 14.1, motivation of investment requires less emphasis on period 1 results and greater emphasis on period 2 results.

Outcome	Compensation to motivate action 3	Compensation to motivate action 2
Period 1: "Poor"	39.45	16.00
Period 1: "Good"	45.15	49.00
Period 2: "Poor"	3.61	16.00
Period 2: "Good"	47.86	49.00

Since the example is a simplified one, the specific numbers are not important, but the patterns would be expected to hold over a wide range of similar situations. Other analyses might expand the model to consider more complex situations. For instance, a three-period analysis where investments can be made in periods 1 and 2 would enable us to examine incentives in a start-up period, a continuing investment period, and a harvesting period. Alternatively, we could make use of *both* periods' outcomes in determining compensation in period 2. For instance, if the manager chooses action 3, there is almost a 50 percent (11/24) probability that the sequence of outcomes will be "poor-good" versus a 2/9 probability for each of the other actions. Therefore, the sequence "poor-good" is more indicative of action 3 than of actions 1 and 2, and should receive a higher compensation. On the other hand, action 3 produces only a 1/24 chance of the sequence "poor-poor," so this should receive a rather low compensation. In general, it is valuable to consider the *sequence* of outcomes in evaluating the manager's performance.

PROBLEMS

14.1. "Good times have brought commensurate rewards to E. Z. Rider, Chairman, and his fellow officers of ABC Corp. who have employment contracts with incentive-compensation clauses. In fiscal 1984, ended Jan. 31, for instance, Mr. Rider's total compensation from the company amounted to $728,673, compared with $426,118 a year earlier.

"Mr. Rider's contract, effective as of Nov. 20, 1982, is for five years, and the principal clause provides for an annual salary of $375,000, plus incentive compensation at the rate of 1% of ABC's net earnings in excess of $20 million up to a maximum of $100 million.

"In fiscal 1984, ABC had net income of $51.5 million, or $6.14 a share, after a $30.1 million gain on debenture exchanges. In the year prior, ABC's net was $26.5 million, or $2.95 a share, after a debenture exchange gain of only $2.3 million and a tax-loss carry-forward of $4.8 million."

Required

A. Describe Mr. Rider's incentive plan with a graph.

B. Describe two general shortcomings of this sort of system from a shareholder's point of view. The bond exchange transaction referred to above works something like this.

Suppose a company issues $1 million of 6% bonds when the market rate is 6%. The bonds will appear as a liability on the balance sheet with a book value of $1 million. Now, if the market interest rate increases to 8%, due to inflation, the market value of the bonds will fall, say, to $850,000. But the book value will remain at $1 million. The company could exchange $850,000 worth of new 8% bonds for the curently outstanding bonds, with the following accounting result.

Dr. old bonds	$1,000,000	
Cr. new bonds		$850,000
Cr. *Gain*		$150,000

The bond exchange would increase the firm's income by $150,000, but this income effect occurs when the bonds are exchanged, not when the interest rates change.

C. Do you feel that the total actual compensation reflects the firm's *current performance?* Why?

D. Suggest one alternative performance evaluation system and discuss its advantages and disadvantages relative to the current system.

14.2. Andrew Baker has recently been put in charge of the control and evaluation function in the Controller's Department. In this position he is responsible for the periodic reporting of variances and other performance measures. Baker also has the responsibility of recommending changes in the measurement and reporting system which will improve motivation and coordination.

The firm is a large manufacturer, with corporate headquarters in Chicago and eighteen production facilities geographically dispersed throughout the country. Each of the eighteen plants operates in its own market, and the plant managers are given considerable autonomy and profit responsibility. Each quarter an income statement and balance sheet is produced for each plant, and is augmented by variances and ratios. The most important factor in the plant manager's performance evaluation is the return on investment (ROI) ratio, which is measured using conventional accounting methods (historical cost, full cost overhead allocation, etc.)

$$\text{ROI} = \frac{\text{Net income for the period}}{\text{Total assets at the beginning of the period}}$$

Baker recognizes the problems inherent in an ROI system like this, but he's not sure what to do about it. In order to get a handle on the problem, he makes up four "representative" investment opportunities as follows.

Project	Initial outlay	Year 1	2	3	4	Net present value @ 10%
1	($10,000)	$13,000				$1,818
2	($15,000)	$17,000				$ 455
3	($30,000)	$19,000	$19,000			$2,975
4	($40,000)	$13,500	$13,500	$13,500	$13,500	$2,793
					TOTAL	$8,041

The firm has a required rate of return of 10%, so the *best* action for the firm would be to accept all four opportunities with an incremental net present value of $8,041.

Required

A. Assume a manager has a one-year time horizon, a current ROI of 20%, and acts to maximize his ROI. What projects will be accepted, and what is the resulting increment in the firm's net present value?

B. Suppose the same manager were evaluated with a residual income measure, using 10% as the required rate of return. What projects will be accepted, and what is the resulting increment in the firm's net present value?

C. Baker is tempted to say that the difference between $8,041 and the answer to A is the opportunity loss due to the present decentralization system. Is that correct? Could the present system be modified to make decentralization more desirable?

14.3. Katie Crihfield has been assigned the problem of developing an evaluation plan for the Director of Research and Development (R&D). The R&D Director makes decisions that affect the level of R&D activity, the success probability of the projects being implemented, and the level of cost efficiency in the R&D department. Like most people engaged in this sort of activity, the R&D Director enjoys the scientific challenges involved in his department's work, and this enthusiasm sometimes leads to significant cost overruns on projects. The objective of the evaluation system that Katie Crihfield is to develop is to encourage the R&D Director to keep the level of activity and probabilities for future success high, but to encourage attention to cost control at the same time.

At the time of evaluation there are usually no measures of the benefits from R&D activity that can be used to evaluate the Director. Cost data is available, but costs are not a good measure of the Director's performance in the two areas defined above. (Activity tends to increase costs, while attention to cost control tends to decrease costs.) For this problem, the following actions and probabilities have been identified. (The cost outcomes are given in increasing order, $C_1 < C_2 < C_3$.) The R&D Director's personal preferences are reflected in the last column.

Action	Cost outcome probabilities C_1	C_2	C_3	Effort disutility
1 Few projects, low cost control	2/3	1/3	0	5
2 Many projects, low cost control	0	1/3	2/3	0
3 Many projects, high cost control	1/3	1/3	1/3	10

In the absence of any evaluation or incentives, the Director's natural inclination would be to choose action 2. In setting up an evaluation based on costs, you may assume that the R&D Director's preferences are reflected in the following function.

$$U(\text{compensation}, \text{effort}) = (\text{compensation})^{1/2} - \text{effort disutility}$$

If the R&D Director were given free reign to choose action 2, he would have to be paid $60,000 to meet the amounts that the firm's competitors would be willing to pay him.

Required

A. Develop a compensation/bonus scheme that will induce the R&D Director to choose action 2. What is the expected compensation that must be paid?

B. Can you do the same as in A for action 3.

C. Suppose the action 3 probabilities of (1/3, 1/3, 1/3) were replaced by (1/6, 2/3, 1/6). Can you find an evaluation scheme that will encourage action 3? Why does this differ from B above?

D. What measures of benefits might be used in this situation? How would they help in motivating the R&D Director to choose a high level of activity *and* to exercise cost control?

14.4. Hapless Industries is a large multinational, diversified corporation, where managers are moved from one job to another with some regularity. A continuing problem for the company is the fact that the development and implementation of long-term, strategic plans frequently suffers from a lack of managerial attention. As an example, consider the following three action choices which have an impact on a division's profitability for two periods.

	Period 1		Period 2		
	Low profits	High profits	Low profits	High profits	Effort disutility
Low effort on short- and long-term	3/4	1/4	1/2	1/2	0
High effort on short-term only	1/4	3/4	1/2	1/2	2
High effort on short- and long term	1/2	1/2	1/8	7/8	3

The manager's choice of action will be reflected by the maximization of the expected value of the following utility function:

$$U(\text{compensation, effort}) = (\text{compensation})^{1/2} - \text{effort disutility}$$

In each period, the manager could receive a salary of \$50,000 in a position that required high effort on short-term activities only.

Required

A. If the manager will only remain in this position for the first period, design an incentive function to encourage him to choose the "short-term effort only" action.

B. If the manager will only remain in this position for the first period, try to design an incentive function to encourage him to choose the "short-term and long-term effort" action.

C. Suppose that central management could receive some other information about the manager's long-term efforts (e.g., a report on R&D costs). How would this help to motivate high effort on both short- and long-term activities?

D. Suppose that the manager expected to stay for both periods. Can you develop an incentive scheme that would motivate high effort on both short- and long-term activities? Do you know of any such incentive arrangements in practice? What types of factors might encourage the manager to stay for the second period?

14.5. It is seldom the case that central management knows the investment opportunities faced by a decentralized manager. Such is the case in Hapless Industries described in problem

14.4. Suppose that the outcome probabilities described in that problem reflect a favorable investment climate, which the manager *may* face. Or, it may be that the manager faces an unfavorable investment climate, in which case central management would want to discourage investment. The outcome probabilities are given below. All other information about the manager's risk and effort preferences and alternative employment opportunities are the same as in problem 14.4.

FAVORABLE INVESTMENT CONDITIONS

	Period 1		Period 2		
	Low profits	High profits	Low profits	High profits	Effort disutility
Low effort on short- and long-term	3/4	1/4	1/2	1/2	0
High effort on short-term only	1/4	3/4	1/2	1/2	2
High effort on short- and long term	1/2	1/2	1/8	7/8	3

UNFAVORABLE INVESTMENT CONDITIONS

	Period 1		Period 2		
	Low profits	High profits	Low profits	High profits	Effort disutility
Low effort on short- and long-term	3/4	1/4	1/2	1/2	0
High effort on short-term only	1/4	3/4	1/2	1/2	2
High effort on short- and long term	1/2	1/2	3/8	5/8	3

Required

A. Suppose that the manager expected to stay for both periods. Can you develop an incentive scheme that would motivate high effort on both short- and long-term activities under the favorable environment *and* high effort on only short-term activities under the unfavorable environment?

B. When the manager has better information about the investment opportunities, is it still valuable to obtain separate information about the manager's long-term efforts (e.g., a report on R&D expenditures)? How would you use that information?

14.6. The Commercial Credit Department of the Maynard Trust Company is made up of approximately 25 Commercial Loan Officers (CLOs). Each CLO has responsibility for developing and maintaining relationships with customers in one or two industries. For established customers, they help plan financing needs, structure loan agreements, and perform the financial analysis that enables the bank to keep informed of the credit-worthiness of its customers. In addition, the CLOs are expected to generate new business in their assigned industries. To do this, they identify potential borrowers in the industry, evaluate their financial condition, make an estimate of their financing needs, and then try to sell the company on borrowing from the Maynard Trust. The mix of short-term and long-term lending depends on the industry, but overall the mix is about 40% short-term (lines of credit, maturities of less than 1 year) and 60% long-term (average maturity of approximately 4 years).

Most CLOs have a Master's degree in business management when they take the position. It's often the case that a CLO will be assigned to a given industry for only a couple of years. After that, they are reassigned to another industry, promoted, or some are hired to take finance staff positions by their customer companies. Therefore, it is common for a CLO to be assigned to an industry with an existing set of customers and loan portfolio.

CLO performance is measured on a variety of dimensions, but a critical element in the evaluation is the performance of his or her loan portfolio. Portfolio performance is measured as the amount loaned to customers times the difference between the interest rate charged to customers and the Commercial Credit Department's cost of funds. In the event a loan is defaulted, the loss is charged to the CLO's portfolio performance. In addition to this financial measure of performance, there are a number of operating activities that are monitored. For instance, the CLO is expected to make at least two contacts with potential new customers every month, and keep the files of existing customers up-to-date.

Required

A. For a CLO who has just been assigned to an industry, make a list of the ways in which his or her performance may be affected by the actions of the previous CLO or by other factors that cannot be controlled. How will these affect the decisions of the new CLO?

B. How would you evaluate CLO performance to minimize the effects of these uncontrollable factors? How much weight would you place on the portfolio's financial performance versus the operating measures?

14.7. One of the major issues in intertemporal allocations is the decision to capitalize, or expense, a cost. The *matching* principle of accrual accounting would argue for recognizing an asset when future benefits have been acquired, providing for a matching of costs with the benefits they produce. On the other hand, the conservatism convention in financial accounting would lead to the immediate expensing of costs which produce no benefits or benefits of uncertain timing and amount. A major example of the conflict between these two principles was the controversy over accounting for oil and gas exploration in the late 1970s.

When a company explores for oil and gas, it does not expect to find a commercially successful property every time. In fact, it is much more common to find dry holes than commercially viable wells. When a company spends $2 million on each of 10 explorations, it may find 9 dry holes and one producing well with expected revenues of $40 million. Under the *successful efforts* method of accounting, the $18 million spent on dry holes would be expensed immediately, and the $2 million spent on the producing well would be capitalized and matched against the $40 million revenues when they are realized. Under the *full cost* method, the $18 million spent on dry holes is considered a normal cost of finding the one producing property, and the entire $20 million would be capitalized and matched against the revenues.

Required

A. Assume that it costs $2 million to explore a propery in year 1, that a successful well will produce $40 million in revenues (realized in years 2 and 3), and that the probability of a well being successful is 1/10. Fill in the following graphs for the *full cost* method, assuming that your company is just starting up in year 1.

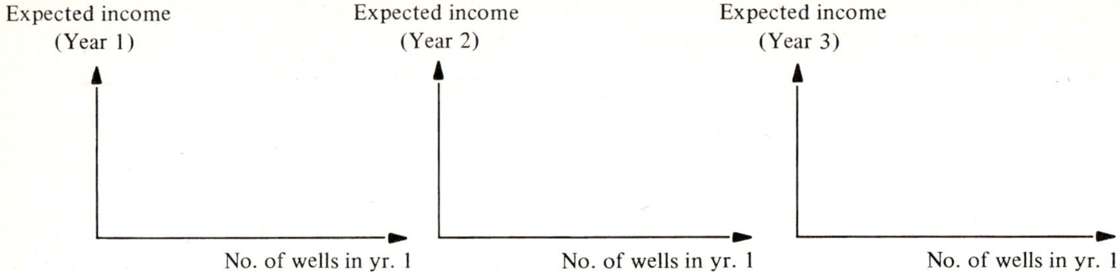

B. Same as part A, but use the *successful efforts* method.

C. Would it be easier to motivate management to devote efforts to increased exploration using the full cost or successful efforts method? Why? Would your answer be the same if the company already had a set of producing wells?

14.8. "One of our biggest headaches is the annual budget setting for the salesforce. We review the past year's performance and the economic forecasts for the coming year before setting a tentative sales target. Then the sales people review the target and respond with a revised target. There's a little negotiating, and we arrive at a budget for the year. It's an important number for the salesforce because their annual bonuses are computed based on the budget. The exact relationship is shown in the graph below.

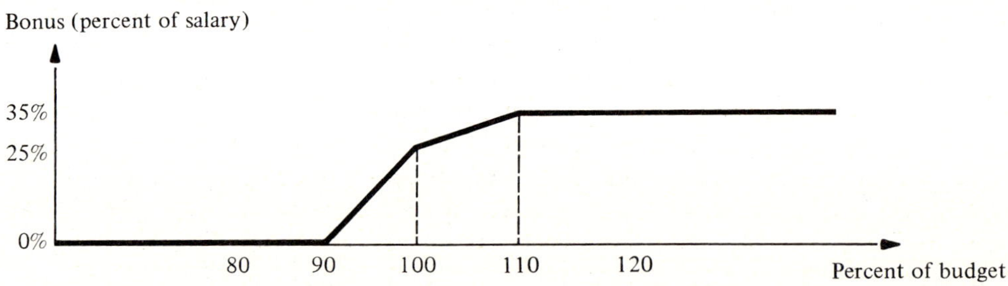

"As you can see, it's important that the budget be set carefully if the salesforce is to be motivated. The problem that we have at present is in the use of prior years' results in setting the preliminary target. The company president almost never accepts a budget that is lower than the past year's actual results, so we usually start out with a target that is somewhat higher than the latest projection for the prior year's sales.

"The problem that we're having is twofold. First, I believe that there are a number of cases where salespeople have been assured of their bonus, say, in November, and then have coasted for the remainder of the year. In fact, there are rumors that some of them have gone so far as to discourage sales in this period, since it wouldn't increase their bonus and it would increase their target for the next year. That sort of behavior is detrimental to the organization on a number of levels. Most notably, it doesn't make us look very well managed to our customers. The second problem has to do with customer development. By setting challenging budgets for the sales personnel, we encourage them to scurry after immediate sales prospects, rather than giving them the opportunity to develop a more long-term approach to their jobs. The salesforce can be an early warning system to alert us to change in customer needs, but I don't think we can simply put more slack in the sales budgets. There are a few sales persons that will use the opportunity to develop future prospects, but it would be naive to think that the majority of them would do so."

Required There are too many salespersons to conduct an in-depth study of each one's territory. How should the prior years' results be used in setting the current year's budget?

Would you recommend a change in the way the bonus is calculated? Try to develop a combination that would both encourage customer development and discourage end-of-year coasting.

14.9. The following information was taken from the proxy statement of Monolithic Industries.

"The executive incentive system administered by the Compensation Committee of the Board of Directors consists of (a) a bonus plan, (b) a performance unit plan, (c) a stock option plan, and (d) grants of restricted stock. Incentive payments under the Company's bonus plan are made annually on the basis of a comparison of managerial performance with predetermined goals. The total amounts of payments under the bonus plan may not be greater than 3% of the amount by which the Company's net income exceeds 8% of common shareholders' equity. In addition, the Compensation Committee grants performance units to executives who are in a position to influence the long-term performance of the Company. Each performance unit has a potential value of $1,000, and will be earned if the Company's performance meets or exceeds the four-year goals set by the Compensation Committee. The current plan provides for a 100% payout on performance units if the four-year earnings per share growth is 12% or greater. If an executive leaves the company, he or she forfeits the performance units, regardless of progress made in the current plan. Stock options are granted by the Compensation Committee to recognize outstanding performance, with the exercise price at least equal to the current market price. Finally, the Compensation Committee makes contingent grants of the Company's stock which are earned if an executive remains in the Company's employ for a specified period (usually five years) or until retirement. These grants are not tied to the attainment of predetermined corporate or individual performance goals."

Required For each of the components of the incentive plan described above, discuss its effect on management's incentives for (i) short-term performance; (ii) long-term performance; (iii) risk-taking.

14.10. "We would like to use stock-based incentives to motivate long-term performance for our upper-level management," says Rosemond Jones, "but the stock price depends on so many factors that are beyond their control. Therefore, it's unlikely to provide much in the way of motivation unless we can find some way to reduce the variability that management cannot control."

Information on the annual stock returns for Bay & Southern Corporation, a diversified conglomerate, are given below, along with a measure of general market returns. At the present time, the stock price of Bay & Southern is $20.00 per share, and there are 70 million shares outstanding.

Year	Bay & Southern return	Average market return
1971	2.5%	11.7%
1972	19.3%	10.5%
1973	−29.5%	−12.4%
1974	−31.9%	−29.9%
1975	28.3%	31.9%
1976	30.1%	18.4%
1977	−1.6%	−12.3%
1978	−5.6%	2.4%
1979	0.9%	12.9%
1980	26.8%	27.6%
1981	−33.5%	−11.2%
1982	19.5%	14.9%

Required

A. Suppose that an executive of Bay & Southern were given 1,000 shares of stock to serve as a long-term incentive. Estimate the standard deviation of the change in stock value over the next year. If the executive could, by concentrating on long-term performance, increase the expected end-of-year share price by $1, would he or she be motivated to do so?

B. Instead of giving 1,000 shares of normal stock, develop a stocklike instrument that starts with the same value as 1,000 shares of normal stock, but does not depend on general market movements. Estimate the standard deviation of the change in the value of this instrument over the next year. Would the executive be more or less motivated to concentrate on long-term performance?

14.11. Photo Guild, Inc. operates a mail-based business in photographic publications (principally books). Subscribers to the company's service receive a monthly brochure describing the currently available publications which are usually offered at prices about 10% below those in retail book stores. If the subscriber wants to purchase an offered publication, he or she returns a post card and the book (with invoice) is shipped from Photo Guild's warehouse.

In order to attract subscribers, it is common for this type of company to offer initial books at a substantial discount and Photo Guild is no exception. For $1.00 (plus a shipping charge), new subscribers may choose any four publications from a list of offerings. Photo Guild's costs for these publications can range from $18 to $32, depending on the subscriber's selection. In return, the new subscriber agrees to purchase a minimum of four books in the next year. The average subscriber remains a member of Photo Guild for 24 months, and during that time he or she will order $175 worth of publications, on average. (Photo Guild's cost of the publications will be about 60% of the price paid by the subscriber.) Most of these purchases will be between the fourth and fourteenth months of membership.

Organizationally, Photo Guild has two divisions. The operations division handles the purchasing, warehousing, shipping, and billing operations, while the sales division is responsible for attracting new subscribers and sales to existing subscribers. Both divisions are treated as profit centers, with the sales division paying a transfer price (cost plus 15%) to the operations division for the publications and services used. Profit targets are set for each division, and the division managers' annual bonuses are determined, in large part, by their profit performance.

The company has been facing increasing competition, so the top management of Photo Guild has set some rigorous sales and profit targets for the current year. Extensive campaigns to attract new subscribers have been, and continue to be, implemented. The president has called you in as an outside consultant to find a way to deal with a problem that he feels jeopardizes the success of the current program. He describes the problem as follows.

"In order for us to survive in this business, it's necessary for everyone to work together in meeting the subscriber's needs. We've got to have new subscribers who will stay subscribers. That means we've got to have attractive publications on a continuing basis, we must provide good service, and most importantly, we must reach the customer in the first place. We have a problem with the profitability measure in the sales division that's best explained by an example. Suppose that a new subscriber chooses four books costing the company $25. That means the sales division has revenue of $1.00, but a cost of $28.75 ($25 plus %15), so they lose $27.75 on that new customer. Of course, we make up that loss if the customer buys enough books in the future, but in the short-term, the sales division's profitability suffers. I can see that the division manager is going to be a little ambivalent about the big push for new subscribers if it hurts his profitability. I'm sure that he could get other job offers if he wanted them—it's a mobile business—so I want to minimize the conflicts if that's possible.

Required

A. Analyze the effects of the current accounting system on the profitability of the sales division. What effect do you think this will have on the division manager's decision making?

B. Develop a system of performance measurement/incentive function that will reduce the conflicting incentives for the manager of the sales division.

14.12. As the Assistant Controller, you have been asked to help in a disagreement between the manager of the consumer division, Laura Brown, and the staff of the personnel department who administer the executive compensation system. The problem revolves around the replacement of a major piece of equipment in the consumer division, which resulted in a gain in the accounting reports. Brown believes that the gain should be included in the computation of her yearly bonus, while the personnel department believes that it should be excluded.

In conversation with you, Laura Brown has expressed the following. ''Look, the money is not the most important thing. Including the gain would give me an extra $4,000 or so, but the company has done well by me, so it's not like I really need the money. But if they don't count the gain, it makes it look like I made a bad decision, and that's not the case. We purchased the old equipment six years ago for $1.2 million, and it's worked just fine. But a new model has been introduced that has increased flexibility to support our expanding product line, and it's more fuel efficient. The old equipment still had five years of good service left, but we didn't need both, so we sold it. It had been depreciated to a book value of about $500,000, but with the inflation we've had its market value was $700,000. I wouldn't say that we planned on that amount of gain, but there's no question that we considered changing price levels when we purchased it six years ago. We also considered these numbers in doing a discounted cash flow analysis for the new equipment, and I've forecasted a net present value of $250,000 over the life of the new equipment. In coming up with that forecast and in making the decision, I tried to be careful to consider possible changes in future prices, but the personnel department wants to tell me that's not part of my job. I can just see me telling my boss that it's not my problem if profits are down because raw material prices are up and they're not part of my job. I wouldn't have a job with *any* parts after that!''

In the personnel department, Peter Gwinn is in charge of the administration of executive compensation. In response to your inquiries, he relates the following. ''I'm not going to argue that anticipating price changes isn't a part of Laura's job. It's not easy to be successful at it, but she is held responsible for it, to a degree. But the calculation of the gain on the equipment sale is too dependent on some arbitrary accounting rules to be used in assessing performance. In particular, the depreciation schedule had been accelerated because of the conservatism of our accountants. The old equipment had an expected life of 14 to 15 years, but they depreciated it over 10 years, and that had a lot to do with the size of the gain. Moreover, there's no way that we can factor the forecasted net present value of $250,000 into the performance evaluation. It's too speculative at this point. Therefore, I don't think we should give her credit for the gain or replacement—it's based on inflation and the depreciation schedule, neither of which she can control.''

The controller has asked you to write up a summary for him, outlining the possible courses of actions with the advantages and disadvantages of each. He says, ''The $4,000 bonus is not enough to worry about. I want to make sure that managers have incentives to do what's best for the company, and that their compensation does not depend too much on things which they can't control.''

Required Write a report for the Controller. Include a recommendation.

REFERENCES

Dearden, J. ''The Case Against ROI Control,'' *Harvard Business Review*. May–June 1967.

Dyckman, T., D. Downes, and R. Magee. *Efficient Capital Markets and Accounting: A Critical Analysis,* Englewood Cliffs, NJ: Prentice-Hall. 1975.

Fama, E. ''Efficient Capital Markets: A Review of Theory and Empirical Evidence,'' *Journal of Finance*. May 1970.

Larcker, D. ''The Association between Performance Plan Adoption and Corporate Capital Investment,'' *Journal of Accounting and Economics*. April 1983.

Rappaport, A. ''Executive Incentives vs. Corporate Growth,'' *Harvard Business Review*. July–August 1978.

Sale, J. ''The Control of Capital Investment in Divisionalized Companies,'' *Management Accounting*. October 1982.

Solomon, E. ''Return on Investment: The Relation of Book Yield to True Yield,'' in R. Jaedicke, Y. Ijiri, and O. Nielson, Eds., *Research in Accounting Measurement,* Chicago, IL: American Accounting Association. 1966.

Stata, R., and M. Maidique. ''Bonus System for Balanced Strategy,'' *Harvard Business Review*. November–December 1980.

Ubelhart, M. ''A New Look at Executive Compensation Plans,'' *Cashflow*. May 1981.

Appendix

Computer Programs

Modern managerial accounting techniques have made increasing use of computing power to produce information for decision making. In fact, the practical application of many of the concepts and models in this text depends on the availability of computational power. Commercial software products can be used to analyze a variety of managerial accounting problems on microcomputers and on time-shared systems. For instance, the decision theory analysis of managerial choices described in Chapters 2 and 3 can be readily entered into one of the many electronic spreadsheet programs, with the cell values defined as the profits or costs that result from a combination of course of action and state of nature. By including the probabilities of the states, the expected payoff for each course of action can be computed, as well as the expected payoff with perfect information (and therefore, the EVPI).

While they are less commonly available on microcomputers, there are a number of statistical packages which can be used to perform the type of analysis described in Chapter 6. Minitab[1] is a friendly, yet powerful, statistical package for the IBM Personal Computer which can do all of the analysis necessary for the problems in Chapter 6.

There are some types of analysis that are beneficial to understanding the concepts covered in the text, but for which no existing programs were available. Therefore, this programming appendix contains listings of four programs written in BASICA for the IBM Personal Computer (and compatibles). A diskette with the four programs (from which copies may be made) is available at no charge to faculty members who adopt the text for classroom use. The first three programs (SERVCOST, LCURVE, and INVRUL) require that 10,000 (10K) bytes of random access memory be available under the BASICA interpreter, while the INCNTV program requires 30,000 (30K) bytes of memory. A printer is not required, but is recommended since it allows the user to make a hard copy of the program results.

[1]Published by Minitab, Inc., 215 Pond Laboratory, University Park, Pennsylvania 16802.

SERVCOST: Service Department Cost Reallocation

This program performs the calculations necessary to determine the variable cost of a unit of service when there are reciprocal service department usages. (A specific example is problem 5.12.) The user must provide information on the service usages of operating departments and of other service departments, as well as the variable costs (per unit) incurred within each service department. The program finds the actual variable costs of service provided to the operating departments.

```
10 CLS
20 PRINT "Program: SERVCOST                                    Version 1.0"
30 PRINT "Author: R. Magee            J.L.Kellogg Graduate School of Management"
40 PRINT:PRINT "Want an explanation (y or n)?";
50 A$=INKEY$:IF A$="" THEN 50
60 IF A$="n" OR A$="N" THEN 190
70 IF A$<>"y" AND A$<>"Y" THEN 50
80 PRINT:PRINT
90 PRINT"     This program will allocate service department costs to operating"
100 PRINT "departments. The user must provide information on reciprocal usages"
110 PRINT "by other service departments, usage by operating departments, and"
120 PRINT "traceable, service department costs. The program will then compute"
130 PRINT "the marginal cost of a unit of service and the marginal cost of a uni
t"
140 PRINT "produced in the operating department. In addition, if budgeted levels
"
150 PRINT "of operating department activity are provided, the program will"
160 PRINT "print out service department budgets."
170 PRINT:PRINT "Press any key to continue."
180 Z$=INKEY$:IF Z$="" THEN 180
190 PRINT:PRINT "Do you want a printed copy of the results (y or n)?";
200 PRN$=INKEY$:IF PRN$="" THEN 200
210 IF PRN$="n" OR PRN$="N" THEN 240
220 IF PRN$<>"y" AND PRN$<>"Y" THEN 200
230 PRINT:INPUT "Input a title for the printed output";TTL$
240 CLS
250 INPUT "Number of Service Departments";S1
260 PRINT:INPUT "Number of Operating Departments";P1
270 DIM A(S1,S1),V(S1),P(P1,S1),B(S1,S1),C(S1,S1),D(S1),E(P1),Q(S1),R(S1),U(P1)
280 DIM NS$(S1),NO$(P1)
290 CLS
300 FOR I=1 TO S1:PRINT "Input a (short) descriptive name of the service"
310 PRINT "        provided by Service Department";I;
320 INPUT NS$(I):NEXT I
330 PRINT
340 FOR I=1 TO P1:PRINT "Input a (short) descriptive name of the output"
350 PRINT "        produced by Operating Department";I;
360 INPUT NO$(I):NEXT I
370 CLS
380 PRINT "Reciprocal Service Department Usages:"
390 PRINT
400 FOR I=1 TO S1
410 PRINT "Service needed by Service Department";I;":"
420 FOR J=1 TO S1
430 PRINT "   Units of ";NS$(J);" needed to produce one unit of ";NS$(I);
440 INPUT A(I,J)
450 IF A(I,J)>=0 THEN 480
460 BEEP:PRINT:PRINT "Usages cannot be negative! Try again!":PRINT
470 GOTO 430
480 NEXT J:PRINT:NEXT I
490 CLS
500 PRINT "Traceable, Variable Service Department Costs:"
```

```
510 PRINT
520 FOR I=1 TO S1
530 PRINT "   Input the traceable variable cost per unit of ";NS$(I)
540 PRINT "               in Service Department";I;
550 INPUT V(I)
560 IF V(I)>=0 THEN 590
570 BEEP:PRINT:PRINT "Variable Costs cannot be negative! Try again!":PRINT
580 GOTO 530
590 NEXT I
600 CLS
610 PRINT "Service Usage by Operating Departments:":PRINT
620 FOR I=1 TO P1
630 PRINT "Service needed by Operating Department";I;":"
640 FOR J=1 TO S1
650 PRINT "   Units of ";NS$(J);" from Service Department";J;" needed"
660 PRINT "           to produce one unit of ";NO$(I);
670 INPUT P(I,J)
680 IF P(I,J)>=0 THEN 710
690 BEEP:PRINT:PRINT "Usages cannot be negative! Try again!":PRINT
700 GOTO 650
710 NEXT J:PRINT:NEXT I
720 PRINT:PRINT "   ...working..."
730 FOR I=1 TO S1
740 FOR J=1 TO S1
750 IF I=J THEN B(I,J)=1-A(I,J) ELSE B(I,J)=-A(I,J)
760 NEXT J
770 C(I,I)=1
780 NEXT I
790 FOR I=1 TO S1:FOR J=1 TO S1
800 IF I=J THEN 860
810 X=B(J,I)/B(I,I)
820 FOR K=1 TO S1
830 B(J,K)=B(J,K)-X*B(I,K)
840 C(J,K)=C(J,K)-X*C(I,K)
850 NEXT K
860 NEXT J
870 NEXT I
880 FOR I=1 TO S1:FOR J=1 TO S1
890 C(I,J)=C(I,J)/B(I,I)
900 NEXT J,I
910 FOR I=1 TO S1:FOR J=1 TO S1
920 D(I)=D(I)+C(I,J)*V(J)
930 NEXT J,I
940 FOR I=1 TO P1:FOR J=1 TO S1
950 E(I)=E(I)+P(I,J)*D(J)
960 NEXT J,I
970 IF PRN$="n" OR PRN$="N" THEN 1120
980 IF PRN$="n" OR PRN$="N" THEN XPR=0 ELSE XPR=1
990 LPRINT "Problem: ";TTL$
1000 LPRINT:LPRINT "                                        Per-Unit Service Department
Usages":LPRINT
1010 LPRINT "Users of ";:FOR J=1 TO S1:LPRINT "     ";:NEXT J:LPRINT "Sources of
Service"
1020 LPRINT "Service     ";:FOR I=1 TO S1:LPRINT USING "Svce ##  ";I;:NEXT I:LPRI
NT
1030 LPRINT "-------     ";:FOR I=1 TO S1:LPRINT "-------  ";:NEXT I:LPRINT
1040 FOR I=1 TO S1:LPRINT USING "Svce ##     ";I;
1050 FOR J=1 TO S1:LPRINT USING "##.####  ";A(I,J);:NEXT J:LPRINT
1060 NEXT I:LPRINT
1070 FOR I=1 TO P1:LPRINT USING "Opng ##     ";I;
1080 FOR J=1 TO S1:LPRINT USING "##.####  ";P(I,J);:NEXT J:LPRINT
1090 NEXT I:LPRINT
1100 LPRINT "Var Cost   ";
```

```
1110 FOR I=1 TO S1:LPRINT USING "$####.##  ";V(I);:NEXT I:LPRINT:LPRINT
1120 CLS
1130 PRINT "Marginal Cost Report:"
1140 IF XPR=1 THEN LPRINT "Marginal Cost Report:"
1150 FOR J=1 TO S1
1160 PRINT "Marginal Cost of a unit of ";NS$(J);" in Department";J;" is $";D(J)
1170 IF XPR=1 THEN LPRINT "Marginal Cost of a unit of ";NS$(J);" in Department";
J;" is $";D(J)
1180 NEXT J:PRINT
1190 IF XPR=1 THEN LPRINT
1200 PRINT "Press any key to continue."
1210 Z$=INKEY$:IF Z$="" THEN 1210
1220 CLS
1230 FOR K=1 TO P1
1240 PRINT "Marginal cost of service to produce a unit of ";NO$(K);" in"
1250 PRINT "        Operating Department";K;" is $";E(K)
1260 IF XPR=1 THEN LPRINT "Marginal cost of service to produce a unit of ";NO$(K
);" in"
1270 IF XPR=1 THEN LPRINT "        Operating Department";K;" is $";E(K)
1280 NEXT K:PRINT
1290 IF XPR=1 THEN LPRINT
1300 PRINT "Press any key to continue."
1310 Z$=INKEY$:IF Z$="" THEN 1310
1320 CLS
1330 PRINT "Do you want to input budgeted levels of Operating Department"
1340 PRINT "   activities, and get Service Department budgets (y or n)?"
1350 A$=INKEY$:IF A$="" THEN 1350
1360 IF A$="n" OR A$="N" THEN END
1370 IF A$<>"y" AND A$<>"Y" THEN 1350
1380 FOR I=1 TO S1:R(I)=0:Q(I)=0:NEXT I
1390 PRINT
1400 PRINT "Forecasted Levels of Activity for Operating Departments:"
1410 IF XPR=1 THEN LPRINT "Forecasted Levels of Activity for Operating Departmen
ts:"
1420 FOR K=1 TO P1
1430 PRINT "  Input forecasted activity (in units of ";NO$(K);") for"
1440 PRINT "     Operating Department";K;
1450 INPUT U(K)
1460 IF U(K)>=0 THEN 1490
1470 BEEP:PRINT:PRINT "Activity levels cannot be negative! Try again!":PRINT
1480 GOTO 1430
1490 IF XPR=1 THEN LPRINT "Forecasted activity for Operating Department";K;":";U
(K);" units of ";NO$(K)
1500 NEXT K
1510 FOR K=1 TO P1:FOR J=1 TO S1:R(J)=R(J)+U(K)*P(K,J):NEXT J,K
1520 FOR I=1 TO S1:FOR J=1 TO S1:Q(I)=Q(I)+R(J)*C(J,I):NEXT J,I
1530 CLS
1540 PRINT "Service Department Budgets:"
1550 IF XPR=1 THEN LPRINT "Service Department Budgets:"
1560 FOR I=1 TO S1
1570 PRINT "  Service Department";I
1580 PRINT "    Units:";Q(I);" (";NS$(I);")"
1590 PRINT "    Traceable Cost:  $";Q(I)*V(I)
1600 IF XPR<>1 THEN 1640
1610 LPRINT "  Service Department";I
1620 LPRINT "    Units:";Q(I);" (";NS$(I);")"
1630 LPRINT "    Traceable Cost:  $";Q(I)*V(I)
1640 NEXT I
1650 PRINT:GOTO 1300
```

LCURVE: Learning Curve Estimation

Estimation of a learning curve can be done with OLS regression only in special cases, as described in Chapter 7. When the learning curve is of the form

$$\text{Cumulative average cost} = v + a(\text{cumulative output}^b)$$

the managerial accountant must know either v or b to use OLS regression. When this is not the case, LCURVE can be used to find estimates of all three parameters—v, a, and b. The user provides the data on costs and output, and initial guesses for the three parameters. LCURVE then uses a nonlinear regression method to refine those guesses until it converges to the estimates of v, a, and b, which best fit the data. (A specific example is problem 7.7.)

```
10 DIM T(3,2),B(3),G(3),V(3,3),U(3,3),D(3),M$(3)
20 M$(1)="v":M$(2)="a":M$(3)="b"
30 A=.00001
40 CLS
50 PRINT "Program: LCURVE                                  Version 1.0"
60 PRINT "Author: R. Magee              J.L.Kellogg Graduate School of Management"

70 PRINT
80 PRINT "Want an explanation (y or n)?"
90 A$=INKEY$:IF A$="" THEN 90
100 IF A$="n" OR A$="N" THEN 260
110 PRINT
120 PRINT "      This program is designed to estimate a learning curve from a set
 of"
130 PRINT "data points provided by the user. The curve is of the form:"
140 PRINT "                      y = v + a * x ^ b"
150 PRINT "where y is the cumulative average cost of production;"
160 PRINT "      x is the cumulative production in units."
170 PRINT
180 PRINT "      The Taylor-Series Expansion approach is used for this nonlinear
estimation"
190 PRINT "problem. The user must enter the data, and then provide initial guess
es for"
200 PRINT "the parameters v,a and b. The program then iterates to refine these"
210 PRINT "estimates. If the program finds that its tolerance limits are met, th
e"
220 PRINT "iterations stop, the final estimates are reported, and the user may m
ake"
230 PRINT "some cost estimates for different levels of production."
240 PRINT:PRINT "Press any key to continue."
250 A$=INKEY$:IF A$="" THEN 250
260 CLS
270 PRINT "Data Entry:":INPUT "      How many observations";N
280 IF N>0 THEN 310
290 BEEP:PRINT:PRINT "Number of Observations must be positive! Try Again!":PRINT

300 GOTO 270
310 DIM Y(N),X(N),F(N),C(N),Z(N,3)
320 PRINT:PRINT "For each observation, input the cumulative average cost and "
330 PRINT "  the cumulative output."
340 FOR I=1 TO N
350 PRINT "Obsn #";I
360 INPUT "  Cum. Avg. Cost";Y(I)
370 INPUT "  Cum. Output";X(I)
380 IF Y(I)>=0 AND X(I)>=0 THEN 420
390 BEEP:PRINT
400 PRINT "Both cost and output must be positive numbers! Try again!":PRINT
```

```
410 GOTO 350
420 NEXT I
430 CLS
440 PRINT "Menu of Options:"
450 PRINT "   1 - Review Existing Data"
460 PRINT "   2 - Modify Existing Data"
470 PRINT "   3 - Estimate Learning Curve Parameters"
480 PRINT "   4 - Quit"
490 PRINT:PRINT "Select Option Number:"
500 O$=INKEY$:IF O$="" THEN 500
510 IF O$="1" THEN 560
520 IF O$="2" THEN 700
530 IF O$="3" THEN 850
540 IF O$="4" THEN END
550 BEEP:GOTO 500
560 ILAST=0:REMAIN=N
570 CLS
580 PRINT "Obsn #          Cumulative Average Cost            Cumulative Output
"
590 PRINT "------          -----------------------            -----------------
"
600 B=ILAST+1
610 IF REMAIN<=20 THEN E=ILAST+REMAIN ELSE E=ILAST+20
620 FOR I=B TO E
630 PRINT USING "  ###                  $  ############.##                ##########
";I,Y(I),X(I)
640 NEXT I
650 PRINT "Press any key to continue."
660 A$=INKEY$:IF A$="" THEN 660
670 ILAST=ILAST+E:REMAIN=REMAIN-E
680 IF REMAIN>0 THEN 570
690 GOTO 430
700 CLS
710 INPUT "Which observation number do you wish to change";K
720 IF K>0 AND K<=N THEN 750
730 BEEP:PRINT:PRINT "Observation numbers go from 1 to";N;"! Try again!":PRINT
740 GOTO 710
750 PRINT:PRINT " Current values for observation";K
760 PRINT "   Cumulative Average Cost: $";Y(K)
770 PRINT "   Cumulative Output: ";X(K);" units"
780 PRINT:INPUT "Input new cost number";Y(K)
790 INPUT "Input new output number";X(K)
800 PRINT:PRINT "Change another observation (y or n)?"
810 A$=INKEY$:IF A$="" THEN 810
820 IF A$="y" OR A$="Y" THEN 700
830 IF A$="n" OR A$="N" THEN 430
840 GOTO 810
850 CLS:PRINT "Initial guesses for parameters: y = v + a ^ b"
860 PRINT:INPUT "Input initial guess for v";T(1,2)
870 PRINT:INPUT "Input initial guess for a";T(2,2)
880 PRINT:INPUT "Input initial guess for b";T(3,2)
890 L=0
900 PRINT
910 L=L+1
920 PRINT "   ...working..."
930 FOR I=1 TO N
940 F(I)=T(1,2)+T(2,2)*X(I)^T(3,2)
950 Z(I,1)=1:Z(I,2)=X(I)^T(3,2):Z(I,3)=(T(2,2)*X(I)^T(3,2))*LOG(X(I))
960 NEXT I
970 FOR I=1 TO 3:FOR J=1 TO 3:V(I,J)=0
980 FOR K=1 TO N:V(I,J)=V(I,J)+Z(K,I)*Z(K,J):NEXT K,J,I
990 FOR I=1 TO 3:FOR J=1 TO 3
```

```
1000 IF I=J THEN U(I,J)=1 ELSE U(I,J)=0
1010 NEXT J,I
1020 FOR I=1 TO 3:FOR J=1 TO 3
1030 IF I=J THEN 1090
1040 X=V(J,I)/V(I,I)
1050 FOR K=1 TO 3
1060 V(J,K)=V(J,K)-X*V(I,K)
1070 U(J,K)=U(J,K)-X*U(I,K)
1080 NEXT K
1090 NEXT J
1100 NEXT I
1110 FOR I=1 TO 3
1120 FOR J=1 TO 3
1130 U(I,J)=U(I,J)/V(I,I)
1140 NEXT J,I
1150 FOR I=1 TO N:C(I)=Y(I)-F(I):NEXT I
1160 FOR I=1 TO 3:D(I)=0
1170 FOR J=1 TO N:D(I)=D(I)+Z(J,I)*C(J)
1180 NEXT J,I
1190 FOR I=1 TO 3:B(I)=0
1200 FOR J=1 TO 3:B(I)=B(I)+U(I,J)*D(J)
1210 NEXT J,I
1220 I9=0
1230 FOR I=1 TO 3:T(I,1)=T(I,2)+B(I):G(I)=B(I)/T(I,2)
1240 IF ABS(G(I))<=A THEN 1260
1250 I9=1
1260 NEXT I
1270 IF I9<.5 THEN 1380
1280 FOR I=1 TO 3:T(I,2)=T(I,1):NEXT I
1290 IF (L MOD 5)<>0 THEN 900
1300 CLS:PRINT L;" iterations completed."
1310 PRINT "Latest estimates (and percentage change at last iteration) are:"
1320 FOR I=1 TO 3:PRINT M$(I);T(I,1);" (";G(I);")":NEXT I
1330 PRINT:PRINT "Continue refinement of estimates (y or n)?"
1340 A$=INKEY$:IF A$="" THEN 1340
1350 IF A$="y" OR A$="Y" THEN 900
1360 IF A$="n" OR A$="N" THEN 1380
1370 GOTO 1340
1380 CLS
1390 IF I9<.5 THEN PRINT "Tolerance limits met."
1400 PRINT:PRINT "Final estimates are:"
1410 FOR I=1 TO 3
1420 PRINT USING "     \ \  ########.####";M$(I),T(I,1)
1430 NEXT I
1440 PRINT:PRINT "Do you want a printed copy of the results (y or n)?"
1450 A$=INKEY$:IF A$="" THEN 1450
1460 IF A$="n" OR A$="N" THEN 1600
1470 IF A$="y" OR A$="Y" THEN 1490
1480 GOTO 1450
1490 LPRINT:LPRINT "Observations used in finding LCURVE estimates:":LPRINT
1500 LPRINT "Obsn #           Cumulative Average Cost           Cumulative Outp
ut"
1510 LPRINT "------           ------------------------           ---------------
--"
1520 FOR I=1 TO N
1530 LPRINT USING "  ###                 $  ############.##               ########
##";I,Y(I),X(I)
1540 NEXT I:LPRINT
1550 LPRINT:LPRINT "Final estimates are:"
1560 XPR=1
1570 FOR I=1 TO 3
1580 LPRINT USING "     \ \  ########.####";M$(I),T(I,1)
```

```
1590 NEXT I
1600 PRINT:PRINT "Do you want to use these parameter estimates to forecast costs
 (y or n)?"
1610 A$=INKEY$:IF A$="" THEN 1610
1620 IF A$="n" OR A$="N" THEN 430
1630 IF A$="y" OR A$="Y" THEN 1650
1640 GOTO 1610
1650 PRINT:INPUT "Input cumulative level of output";X9
1660 Y9=T(1,1)+T(2,1)*X9^T(3,1):T9=X9*Y9
1670 PRINT USING "   Cum. Avg. Cost $#########   ;   Cum. Total Cost $#########"
;Y9,T9
1680 IF XPR<.5 THEN 1700
1690 LPRINT:LPRINT USING "Cum Output ######  ;  Cum Avg Cost $#########  ;  Cum
Total Cost $#########";X9,Y9,T9
1700 GOTO 1600
```

INVRUL: Cost Variance Investigation Rule

This program assists the user in finding a variance investigation rule as described in Chapters 9 and 10, where all variances in excess of a critical value will be investigated. (Specific examples are problems 9.8, 9.10, and 10.4.) The user provides estimates of the probability distributions (assumed to be normal) of costs when the operation is in control and when it is operating with a controllable inefficiency. In addition, the cost of conducting an investigation and the probability of an inefficiency developing must be provided. Then the program computes the expected cost per period for investigation rules suggested by the user, and, in turn, the program suggests what values the user might try next. This program can also be used to determine the value of obtaining further information about uncertain parameters (e.g., the expected cost when out of control), and the value of improved variances as described in Chapter 10.

```
10 DIM D(2),E(2),F(2),U(2),S(2),C(2),H(2)
20 CLS
30 PRINT "Program: INVRUL                                Version 1.0"
40 PRINT "Author: R. Magee         J.L.Kellogg Graduate School of Management"
50 PRINT
60 PRINT "Want an explanation (y or n)?";
70 B$=INKEY$:IF B$="" THEN 70
80 IF B$="n" OR B$="N" THEN 300
90 IF B$<>"y" AND B$<>"Y" THEN 50
100 PRINT "     This program will assist the user in finding an efficient"
110 PRINT "cost variance investigation strategy using the Dittman and Prakash"
120 PRINT "method which is described in Chapter 9 of the text."
130 PRINT "The program will ask for the parameters of the cost process,"
140 PRINT "and will then require the user to describe the strategies"
150 PRINT "he or she wishes to consider. All strategies are of the "
160 PRINT "form 'investigate if costs exceed XBAR' and therefore, the"
170 PRINT "user must describe the values of XBAR he or she wishes to"
180 PRINT "examine. This is done by inputting the lowest value, the"
190 PRINT "highest value, and the increment to be used between the two"
200 PRINT "values. (The increment must be an integer no smaller than 1.)"
210 PRINT "     The program will then print out the expected cost per"
220 PRINT "period and the first derivative for each strategy, to aid "
230 PRINT "the user in searching for the best value of XBAR. (The first"
240 PRINT "derivative should be negative below the best XBAR, and positive"
250 PRINT "above. The program will also suggest where the user might look"
260 PRINT "further for the best value of XBAR.)"
270 PRINT
280 PRINT "Press any key to continue";
```

```
290 A$=INKEY$: IF A$="" THEN 290
300 CLS
310 PRINT "                              Input of Problem Information"
320 PRINT "                              ----------------------------":PRINT
330 PRINT "Probability Distribution of Costs:"
340 PRINT "   IN CONTROL"
350 INPUT "    mean";U(1)
360 INPUT "    standard deviation";S(1)
370 IF S(1)>=0 THEN 400
380 BEEP:PRINT "A standard deviation cannot be negative!!!  Try again."
390 GOTO 360
400 PRINT
410 PRINT "   OUT OF CONTROL"
420 INPUT "    mean";U(2)
430 INPUT "    standard deviation";S(2)
440 IF S(2)>=0 THEN 470
450 BEEP:PRINT "A standard deviation cannot be negative!!!  Try again."
460 GOTO 430
470 PRINT
480 INPUT "Expected Cost of Conducting an Investigation";K
490 PRINT
500 PRINT "Probability that an IN CONTROL cost process will stay"
510 INPUT "     that way the following period";G
520 IF G>=0 AND G<=1 THEN 550
530 BEEP:PRINT "A probability must be between zero(0) and one(1)!!!  Try again.
540 GOTO 500
550 CLS:PRINT "Review of Problem Information:"
560 PRINT "                                Characteristics of Costs Per Period"
570 PRINT "                             Expected Cost          Standard Deviation"
580 PRINT USING "   In-Control          $############          $#############";U(1
),S(1)
590 PRINT USING "   Out-of-Control      $############          $#############";U(2
),S(2)
600 PRINT:PRINT USING "  Expected Cost per Investigation:    $########";K
610 PRINT:PRINT "   Probability of an In-Control Process Remaining In-Control"
620 PRINT USING "      the Next Period:   #.####";G
630 PRINT
640 PRINT "Options:"
650 PRINT "  1 - change expected cost when in-control"
660 PRINT "  2 - change standard deviation of cost when in-control"
670 PRINT "  3 - change expected cost when out-of-control"
680 PRINT "  4 - change standard deviation of cost when out-of-control"
690 PRINT "  5 - change expected cost of investigation"
700 PRINT "  6 - change of probability of staying in the in-control state"
710 PRINT:PRINT "  7 - search for best investigation strategy"
720 PRINT:INPUT "Choice";OPT
730 IF OPT=7 THEN 870
740 IF OPT<>6 THEN 760
750 INPUT "New Probability of In-Control Process Staying In-Control";G:GOTO 550
760 IF OPT<>5 THEN 780
770 INPUT "New Cost of Making an Investigation";K:GOTO 550
780 IF OPT<>4 THEN 800
790 INPUT "New Standard Deviation of Cost When Out-of-Control";S(2):GOTO 550
800 IF OPT<>3 THEN 820
810 INPUT "New Expected Cost When Out-of-Control";U(2):GOTO 550
820 IF OPT<>2 THEN 840
830 INPUT "New Standard Deviation of Cost When In-Control";S(1):GOTO 550
840 IF OPT<>1 THEN 860
850 INPUT "New Expected Cost When In-Control";U(1):GOTO 550
860 BEEP:GOTO 550
870 CLS
880 PRINT "Do you want a printed copy of the results (y or n)?";
```

```
890 PRN$=INKEY$:IF PRN$="" THEN 890
900 IF PRN$="n" OR PRN$="N" THEN 1030
910 IF PRN$<>"y" AND PRN$<>"Y" THEN 880
920 PRINT"    Turn on the printer, then hit any key to continue."
930 A$=INKEY$: IF A$="" THEN 930
940 LPRINT:LPRINT:LPRINT "Review of Problem Information:"
950 LPRINT "                              Characteristics of Costs Per Period"
960 LPRINT "                           Expected Cost          Standard Deviation"
970 LPRINT USING "   In-Control          $############          $#############";U(
1),S(1)
980 LPRINT USING "   Out-of-Control      $############          $#############";U(
2),S(2)
990 LPRINT:LPRINT USING "   Expected Cost per Investigation:    $########";K
1000 LPRINT:LPRINT "   Probability of an In-Control Process Remaining In-Control

1010 LPRINT USING "      the Next Period:   #.####";G
1020 LPRINT
1030 IF ((1-G)*K)>=(G*(U(2)-U(1))) THEN 1600
1040 PRINT
1050 PRINT "Values of XBAR to be tried:"
1060 INPUT "     Minimum";X1
1070 INPUT "     Maximum";X2
1080 INPUT "     Increment";X3
1090 IF X3>=1 THEN 1120
1100 BEEP
1110 GOTO 1080
1120 PRINT
1130 PRINT " XBAR     EXPECTED COST     1ST DERIVATIVE"
1140 PRINT " ----     -------------     --------------"
1150 IF PRN$="n" OR PRN$="N" THEN 1190
1160 LPRINT
1170 LPRINT " XBAR     EXPECTED COST     1ST DERIVATIVE"
1180 LPRINT " ----     -------------     --------------"
1190 N=1+(X2-X1)/X3
1200 Z9=X1-1
1210 FOR M=1 TO N
1220 X=X1+(M-1)*X3
1230 FOR J=1 TO 2
1240 C(J)=1/(S(J)*SQR(2*3.14159))
1250 H(J)=S(J)/20
1260 Y1=X+H(J)
1270 F(J)=C(J)*EXP(-(X-U(J))^2/(2*S(J)^2))
1280 D(J)=F(J)
1290 Y1=Y1-2*H(J)
1300 Y2=Y1-H(J)
1310 F(J)=F(J)+4*C(J)*EXP(-(Y1-U(J))^2/(2*S(J)^2))
1320 F(J)=F(J)+2*C(J)*EXP(-(Y2-U(J))^2/(2*S(J)^2))
1330 IF Y2<=(U(J)-4*S(J)) THEN 1350
1340 GOTO 1290
1350 F(J)=(H(J)/3)*F(J)+C(J)*EXP(-(Y2-H(J)-U(J))^2/(2*S(J)^2))
1360 NEXT J
1370 P=(1-F(2))/(1-G*F(2))
1380 C=U(2)+P*(K-G*(U(2)-U(1))-G*K*F(1))
1390 C1=P*(-G*K*D(1))
1400 C1=C1-D(2)*(1-G)*(K-G*(U(2)-U(1))-G*K*F(1))/(1-G*F(2))^2
1410 PRINT USING "######    $#########.###     $####.########";X,C,C1
1420 IF PRN$="n" OR PRN$="N" THEN 1440
1430 LPRINT USING "######    $#########.###     $####.########";X,C,C1
1440 IF C1>0 THEN 1460
1450 Z9=X
1460 NEXT M
1470 IF M=2 THEN 1550
```

```
1480 IF Z9>=X1 THEN 1510
1490 PRINT "The best strategy appears to be less than or equal to ";X1
1500 GOTO 1550
1510 IF Z9<X2 THEN 1540
1520 PRINT "The best strategy appears to be greater than or equal to ";X2
1530 GOTO 1550
1540 PRINT "The best strategy appears to be between the values of ";Z9;" and ";(
Z9+X3)
1550 PRINT
1560 INPUT "Do you wish to continue looking for a policy (y or n)";B$
1570 IF B$="y" OR B$="Y" THEN 1040
1580 IF B$="n" OR B$="N" THEN 1690
1590 BEEP:GOTO 1560
1600 BEEP:PRINT "      The characteristics of the cost process you describe are"
1610 PRINT "such that it never pays to investigate. That is, the expected"
1620 PRINT "benefit from investigation never exceeds the cost."
1630 IF PRN$="n" OR PRN$="N" THEN 1670
1640 LPRINT "      The characteristics of the cost process you describe are"
1650 LPRINT "such that it never pays to investigate. That is, the expected"
1660 LPRINT "benefit from investigation never exceeds the cost."
1670 PRINT:PRINT "Press any key to continue.";
1680 A$=INKEY$:IF A$="" THEN 1680
1690 CLS:PRINT:PRINT "Options:"
1700 PRINT "  1 - Modify Existing Problem Information"
1710 PRINT "  2 - Input New Problem Information"
1720 PRINT:PRINT "  3 - END INVRUL SESSION"
1730 PRINT:INPUT "Choice";OPT
1740 IF OPT=1 THEN 550
1750 IF OPT=2 THEN 300
1760 IF OPT=3 THEN END
1770 BEEP:GOTO 1690
```

INCNTV: Incentive Analysis

This program enables the user to perform a simple *agency analysis* of situations where the choice of action has been delegated to an agent. (Specific examples are problems 11.6 and 14.3.) The user must describe the possible courses of action the agent might take, the number of possible performance outcomes, the impact of each course of action on the probability distribution of the performance outcomes, and the agent's natural preferences for the courses of action. The program assumes that the agent is risk-averse, and that his or her preference for a payoff of $\$x (x > 0)$ after taking action a is reflected in the function:

$$U[\$x,a] = x^{1/2} - \text{disutility for action } a$$

In this setting, a compensation function is a schedule of the amount the agent will be paid for each of the possible performance outcomes.

There are two types of analysis the user may perform. First, the user may put in a compensation function by entering the amount of compensation to be paid for each possible performance outcome. Then the program will determine which course of action will be motivated by that compensation, and it also checks to see whether the agent is being paid enough to accept the job. In the second type of analysis, the user specifies a course of action, and the program searches for the most efficient compensation function that motivates the specified course of action.

INCNTV *can* be used (with care) to examine two-period incentive problems as described in Chapter 14 and its Appendix. In this situation, the courses of action must describe the agent's decisions for two periods, and the performance outcomes must span both periods. The probabilities of the performance outcomes must sum to 2, and the minimum expected utility must cover both periods. Some of the program output will not be easily interpreted, but the compensation functions are valid.

```
10 CLS
20 PRINT "Program Title: INCNTV              Version 1.1"
30 PRINT "Author: R. Magee        J.L.Kellogg Grad. School of Mgmt."
40 PRINT
50 PRINT "      INCNTV is an interactive program which aids the user in "
60 PRINT "determining an optimal incentive function for a decision maker who"
70 PRINT "has been employed by a principal to act as a decision-making agent."
80 PRINT "The program assumes that the decision maker's utility function"
90 PRINT "is represented by the square root of his monetary payment minus"
100 PRINT "an effort aversion term. The agent/decision maker will choose the"
110 PRINT "action which maximizes the following:"
120 PRINT
130 PRINT "        E(SQR(Compensation))-Effort Aversion"
140 PRINT
150 PRINT "      The user must provide the list of actions (maximum 10)"
160 PRINT "and possible outcomes (maximum 15). For each possible action,"
170 PRINT "the decision maker's effort aversion must be given, and for"
180 PRINT "every action/outcome combination, the user must provide the"
190 PRINT "probability of the outcome given the action. In addition, the"
200 PRINT "user must specify the expected payoff to the principal (before"
210 PRINT "agent compensation) for each performance outcome, and the"
220 PRINT "decision maker's minimum expected utility."
230 PRINT
240 PRINT "Press any key to continue";
250 Z$=INKEY$: IF Z$="" THEN 250
260 CLS
270 PRINT "      Based on this information, the user may perform two types of"
280 PRINT "analysis. If the user specifies an action, the program will find"
290 PRINT "the compensation function that will motivate the chosen action which"

300 PRINT "has the lowest expected cost to the principal. Alternatively, the"
310 PRINT "user may specify a compensation function by typing in the amount"
320 PRINT "to be paid to the agent for each performance outcome. The program"
330 PRINT "will then find the action that would be motivated by that compen-"
340 PRINT "sation function."
350 PRINT
360 PRINT "Press any key to continue";
370 Z$=INKEY$:IF Z$="" THEN 370
380 CLS
390 REM
400 REM input of variables
410 REM
420 INPUT "Do you want a printed copy of the results (y or n)";PRN$
430 PRINT
440 IF PRN$="y" THEN 490
450 IF PRN$="n" THEN 490
460 PRINT CHR$(7)
470 PRINT "Please use lower case y or n!"
480 GOTO 420
490 IF PRN$="n" THEN 530
500 INPUT "Do you want to give a title name for the output (y or n)";ZTL$
510 IF ZTL$<>"y" THEN 540
520 INPUT "Type in title name";TTL$
530 PRINT
540 INPUT "How many action alternatives does that agent have (max 10)";M1
550 IF M1<=10 AND M1>=1 THEN 580
```

```
560 PRINT CHR$(7)
570 GOTO 540
580 PRINT
590 INPUT "How many performance outcomes are possible (max 15)";M2
600 IF M2<=15 AND M2>=1 THEN 630
610 PRINT CHR$(7)
620 GOTO 590
630 N=M1+M2
640 ML1=M1-1
650 N2=2*N
660 OPTION BASE 1
670 DIM V(10),P(15,10),T$(10)
680 DIM M(25,25),Q(25),B(25,25),W(25),Z(25),A(25),S(50)
690 DIM C(15),OT$(15),PAYOFF(15)
700 PRINT
710 CLS
720 PRINT "     You must enter information which reflects the agent's other"
730 PRINT "employment opportunities and his inherent preferences for the differe
nt"
740 PRINT "courses of action. To find the 'minimum expected utility required,'
750 PRINT "take the square root of the amount of money that you would have to"
760 PRINT "pay the agent to take the action which he favors most. For example,"
770 PRINT "if action 1 is the one most favored by the agent, and if you would"
780 PRINT "have to pay $14,400 to get the agent to take the job, then the "
790 PRINT "'minimum expected utility' is 120 (the square root of 14,400)."
800 PRINT:INPUT "What is the minimum expected utility required";UMIN
810 PRINT
820 PRINT "     The 'action disutility' reflects the agent's distaste for"
830 PRINT "courses of action, relative to the most preferred action. Therefore,"

840 PRINT "the action disutility for the most preferred action (action 1 in the"

850 PRINT "example above) is 0 (zero). For other actions, action disutility is"
860 PRINT "measured in 'utiles,' and reflects the amount of additional monetary"

870 PRINT "utility that is required to compensate the agent for his dislike of"
880 PRINT "the course of action. For instance, if we could insure that the agent
"
890 PRINT "would take action 2 by paying $16,900 and observing his choice of act
ion,"
900 PRINT "the action disutility would be 10, the difference between 130 (the sq
uare"
910 PRINT "root of 16,900) and the 120 required for the most preferred action."
920 FOR I=1 TO M1
930 PRINT "   input the name of action";I;
940 INPUT T$(I)
950 INPUT "   what is the 'action disutility' for this action";V(I)
960 NEXT I
970 CLS
980 PRINT "Input description and the gross payoff (before compensation) for"
990 PRINT "     each performance outcome."
1000 FOR I=1 TO M2
1010 PRINT
1020 PRINT "Input description of outcome number ";I;
1030 INPUT OT$(I)
1040 PRINT "Input the gross payoff for outcome number ";I;
1050 INPUT PAYOFF(I)
1060 NEXT I
1070 FOR I=1 TO M1
1080 CLS
1090 PRINT "Input the outcome probabilities if the agent takes action";I;"(";T$(
I);")"
```

```
1100 P9=0!
1110 FOR J=1 TO M2
1120 PRINT " Probability of outcome";J;" (";OT$(J);")";
1130 INPUT P(J,I)
1140 P9=P9+P(J,I)
1150 NEXT J
1160 IF P9>1.00001 THEN 1190
1170 IF P9<.99999 THEN 1190
1180 GOTO 1220
1190 INPUT "The probabilities don't sum to 1.0! Re-enter data (y or n)";Z$
1200 IF Z$="Y" THEN 1080
1210 IF Z$="y" THEN 1080
1220 PRINT
1230 NEXT I
1240 IF PRN$="n" THEN 1620
1250 LPRINT "                    INCENTIVE COMPENSATION SUMMARY"
1260 LPRINT "                    ------------------------------"
1270 LPRINT
1280 IF ZTL$<>"y" THEN 1310
1290 LPRINT "Title: ";TTL$
1300 LPRINT
1310 FOR I=1 TO M1
1320 LPRINT "Action";I;":  ";T$(I)
1330 NEXT I
1340 LPRINT
1350 FOR I=1 TO M2
1360 LPRINT "Outcome";I;":  ";OT$(I);"($";PAYOFF(I);")"
1370 NEXT I
1380 LPRINT
1390 LPRINT "      Summary of Outcome Probabilities for Actions"
1400 LPRINT
1410 LPRINT "Outcome/Action";
1420 FOR I=1 TO ML1
1430 LPRINT USING "  ##  ";I;
1440 NEXT I
1450 LPRINT USING "  ##  ";M1
1460 FOR J=1 TO M2
1470 LPRINT USING "  ##          ";J;
1480 FOR I=1 TO ML1
1490 LPRINT USING " #.###";P(J,I);
1500 NEXT I
1510 LPRINT USING " #.###";P(J,M1)
1520 NEXT J
1530 LPRINT
1540 LPRINT "act'n disutlty";
1550 FOR I=1 TO ML1
1560 LPRINT USING " ###.#";V(I);
1570 NEXT I
1580 LPRINT USING " ###.#";V(M1)
1590 LPRINT
1600 LPRINT "Minimum Expected Utility Required:  EUM=";UMIN
1610 LPRINT
1620 CLS
1630 PRINT "Select one option from the following:"
1640 PRINT "  1 - find the best incentive to motivate a chosen action"
1650 PRINT "  2 - find the action motivated by a given incentive function"
1660 PRINT "  3 - modify existing problem data"
1670 PRINT "  4 - end"
1680 INPUT "Input option number";OPT
1690 IF OPT=3 THEN 5230
1700 IF OPT=2 THEN 4560
1710 IF OPT=1 THEN 1740
```

```
1720 IF OPT<>4 THEN 1620
1730 END
1740 CLS
1750 PRINT "                    SUMMARY"
1760 PRINT "Outcome/Action";
1770 FOR I=1 TO ML1
1780 PRINT USING "  ##   ";I;
1790 NEXT I
1800 PRINT USING "  ##   ";M1
1810 FOR J=1 TO M2
1820 PRINT USING "  ##          ";J;
1830 FOR I=1 TO ML1
1840 PRINT USING " #.###";P(J,I);
1850 NEXT I
1860 PRINT USING " #.###";P(J,M1)
1870 NEXT J
1880 PRINT "act'n disutlty";
1890 FOR I=1 TO ML1
1900 PRINT USING " ###.#";V(I);
1910 NEXT I
1920 PRINT USING " ###.#";V(M1)
1930 INPUT "Select an action number to be motivated";JSTAR
1940 IF JSTAR<1 THEN 1930
1950 IF JSTAR>M1 THEN 1930
1960 REM
1970 REM initialize the matrix variables for optimization
1980 REM
1990 CLS
2000 PRINT "     ...working..."
2010 FOR I=1 TO  N
2020 Q(I)=0!
2030 FOR J=1 TO N
2040 M(I,J)=0!
2050 NEXT J,I
2060 K=1
2070 FOR J=1 TO M1
2080 IF J=JSTAR THEN 2160
2090 M2K=M2+K
2100 Q(M2K)=V(J)-V(JSTAR)
2110 FOR I=1 TO M2
2120 M(M2K,I)=P(I,JSTAR)-P(I,J)
2130 M(I,M2K)=-M(M2K,I)
2140 NEXT I
2150 K=K+1
2160 NEXT J
2170 Q(N)=-UMIN-V(JSTAR)
2180 FOR I=1 TO M2
2190 M(I,I)=2*P(I,JSTAR)
2200 M(N,I)=P(I,JSTAR)
2210 M(I,N)=-M(N,I)
2220 NEXT I
2230 FOR I=1 TO N
2240 FOR J=1 TO N
2250 B(I,J)=1!
2260 IF I=J THEN 2280
2270 B(I,J)=0!
2280 NEXT J,I
2290 GOTO 2410
2300 IF IR=1000 THEN 2370
2310 GOTO 2830
2320 IF IR=1000 THEN 2370
2330 GOTO 3140
```

```
2340 IF IR=1000 THEN 2370
2350 GOTO 3510
2360 GOTO 2310
2370 INPUT "Do you want to try another action (y or n)";Z$
2380 IF Z$="Y" THEN 1740
2390 IF Z$="y" THEN 1740
2400 GOTO 1620
2410 REM
2420 REM find the initial almost complementary solution by
2430 REM      adding an artificial variable Z0.
2440 REM
2450 I=1
2460 J=2
2470 IF Q(I)<=Q(J) THEN 2490
2480 I=J
2490 J=J+1
2500 IF J<=N THEN 2470
2510 REM
2520 IR=I
2530 T1=-Q(IR)
2540 IF T1<=0! THEN 2780
2550 FOR I=1 TO N
2560 Q(I)=Q(I)+T1
2570 NEXT I
2580 Q(IR)=T1
2590 REM
2600 FOR J=1 TO N
2610 B(J,IR)=-1!
2620 W(J)=Q(J)
2630 Z(J)=0!
2640 S(J)=1
2650 L=N+J
2660 S(L)=J
2670 NEXT J
2680 NL1=1
2690 L=N+IR
2700 NL2=IR
2710 S(IR)=3
2720 S(L)=0
2730 W(IR)=0!
2740 Z0=Q(IR)
2750 L1=1
2760 REM
2770 GOTO 2300
2780 PRINT "Problem has a trivial complementary solution with"
2790 PRINT "   W=Q and Z=0."
2800 IR=1000
2810 GOTO 2300
2820 REM
2830 REM find the new basis column to enter in terms of the current basis.
2840 REM
2850 IF (L1 MOD 3)<>0 THEN 2910
2860 PRINT "     ...working..."
2870 REM
2880 REM if NL1 is neither 1 nor 2 then the variable Z0 leaves the
2890 REM      basis indicating termination with a complementary solution.
2900 REM
2910 IF NL1=1 THEN 2970
2920 IF NL1=2 THEN 3080
2930 CLS
2940 PRINT "Complementary Solution found on iteration number:";L1
2950 IR=1000
```

```
2960 GOTO 3740
2970 NE1=2
2980 NE2=NL2
2990 REM
3000 FOR I=1 TO N
3010 T1=0!
3020 FOR J=1 TO N
3030 T1=T1-B(I,J)*M(J,NE2)
3040 NEXT J
3050 A(I)=T1
3060 NEXT I
3070 GOTO 2320
3080 NE1=1
3090 NE2=NL2
3100 FOR I=1 TO N
3110 A(I)=B(I,NE2)
3120 NEXT I
3130 GOTO 2320
3140 REM
3150 REM find the pivot row for the next iteration by the use of
3160 REM     (simplex-type) minimum ratio rule.
3170 REM
3180 I=1
3190 IF A(I)>.0000001 THEN 3230
3200 I=I+1
3210 IF I>N THEN 3390
3220 GOTO 3190
3230 T1=Q(I)/A(I)
3240 IR=I
3250 I=I+1
3260 IF I>N THEN 3340
3270 IF A(I)>0! THEN 3290
3280 GOTO 3250
3290 T2=Q(I)/A(I)
3300 IF T2>=T1 THEN 3250
3310 IR=I
3320 T1=T2
3330 GOTO 3250
3340 GOTO 2340
3350 REM
3360 REM failure of the ratio rule indicates termination with
3370 REM      no complementary solution.
3380 REM
3390 IF PRN$="n" THEN 3460
3400 LPRINT
3410 LPRINT
3420 LPRINT
3430 LPRINT "There does not appear to be a way to motivate action";JSTAR;"."
3440 LPRINT
3450 LPRINT
3460 PRINT "Problem has no complementary solution!"
3470 PRINT "   Iteration no.";L1
3480 PRINT "There does not appear to be a way to motivate action";JSTAR;"."
3490 IR=1000
3500 GOTO 2340
3510 REM
3520 REM perform the pivot operation by updating the inverse of
3530 REM     the basis and the Q vector.
3540 REM
3550 FOR I=1 TO N
3560 B(IR,I)=B(IR,I)/A(IR)
3570 NEXT I
```

```
3580 Q(IR)=Q(IR)/A(IR)
3590 FOR I=1 TO N
3600 IF IR=I THEN 3650
3610 Q(I)=Q(I)-Q(IR)*A(I)
3620 FOR J=1 TO N
3630 B(I,J)=B(I,J)-B(IR,J)*A(I)
3640 NEXT J
3650 NEXT I
3660 REM
3670 NL1=S(IR)
3680 L=N+IR
3690 NL2=S(L)
3700 S(IR)=NE1
3710 S(L)=NE2
3720 L1=L1+1
3730 GOTO 2360
3740 REM
3750 REM print the solution and a graphics plot.
3760 REM
3770 FOR I=1 TO M2
3780 C(I)=0!
3790 NEXT I
3800 CMAX=-1
3810 IF PRN$="n" THEN 3880
3820 LPRINT
3830 LPRINT
3840 LPRINT
3850 LPRINT "Least-Cost Incentive Function to Motivate Action";JSTAR;"-";T$(JSTA
R)
3860 LPRINT "Outcome Number    Probability       Compensation"
3870 LPRINT "--------------    -----------       ------------"
3880 PRINT "Least-cost Incentive Function to Motivate Action";JSTAR;"-";T$(JSTAR
)
3890 PRINT "Outcome Number    Probability       Compensation"
3900 PRINT "--------------    -----------       ------------"
3910 I=N+1
3920 J=1
3930 K1=S(I)
3940 K2=S(J)
3950 IF Q(J)>=0! THEN 3970
3960 Q(J)=0!
3970 IF K2=1 THEN 4010
3980 IF K1>M2 THEN 4010
3990 IF P(K1,JSTAR)<.0000001 THEN 4010
4000 C(K1)=Q(J)^2
4010 I=I+1
4020 J=J+1
4030 IF J<=N THEN 3930
4040 EXPC=0!
4050 EUM=0!
4060 EPAYOFF=0!
4070 EGPAYOFF=0!
4080 FOR I=1 TO M2
4090 PRINT USING "       ##              #.###          $########.###";I,P(I,JSTAR)
,C(I)
4100 IF PRN$="n" THEN 4120
4110 LPRINT USING "       ##              #.###          $########.###";I,P(I,JSTAR
),C(I)
4120 EXPC=EXPC+P(I,JSTAR)*C(I)
4130 EPAYOFF=EPAYOFF+P(I,JSTAR)*(PAYOFF(I)-C(I))
4140 EGPAYOFF=EGPAYOFF+P(I,JSTAR)*PAYOFF(I)
4150 EUM=EUM+SQR(C(I))*P(I,JSTAR)
```

```
4160 IF C(I)<CMAX THEN 4180
4170 CMAX=C(I)
4180 NEXT I
4190 PRINT USING "Expected Compensation is $#########.##;  First-Best Compensatio
n is $#########.##";EXPC,((UMIN+V(JSTAR))^2)
4200 PRINT USING "Expected Payoff to Principal: Gross $#########.##; Net $########
#.##";EGPAYOFF,EPAYOFF
4210 IF PRN$="n" THEN 4240
4220 LPRINT USING "Expected Compensation is $#########.##;  First-Best Compensati
on is $#########.##";EXPC,((UMIN+V(JSTAR))^2)
4230 LPRINT USING "Expected Payoff to Principal: Gross $#########.##; Net $#######
##.##";EGPAYOFF,EPAYOFF
4240 IF (EUM-V(JSTAR))<(UMIN+.0001) THEN 4290
4250 PRINT "Minimum Expected Utility constraint is not binding. EUM=";(EUM-V(JST
AR))
4260 IF PRN$="n" THEN 4280
4270 LPRINT "Minimum Expected Utility Constraint is not binding. EUM=";(EUM-V(JS
TAR))
4280 GOTO 4320
4290 PRINT "Minimum Expected Utility constraint is binding."
4300 IF PRN$="n" THEN 4320
4310 LPRINT "Minimum Expected Utility constraint is binding."
4320 INPUT "Do you want a graphics display of the contract (y or n)";Z$
4330 IF Z$="y" THEN 4360
4340 IF Z$="Y" THEN 4360
4350 GOTO 4550
4360 CLS
4370 PRINT "$ of Compensation                              **** 1st best ($";(UMIN+V(JS
TAR))^2;")"
4380 IF PRN$<>"n" THEN LPRINT:LPRINT:LPRINT "$ of Compensation
     **** 1st best ($";(UMIN+V(JSTAR))^2;")" ELSE 4390
4390 NBL=INT(60/M2)-2:FBEST=(UMIN+V(JSTAR))^2
4400 FOR ROW=1 TO 20:PRINT "  :";:IF PRN$<>"n" THEN LPRINT "  :"; ELSE 4410
4410 G$=" "
4420 IF FBEST>((20-ROW)*1.2*CMAX/20) THEN G$="*":FBEST=-9999
4430 IF ROW=20 THEN G$="_"
4440 FOR J=1 TO M2
4450 FOR I=1 TO NBL:PRINT G$;:IF PRN$<>"n" THEN LPRINT G$;ELSE 4460
4460 NEXT I
4470 IF C(J)>((20-ROW)*1.2*CMAX/20) THEN PRINT "XX"; ELSE PRINT G$;G$;
4480 IF PRN$="n" THEN 4500
4490 IF C(J)>((20-ROW)*1.2*CMAX/20) THEN LPRINT "XX"; ELSE LPRINT G$;G$;
4500 NEXT J:PRINT:IF PRN$<>"n" THEN LPRINT
4510 NEXT ROW
4520 PRINT "                                                    Performance Outcom
es"
4530 IF PRN$="n" THEN 4550
4540 LPRINT "                                                    Performance Outco
mes":LPRINT:LPRINT
4550 GOTO 2320
4560 CLS
4570 PRINT "For each outcome, input the compensation to be paid:"
4580 FOR I=1 TO M2
4590 PRINT "Compensation for outcome ";I;"(";OT$(I);")";
4600 INPUT C(I)
4610 IF C(I)>=0 THEN 4640
4620 PRINT CHR$(7):PRINT"  Compensation cannot be negative!"
4630 GOTO 4590
4640 NEXT I
4650 EUMAX=-999999!
4660 EPMAX=-999999!
4670 AMAX=0
```

```
4680 IF PRN$="n" THEN 4760
4690 LPRINT: LPRINT
4700 LPRINT "              Proposed Compensation Function"
4710 LPRINT "              ------------------------------"
4720 FOR I=1 TO M2
4730 LPRINT USING "Outcome No. ##  (\        \)   $########.##";I,OT$(I),C(I)
4740 NEXT I
4750 LPRINT
4760 PRINT
4770 FOR I=1 TO M1
4780 EUM=-V(I)
4790 EP=0!
4800 FOR J=1 TO M2
4810 EUM=EUM+SQR(C(J))*P(J,I)
4820 EP=EP+(PAYOFF(J)-C(J))*P(J,I)
4830 NEXT J
4840 PRINT USING "Action ##  Expected Utility of Agent = ######.##";I,EUM
4850 IF PRN$="n" THEN 4870
4860 LPRINT USING "Action ##  Expected Utility of Agent = ######.##";I,EUM
4870 IF EUM<(EUMAX-.0000001) THEN 4930
4880 IF EUM>(EUMAX+.0000001) THEN 4910
4890 IF EP<EPMAX THEN 4930
4900 AMAX=I
4910 AMAX=I
4920 EUMAX=EUM
4930 NEXT I
4940 PRINT
4950 PRINT "The agent would choose action ";AMAX;"  (";T$(AMAX);")."
4960 IF PRN$="n" THEN 4980
4970 LPRINT "The agent would choose action ";AMAX;"  (";T$(AMAX);")."
4980 IF EUMAX>=UMIN THEN 5070
4990 PRINT "However, the agent's expected utility constraint is not met."
5000 PRINT
5010 IF PRN$="n" THEN 5040
5020 LPRINT "However, the agent's expected utility constraint is not met."
5030 LPRINT
5040 PRINT "Press any key to continue."
5050 Z$=INKEY$: IF Z$="" THEN 5050
5060 GOTO 5190
5070 EPAYOFF=0
5080 EGPAYOFF=0
5090 FOR I=1 TO M2
5100 EPAYOFF=EPAYOFF+P(I,AMAX)*(PAYOFF(I)-C(I))
5110 EGPAYOFF=EGPAYOFF+P(I,AMAX)*PAYOFF(I)
5120 NEXT I
5130 PRINT USING "Expected Payoff to Principal: Gross $########.##; Net $#######
#.##";EGPAYOFF,EPAYOFF
5140 IF PRN$="n" THEN 5160
5150 LPRINT USING "Expected Payoff to Principal: Gross $########.##; Net $######
##.##";EGPAYOFF,EPAYOFF
5160 PRINT
5170 PRINT "Press any key to continue."
5180 Z$=INKEY$: IF Z$="" THEN 5180
5190 CLS
5200 INPUT "Do you want to input another compensation function (y or n)";Z$
5210 IF Z$="y" THEN 4560
5220 GOTO 1620
5230 CLS
5240 PRINT "Possible data modifications:"
5250 PRINT "  0 - title"
5260 PRINT "  1 - effort disutilities"
5270 PRINT "  2 - outcome payoffs"
```

```
5280 PRINT "  3 - performance outcome probabilities"
5290 PRINT "  4 - minimum expected utility required by agent"
5300 PRINT:PRINT "  5 - printout of new values and return to main menu"
5310 PRINT:PRINT "  6 - return to main menu"
5320 PRINT: INPUT "Choose option number";OPT
5330 IF OPT=6 THEN 1620
5340 IF OPT<>5 THEN 5400
5350 IF PRN$="y" THEN 1250
5360 INPUT "Do you wish to get printed output from now on (y or n)";PRN$
5370 IF PRN$="y" THEN 1250
5380 IF PRN$="n" THEN 5230
5390 PRINT CHR$(7):GOTO 5360
5400 IF OPT=4 THEN 5460
5410 IF OPT=3 THEN 5500
5420 IF OPT=2 THEN 5610
5430 IF OPT=1 THEN 5680
5440 IF OPT=0 THEN 5750
5450 GOTO 5230
5460 CLS
5470 PRINT "Current minimum expected utility is";UMIN;". Input new value";
5480 INPUT UMIN
5490 GOTO 5230
5500 CLS
5510 INPUT "Input action number";ACT
5520 INPUT "Input performance outcome number";PERF
5530 PRINT "   Current probability is";P(PERF,ACT)
5540 INPUT "   Input new value";P(PERF,ACT)
5550 P9=0!
5560 FOR I=1 TO M2:P9=P9+P(I,ACT):NEXT I
5570 PRINT:PRINT "Sum of probabilities for this action is";P9
5580 PRINT:INPUT "Do you want to change other probabilities (y or n)";Z$
5590 IF Z$="y" THEN 5500
5600 IF Z$="n" THEN 5230 ELSE 5580
5610 CLS
5620 INPUT "Input performance outcome number";PERF
5630 PRINT "   Current expected payoff for ";OT$(PERF);" is";PAYOFF(PERF)
5640 INPUT "   Input new value";PAYOFF(PERF)
5650 PRINT:INPUT "Do you want to change other outcome payoffs (y or n)";Z$
5660 IF Z$="y" THEN 5610
5670 IF Z$="n" THEN 5230 ELSE 5650
5680 CLS
5690 INPUT "Input action number";ACT
5700 PRINT "   Current effort disutility for ";T$(ACT);" is";V(ACT)
5710 INPUT "   Input new value";V(ACT)
5720 PRINT:INPUT "Do you want to change other effort disutilities (y or n)";Z$
5730 IF Z$="y" THEN 5680
5740 IF Z$="n" THEN 5230 ELSE 5720
5750 CLS
5760 PRINT "Current title is: ";TTL$
5770 INPUT "   Input new title";TTL$
5780 GOTO 5230
```

Index